Oracle 11g

Fourth Edition

Developing AJAX Applications with PL/SQL Server Pages

Rajeev Kaula

College of Business Administration
Missouri State University

Learning Solutions

Boston   Burr Ridge, IL   Dubuque, IA   New York   San Francisco   St. Louis
Bangkok   Bogotá   Caracas   Lisbon   London   Madrid
Mexico City   Milan   New Delhi   Seoul   Singapore   Sydney   Taipei   Toronto

Oracle 11g
Developing AJAX Applications with PL/SQL Server Pages

10 11 12 13 14 15 QVS/QVS 19 18 17 16 15

ISBN-13: 978-0-07-340877-4
ISBN-10: 0-07-340877-8

Learning Solutions Specialist: Tricia Wagner
Production Editor: Jennifer Pickel
Cover Design: Paul Illian
Printer/Binder: Quad/Graphics

BRIEF
CONTENTS

TABLE OF
CONTENTS

PREFACE

PL/SQL Server Pages technology enables the building of Web applications by using Oracle's primary database language PL/SQL as a server-side scripting language. Such Web applications have evolved from traditional round-trip updates of Web pages to a more desktop application style of Web page processing. One of the key concept and technology that has facilitated the movement toward desktop application interface among Web applications is AJAX. AJAX stands for asynchronous Javascript and XML. AJAX in nutshell merges server-side script language like PL/SQL with client-side scripting language Javascript along with the XML language.

This book outlines the structure of PL/SQL language for developing database applications, including its extension as a server-side Web scripting language. It also covers the basics of Oracle SQL, HTML, Oracle XML, Javascript, and AJAX. It simplifies the concepts necessary to develop simple Web applications as well as more complex AJAX applications. Developing intense desktop application type activity in Web applications is beyond the scope of this book. Instead the focus is on providing an understanding of the basic concepts to ensure better development of such applications.

INTENDED TEXT BOOK AUDIENCE

This text book is written with the objective of providing the students or professionals with the knowledge of how to develop and manipulate a relational database through the medium of the Internet. It provides a hands-on approach toward applying the database application concepts for Web development. The ease with which SQL interacts with PL/SQL and the utilization of SQL in PL/SQL Server Pages allows students to (i) simplify database application logic, and (ii) understand the Web application framework. In an academic environment, the book can be adopted in any class or course that emphasizes relational database application concepts and/or Web application development.

FEATURES OF THE TEXT BOOK

The text book goes beyond mere refinements of database or Web application concepts. It contains many distinct features and presents concepts in a significantly new way. These features together provide a complete package for Web application development. The major features along with their coverages are listed below.

- Web Application Coverage: Explain important concepts in the design of Oracle based Web applications. These explanations cover the HTML language for Web layout, PL/SQL for server-side scripting, and Javascript and XML for AJAX development.

- SQL Coverage: In depth coverage of SQL to ensure that developers or students have a sound understanding of the language for proper manipulation of relational databases.

- PL/SQL Coverage: Detail coverage of PL/SQL language concepts to ensure that developers as well as students comprehend the nature of application logic necessary to manipulate database content successfully.

- XML Coverage: Details on generating XML from relational database through the PL/SQL language.

- Problem-Solving Guidelines: Hands-on explanation of concepts and examples to solve problems. Developers need guidelines to solve problems in a systematic manner. The text book provides running examples of various concepts as well as detailed tutorials on their application.

- Sample Databases: There are four databases utilized throughout the text book. These databases offer varying Web application scenarios. To ensure consistency in problem solving skills, one database (Superflex Apartment) is used in general for examples and tutorials, while the other databases provide the developers or students the opportunity to apply their problem-solving skills to Web application situations.

- Problem Solving Exercises: The review questions and exercises, as well as the problem solving exercises at the end of chapter focus, and test the readers ability to apply the chapter material in a meaningful way. These exercises further extend the practice of designing and implementing Web applications.

ORGANIZATION OF THE BOOK

The text book explains the various concepts through many examples and tutorials. Testing of these concepts is performed through review questions, review exercises, and problem solving exercises. The nature and depth of topics covered in the book accomplishes the following objectives:

- Allow familiarity with the Internet and Web application concepts and their working setup.

- Understand Oracle SQL statements to create, retrieve, and manipulate a relational database.

- Understand Oracle PL/SQL database language as a basis to develop applications that interact and manipulate relational databases.

- Learn the basic features of a Web page and Web site through HTML statements.

- Provide a hands-on understanding of how to create basic AJAX style Web applications using PL/SQL, Javascript and XML.

Chapter 1 introduces the Internet, Web application and relational database concepts. The chapter also introduces the four sample databases that are used throughout the text book. These databases provide a semblance of realistic data values and relationships to enhance learning.

Chapter 2 covers the SQL language in three parts (Lesson A, Lesson B, and Lesson C). Lesson A describes the SQL statements to create, maintain, and install a relational database. Lesson B describes the SQL statements to manipulate a relational database. Lesson C explores Oracle specific SQL functions as well as advanced features of SQL.

Chapter 3 introduces the PL/SQL language in three parts (Lesson A, Lesson B, and Lesson C). Lesson A provides the basic features of the language and its associated programs. Lesson B details the understanding of PL/SQL programs like procedures and functions. Lesson C covers some advanced PL/SQL program features like packages, triggers, and dynamic SQL.

Chapter 4 introduces Web design in two parts (Lesson A and Lesson B). Lesson A covers the essential Web application design concepts, as well as the necessary HTML statements. The lesson also provides a set of three Web page layout templates that are utilized in later chapters to explain Web application and PL/SQL Server Pages concepts. Lesson B introduces Document Object Model (DOM) and explains its use toward AJAX style Web application development.

Chapter 5 introduces PL/SQL server page in two parts (Lesson A and Lesson B). Lesson A explains the PL/SQL server pages statements and the mechanisms to embed such statements in Web page layout. Lesson B shows how to display tabular data in a Web page.

Chapter 7 covers the use of Web form to input as well as modify database values in two parts (Lesson A and Lesson B) . Lesson A introduces Web form features as well as its use for collecting data for input in a database. Lesson B focuses on modifying existing database data through Web forms.

Chapter 8 outlines the essential features of Javascript. This coverage is from the standpoint of completing AJAX development. Chapter 10 covers the essential features of Oracle XML. This coverage focuses simply on transforming database data into XML format, necessary for AJAX operations.

Chapter 9 covers the details of AJAX concepts in two parts (Lesson A and Lesson B). Lesson A introduces the AJAX concept and its operations with Text formatted data. Lesson B covers the AJAX operations with XML formatted data.

Chapter 10 explore some of the additional Web application concepts like cookie and database locks in two parts (Lesson A and Lesson B). Lesson A focuses on use of cookies with PSP, while Lesson B explores the database lock mechanisms within a Web application setting.

The appendices at the end of the book further enhance a professional or students ability to develop such Web applications. These enhancements are in the form of setting up of database access descriptor (Appendix A), making portable PL/SQL Web applications (Appendix B), outlining of additional Oracle Web utilities (Appendix C), and essential mechanisms or source to upload and download files to and from PL/SQL Web application (Appendix D). Appendix E provides a brief working explanation on Oracle's free PL/SQL editor SQL Developer.

The text book utilizes the Oracle SQL Developer for SQL and PL/SQL language development. There are numerous examples and tutorials in the book to explain various concepts. Each chapter ends with Chapter Summary, Review Questions, Review Exercises, and Problem Solving Exercises. These are supposed to test the readers understanding of the concepts covered in the chapter.

TEACHING PATHS

The text book has two major components – database manipulation and Web development. Accordingly, it can be covered in one or two semester sequence. Students having prior knowledge of SQL language can cover the text book in one semester. If students have no exposure to SQL language, then Chapter 2 and Chapter 3 can be covered in more details in the first semester, while the remaining chapters can be covered in the second semester.

The Web development component of the text book can be utilized in any class where students have little or no exposure to Web design. For students with some understanding of HTML statements, the book can be incorporated with any Web (HTML) editor as Web application design features are also explained with relevant HTML tags.

ACKNOWLEDGMENT

I would like to thank my students and colleagues in providing important inputs and comments. I also appreciate the invaluable assistance I received from Oracle Meta-link support groups. Finally, I would like to take this opportunity to thank my family for having the eternal patience to withstand the sight of continuous work on the project. My wife Radhika, and children Ritika and Sharika have been a source of inspiration to accomplish something worthwhile. I also appreciate the promptness of McGraw-Hill in ensuring smooth publication of the book.

This text book will be revised for future editions. I would greatly appreciate comments and observations on the content, coverage, organization, examples, as well as errors.

Rajeev Kaula
Springfield, MO (USA)
E-Mail: rajeevkaula@missouristate.edu

READ THIS BEFORE YOU BEGIN

Data Files

To work through the examples and complete the tutorials and exercises in this book, data files need to be utilized. These data files are located on the Web at URL http://www.faculty.missouristate.edu/r/rajeevkaula.

Software Instructions

Those wishing to install the Oracle 11g database should first get the software from Oracle or download it from Oracle Technology Network (http://www.oracle.com/technology/index.html). Academic institutions associated with Oracle Academy receive the software automatically. Information on the installation of Oracle 11g database is available on Oracle Web site. Additional details are also available at http://www.faculty.missouristate.edu/r/rajeevkaula.

Oracle SQL Developer can also be downloaded from Oracle Technology Network (http://www.oracle.com/technology/index.html).

For those wishing to use an HTML editor with the book, there is a free editor (HTML Kit) available. To download HTML Kit use the URL http://www.chami.com/html-kit/.

CHAPTER 1

Internet and PL/SQL Server Pages

- Internet
- Web Application
- Relational Model
- Sample Databases

INTRODUCTION

Internet is a worldwide collection of computer networks that are connected to each other for the purpose of sharing and exchanging of information. The *World Wide Web* (or simply the *Web*) is part of the Internet that provides information to computers connected to the Internet. The Web organizes its resources in a common way so that the information can be easily stored, transferred, and displayed among the various types of computers connected to it. Businesses use the Web regularly for everything from advertising to retailing.

The exchange of information on the Web is done through an electronic document called a *Web page*. Each page contains information ranging from simple text to complex multimedia. A *Web site* is a set of related Web pages that are linked together. A Web site has some goal or purpose, and the Web pages within the site are developed for achieving this objective. For example, a retail company Web site will have Web pages to enable selling of products. Web pages in this case will include display of products, ordering of products, servicing of order, customer support operations, and so on.

Web pages on the Internet are classified as *static* or *dynamic*. A static Web page displays the same content during a session. A dynamic Web page content changes frequently during a session. Dynamic Web pages generally use database to display varying information.

Internet Protocols

There are two protocols that are important for working on the Internet.
- TCP/IP.
- HTTP.

TCP/IP represents protocols TCP and IP, that work together to govern the connection and transmission of information. TCP stands for Transmission Control Protocol, while IP stands for Internet Protocol. Messages sent according to this protocol contain a *header* along with the information that is being sent. This header provides instructions for transmitting the data.

1

When information/message is sent across the Internet, it is in the form of a TCP/IP *envelope*. This envelope contains information on the sender, the receiver, and other instructions to ensure that the message is sent and received correctly.

Each machine connected to the Internet, is assigned an address referred as an *IP address* or *Internet Protocol address*. This IP address is used in TCP/IP when specifying the source and destination for the transmission. An IP address is a 32-bit number, which is expressed as four numbers separated by decimal points. An example of an IP address is 146.7.120.236, wherein each number can range from 0 to 255. Since it is not easy to remember numeric addresses, naming schemes have been developed as an alias for the numeric IP address. For example, the 146.7.120.236 can have the alias gl388.missouristate.edu.

HTTP protocol is designed specifically for Web pages. HTTP stands for Hypertext Transfer Protocol. This protocol is a familiar prefix for Web page addresses.

Web Architecture

Web architecture is the setup of hardware and software to facilitate Internet working. There are two types of Web architectures – a two-tier architecture and a three-tier architecture. The two-tier architecture is sufficient for displaying static Web pages. To display dynamic Web pages, the three-tier architecture is required.

The two-tier architecture consists of multiple computers (referred as clients) connected to a server computer as shown in Figure 1-1. The client computers have a software referred as *Web Browser*, while the server computer contains a *Web Server* software.

The basic role of a Web browser is to take requests for Web pages from users, and then display those pages within the browser window. This is also referred as *rendering* of a Web page. To get the Web page, the browser needs an address (called as URL) of where the Web page is stored. Once that address is provided, the browser locates the Web page on the Internet, retrieves it, and displays it in the browser's window.

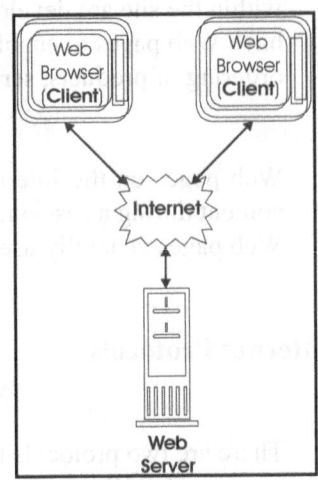

Figure 1-1 Two-tier Architecture

The URL stands for Uniform Resource Locator. Each Web page has a unique URL, and to view a Web page its URL must be known. For example, the following URL retrieves database related information from the www.oracle.com Web site.

```
http://www.oracle.com/database/index.html
```

The browser divides the URL into three parts. The first part of the URL is the HTTP protocol keyword represented as http://. This indicates that the Web page should be retrieved using the HTTP protocol. An extension of HTTP protocol is HTTPS. HTTPS protocol is used for additional security in the form of a Secure Socket Layer (SSL) on top of the HTTP protocol.

The second part of the URL is the *domain*. In this example it is "`www.oracle.com`" which identifies a (server) machine on the Internet. A domain ends with characters that give a general indication of the site's purpose, such as .com, .org, .net, .gov, .edu, and so on. There are also many country suffixes such as .uk for United Kingdom, .de for Germany, and so on.

The middle portion of the domain provides specific information on the site being accessed. In the above example it is "oracle" which stands for Oracle corporation. For name recognition, most organizations use their own name, or a familiar abbreviation for it.

The leftmost part of the domain is the actual machine name (Web server), or hostname. Many organizations use "www" as a convention, instead of a specific machine name. When a request arrives for a page on the "www" machine, the company's network has configuration files redirects such requests to the appropriate machine. Using "www" instead of a specific machine makes it easier for a company to move pages from one machine to another.

As machines on the Internet are identified by an IP address which are four numbers separated by decimal points, one can also use this numeric IP address in URL for machine identification. But it is better to use aliases like "www.oracle.com" instead of some numeric IP address as it is easier to remember. Also, another advantage of using alias is that the system administrators can associate an alias with another IP address if required without affecting the access to the site on the Internet.

When an alias is used instead of the numeric IP address in a URL, the browser has to translate the alias into a numeric IP address before it can request a Web page. To resolve the alias numeric IP address, the browser contacts a specific type of server known as a Domain Name System server, or DNS server. The browser often may have to contact several DNS servers to translate a domain name into its corresponding numeric IP address. Companies may sometimes have an internal DNS server, which must be contacted to provide further translation of domain within a company.

The third part of the URL, to the right of the domain name, is optional. It refers to the specific resource being requested. This resource can be a file name or a path to a file name. In the example, it is "`/database/index.html`" which refers to the resource called "index.html" file located in a folder called "database." *If the URL does not contain this third part, then a default page is displayed.* Most Web sites have an initial page with an address that contains only the domain name, for ease in remembering the URL.

Once the browser reads the URL, and identifies the IP address of the machine to contact, as well as the specific path and resource requested, it initiates the request. It connects to the IP address using a specific point of connection on the target server called a *port*. Port is an entry point (identified as a number) that is configured on the server machine to handle incoming requests. Generally, systems administrators configure their machines to use port 80 as the default for HTTP Web documents. For this reason, the port number is usually not included in the URL, but the port can be included (after the domain) if needed by ending the domain name by a colon followed by the port number. The above URL example could also be written as:

```
http://www.oracle.com:80/database/index.html
```

Through the connection that it has established, the browser sends a request called a GET request, for the Web page. The Web server processes the request by looking for the folder and the file requested. If the request is for a static Web page, it is transmitted back to the browser immediately. On the other hand, requests for dynamic Web pages may take longer as the Web page may have to be generated. The URL in this case may invoke the scripts that produces the page dynamically, and then transmit the completed page to the browser. If the server cannot find the resource being requested, it returns an error message to the browser. A Web server also manages a Web site besides transferring Web contents to a Web browser.

Although the user apparently requests a single Web page, that Web page may in turn initiate additional requests for files to complete the Web page. When rendering a Web page, the browser may find that the page contains several other files (like image files, audio files, etc.) which need to be also retrieved. Once the browser has received all the additional files, it assembles the Web page for display in the browser window. Examples of Web browsers are Internet Explorer, Firefox, Opera, Safari, and so on. Figure 1-2 displays the interaction between the Web browser and the Web server.

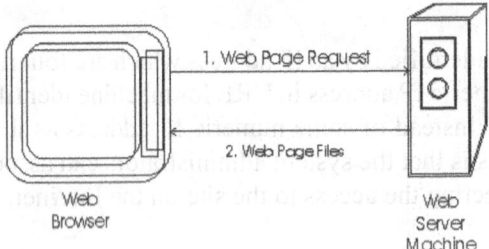

Figure 1-2   Web browser and Web
server interaction

To incorporate dynamic (or database) content in Web pages the two-tier architecture is extended to a three-tier architecture as shown in Figure 1-3. Three-tier architecture is split into three parts: the client, the Web/Application server, and the database server (DBMS).

The database level is the DBMS software (Database Management System Software) that provides the database information for the Web page. The Web/application server is referred as the *middle-tier*. The middle-tier Web server listens for requests for Web pages from the clients Web browser. When the client machines' Web browser requests Web pages from the middle-tier, the Web server routes the request to the application server for processing. The application server facilitates retrieval of information from the database server. Once the request is processed, the Web server sends the Web page to the browser that requested it. Web servers and application servers maybe on separate machines or same machine.

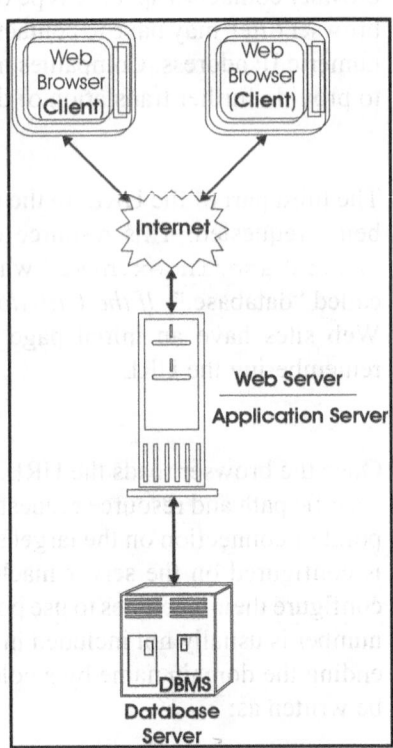

Figure 1-3   Three-tier
Architecture

Web Application

A Web application is an application deployed on the Web. It is a Web page or a series of Web pages. Web applications generally utilize dynamic Web pages to enhance application interactivity. The purpose of a Web application is to allow organizations and users to accomplish various tasks like obtaining information, shopping, customer relationship, and so on. Web applications have evolved from traditional round-trip updates of Web pages to a more desktop application style of Web page processing. Deploying an application on the Web gives an organization a way (i) to extend its reach beyond the borders of the organization, and (ii) perform various organizational activities in an optimal way.

A variation of Internet is called as *Intranet*. Intranet is an internal network like an Internet, but available within the organization. An Intranet allows employees to share information, e-mail, and perform other activities. A Web application on the Intranet allows an organization to utilize the power of the Internet to accomplish organizational tasks.

Web Development

Each Web page is written in a language called HTML (Hypertext Markup Language). HTML is not a programming language, but a language that consists of markers (or tags) that specify how content would appear in a Web browser. Creating a Web page with HTML can be quite tedious. To simplify Web page development, many Web authoring software like NetObjects Fusion and Dreamweaver have emerged. These software require little understanding of HTML to construct Web pages and associated Web sites.

HTML is sufficient for developing static Web pages. However, if the Web page contains database data, HTML is not appropriate. Consequently, database driven dynamic Web pages require regular programming language syntax to be mixed with HTML markers. For example, Visual Basic is a programming language that can be mixed with HTML to create Active Server Pages (ASP).

The programming language within a Web page is also referred as a *scripting* language. There are many scripting languages. Some scripting languages work within the browser (referred as client-side languages), while other scripting languages work at the server level (referred as server-side languages). For example, Javascript is a programming language that executes within a browser on the client machine. VBScript on the other hand is a programming language that executes within the server where the result of its operations are formatted in HTML and delivered to the client machine Web browser. Server-side scripts are useful if the application will be accessed by many users through different kinds of browsers.

To provide desktop like capabilities in Web applications, server-side scripts are complemented with (i) client-side scripts like Javascript, and (ii) XML type data formats. The Javascript language facilitates desktop like handling of Web applications within the Web browser window, while the XML language provides the data format to ease the transfer of data from the database server to the Web browser. The AJAX (asynchronous Javascript and XML) concept encapsulates the mechanism for providing desktop applications like framework for Web applications.

SQL is an essential component in the development of database driven dynamic Web pages. It is an industry standard database language to create and manipulate a relational database. To enhance database actions, Oracle developed a language PL/SQL (or Procedural Language/Structured Query Language) that extended the SQL language. PL/SQL added sophisticated logic control structures to the SQL language. Currently, PL/SQL is also the Oracle's primary database language.

Oracle developed a server-side script approach to facilitate database driven dynamic Web pages called as *PL/SQL Server Pages (PSP)*. The PL/SQL server page uses the database language PL/SQL as a scripting language along with HTML to generate database driven Web pages. Since PL/SQL is optimized for database operations, the resulting Web pages are more efficient in database interactivity. PL/SQL server pages are stored within the Oracle server (DBMS). To enhance the utility of a Web page, it is possible to embed Javascript or other client-side script code in a PL/SQL server page.

Since PL/SQL is compiled and stored directly in the database, it has the distinct advantage of being fast. It does not require compilation or interpretation at runtime, and it interacts with the database server quickly. Other technologies like ASP, JSP, Perl, etc. that generate database driven Web pages require many trips to and from the database server while generating the Web page. As PL/SQL is resident within the database, such back-and-forth trips are avoided. Further, when dealing with large volumes of data, having the logic within the database speeds up the processing and the generation of Web pages. Besides, it is also possible to utilize the security of the database for Web applications.

In this book, elementary HTML is utilized to compose Web pages and outline the creation of PL/SQL server pages. To ensure understanding of AJAX concepts, the book covers the essential features of Javascript and XML language. Any HTML editor can be utilized to compose Web pages with PSP and AJAX capabilities.

RELATIONAL MODEL

Knowledge of relational model is necessary to design PL/SQL server pages and facilitate its interaction with Oracle DBMS. A relational model is a data model for representing organizational data requirements. Since a relational model does not transform user/work requirements easily into its structure, another logical model like *entity-relationship* model is utilized as a front-end to capture data requirements more appropriately. The data model defined through the entity-relationship model is then transformed into a relational model. A brief overview of the relational model is now provided.

Relational model organizes and structures data in the form of two-dimensional tables called as *relation*. For example, the following table APARTMENT has many rows and columns.

APARTMENT

APT_NO	APT_TYPE	APT_STATUS	APT_UTILITY	APT_DEPOSIT_AMT	APT_RENT_AMT
100	0	V	Y	200	300
101	0	V	N	200	300
102	0	V	Y	200	300
...	...	...	...	...	...

The rows of the table are referred as *tuples*, while the columns are referred as *attributes*. Attributes are also referred as fields sometimes. Each table supposedly refers to some entity in the users work environment. There are some basic rules that need to be followed while defining tables.

1. A table name is unique in the database.
2. Attribute names are unique within a table.
3. No two tuples will be the same. In other words, duplicate rows are not allowed.
4. All attributes in a tuple are single valued only. In other words, an attribute cannot have more than one value in each row.
5. There is no ordering among tuples or attributes.
6. Each table should have a *primary key*. Primary key is one or more attribute whose values are unique for each row of the table.

The final structure of a table is derived through the process of *normalization*. Normalization is a concept that enables a stable grouping of attributes such that a tables' structure does not become inconsistent during data manipulation. Normalization is outside the purview of this book. Normalization also facilitates the identification of attributes that form the key structure of a table.

Tables in a relational model are connected to each other through the concept of database *relationships*. These database relationships (also called as *binary relationships*) define the logical link between two tables at a time. There are three forms of database relationships:

*   one-to-one (1:1).
*   one-to-many (1:N).
*   many-to-many (M:N).

All relationships are defined (logically) through the concept of *foreign key*. Foreign key is an attribute in one table that contains values which are also the primary key values in another table. For example in Figure 1-4, APT_NO is the key of the table APARTMENT in the Superflex Apartment database. Now if the RENTAL table has APT_NO as a foreign key attribute in its structure, it means that it can only have values that exist for APT_NO attribute in the APARTMENT table. Foreign key attribute names need not be the same as their related primary key names.

One-to-one (1:1) relationship exists if a row/tuple of one table is related to only one row/tuple of another table. To represent 1:1 relationship, foreign key will appear in either of the two tables (but not both). For example the relationship between the APARTMENT and RENTAL tables shown in Figure 1-4 is 1:1. The foreign key (APT_NO) attribute appears in the RENTAL table.

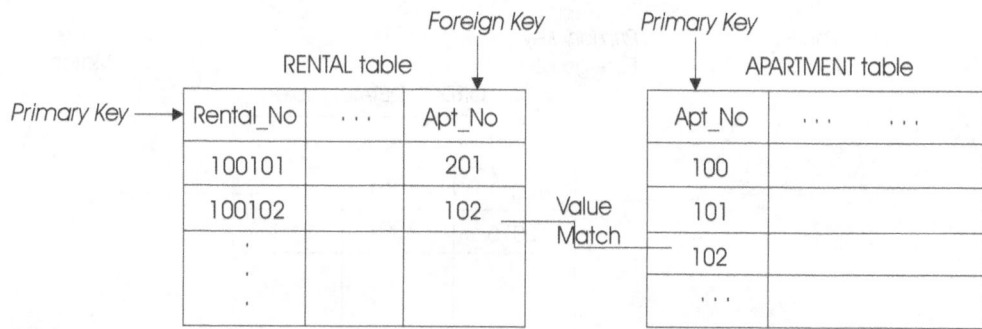

Figure 1-4 1:1 Relationship Representation

One-to-many (1:N) relationship exists if a row/tuple of one table is related to many rows/tuples of another table. To represent 1:N relationship, foreign key is placed in the table that represents the many part of the relationship. For example in Figure 1-5, the relationship between RENTAL and RENTAL_INVOICE tables of Superflex Apartment database is 1:N. RENTAL_INVOICE table represents the many part of the relationship. So, the foreign key (RENTAL_NO) appears in the RENTAL_INVOICE table.

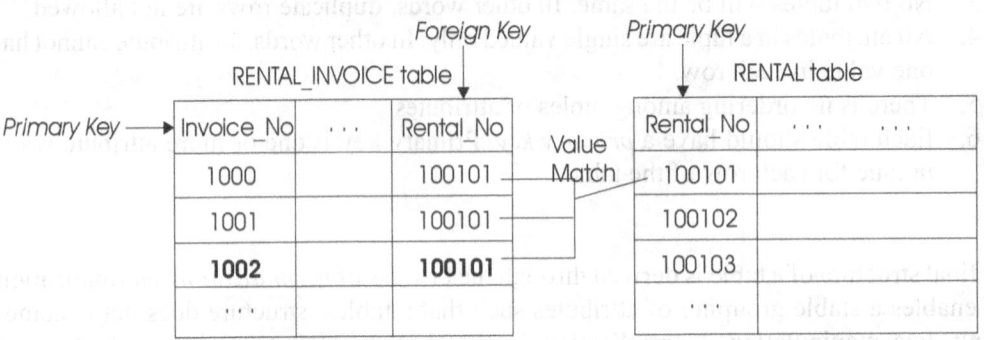

Figure 1-5   1:N Relationship Representation

Many-to-many (M:N) relationship exists if a row/tuple of one table is related to many rows/tuples of another table and vice-versa. To represent M:N relationship, a new table is created. This new table (referred as an intersection table) has the primary key attributes of the table s that have M:N relationship. The attributes of the intersection table are also the primary keys as well as foreign keys. For example Figure 1-6 shows the M:N relationship between the PRODUCT table and PRODUCT_ORDER table of Outdoor Clubs & Product database through an intersection table called ORDER_DETAILS. ORDER_DETAILS table consists of only two attributes ORDER_ID and PRODUCT_ID. These two attributes together are now the primary key of the intersection table as well as individually also the foreign keys.

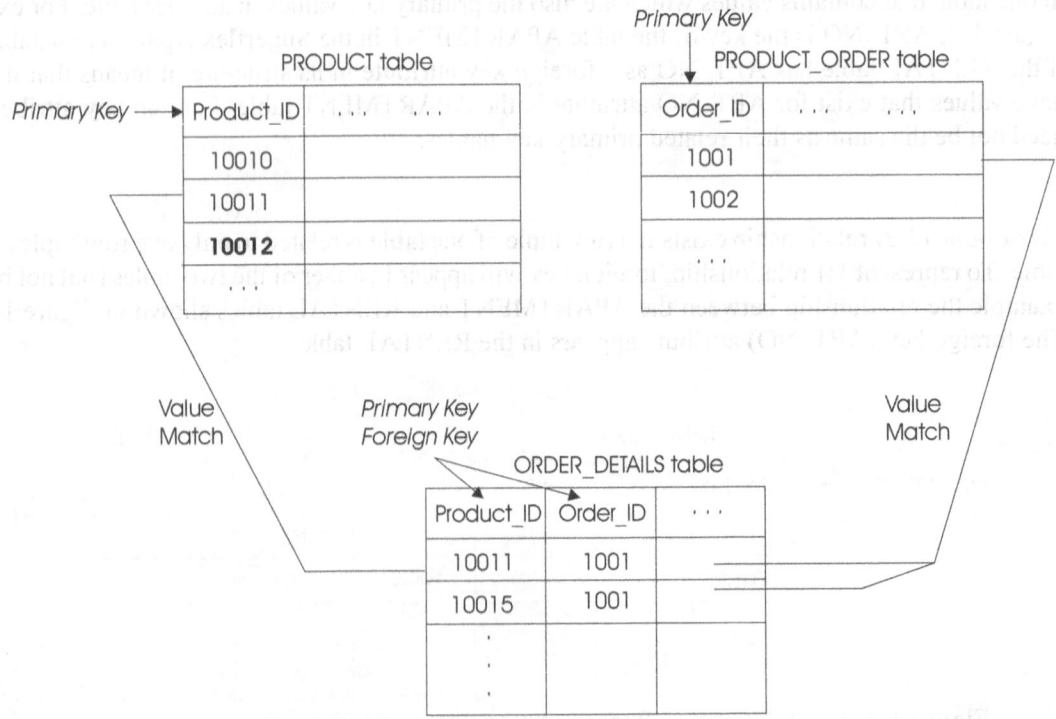

Figure 1-6   N:M Relationship Representation

SAMPLE DATABASES

In this book there are four sample databases – Superflex Apartment Database, Outdoor Clubs & Product Database, Sentiments Anywhere Database, and Travel Database. These data models are utilized to explain the use of database with respect to PL/SQL language and PL/SQL server pages.

Superflex Apartment

Superflex Apartment is a hypothetical database of an apartment complex. The Entity-Relationship Model of the database is shown in Figure 1-7.

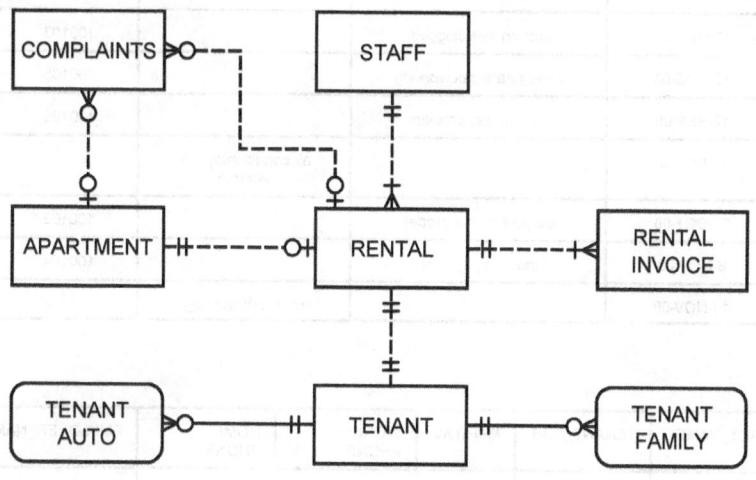

Figure 1-7

The relational model of the database in the form of tables is now provided followed by attribute description. The primary keys of a relations are shown in boldface, while the foreign keys appear in italics. An attribute that is both the primary key and foreign key appears as boldface and italics.

APARTMENT

APT_NO	APT_TYPE	APT_STATUS	APT_UTILITY	FLOORING	BALCONY	APT_DEPOSIT_AMT	APT_RENT_AMT
100	0	R	Y	Carpet	N	200	300
101	0	R	N	Carpet	N	200	300
102	0	R	Y	Carpet	N	200	300
103	1	V	N	Carpet	N	300	400
104	1	R	Y	Carpet	N	300	400
200	2	V	Y	Hardwood	Y	400	500
201	2	R	Y	Carpet	N	400	500
202	3	V	Y	Hardwood	Y	500	700
203	3	R	Y	Hardwood	Y	500	700

RENTAL

RENTAL_NO	RENTAL_DATE	RENTAL_STATUS	LEASE_TYPE	LEASE_START	LEASE_END	STAFF_NO	APT_NO
100101	12-MAY-07	O	One	01-JUN-07	31-MAY-08	SA200	201
100102	21-MAY-07	O	Six	01-JUN-07	30-NOV-07	SA220	102
100103	12-OCT-07	O	Six	01-NOV-07	30-APR-08	SA240	203
100104	06-MAR-08	O	One	01-APR-08	31-MAR-09	SA210	101
100105	15-APR-08	O	One	01-MAY-08	30-APR-09	SA220	104
100106	15-JUL-08	S	One	01-AUG-08	31-JUL-09	SA200	100

COMPLAINTS

COMPLAINT_NO	COMPLAINT_DATE	RENTAL_COMPLAINT	APT_COMPLAINT	RENTAL_NO	APT_NO	STATUS
10010	12-DEC-07	kitchen sink clogged		100103	203	F
10011	17-AUG-08	water heater not working		100105	104	F
10012	17-SEP-08	room heater problem		100105	104	P
10013	17-SEP-08		air conditioning not working		103	
10014	20-OCT-08	car parking not proper		100103		P
10015	8-NOV-08	delay in payment		100104		F
10016	16-NOV-08		utility not working		202	

TENANT

TENANT_SS	TENANT_NAME	TENANT_DOB	MARITAL	WORK PHONE	HOME PHONE	EMPLOYER_NAME	GENDER	RENTAL_NO
123456789	Jack Robin	21-JUN-60	M	4173452323	4175556565	Kraft Inc.	M	100101
723556089	Mary Stackles	02-AUG-80	S	4175453320	4176667565	Kraft Inc.	F	100102
450452267	Ramu Reddy	11-APR-62	M	4178362323	4172220565	MSU	M	100103
223056180	Marion Black	25-MAY-81	S	4174257766	4176772364	MSU	M	100104
173662690	Venessa Williams	12-MAR-70	M	4175557878	4173362565	Kraft Inc.	F	100105

TENANT_AUTO

TENANT_SS	LICENSE_NO	AUTO_MAKE	AUTO_MODEL	AUTO_YEAR	AUTO_COLOR
123456789	SYK332	Ford	Taurus	1999	Red
123456789	TTS430	Volvo	GL 740	1990	Green
723556089	ABC260	Toyota	Lexus	2000	Maroon
450452267	LLT322	Honda	Accord	2001	Blue
450452267	KYK100	Toyota	Camry	1999	Black
223056180	FLT232	Honda	Civic	1999	Red
173662690	LLT668	Volvo	GL 980	2000	Velvet

TENANT_FAMILY

TENANT_SS	FAMILY_SS	NAME	SPOUSE	CHILD	GENDER	DOB
123456789	444663434	Kay Robin	Y	N	F	21-JUN-65
450452267	222664343	Sarla Reddy	Y	N	F	11-JUN-65
450452267	222663434	Anjali Reddy	N	Y	F	10-AUG-90
173662690	111444663	Terry Williams	Y	N	F	21-MAR-68
173662690	242446634	Tom Williams	N	Y	M	20-MAY-91

RENTAL_INVOICE

INVOICE_NO	INVOICE_DATE	INVOICE_DUE	CC_NO	CC_TYPE	CC_EXP_DATE	RENTAL_NO
1000	12-MAY-07	500	1234567890123456	visa	01-DEC-10	100101
1001	30-JUN-07	500	1234567890123456	visa	01-DEC-10	100101
1002	30-JUL-07	500	1234567890123456	visa	01-DEC-10	100101
1003	30-AUG-07	500	1234567890123456	visa	01-DEC-10	100101
1004	30-SEP-07	500	1234567890123456	mastercard	01-DEC-10	100101
1005	30-OCT-07	500	1234567890123456	mastercard	01-DEC-10	100101
1006	30-NOV-07	500	1234567890123456	visa	01-DEC-10	100101
1007	30-DEC-07	500	1234567890123456	visa	01-DEC-10	100101
1008	30-JAN-08	500	1234567890123456	visa	01-DEC-10	100101
1009	21-MAY-07	300	3343567890123456	mastercard	01-OCT-11	100102
1010	30-JUN-07	300	3343567890123456	mastercard	01-OCT-11	100102
1011	30-JUL-07	300	3343567890123456	mastercard	01-OCT-11	100102
1012	30-AUG-07	300	3343567890123456	mastercard	01-OCT-11	100102
1013	30-SEP-07	300	3343567890123456	mastercard	01-OCT-11	100102
1014	30-OCT-07	300	3343567890123456	mastercard	01-OCT-11	100102
1015	30-NOV-07	300	3343567890123456	mastercard	01-OCT-11	100102
1016	12-OCT-07	700	8654567890123296	discover	01-NOV-11	100103
1017	30-NOV-07	700	8654567890123296	discover	01-NOV-11	100103
1018	06-MAR-08	500	7766567890123203	visa	01-SEP-10	100104
1019	30-APR-08	300	7766567890123203	visa	01-SEP-10	100104
1020	30-MAY-08	300	7766567890123203	visa	01-SEP-10	100104
1021	30-JUN-08	300	7766567890123203	visa	01-SEP-10	100104
1022	30-JUL-08	300	7766567890123203	visa	01-SEP-10	100104
1023	15-APR-08	700	6599567890126211	visa	01-DEC-12	100105
1024	30-MAY-08	400	6599567890126211	visa	01-DEC-12	100105
1025	30-JUN-08	400	6599567890126211	discover	01-DEC-11	100105
1026	30-JUL-08	400	6599567890126211	discover	01-DEC-11	100105

STAFF

STAFF_NO	FIRST_NAME	LAST_NAME	POSITION	STATUS	GENDER	DOB	SALARY
SA200	Joe	White	Assistant	T	M	07/08/82	24000
SA210	Ann	Tremble	Assistant	T	F	06/12/81	26000
SA220	Terry	Ford	Manager	P	M	10/20/67	53000
SA230	Susan	Brandon	Supervisor	P	F	03/10/77	46000
SA240	Julia	Roberts	Assistant	T	F	09/12/82	28000

APARTMENT table: This table contains data on apartments. Its attributes are:

APT_NO:	Unique apartment numbers. Also primary key.
APT_TYPE:	Type of apartment. Values are 0, 1, 2, 3. 0 indicates studio apartment; 1 indicates one-bedroom apartment; 2 indicates two-bedroom apartment; 3 indicates a three-bedroom apartment.
APT_STATUS:	Rental status of an apartment. Values are V (for vacant) or R (for rented).
APT_UTILITY:	Availability of utilities in an apartment. Values are Y (utilities available) or N (utilities not available).
FLOORING:	Nature of flooring in an apartment. Values are Hardwood or Carpet.
BALCONY:	Availability of balcony in an apartment. Values are Y (balcony available) or N (balcony not available).
APT_DEPOSIT_AMT:	Amount required as deposit for the apartment.
APT_RENT_AMT:	Rent for the apartment.

RENTAL table: This table contains data on rentals of various apartments. Its attributes are:

RENTAL_NO:	Unique rental number. Also primary key.
RENTAL_DATE:	Date rental contract signed.
RENTAL_STATUS:	Status of rental. Values are S (rental signed but not occupied) or O (for apartment occupancy).
LEASE_TYPE:	Type of lease. Values are One (for one year lease) or Six (for six monthly lease).
LEASE_START:	Date the current lease starts.
LEASE_END:	Date the current lease ends.
STAFF_NO:	The staff employee who handled the rental. Also foreign key to staff table.
APT_NO:	The apartment number assigned to this rental number. Also foreign key to apartment table.

COMPLAINTS table: This table contains data on complaints filed by tenants as well as employees regarding apartments. Its attributes are:

COMPLAINT_NO:	Unique complaint number. Also primary key.
COMPLAINT_DATE:	Date the complaint is filed.
RENTAL_COMPLAINT:	Description of the complaint regarding the rental.
APT_COMPLAINT:	Description of the complaint regarding the apartment.
RENTAL_NO:	The rental number of the complaint. Also foreign key to rental table.
APT_NO:	The apartment number of the complaint. Also foreign key to apartment table.
STATUS:	Status of the complaint. Values are F (fixed the complaint), P (complaint pending), or NULL (complaint situation not determined).

TENANT table: This table contains data on details of tenants in whose name the rental exists. Its attributes are:

TENANT_SS:	The social security number of the tenant. Also the primary key.
TENANT_NAME:	The full name of the tenant.
TENANT_DOB:	The date of birth of the tenant.
MARITAL:	Marital status of the tenant. Values are M (for married) or S (for single).
WORK_PHONE:	Phone number of the tenant work place.
HOME_PHONE:	Phone number of the tenant apartment (home).
EMPLOYER:	The employer name of the tenant.
GENDER:	Gender of the tenant. Values are M (for male) or F (for female).
RENTAL_NO:	Rental number of the tenant. Also foreign key.

TENANT_AUTO table: This table contains data on automobiles parked belonging to a tenant. Its attributes are:

TENANT_SS:	The social security number of the tenant. Also primary key as well as foreign key to tenant table.
LICENSE_NO:	The plate number of the automobile. Also primary key.
AUTO_MAKE:	The manufacturer of the automobile.
AUTO_MODEL:	The model name of the automobile.
AUTO_YEAR:	The year of the model.
AUTO_COLOR:	The color of the automobile.

TENANT_FAMILY table: This table contains data on other person details who are sharing the apartment with the tenant. Its attributes are:

TENANT_SS:	The social security number of the tenant. Also primary key as well as foreign key to tenant table.
FAMILY_SS:	The social security number of the other person. Also primary key.
NAME:	The full name of the person.
SPOUSE:	Identification of whether the person is a spouse of the tenant. The values are Y (yes) or N (no).
CHILD:	Identification of whether the person is a child of the tenant. The values are Y (yes) or N (no).
GENDER:	Gender of the person. Values are M (for male) or F (for female).
DOB:	The date of birth of the person.

RENTAL_INVOICE table: This table contains data on payment of rent by tenants. Its attributes are:

INVOICE_NO:	Unique invoice number. Also primary key.
INVOICE_DATE:	Date on which invoice generated.
INVOICE_DUE:	Amount due for the rent.
CC_NO:	Credit card number for the payment.
CC_TYPE:	Type of credit card used toward payment.
CC_EXP_DATE:	Date of expiration on the credit card.
RENTAL_NO:	Rental number associated with the payment. Also foreign key to rental table.

STAFF table: This table contains data on employees who work at Superflex Apartments. Its attributes are:

STAFF_NO:	Unique staff numbers. Also primary key.
FIRST_NAME:	First name of staff employee.
LAST_NAME:	Last name of staff employee.
POSITION:	Job title of staff employee.
STREET:	Street address.
CITY:	City name.
STATE:	State name.
ZIP:	Zip code.
PHONE:	Home phone number.

Outdoor Clubs & Product

Outdoor Clubs & Product is a hypothetical database of a sporting agency that provides services in the form of enrollment in outdoor clubs as well as outdoor sport products. The Entity-Relationship Model of the database is shown in Figure 1-8.

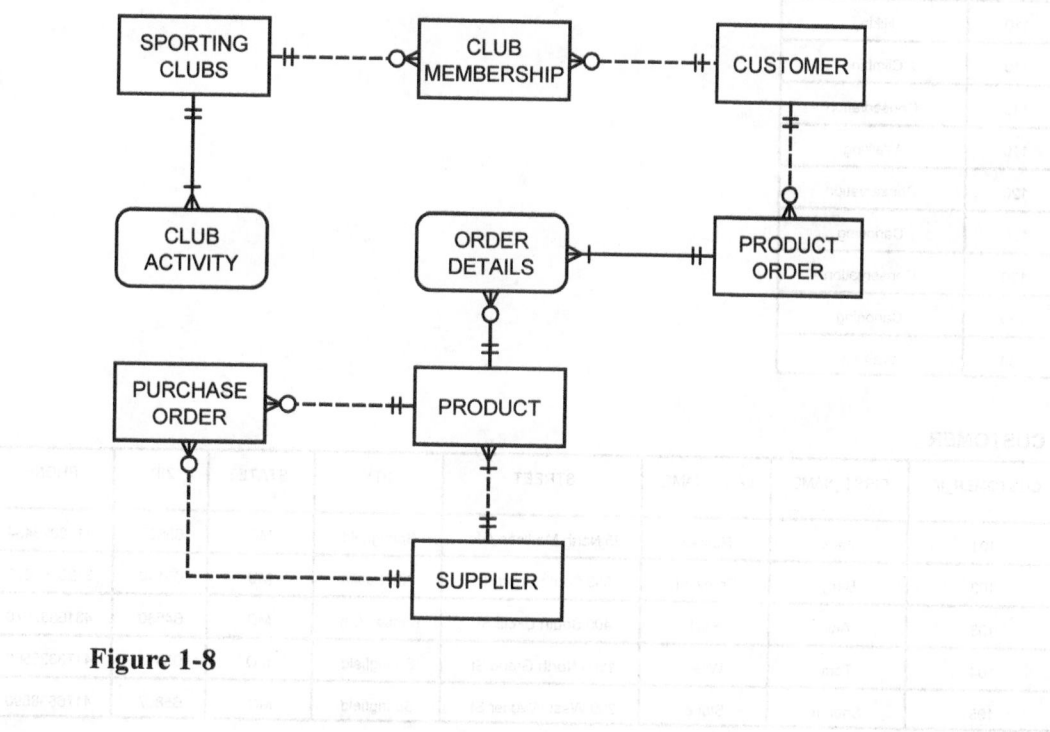

Figure 1-8

The relational model of the database in the form of tables is now provided followed by attribute description. The primary keys of a relations are shown in boldface, while the foreign keys appear in italics. An attribute that is both the primary key and foreign key appears as boldface and italics.

SPORTING_CLUBS

CLUB_ID	NAME	STREET	CITY	STATE	ZIP	PHONE
100	Hillside Mountain Club	1 Winona St	Wichita	KS	34342	3163997676
110	Branson Climbing Club	2 Sherwood Dr.	Branson	MO	65670	4174485676
120	Cherokee Rafting Club	44 Kent Ave.	St. Charles	MO	66572	3147780870
130	White Plains Club	225 Tracy St.	New York	NY	13567	2126678090

SUPPLIER

SUPPLIER_ID	NAME	STREET	CITY	STATE	ZIP	PHONE
S500	Hillside Ski	2717 S Western Ave	Los Angeles	CA	90006	7146654959
S510	Tiger Mountain	2600 S Vermont Ave	Los Angeles	CA	90006	7143327878
S520	Asha Outdoor	44 S. LaSalle St.	Chicago	IL	60603	3125554678
S530	Sheraton Recreation	225 Tracy St.	New York	NY	13567	2128889569

CLUB_ACTIVITY

CLUB_ID	ACTIVITY
100	Hiking
100	Climbing
100	Walking
110	Hiking
110	Climbing
110	Conservation
110	Walking
120	Conservation
120	Canoeing
130	Conservation
130	Canoeing
130	Walking

CUSTOMER

CUSTOMER_ID	FIRST_NAME	LAST_NAME	STREET	CITY	STATE	ZIP	PHONE
101	Jack	Russell	25 North Madison Ave.	Springfield	MO	65807	4178823434
102	Betty	Trumbell	550 South Court Dr.	St. Louis	MO	63140	3125556670
103	Anil	Kaul	400 South Circle St.	Kansas City	MO	64530	4316667070
104	Tom	Wiley	1500 North Grand St.	Springfield	MO	65810	4178825560
105	Sharon	Stone	200 West Wagner St.	Springfield	MO	65807	4176668890

PRODUCT

PRODUCT_ID	PRODUCT_NAME	QUANTITY_IN_STOCK	REORDER_POINT	PRICE	SUPPLIER_ID	REORDER_QTY
10010	Beginner's Ski Boot	20	5	9.75	S500	25
10011	Intermediate Ski Boot	18	5	12.99	S500	20
10012	Pro Ski Boot	21	7	15.49	S510	25
10013	Beginner's Ski Pole	15	3	25.49	S500	20
10014	Intermediate Ski Pole	20	3	29.99	S520	22
10015	Pro Ski Pole	21	5	34.99	S530	25
10016	Road Bicycle	15	4	34.95	S520	18
10017	Mountain Bicycle	19	4	49.99	S520	20
10018	Tire Pump	8	2	7.99	S530	10
10019	Water Bottle	25	4	2.49	S510	25
10020	Bicycle Tires	30	5	4.99	S500	33
10021	Bicycle Helmet	23	6	10.95	S510	25

CLUB_MEMBERSHIP

MEMBERSHIP_ID	MEMBERSHIP_DATE	DURATION	AMOUNT	PAYMENT_TYPE	CLUB_ID	CUSTOMER_ID
10010	12-JUN-08	4	200	CC	100	101
10020	15-JUN-08	2	100	Check	110	102
10030	21-JUN-08	5	250	Check	120	103

PRODUCT_ORDER

ORDER_ID	ORDER_DATE	SHIP_DATE	PAYMENT_TYPE	TOTAL	CUSTOMER_ID
1001	27-MAY-08	01-JUN-08	CC	130.95	102
1002	28-MAY-08	02-JUN-08	CC	134.85	103
1003	28-MAY-08	03-JUN-08	Check	12.45	104
1004	05-JUN-08	10-JUN-08	CC	44.43	105
1005	06-JUN-08	08-JUN-08	Check	52.48	103
1006	08-JUN-08	12-JUN-08	CC	131.94	104

PURCHASE_ORDER

PO_NO	PO_DATE	PRODUCT_ID	QUANTITY	SUPPLIER_ID
PO11	25-MAY-08	10011	20	S500
PO12	12-MAY-08	10015	25	S530
PO13	25-JUN-08	10011	20	S500
PO14	25-JUN-08	10018	10	S530
PO15	10-JUL-08	10015	25	S530
PO16	21-JUL-08	10019	25	S510

ORDER_DETAILS

ORDER_ID	PRODUCT_ID	QUANTITY
1001	10011	2
1001	10015	3
1002	10011	5
1002	10016	2
1003	10019	5
1004	10018	3
1004	10011	1
1004	10019	3
1005	10017	1
1005	10019	1
1005	10021	1
1006	10012	4
1006	10015	2

SPORTING_CLUBS table: This table contains data on mountain clubs. Its attributes are:

CLUB_ID:	Unique club number. Also primary key.
NAME:	Name of the mountain club.
STREET:	Street address.
CITY:	City name.
STATE:	State name.
ZIP:	Zip code.
PHONE:	Business phone number.

SUPPLIER table: This table contains details on the suppliers who provide outdoor sport products to the sporting agency for sale. Its attributes are:

SUPPLIER_ID:	Unique supplier number. Also primary key.
NAME:	Name of the supplier.
STREET:	Street address.
CITY:	City name.
STATE:	State name.
ZIP:	Zip code.
PHONE:	Business phone number.

CLUB_ACTIVITY table: This table contains data on activities offered by sporting club. Its attributes are:

CLUB_ID:	Unique club number. Also primary key as well as foreign key to sporting_clubs table.
ACTIVITY:	Name of the sporting activity. Also primary key.

CUSTOMER table: This table contains details on customers. Its attributes are:

CUSTOMER_ID:	Unique customer number. Also primary key.
FIRST_NAME:	First name of the customer.
LAST_NAME:	Last name of the customer.
STREET:	Street address.
CITY:	City name.
STATE:	State name.

ZIP:	Zip code.
PHONE:	Home phone number.

PRODUCT table: This table contains list of products being sold. Its attributes are:

PRODUCT_ID:	Unique product number. Also primary key.
PRODUCT_NAME:	Name of the product.
QUANTITY_IN_STOCK:	The number of product quantity in stock.
REORDER_POINT:	The number of product quantity to re-order the product.
PRICE:	The price of the product.
SUPPLIER_ID:	The supplier number who provided the outdoor product. Also foreign key to supplier table.
REORDER_QTY:	The quantity of the product that should be ordered from the supplier in a typical purchase order.

CLUB_MEMBERSHIP table: This table contains details on club membership. Its attributes are:

MEMBERSHIP_ID:	Unique membership number. Also primary key.
MEMBERSHIP_DATE:	Date membership acquired.
DURATION:	Duration of membership (in months).
AMOUNT:	Membership amount paid.
PAYMENT_TYPE:	Method of membership payment. Values are credit card (CC) or check (Check).
CLUB_ID:	The club number for the membership. Also foreign key to sporting_clubs table.
CUSTOMER_ID:	The customer number for the membership. Also foreign key to customer table.

PRODUCT_ORDER table: This table contains details on order placed for different products. Its attributes are:

ORDER_ID:	Unique order number. Also primary key.
ORDER_DATE:	Date order received.
SHIP_DATE:	Date order shipped.
PAYMENT_TYPE:	Method of order payment. Values are credit card (CC) or check (Check).
TOTAL:	Total amount of the order.

CUSTOMER_ID: The customer number for the order. Also foreign key to customer table.

PURCHASE_ORDER table: This table providing details on products that are re-ordered from suppliers. Its attributes are:

PO_NO: Unique purchase order number. Also primary key.

PO_DATE: Date of purchase order.

PRODUCT_ID: The product number of the outdoor product being re-ordered. Also foreign key to product table.

QUANTITY: The quantity of the product that is being re-ordered from the supplier.

SUPPLIER_ID: The supplier number who provides the outdoor product. Also foreign key to supplier table.

ORDER_DETAILS table: This table contains data on the quantity of product within an order. Its attributes are:

ORDER_ID: Unique order number. Also primary key as well as foreign key to product_order table.

PRODUCT_ID: Unique product number. Also primary key as well as foreign key to product table.

QUANTITY: Quantity of product ordered.

Sentiments Anywhere

Sentiments Anywhere is a hypothetical database of an online company offering sentiments for different occasions. The Entity-Relationship Model of the database is shown in Figure 1-9.

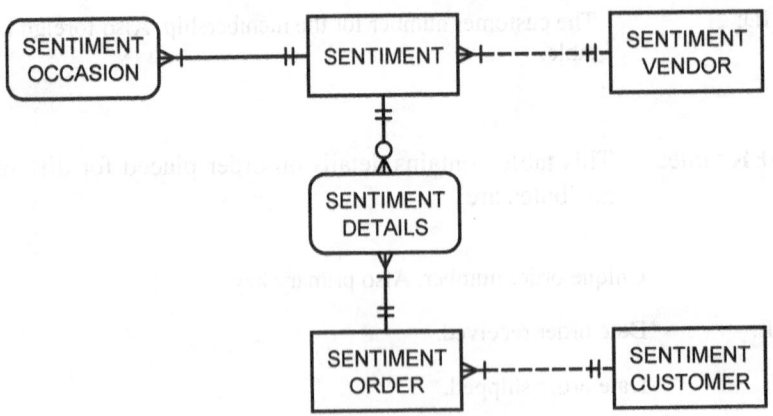

Figure 1-9

The relational model of the database in the form of tables is now provided followed by attribute description. The primary keys of a relations are shown in boldface, while the foreign keys appear in italics. An attribute that is both the primary key and foreign key appears as boldface and italics.

SENTIMENT_CUSTOMER

CUSTOMER_ID	FIRST_NAME	LAST_NAME	STREET	CITY	STATE	ZIP	PHONE
101	Tracy	Bussell	125 N. Madison Ave.	St. Louis	MO	63140	3128823434
102	Lacy	George	550 South Court Dr.	Springfield	MO	65810	4175556670
103	Sania	Raina	420 South Circle St.	Kansas City	MO	64530	4316667171
104	Tom	Peters	2500 S. Grand St.	Springfield	MO	65810	4178625577
105	Sharon	Key	1200 West Wagner St.	Springfield	MO	65807	4176648450

SENTIMENT_VENDOR

VENDOR_ID	NAME	STREET	CITY	STATE	ZIP	PHONE
1	Flower Fresh	123 Jackson Street	New York	NY	10042	6078823434
2	Rose Way	121 Gold Street	New York	NY	10038	6075556670
3	Small Treats	300 Baronne Street	New Orleans	LA	70115	5046667070
4	Wonder Works	155 St. Charles Ave.	New Orleans	LA	70130	5048825560

SENTIMENT_ORDER

ORDER_ID	ORDER_DATE	SHIP_DATE	PAYMENT_TYPE	SUBTOTAL	SHIPPING	CUSTOMER_ID
1001	27-MAY-08	01-JUN-08	CC	86.97	6.00	101
1002	28-MAY-08	02-JUN-08	CC	104.97	8.50	102
1003	28-MAY-08	03-JUN-08	Check	34.95	6.00	103
1004	05-JUN-08	10-JUN-08	CC	189.82	6.00	103
1005	06-JUN-08	08-JUN-08	Check	184.93	8.50	104
1006	08-JUN-08	12-JUN-08	CC	99.97	8.50	105

SENTIMENT

SENTIMENT_ID	NAME	PRICE	TYPE	ECOLOGY	Vendor_ID	Min_Stock	In_Stock
100	Floral Embrace	49.99	Flowers	N	2	3	10
101	Red Bouquet	36.99	Flowers	N	2	4	12
102	Musical Bouquet	49.99	Flowers	O	1	2	15
103	Pink Perfection	44.99	Flowers	N	1	3	17
104	Rose Elegance	34.99	Flowers	N	1	4	18
105	First Bloom Bouquet	45.99	Flowers	O	1	2	14
106	Rose Lover's Bouquet	45.99	Flowers	N	2	3	16
107	White Glow	89.95	Flowers	O	2	3	19
108	Balloon Bouquet	34.95	Flowers	N	2	4	12
109	Recovery Bouquet	39.99	Flowers	N	1	4	14
110	July Lily's	29.95	Flowers	N	1	2	13
111	Rustic Wildflower	34.95	Flowers	N	1	3	17
112	Simple Thanks	29.95	Flowers	N	1	4	19
113	Happy Bearwish	24.99	Gift	N	3	4	21
114	Home Candle Set	24.99	Gift	N	4	4	18
115	Sentiment Box	29.95	Gift	N	3	3	22
116	Promises Small Tray	34.95	Gift	N	3	2	15
117	Heart Wreath	34.95	Gift	N	4	3	19
118	Bear Love	29.99	Gift	N	4	3	20
119	Smiling Joe	24.99	Gift	N	3	2	18
120	Vanity Dish	34.95	Gift	N	3	4	24

SENTIMENT_DETAILS

ORDER_ID	SENTIMENT_ID	QUANTITY
1001	101	1
1001	113	2
1002	103	1
1002	118	2
1003	108	1
1004	118	3
1004	115	1
1004	116	2
1005	102	1
1005	103	1
1005	107	1
1006	100	1
1006	113	2

SENTIMENT_OCCASION

SENTIMENT_ID	OCCASION
100	Birthday
100	Anniversary
101	Birthday
101	Thank You
102	Birthday
102	Get Well
103	Birthday
103	Anniversary
103	Wedding
104	Anniversary
105	Anniversary
105	Wedding
106	Wedding
107	Wedding
108	Get Well
109	Get Well
110	Thank You
111	Thank You
112	Thank You
113	Birthday
113	Get Well
114	Birthday
114	Get Well
114	Anniversary
115	Birthday
115	Wedding
115	Thank You
116	Wedding
117	Anniversary
118	Anniversary
119	Get Well
120	Thank You
120	Anniversary

SENTIMENT_CUSTOMER table: This table contains details on customers. Its attributes are:

CUSTOMER_ID: Unique customer number. Also primary key.

FIRST_NAME: First name of the customer.

LAST_NAME: Last name of the customer.

STREET:	Street address.
CITY:	City name.
STATE:	State name.
ZIP:	Zip code.
PHONE:	Home phone number.

SENTIMENT_VENDOR table: This table contains details on vendors. Its attributes are:

VENDOR_ID:	Unique vendor number. Also primary key.
NAME:	Name of the vendor company.
STREET:	Street address.
CITY:	City name.
STATE:	State name.
ZIP:	Zip code.
PHONE:	Vendor phone number.

SENTIMENT_ORDER table: This table contains details on order placed for different sentiments. Its attributes are:

ORDER_ID:	Unique order number. Also primary key.
ORDER_DATE:	Date order received.
SHIP_DATE:	Date order shipped.
PAYMENT_TYPE:	Method of order payment. Values are credit card (CC) or check (Check).
SUBTOTAL:	Total amount of the order.
SHIPPING:	Shipping and handling cost.
CUSTOMER_ID:	The customer number for the order. Also foreign key to sentiment_customer table.

SENTIMENT table: This table contains details on sentiments offered. Its attributes are:

SENTIMENT_ID:	Unique customer number. Also primary key.
NAME:	Name of the sentiment.
PRICE:	Price of the sentiment.
TYPE:	Type of sentiment. Values are Flowers or Gift.

ECOLOGY:	A sentiment's ecology. Values are Organic (O) or Normal (N).
VENDOR_ID:	Vendor number who is the supplier of the sentiment. Also foreign key to sentiment_vendor table.
MIN_STOCK:	Minimum units of sentiment before re-purchasing from vendor.
IN_STOCK:	The current units of sentiment in inventory.

SENTIMENT_DETAILS table: This table contains data on the quantity of sentiments within an order. Its attributes are:

ORDER_ID:	Unique order number. Also primary key as well as foreign key to sentiment_order table.
SENTIMENT_ID:	Unique sentiment number. Also primary key as well as foreign key to sentiment table.
QUANTITY:	Quantity of sentiment ordered.

SENTIMENT_OCCASION table: This table contains data on the various occasions for which a sentiment can be utilized. Its attributes are:

SENTIMENT_ID:	Unique sentiment number. Also primary key as well as foreign key to sentiment table.
OCCASION:	Name of the occasion. Also primary key.

Travel Anywhere

Travel Anywhere is a short hypothetical database for an online travel agency. The Entity-Relationship Model of the database is shown in Figure 1-10.

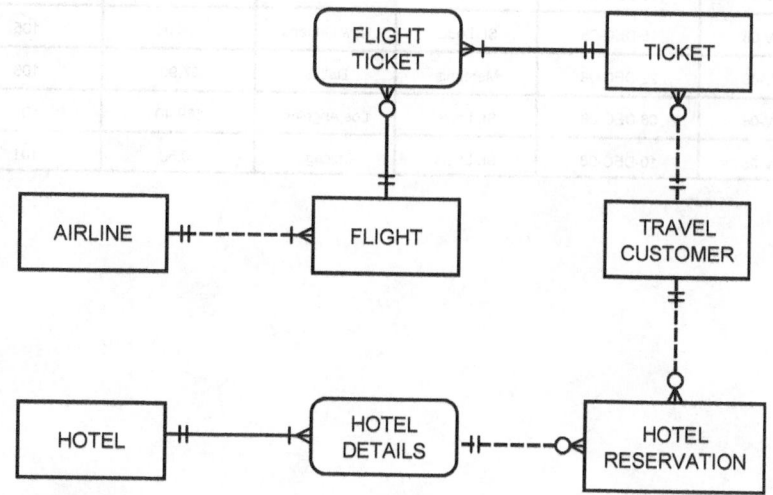

Figure 1-10

The relational model of the database in the form of tables is now provided followed by attribute description. The primary keys of a relations are shown in boldface, while the foreign keys appear in italics. An attribute that is both the primary key and foreign key appears as boldface and italics.

TRAVEL_CUSTOMER

CUSTOMER_ID	FIRST_NAME	LAST_NAME	STREET	CITY	STATE	ZIP	PHONE	AGE	MEALS	ASST
101	Jack	Russell	25 North Madison Ave.	Springfield	MO	65807	4178823434	35	R	
102	Betty	Trumbell	550 South Court Dr.	St. Louis	MO	63140	3125556670	62	V	Y
103	Tracy	Bussell	125 N. Madison Ave.	St. Louis	MO	63140	3128823434	28	R	
104	Lacy	George	550 South Court Dr.	Springfield	MO	65810	4175556670	44	R	
105	Sania	Raina	420 South Circle St.	Kansas City	MO	64530	4316667171	31	V	
106	Tom	Peters	2500 S. Grand St.	Springfield	MO	65810	4178625577	28	R	
107	Sharon	Key	1200 West Wagner St.	Springfield	MO	65807	4176648450	66	S	Y

AIRLINE

NAME	STREET	CITY	STATE	ZIP	PHONE
Tranworld	125 S. LaSalle Ave.	Chicago	IL	60611	3128879025
Global	440 S. Lindberg	St. Louis	MO	63140	3142326554

TICKET

TICKET_NO	ISSUED_DATE	FLIGHT_DATE	ORIGIN_CITY	DEST_CITY	QUOTED_FARE	CUSTOMER_ID
100501	28-OCT-08	12-DEC-08	St. Louis	Amsterdam	968.00	101
100502	30-OCT-08	14-DEC-08	Memphis	Tokyo	937.20	102
100503	02-NOV-08	22-NOV-08	Chicago	Frankfurt	447.70	103
100504	02-NOV-08	28-NOV-08	Chicago	New York	82.50	101
100505	03-NOV-08	10-DEC-08	Memphis	Las Vegas	271.70	104
100506	05-NOV-08	15-DEC-08	St. Louis	New Orleans	110.00	105
100507	05-NOV-08	22-DEC-08	Memphis	Dallas	97.90	106
100508	08-NOV-08	08-DEC-08	St. Louis	Los Angeles	169.40	107
100509	08-NOV-08	10-DEC-08	St. Louis	Chicago	60.50	101

FLIGHT

FID	FLIGHT_NO	ORG_CITY	DEST_CITY	AIR_MILES	FARE	SEATS_AVAIL	MODEL	*NAME*	ORG_REGION	DEST_REGION
1	TW122	Detroit	Los Angeles	1500	120	14	767	Tranworld	America	America
2	TW142	Detroit	Amsterdam	3500	760	15	747	Tranworld	America	Europe
3	TW162	Detroit	Seoul	5500	700	11	747	Tranworld	America	Asia
4	TW182	Los Angeles	Memphis	1250	155	2	767	Tranworld	America	America
5	TW202	Detroit	New York	1250	55	6	A300	Tranworld	America	America
6	TW222	St. Louis	Detroit	750	45	5	737	Tranworld	America	America
7	TW242	Memphis	Detroit	750	82	18	A300	Tranworld	America	America
8	TW262	Los Angeles	Tokyo	4570	650	12	747	Tranworld	America	Asia
9	TW282	Amsterdam	Rome	2570	216	3	767	Tranworld	Europe	Europe
10	TW302	Tokyo	Hong Kong	1750	103	8	747	Tranworld	Asia	Asia
11	TW322	Seoul	Hong Kong	2750	148	6	747	Tranworld	Asia	Asia
12	TW342	Los Angeles	Las Vegas	750	45	3	737	Tranworld	America	America
13	TW362	Detroit	New Orleans	1500	79	8	767	Tranworld	America	America
14	TW382	Detroit	Orlando	1670	120	4	A300	Tranworld	America	America
15	GL155	Chicago	New York	1750	75	15	767	Global	America	America
16	GL175	Chicago	London	4050	445	11	A330	Global	America	Europe
17	GL195	Chicago	Seoul	4500	670	7	747	Global	America	Asia
18	GL215	Dallas	Detroit	1250	68	3	737	Global	America	America
19	GL235	Dallas	Frankfurt	3750	475	7	A330	Global	America	Europe
20	GL255	Dallas	Tokyo	5750	620	8	747	Global	America	Asia
21	GL275	New York	Frankfurt	3870	332	16	767	Global	America	Europe
22	GL295	Frankfurt	Rome	1200	178	3	767	Global	Europe	Europe
23	GL315	London	Rome	1670	140	1	A330	Global	Europe	Europe
24	GL335	Memphis	Dallas	750	89	1	737	Global	America	America
25	GL355	St. Louis	Chicago	750	55	5	737	Global	America	America
26	GL375	Chicago	Los Angeles	1250	99	5	A330	Global	America	America
27	GL395	Chicago	Las Vegas	1050	49	6	767	Global	America	America
28	GL415	Dallas	New Orleans	750	55	5	737	Global	America	America
29	GL435	St. Louis	Dallas	750	45	12	737	Global	America	America
30	GL455	Dallas	Orlando	1050	89	5	737	Global	America	America

FLIGHT_TICKET

FID	TICKET_NO
6	100501
2	100501
7	100502
1	100502
8	100502
15	100503
21	100503
15	100504
7	100505
1	100505
12	100505
29	100506
28	100506
24	100507
25	100508
26	100508
25	100509

HOTEL

HOTEL_ID	HOTEL_NAME	STREET	CITY	STATE	ZIP	PHONE
10	Iberville Suites	123 Baronne St.	New Orleans	LA	70115	5042237642
11	Iberville Suites	20 Gold Street	New York	NY	10038	2128879056
12	Imperial Palace	5200 Paradise Road	Las Vegas	NV	89119	7024823156
13	Imperial Palace	350 South Orange Ave.	Orlando	FL	32801	3216677878
14	La Quinta	1605 Sand Lake Road	Orlando	FL	32809	3218776432
15	La Quinta	175 St. Charles Ave.	New Orleans	LA	70130	5047789090
16	La Quinta	4500 Paradise Road	Las Vegas	NV	89119	7025528856
17	Iberville Suites	900 Canal Street	New Orleans	LA	70112	5042228989
18	Iberville Suites	140 St. Charles Ave.	New Orleans	LA	70130	5041123030
19	Iberville Suites	135 Lafayette Street	New York	NY	10013	2125550770
20	Imperial Palace	4940 North Rancho	Las Vegas	NV	89130	7021223058
21	La Quinta	300 E. Flamingo Road	Las Vegas	NV	89109	7028884155

HOTEL_DETAILS

HOTEL_ID	BED_TYPE	RATE	ROOMS
10	DT	125	12
10	DQ	155	5
11	DT	150	5
11	DQ	195	1
12	DT	55	8
12	DQ	68	5
13	DT	130	1
13	DQ	144	10
14	DT	135	15
14	DQ	165	2
15	DT	80	2
15	DQ	100	4
16	DT	45	3
16	DQ	65	10
17	DT	115	2
17	DQ	135	1
18	DT	105	15
18	DQ	120	8
19	DT	145	15
19	DQ	167	12
20	DT	45	12
20	DQ	60	3
21	DT	48	6
21	DQ	60	2

HOTEL_RESERVATION

RESERVE_NO	RESERVE_DATE	ARRIVAL_DATE	DEP_DATE	BABY_CRIB	NUM_ADULTS	NUM_KIDS	CUSTOMER_ID	HOTEL_ID	BED_TYPE
100601	02-NOV-08	28-NOV-08	30-NOV-08	N	1	0	101	19	DQ
100602	03-NOV-08	10-DEC-08	16-DEC-08	N	2	1	104	12	DT
100603	05-NOV-08	15-DEC-08	22-DEC-08	N	2	0	105	17	DQ
100604	12-DEC-08	22-DEC-08	28-DEC-08	N	1	0	107	14	DQ
100605	02-DEC-08	23-DEC-08	30-DEC-08	N	2	1	104	14	DT

TRAVEL_CUSTOMER table: This table contains details on customers who buy air or hotel rates from the travel agency. Its attributes are:

CUSTOMER_ID: Unique customer number. Also primary key.

FIRST_NAME: First name of the customer.

LAST_NAME:	Last name of the customer.
STREET:	Street address.
CITY:	City name.
STATE:	State name.
ZIP:	Zip code.
PHONE:	Home phone number.
AGE:	The age of the traveling customer.
MEALS:	The request for meals during the flight. Values are regular (R), or vegetarian (V), or kids (K), or special (S). Default is regular (R).
ASST:	Request for airport or hotel assistance.

AIRPLANE table: This table contains details on the airlines listed with the travel agency. Its attributes are:

NAME:	Name of the airline. Also primary key.
STREET:	Street address.
CITY:	City name.
STATE:	State name.
ZIP:	Zip code.
PHONE:	Business phone number.

TICKET table: This table contains details on ticket issued for air travel. Its attributes are:

TICKET_NO:	Unique ticket number. Also primary key.
ISSUED_DATE:	Date the ticket is issued.
FLIGHT_DATE:	Date of the flight.
ORG_CITY:	Name of the origin (departure) city.
DEST_CITY:	Name of the final destination (arrival) city.
QUOTED_FARE:	The final fare of flights on this ticket. This fare is 10% above the fare provided by the airline.
CUSTOMER_ID:	The customer number of the travel customer. Also foreign key to travel_customer.

FLIGHT table: This table contains details on air flights by various airlines. Its attributes are:

FID:	Unique flight identification number. Also primary key.
FLIGHT_NO:	Unique flight number.
ORG_CITY:	Name of the origin (departure) city.
DEST_CITY:	Name of the destination (arrival) city.
AIR_MILES:	The number of frequent flyer miles accrued for the flight.
FARE:	Fare of the flight as provided by the airline to the travel agency.
SEATS_AVAIL:	The number of seats available.
MODEL:	The type of airplane utilized for the flight.
NAME:	Name of the airline. Also foreign key to airline table.
ORG_REGION:	Geographic region of the origin (departure) city.
DEST_REGION:	Geographic region of the destination (arrival) city.

FLIGHT_TICKET table: This table provides details on flights attached to a ticket. Its attributes are:

FID:	Flight identification number. Also primary key as well as foreign key to flight table.
TICKET_NO:	Ticket number. Also primary key as well as foreign key to ticket table.

HOTEL table: This table contains details on hotels listed with the travel agency. Its attributes are:

HOTEL_ID:	Unique hotel number. Also primary key.
HOTEL_NAME:	Name of the hotel.
STREET:	Street address.
CITY:	City name.
STATE:	State name.
ZIP:	Zip code.
PHONE:	Hotel phone number.

HOTEL_DETAILS table: This table contains additional details on hotels listed with the travel agency. Its attributes are:

HOTEL_ID:	Unique hotel number. Also primary key as well as foreign key to hotel table.
BED_TYPE:	The type of room bed available. Also primary key. Values are double twins (DT) or double queens (DQ).

RATE:	Room rate per night at the hotel.
ROOMS:	The number of rooms currently available at the hotel.

HOTEL_RESERVATION table: This table contains details on hotel reservation performed by the travel agency. Its attributes are:

RESERVE_NO:	Unique reservation number. Also primary key.
RESERVE_DATE:	Date of reservation.
ARRIVAL_DATE:	Date of arrival at the hotel.
DEP_DATE:	Date of departure from the hotel.
BABY_CRIB:	Specification on need for crib for accompanying baby. Values are yes (Y) or no (N).
NUM_ADULTS:	The number of adults staying in the room.
NUM_KIDS:	The number of kids staying in the room.
CUSTOMER_ID:	The customer number of the travel customer. Also foreign key to travel_customer table.
HOTEL_ID:	The hotel number of the reservation. Also foreign key to hotel_details table.
BED_TYPE:	The type of reserved room bed. Also foreign key to hotel_details table.

LANGUAGE SYNTAX CONVENTION

The convention used in this book to describe the syntax of language or statements is as follows:

- command (reserved) words appear in uppercase letters.
- user entries appear in lower case letters and italics.

In general, Oracle commands are not case sensitive.

CHAPTER SUMMARY

▸ Internet is a worldwide collection of computer networks that are connected to each other to facilitate sharing and exchange of information.

▸ The World Wide Web (or simply the Web) is part of the Internet that provides information to computers connected to the Internet.

▸ The exchange of information on the Web is done through an electronic document called a Web page.

▸ A Web site is a related set of Web pages that are linked together.

▸ There are two protocols that are important for working on the Internet – TCP/IP and HTTP.

▸ TCP stands for Transmission Control Protocol, while IP stands for Internet Protocol.

▸ Each machine connected to the Internet, is assigned an address referred as an *IP address* or *Internet Protocol address*.

▸ HTTP protocol is designed specifically for Web pages. HTTP stands for Hypertext Transfer Protocol.

▸ The basic role of a Web browser is to take a request for a Web page from a user, and then display that page to the user.

▸ The URL stands for Uniform Resource Locator. Each Web page has a unique URL.

▸ The browser divides the URL into three parts – the HTTP protocol, the domain name, the name of the resource being requested.

▸ As machines on the Internet are identified by an IP address which are four numbers divided by decimal points, one can use the numeric IP address also in URL for machine identification.

▸ Port is an entry point (identified as a number) that is configured on the server machine to handle incoming requests.

▸ Web pages on the Internet can be referred as *static* or *dynamic* (content-driven).

▸ A static Web page displays the same content during a session.

▸ A content-driven dynamic Web page displays content from database that changes frequently.
▸ A Web application is an application deployed on the Web.

▸ Web architecture is the setup of hardware and software to facilitate Internet working.

▸ There are two types of Web architectures – a two-level architecture and a three-level architecture.

▸ The two-level architecture is sufficient for displaying static Web pages. It involves the Web browser and the Web server.

▸ The three-level architecture is required to display dynamic Web pages. It involves the Web browser, the Web server, the Application server, and the database server.

▸ Each Web page is written in a language called HTML (Hypertext Markup Language).

▸ HTML is sufficient for developing static Web pages.

▸ HTML is not sufficient for dynamic Web pages that contain database data. Consequently, database content-driven dynamic Web pages require regular programming language syntax to be mixed with HTML markers.

▸ The programming language within a Web page is sometimes also referred as a scripting language.

▸ Some scripting languages work within the browser and so are referred as client-side scripting languages.

▸ Some scripting languages work at the server level and so are referred as server-side scripting languages.

▸ Oracle extended its primary database language PL/SQL to server as a server-side scripting language.

▸ Dynamic Web pages created through the use of PL/SQL database language are called PL/SQL Server Pages (PSP).

▸ A relational model is a data model for representing organization data requirements.

▸ Relational model organizes and structures data in the form of two-dimensional tables called as relation (or table).

▸ Each table supposedly refers to some entity in users work environment.

▸ The rows of the table are referred as tuples, while the columns are referred as attributes. Attributes are also referred as fields sometimes.

▸ Each table should have a primary key. Primary key is one or more attribute whose values are unique for each row of the table.

▸ Tables in a relational model are connected to each other through the concept of database relationships.

▸ All relationships are defined (logically) through the concept of foreign key.

▸ The Superflex Apartment is a hypothetical database of an apartment complex. It contains the following tables: Apartment, Rental, Rental_Invoice, Complaints, Staff, Tenant, Tenant_Auto, and Tenant_Family.

▸ Outdoor Clubs & Product is a hypothetical database of a sporting agency that provides services in the form of enrollment in outdoor clubs as well as outdoor sport products. It contains the following tables: Sporting_Clubs, Club_Activity, Supplier, Product, Customer, Club_Membership, Product_Order, Purchase_Order, and Order_Details.

- Sentiments Anywhere is a hypothetical database of an online company offering sentiments for different occasions. It contains the following tables: Sentiment, Sentiment_Vendor, Sentiment_Customer, Sentiment_Order, Sentiment_Details, and Sentiment_Occasion.

- Travel Anywhere is a hypothetical database of an online travel agency. It contains the following tables: Airline, Flight, Travel_Customer, Ticket, Flight_Ticket, Hotel, Hotel_Reservation, and Hotel_Details.

REVIEW QUESTIONS

1. What is a Web page? How is it relevant in the Internet setup?

2. What is the role of application server in Internet setup?

3. What are the different types of scripting languages? How do they function?

4. How is a dynamic Web page different from a static Web page?

5. What is the scripting method for PL/SQL server pages?

6. How does PL/SQL server pages create Web sites?

7. List the rules for composing relations.

8. What is a primary key and foreign key?

9. Describe the various database relationships.

10. Explain the relevance of logical data models like entity-relationship model with the relational model.

REVIEW EXERCISES

1. _____ is a collection of computer networks to facilitate sharing and exchange of information.

2. The protocol of the Internet is _____.

3. The protocol to request a Web page from a browser is _____.

4. Exchange of information on the Web is done through a document called _____ page.

5. A set of related Web pages is called as a Web _____.

6. A Web page is displayed in a Web _____.

7. Each Web page has a unique _____.

8. The domain within a URL identifies each _____ on the Internet.

9. Machines on the Internet are identified by an _____ address.

10. A variation of the Internet available within an organization is called _____.

11. The port for the URL below is _____.

     http://www.amazon.com/index.html

12. Web pages on the Internet can be _____ and _____.

13. The Web architecture for static pages is _____ level.

14. The Web architecture of dynamic pages is _____ level.

15. Dynamic content in a Web page generally involves the use of _____.

16. Application server manages the interaction of the _____ with the _____.

17. Each Web page is written in _____ language.

18. HTML is sufficient for developing _____ Web pages.

19. Programming language is required for developing _____ Web pages.

20. The programming language within a Web page is also referred as a _____ language.

21. Scripting languages that execute within the browser are referred as _____ languages.

22. Scripting languages that execute on the server are referred as _____ languages.

23. PL/SQL Server Pages uses Oracle's _____ language as a _____ scripting language.

24. Each relation or table in relational model refers to an _____.

25. Attribute(s) values in a table that are unique for each row are referred as _____.

26. Relationships in a relational model are defined through the concept of _____.

27. When one row on one table is related to only one row of another table, the relationship is referred as _____.

28. When one row on one table is related to many rows of another table, the relationship is referred as _____.

29. When one row on one table is related to many rows of another table, and vice-versa, the relationship is referred as _____.

CHAPTER 2
(LESSON A)

SQL in PL/SQL

- Create tables
- Maintain database structure
- Script files

Relational model is a simple data model to store and structure data for information systems. The database language to store and manipulate data in a relational model is called SQL (structured query language). SQL is also an ANSI standard language for relational database processing. Oracle uses SQL within the framework of its PL/SQL language for application development. The SQL language in this case accomplishes the transfer and retrieval of data from the database.

There are many SQL and PL/SQL editors in the marketplace. Oracle 11g provides an editor called SQL Developer to facilitate SQL and PL/SQL language development. In this book, SQL Developer is emphasized for working with SQL and PL/SQL languages.

SQL has two major components referred as Data Definition Language (DDL) and Data Manipulation Language (DML). DDL consists of statements to create the structure of tables and their relationships. It also consists of other statements to control the administration of relational databases. DML consists of statements to manipulate data in existing tables. It consists of statements to insert a row in a table, delete rows from a table, update attribute values in a table or retrieve data from tables. The DDL statements are explained first, followed by the DML statements. Oracle generally refers to entries in its database as *objects*.

DDL statements at the user level deal with the creation and maintenance of tables, views, indexes, and so on. In this lesson, basic DDL statements are outlined.

All database object names like table names, attribute names, etc. in Oracle must follow the naming standard as shown in Table 2-1.

Naming Standard	Invalid Names Example
Spaces not allowed in between words.	Customer Order
Hyphens not allowed between words.	Customer-Order
Must begin with a letter	9Customer
Cannot exceed 30 characters	employee_social_security_numbers_column

Table 2-1: Oracle Naming Rules

37

> This lesson utilizes the table structure of Superflex Apartment database and Outdoor Clubs & Product database to explain examples.

CREATE TABLE

The SQL statement to create a new table is defined below. The constraint declarations are optional.

```
CREATE TABLE tablename
(attribute1 data type & size [CONSTRAINT constraint declaration],
attribute2 data type & size [CONSTRAINT constraint declaration],
. . .
[CONSTRAINT constraint declaration . . .]);
```

All SQL statements in Oracle are terminated by a semi-colon (;) sign.

Data Types

When a table is created, each attribute is assigned a data type, which specifies what kind of data will be stored for that attribute. Data types also serve the purpose of error checking. For example, one cannot store name "Jack" into an attribute assigned a DATE data type. Further, data types cause storage space to be more efficiently utilized by optimizing the way specific types of data are stored. The convention to define a data type is *attributename datatype-and-size*. For example, `name varchar2(20)`. The main Oracle data types include characters, numbers, dates, and large objects.

Character Data Types

Character data types consists of alphabets and numbers. Character data type value cannot be used in calculations. There are four character data types – VARCHAR2, CHAR, NVARCHAR2, and NCHAR. Any character data type specification also includes the data size.

CHAR

The CHAR data type holds fixed-length character data up to a maximum size of 2000 characters. Char data type should be used for only fixed-length data having a restricted set of values. If no data size is defined, the default size for a CHAR data type is one character. Using the CHAR data type on attributes that might not fill the complete width forces the DBMS to add trailing blank spaces. For example, if TENANT_NAME in TENANT table is declared as CHAR(20), and a data value of "Mary Stackles" is inserted, then the actual value will be stored as "Mary Stackles" plus 7 blank spaces to the right of the last character. If the inserted data is wider than the specified size, an error occurs.

VARCHAR2

The VARCHAR2 data type stores variable length character data up to a maximum of 4,000 characters. If the inserted data values are smaller than the specified size, only the inserted values are stored, and the trailing blank spaces are not added to the end of the entry to make it fill the specified attribute size. For example, if TENANT_NAME in TENANT table is declared as VARCHAR2(20), and a data value of "Mary Stackles" is inserted, then the actual value will also be stored as "Mary Stackles." If the inserted data is wider than the specified size, an error occurs.

NVARCHAR2

NVARCHAR2 data type is used to store data in non-English alphabets. Each non-English character is encoded using a Unicode coding scheme. Unicode is a standardized technique that provides a way to encode data in non-English languages. Otherwise it is similar to VARCHAR2 data type. The general syntax is *attributename* NVARCHAR2*(size)*.

NCHAR

NCHAR data type is used to store data in non-English alphabets. Each non-English character is encoded using a Unicode coding scheme. Unicode is a standardized technique that provides a way to encode data in non-English languages. Otherwise it is similar to CHAR data type. The general syntax is *attributename* NCHAR*(size)*.

Number Data Types

The NUMBER data types store positive, negative, fixed, and floating-point numbers betweeen 10^{-130} and 10^{125} with precision up to 38 decimal places. Precision is the total number of digits both to the left and to the right of the decimal point. The NUMBER data type is used for all numeric data. Whenever the NUMBER data type is declared, the precision and scale should be also specified. Scale is the number of digits to the right of the decimal point. The three NUMBER data types are integer, fixed-point, and floating-point. Also, variations of NUMBER data type exist in the form of DEC, DECIMAL, DOUBLE PRECISION, FLOAT, INTEGER, INT, NUMERIC, REAL, and SMALLINT.

INTEGERS

An integer is a whole number with no digits to the right of the decimal point. Using the NUMBER data type, only the total number of digits are specified. For example, the TENANT_SS attribute in TENANT table stores only numeric numbers, so it is declared as NUMBER(9). Alternately the declaration can also be TENANT_SS INT.

FIXED-POINT NUMBERS

A fixed-point number contains a specific number of decimal places. For example, a potential COST attribute can be declared as NUMBER(5,2). NUMBER(5,2) specification indicates that all values will have two digits to the right of the decimal point, and there are a total number of five digits. For example valid COST values are 25.95, 125.50, and so on.

FLOATING-POINT NUMBERS

A floating-point number is a number with variable number of decimal places. The decimal point can appear anywhere, from before the first digit to after the last digit, or can be omitted. Floating point values are defined by not specifying either the precision or scale in the field declaration. For example, a potential STUDENT_GPA attribute can be declared of the type NUMBER. The possible values can be like 2.575, 3.5, or 3.0.

DATE Data Type

The DATE data type stores dates from January 1, 4712 B.C. to December 31, 9999 A.D. The DATE data type stores the century, year, month, day, hour, minute, and second. The default date format is DD-MON-YY which stands for day of the month (DD), followed by month (MON), and the last two digits of the year (YY). The default time format is HH:MI:SS A.M., which indicates the hours (HH), minutes (MI), and seconds (SS) using the 12-hour clock. If no time is specified in a DATE data type, the default time value is stored as 12:00:00 A.M. If no date is specified when a time is entered in a DATE data type, the default date is the first day of the current month. For example, the TENANT_DOB attribute in TENANT table is declared as DATE data type. DATE values are stored in a standard internal format in the database, so no length specification is required.

Large Object (LOB) Data Types

LOB data types can be used to store binary data, such as digitized sounds or images, or references to binary files from a word processor or spreadsheet. There are four LOB data types – BLOB, CLOB, BFILE, and NCLOB. Each of LOB data types is briefly described below in Table 2-2.

Large Object (LOB) Data Type	Description
BLOB	Binary LOB, stores up to 4 GB of binary data.
CLOB	Character LOB, stores up to 4 GB of character data.
BFILE	Binary File, storing a reference to a binary file located outside the database.
NCLOB	Character LOB that supports 2-byte character codes in the database.

Table 2-2: Various LOB Data Types

Constraints

Constraints are rules that restrict the data values that can be entered for an attribute. There are two types of constraints – *integrity constraints* and *value constraints*. Integrity constraints are used to define primary key and foreign key specifications. Value constraints are limitations placed on attribute values such as unique values (NOT NULL), range of values, and so on. *All constraints are uniquely named in the database*. They can be placed alongside the data type declaration of an individual attribute or after all the attributes of a table have been defined.

Integrity Constraint

The general syntax for defining a *primary key constraint* after an attribute data type declaration is CONSTRAINT *constraint-name* PRIMARY KEY. For example, the following syntax creates the table SPORTING_CLUBS.

```
create table sporting_clubs
(club_id number(3)constraint sporting_clubs_pk primary key,
name varchar2(30),
street varchar2(30),
city varchar2(15),
state char(2),
zip number(5),
phone varchar2(10));
```

The syntax for separate primary key constraint declaration is CONSTRAINT *constraint-name* PRIMARY KEY (*attribute-name*). This syntax is generally used whenever the primary key consists of more than one attribute – called as *composite primary key*. For example, the following syntax creates the table TENANT_AUTO, where the primary key consists of two attributes. Keep in mind that the constraint name "tenant_auto_pk" must be unique in the database.

```
create table tenant_auto
(tenant_ss number(9),
license_no varchar2(6),
auto_make varchar2(15),
auto_model varchar2(15),
auto_year number(4),
auto_color varchar2(10),
constraint tenant_auto_pk primary key (tenant_ss,license_no));
```

The general syntax for defining a *foreign key constraint* after an attribute data type declaration is CONSTRAINT *constraint-name* REFERENCES *table name*. The foreign key attribute value has to match the primary key value of the referenced table. For example, the following syntax creates the table RENTAL_INVOICE with one foreign key.

```
create table rental_invoice
(invoice_no number(6) constraint rental_invoice_pk primary key,
invoice_date date,
invoice_due number(4),
cc_no number(16),
cc_type varchar2(10),
cc_exp_date date,
rental_no number(6) constraint rental_invoice_fk references rental);
```

In the above example, "rental" is another table, whose primary key value will be checked with the values inserted for rental_no attribute in this table.

The syntax for separate foreign key constraint declaration is CONSTRAINT *constraint name* FOREIGN KEY (*attribute-name*) REFERENCES *table name* [(*primary-key-attribute*)]. The primary-key-attribute entry is the name of the primary key of the referenced table. For example, the following syntax modifies the previous syntax to create RENTAL_INVOICE table with the foreign key declaration at the end of the attribute declarations.

```
create table rental_invoice
(invoice_no number(6) constraint rental_invoice_pk primary key,
invoice_date date,
invoice_due number(4),
cc_no number(16),
cc_type varchar2(10),
cc_exp_date date,
rental_no number(6),
constraint rental_invoice_fk FOREIGN KEY (rental_no)
references rental(rental_no));
```

When defining foreign keys, it is possible to indicate update and delete referential integrity actions. These actions are specified using the ON UPDATE and ON DELETE expressions. Oracle does not support ON UPDATE specification. The default behavior for preserving referential integrity constraints is to allow no change to the primary key if the related child row exists, and to disallow any deletion if related child rows exist.

There are three possibilities with respect to ON DELETE actions – RESTRICT, CASCADE, and SET NULL. RESTRICT will not allow deletion of a referenced key in the referenced table at all. This is the default option and so is not explicitly allowed. CASCADE will allow the deletion by deleting all dependent references to the table. SET NULL will delete the entry in the foreign key table and then set the dependent values to null. The SET NULL option indicates a optional relationship.

These actions are added after the REFERENCES clause of the CREATE TABLE statement as shown below.

```
create table rental_invoice
(invoice_no number(6) constraint rental_invoice_pk primary key,
invoice_date date,
invoice_due number(4),
cc_no number(16),
cc_type varchar2(10),
cc_exp_date date,
rental_no number(6) constraint rental_invoice_fk references rental
on delete cascade);

create table complaints
(complaint_no number(6) constraint complaints_pk primary key,
complaint_date date,
rental_complaint varchar2(100),
apt_complaint varchar2(100),
rental_no number(6) constraint complaints_fk1 references rental on delete
set null,
apt_no number(3) constraint complaints_fk2 references apartment,
status char(1) constraint complaint_status_ck check ((status = 'F') or
(status = 'P') or (status = NULL)));
```

Value Constraint

Value constraints are attribute-level constraints which restrict the nature of data values that can be entered into an attribute. Constraint specification in this category include whether an attribute can or cannot be blank or NULL, what can be the default value, what specific values or ranges can be inserted (called CHECK condition), and so on. Multiple constraints for an attribute can be defined one after the other. Some of the major value constraints are described now.

UNIQUE

The UNIQUE constraint is identical to the PRIMARY KEY constraint except that NULL values are allowed. A table can have only one PRIMARY KEY constraint, but more than one UNIQUE constraint. Further, a FOREIGN KEY generally references a PRIMARY KEY, but it can also reference an attribute with UNIQUE constraint.

For example, the following syntax creates the SPORTING_CLUB_SP table with UNIQUE constraint.

```
create table sporting_club_sp
(club_id number(3) constraint sporting_club_sp_pk primary key,
name varchar2(30) constraint sporting_club_sp_name unique,
address varchar2(50));
```

It is possible to have concatenated attributes defined as UNIQUE constraint. For example, TENANT_AUTO table may be modified as follows:

```
create table tenant_auto
(tenant_ss number(9) constraint tenant_auto_fk references tenant,
license_no varchar2(6),
auto_make varchar2(15),
auto_model varchar2(15),
auto_year number(4),
auto_color varchar2(10),
constraint tenant_auto_pk primary key (tenant_ss,license_no),
constraint tenant_auto_lic_year (license_no,auto_year) unique);
```

NOT NULL

NOT NULL constraint guarantees that an attribute has a value in a row. For example, the SPORTING_CLUB_NL table defined with NOT NULL constraint.

```
create table sporting_club_nl
(club_id number(3) constraint sporting_club_sp_pk primary key,
name varchar2(30) constraint sporting_club_sp_name not null,
address varchar2(50));
```

DEFAULT

The DEFAULT constraint is utilized to assign a default value to an attribute. In this case during the INSERT operation it is not necessary to provide a value for the attribute.

CHECK

A CHECK constraint defines a discrete list of values that an attribute can contain. This list of values can be literally expressed within the constraint definition or expressed through a conditional expression.

A CHECK constraint can also define a rule that is constructed from multiple attributes of a table. In this case, the constraint must be declared as a separate constraint clause, instead of being attached to a specific attribute. For example, a CHECK constraint can be added to the RENTAL table that ensures that the difference between LEASE_START attribute and LEASE_END attribute is six months or twelve months.

```
create table rental
(rental_no number(6) constraint rental_pk primary key,
rental_date date,
rental_status char(1),
lease_type varchar2(3),
lease_start date,
lease_end date,
apt_no number(3) constraint rental_apt_fk references apartment,
constraint rental_duration_ck check (((lease_end - lease_start) = 6) or ((lease_end
- lease_start) = 12)));
```

CHECK constraint conditional expression attributes are limited to its table. If the conditional expression depends on values in other tables or needs to reference values before/after the changes on the attribute, the CHECK constraint should not be used. Instead in such situations PL/SQL TRIGGERS should be considered.

For example, the following syntax shows another creation of the RENTAL table with the following constraint specifications:
- attribute RENTAL_DATE cannot have NULL values.
- attribute RENTAL_STATUS can have values that are either S or O or C or V.
- attribute LEASE_TYPE will have a default value of One.
- attribute LEASE_TYPE can also have values One or Six.

```
create table rental
(rental_no number(6) constraint rental_pk primary key,
rental_date date constraint rental_date_nn NOT NULL,
rental_status char(1)constraint rental_status_ck check ((rental_status = 'S') or
(rental_status = 'O') or (rental_status = 'C') or (rental_status = 'V')),
lease_type varchar2(3) default 'One' constraint lease_type_ck check ((lease_type
= 'One') or (lease_type = 'Six')),
lease_start date,
lease_end date,
apt_no number(3) constraint rental_apt_fk references apartment);
```

The following syntax is an alternative to defining the same value constraints for the RENTAL table after the listing of attributes.

```
create table rental
(rental_no number(6) constraint rental_pk primary key,
rental_date date constraint rental_date_nn NOT NULL,
rental_status char(1),
cancel_date date,
lease_type varchar2(3) default 'One',
lease_start date,
lease_end date,
apt_no number(3) constraint rental_apt_fk references apartment,
constraint rental_status_ck check ((rental_status = 'S') or (rental_status = 'O')
or (rental_status = 'C') or (rental_status = 'V')),
```

```
constraint lease_type_ck check ((lease_type = 'One') or (lease_type = 'Six'));
```

MAINTAIN DATABASE STRUCTURE

Once the table has been created additional SQL statements are needed to maintain the database. Such statements change the structure of the table, remove the table from the database, or rename existing table name. The change in table structure is accomplished through the ALTER statement, while the removing of the table from database is done through the DROP statement. The renaming is done through the RENAME statement.

ALTER Statement

The ALTER statement performs many functions. It can be used to add an attribute to an existing table, modify the data type declaration of an existing attribute, add new constraints in a table, drop existing constraints from a table, and drop an attribute from a table.

The syntax of ALTER statement to add an attribute is:

> ALTER TABLE tablename
> ADD *attribute-name   data-type-and-size* [*constraint specification*];

For example, the following SQL statement adds an attribute ESTABLISHED to the SPORTING_CLUBS table.

```
ALTER TABLE sporting_clubs
ADD established number(4);
```

The syntax of ALTER statement to modify an attribute's data type declaration is:

> ALTER TABLE tablename
> MODIFY *attribute-name   new-data-type-and-size*;

Modification of an attribute's data type declaration is allowed only if existing data in the attribute being modified is compatible with the new specification. For example, one can change a VARCHAR2 data type to a CHAR data type, but not to a NUMBER data type.

For example, the following SQL statement modifies the data type of attribute ESTABLISHED (added in the previous SQL statement) in the SPORTING_CLUBS table.

```
ALTER TABLE sporting_clubs
MODIFY established varchar2(4);
```

The syntax of ALTER statement to drop a constraint is:

```
ALTER TABLE tablename
DROP CONSTRAINT  constraint-name ;
```

For example, the following SQL statement drops the foreign key constraint in the RENTAL table.

```
ALTER TABLE rental
DROP CONSTRAINT rental_apt_fk2;
```

The syntax of ALTER statement to add a constraint specification is:

```
ALTER TABLE tablename
ADD CONSTRAINT constraint-specification ;
```

For example, the following SQL statement adds a foreign key constraint to the RENTAL table.

```
ALTER TABLE rental
ADD CONSTRAINT rental_apt_fk FOREIGN KEY (apt_no) references apartment;
```

The syntax of ALTER statement to drop an attribute from a table is:

```
ALTER TABLE tablename
DROP COLUMN attribute-name;
```

For example, the following SQL statement drops the attribute ESTABLISHED (added in the previous SQL statement) from the SPORTING_CLUBS table.

```
ALTER TABLE sporting_clubs
DROP COLUMN established;
```

DROP Statement

DROP statement is used to remove the table from the database. This is a serious statement, because once the table is dropped, all the data that may have existed in the table is also deleted. The syntax of DROP statement is:

```
DROP TABLE tablename [CASCADE CONSTRAINTS];
```

This command will not be successful if the table being dropped contains attributes referenced as foreign keys in other tables. In this case, one can either drop all of the tables that contain the foreign key references first, or drop the foreign key constraints in all of the associated tables using the CASCADE CONSTRAINTS option. When the DROP TABLE command is issued with the CASCADE CONSTRAINTS option, the system first drops all of the constraints associated with the table, and then drops the table. This allows the table to be dropped in any order, regardless of the foreign key constraints.

RENAME Statement

The RENAME statement allows the renaming of existing tables. The syntax is:

RENAME *old-tablename* TO *new-tablename*;

For example, the following syntax renames sporting_clubs table to outdoor_clubs table.

```
RENAME sporting_clubs TO outdoor_clubs;
```

Table 2-4 below shows the scope of SQL statements performing database maintenance.

Actions	Scope
Drop Tables	Dropping a table from a user schema; allowed only if the table does not contain any attributes that are referenced as foreign keys in other tables.
Increasing Attribute data type size	Allowed only if existing data in the attribute being modified is compatible with the new specification.
Decreasing Attribute data type size	Allowed only if the existing attribute values are NULL.
Adding Constraints	Adding a primary key constraint to an existing attribute allowed only if the attribute values are unique and not NULL.
	Adding a foreign key constraint is allowed only if the current attribute values are NULL or exist in the referenced table.
Adding UNIQUE Constraint	Allowed only if the current attribute values are all unique.
Adding CHECK Constraint	Allowed, but the constraint is only applied to new values that are inserted.
Changing DEFAULT value	Allowed, but the change is only applied to new values that are inserted.

Table 2-4: Database Action Scope

DATA MANIPULATION

Data manipulation statements deal with the insertion of rows in a table, modification of attribute values within a table, and deletion of rows from a table. The insertion of rows in a table is accomplished through the INSERT statement; the modification of attribute values within a table is accomplished through the UPDATE statement; and the deletion of rows from a table is accomplished through the DELETE statement.

INSERT Statement

Rows can be inserted into a table one row at a time. The INSERT statement works in two ways: (i) to insert all attribute values into a row at once, or (ii) to insert only selected attribute values. The basic syntax of INSERT statement is:

```
INSERT INTO tablename [(attribute1-name, attribute2- name, . . .)]
VALUES (attribute1-value, attribute 2-value, . . .);
```

When all attribute values are being inserted, the optional listing of attribute names is not needed. *Also, when all table attribute values are being inserted in a row, the listing of attribute values should follow the existing sequence of attributes in the table (defined through the CREATE TABLE statement).*For example, the following SQL statement inserts a row in SPORTING_CLUBS table.

```
insert into sporting_clubs
values(100, 'Hillside Mountain Club','1 Winona St',
'Wichita','KS',34342,'3163997676');
```

If an attribute does not have a value, a NULL keyword value should be used instead as a substitute for the blank value. For example, the following SQL statement inserts a row in SPORTING_CLUBS table where values for only two out of seven attributes are available.

```
insert into sporting_clubs
values(400, 'Vintage Club', null, null, null, null, null);
```

If data for all attribute values will not be inserted, then those attributes for which data is available should be listed. In this case the sequence of attribute names in the syntax and their corresponding values should match. For example, the following SQL statement inserts a row with values for only two attributes in SPORTING_CLUBS table.

```
insert into sporting_clubs (club_id, name)
values(200, 'Branson Climbing Club');
```

Insert Text with Quotation Mark

To insert text with quotation mark, one needs to enter the single quotation mark twice. For example, the following SQL statement inserts a row in the SPORTING_CLUBS table, where the NAME attribute has a quotation string.

```
insert into sporting_clubs (club_id, name)
values(600, 'Jimmy''s Climbing Club');
```

Insert Values with Decimals

To insert values with decimals, the decimal point should be inserted with the value. For example, the following SQL statement inserts a row in the PRODUCTS table, where the PRICE attribute has a decimal value.

```
insert into product (product_id,product_name,price)
values(10025,'Back Pack SX',6.49);
```

Insert Values in DATE Data Type

Date values are character strings. To insert values in DATE data type, format masks have to be used. Oracle keeps date values in an internal format. The TO_DATE function is used to transfer the date value (character string) into the internal format. The general syntax of the TO_DATE function is TO_DATE('<date character string>', '<date format mask>'). Various date format masks exist in Oracle as shown in Table 2-5 below.

Format	Description	Example
MONTH	Name of month	June
MON	Three-letter abbreviation for month name.	JUN
MM	Two-digit numeric value of the month.	06
D	Numeric value for day of the week.	Wednesday = 4
DD	Numeric value for the day of the month (01-31).	25
DDD	Numeric value for the day of the year (01-366).	150
DAY	Name of the day of the week upto 9 characters.	Wednesday
DY	Three-letter abbreviation for day of the week.	WED
YYYY	Displays the four-digit year	2008
YYY or YY or Y	Displays the last three, two, or single digit of the year.	008, 08, 8
YEAR	Spells out the year.	TWO THOUSAND EIGHT
HH	Displays hours of the day using 12-hour clock.	06
HH24	Displays hour of the day using 24-hour clock.	17

Table 2-5: Date Format Masks

Format	Description	Example
MI	Displays minutes (0-59)	45
SS	Displays seconds (0-59)	35

Table 2-5: Date Format Masks

Format masks can be created by including front slashes, hyphens, and colons as separators between different date elements. For example, the format mask MM/DD/YY for October 15, 2008 would appear as 10/15/08. It is possible to include additional characters such as commas, periods, and blank spaces. For example, the format mask DAY, MONTH DD, YYYY for January 15, 2008 would appear as TUESDAY, JANUARY 15, 2008. Time mask can be like HH:MI:SS to stand for 04:35:50.

To insert date values, the TO_DATE function can be defined as `TO_DATE('5/15/2008', 'MM/DD/YYYY')` for character string '05/15/2008.' Similarly '22-AUG-2008' would be represented as `TO_DATE('22-AUG-2008', 'DD-MON-YYYY')`.

The following SQL statement inserts a row in the TENANT_FAMILY table having a date data type.

```
insert into tenant_family
values(123456789,444663434,'Kay Robin', 'Y', 'N','F',
to_date('6/21/1965','mm/dd/yyyy'));
```

To insert time values in a date attribute, use either the 24-hour clock or the 12-hour clock. The following examples show the use of 24-hour clock and 12-hour clock to insert a new row in RENTAL table.

```
insert into rental (rental_no,rental_date)
Values(100110,to_date('15:30','hh24:mi'));

insert into rental (rental_no,rental_date)
Values(100111,to_date('2:30','hh:mi pm'));
```

UPDATE Statement

An important manipulation operation is modifying existing data using the UPDATE statement. The syntax for UPDATE is

```
UPDATE tablename
SET attribute1 = new-value1 [, attribute2 = new-value2, . . .]
[WHERE search condition ];
```

It is possible to update multiple attributes in a table using a single UPDATE statement, but only one table can be updated at one time. Search conditions can be specified in the WHERE clause to make the update operation row specific. If the search condition is not specified, all rows of the table will have the new attribute value.

The general syntax of the search condition is:

> *attribute-name comparison-operator expression/value*

Every search condition is evaluated as either TRUE or FALSE. *Search condition values are case sensitive, where the character expressions must be enclosed in single quotation.* The Table 2-6 below lists common comparison operators used in SQL.

Operator	Description	Example
=	Equal To	`lease_type = 'One'`
>	Greater Than	`apt_deposit_amt > 300`
<	Less Than	`apt_deposit_amt < 300`
>=	Greater Than or Equal To	`invoice_no >= 1040`
<=	Less Than or Equal To	`invoice_no <= 1040`
<>, !=, ^=	Not Equal To	`lease_type <> 'Six'`

LIKE	Pattern Matching Text Strings	`tenant_name like 'M%'`
		`where % implies wildcard character`
		`indicating that part of the string`
		`can contain any characters.`
		
		`auto_make like '_o%'`
		`where _ implies a single character`
		`substitution.`

BETWEEN	Range Comparison	`apt_rent_amt between 300 and 600`
		`(similar to apt_rent_amt >= 300 and`
		`apt_rent_amt <= 600)`

IN	Determine if value part of a set.	`cc_type in ('visa', 'discover')`
NOT IN	Determine if value is not part of a set.	`cc_type not in ('visa', 'discover')`

Table 2-6: Comparison Operators

The following SQL statements illustrate the working of the UPDATE statement.

1. Update attribute AUTO_MAKE value in the TENANT_AUTO table.

    ```
    update tenant_auto
    set auto_make = 'Toyota'
    where license_no = 'SYK332';
    ```

2. Update attribute AUTO_MAKE and AUTO_COLOR values in TENANT_AUTO table.

    ```
    update tenant_auto
    set auto_make = 'Volvo', auto_color = 'Green '
    where license_no = 'ABC260';
    ```

Multiple search conditions can be combined using AND and OR operators. When AND operator is used to combine two search conditions, both conditions must be true for the UPDATE statement to satisfy the search condition. When the OR operator is used to combine two search conditions, only one of the condition must be true for the UPDATE statement to satisfy the search condition. For example, the following SQL statement will update the TENANT_AUTO table using the AND operator.

```
update tenant_auto
set auto_model = 'S70', auto_color = 'Black '
where license_no = 'TTS430' and tenant_ss = '123456789 ';
```

DELETE Statement

DELETE statement deletes rows from an existing table. Deleting rows is a dangerous operation, because if the values are accidently deleted and committed, it may be difficult to recover the deleted rows. The syntax of the DELETE statement is:

```
DELETE FROM tablename
[WHERE search condition ];
```

Always include the WHERE clause in the DELETE statement to ensure that the correct rows are deleted. If the WHERE clause is omitted, all table rows are deleted.

For example, the following SQL statement will delete two rows from the COMPLAINTS table where the rental_no is 100103.

```
delete from complaints
where rental_no = '100103';
```

SAVING MANIPULATION CHANGES

When data is inserted in a table, the new row is not immediately visible to other users. The reason being that Oracle does not save the new insertions in the database even though it generates the message that the row was successfully created. To save the new insertions permanently in the database, another statement called COMMIT has to be used. For example, the following two SQL statements will save the inserted row permanently in the database.

```
insert into sporting_clubs (club_id, name)
values(200, 'Branson Climbing Club');

commit;
```

The COMMIT statement also has to be used with other manipulation statements like DELETE and UPDATE. *In other words, no INSERT, DELETE, or UPDATE operation in Oracle database is permanent unless the COMMIT statement is executed.* The COMMIT statement does not have to be executed after each manipulation statement. It can be done anytime in a session. However, it is a good idea to explicitly commit changes often so that the data will be available to other users, and the changes are saved in a timely manner.

Once data has been saved (commit executed) it cannot be changed. To overcome situations when some manipulation statement results need to be cancelled, a statement called ROLLBACK is used. ROLLBACK undoes the changes since the last successful COMMIT execution. It is a way to remove the changes done previously in the session. For example, the following INSERT statement will not be saved once the ROLLBACK statement is executed.

```
insert into sporting_clubs (club_id, name)
values(300, 'Jackie Hill Club');

rollback;
```

It is possible to rollback selectively using the SAVEPOINTS statement. SAVEPOINT is a kind of marker that allows for partial rollback. The syntax of SAVEPOINT is

```
SAVEPOINT <savepoint name>
```

The savepoint name can be any name. Multiple SAVEPOINTS can be created in a session, and then the ROLLBACK statement can remove changes upto a particular savepoint name. For example, consider the following list of INSERT statements. The last INSERT statement will not be saved once the ROLLBACK statement is executed.

```
insert into sporting_clubs (club_id, name)
values(400, 'Virginia Club');

savepoint marker1;

insert into sporting_clubs (club_id, name)
values(500, 'Mountain View Club');

savepoint marker2;


insert into sporting_clubs (club_id, name)
values(600, 'Tommy Virginia Club');

rollback to marker2;
```

LOCK TABLE Statement

When DML statements are issued, the database by default performs a row level lock, so that no other user can change the same rows. In addition, a lock is indicated on the table so other users cannot attempt to lock the whole table while the row lock is active. This lock is a *shared lock*, which allows other users to view the data stored in the table without altering the structure of the table or performing other table operations.

It is possible to explicitly lock a table in share mode through the LOCK TABLE statement. The syntax is: LOCK TABLE *tablename* IN SHARE MODE;.

When DDL operations are performed, Oracle places an *exclusive lock* on the table so that no other user can alter the table or try to manipulate the contents of the table. Besides, if an exclusive lock exists on a table, no other user can obtain an exclusive or shared lock on the same table. Also if a shared lock is placed on a table, no other user can place an exclusive lock on the same table. To lock a table in exclusive mode the syntax is: LOCK TABLE *tablename* IN EXCLUSIVE MODE;.

SCRIPT FILE

A script is a text file that contains a list of SQL statements. Figure 2-1 is an example of a script file (sporting_script.sql) to create the SPORTING_CLUBS table and insert rows.

```
drop table sporting_clubs;

create table sporting_clubs
(club_id number(3)constraint sporting_clubs_pk primary key,
name varchar2(30),
street varchar2(30),
city varchar2(15),
state char(2),
zip number(5),
phone varchar2(10));

insert into sporting_clubs
values(100, 'Hillside Mountain Club', '1 Winona St', 'Wichita',
'KS',34342,'3163997676');
insert into sporting_clubs
values(200, 'Branson Climbing Club', '2 Sherwood Dr.', 'Branson',
'MO',65670,'4174485676');
insert into sporting_clubs
values(300, 'Cherokee Rafting Club', '44 Kent Ave.','St. Charles',
'MO',66572,'3147780870');
insert into sporting_clubs
values(400, 'White Plains Club', '225 Tracy St.','New York',
'NY',13567,'2126678090');

commit;
```

Figure 2-1   Script file

The SQL statements within a script file are executed in the SQL editor in the sequence of their listing. Script files can contain any SQL statement from creating or modifying tables, to retrieving, inserting, updating and deleting rows from the tables. Usually script files have a .sql extension if created from within a SQL editor. Otherwise script files with .txt extensions can be created through other text editors or word processors. All SQL statements in script files must end with a semi-colon (;). For example, the four databases in the book have associated script files that create their respective databases.

CHAPTER SUMMARY

▸ The database language to work with the relational model is SQL (structured query language).

▸ SQL allows for the storage and manipulation of data within a relational model. It is also an ANSI standard language for relational database processing.

▸ Oracle provides tools for SQL and PL/SQL working like SQL Developer.

▸ SQL has two components called as Data Definition Language (DDL) and Data Manipulation Language (DML).

▸ DDL consists of statements to create the structure of relations and relationships. It also consists of other administrative statements to control the setup of relational databases.

▸ DML consists of statements to manipulate data in existing relations/tables. It consists of statements to insert a row in table, delete rows from table, update attribute values in a table or retrieve data from tables.

▸ Oracle generally refers to entries in the database as objects.

▸ All database object names like table names, attribute names, etc. in Oracle must follow a naming standard.

▸ The main Oracle data types include characters, numbers, dates, and large objects.

▸ The character data types include varchar2, char, nvarchar2, and nchar.

▸ The number data type can be used for all numeric data.

▸ Large objects data types can be used to store binary data, such as digitized sounds or images, or references to binary files from a word processor or spreadsheet.

▸ Database tables have constraints defined. These constraints are rules that restrict the data values that can be entered for an attribute.

▸ There are two types of constraints – integrity constraints and value constraints.

▸ Integrity constraints are used to define primary key and foreign keys.

▸ When defining foreign keys, it is possible to indicate update and delete referential integrity actions like RESTRICT, CASCADE, and SET NULL.

▸ Value constraints are limitations placed on attribute values such as unique values, range of values, and so on.

▸ The SQL statement to create a new table/relation is CREATE TABLE statement.

▸ SQL statements to maintain the database are ALTER, DROP and RENAME.

- ▸ Rows are inserted into a table one row at a time through the INSERT statement.

- ▸ Updating existing data in a table is done using the UPDATE statement.

- ▸ The DELETE statement deletes rows from an existing table.

- ▸ To save the results of INSERT, UPDATE and DELETE statements another statement called COMMIT has to be used.

- ▸ A script is a text file that contains a sequence of SQL statements.

REVIEW QUESTIONS

1. List the various data types supported in SQL.

2. What the rules for naming objects in Oracle?

3. What is the difference between CHAR and VARCHAR2 data type?

4. Explain the two integrity constraints.

5. What actions can be performed using the ALTER statement?

6. How are manipulation changes saved permanently in the database? Explain.

7. Explain the purpose of ROLLBACK statement.

8. What are script files? Describe the nature of their content.

REVIEW EXERCISES

1. The two components of SQL are _____ and _____.

2. The data type to store variable length character data is _____.

3. The data type for numeric value 12.45 should be _____.

4. The data type for numeric value 22335 should be _____.

5. Complete the syntax for creating a table supplier where supplier_no is the primary key.

```
create table supplier
(supplier_no number(3) _____,
sname varchar2(15),
scity varchar2(10));
```

6. Complete the syntax for creating a table supplier_invoice where supplier_no is the foreign key to the table supplier.

```
create table supplier
(supplier_inv number(3),
invoice_date date,
invoice_total number(4,2),
supplier_no number(3) _____ );
```

7. The _____ value constraint keyword guarantees that an attribute always has a value.

8. The _____ value constraint keyword specifies a discrete list of values an attribute can have.

9. The syntax to drop constraint customer_fk from table customer is:
    _____
```
drop constraint customer_fk;
```

10. The syntax to modify the data type of attribute invoice_total to number(7,2) in table supplier is:
```
alter table supplier
```
_____;

11. Complete the following syntax to drop a table having foreign keys links automatically removed.
```
drop table supplier _____;
```

12. To save the new insertions permanently in the database a _____ statement should be executed.

13. A text file that contains a sequence of SQL statement is called _____ file.

PROBLEM SOLVING EXERCISES

> Run the script file outdoorDB_v4.sql to load the Outdoor Clubs & Product database to complete some of the exercises.

Ex2A-1.   Create a table KR_CUSTOMER with the following attributes as shown below.

Name	City	Status
Jackie Foods	Memphis	P
Tom Construction	Kansas City	R
Indie Professional	Memphis	P

Name attribute is the primary key of the table. Choose appropriate data types for attributes.

Ex2A-2.   Create a table KR_SALESPERSON with the following attributes as shown below.

Name	Age	Salary
Tom Selleck	40	50150
Jeremy Mack	35	100300
Anita Raina	38	65500
Kerry Kao	28	35600
Joe Walton	45	110500

Name attribute is the primary key of the table. Choose appropriate data types for attributes.

Ex2A-3.   Create a table KR_ORDER with the following attributes as shown below.

Order_Number	Customer_Name	Salesperson_Name	Amount
100	Jackie Foods	Anita Raina	700
200	Indie Professional	Tom Selleck	1200
300	Tom Construction	Joe Walton	1500
400	Jackie Foods	Tom Selleck	850
500	Indie Professional	Jeremy Mack	455
600	Jackie Foods	Joe Walton	1500
700	Tom Construction	Anita Raina	860

Order_Number attribute is the primary key of the table. Customer_Name is a foreign key linked to KR_Customer table. Salesperson_Name is a foreign key linked to KR_Salesperson table. Choose appropriate data types for attributes.

Ex2A-4. Create a script file ex2a_4.sql that inserts rows in the above tables.

Ex2A-5. Create a script file ex2a_5.sql that inserts the following rows in SPORTING_CLUBS table of Outdoor Clubs & Product database. The attribute names are the column heading.

Club_ID	Name
150	Central Climbing Club
160	Steinbeck Sports Club

Ex2A-6. Modify the price of Product_ID 10011 to 15.75 in the PRODUCT table of Outdoor Clubs & Product database.

Ex2A-7. Modify the price of Product_ID 10020 to 6.99 in the PRODUCT table of Outdoor Clubs & Product database.

Ex2A-8. Create a script file ex2a_8.sql that inserts the following rows in KR_ORDER table. The attribute names are the column heading.

Order_Number	Customer_Name	Amount
800	Jackie Foods	550
900	Indie Professional	780

Ex2A-9. Delete Order_Number 500 from KR_ORDER table.

Ex2A-10. Change the data type of Customer_Name attribute in KR_ORDER table.

Ex2A-11. Change the data type of Salesperson_Name attribute in KR_ORDER table.

Ex2A-12. Add an attribute "Fee" with numeric data type in the SPORTING_CLUBS table. Issue SQL Update statements that insert appropriate values for the Fee attribute.

Ex2A-13. Add an attribute "Club_Created" with date data type in the SPORTING_CLUBS table. Issue SQL Update statements that insert appropriate values for the Club_Created attribute.

Ex2A-14. Delete rows from the PURCHASE_ORDER table for supplier "Hillside Ski."

Ex2A-15. Delete rows from the SPORTING_CLUBS table for all clubs in state "NY."

SQL in PL/SQL

- SQL Query
- Database Views

SQL query is a powerful mechanism to retrieve information from a relational database. These queries range from simple listing of attributes to more complex criteria for retrieval involving multiple tables. There are also concepts like Views that provide an alternative setup to query from the database.

> This lesson utilizes the table structure of Superflex Apartment database to explain examples.

SQL QUERY

All retrieval of data from tables (also referred as a *database query*) is done using the SELECT statement. Retrieval of data can be from a single table or it can involve multiple tables. Since the complete syntax of SELECT statement is quite complex, it will be explained gradually. The explanation will start with the minimal set, which will then be built upon with more complex extensions. Initially the focus is on querying from a single table. Later on, multi-table querying will be explained. The basic syntax of the SELECT query statement is as follows:

```
SELECT attributename1, attributename2, . . .
FROM tablename1;
```

There are two main keywords SELECT and FROM that are required in all query statements. The SELECT keyword clause contains a list of attributes that are desired in output, while the FROM keyword clause lists the table name from which the attributes values of the SELECT keyword clause will be generated. The result of any query is formatted as a tabular display with attribute names appearing as column names. For example, the following SQL query retrieves the TENANT_NAME and EMPLOYER_NAME attribute values from the TENANT table. The result appears below the query.

```
select tenant_name, employer_name
from tenant;

TENANT_NAME                     EMPLOYER_NAME
------------------------------  -------------------------
Jack Robin                      Kraft Inc.
Mary Stackles                   Kraft Inc.
Ramu Reddy                      MSU
Marion Black                    MSU
Venessa Williams                Kraft Inc.
```

SELECT Keyword

There are many optional entries in the SELECT keyword clause to help generate output. These entries are separately explained to enable better understanding of the complete syntax of the SELECT clause.

- * symbol.
- DISTINCT keyword.
- Mathematical expressions.
- Alias for attribute names.
- Concatenation symbols.

The asterisk (*) symbol can be used if the query lists all attributes values from a table. In other words, instead of listing all the attribute names of a table in the SELECT keyword clause, the symbol * can be used instead. Further, if the symbol * is used in the SELECT keyword clause, it should be the only entry. For example, the following SQL query retrieves all attributes of TENANT_AUTO table. The results appear below the query.

```
select * from tenant_auto;

TENANT_SS LICENS AUTO_MAKE        AUTO_MODEL       AUTO_YEAR AUTO_COLOR
--------- ------ ---------------  ---------------  --------- ----------
123456789 SYK332 Ford             Taurus               1999 Red
123456789 TTS430 Volvo            GL 740               1990 Green
723556089 ABC260 Toyota           Lexus                2000 Maroon
450452267 LLT322 Honda            Accord               2001 Blue
450452267 KYK100 Toyota           Camry                1999 Black
223056180 FLT232 Honda            Civic                1999 Red
173662690 LLT668 Volvo            GL 980               2000 Velvet
```

The DISTINCT keyword ensures unique rows in the query output by dropping the duplicate rows. Two rows are considered duplicate if all attribute values match. The syntax of the SELECT keyword clause now is as follows:

SELECT [DISTINCT] *attributename1, attributename2, . . .*
FROM *tablename1*;

The following SQL queries show the results of using the DISTINCT keyword. The first query shows the listing of AUTO_MAKE attribute values from the TENANT_AUTO table. Since there are many duplicate values, the second query using the DISTINCT keyword shows the values without the duplication. The results follow the query.

```
select auto_make from tenant_auto;

AUTO_MAKE
---------------
Ford
Volvo
Toyota
Honda
Toyota
Honda
Volvo
```

```
select distinct auto_make from tenant_auto;

AUTO_MAKE
---------------
Ford
Honda
Toyota
Volvo
```

The use of mathematical expressions along with attribute names improves the versatility of the SELECT clause. The attributes in the expression should be table attributes. Each row of attribute value is considered during the computing of the expression. The syntax of the SELECT keyword clause now is as follows:

SELECT [DISTINCT] *attribute1, expression, attribute2* . . .
FROM *tablename1*;

The following SQL query shows the output using an expression entry. The expression tries to tabulate the yearly rental amount for each apartment. The results follow the query.

```
select apt_no, apt_rent_amt*12
from apartment;

  APT_NO APT_RENT_AMT*12
--------- ----------------
     100             3600
     101             3600
     102             3600
     103             4800
     104             4800
     200             6000
     201             6000
     202             8400
     203             8400
```

The use of *alias* for attribute names is for renaming the attribute names listed in the SELECT clause. This renaming of attributes is especially useful when mathematical expressions are listed in the SELECT keyword clause. Aliases are given in the SELECT keyword clause by using:

- the keyword AS followed by the new name, or
- having a space after the attribute name and following it with the new name, or
- enclosing the new name within double quotes.

The syntax of the SELECT keyword clause now is as follows:

SELECT [DISTINCT] *attribute1* [AS *newname*], *expression* [*newname*], . . .
FROM *tablename1*;

The following SQL queries show the use of an alias for the expression entry. The results follow the query.

```
select apt_no apartment, apt_rent_amt*12 as yearly_rent
from apartment;

APARTMENT YEARLY_RENT
--------- -----------
      100        3600
      101        3600
      102        3600
      103        4800
      104        4800
      200        6000
      201        6000
      202        8400
      203        8400


select apt_no "apartment", apt_rent_amt*12 as yearly_rent
from apartment;

apartment YEARLY_RENT
--------- -----------
      100        3600
      101        3600
      102        3600
      103        4800
      104        4800
      200        6000
      201        6000
      202        8400
      203        8400
```

Use of the concatenation symbols || in the SELECT clause allows mixing of text and attribute values to generate more formal output. For example, the following SQL query displays the RENTAL_NO and APT_NO attribute values like a text statement. The results follow the query.

```
select 'Rental Number '||rental_no||' belongs to apartment '||apt_no "Rental Statements"
from rental;

Rental Statements
---------------------------------------------------------------------------------------
Rental Number 100101 belongs to apartment 201
Rental Number 100102 belongs to apartment 102
Rental Number 100103 belongs to apartment 203
Rental Number 100104 belongs to apartment 101
Rental Number 100105 belongs to apartment 104
Rental Number 100106 belongs to apartment 100
```

Use of the concatenation symbol allows for any type of special formatting that may be required, like that for showing social security number as 123-456-7890 or phone number as (123) 456-7890.

WHERE Keyword

A common extension of the SQL query statement involves search conditions. Inclusion of search conditions in a database query is done through the WHERE keyword clause. The search conditions are similar to those shown in Table 2-6. Every search condition is evaluated as either TRUE or FALSE. Search condition values are case sensitive, where character expressions must be enclosed in single quotation. The Table 2-7 lists common comparison operators used in SQL with associated examples of the WHERE clause.

Operator	Description	Example
=	Equal To	`lease_type = 'One'`
>	Greater Than	`apt_deposit_amt > 300`
<	Less Than	`apt_deposit_amt < 300`
>=	Greater Than or Equal To	`invoice_no >= 1040`
<=	Less Than or Equal To	`invoice_no <= 1040`
<>, !=, ^=	Not Equal To	`lease_type <> 'Six'`

LIKE	Pattern Matching Text Strings	`tenant_name like 'M%'`
		where % implies wildcard character indicating that part of the string can contain any characters.
		
		`auto_make like '_o%'`
		where _ implies a single character substitution.

BETWEEN	Range Comparison	`apt_rent_amt between 300 and 600` (similar to `apt_rent_amt >= 300 and apt_rent_amt <= 600`)
IN	Determine if value part of a set.	`cc_type in ('visa', 'discover')`
NOT IN	Determine if value is not part of a set.	`cc_type not in ('visa', 'discover')`

Table 2-7: Search Conditions

The attributes in the search condition should be from the table listed in the FROM keyword clause of the query. The general syntax of the SQL query statement with the search condition is as follows:

```
SELECT [DISTINCT] attribute1, attribute2, . . .
FROM tablename1
[WHERE search-condition];
```

The following SQL queries are examples involving the WHERE keyword clause. The results follow the query.

1. Retrieve APT_NO and APT_UTILITY values for all one-bedroom apartments in the APARTMENT table. The search condition attribute is APT_TYPE value of 1.

```
select apt_no, apt_utility
from apartment
where apt_type = 1;

    APT_NO A
--------- -
       103 N
```

104 Y

2. Retrieve APT_NO and APT_STATUS values for all one-bedroom apartments in the APARTMENT table which have utilities installed. The search condition attribute is APT_TYPE attribute value of 1, and APT_UTILITY attribute value of 'Y' (indicates installation of utilities in an apartment).

```
select apt_no, apt_status
from apartment
where apt_type = 1
and apt_utility = 'Y';

   APT_NO A
--------- -
      104 R
```

3. Retrieve TENANT_NAME values starting with character 'M' and having TENANT_DOB values beyond 1979 from the TENANT table.

```
select tenant_name
from tenant
where tenant_name like 'M%'
and tenant_dob > '01-Jan-1980';

TENANT_NAME
-------------------------
Mary Stackles
Marion Black
```

Searching for NULL values

Sometimes the search condition of a query has to find rows where the value of an attribute is NULL. In this case the syntax for the search condition is WHERE attribute-name IS [NOT] NULL. For example, the following SQL query finds rows in the COMPLAINTS table where the STATUS attribute value is NULL. The results follow the query.

```
select complaint_no, rental_no
from complaints
where status is null;

COMPLAINT_NO          RENTAL_NO
--------------------- ---------------------
10012                 100105
10013
10014                 100103
10016
```

ORDER BY Keyword

Next extension of the SQL query statement involves the sorting of query output. By default, the output of a query will be displayed as the rows are selected. However, any re-ordering of the output rows can be accomplished through the ORDER BY keywords in ascending or descending sequence. The ORDER BY keyword clause requires a minimum of one attribute name from the attribute list that appears in the SELECT keyword clause as a sort key. The general syntax of the query with the sorting keyword clause is as follows:

```
SELECT [DISTINCT] attribute1, attribute2, . . .
FROM tablename1
[WHERE search-condition ]
[ORDER BY  attribute1 [DESC] [attribute2  [DESC]...]];
```

The ORDER BY keyword clause should be the last keyword clause of the SQL query statement. If more than one attribute is listed in the ORDER BY keyword clause, a multi-key sorting is performed. The default sorting order is ascending. The keyword for ascending is ASC. To enable the descending sorting, the DESC keyword must follow the attribute name. Rows are sorted in numeric order if the sort attribute (key) is having a NUMBER data type. The alphabetic order is adopted if the sort attribute (key) is having a CHAR or VARCHAR2 data type.

The following SQL query shows the results using the ORDER BY keyword clause. The query lists AUTO_YEAR and AUTO_MAKE values from TENANT_AUTO table. Since the AUTO_YEAR values in the table are not arranged in any particular sequence, the ORDER BY keyword clause is used to arrange the output in ascending sequence. The results follow the query.

```
select auto_make, auto_year
from tenant_auto
where auto_year > 1995
order by auto_year;

AUTO_MAKE        AUTO_YEAR
---------------  ---------
Ford                  1999
Toyota                1999
Honda                 1999
Toyota                2000
Volvo                 2000
Honda                 2001
```

Built-in Functions

There are five built-in functions that can be used in the SQL query statement. These functions and their descriptions are shown in Table 2-8.

Function	Description
COUNT(*)	Returns the number of rows.
COUNT([DISTINCT] *attribute-name*)	Returns the number of (distinct) values taken by the attribute.
SUM(*attribute-name*)	Returns the total of all values for the attribute.
AVG(*attribute-name*)	Returns the average of all values for the attribute.
MAX(*attribute-name*)	Returns the highest value of the attribute.
MIN(*attribute-name*)	Returns the lowest value of the attribute.

Table 2-8: SQL Built-in Functions

These functions should be the only entries in the SELECT keyword clause. If attributes need to be placed along with the built-in functions in the SELECT keyword clause, the GROUP BY keyword clause (explained later) should be utilized. These functions can be used with search conditions, in which case the function is applied after the rows have been selected through the search criteria. However, the built-in function cannot be substituted for an expression or value in a search condition involving the WHERE keyword clause. Each functions working is now shown through SQL query examples. The results follow the query.

1. Count the number of rows in the APARTMENT table using the count(*) function.

```
select count(*)
from apartment;

 COUNT(*)
---------
        9
```

2. Count the number of rows having different values for APT_TYPE attribute in the APARTMENT table using the count(distinct attribute-name) function.

```
select count(distinct apt_type)
from apartment;

COUNT(DISTINCTAPT_TYPE)
-----------------------
                      4
```

3. Sum the invoices billed (INVOICE_DUE attribute) to credit card "visa" (CC_TYPE attribute value) in the RENTAL_INVOICE table using the sum(attribute-name) function.

```
select sum(invoice_due)
from rental_invoice
where cc_type = 'visa';

SUM(INVOICE_DUE)
----------------------
6300
```

4. Calculate the average of the invoices billed (INVOICE_DUE attribute) to credit card "mastercard" (CC_TYPE attribute value) in the RENTAL_INVOICE table using the avg(attribute-name) function.

```
select avg(invoice_due)
from rental_invoice
where cc_type = 'mastercard';

AVG(INVOICE_DUE)
----------------------
344.4444444444444444444444444444444444444444
```

5. Find the highest rental amount (APT_RENT_AMT attribute) in the APARTMENT table using the max(attribute-name) function.

```
select max(apt_rent_amt)
from apartment;

MAX(APT_RENT_AMT)
----------------------
700
```

6. Find the lowest rental amount (APT_RENT_AMT attribute) in the APARTMENT table using the min(attribute-name) function.

```
select min(apt_rent_amt)
from apartment;

MIN(APT_RENT_AMT)
----------------------
300
```

GROUP BY Keyword

This extension of the SQL query statement involves the use of GROUP BY keyword clause to perform grouping of selected rows based on similar attribute values. The general syntax of the SQL query statement along with the GROUP BY keyword clause is as follows:

```
SELECT [DISTINCT] attribute1, [ attribute2 ], [ built-in function ], . . .
FROM tablename1
[WHERE search condition ]
[GROUP BY  attribute1, [ attribute2 ] . . .
[ORDER BY  attribute1 [DESC] [ attribute2  [DESC]...]];
```

The attributes in the GROUP BY keyword clause should be from those that are listed in the SELECT keyword clause. If more than one attribute is listed in the GROUP BY keyword clause, then there is an outer grouping of similar values, and for each such group value, an inner grouping of values for the other attribute occurs. There can be many attributes in the GROUP BY keyword clause, but each such attribute must also be in the SELECT keyword clause list.

It is possible to have a built-in function in the SELECT keyword clause along with the other attribute entries. The built-in function now applies to the selected group. The following SQL query examples show the working of GROUP BY keyword clause. The results follow the query.

1. List the number of different types of car makes in the TENANT_AUTO table.

    ```
    select auto_make, count(*)
    from tenant_auto
    group by auto_make;

    AUTO_MAKE        COUNT(*)
    ---------------  ---------
    Ford                    1
    Honda                   2
    Toyota                  2
    Volvo                   2
    ```

2. List the different car makes in the TENANT_AUTO table.

    ```
    select auto_make
    from tenant_auto
    group by auto_make;

    AUTO_MAKE
    ---------------
    Ford
    Honda
    Toyota
    Volvo
    ```

3. List the different types of car makes and count the different models for each such car in the TENANT_AUTO table.

    ```
    select auto_make, auto_model, count(*)
    from tenant_auto
    group by auto_make, auto_model;

    AUTO_MAKE        AUTO_MODEL       COUNT(*)
    ---------------  ---------------  ---------
    Ford             Taurus                  1
    Honda            Accord                  1
    Honda            Civic                   1
    Toyota           Camry                   1
    Toyota           Lexus                   1
    Volvo            GL 740                  1
    Volvo            GL 980                  1
    ```

The GROUP BY keyword clause can be extended with the HAVING keyword clause. The HAVING keyword clause is used to specify a search condition on the groups created through the GROUP BY keyword clause. *The HAVING keyword clause must occur only with the GROUP BY keyword clause*, and follows the GROUP BY keyword clause syntax. The syntax of the HAVING keyword clause along with the GROUP BY keyword clause is:

    GROUP BY *attribute1* [, *attribute2* . . .]
    HAVING *search-condition*

For example, the following SQL query lists only those car makes with two or more entries in the TENANT_AUTO table. The results follow the query.

```
select auto_make, count(*)
from tenant_auto
group by auto_make
having count(*) > 1;

AUTO_MAKE         COUNT(*)
---------------   ---------

Honda                   2
Toyota                  2
Volvo                   2
```

DECODE Function

The DECODE function in the SELECT keyword clause is similar to the CASE or IF..THEN..ELSE structures found in programming languages. The function compares an attribute or search value to values in the list. If a match is found, then the specified output value is returned. If no match is found, then the default value is returned. If no default value is defined, a NULL value is returned as the result.

The syntax for the DECODE function is DECODE(*MatchValue, List1, Result1, List2, Result2, ..., Default*). MatchValue is the search value. List1 represents the first value in the list. Result1 represents the output value to be returned if List1 and MatchValue are equivalent. List2 and Result2 pair follow the logic similar to List1 and Result1, and so on. The Default is the output value if no match is found.

For example, the following SQL query displays the status of various apartments. The status is whether the apartment is vacant or rented. The results follow the query.

```
select apt_no,
decode(apt_status,'R','Rented','V','Vacant','Not Available') "Status"
from apartment;

APT_NO Status
--------- -------------
    100 Rented
    101 Rented
    102 Rented
    103 Vacant
    104 Rented
    200 Vacant
    201 Rented
    202 Vacant
    203 Rented
```

CASE Function

The CASE function in the SELECT keyword clause provides functionality similar to DECODE function. The syntax for the CASE function is

```
CASE attribute  WHEN List1 THEN Result1
                [WHEN List2 THEN Result2
                 WHEN ... ]
                ELSE Default
END
```

The CASE attribute is the one whose value will be considered. List1 represents the first value in the list. Result1 represents the output to be returned if List1 matches the attribute value. The other list and result entries have similar logic. The Default is the value to return if no match is found. For example, the following SQL query displays the status of various apartments. The status is whether the apartment is vacant or rented. The results follow the query.

```
select apt_no, (case apt_status when 'R' then 'Rented'
when 'V' then 'Vacant'
else 'Data Error!' end) "Status"
from apartment;
```

```
APT_NO Status
--------- -----------
   100 Rented
   101 Rented
   102 Rented
   103 Vacant
   104 Rented
   200 Vacant
   201 Rented
   202 Vacant
   203 Rented
```

Multi-Table Query

Queries involving more than one table require proper linking of tables. Linking of tables is accomplished through two approaches – join or subquery. Joins can be of two types – inner join and outer join. It is possible to have both approaches in the same SQL query statement.

Subquery

A subquery is created when there is another query inside a SQL query statement. The inside query is called the subquery, while the main query is called the outer query. *The subquery is used to fulfill a search condition in the outer query*. The purpose of creating subqueries is to limit the processing of the outer query by using the subquery to create intermediate results. Subqueries can return one of more values and can also be nested with additional subqueries themselves. The general syntax of the subquery approach is:

```
SELECT attribute1, attribute2, . . .
FROM tablename
WHERE search-attribute {[=] | [IN]} (SELECT attribute
                                     FROM tablename
                                     [WHERE  search conditions])
   . . .;
```

The first SELECT statement query is called the outer query. The second SELECT statement query within the parenthesis is called the subquery. The search attribute in the WHERE keyword clause of the outer query is linked with the attribute values returned by the subquery SELECT keyword clause. There are two operators (= or IN) linking the outer query search attribute with the subquery. If the subquery will return a single value then the = operator can be used. But if subquery returns multiple values, then the IN operator should be used.

The subquery should *not* have more than one attribute in the SELECT keyword clause. The subquery can also contain a subquery (called as nested subquery) by becoming the outer query for another subquery associated with its search condition. It is possible for the outer query to have more than one subquery associated with different search attributes in its search condition.

The use of subquery occurs when the condition attribute of a SQL query is in one table, while the output attributes are in a separate table. The linking of the outer query table with the inner query table occurs over attributes that share a common domain. This common domain concept generally applies to the primary key and foreign key combinations. In other words, the WHERE search attribute of the outer query and the SELECT attribute of the subquery should correspond to the primary key and foreign key combinations. Many times the output attribute table and the condition attribute table have no direct primary or foreign key link. In this case other tables that can facilitate the link are utilized. The following SQL query examples illustrate the use of the subquery approach. The results follow the query.

1. List the TENANT_NAME and TENANT_DOB attribute values for those tenants that drive Volvo cars.

   ```
   select tenant_name, tenant_dob
   from tenant
   where tenant_ss in (select tenant_ss
   from tenant_auto
   where auto_make = 'Volvo');

   TENANT NAME                    TENANT DOB
   ------------------------       --------------------------
   Jack Robin                     21-JUN-60
   Venessa Williams               12-MAR-70
   ```

2. List the TENANT_NAME and TENANT_DOB attribute values for those tenants who live in apartment 203.

   ```
   select tenant_name, tenant_dob
   from tenant
   where rental_no = (select rental_no
   from rental
   where apt_no = 203);

   TENANT NAME                    TENANT DOB
   ------------------------       --------------------------
   Ramu Reddy                     11-APR-62
   ```

3. List the TENANT_NAME and TENANT_DOB attribute values for those tenants who have apartment utilities installed (i.e. APT_UTILITY is 'Y').

```
select tenant_name, tenant_dob
from tenant
where rental_no in (select rental_no from rental
where apt_no in (select apt_no from apartment
where apt_utility = 'Y'));
```

TENANT_NAME	TENANT_DOB
Jack Robin	21-JUN-60
Mary Stackles	02-AUG-80
Ramu Reddy	11-APR-62
Venessa Williams	12-MAR-70

Subquery with an aggregate function in SELECT statement

It is possible to use a subquery within a SELECT statement. For example, the following query lists all staff whose salary is greater than the average salary, along with the display of the difference. The results follow the query.

```
select staff_no, first_name, last_name,
salary-(select avg(salary) from staff) as SalaryDiff
from staff
where salary > (select avg(salary) from staff);
```

STAFF_NO	FIRST_NAME	LAST_NAME	SALARYDIFF
SA220	Terry	Ford	17600
SA230	Susan	Brandon	10600

Join (Inner Join)

Join (inner join) in database query is an alternative approach to perform a multi-table query. In the traditional approach there are two entries essential in the join approach. The first entry requires the query to list all the tables involved in the FROM keyword clause. The second entry involves the use of the WHERE keyword clause to define the search conditions that link the involved tables through a special type of search condition called as *join condition*. The linking of tables occurs over attributes that share a common domain. This common domain concept generally applies to the primary key and foreign key combinations. In other words, the search attribute of one table and the value attribute of the second table should correspond to the primary key and foreign key combinations. The general syntax of the join approach is:

```
SELECT attribute1, attribute2, . . .
FROM tablename1, tablename2, . . .
WHERE tablename1.attribute = tablename2.attribute
and  search conditions . . .;
```

The above syntax illustrates what is called as an *inner join (or equality join or equijoin)* where the join is based on values in one table being equal to values in another table. Generally the tablename prefix before the attribute name is not required if the attributes in the tables involved in the query are uniquely named. Otherwise it is necessary to have the tablename prefix before the attribute names to provide a more specific reference. If the join condition is excluded by mistake, the query will still give results, but the outcome will be voluminous based on the relational algebra concept of *cartesian product*. In cartesian product every row in one table is joined with every row of the other table.

The attributes in the SELECT keyword clause can be from any of the tables listed in the FROM keyword clause. The join condition attributes need not be listed in the SELECT keyword clause. The linking of tables occurs two tables at a time. If more than two tables are involved in the query, then there will be tables that will serve as intermediary between the other tables. For example, say the FROM keyword clause has tableA, tableB, and tableC. In such case tableA may link with tableB, and tableB many link with tableC to form a chain of interconnected tables for the query. Many times the output attribute table and the condition attribute tables have no direct primary key or foreign key link. In these cases other tables that can facilitate the link are utilized.

The join condition can be stated in any order in the WHERE keyword clause along with other search conditions. The following SQL query examples illustrate the use of join approach. The results follow the query.

1. List the TENANT_NAME, TENANT_DOB, and LICENSE_NO attribute values for those tenants that drive Volvo cars.

```
select tenant_name, tenant_dob, license_no
from tenant, tenant_auto
where tenant.tenant_ss = tenant_auto.tenant_ss
and auto_make = 'Volvo';
```

TENANT_NAME	TENANT_DOB	LICENSE_NO
Jack Robin	21-JUN-60	TTS430
Venessa Williams	12-MAR-70	LLT668

2. List the TENANT_NAME, LEASE_END, and APT_NO attribute values for those tenants who live in Studio types apartments (i.e. APT_TYPE is 0).

```
select tenant_name, lease_end, apartment.apt_no
from tenant, rental, apartment
where tenant.rental_no = rental.rental_no
and rental.apt_no = apartment.apt_no
and apt_type = 0;
```

TENANT_NAME	LEASE_END	APT_NO
Mary Stackles	30-NOV-07	102
Marion Black	31-MAR-09	101

There are two alternatives to the traditional implementation of inner join as described above. The first alternative involves the use of INNER JOIN keyword, while the second alternative utilizes the NATURAL JOIN keyword. The SQL query statement syntax involving INNER JOIN keyword is:

```
SELECT attribute1, attribute2, . . .
FROM tablename1 INNER JOIN  tablename2
ON join-condition1
[INNER JOIN tablename3 ON join-condition2 . . .]
```

WHERE *search-conditions* . . .;

In the above syntax, the join-condition1 entry is similar to the join condition linking tablename1 and tablename2 in the WHERE keyword clause of the traditional syntax, i.e. *tablename1.attribute = tablename2.attribute*. The join-condition2 entry for tablename3 should now link tablename3 through its associated ON keyword entry with tablename1 or tablename2. For example, the previous two SQL queries with the new syntax are as follows:

```
select tenant_name, tenant_dob, license_no
from tenant inner join tenant_auto
on tenant.tenant_ss = tenant_auto.tenant_ss
where auto_make = 'Volvo';
```

TENANT_NAME	TENANT_DOB	LICENSE_NO
Jack Robin	21-JUN-60	TTS430
Venessa Williams	12-MAR-70	LLT668

```
select tenant_name, lease_end, apartment.apt_no
from tenant inner join rental
on tenant.rental_no = rental.rental_no
inner join apartment on rental.apt_no = apartment.apt_no
where apt_type = 0;
```

TENANT_NAME	LEASE_END	APT_NO
Mary Stackles	30-NOV-07	102
Marion Black	31-MAR-09	101

The SQL query statement syntax involving NATURAL JOIN keyword is:

SELECT *attribute1*, *attribute2*, . . .
FROM *tablename1* NATURAL JOIN *tablename2* [NATURAL JOIN *tablename3* . . .]
WHERE *search conditions* . . .;

In this syntax, the DBMS automatically accomplishes the linking of tables around the NATURAL JOIN keyword using the primary key and foreign key specifications as defined during table definitions. For example, the two SQL queries previously based on inner join, with the new syntax are as follows:

```
select tenant_name, tenant_dob, license_no
from tenant natural join tenant_auto
where auto_make = 'Volvo';
```

TENANT_NAME	TENANT_DOB	LICENSE_NO
Jack Robin	21-JUN-60	TTS430
Venessa Williams	12-MAR-70	LLT668

```
select tenant_name, lease_end, apt_no
from tenant natural join rental natural join apartment
where apt_type = 0;
```

TENANT_NAME	LEASE_END	APT_NO
Mary Stackles	30-NOV-07	102

```
Marion Black            31-MAR-09              101
```

Outer Join

Outer join extends the inner join approach by also returning rows that do not have a match as specified in the join condition. There are three forms of outer join – left outer join, right outer join, and full outer join. Left outer join and right outer join list the unmatched rows of only one table, while the full outer join lists unmatched rows of both tables. In outer join, one table is declared as an outer table, while the other table is declared as an inner table. The outer table is the one from which the unmatched rows will be listed. In the Oracle traditional approach the outer join can be set through the plus (+) symbol. Alternative to the traditional outer join symbol involves the use of specific outer join keywords like left join, right join, and full join.

The Oracle traditional plus symbol (+) serves as an outer join marker to frame the outer join condition. The syntax for this approach involves placing the plus (+) symbol with the join condition in the WHERE keyword clause as *outer-tablename.attribute=inner-tablename.attributename* (+). In this syntax, a NULL value is inserted for the attributes in the inner-tablename that do not have matching rows in the outer-tablename. The plus (+) symbol can be placed on either side of the equality (=) operator, wherein the tablename.attribute having the sign becomes the inner-tablename. The use of + outer join marker yields only the left outer join or the right outer join.

For example the following query retrieves the RENTAL_NO, APT_NO, and APT_TYPE attribute values for all apartments with utilities installed (i.e. APT_UTILITY value is 'Y'). This query with inner join will only return rows that match APT_NO values in tables APARTMENT and RENTAL. The results follow the query.

```
select rental_no, apartment.apt_no, apt_type
from apartment, rental
where apartment.apt_no = rental.apt_no
and apt_utility = 'Y';

RENTAL_NO    APT_NO   APT_TYPE
---------  ---------  ---------
   100101       201          2
   100102       102          0
   100103       203          3
   100105       104          1
   100106       100          0
```

If we also want apartments that still do not have rentals, then the outer join feature is utilized. The above query is now modified as an outer join query.

```
select rental_no, apartment.apt_no, apt_type
from apartment, rental
where apartment.apt_no = rental.apt_no (+)
and apt_utility = 'Y';

RENTAL_NO    APT_NO   APT_TYPE
---------  ---------  ---------
   100106       100          0
   100102       102          0
```

```
100105          104          1
                200          2
100101          201          2
                202          3
100103          203          3
```

Left Join Keyword

Left outer join includes all rows that match the join condition along with those rows in the first (left) table that are unmatched with rows from the second (right) table. The LEFT JOIN keyword appears in the FROM keyword clause for left outer join. The SQL query statement syntax is:

```
SELECT attribute1, attribute2, . . .
FROM tablename1 LEFT JOIN  tablename2
ON join-condition1 [...]
WHERE search-conditions . . .;
```

In the above syntax, unmatched rows of tablename2 are filled with NULLs. For example, to show rentals that have registered complaints along with those that do not have any complaints, the following query lists the RENTAL_NO and COMPLAINT_NO values from RENTAL and COMPLAINTS table.

```
select rental.rental_no,complaint_no
from rental left join complaints
on rental.rental_no=complaints.rental_no;

RENTAL_NO                   COMPLAINT_NO
----------------------      ----------------------
100103                      10010
100105                      10011
100105                      10012
100103                      10014
100104                      10015
100102
100106
100101
```

Right Join Keyword

Right outer join includes all rows that match the join condition along with those rows in the second (right) table that are unmatched with rows from the first (left) table. The RIGHT JOIN keyword appears in the FROM keyword clause for right outer join. The SQL query statement syntax is:

```
SELECT attribute1, attribute2, . . .
FROM tablename1 RIGHT JOIN  tablename2
ON join-condition1 [...]
WHERE search-conditions . . .;
```

In the above syntax, unmatched rows of tablename1 are filled with NULLs. For example, to show complaints that have been registered by rentals along with those that do not have any associated rentals, the following query lists the RENTAL_NO and COMPLAINT_NO values from RENTAL and COMPLAINTS table.

```
select rental.rental_no,complaint_no
from rental right join complaints
on rental.rental_no=complaints.rental_no;
```

RENTAL_NO	COMPLAINT_NO
100103	10010
100105	10011
100105	10012
	10013
100103	10014
100104	10015
	10016

Full Join Keyword

Full outer join includes all rows that match the join condition along with those rows that are unmatched in both tables. The FULL JOIN keyword appears in the FROM keyword clause for full outer join. The SQL query statement syntax is:

> SELECT *attribute1*, *attribute2*, . . .
> FROM *tablename1* FULL JOIN *tablename2*
> ON join-condition1 [...]
> WHERE *search-conditions* . . .;

In the above syntax, the unmatched rows in both tables are filled with NULLs. For example, to show complaints that have been registered by rentals along with those that do not have any associated rentals, and vice-versa, the following query lists the RENTAL_NO and COMPLAINT_NO values from RENTAL and COMPLAINTS table.

```
select rental.rental_no,complaint_no
from rental full join complaints
on rental.rental_no=complaints.rental_no;
```

RENTAL_NO	COMPLAINT_NO
100103	10010
100105	10011
100105	10012
100103	10014
100104	10015
100102	
100106	
100101	
	10013
	10016

Self Join

Sometimes a query may require the same table to be queried more than once. This type of query is called a *self-join*. To perform self-join a table alias may need to be created. A table alias is an alternate name given to a table in the FROM keyword clause. The syntax of table alias is: *tablename aliasname*. When a table alias is defined, then the alias name should be used in the query instead of the table name. *Table alias can be used also in a regular query.*

Inequality Join

Inequality join occurs when the join condition is not based on the equality of values. In this case the join operator can be any other operator instead of the = operator.

Exists Subquery

EXISTS and NOT EXISTS are logical operators associated with a subquery in the WHERE keyword clause whose values are either true or false depending on the presence or absence of rows in the subquery. In this case the subquery is related to the outer query through its search condition. If the subquery returns one or more rows, then the EXIST condition evaluates as true, and the related row in the outer query is retrieved. If the subquery returns no rows, then the EXIST condition evaluates as false, and the related row in the outer query is not retrieved.

Even though a subquery is utilized in the SQL query statement, the operation of the subquery is different. The subquery is not fulfilling a search condition of the outer query in the traditional sense. The DBMS selects a row of the outer query and then executes the subquery to see if there is any row returned by it. If there is a row returned, the EXIST condition is considered true, and the row of the outer query is placed for output. Essentially the subquery is executed for each row of outer query.

For example consider the SQL query to retrieve RENTAL_NO attribute values for those tenants who have paid with different credit cards (CC_TYPE attribute). The results follow the query.

```
select distinct rental_no
from rental_invoice a
where exists
(select * from rental_invoice b
where a.rental_no = b.rental_no
and a.cc_type <> b.cc_type);

RENTAL_NO
---------
   100101
   100105
```

Similarly if we want to retrieve RENTAL_NO attribute values for those tenants who have not paid with different credit cards (CC_TYPE attribute), the query and its result are as follows:

```
select distinct rental_no
from rental_invoice a
where not exists
(select * from rental_invoice b
where a.rental_no = b.rental_no
and a.cc_type <> b.cc_type);

RENTAL_NO
---------
   100102
   100103
   100104
```

ANY and ALL Keywords

Keywords ANY and ALL may be used with a set of values in the WHERE keyword clause. If the values in the condition are preceded by keyword ALL, the condition will only be true if satisfied by all values. If the values in the condition are preceded by keyword ANY, the condition will only be true if satisfied by any (one or more) values. If the values are generated through a subquery, and the subquery is empty, then ALL condition returns true while the ANY condition returns false. It is possible to use the keyword SOME instead of ANY. The following SQL query examples explain the working of ANY or ALL keywords. The results follow the query.

1. List all credit cards that have been used for amounts greater than 300, 400, 500.

```
select distinct cc_type
from rental_invoice
where invoice_due > all (300,400,500);

CC_TYPE
----------
visa
discover
```

2. List all credit cards that have been used for any amount greater than 300, 400, 500.

```
select distinct cc_type
from rental_invoice
where invoice_due > any (300, 400,500);

CC_TYPE
----------
visa
mastercard
discover
```

3. List the credit card that has been used the most (in terms of dollar payments).

```
select cc_no, cc_type, sum(invoice_due)
from rental_invoice
group by cc_no, cc_type
having sum(invoice_due) >= all
(select sum(invoice_due)
from rental_invoice
group by cc_no,cc_type);
```

```
CC_NO                      CC_TYPE     SUM(INVOICE_DUE)
------------------------   ----------  ----------------------
1234567890123456           visa        3500
```

4. List the credit card that has not been used the most (in terms of dollar payments).

```
select cc_no, cc_type, sum(invoice_due)
from rental_invoice
group by cc_no, cc_type
having sum(invoice_due) < any
(select sum(invoice_due)
from rental_invoice
group by cc_no,cc_type);
```

```
CC_NO                      CC_TYPE     SUM(INVOICE_DUE)
------------------------   ----------  ----------------------
8654567890123296           discover    1400
6599567890126211           visa        1100
6599567890126211           discover    800
1234567890123456           mastercard  1000
3343567890123456           mastercard  2100
7766567890123203           visa        1700
```

Set Operators

Sometimes there might be a need to combine query results of two separate queries. Common set operators like UNION, UNION ALL, INTERSECT, and MINUS can be utilized to combine the results of two separate queries into a single result. Table 2-9 explains their purpose.

Set Operator	Description
UNION	Returns all rows from both queries, but displays duplicate rows once.
UNION ALL	Returns all rows from both queries, but displays all duplicate rows.
INTERSECT	Returns only rows common to both queries.
MINUS	Returns the rows returned by first query minus the common rows returned by the second query.

Table 2-9: SQL Set Operators

The general syntax of the set operators is *query1 set-operator query2;*. The rules for using the set operators are:

1. Both queries must have the same number of attributes in the SELECT keyword clause.
2. The data type of corresponding attributes in the SELECT keyword clause of both the queries have to match.

For example the following SQL query generates a list of all tenants social security numbers, name, and date of births in the apartment complex using the UNION operator. The results follow the query.

```
select tenant_ss, tenant_name, tenant_dob
from tenant
union
select family_ss, name, dob
from tenant_family;
```

```
TENANT_SS            TENANT_NAME            TENANT_DOB
------------------   ---------------------  -------------------------
111444663            Terry Williams         21-MAR-68
123456789            Jack Robin             21-JUN-60
173662690            Venessa Williams       12-MAR-70
222663434            Anjali Reddy           10-AUG-90
222664343            Sarla Reddy            11-JUN-65
223056180            Marion Black           25-MAY-81
242446634            Tom Williams           20-MAY-91
444663434            Kay Robin              21-JUN-65
450452267            Ramu Reddy             11-APR-62
723556089            Mary Stackles          02-AUG-80
```

DATABASE VIEWS

Database views are sort of pseudo tables that do not actually store data. A view stores a query, and is then used to access data in the underlying tables (referred as *base tables*). Figure 2-2 shows the basic processing of a view.

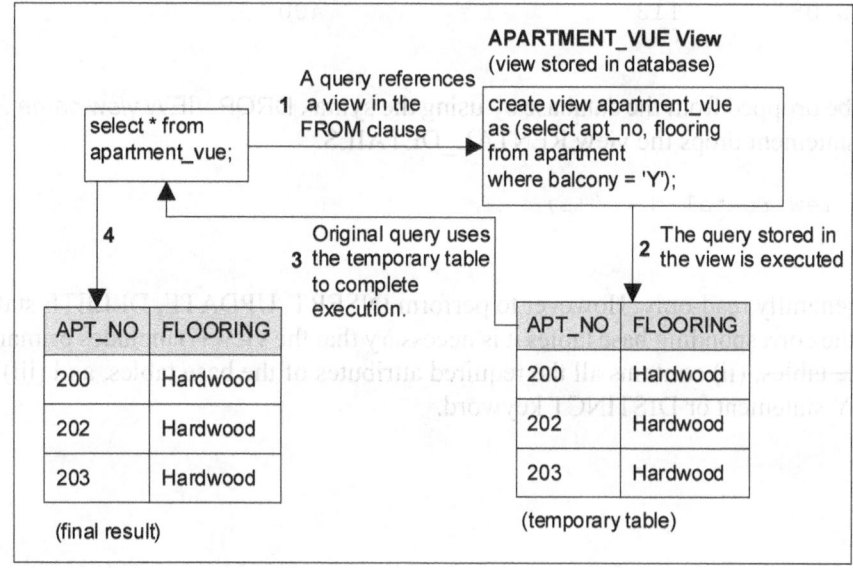

Figure 2-2

When a query references a view, the query contained in the view is processed and the results are treated as a virtual or temporary table. Views can assist users who do not have the training to create complex SQL queries, as well as restrict users to sensitive data. The general syntax is:

CREATE VIEW *view-name* [(*column1, column2, ...*)]
AS *database-query;*

The view-name should be unique within the database. The optional column names (column1, column2, ...) are utilized if the columns of the view will have different names from the corresponding SELECT keyword clause entries in the database query. Views have restrictions with regard to certain data manipulation operations like insert, update or delete.

For example the following SQL query creates a view RENTAL_DETAILS based on a SQL query that retrieves RENTAL_NO, APT_NO, APT_TYPE, and APT_RENT_AMT attribute values from the RENTAL and APARTMENT tables.

```
create view rental_details as
(select rental_no, rental.apt_no, apt_type, apt_rent_amt
from rental, apartment
where rental.apt_no = apartment.apt_no);
```

Once the view has been created it can be queried just like any other table. For example, the following query retrieves data from the RENTAL_DETAILS view. The results follow the query.

```
select * from rental_details;

RENTAL_NO    APT_NO  APT_TYPE APT_RENT_AMT
---------    ------  -------- ------------
   100101       201         2          500
   100102       102         0          300
   100103       207         3          700
   100104       104         0          300
   100105       113         1          400
```

Views can be dropped from the database by using the syntax DROP VIEW *view name*;. For example, the following statement drops the view RENTAL_DETAILS.

```
drop view rental_details;
```

A view is generally read-only. However to perform INSERT, UPDATE, DELETE statements on views that affect the corresponding base tables it is necessary that the view (i) includes primary key (or foreign key) of base tables, (ii) contains all the required attributes of the base tables, and (iii) does not include GROUP BY statement or DISTINCT keyword.

Inline View

Inline view is a temporary table generated through a subquery in the FROM clause. The subquery data can thereafter be referenced by the SELECT and WHERE clauses of the query. It is temporary because the data from the subquery is not stored in the database. The syntax is:

```
SELECT column1, column2, ...
FROM (subquery)
WHERE condition;
```

The following SQL query retrieves the APT_NO and RENT attribute values from an inline view in the form of a subquery on the apartment table. The results follow the query.

```
select apt_no, rent
from (select apt_no, apt_rent_amt rent
from apartment
order by apt_rent_amt desc)
where apt_no like '2%';


APT_NO                      RENT
----------------------  ----------------------
202                         700
203                         700
200                         500
201                         500
```

Materialized View

A materialized view stores the data defined by the view query, so that the data can be retrieved without executing the view query again. In other words, a materialized view allows replication of data. There are many reasons for storing duplicate data as materialized view:

- Complex queries on large databases may require a significant amount of processing, which can then affect the transactional processing of the system. Replicating data for reporting and analysis allows better transactional processing.
- Remote users can improve query performance by replicating data to a local database.
- Data analysis needs may require data to be frozen for specific time for comparison purposes.

Of course there are also some drawbacks to materialized views, like additional storage space is required to store view data, and modifications to materialized views require synchronization with base tables. The syntax for materialized view is:

CREATE MATERIALIZED VIEW *view-name* [(*column1, column2, ...*)]
[REFRESH COMPLETE]
[START WITH start-date NEXT refresh-date]
AS *database-query;*

where REFRESH COMPLETE stores a new copy of the view query results; and START WITH clause specifies the timing for view refresh.

The following SQL query creates a materialized view RENTAL_DETAILS_VUE based on a SQL query that retrieves RENTAL_NO, APT_NO, APT_TYPE and APT_RENT_AMT attribute values from the RENTAL and APARTMENT tables.

```
create materialized view rental_details_vue
refresh complete
start with sysdate next sysdate+7
as (select rental_no, rental.apt_no, apt_type, apt_rent_amt
from rental, apartment
where rental.apt_no = apartment.apt_no);
```

Views can be dropped from the database by using the syntax DROP MATERIALIZED VIEW *view name*;. For example, the following statement drops the view RENTAL_DETAILS_VUE.

```
drop materialized view rental_details_vue;
```

CHAPTER SUMMARY

- All retrieval of data from tables (also referred as a SQL database query) is done using the SELECT statement.

- The retrieval can be from a single table or it can involve multiple tables.

- There are many ways by which output can be specified in the SELECT keyword clause.

- Also there are many extensions of the basic query syntax. These extensions involve the use of additional keywords and associated keyword clauses like WHERE keyword clause, ORDER BY keyword clause, and GROUP BY keyword clause.

- There are also built-in functions that are standard to query statement.

- At the advanced level, database developers can develop their own custom functions to be used within a query statement.

- Queries involving more than one table require proper linking of tables.

- Linking of tables is accomplished through two approaches – join or subquery.

- Joins can are of two major types – inner join and outer join.

- Common set operators like UNION, UNION ALL, INTERSECT, and MINUS can be utilized to combine the results of two separate queries into a single result.

- To implement IF..THEN..ELSE types of logic structures the DECODE and CASE functions are utilized.

- Database views are sort of pseudo tables that are created to present a particular "display" of database content.

- Views can assist users who do not have the training to create complex SQL queries, as well as restrict users to sensitive data.

- An inline view is a subquery in the FROM clause, whose results can by used only by the current query.

- A materialized view physically stores the view query results.

REVIEW QUESTIONS

1. List the basic keywords necessary to develop a SQL query.

2. What are the different ways to give custom names to output columns?

3. What is the purpose of WHERE keyword clause?

4. How is the query output sorted? Explain.

5. Explain the various built-in functions provided by SQL.

6. Provide the rationale for the HAVING keyword in SQL query.

7. How many attributes can be listed in the SELECT keyword clause of a subquery?

8. Explain the difference between inner joins and outer joins.

9. Describe the purpose and structure of database views.

10. Describe an inline view.

11. What is a materialized view. Compare its advantages and disadvantages.

REVIEW EXERCISES

1. The basic syntax of the SELECT statement requires two keywords _____ and _____.

2. Entry in the SELECT keyword clause that shows all attributes from a table is _____.

3. Entry in the SELECT keyword clause that ensures unique rows in query result is _____.

4. The keywords of a keyword clause in the SELECT query statement that sorts the query output is _____.

5. The built-in function that counts the number of rows in a table is _____.

6. There are _____ built-in functions that can be used in a query statement.

7. The keywords of a clause in the SELECT query statement that performs grouping of selected rows based on similar attribute values is _____.

8. The keywords of a clause in the SELECT query statement that specifies a search condition on the groups created is _____.

9. Queries involving more than one table require proper _____ of tables.

10. The _____ is used to fulfill a search condition in the outer query.

11. The condition to join tables in a query is specified in the _____ WHERE keyword clause.

12. The _____ function in the SELECT keyword clause takes a specific value and compares it to values in the list.

13. _____ outer join includes all rows that match the join condition along with those rows in the first (left) table that are unmatched with rows from the second (right) table.

14. _____ outer join includes all rows that match the join condition along with those rows in the second (right) table that are unmatched with rows from the first (left) table.

15. _____ outer join includes all rows that match the join condition along with those rows that are unmatched in both tables.

16. The keywords to create a view is _____ _____.

17. Views can be dropped from the database using the _____ _____ keywords.

18. _____ view is a temporary table generated through a subquery in the FROM clause.

19. A _____ view stores the data defined through the view query.

20. A _____ view allows replication of data.

PROBLEM SOLVING EXERCISES

> Run the script file outdoorDB_v4.sql to load the Outdoor Clubs & Product database to complete the following exercises.

Ex2B-1.   List the PRODUCT_ID, PRODUCT_NAME, and PRICE values from the PRODUCT table.

Ex2B-2.   List the PRODUCT_ID, PRODUCT_NAME, and PRICE values from the PRODUCT table where PRICE is greater than 10.

Ex2B-3.   How many customers are listed in the CUSTOMER table.

Ex2B-4.   List the FIRST_NAME, LAST_NAME for all customers who have placed a product order. (Use subquery).

Ex2B-5.   List the FIRST_NAME, LAST_NAME for all customers who have placed a product order. (Use join).

Ex2B-6.   List the mountain club NAME, DURATION, FIRST_NAME, LAST_NAME for customers who have club membership.

Ex2B-7.   How many product orders are there for each PAYMENT_TYPE.

Ex2B-8.   What is average quantity for each product order.

Ex2B-9.   List all product name which end with word "Pole."

Ex2B-10. List the customer name (FIRST_NAME, LAST_NAME) along with their club MEMBERSHIP_ID. If a customer does not have club membership, the output should show null.

Ex2B-11. List all products (PRODUCT_NAME) along with the number of times each product has been re-ordered.

Ex2B-12. List the SUPPLIER_ID, supplier NAME, and the number of products each supplier has provided.

Ex2B-13. List the SUPPLIER_ID, supplier NAME, and the number of products each supplier has provided. However, only those suppliers who have supplied more than two products should be listed.

Ex2B-14. List all products (PRODUCT_ID, PRODUCT_NAME) and their remaining stock (QUANTITY_IN_STOCK - REORDER_POINT).

Ex2B-15. List all products (PRODUCT_ID, PRODUCT_NAME) and their remaining stock (QUANTITY_IN_STOCK - REORDER_POINT). List only those rows whose remaining stock is more than the average REORDER_QTY value.

Ex2B-16.   Create a database view PRODUCT_VIEW containing PRODUCT_NAME, PRICE, supplier NAME, and supplier CITY attributes.

Ex2B-17.   Query the previously created database view PRODUCT_VIEW to list all PRODUCT_NAME, and supplier NAME located in Los Angeles.

Ex2B-18.   Create a database view CUSTOMER_VIEW containing FIRST_NAME, LAST_NAME, ORDER_ID, PRODUCT_NAME, QUANTITY attributes.

Ex2B-19.   Query the previously created database view CUSTOMER_VIEW to list those customers (FIRST_NAME, LAST_NAME) who have ordered more than two products.

Ex2B-20.   Query the previously created database view CUSTOMER_VIEW to list average quantity per PRODUCT_NAME.

> Run the script file superflexDB_v4.sql to load the Superflex Apartment database to complete the following exercises.

Ex2B-21.   List the name of each child that is in a rental unit.

Ex2B-22.   List the INVOICE_NO for each invoice from November 2007.

Ex2B-23.   List the APT_NO for each apartment that is currently vacant.

Ex2B-24.   For each apartment, list the apartment number and rental amount. Order this in descending order based on rental amount.

Ex2B-25.   For each AUTO_MAKE, list the number (count) for each make.

Ex2B-26.   List the length of the lease for each rental.

Ex2B-27.   For each apartment (APT_NO), list the name of each tenant.

Ex2B-28.   List the number of payments made on each credit card, including the credit card type.

Ex2B-29.   List the number of automobiles for each RENTAL_NO and APT_NO.

Ex2B-30.   List the amount of rent collected per month if all apartments are rented (and the tenants pay their rent).

Ex2B-31.   List the amount of rent collected based on the apartment that are rented (and the tenants pay their rent).

Ex2B-32.   List the APT_NO for the most expensive apartments.

Ex2B-33.   List the number of complaints by RENTAL_NO.

Ex2B-34.   List the RENTAL_NO that has the most complaints.

Ex2B-35.   List the TENANT_NAME of the oldest tenant.

Ex2B-36.   List the number of tenants in each apartment. Make sure you also count the tenant and include any empty apartments.

Ex2B-37.   List the name of any member of the tenant family that is older than the tenant itself.

SQL in PL/SQL

- Sequences and Format Masks
- Oracle SQL Functions
- Index and Privileges
- Query Data Dictionary

Aside from simple retrieval of table attributes values, Oracle provides various built-in functions to further enhance retrieval and manipulation of information. This lesson explores such additional features available in Oracle. It also looks at ways in which the Oracle data dictionary can be queried to retrieve user and schema specific information.

> This lesson utilizes the table structure of Superflex Apartment database and Outdoor Clubs & Product database to explain examples.

SEQUENCES

Sequences are database objects that automatically generate sequential list of numbers (integers). They are useful for creating unique primary key attributes or serve the basis for creating unique surrogate keys. Attributes using values from sequences must have a NUMBER data type. The general syntax to create a sequence is as follows (curly brackets indicate one of the two options can be used but not both):

```
CREATE SEQUENCE sequence-name
[INCREMENT BY number ]
[START WITH  start-value ]
[{MAXVALUE  final-value | NOMAXVALUE}]
[{MINVALUE  minimum-value | NOMINVALUE}]
[{CYCLE | NOCYCLE}]
[{CACHE number-of-sequence-values-to-cache | NOCACHE}]
[{ORDER | NOORDER}];
```

Every sequence must have a unique name and must follow the Oracle naming convention. The CREATE SEQUENCE keyword clause is the only required clause in creating a sequence; the rest of the clauses are optional. Creating a sequence is a DDL statement. Table 2-10 describes the optional clauses.

Keyword	Description	Default Value
INCREMENT BY	Value by which sequence incremented.	INCREMENT BY 1
START WITH	The sequence start value.	START WITH 1
MAXVALUE	The maximum value to which sequence can increment.	NOMAXVALUE, which allows sequence to be incremented to 1* 1027
MINVALUE	The minimum value for a decrementing sequence.	NOMINVALUE
CYCLE	Indicates that when the sequence reaches its MAXVALUE, it cycles back and starts again from the MINVALUE.	NOCYCLE, which indicates that sequence should stop at the MAXVALUE
CACHE	Whenever a sequence value is requested, the server automatically generates several sequence values and saves them in the server memory area called a cache to improve system performance.	20 sequence numbers are cached.
NOCACHE	Directs the server not to cache any sequence values.	
ORDER	Ensures that the sequence numbers are granted in exact order in which requested.	NOORDER, which indicates no order in number generation.

Table 2-10: Sequence Syntax Keywords

For example, the following SQL statement creates a sequence CLUB_ID_SEQUENCE that starts with 100 and increments by 10.

```
create sequence club_id_sequence
start with 100
increment by 10;
```

Sequences can be used to insert attribute values by using the convention of *sequence-name*.NEXTVAL in the INSERT statement. The following example inserts a row in the SPORTING_CLUBS table using the CLUB_ID_SEQUENCE created before.

```
insert into sporting_clubs
values(club_id_sequence.nextval, 'Hillside Mountain Club', '1 Winona St',
'Wichita', 'KS', 34342,'3163997676');
```

It is possible to determine what the current sequence value is by running a SQL query with CURRVAL keyword on the DUAL system table. The syntax of the statement is:

SELECT *sequence-name*.CURRVAL FROM DUAL;

For example, the following SQL query statement provides the status of the club_id_sequence sequence. The results follow the query.

```
select club_id_sequence.currval
from dual;

   CURRVAL
 ---------
       100
```

It is also possible to determine what the next sequence value is going to be by running a SQL query with NEXTVAL keyword on the DUAL system table. The syntax of the statement is:

SELECT *sequence-name*.NEXTVAL FROM DUAL;

For example, the following SQL query statement provides the next sequence value of the club_id_sequence sequence. The results follow the query.

```
select club_id_sequence.nextval
from dual;

   NEXTVAL
 ---------
       110
```

Once the next sequence value has been generated, the previous sequence value cannot be accessed using the sequence statement. This restriction prevents a user from accidently using the same sequence value as the primary key for two different rows. The CURRVAL keyword statement can only be used in the same database user session and immediately after using the NEXTVAL keyword statement. For example, lets confirm the CURRVAL database session restrictions by exiting the SQL editor, starting it again, and then try to use the CURRVAL statement. The results that follow the query show the error.

```
select club_id_sequence.currval from dual;

ERROR at line 1:
ORA-08002: sequence CLUB_ID_SEQUENCE.CURRVAL is not yet defined in this session
```

Sequences are dropped from the database by using the following statement.

DROP SEQUENCE *sequence-name*;

ORACLE SQL FUNCTIONS

There are many SQL functions that exist in Oracle database. These functions are in addition to the standard SQL built-in functions.

Date Functions

The SYSDATE function retrieves the current system date and time from the database server. There are many variations of SYSDATE function. To just retrieve the current date or time, the following SQL query on DUAL table can be used as shown below. The results follow the query.

```
select sysdate from dual;

SYSDATE
-------------------------
10-MAY-08
```

If you retrieve the SYSDATE value along with other attributes you can omit DUAL from the FROM keyword clause. For example, the following SQL query retrieves the CLUB_ID, NAME, and SYSDATE information from SPORTING_CLUBS table. The results follow the query.

```
select club_id, name, sysdate
from sporting_clubs;

   CLUB_ID NAME                                SYSDATE
---------- ---------------------------------- ---------
       100 Hillside Mountain Club             10-MAY-08
       110 Branson Climbing Club              10-MAY-08
       120 Cherokee Rafting Club              10-MAY-08
       130 White Plains Club                  10-MAY-08
```

When creating database reports, it may be useful to perform arithmetic calculations on dates. These calculations can utilize the Oracle date functions like ADD_MONTHS, LAST_DAY, and MONTHS_BETWEEN. Table 2-11 provides descriptions of these functions.

Function	Description
ADD_MONTHS(*input date*, *number of months to add*)	Returns a date that is specific number of months after the input date.
LAST_DAY(*input date*)	Returns a date that is the last day of the month for the entered input date.
MONTHS_BETWEEN(*input date1*, *input date2*)	Returns the number of months between two dates (including fractions).

Table 2-11: Oracle Date Functions

The use of the above functions are explained by the following SQL query examples. The results follow the query.

1. Display the extension of apartment renewal dates by two months.

```
select rental_no, add_months(lease_end,2) as new_renewals
from rental;
```

```
RENTAL_NO                NEW_RENEWALS
-----------------------  -------------------------
100101                   31-JUL-08
100102                   31-JAN-08
100103                   30-JUN-08
100104                   31-MAY-09
100105                   30-JUN-09
100106                   30-SEP-09
```

2. Display the last day of the current month.

```
select last_day(sysdate)
from dual;

LAST_DAY(SYSDATE)
-------------------------
31-MAY-08
```

3. Display the last date of the month before which the complaint number 10011 has to be completed.

```
select last_day(complaint_date)
from complaints
where complaint_no = 10011;

LAST_DAY(COMPLAINT_DATE)
-------------------------
31-AUG-08
```

4. Display the number of months between the date the lease ends and an input date for rental number 100102. There are two queries showing the positive and negative results. If the first date is greater than the second date, the result is positive otherwise it is negative.

```
select months_between(lease_end,to_date('9/30/07','mm/dd/yy'))
from rental
where rental_no = 100102;

MONTHS_BETWEEN(LEASE_END,TO_DATE('9/30/07','MM/DD/YY'))
----------------------------------------------------------
2


select months_between(to_date('9/30/07','mm/dd/yy'),lease_end)
from rental
where rental_no = 100102;

MONTHS_BETWEEN(TO_DATE('9/30/07','MM/DD/YY'),LEASE_END)
----------------------------------------------------------
-2
```

Other types of date arithmetic can involve the use of WHERE keyword clause. For example, a SQL query to display the rental number and apartment number of those rentals that are due 60 days after the entered date of 9/30/08. The results follow the query.

```
select rental_no, apt_no
from rental
where lease_end >= to_date('9/30/08','mm/dd/yy')+60;

RENTAL_NO                APT_NO
-----------------------  -------------------------
100104                   101
```

```
100105                        104
100106                        100
```

The WHERE keyword clause can use the number of days value after the specific date using the sign +, and before the specific date using the sign -. For example, a SQL query to display the rental number and apartment number of those rentals that are due 60 days before the entered date of 9/30/08. The results follow the query.

```
select rental_no, apt_no
from rental
where lease_end <= to_date('9/30/08','mm/dd/yy')-60;

RENTAL_NO                     APT_NO
--------------------          ----------------------
100101                        201
100102                        102
100103                        203
```

The WHERE keyword clause can also contain a condition involving attributes having date data types. For example, a SQL query to list customer names who have products shipped in less than 5 days. The results follow the query.

```
select first_name, last_name
from customer
where customer_id in
(select customer_id
from product_order
where (ship_date-order_date) < 5);

FIRST_NAME  LAST_NAME
----------  ----------
Anil        Kaul
Tom         Wiley
```

Number Functions

There are many Oracle SQL functions to manipulate retrieved data called as single-row functions. These functions return a single result for each row of data retrieved. Table 2-12 describes some of these functions.

Function	Description	Example
ABS(*number*)	Returns the absolute value of a number.	ABS(25) = 25
CEIL(*number*)	Returns the value of a number rounded to the next highest integer.	CEIL(65.99) = 66
FLOOR(*number*)	Returns the value of a number rounded down to the integer value.	FLOOR(65.99) = 65

Table 2-12: Oracle Number Functions

Function	Description	Example
MOD(*number*, *divisor*)	Returns the remainder of a number and its divisor.	MOD(17,10) = 7
POWER(*number*, *power*)	Represents the value representing a number raised to the specified power.	POWER(3,2) = 9
ROUND(*number*, *precision*)	Returns a number rounded to a specified precision.	ROUND(35.99,0) = 36
SIGN(*number*)	Returns a value 1 if the number is positive, value -1 if the number is negative, value 0 if the number is zero.	SIGN(25) = 1
TRUNC(*number*, *precision*)	Returns a number truncated to the specified precision. Default precision is 0.	TRUNC(34.95,1) = 34.9

Table 2-12: Oracle Number Functions

To use these numeric functions, enter the function in the SELECT keyword clause. For example, the following SQL query displays the absolute value of the number of months between the date the lease ends and an input date for rental number 100102. The results follow the query. Without the ABS function the result would have been negative.

```
select abs(months_between(lease_end,to_date('3/15/08','mm/dd/yy')))
from rental
where rental_no = 100102;

ABS(MONTHS_BETWEEN(LEASE_END,TO_DATE('3/15/08','MM/DD/YY')))
-----------------------------------------------------------
3.51612903225806451612903225806451612903
```

Character Functions

There are a number of character functions provided by Oracle SQL. These functions provide ways to manipulate display of text data. Table 2-13 describes some of these functions. These functions allow substitution of attribute names for string values or string constants.

Function	Description	Example	Example Result
CONCAT(*string1*, *string2*)	Combines two strings.	concat('Ford','Taurus')	FordTaurus
INITCAP(*string*)	Returns the string with initial letter only in upper case.	initcap('DR')	Dr
LENGTH(*string*)	Returns the length of the input string.	length('Jack')	4

Table 2-13: Oracle Character Functions

Function	Description	Example	Example Result
LPAD(*string, number of characters to add, padding characters*)	Returns the value of the string with sufficient padding of the entered character on the left side.	lpad('Jack',8,'*')	****Jack
RPAD(*string, number of characters to add, padding characters*)	Returns the value of the string with sufficient padding of the entered character on the right side.	rpad('Jack',8,'*')	Jack****
REPLACE(*string, search string, replacement string*)	Returns the string with every occurrence of the search string replaced with the replacement string.	replace('Toyota','o','d')	Tdydta
SUBSTR(*string, start position, length*)	Returns a subset of the input string, starting at the start position and of the specified length.	substr('Velvet',1,3)	Vel
UPPER(*string*)	Returns the input string in upper case.	upper('Fall')	FALL
LOWER(*string*)	Returns the input string in lower case.	lower('Fall')	fall

Table 2-13: Oracle Character Functions

To use these character functions, enter the function in the SELECT keyword clause. For example, the following SQL query combines the values of automobile make and the year of the vehicle from the TENANT_AUTO table. The results follow the query.

```
select concat(auto_make,auto_year)
from tenant_auto;

CONCAT(AUTO_MAKE,AUTO_YEAR)
-----------------------------------------------------
Ford1999
Volvo1990
Toyota2000
Honda2001
Toyota1999
Honda1999
Volvo2000
```

It is possible to embed format masks with data values such as social security numbers or telephone numbers using the concatenation || symbol. For example the following SQL query lists the TENANT_NAME, RENTAL_NO, and WORK_PHONE of tenants using phone formatting. The results follow the query.

```
select tenant_name, rental_no,
'('||substr(work_phone,1,3)||')'||substr(work_phone,4,3)||'-'||s
ubstr(work_phone,7,10) "Work Phone"
from tenant;
```

```
TENANT_NAME                RENTAL_NO Work Phone
------------------------   --------- -------------
Jack Robin                    100101 (417)345-2323
Mary Stackles                 100102 (417)545-3320
Ramu Reddy                    100103 (417)836-2323
Marion Black                  100104 (417)425-7766
Venessa Williams              100105 (417)555-7878
```

FORMAT MASKS

Data stored in database tables can be displayed using a variety of output formats. Various date format masks exist in Oracle as shown in Table 2-14.

Format	Description	Example
MONTH	Name of month	June
MON	Three-letter abbreviation for month name.	JUN
MM	Two-digit numeric value of the month.	06
D	Numeric value for day of the week.	Wednesday = 4
DD	Numeric value for the day of the month (01-31).	25
DDD	Numeric value for the day of the year (01-366).	150
DAY	Name of the day of the week upto 9 characters.	Wednesday
DY	Three-letter abbreviation for day of the week.	WED
YYYY	Displays the four-digit year	2003
YYY or YY or Y	Displays the last three, two, or single digit of the year.	003, 03, 3
YEAR	Spells out the year.	TWO THOUSAND THREE
HH	Displays hours of the day using 12-hour clock.	06
HH24	Displays hour of the day using 24-hour clock.	17
MI	Displays minutes (0-59)	45
SS	Displays seconds (0-59)	35

Table 2-14: Date Format Masks

Format masks can be created by including front slashes, hyphens, and colons as separators between different date elements. For example, the format mask MM/DD/YY would appear as 10/15/03. It is possible to include additional characters such as commas, periods, and blank spaces. For example, the format mask DAY, MONTH DD, YYYY would appear as FRIDAY,JANUARY 15,2003. Time mask can be like HH:MI:SS to stand for 04:35:50.

Some of the numeric format masks are shown in Table 2-15.

Format Mask	Description	Example
99999	Number of 9s determine display width.	34345
099999	Displays leading zeros.	034345
$99999	Prefix a dollar before the value.	$34345
99999MI	Displays "-" before negative values.	-34345
99999PR	Displays negative values in angle brackets.	<34345>
99,999	Displays a comma in the indicated position.	34,345
99999.99	Displays a decimal point in the indicated position.	34345.00

Table 2-15: Numeric Format Masks

Format Output with TO_CHAR Function

Whenever data is retrieved from NUMBER or DATE data type attributes, the data values appear using the default date and number formats. The format masks can be utilized to display data in a different format. Such display is accomplished through the the TO_CHAR function. The TO_CHAR function has the following syntax: TO_CHAR(*data value*, '*format mask*'). The following SQL query examples illustrate the use of this function. The results follow the query.

1. List the RENTAL_NO attribute value and the date the lease started (LEASE_START attribute) from the RENTAL table.

    ```
    select rental_no, to_char(lease_start,'mm/dd/yyyy') as lease_start_date
    from rental;

    RENTAL_NO               LEASE_START_DATE
    ----------------------- ----------------
    100101                  06/01/2007
    100102                  06/01/2007
    100103                  11/01/2007
    100104                  04/01/2008
    100105                  05/01/2008
    100106                  08/01/2008
    ```

2. List the APT_NO attribute value and an apartment's deposit amount (APT_DEPOSIT_AMT attribute) with $ sign having no utility from the APARTMENT table.

    ```
    select apt_no, to_char(apt_deposit_amt,'$999.99') deposit
    from apartment
    where apt_utility = 'N';

        APT_NO DEPOSIT
    --------- --------
           101 $200.00
           103 $300.00
    ```

3. List the RENTAL_NO attribute and RENTAL_DATE attribute time values from the RENTAL table.

```
select rental_no,to_char(rental_date,'hh:mi pm') rental_date
from rental;

RENTAL_NO                RENTAL_DATE
-----------------------  -----------
100101                   12:00  am
100102                   12:00  am
100103                   12:00  am
100104                   12:00  am
100105                   12:00  am
100106                   12:00  am
```

ROWNUM

ROWNUM is an Oracle attribute for listing row numbers. ROWNUM attribute can appear in the SELECT keyword clause along with other attributes names, or be part of a condition in the WHERE keyword clause. For example the following SQL queries show the ROWNUM attribute in SELECT or WHERE keyword clause. The results follow the query.

```
select rownum,first_name,last_name
from customer;

   ROWNUM FIRST_NAME LAST_NAME
--------- ---------- ----------
        1 Jack       Russell
        2 Betty      Trumbell
        3 Anil       Kaul
        4 Tom        Wiley
        5 Sharon     Stone

select first_name,last_name from customer where rownum > 3;

FIRST_NAME LAST_NAME
---------- ----------
0 rows selected

select first_name,last_name from customer where rownum < 6;

FIRST_NAME LAST_NAME
---------- ----------
Jack       Russell
Betty      Trumbell
Anil       Kaul
Tom        Wiley
Sharon     Stone

select first_name,last_name from customer where rownum <3;

FIRST_NAME LAST_NAME
---------- ----------
Jack       Russell
Betty      Trumbell
```

There are rules on the use of ROWNUM attribute.

1. The WHERE keyword clause with ROWNUM must contain an inequality. Further the inequality must be < or <=. It will not work with >, >=, =, <>.

2. The ROWNUM in the SELECT keyword clause must not appear with *.
   eg. `select rownum, * from ...`

INDEX

Indexes are created to improve query performance. An index is a table that has two attributes. One attribute stores a data value, while the other attribute stores the row or physical location in the table where the value exists. To facilitate the location of data value in a table, every table has a pseudocolumn called ROWID that specifies the internal location of the row. It is possible to find the ROWID of table rows by running the following SQL query. The results follow the query.

```
select rowid, auto_year from tenant_auto;

ROWID                AUTO_YEAR
------------------   ----------
AAAHZpAAJAAAABAAAA      1999
AAAHZpAAJAAAABAAAB      1990
AAAHZpAAJAAAABAAAC      2000
AAAHZpAAJAAAABAAAD      2001
AAAHZpAAJAAAABAAAE      1999
AAAHZpAAJAAAABAAAF      1999
AAAHZpAAJAAAABAAAG      2000
```

The ROWID column shows the encoded values that correspond to the physical location where each row is stored on the database server. Once the index is created, it is easy for the server to search index for specific database values like auto_year in the above query.

Oracle automatically creates an index for the primary key of the table. Indexes should be created on attributes that are often specified in query search conditions or foreign key values. DBMS automatically maintains the indexes. Every change in the database value stored in an index is automatically modified in the index. Also, indexes should be created after the table has been populated. A table can have an unlimited number of indexes. Indexes add considerable overhead to insert, update and delete operations. In general indexes should be utilized for tables that have many rows.

To create an index the following statement should be used:

CREATE INDEX *index-name* ON *table-name* (*index-column1*, [*index-column2*, . . .]);

For example,

```
create index tenant_auto_year
on tenant_auto (auto_year);
```

Multiple attributes (up to 16) can be utilized for index specification (called composite indexes). In such specification the first attribute is the primary search column, followed by the next attribute/column, and so on.

```
create index rental_invoice_cc_details
on rental_invoice (cc_type,cc_exp_date,cc_amt);
```

Indexes can be dropped if the applications no longer use the queries that are aided by the index or if the index does not improve query performance. The statement to drop an index is:

DROP INDEX *index-name*;

For example, the above indexes can be dropped by the following SQL statements.

```
drop index tenant_auto_year;

drop index rental_invoice_cc_details;
```

GRANTING PRIVILEGES

Privileges allow Oracle users to execute certain SQL statements. Two types of privileges exist in the database: system privileges and object privileges. System privileges allows users to perform DDL operations, while object privileges allow users to perform DML operations. These privileges are assigned by the database administrator (DBA). However some privileges can be setup by the users themselves.

The simplified command to grant privileges is:

GRANT *privilege1*, [*privilege2*, ...]
[ON *objectname*]
TO *username*;

Privileges can range from SELECT, INSERT, UPDATE, DELETE, EXECUTE, and ALTER to administration specific privilege. Objectname is the name of database object like table, procedure, and views on which the privilege will apply. Username is the userid of the user who will have the privilege.

For example, command to grant SELECT and INSERT privileges on table CUSTOMER to user "thomas" is as follows.

```
grant select, insert on customer to thomas;
```

To remove the granted privilege, the REVOKE command should be used. The syntax of REVOKE command is:

REVOKE *privilege1*, [*privilege2*, ...]
[ON *objectname*]
FROM *username*;

For example, the following SQL statement removes the INSERT privilege from user "thomas."

```
revoke insert on customer from thomas;
```

SYNONYMS

In general it is not possible for users to access database objects in each other's account or schema. However, owners can grant privileges to other users to enable other users to use their database objects. For example, user "scott" can grant SELECT privileges to user "rajeev" as follows:

```
grant select on dept to rajeev;
```

To remove privilege granted previously, the following SQL statement should be issued.

```
revoke select on scott.dept from rajeev;
```

To access a database object owned by another user, by default the object name must have a prefix of owner's username. For example, if user "rajeev" wishes to access data in DEPT table of user "scott," the following SQL query can be used. The results follow the query.

```
select * from scott.dept;

    DEPTNO DNAME          LOC
--------- -------------- --------------
        10 ACCOUNTING     NEW YORK
        20 RESEARCH       DALLAS
        30 SALES          CHICAGO
        40 OPERATIONS     BOSTON
```

To overcome this default specification, SYNONYM is defined. A SYNONYM is an alternate name for an object that references the owner name, as well as the object name. There are two types of synonyms: public synonym and private synonym.

A public synonym can be created only by a DBA or by a user who has the privilege to create public synonym. After a public synonym is created, all database users can use the synonym to reference the database object, as long as they have sufficient privileges to access the object. The command to create a public synonym is:

CREATE PUBLIC SYNONYM *synonoym-name* FOR *owner-name.table-name*;

For example, a DBA creates a public synonym for table DEPT that exists in username "scott" as follows:

```
create public synonym public_dept
for scott.dept;
```

Now any user who has privileges to view data in scott.dept table can use the public synonym in a SQL query as follows. The results follow the query.

```
select *
from public_dept;

    DEPTNO DNAME           LOC
    --------- --------------- -------------
        10 ACCOUNTING      NEW YORK
        20 RESEARCH        DALLAS
        30 SALES           CHICAGO
        40 OPERATIONS      BOSTON
```

A public synonym can be dropped by the DBA as follows:

```
drop public synonym public_dept;
```

Private synonyms are created by users who have the privilege to access data in the other username to simplify their reference. When a user creates a private synonym, only that user can use that synonym. The command to create a private synonym is:

CREATE SYNONYM *synonoym-name* FOR *owner-name.table-name*;

For example, user "rajeev" creates a private synonym for scott.dept table, and use the private synonym in a query as follows. The results follow the query.

```
create synonym private_dept for scott.dept;

Synonym created.

select *
from private_dept;

    DEPTNO DNAME           LOC
    --------- --------------- -------------
        10 ACCOUNTING      NEW YORK
        20 RESEARCH        DALLAS
        30 SALES           CHICAGO
        40 OPERATIONS      BOSTON
```

A private synonym can be dropped by the user as follows:

```
drop synonym private_dept;
```

QUERY DATA DICTIONARY

The Oracle data dictionary consists of tables that contain information about the structure of the database. The Oracle DBMS updates the data dictionary tables automatically as users create, update, or delete database objects. As a general rule, users and database administrators do not generally view, update, or delete information in the data dictionary tables. Rather, they interact with the data dictionary using pre-defined views.

The data dictionary views are divided into three general categories based on user's privileges.
- USER – which shows objects the user has created.
- ALL – which shows objects user has created as well as those objects to which user has privileges.
- DBA – which allows users with DBA privileges to view information about all database objects.

The category prefix is applied to the view names. Some of the view names are shown in the Table 2-16.

View Name	Description
USER_OBJECTS	Details on all database objects like tables, procedures, and so on.
USER_TABLES	Details on database tables.
USER_VIEWS	Details on database views.
USER_SEQUENCES	Details on database sequences.
USER_CONSTRAINTS	Details on table constraints.
USER_CONS_COLUMNS	Details on table columns that have constraints.
USER_SOURCE	Source code of user objects.
USER_TAB_COLUMNS	Details on all table columns.

Table 2-16: Data Dictionary View Names

For example, the following SQL statements shows the contents from different data dictionary views. The results follow the query.

```
select sequence_name from user_sequences;

SEQUENCE_NAME
------------------------------
APARTMENT_SEQUENCE1
APARTMENT_SEQUENCE2
CLUB_SEQUENCE
COUNTER_HOME_SEQUENCE
RENTAL_COMPLAINT_SEQUENCE
RENTAL_INVOICE_SEQUENCE
RENTAL_SEQUENCE

select table_name from user_tables;

TABLE_NAME
------------------------------
APARTMENT
COUNTER_TABLE
MOUNTAIN_CLUBS
RENTAL
RENTAL_COMPLAINT
RENTAL_INVOICE
TENANT
```

```
TENANT_AUTO
TENANT_FAMILY

select table_name, constraint_name, constraint_type
from user_constraints;

TABLE_NAME                CONSTRAINT_NAME               CCONSTRAINT_TYPE
------------------------- ----------------------------- ----------------
APARTMENT                 APARTMENT_STATUS_CK           C
APARTMENT                 APARTMENT_UTILITY_CK          C
APARTMENT                 APARTMENT_PK                  P
APARTMENT                 APARTMENT_TYPE_CK             C
CLUB_MEMBERSHIP           MEMBERSHIP_PAYMENT_TYPE_CK    C
CLUB_MEMBERSHIP           CLUB_MEMBERSHIP_PK            P
CLUB_MEMBERSHIP           CLUB_MEMBERSHIP_FK1           R
CLUB_MEMBERSHIP           CLUB_MEMBERSHIP_FK2           R
CUSTOMER                  CUSTOMER_PK                   P
FLIGHT_DETAILS            FLIGHT_DETAILS_PK             P
HOTEL_DETAILS             HOTEL_DETAILS_PK              P
MOUNTAIN_CLUBS            MOUNTAIN_CLUBS_PK             P
ORDER_DETAILS             ORDER_DETAILS_PK              P
ORDER_DETAILS             ORDER_DETAILS_FK1             R
ORDER_DETAILS             ORDER_DETAILS_FK2             R
PRODUCT                   PRODUCT_PK                    P
PRODUCT_ORDER             PROD_ORDER_PAYMENT_TYPE_CK    C
...
```

The values for the available constraint type are as follows:

P is a primary key.

U is unique.

R is a foreign key.

C is a check constraint.

V is a WITH CHECK OPTION for views.

To determine the attribute names that exist in a database view/table, the DESCRIBE statement is used. The syntax of the DESCRIBE statement is: DESCRIBE `table or view name`; For example, the following SQL statements show the attribute list for APARTMENT table followed by the USER_CONSTRAINTS view.

```
describe apartment;

Name                                Null?      Type
----------------------------------- ---------- ----
APT_NO                              NOT NULL   NUMBER(3)
APT_TYPE                                       NUMBER(1)
APT_STATUS                                     CHAR(1)
APT_UTILITY                                    CHAR(1)
APT_DEPOSIT_AMT                                NUMBER(3)
APT_RENT_AMT                                   NUMBER(3)

describe user_constraints;

Name                                Null?      Type
----------------------------------- ---------- ----
OWNER                              NOT NULL   VARCHAR2(30)
CONSTRAINT_NAME                    NOT NULL   VARCHAR2(30)
CONSTRAINT_TYPE                               VARCHAR2(1)
TABLE_NAME                         NOT NULL   VARCHAR2(30)
SEARCH_CONDITION                              LONG
```

```
R_OWNER                          VARCHAR2(30)
R_CONSTRAINT_NAME                VARCHAR2(30)
DELETE_RULE                      VARCHAR2(9)
STATUS                           VARCHAR2(8)
DEFERRABLE                       VARCHAR2(14)
DEFERRED                         VARCHAR2(9)
VALIDATED                        VARCHAR2(13)
GENERATED                        VARCHAR2(14)
BAD                              VARCHAR2(3)
RELY                             VARCHAR2(4)
LAST_CHANGE                      DATE
```

CHAPTER SUMMARY

▸ Sequences are database objects that automatically generate sequential list of numbers (integers).

▸ Sequences are useful for creating unique primary key attributes or serve the basis for creating unique surrogate keys.

▸ There are many SQL functions in Oracle to perform date arithmetic, single-row numeric functions, and character functions to manipulate display of text data.

▸ Data stored in database tables can be displayed using a variety of output formats including date formats.

▸ There is an Oracle attribute called rownum for listing and querying through row numbers.

▸ Indexes are created in database to improve query performance.

▸ Grant statement provides many data administration functions.

▸ Synonyms serve as an alternate name for tables in database.

▸ There are two types of synonyms: public synonym and private synonym.

▸ The Oracle data dictionary consists of tables that contain information about the structure of the database.

▸ The Oracle DBMS updates the data dictionary tables automatically as users create, update, or delete database objects.

▸ As a general rule, users and database administrators do not generally view, update, or delete information in the data dictionary tables. Rather, they interact with the data dictionary using pre-defined views.

▸ The data dictionary views are divided into three general categories based on user's privileges – USER, ALL, DBA.

REVIEW QUESTIONS

1. Outline the purpose and working of sequences.

2. Which Oracle Date function gives the number of months between two dates? Explain.

3. Outline the purpose of Oracle Number functions. Give at least two examples.

4. Explain the working of CONCAT function.

5. Explain the usefulness of TO_CHAR function.

6. What are the three Oracle data dictionary views? Explain their purpose.

7. Describe three Oracle data dictionary view names.

_____

REVIEW EXERCISES

1. _____ are database objects that automatically generate sequential list of numbers.

2. The function that retrieves the current system date and time from the database is called _____.

3. The function to apply format masks for display of database data is _____.

4. The command to show the attribute list for a table is _____.

5. The Oracle attribute for listing row numbers in a table is _____.

6. _____ is created to improve query performance.

7. A _____ is an alternate name for an object that references the owner name as well as the object name.

8. The two types of synonyms are _____ and _____.

9. Complete the syntax to retrieve list of tables existing in an Oracle user account.

    ```
    select table_name from _____;
    ```

10. Complete the syntax to retrieve list of sequences existing in an Oracle user account.

    ```
    select sequence_name from _____;
    ```

PROBLEM SOLVING EXERCISES

> Run the script file outdoorDB_v4.sql to load the Outdoor Clubs & Product database to complete the exercises.

Ex2C-1.   Create a script file ex2c_1.sql that
(i) creates a sequence KR_ORDER_SEQUENCE, starting at 1000. The sequence increments by 100.
(ii) Use this sequence to insert the following rows in KR_ORDER table created in Chapter 2 (Lesson A) Exercises.

Order_Number	Customer_Name	Salesperson_Name	Amount
1000	Jackie Foods	Anita Raina	700
1100	Indie Professional	Tom Selleck	1200
1200	Tom Construction	Joe Walton	1500
1300	Jackie Foods	Tom Selleck	850

Ex2C-2.   List the MEMBERSHIP_ID, CUSTOMER_ID, and the dates on which the club memberships expire.

Ex2C-3.   List ORDER_ID, ORDER_DATE, and shipping time (the number of days it takes to ship order).

Ex2C-4.   List only those ORDER_ID, ORDER_DATE, and shipping time (the number of days it takes to ship order) where the shipping time is greater than the average such time.

Ex2C-5   List the FIRST_NAME, LAST_NAME of customers who had their products shipped in less than 5 days.

Ex2C-6.   List the first four PRODUCT_NAME.

Ex2C-7.   List the first two ORDER_ID values where the payment type is credit card.

Ex2C-8.   List the attributes and their data types for PRODUCT_ORDER and CUSTOMER tables in Outdoor Clubs & Product Database.

Ex2C-9.   Show all the constraints in the database.

Ex2C-10. Show all the constraints in the ORDER_DETAILS table of Outdoor Clubs & Product Database.

Ex2C-11. Show all the tables in the database.

CHAPTER 3
(LESSON A)

PL/SQL Language

- PL/SQL Language Structure
- PL/SQL Variables and Statements
- Anonymous PL/SQL Program Unit
- SQL Query Cursors

SQL has no structured logic capabilities. Generally, the structured logic of an application is provided by programming languages like C or Cobol. Such languages also have a SQL component (sometimes called as embedded SQL) to retrieve or transfer database data. Oracle developed a language native to its database called PL/SQL for application building as well as database operations. This lesson provides an introduction to PL/SQL structure and its application building capabilities.

PL/SQL is an extension of the SQL database language with structured logic capabilities. While SQL enables development of individual queries, PL/SQL provides the ability to combine such SQL queries for more complex database retrieval and manipulation. The interaction of SQL with PL/SQL is seamless. PL/SQL allows the data manipulation and query statements of SQL to be included within its block structure, thereby making PL/SQL a powerful transaction processing language. Aside from procedural capabilities, the other benefits of PL/SQL can be categorized as:
- Modular program development.
- Define identifiers and then use them in SQL and procedural statements.
- Efficient handling of database errors.
- Portable PL/SQL program units for execution in any host environment that supports the Oracle setup.
- Integration with other Oracle development tools.
- Improve performance of an application since PL/SQL performs database operations very efficiently.
- Support for object-oriented programming.
- Web database interactivity.

PL/SQL PROGRAM UNIT STRUCTURE

A PL/SQL program unit consists of a standard structure referred as a *PL/SQL block*. It consists of three sections – declarative, executable, and exception handling. The PL/SQL block structure with sections and related keywords is shown in Figure 3-1. Each declaration ends with a semi-colon (;). Each SQL or PL/SQL statement also ends with a semi-colon (;).

```
[DECLARE
... variables, user-defined exceptions ...]

BEGIN
... SQL and PL/SQL statements ...

[EXCEPTION
... error-handling statements  (SQL and PL/SQL statements) ...]

END;
```

Figure 3-1

Table 3-1 below provides a brief description of the sections along with each sections inclusion status within a PL/SQL block.

Block Section	Section Description
Declarative *(Optional)*	Specified with the keyword DECLARE. This section defines all the variables and user-defined exceptions that will be referenced within the Executable section. The variables in this section may store database values like rental_no attribute value, a table row, or some temporary value.
Executable *(Mandatory)*	Specified within the BEGIN and END keywords. This section is the heart of the PL/SQL block. It contains all the processing logic involving SQL and PL/SQL statements.
Exception Handling *(Optional)*	Specified with the EXCEPTION keyword. This section includes actions (or error handlers) when errors arise within the Executable section.

Table 3-1: PL/SQL Block Description

The PL/SQL program units are categorized into named or anonymous(unnamed) units. The standard PL/SQL block of Figure 3-1 is also referred as an anonymous PL/SQL program unit. If a named PL/SQL program unit is developed, the top line of the PL/SQL block will include a header line. The header line defines the name and the type of the program unit as well as any parameters (values) it is supposed to receive or return. These PL/SQL program units can be developed based on the needs of the development environment. Table 3-2 provides a brief description of these program units.

PL/SQL Program Unit	Description
Anonymous Block	Unnamed PL/SQL block that can be embedded within an application or run through a SQL editor.
Stored Procedure or Function	Named PL/SQL block in the database that can accept input and can be invoked repeatedly.
Application Procedure or Function	Named PL/SQL block in an application that can accept input and can be invoked repeatedly.

Table 3-2: PL/SQL Program Unit Descriptions

PL/SQL Program Unit	Description
Package	Named PL/SQL module that groups related procedures, functions, and identifiers together.
Database Trigger	A PL/SQL block that is associated with a database table and is executed in response to a database event.
Application Trigger	A PL/SQL block that is executed in response to an application event.

Table 3-2: PL/SQL Program Unit Descriptions

This lesson utilizes anonymous block program units to explain the working of PL/SQL language structure. The following lessons cover the named program units.

Nature of PL/SQL Program Unit Interaction with the Database Server

Even though the PL/SQL program units are stored in Oracle DBMS, they are relatively separate modules within the server. The interaction of PL/SQL program units with the database server is channeled through the PL/SQL Engine. This interaction is through the SQL statements as shown in Figure 3-2.

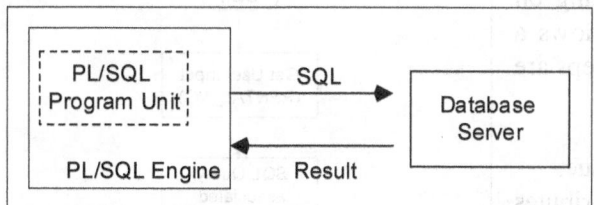

Figure 3-2

PL/SQL program units primarily deal with database data. One of the key elements during this interaction pertains to the handling of SQL operations. The database server processes and returns the result of each SQL statement back to the PL/SQL program unit. The server does not hold the result, while the program unit continues processing. This implies that for SQL statements like INSERT, UPDATE, DELETE where the results are either success or failure due to error, the PL/SQL program unit does not have to store anything. However, in case of SQL query, the entire query output is returned to the program unit. It is the job of the PL/SQL program unit to store the query results for processing.

Structured Logic Overview

Irrespective of the purpose of any programming language, all languages in general have similar logic structures. PL/SQL language also follows the standard logic structures. Since PL/SQL is a database language, most of the PL/SQL logic structures typically involve database content. These logic structures are now reviewed within the database context using flowchart diagrams.

SEQUENCE LOGIC

Every program unit has a sequence of actions. Such actions are expressed through the sequence of PL/SQL language statements. The flowchart of Figure 3-3 shows a typical sequence logic. The logic steps are as follows:

1. User inputs RENTAL_NO attribute value.
2. SQL query on the TENANT table attributes TENANT_SS, TENANT_NAME and EMPLOYER_NAME for input RENTAL_NO. The database server returns the query output row values that are stored as a variable in the program unit.
3. Fetch the stored TENANT output row for processing.
4. Display the output row TENANT_SS, TENANT_NAME and EMPLOYER_NAME attribute values.

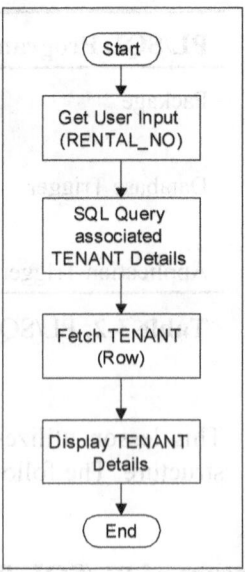

Figure 3-3

DECISION/SELECTION LOGIC

Program units may include decision/selection logic that outlines sequences of actions depending on some question or condition. Figure 3-4 shows a simple decision logic situation. The logic steps are as follows:

1. User inputs RENTAL_NO attribute value.
2. SQL query on the TENANT table attributes TENANT_SS, TENANT_NAME and EMPLOYER_NAME for input RENTAL_NO. The database server returns the query output row values that are stored as a variable in the program unit.
3. Fetch the stored TENANT output row for processing.
4. Check if the stored EMPLOYER_NAME value is "MSU."
   - If the EMPLOYER_NAME is "MSU" display stored TENANT_SS, TENANT_NAME values along with text "Academic."
   - If the EMPLOYER_NAME is not "MSU" display stored TENANT_SS, TENANT_NAME values along with text "Professional."

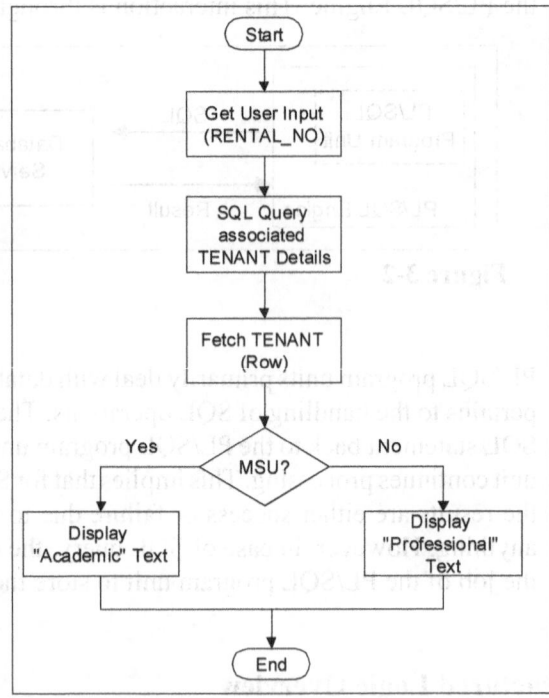

Figure 3-4

ITERATION LOGIC

Program units may include looping/iteration logic that repeat actions. Figure 3-5 shows a simple iteration logic. The logic steps are as follows:

1. SQL query on STAFF table attributes STAFF_NO, FIRST_NAME, and LAST_NAME. The database server returns multiple rows of output. The output rows are stored in the program unit as a variable.
2. Fetch the first row of stored STAFF output row for processing.
3. SQL update operation on the STAFF table to increment the SALARY attribute value by 10% for the fetched STAFF_NO value.
4. Display the stored FIRST_NAME and LAST_NAME attribute values.
5. Check if there is another row of output to be processed.
    -   If there is another row of output to be processed, fetch the row, and complete step 3 and 4.
    -   If there is no row remaining for processing, exit the program unit processing.

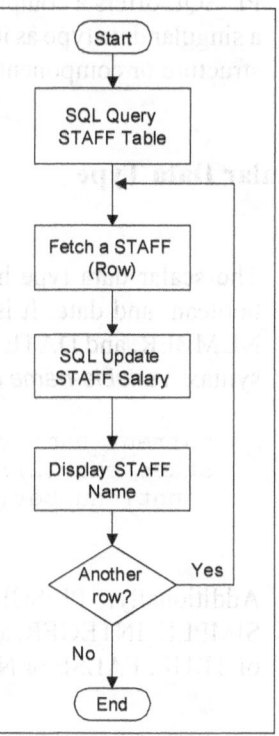

Figure 3-5

PL/SQL VARIABLES AND DATA TYPES

In PL/SQL program units variables are needed to hold values for use in program logic. PL/SQL is a strongly typed language, which means that all variables must be declared prior to their use in the executable section of the program. For example, if a SELECT statement is included in a program unit, variables are needed to hold the data retrieved from the database. On the other hand, if the program unit performs a calculation, a variable is needed to hold the resulting value.

Each variable in the PL/SQL program unit has a data type. The type of data that needs to be stored determines the type of variable needed. The data type also dictates the storage format, restrictions on how the variable can be used, and the valid values which may be placed for that variable. Since SQL is embedded within the PL/SQL language, the SQL names and data types can be used within PL/SQL. All PL/SQL variable names must follow the Oracle naming standard as shown in Table 3-3 below.

Naming Standard	Invalid Names Example
Spaces not allowed in between words.	Customer Order
Hyphens not allowed between words.	Customer-Order
Must begin with a letter	9Customer
Cannot exceed 30 characters	employee_social_security_numbers_column
Exclude PL/SQL reserved words	declare

Table 3-3: PL/SQL Variable Names Convention

PL/SQL offers a comprehensive set of predefined scalar and composite data types. A scalar data type is a singular data type as it is not made up of other variable components. A composite data type has internal structure or components. The major data types are explained in this lesson.

Scalar Data Type

The scalar data type holds a single value, and falls into one of four categories: number, character, boolean, and date. It is similar to data types available for table attributes like CHAR, VARCHAR2, NUMBER, and DATE (explained in Chapter 2, Lesson A). All variable declarations have the following syntax *variable-name data-type-and-size*;. Some examples of variable declarations are:

```
current_name varchar2(30);
state char(2);
count1 number(3);
```

Additionally, PL/SQL language includes data types like BOOLEAN, BINARY_INTEGER, SIMPLE_INTEGER, and PLS_INTEGER. Boolean is a "logical" data type. It can be assigned the value of TRUE, FALSE or NULL.

The BINARY_INTEGER data type allows you to store signed integers. The range of magnitude of a binary_integer is $-2^{31} + 1$ through $2^{31} - 1$.

Variables declared as PLS_INTEGER also store signed integers. The magnitude range for this data type is -2147483647 through 2147483647. Oracle recommends pls_integer for all integer calculations which do not fall outside of its range. Pls_integer values require less storage than number values, and operations on pls_integer use machine arithmetic, making them more efficient.

Variables declared as pls_integer and binary_integer have the same range, but they are treated differently. When a calculation involving pls_integer overflows, PL/SQL raises an exception. However, similar overflow involving binary_integers will not raise an exception if the result is being assigned to a number variable.

Variable Initialization

Sometimes a starting or initial value is needed for a variable. This is accomplished in PL/SQL through initialization during variable declaration. Initialization means that the variable will already contain a value when the executable section of the program unit (BEGIN/END section) starts processing the program logic. Some examples of variable declarations with initialization are:

```
current_name varchar2(30) default 'Jack Trench';
state char(2) default 'MO';
count1 number(3) default 123;
status boolean default FALSE;
```

Assignment operator symbol ":=" (explained later) can also be used in place of keyword DEFAULT to accomplish the same result. In practice the assignment operator symbol is more widely used.

NOT NULL and CONSTANT

The NOT NULL option will require that the variable always contain a value. This value can change during the program unit execution, but the variable must always contain a value. For example, the following declaration initializes variable "current_name" with NOT NULL option, thereby implying that this variable must always store some value.

```
current_name varchar2(30) not null default 'Jack Trench';
```

The CONSTANT option can be added to the variable declaration to require the variable to always contain a specific value within the program unit. In other words, the CONSTANT option can keep the value of the variable from being changed within the program unit. For example, the following declaration initializes variable state with a fixed value "MO" throughout the program unit.

```
state constant char(2) default 'MO';
```

Reference Data Type

There are two special data types in PL/SQL called as *reference data types* that allow a PL/SQL variable to have (i) direct reference and use of a table attribute data type, or (ii) provide a way to reference a table row or a row of output from a SQL query. Reference data types reduce errors when database values have to be stored in variables. It ensures that the developer does not have to check the data type of a database table attribute to be sure that it matches correctly with the declared variable. Further if changes are made to the database structure, such as making an attribute size longer, the developer does not have to be concerned with modifying the variable declaration.

Direct Reference to a Table Attribute Data Type

The syntax of reference data type that refers to the data type of a table attribute in database is:

variablename   tablename.attributename%TYPE;

For example, the following declaration for a variable named "current_apt_no" stores data similar to APT_NO attribute in APARTMENT table:

```
current_apt_no apartment.apt_no%type;
```

Reference a Table Row or a SQL Query Output Row

The syntax of reference data type that refers to an entire row of a table or SQL query output is:

> *variablename   table or query name*%ROWTYPE;

The query name involves the use of a concept called cursor (explained later). For example, the declaration for a variable named RENTAL_ROW that will store one row of RENTAL table will be written in a PL/SQL program unit as:

```
rental_row rental%rowtype;
```

Since RENTAL_ROW variable stores a row of rental table, each attribute of the RENTAL table will be accessed using the syntax *variable-name.attribute-name*. So, to access the LEASE_TYPE attribute value the syntax will be `rental_row.lease_type`. Rowtype declarations are also used to define table-based records (explained later).

Composite Data Types

Variables can be defined that store multiple scalar values using more complex data types called as collections and records. Collections consist of associative arrays, nested tables, varrays, and PL/SQL record.

Associative Arrays

An associative array data type (also known as index-by tables) is similar to a one-dimensional array. It consists of two elements – a primary key that indexes the table, and the actual value having its own data type. A variable having associative array data type is declared using the following syntax:

> TYPE *typename* IS TABLE OF *scalar data type* [NOT NULL]
>   INDEX BY [BINARY_INTEGER | PLS_INTEGER | VARCHAR2(size-limit)];
> *variablename typename*;

For example, variables AUTO_MAKE_TABLE and AUTO_MODEL_TABLE can be declared to store the AUTO_MAKE and AUTO_MODEL values from TENANT_AUTO table as follows:

```
TYPE auto_type IS TABLE OF varchar2(10)
   INDEX BY BINARY_INTEGER;
auto_make_table auto_type;
auto_model_table auto_type;
```

To fill the table, values should be assigned directly with the assignment operator (:=) using the syntax *plsql-arrayname(key) := value*. Table 3-4 shows the sample values of auto_make_table. The first key value does not have to be 1, and the associated values do not have to be inserted sequentially. To reference an item in the associative array the syntax should be *plsql-arrayname(key)*. The following anonymous block unit fills the associative array auto_make_table.

Key	Value
1	Ford
2	Volvo
3	Toyota
4	Honda

Table 3-4: Table Data Type Values

```
declare
TYPE auto_type IS TABLE OF varchar2(10)
   INDEX BY BINARY_INTEGER;
auto_make_table auto_type;
begin
auto_make_table(1) := 'Ford';
auto_make_table(2) := 'Volvo';
auto_make_table(3) := 'Toyota';
auto_make_table(4) := 'Honda';
end;
```

For example auto_make_table(2) will reference the second value "Volvo." The elements in an associative array are not stored in any particular order, and the key values need not be sequential. The only restriction on the key values are that they must be integers and unique within the array table structure. Associative array table values are stored in the memory of the database server. It can grow as large as needed, depending on available server memory.

Associative array tables can also be used to store multiple values called as *table of records*. Such tables are useful for storing lookup information from database tables that are used many times within a program unit. By storing the information in an associative array table, the program unit does not have to repeatedly query the database, which improves processing performance. The table declaration now uses the ROWTYPE reference datatype as shown below.

```
TYPE complaint_type IS TABLE OF complaints%rowtype
   INDEX BY BINARY_INTEGER;
complaint_table complaint_type;
```

In the above declaration the `complaint_type` data type holds a row of COMPLAINTS table. A table of records in filled programmatically similar to a table of single value, but now it will expand horizontally with all attributes of the table.

There are many special keywords attached to an associative array that helps in its manipulation. These features are explained in the Table 3-5.

Keyword	Description	Examples	Results
COUNT	Returns the number of rows in the table	auto_make_table.count	4
DELETE (*row key*)	Deletes a specific table row or a range of rows.	auto_make_table.delete	Deletes all rows.
DELETE(*first key to be deleted, last key to be deleted*)		auto_make_table.delete(2)	Deletes row with index value 2.
		auto_make_table.delete(1,2)	Deletes rows with index values 1 through 2.
EXISTS(*row key*)	Returns TRUE or FALSE if the specified row exists.	IF auto_make_table.exists(2)	Returns TRUE if the item associated with key value 2 exists.
FIRST	Returns the key value of the first item in the table.	auto_make_table.first	1
LAST	Returns the key value of the last item in the table.	auto_make_table.last	4
NEXT(*row key*)	Returns the value of the key of next row after the specified row.	auto_make_table.next(2)	If current row key = 2, returns 3
PRIOR(*row key*)	Returns the value of the key of row before the specified row.	auto_make_table.prior(3)	If current row key = 3, returns 2

Table 3-5: PL/SQL Table Processing Keywords

Nested Tables

Nested tables represent sets of values. They are also one-dimensional arrays with no upper bound. One can model multi-dimensional arrays by creating nested tables whose elements are also nested tables. They use sequential numbers as subscripts.

Nested tables can also be stored in database tables and manipulated through SQL. Within the database, nested tables are column types that hold sets of values. Oracle stores the rows of a nested table in no particular order. When a nested table is retrieved from the database into a PL/SQL variable, the rows are given consecutive subscripts starting at 1. That gives array-like access to individual rows.

Nested tables differ from arrays in two important ways: (i)the size of a nested table can increase dynamically, and (ii) they might not have consecutive subscripts. One can delete elements from a nested table using the built-in procedure DELETE. The built-in function NEXT lets you iterate over all the subscripts of a nested table, even if the sequence has gaps.

The syntax to define a PL/SQL type for nested tables is:

```
TYPE typename IS TABLE OF scalar data type [NOT NULL];
variablename typename;
```

Varrays

Varrays (short for variable-size arrays) hold a fixed number of elements (although you can change the number of elements at runtime). They use sequential numbers as subscripts. You can define equivalent SQL types, allowing varrays to be stored in database tables. They can be stored and retrieved through SQL, but with less flexibility than nested tables.

A varray has a maximum size, which you specify in its type definition. Its index has a fixed lower bound of 1 and an extensible upper bound. A varray can contain a varying number of elements, from zero (when empty) to the maximum specified in its type definition.

The syntax to define a PL/SQL type for varrays is:

```
TYPE typename IS {VARRAY | VARYING ARRAY} (size_limit)
  OF scalar data type [NOT NULL];
variablename typename;
```

where size_limit is a positive integer literal representing the maximum number of elements in the array.

Until nested tables or varrays are initialized, they are atomically null: the collection itself is null, not its elements. To initialize a nested table or varray, a constructor is utilized. This constructor is a system-defined function with the same name as the collection type. This function "constructs" collections from the elements passed to it. This constructor must be explicitly called for each varray and nested table variable.

To store nested tables and varrays inside database tables, it is necessary to declare SQL types using the CREATE TYPE statement. The SQL types can be used as columns or as attributes of SQL object types.

PL/SQL Record

A PL/SQL record is a composite data structure, similar to a record structure in a high-level programming language. PL/SQL records can be table based, cursor based, or programmer defined. These composite data structures utilize the cursor concept (explained later) for storing values.

TABLE-BASED RECORD

A table-based record represents the structure of a table row. This is useful in situations when the application is reading (or writing) rows from (to) database tables. The individual attributes are accessed using the dot notation. The syntax for a table-based record is:

> *variable-name   table-name*%ROWTYPE;

For example, the program unit below declares a variable `tenant_rec` that stores one row of TENANT table. The SQL query in the begin/end block of the program will transfer all attribute values for the specific row to variable `tenant_rec`. To access individual row values the syntax should be *variable-name.attribute-name*.   So, to access the MARITAL attribute value the syntax will be `tenant_rec.marital`.

```
declare
tenant_rec tenant%rowtype;
begin
select *
into tenant_rec
from tenant
where tenant_ss = 123456789;
end;
```

PROGRAMMER-DEFINED RECORD

A programmer-defined record is similar to records in high-level programming language. To declare a record variable, a type declaration must be made first followed by the variable name. The syntax is:

```
TYPE record-variable-type-name IS RECORD
    (field-1  datatype,
     field-2  datatype,
     .
     .
     .
     field-i  datatype);
    record-variable  record-variable-type-name;
```

For example, the program unit below declares a variable `tenant_rec` that stores a record of the type `my_tenant_type`. The record will hold three variable values. The SQL query in the executable section of the program unit will transfer three attribute values for the specific row to variable `tenant_rec`. To access individual values the syntax should be *variable-name.record-type-variable*. So, to access the EMPLOYER attribute value the syntax will be `tenant_rec.employer`.

```
declare
type my_tenant_type is record
    (ss tenant.tenant_ss%type,
    name tenant.tenant_name%type,
    employer varchar2(20));
tenant_rec my_tenant_type;
begin
```

```
select tenant_ss, tenant_name, employer_name
into tenant_rec
from tenant
where tenant_ss = 123456789;
end;
```

CURSOR-BASED RECORD

Cursor-based records are described as explicit cursors record later in the chapter.

SQL STATEMENTS IN PROGRAM UNIT

Due to the seamless integration of SQL within a PL/SQL program unit, SQL statements can be directly specified within the executable section of a PL/SQL block.

DATA MANIPULATION

Data manipulation statements are often required in applications. For example, when a new RENTAL row is created, data related to it needs to be stored in the database. DML statements can be embedded directly into the executable section of the PL/SQL block. The following examples show different DML statements within a PL/SQL block. It is possible to combine multiple DML operations in one PL/SQL block.

1. A PL/SQL anonymous block unit that inserts a new row in RENTAL table.

```
begin
insert into rental (rental_no, rental_date, staff_no, apt_no)
values(rental_sequence.nextval,sysdate,'SA200',103);
commit;
end;
```

2. A PL/SQL anonymous block unit that modifies the STAFF_NO value for RENTAL_NO 100103 in RENTAL table.

```
begin
update rental
set staff_no = 'SA200'
where rental_no = 100103;
commit;
end;
```

3. A PL/SQL anonymous block unit that deletes COMPLAINT_NO 10010 from the COMPLAINTS table.

```
begin
delete from complaints
where complaint_no = 10010;
commit;
end;
```

SQL QUERY

SQL query statements can be embedded in the executable section of a PL/SQL block to retrieve data from the database for use in the block. When a SQL query is included in a PL/SQL block, the SELECT clause is followed by a INTO clause. The INTO clause lists the variables that are to hold the values that are returned by the database server. A SQL query embedded within the executable section of the PL/SQL block must return only one row. The Handling SQL Query Cursors section has more details on how SQL queries are handled in PL/SQL block.

The following PL/SQL anonymous program unit retrieves one row of STAFF_NO and APT_NO attribute values for RENTAL_NO 100103 from the RENTAL table.

```
declare
staff_no_text rental.staff_no%type;
apt_no_text rental.apt_no%type;
begin
select staff_no, apt_no
into staff_no_text, apt_no_text
from rental
where rental_no = 100103;
end;
```

Details on running anonymous PL/SQL program unit in SQL Developer is provided in Appendix E.

LOGIC STRUCTURES & PL/SQL STATEMENTS

Standard programming logic structures can be implemented through relevant PL/SQL statements. Such statements consists of assignment statements, selection statements, and iteration statements. Besides the logic structure statements there are also comment statements, display statements, and special statements. PL/SQL statements can span many lines, but must terminate with a semi-colon. PL/SQL statements can be executed in a PL/SQL editor or any other Oracle development environment based on the PL/SQL language.

The anonymous PL/SQL program units can be entered directly in a PL/SQL editor. Since each PL/SQL statement ends with a semi-colon, a PL/SQL editor recognizes a PL/SQL program unit by entry of keywords like DECLARE, and so does not execute statements even if they end with semi-colon.

Comment Statement

Comment statements are not executed, but utilized for documentation purposes. Comments can be inserted anywhere in the program. There are two types of comment statements – single line or multi-line. Single line comment statements have two hyphens (- -) at the beginning of the line. Multi-line comments start with the symbols /* and end with symbols */. For example the following code shows the two types of comments.

```
-- This is a single line comment statement.
/* This is a multiple line comment statement. It can be created
   anywhere in the program */
```

Display Statement

Display statements in PL/SQL show variable data or text string in a PL/SQL editor. The general display statement is DBMS_OUTPUT.PUT_LINE. DBMS_OUTPUT is a standard Oracle built-in package that users can access. This package has a PUT_LINE program unit that displays the content in one line. There are many other program units in the package which provide different options for displaying variable data or text string. The syntax of the statement is:

DBMS_OUTPUT.PUT_LINE({*variable* | *text string* } [|| { *variable* | *text string* } ...]);

The text string values must be enclosed in quotation marks. The concatenation symbol is used to separate entries in the statement. Prior to the use of DBMS_OUTPUT statement in program units, it is necessary to set the SET SERVEROUTPUT option. The SET SERVEROUTPUT option has to be done once per editor session. If the SERVEROUTPUT option has not been set during the session, the DBMS_OUTPUT statements in program units will display nothing. The following anonymous block program unit displays a variable data and text string.

```
declare
last_name varchar2(5) default 'Kay';
begin
dbms_output.put_line('Last Name is ' ||last_name);
end;
```

Details on enabling DBMS OUTPUT in SQL Developer is provided in Appendix E.

Assignment Statement

The assignment statement assigns a value to a variable. In PL/SQL, the assignment operator is :=. The name of the variable is on the left side of the assignment operator, while the value is placed on the right side of the operator. The value can be a literal (actual value), or another variable, or an arithmetic expression. The assignment operator can also be used to initialize variables in the declaration section of the program. The following examples show different ways of using the assignment statement in anonymous block program unit.

1. Assign a literal value to a variable last_name.

```
declare
last_name varchar2(5);
begin
last_name := 'Kay';
end;
```

2. Assign a variable temp_name to a variable first_name.

```
declare
first_name varchar2(5);
temp_name char(5);
begin
temp_name := 'Jack';
first_name := temp_name;
end;
```

3. Initialize variables in the declaration section of a program.

```
declare
state char(2) := 'MO';
count1 number(2) := 10;
begin
-- plsql statements
end;
```

4. Assign a database SEQUENCE, CURRVAL and NEXTVAL values to variable temp_curr and temp_next.

```
declare
temp_curr integer;
temp_next integer;
begin
temp_curr := apartment_sequence1.currval;
temp_next := apartment_sequence1.nextval;
end;
```

The sequence pseudo-columns can also be referenced directly, which means that one can bypass the intermediate variable assignment if necessary.

Sequence Logic

The sequence programming logic flowchart is now shown in Figure 3-6 along with the accompanying anonymous block program unit. The program unit simply assigns and displays variable data.

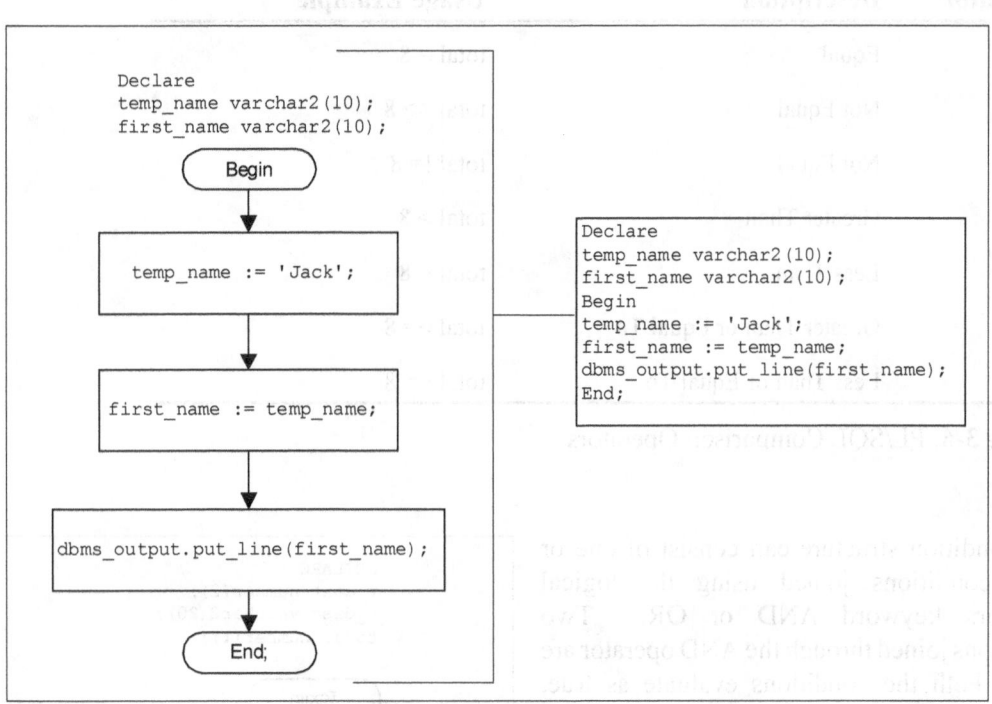

Figure 3-6

Selection Logic

The PL/SQL selection logic is a structured programming construct that changes the default sequential processing of statements. In this case, the logic sequences the processing statements based on the result of some condition or decision that is evaluated as true or false. PL/SQL language provides a IF/THEN statement that implements the selection logic. The syntax of PL/SQL selection logic statement is:

```
IF condition THEN
    ... PL/SQL statements (if condition is true) ...
[ELSE
    ... PL/SQL statements (if condition is false) ...]
END IF;
```

Every IF keyword must have a corresponding END IF keyword. The condition can either use a condition structure involving a comparison operator or a Boolean variable. The condition structure has the syntax *variablename comparison-operator value*. Table 3-6 provides a list of comparison operators and their usage example.

Operator	Description	Usage Example
=	Equal	total = 8
<>	Not Equal	total <> 8
!=	Not Equal	total != 8
>	Greater Than	total > 8
<	Less Than	total < 8
>=	Greater Than or Equal To	total >= 8
<=	Less Than or Equal To	total <= 8

Table 3-6: PL/SQL Comparison Operators

The condition structure can consist of one or more conditions joined using the logical operators keyword AND or OR. Two conditions joined through the AND operator are true if both the conditions evaluate as true, while conditions joined through the OR operator are true if either of the conditions evaluate as true. The following are examples of selection statements in anonymous block program unit.

1. Assign a numeric value 10 to variable t_cost if the condition is true, else assign a text value to variable t_desc. The program unit logic is shown in Figure 3-7.

```
declare
t_cost number(2);
t_desc varchar2(20);
total number(1);
begin
total := 8;
if total >= 8 then
    t_cost := 10;
else
    t_desc := 'condition not met';
end if;
end;
```

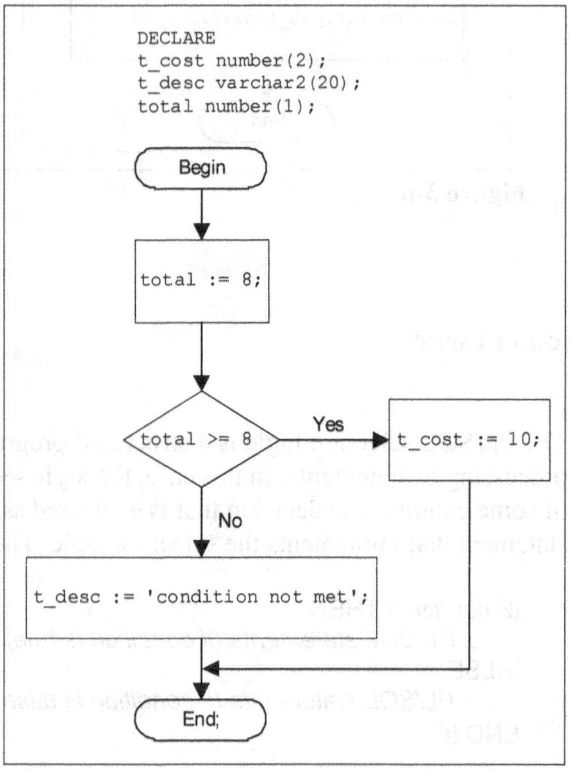

```
DECLARE
t_cost number(2);
t_desc varchar2(20);
total number(1);
```

Begin

```
total := 8;
```

total >= 8 — Yes → t_cost := 10;

No

t_desc := 'condition not met';

End;

Figure 3-7

2. Assign a text value to variable t_check if the boolean condition is true. The boolean value is defined for variable test_flag through its initialization using the assignment operator in the declaration section of the program unit. The program unit results in t_check variable having the text 'test_flag is true.'

```
declare
t_check varchar2(20);
test_flag boolean := TRUE;
begin
```

```
if test_flag = TRUE then
    t_check := 'test_flag is true';
else
    t_check := 'test_flag is false';
end if;
end;
```

3. Assign a text value to variable x_found if auto_maker and auto_style variables have correct values using the AND operator. Reference data types are used to complete declarations of variables auto_maker and auto_style. Also assignment operator is used to initialize the variables in the declaration section. The program unit results in x_found variable having the text 'Correct Match.'

```
declare
x_found varchar2(20);
auto_maker tenant_auto.auto_make%type := 'Toyota';
auto_style tenant_auto.auto_model%type := 'Lexus';
begin
if (auto_maker = 'Toyota' and auto_style = 'Lexus') then
    x_found := 'Correct Match';
end if;
end;
```

4. Assign a text value to variable x_found if auto_maker and auto_style variables have correct values using the OR operator. Reference data types are used to complete declarations of variables auto_maker and auto_style. Also the assignment operator is used to initialize the variables in the declaration section. The program unit results in x_found variable having the text 'Correct Match.'

```
declare
x_found varchar2(20);
auto_maker tenant_auto.auto_make%type := 'Toyota';
auto_style tenant_auto.auto_model%type := 'Lexus';
begin
if (auto_maker = 'Toyota' or auto_style = 'Camry') then
    x_found := 'Correct Match';
else
    x_found := 'Match not correct';
end if;
end;
```

5. Assign a text value to variable x_found if auto_maker and auto_style variables have correct values using the AND operator. Reference data types are used to complete declarations of variables auto_maker and auto_style. Also the assignment operator is used to initialize the variables in the declaration section. In this case the variable x_found gets the text value 'Match not correct.'

```
declare
x_found varchar2(20);
auto_maker tenant_auto.auto_make%type := 'Toyota';
auto_style tenant_auto.auto_model%type := 'Lexus';
begin
if (auto_maker = 'Ford' and auto_style = 'Taurus') then
    x_found := 'Correct Match';
else
    x_found := 'Match not correct';
end if;
end;
```

The IF/THEN/ELSE statements can be *nested*. Nested statements involve using another IF/THEN/ELSE combination within an existing IF/THEN/ELSE statement. For example, assign a text value to variable x_found if auto_maker and auto_style variables have correct values using the logical operators. Another IF clause is inserted if the first IF condition is true. In this case the variable x_found gets the text value 'Match is Toyota.'

```
declare
x_found varchar2(20);
auto_maker tenant_auto.auto_make%type := 'Toyota';
auto_style tenant_auto.auto_model%type := 'Lexus';
begin
if (auto_maker = 'Toyota' or auto_maker = 'Ford') then
   if auto_style = 'Taurus' then
      x_found := 'Match is Ford';
   else
      x_found := 'Match is Toyota';
   end if;
else
   x_found := 'Match not correct';
end if;
end;
```

A variation of the IF/THEN/ELSE statement is the IF/ELSIF statement. The IF/ELSIF statement allows the testing of many different conditions and is similar to CASE or SELECT CASE statements used in other programming languages. The syntax of the statement is:

```
IF condition1 THEN
      ... PL/SQL statements (if condition1 is true) ...
[ELSIF condition2 THEN
      ... PL/SQL statements (if condition2 is true) ...]
[ELSIF condition3 THEN
      ... PL/SQL statements (if condition3 is true) ...]
...
ELSE
      ... PL/SQL statements (if none of the conditions are true) ...
END IF;
```

For example, assign a text value to variable x_found if auto_maker and auto_style variables have correct values using the IF/ELSIF statement. In this case the variable x_found gets the text value 'Match is Lexus.'

```
declare
x_found varchar2(20);
auto_maker tenant_auto.auto_make%type := 'Toyota';
auto_style tenant_auto.auto_model%type := 'Lexus';
begin
if auto_maker = 'Honda' then
   x_found := 'Match is Honda';
elsif auto_style = 'Taurus' then
   x_found := 'Match is Taurus';
elsif auto_style = 'Lexus' then
   x_found := 'Match is Lexus';
else
   x_found := 'Match not correct';
end if;
end;
```

Iteration Logic

Iteration logic is a structured programming construct where one or more action statements are executed repeatedly. These action statements can represent simple sequence logic to more complex logic involving combination of sequence, selection, and even iteration logic. The repetition of action statements within the iteration logic can be for a fixed number of times, or can be based on the result of a condition. In PL/SQL language, the iteration statements are performed using different types of keywords.

Iteration logic statement using some condition as a basis for repeating action statement are expressed in three ways. The first two syntax statement involves the keyword LOOP, while the third syntax statement involves the keyword WHILE. The fourth syntax statement performs repetition of action statements a fixed number of times.

```
1.  LOOP
        ... PL/SQL statements ...
        [CONTINUE [WHEN condition]]
        IF condition THEN
          EXIT;
        END IF;
        ... PL/SQL statements ...
    END LOOP;
```

```
2.  LOOP
        ... PL/SQL statements ...
        [CONTINUE [WHEN condition]]
        EXIT WHEN condition;
        ... PL/SQL statements ...
    END LOOP;
```

```
3.  WHILE condition
        LOOP
        ... PL/SQL statements ...
        [CONTINUE [WHEN condition]]
    END LOOP;
```

```
4.  FOR variable IN <start value> .. <end value>
        LOOP
        ... PL/SQL program statements ...
    END LOOP;
```

One of the main difference in the first three statements is the manner in which the exit condition is tested. Generally when an EXIT statement is encountered, the loop completes immediately and control passes to the statement immediately after END LOOP. In the LOOP/EXIT combination, the EXIT keyword can be anywhere between the LOOP and END LOOP keyword. This setup gives the flexibility to place the exit condition in between the LOOP and END LOOP keywords in three different ways.

1. Test the exit condition first before any programming statement is executed (referred in programming as *pretest loop*).
2. Perform some statements and then test the exit condition.

3. Test the exit condition last, after all programming statements have been executed once (referred in programming as *posttest loop*).

The WHILE/LOOP statement on the other hand is always a pretest loop in which the exit condition is evaluated before any program statement is executed. The CONTINUE keyword exits the current iteration of a loop and transfers control to the next iteration (in contrast with the EXIT statement, which exits a loop and transfers control to the end of the loop). The CONTINUE statement has two forms: the unconditional CONTINUE and the conditional CONTINUE WHEN. In case of CONTINUE WHEN keyword, the condition in the WHEN clause is evaluated. If the condition is true, the current iteration of the loop completes and control passes to the next iteration.

To illustrate working of iteration logic with database, create a table abc and then insert rows in the table with iteration logic statements. The program unit logic is shown in Figure 3-8.

```
create table abc (sno number(2));

declare
tcount number(2) :=10;
begin
loop
insert into abc values (tcount);
tcount := tcount + 1;
exit when tcount > 15;
dbms_output.put_line('Value inserted '||tcount);
end loop;
end;
```

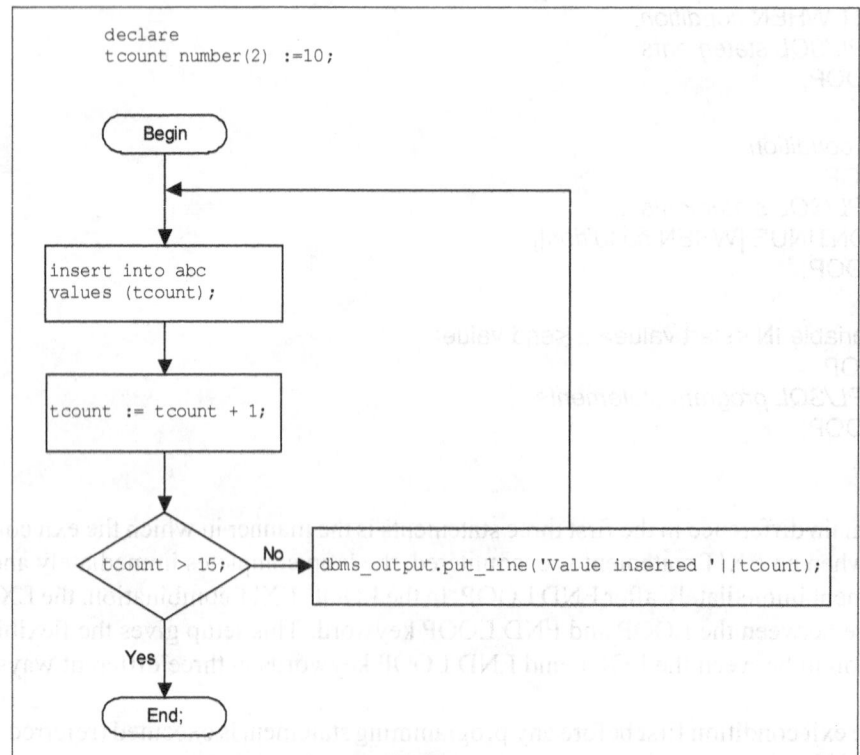

Figure 3-8

To illustrate additional examples of iteration logic create a table COUNTER_TABLE having one attribute COUNTER2 using the following SQL statement.

```
CREATE TABLE counter_table
(counter2 number(2));
```

1. Use the LOOP statements to insert rows in the table COUNTER_TABLE upto value 8 using the EXIT clause.

```
declare
count_loop number(2) := 1;
begin
loop
insert into counter_table
   values (count_loop);
dbms_output.put_line('Row Number '||count_loop);
if count_loop = 8 then
   exit;
end if;
count_loop := count_loop + 1;
end loop;
end;
```

2. Use the LOOP statements to insert rows in the table COUNTER_TABLE with CONTINUE keyword upto value 8 using the EXIT clause. There are two dbms_output statements. The first dbms_output statement will be displayed all the time. Due to the CONTINUE WHEN condition, the second dbms_output message will be displayed after the second iteration.

```
declare
count_loop number(2) := 1;
begin
loop
insert into counter_table
   values (count_loop);
dbms_output.put_line('Row Number '||count_loop);
continue when count_loop < 3;
if count_loop = 8 then
   exit;
end if;
dbms_output.put_line('After Continue '||'Row Number '||count_loop);
count_loop := count_loop + 1;
end loop;
end;
```

3. Use the LOOP statements to insert rows in the table COUNTER_TABLE upto value 17 using the EXIT WHEN clause.

```
declare
count_loop number(2) := 10;
begin
loop
exit when count_loop = 18;
insert into counter_table
   values (count_loop);
dbms_output.put_line('Row Number '||count_loop);
count_loop := count_loop + 1;
end loop;
end;
```

4. Use the WHILE/LOOP statements to insert rows in the table COUNTER_TABLE upto value 27.

```
declare
count_loop number(2) := 20;
begin
while count_loop < 28
loop
insert into counter_table
   values (count_loop);
dbms_output.put_line('Row Number '||count_loop);
count_loop := count_loop + 1;
end loop;
end;
```

The repetition of PL/SQL statements for a fixed number of times is done through the FOR keyword statement. This implementation of iteration statement requires a variable to count the number of iterations. The syntax of this implementation of iteration statement is:

```
FOR variable IN <start value> .. <end value>
LOOP
   ... PL/SQL program statements ...
END LOOP;
```

The variable in the syntax can be any valid PL/SQL variable. The start value is the initialization value for the defined variable, and the end value is the final value for the variable. Each time the PL/SQL statements between the LOOP and END LOOP keywords are executed, the variable is automatically incremented by 1. For example, the following syntax insert rows in the table COUNTER_TABLE from value 50 upto 60 using the FOR/LOOP statement.

```
begin
for count_loop in 50 .. 60
loop
INSERT INTO counter_table
   VALUES (count_loop);
end loop;
end;
```

CASE Statement

CASE statement is another type of conditional control. The syntax is as follows:

```
CASE selector
   WHEN expression-1 THEN statement-1;
   WHEN expression-2 THEN statement-2;

   . . .
   WHEN expression-n THEN statement-n;
   [ELSE statement-i;]
END CASE;
```

A *selector* is a value or a variable. Based on the *selector*, the program unit determines which WHEN clause should be executed. Each WHEN clause has an *expression* that is evaluated against the *selector*, and if the comparison is true the *statement* is executed. The *selector* is evaluated only once. The WHEN clauses are evaluated sequentially. Whenever a WHEN clause *expression* matches with the *selector*, the other WHEN clauses following it are ignored. If no WHEN clause *expression* matches the value of the *selector*, the ELSE clause is executed.

SEARCHED CASE Statement

A searched CASE statement has search conditions that yield boolean values of TRUE, FALSE or NULL. The syntax is as follows:

```
CASE
    WHEN search-condition-1 THEN statement-1;
    WHEN search-condition-2 THEN statement-2;
    . . .
    WHEN search-condition-n THEN statement-n;
    [ELSE statement-i;]
END CASE;
```

When a particular *search-condition* evaluates as true, the *statement* associated with this condition is executed. If no *search-condition* yields true, then the *statement* associated with the ELSE clause is executed.

LABEL Statement

Any executable statement in PL/SQL program unit can be *labeled*. To label a particular section of PL/SQL block simply add <<your_label_name_here>> in front of that section. The label name cannot be more than 30 characters and has to start with a letter. No need to end the label with a semi-colon (;). Labels can be the target of a GOTO statement , EXIT statement, references to variables with the same name, nested loops identification, and so on. For example the following nested loop with labels improves readability.

```
declare
    s1 integer := 0;
    i1 integer := 0;
    j1 integer;
begin
    <<outer_loop>>
    loop
        i1 := i1 + 1;
        j1 := 0;
        <<inner_loop>>
        loop
            j1 := j1 + 1;
            s1 := s1 + i1 * j1; -- Sum several products
            exit inner_loop when (j1 > 5);
            exit outer_loop when ((i1 * j1) > 15);
        end loop inner_loop;
    end loop outer_loop;
    dbms_output.put_line('The sum of products equals: ' || to_char(s1));
end;
```

Interactive PL/SQL Anonymous Program Unit

It is possible to create interactive anonymous program units. To generate such interactivity, substitution variables are utilized. Substitution variables can replace values in any SQL query clause in PL/SQL program units. These substitution variables at runtime prompt the user for values. There are two substitution variable types:

1. Single ampersand (&) defined as &*variable-name*.
2. Double ampersand (&&) defined as &&*variable-name*.

Single ampersand (&) in a PL/SQL program unit indicates a variable that holds a value during program runtime. Double ampersand (&&) in a PL/SQL program unit is a variable that retains its value for the session until the variable is reset or deleted.

The following anonymous PL/SQL program unit prompts the user for RENTAL_NO and RENTAL_COMPLAINT attribute values input, and then inserts a row in COMPLAINTS table.

```
declare
complaint_desc complaints.rental_complaint%type;
rental_no_in complaints.rental_no%type;
begin
insert into complaints (complaint_no,complaint_date,rental_complaint, rental_no)
values(complaints_sequence.nextval,sysdate,&complaint_desc,&rental_no_in);
commit;
end;
```

In the above program unit &complaint_desc and &rental_no_in are variables defined within SQL editor to make the program unit interactive.

HANDLING SQL CURSORS

A cursor is a variable or reference name given to a SQL query that retrieves database data. The cursor concept is the primary approach to retrieve database data in a PL/SQL program unit. There are two types of cursors – implicit cursor and explicit cursor. Implicit cursor is declared automatically whenever a SQL statement is issued within the BEGIN and END keywords (executable section) of a PL/SQL program unit. Consequently all DML (INSERT, UPDATE, DELETE statements) and SQL query statements in executable section of a PL/SQL program unit are implicit cursors. Explicit cursors on the other hand is a SQL query that is defined in the DECLARE section of the program unit. The explicit cursor can handle any number of output rows returned by the database server.

Implicit Cursor

An implicit cursor is created automatically whenever a DML or SQL query is executed within the executable section of a PL/SQL program unit. For purposes of implicit cursor, the standard SQL query syntax is modified to include an INTO clause. The INTO clause indicates the variables that are to hold the values that are retrieved from the database. An implicit cursor SQL query must generate only one row of output. The INTO keyword clause provides a way to define local variables in the PL/SQL program unit that will hold the attribute values returned by the database server. The number of variables in the INTO clause should be the same as the number of attributes in the SELECT keyword clause. The transfer of attribute values listed in the SELECT keyword clause to the variables in the INTO clause will follow the sequence of their corresponding list. The implicit cursor SQL query syntax is as follows:

```
SELECT attribute1, attribute2, ...
INTO variable1, variable2, ...
FROM tablename ...
...;
```

For example, the following anonymous PL/SQL program unit contains an implicit cursor query that retrieves the values of AUTO_MAKE and AUTO_MODEL attribute values for LICENSE_NO 'SYK332' from the TENANT_AUTO table. The program unit declaration section has variables make_in and model_in. Once the SQL query is executed by the database server, the AUTO_MAKE value is stored in the make_in variable, while the AUTO_MODEL value is stored in the model_in variable. The program unit logic is shown in Figure 3-9.

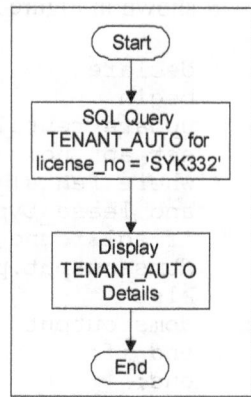

Figure 3-9

```
declare
make_in tenant_auto.auto_make%type;
model_in tenant_auto.auto_model%type;
begin
select auto_make, auto_model
into make_in, model_in
from tenant_auto
where license_no = 'SYK332';
dbms_output.put_line('Auto make is '||make_in||
' and model is '||model_in);
end;
```

There are implicit cursor attributes that provide useful information on the execution of SQL query or data manipulation statements. These implicit cursor attributes are: %FOUND, %ISOPEN, %NOTFOUND, and %ROWCOUNT. Any reference to these attributes in the PL/SQL program unit requires the SQL prefix in reference to the cursor as a SQL cursor. Table 3-7 describes these keyword attributes.

Keyword Attribute	Description
SQL%NOTFOUND	Evaluates as TRUE if an INSERT, UPDATE, or DELETE statement affected no rows, or a SELECT INTO statement returned no rows. Otherwise, it yields FALSE. This keyword attribute is the logical opposite of %FOUND.
SQL%FOUND	Evaluates as TRUE if an INSERT, UPDATE, or DELETE statement affected one or more rows, or a SELECT INTO statement returned one or more rows. Otherwise, it yields FALSE.
SQL%ROWCOUNT	Returns the number of rows affected by an INSERT, UPDATE, or DELETE statement, or returned by a SELECT INTO statement.
SQL%ISOPEN	Always yields FALSE because Oracle closes the SQL cursor automatically after executing its associated SQL statement.

Table 3-7: Implicit Cursor Keyword Attributes

The implicit cursor attributes are not substitutes for DBMS errors. The following examples of interactive anonymous PL/SQL block program unit illustrates the use of such attributes.

1. An implicit cursor with a SQL Update statement. The Update statement changes the existing APT_NO value with the corresponding input value, for an input RENTAL_NO which has a LEASE_TYPE of "Six" months. The SQL%FOUND attribute checks if the Update was successful. The program unit logic is shown in Figure 3-10.

```
declare
begin
update rental
set apt_no = &in_apt_no
where rental_no = &rental_no
and lease_type = 'Six';
if sql%found then
dbms_output.put_line('Update Successful');
else
dbms_output.put_line('Update Failed');
end if;
end;
```

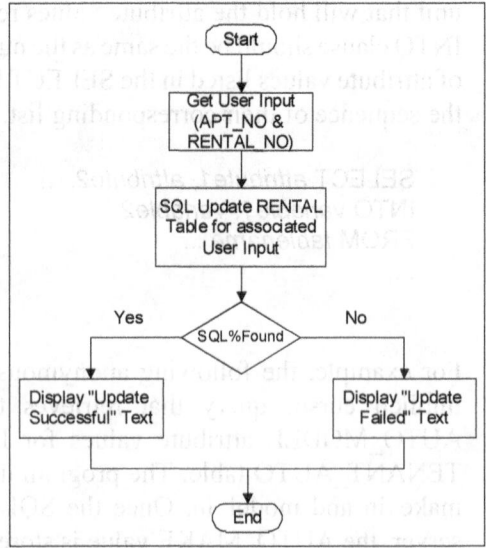

Figure 3-10

2. An implicit cursor with a SQL query. The SQL query outputs the TENANT_NAME attibute value from the TENANT table for EMPLOYER_NAME having "MSU" value and the RENTAL_NO having an input value. The SQL%FOUND attribute checks whether the SQL Query successfully retrieves a row from the database. The program unit logic is shown in Figure 3-11.

```
declare
name tenant.tenant_name%type;
begin
select tenant_name
into name
from tenant
where rental_no = &rental_no
and employer_name = 'MSU';
if sql%found then
dbms_output.put_line('Retrieval
Successful');
else
dbms_output.put_line('Retrieval Failed');
end if;
end;
```

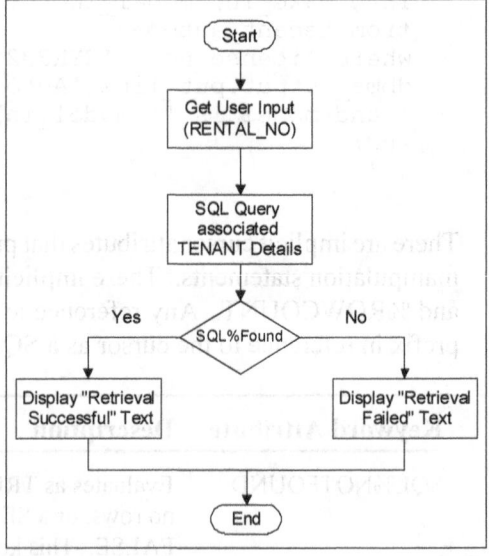

Figure 3-11

Explicit Cursor

Explicit cursors are variable names given to a SQL query in the declare section of the program unit. Once the explicit cursor has been defined, it is processed in the BEGIN and END keywords (executable section) of the program unit. The syntax of the explicit cursor definition is:

```
CURSOR cursor-name IS
SELECT attribute1, ...
FROM tablename...
[WHERE  search condition  ...] ...;

variable1  cursor name%rowtype;
```

The cursor name is a PL/SQL variable name followed by the regular SQL query statement. Along with the cursor declaration, a local variable need to be declared having the rowtype reference data type. The local variable is necessary to facilitate the cursor processing later.

Once the cursor has been defined, the processing of the cursor (shown also through the flowchart in Figure 3-12) is as follows:

1. Open the cursor:
   a. Opening the cursor essentially (i) executes the SQL query statement attached to the cursor-name variable, and (ii) stores the query output rows returned from the database server under the cursor-name variable.
2. Fetch the stored cursor row into the local variable having the rowtype reference data type:
   a. Fetching the cursor row essentially loads the current (or first) row of the cursor, and transfers the row content to the rowtype local variable.
   b. Once the row has been transferred to the rowtype local variable, the individual attribute values of the cursor row can be now accessed using the syntax *rowtype-local-variable.attribute*.
   c. This fetching of cursor rows is done sequentially till the end of SQL output rows in cursor is reached.
   d. An exit condition to test the end of cursor rows is included in the **Figure 3-12** processing.
3. Close the cursor:
   a. Closing the cursor releases the SQL query results. To get the query results again, the cursor has to be reopened again.

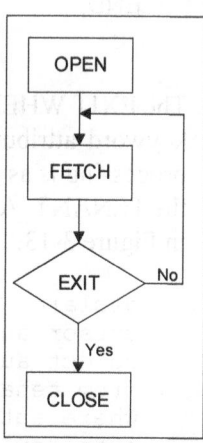

Figure 3-12

Similar to implicit cursor attributes, there are explicit cursor attributes that provide useful information to further facilitate its processing. These explicit cursor attributes are: %FOUND, %ISOPEN, %NOTFOUND, and %ROWCOUNT. Any reference to these attributes in the PL/SQL program unit requires the cursor name prefix in reference to the defined cursor. Table 3-8 describes these keyword attributes.

Keyword Attributes	Description
cursor-name%NOTFOUND	Evaluates as TRUE if a cursor has no further rows to fetch, and FALSE when there are rows remaining.
cursor-name%FOUND	Evaluates as TRUE if a cursor has rows remaining to fetch, and FALSE when there are no rows remaining.
cursor-name%ROWCOUNT	Returns the number of rows that a cursor has fetched so far.
cursor-name%ISOPEN	Returns TRUE if the cursor is open, and FALSE if cursor is closed.

Table 3-8: Explicit Cursor Keyword Attributes

There are two ways to perform explicit cursor processing. The first syntax is:

```
BEGIN
OPEN cursor-name;
LOOP
FETCH cursor-name INTO rowtype-variable;
EXIT WHEN cursor-name%NOTFOUND;
... pl/sql statements ...
END LOOP;
CLOSE cursor-name;
END;
```

The EXIT WHEN clause checks for the end of cursor rows. The cursor-name%NOTFOUND is a cursor keyword attribute that determines the defined cursor's end of rows. An example of explicit cursor processing is as follows: List the AUTO_MAKE, AUTO_MODEL attribute values of all cars listed in the TENANT_AUTO table that belong of model year 2000 and beyond. The program unit logic is shown in Figure 3-13.

```
declare
cursor auto_cursor is
select auto_make, auto_model
from tenant_auto
where auto_year > 1999;
auto_row auto_cursor%rowtype;
begin
open auto_cursor;
loop
fetch auto_cursor into auto_row;
exit when auto_cursor%notfound;
dbms_output.put_line('Make is '
||auto_row.auto_make|| ' and model is '
||auto_row.auto_model);
end loop;
close auto_cursor;
end;
```

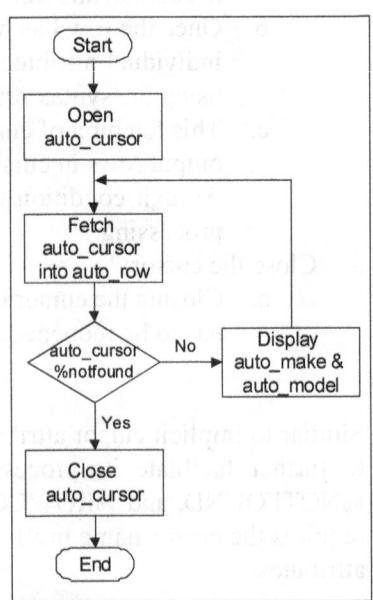

Figure 3-13

The second syntax uses a variation of the PL/SQL iteration logic FOR LOOP statement for cursor processing as follows:

```
BEGIN
FOR rowtype-variable IN cursor-name
LOOP
... pl/sql statements ...
END LOOP;
END;
```

With this syntax, there is no need to explicitly open the cursor, fetch the cursor rows, check for the end condition, and close the cursor. The PL/SQL engine implicitly performs these operations now. However the cursor values cannot be referenced outside the cursor FOR loop. The example of the first program unit for explicit cursor is now re-written for this second program unit as follows:

```
declare
cursor auto_cursor is
select auto_make, auto_model
from tenant_auto
where auto_year > 1999;
auto_row auto_cursor%rowtype;
begin
for auto_row in auto_cursor
loop
dbms_output.put_line('Make is '||auto_row.auto_make||
                     ' and model is '||auto_row.auto_model);
end loop;
end;
```

Cursor Processing Guidelines

PL/SQL language provides for complex data retrieval and processing. Often times this may involve multiple cursors, where the results of one cursor query may be the condition for another cursor query. Figure 3-14 shows a schematic view of nested cursor data retrieval. The basic approach to perform SQL query processing using cursors within a program unit should be:

1. Determine what data needs to be retrieved. This includes the attribute names and their respective tables.
2. Determine how many SQL queries (cursors) will be required to facilitate complete retrieval.
3. In case of multi-query retrieval, determine the nature of each query type, ie. whether it is an implicit cursor query or an explicit cursor query.
4. In case of multi-query retrieval sequencing of SQL queries is important – referred as *cursor nesting*. Such nesting is accomplished through notion of placing the attribute value of one cursor query as the search value of the second cursor query's search condition, and so on.

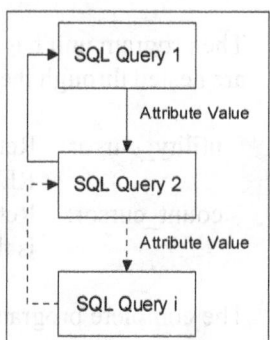

Figure 3-14

For example, lets say a PL/SQL program unit is supposed to list apartments which have utility, and for such apartments display the credit card payment count summary. The program unit should list as output attribute RENTAL_NO, APT_NO, APT_UTILITY, and CC_TYPE values along with a count of the number of times the specific credit card has been used for payment. Figure 3-15 shows the flowchart logic of the nested cursor processing example.

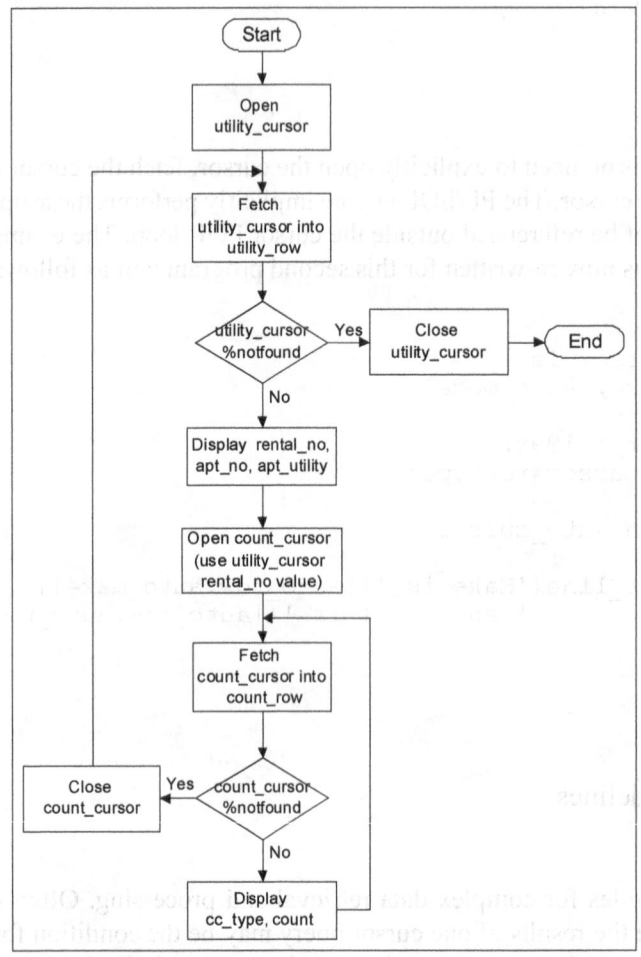

Figure 3-15

The program unit has two explicit cursors – utility_cursor and count_cursor. These two explicit cursors are nested through the RENTAL_NO value of utility_cursor. The explicit cursor queries are as follows:

utility_cursor: Retrieve RENTAL_NO, APT_NO, and APT_UTILITY from APARTMENT and RENTAL tables.

count_cursor: Retrieve CC_TYPE, COUNT(*) from RENTAL_INVOICE where the RENTAL_NO is the same as RENTAL_NO of utility_cursor.

The complete program unit is as follows.

```
declare
cursor utility_cursor is
```

```
select rental_no,apartment.apt_no apartment_no,apt_utility
from apartment,rental
where rental.apt_no = apartment.apt_no;
utility_row utility_cursor%rowtype;

cursor count_cursor is
select cc_type, count(*) as Card_Used
from rental_invoice
where rental_no = utility_row.rental_no
group by cc_type;

count_row count_cursor%rowtype;
cc_type_in char(10);

begin
open utility_cursor;
loop
  fetch utility_cursor into utility_row;
  exit when utility_cursor%notfound;
  dbms_output.put_line('Rental '||utility_row.rental_no||
            ' for Apartment '||utility_row.apartment_no||
            ' with Utility '||utility_row.apt_utility);
  dbms_output.put_line(' CC Number '||'Times Card Used');
  dbms_output.put_line(' --------- '||'---------------');
  open count_cursor;
  loop
    fetch count_cursor into count_row;
    exit when count_cursor%notfound;
    cc_type_in := count_row.cc_type;
    dbms_output.put_line(cc_type_in||'          '|| count_row.card_used);
  end loop;
  close count_cursor;
end loop;
close utility_cursor;
end;
```

Database Access Using Cursors

Aside from explicit cursor processing explained before there are other forms of cursor processing available in PL/SQL. These can be in the form of parameterized cursors, cursor variables, or cursors for updates.

Parameterized Cursors

Explicit cursors can be defined in PL/SQL that take input parameters. This feature makes the cursor more flexible. The syntax for declaring a PL/SQL explicit cursor with parameters is:

```
CURSOR cursor name (parameter1 IN datatype, [parameter2 IN datatype, ...])
[RETURN return_spec] IS
select statement;
```

For example, the following cursor declaration has an input parameter that is utilized in the cursor query. The cursor query fetches TENANT_NAME and EMPLOYER_NAME attribute values from the TENANT and TENANT_AUTO tables where the AUTO_COLOR matches the input parameter value.

```
cursor tenant_cursor (color_in tenant_auto.auto_color%type) is
    select tenant_name, employer_name
    from tenant, tenant_auto
    where tenant.tenant_ss = tenant_auto.tenant_ss
    and auto_color = color_in;
```

If a cursor loop is used to process the cursor, it will be done as follows:

```
for tenant_row in tenant_cursor('Red')
loop
...
end loop;
```

Cursor Variables

Cursor variables are special type of explicit cursors. For these variables there is no need to have a SQL query associated with them at the time of declaration. Consequently different SQL queries can be associated with cursor variables at different times in the program unit. Furthermore, cursor variables can be passed as parameters to other program units. This results in the cursor being opened in one program unit, possibly a few rows being fetched in that program unit, and the rest of the processing happening in another program unit.

Creating a cursor variable includes a TYPE statement for a REF CURSOR data type and a variable declaration using this data type. The processing is handled like an explicit cursor using the OPEN, FETCH, and CLOSE statements. However, the OPEN statement for the cursor variable provides the query to be processed. The syntax to define the cursor variable is:

```
TYPE cursor-variable-type-name IS REF CURSOR
    [RETURN return-type];
cursor-variable        cursor-variable-type-name;
```

The RETURN clause is used to constrain the type of SELECT statement that will be associated with the cursor at a later time. If the RETURN clause is missing, any SELECT statement can be associated with the cursor. Cursor variables that are declared with the RETURN clause are sometimes referred to as *constrained cursor variables*.

The syntax to OPEN cursor variables with a SQL query is:

```
OPEN cursor-variable FOR sql-statement;
```

If the cursor variable is a constrained variable, the return type of the variable must be consistent with the select list used in the query of the OPEN statement. Otherwise, a *rowtype_mismatch* exception will be generated by the system. The SQL query statement must be explicitly stated; it should not be a value of a string variable. Once opened, a cursor variable works in the same manner as explicit cursors.

For example, the following interactive anonymous PL/SQL program unit opens and displays data from different queries based on input "enter_name" value.

```
declare
type cur_type is ref cursor;
c1 cur_type;
apartment_rec apartment%rowtype;
rental_rec rental%rowtype;
family_rec tenant_family%rowtype;
tname varchar2(10);

begin
tname := &enter_name;
if tname = 'APARTMENT' then
open c1 for select * from apartment;
elsif tname = 'RENTAL' then
open c1 for select * from rental;
elsif tname = 'FAMILY' then
open c1 for select * from tenant_family;
else
dbms_output.put_line('Make proper selections.');
end if;

if tname = 'APARTMENT' then
loop
fetch c1 into apartment_rec;
exit when c1%notfound;
dbms_output.put_line(apartment_rec.apt_no||' '|| apartment_rec.apt_utility);
end loop;
end if;

if tname = 'RENTAL' then
loop
fetch c1 into rental_rec;
exit when c1%notfound;
dbms_output.put_line(rental_rec.rental_no||' '||rental_rec.lease_end);
end loop;
end if;

if tname = 'FAMILY' then
loop
fetch c1 into family_rec;
exit when c1%notfound;
dbms_output.put_line(family_rec.name||' '||family_rec.dob);
end loop;
end if;
end;
```

Cursor for Update

In many instances it may be necessary to retrieve rows from the database and perform processing on each row, including data manipulation (UPDATE or DELETE) operations. Cursor for Update is an extension of explicit cursor, that allows the Oracle server to keep track of which physical database row (ROWID) corresponds to each row in the cursor through the FOR UPDATE clause in the cursor declaration. This instructs the server to lock the rows retrieved with the cursor query for incoming updates via the cursor, and to keep track of the physical row (ROWID) of the database table to which each row in the cursor corresponds. The cursor syntax is as follows:

```
CURSOR cursor-name IS
select-statement FOR UPDATE [NOWAIT];
```

The NOWAIT option controls what will occur if the rows being retrieved by the cursor are already locked by another transaction. If this option is excluded, the statement will wait indefinitely for the rows to unlock and become available. The NOWAIT option raises the Oracle error that the desired rows are currently locked.

In addition, at the time of Update or Delete operations, the WHERE CURRENT OF cursor clause may be added to instruct the server to update/delete the physical row of the table that corresponds to the row of the cursor that is currently being processed. The syntax for UPDATE operations is as follows:

```
UPDATE table-name
SET new-values
WHERE CURRENT OF cursor-name;
```

The syntax for DELETE operations are as follows:

```
DELETE FROM table-name
WHERE CURRENT OF cursor-name;
```

The following PL/SQL anonymous block program unit fetches the POSITION and SALARY attributes from the STAFF table, and based on the POSITION attribute value, outlines different salary increments. The "Assistant" is given a 20% salary increment, the "Manager" is given a 40% salary increment, while the "Supervisor" is given a 50% salary increment.

```
declare
cursor staff_cursor is
select position, salary
from staff
for update nowait;
staff_row staff_cursor%rowtype;
increment staff.salary%type;
begin
for staff_row in staff_cursor
loop
if staff_row.position = 'Assistant' then
increment := staff_row.salary * 1.20;
end if;
if staff_row.position = 'Manager' then
increment := staff_row.salary * 1.40;
end if;
```

```
    if staff_row.position = 'Supervisor' then
    increment := staff_row.salary * 1.50;
        end if;
        update staff
        set salary = increment
    where current of staff_cursor;
    end loop;
    commit;
    end;
```

CHAPTER SUMMARY

- ▸ PL/SQL is a database programming language for Oracle database.

- ▸ PL/SQL is also an extension of the SQL database language with structured logic capabilities.

- ▸ The interaction of SQL with PL/SQL is seamless.

- ▸ PL/SQL allows the data manipulation and query statements of SQL to be included within the its program block structure, thereby making PL/SQL a powerful transaction processing language.

- ▸ A PL/SQL program consists of a standard structure referred as PL/SQL block consisting of three sections – declarative, executable, and exception handling.

- ▸ The PL/SQL block is the basis for different PL/SQL programs like anonymous blocks, procedure, functions, packages, and triggers.

- ▸ PL/SQL is a strongly typed language, which means that all variables must be declared prior to their use in the executable section of the program.

- ▸ Since SQL is embedded within the PL/SQL language, the SQL names and data types can be used within PL/SQL.

- ▸ PL/SQL language includes a BOOLEAN data type, along with two special data types called as reference data types.

- ▸ Reference data types allow a PL/SQL variable to have (i) direct reference and use of a table attribute data type, or (ii) provide a way to reference a row of output from a SQL query.

- ▸ It is also possible to define a variable that stores multiple scalar values using more complex data types referred as collections.

- ▸ There is a record data structure, similar to a record structure in a high-level programming language. PL/SQL records can be table based, cursor based, or programmer defined.

- ▸ PL/SQL statements consists of comment statements, assignment statements, selection statements, display statements, iteration statements, and special statements like CASE.

- ▸ PL/SQL uses a special concept called as cursor which is implemented as a variable for a SQL query that retrieves database data.

- ▸ There are two types of cursors in PL/SQL – implicit cursor and explicit cursor.

- ▸ The implicit cursor handles only one row of result returned by the database server.

- ▸ Explicit cursor is a SQL SELECT statement that is defined in declare section of the program. The explicit cursor can handle any number of rows returned by the database server.

- Parameterized cursors are explicit cursors that take input parameters.

- Cursor variables are special type of explicit cursors that do not have a SQL query associated at the time of declaration.

- Cursor variables allow association of different SQL queries at different times in the program.

- Cursor for Update is an extension of explicit cursor that besides retrieving rows from the database allows data manipulation operations on each processed cursor row.

- Cursor for Update allows the Oracle server to keep track of which physical database row (ROWID) corresponds to each row in the cursor.

REVIEW QUESTIONS

1. What are the different parts of a PL/SQL block?

2. Define the two reference data types.

3. How many types of PL/SQL program units can be created?

4. What PL/SQL statement implements decision logic?

5. What PL/SQL statement implements iteration logic?

6. Describe an implicit cursor.

7. Explain an explicit cursor.

8. What are nested cursors?

9. What statement is used to display PL/SQL program unit output?

10. What are paremeterized cursors?

11. Describe use of cursor variables?

12. Explain rationale of cursor for update?

REVIEW EXERCISES

1. PL/SQL is a database programming language that extends the _____ language with structured logic capabilities.

2. The keyword for the declaration section of a typical PL/SQL program is _____.

3. The keyword for the executable section of a typical PL/SQL program is _____.

4. The keyword for the exception section of a typical PL/SQL program is _____.

5. An _____ _____ is a PL/SQL program that has no name, but can be run through SQL Plus.

6. A _____ is a named PL/SQL program that can accept input and can be invoked repeatedly.

7. A _____ is a named PL/SQL program that will always return some value.

8. A _____ is a named PL/SQL program that is associated with a database table, and is executed in response to a database event.

9. The following declaration refers the data type of invoice_name variable to _____ attribute.

   ```
   invoice_name customer.last_name%type;
   ```

10. A PL/SQL _____ data type is similar to a one-dimensional array.

11. The following PL/SQL statement assigns _____ to _____.

    ```
    last_name := temp_name;
    ```

12. Complete the following syntax:

    ```
    if total >= 10 then
    t_desc := 'condition met';
    else t_desc := 'condition not met';
    _____ ;
    ```

13. Complete the following syntax:

    ```
    loop
    insert into counter_table values (count_loop);
    _____ ;
    ```

14. An _____ cursor is a SQL query statement defined within the BEGIN/END block of the program.

15. An _____ cursor can handle only one row of result returned by the database server.

16. An _____ cursor is a SQL query statement defined in the declare section of the program.

17. An _____ cursor can handle any number of rows returned by the database server.

18. Complete the following syntax:

```
loop
fetch customer_cursor into customer_row;
exit when _____;
end loop;
```

19. The name of the cursor being processed below is _____.

```
for invoice_row in customer_order
loop
dbms_output.put_line('Inside Cursor');
end loop;
```

20. The following statements pertain to the processing of an _____ cursor.

```
for invoice_row in customer_order
loop
dbms_output.put_line('Inside Cursor');
end loop;
```

PROBLEM SOLVING EXERCISES

> Run the script file outdoorDB_v4.sql to load the Outdoor Clubs & Product database to complete the exercises.

Ex3A-1.   Create a PL/SQL anonymous block program unit that displays for each sporting club, membership details in the form of membership_id, membership_date, first_name, last_name, and duration attribute values. For those sporting clubs that do not yet have any membership, "No Membership Yet" message should be displayed. Save the PL/SQL anonymous block program unit as a script file with filename ex3a1.

Ex3A-2.   Create a PL/SQL anonymous block program unit that displays product_name attribute values from the product table, and a status text based on the price attribute value. Save the PL/SQL anonymous block program unit as a script file with filename ex3a2. The rules for categorizing the price status text display are:

Price Range	Price Status
< $5.00	Low
Between 5 and 20	Medium
> 20	High

The program unit output is as follows:

```
Product Name Price Status
------------ ---------------
             Low
             Medium
             High
```

Ex3A-3.   Create a PL/SQL anonymous block program unit that counts how many products listed in the product table fall within the price range categories shown below. Save the PL/SQL anonymous block program unit as a script file with filename ex3a3. The rule for categorizing price ranges are:

Price Range	Price Status
< $5.00	Low
Between 5 and 20	Medium
> 20	High

The program unit output is as follows:

```
Product Count Price Status
------------- ----------------
              Low
              Medium
              High
```

Ex3A-4.   Create a PL/SQL anonymous block program unit that displays the product_name and price attribute values for those products that have been ordered in quantities of more than 3. Save the PL/SQL anonymous block program unit as a script file with filename ex3a4.

Ex3A-5.   Create a PL/SQL anonymous block program unit that lists the product_name attribute value and a *demand status* text display. The *demand status* text display is determined by counting the number of times a product has been ordered so far. The *demand status* text display will be either "Low Demand" or "High Demand". Low Demand is displayed if the product has been ordered less than 2 times. High Demand is displayed if the product has been ordered more than 2 times. Save the PL/SQL anonymous block program unit as a script file with filename ex3a5.

Ex3A-6.   Create a PL/SQL anonymous block program unit that displays the activity attribute values listed in the club_activity table along with a count of the clubs in the sporting_clubs table that provide the activity. Save the PL/SQL anonymous block program unit as a script file with filename ex3a6.

Ex3A-7.   Create a PL/SQL anonymous block program unit that displays the activity attribute value listed in the club_activity table along with the name of the clubs in the sporting_clubs table that provide the activity. Save the PL/SQL anonymous block program unit as a script file with filename ex3a7. A partial display of output is shown below:

```
Hiking
---------
   Hillside Mountain Club
   Branson Climbing Club

Canoeing
---------
   Cherokee Rafting Club
   White Plains Club
```

Ex3A-8.   Create a PL/SQL anonymous block program unit which uses the following values to complete a product order for an existing customer. The program unit should use variables for input values.

Product Order Details	
Order_No	Use sequence *product_order_sequence* for value.
Order_Date	SYSDATE
Ship_Date	5 days after Order_Date

Payment_Type	CC

Customer Details	
First Name	Anil
Last Name	Kaul

Product Details	
Product_ID	Quantity
1018	1
1019	2

Check with the database script file to ascertain the correct table attributes, data types as well as the sequence of operations.

After the successful completion of the above product order, display the values from the database as follows:

```
Order ID:
Cust_ID:
Total:
Product ID:
Quantity:
Product ID:
Quantity:
```

Save the PL/SQL anonymous block program unit as a script file with filename ex3a8.

Ex3A-9.   Create a PL/SQL anonymous block program unit which uses the following values to complete a product order for a new customer. The program unit should use variables for input values.

Product Order Details	
Order_No	Use sequence *product_order_sequence* for value.
Order_Date	SYSDATE
Ship_Date	5 days after Order_Date
Payment_Type	CC

Customer Details	
First Name	Brad
Last Name	Pitt
City	Kansas City

State	MO	
Product Details		
Product_ID	Quantity	
1020	2	
1021	1	

Check with the database script file to ascertain the correct table attributes, data types as well as the sequence of operations. Use the sequence customer_sequence to create the new customer.

After the successful completion of the above product order, display the values from the database as follows:

```
Order ID:
Cust_ID:
Total:
Product ID:
Quantity:
Product ID:
Quantity:
```

Save the PL/SQL anonymous block program unit as a script file with filename ex3a9.

Ex3A-10. Create a PL/SQL anonymous block program unit that displays the first_name and last_name attribute value listed in the customer table along with a list of activity values for the sporting club for which the customer has club membership. Save the PL/SQL anonymous block program unit as a script file with filename ex3a10.

PL/SQL Language

- PL/SQL Stored Procedure
- PL/SQL Stored Function
- PL/SQL Exceptions

P L/SQL program units in the database are identified by their name and type. The anonymous PL/SQL block program unit structure is extended by giving it a name and specifying its type. This lesson introduces the PL/SQL stored procedure and function program units, along with the working of the exception section of the PL/SQL block.

This lesson utilizes the table structure of Superflex Apartment database to explain examples.

PL/SQL PROCEDURE

A PL/SQL stored procedure is a named PL/SQL block structure that is stored on the database server. It can receive multiple input parameters (values), can return multiple output values, or can return no output values. A procedure is defined through the header statement attached to a PL/SQL block. The general syntax of a stored procedure is:

```
CREATE [OR REPLACE] PROCEDURE procedure name
        [( parameter1  mode  datatype, parameter2  mode  datatype, ...)] {IS|AS}
... declaration statements ...
BEGIN
... pl/sql program statements ...
END;
```

The *procedure name* must conform to Oracle naming standard. The parameter list is optional. The *parameters* can be variables or constants. The parameter *mode* defines how the parameter values can be changed in the program unit. The mode of the parameter can be IN, OUT, or IN OUT. Table 3-9 describes the different modes.

Parameter Mode	Description
IN	Parameter is passed to the procedure as a read-only (input) value that cannot be changed in the program unit.
OUT	Parameter is passed to the procedure as a write-only (output) variable. It can appear on the left side of an assignment statement in the program unit.
IN OUT	Combination of IN and OUT modes. The parameter value is passed with some input value which can then be changed in the program unit as an assignment variable.

Table 3-9: Procedure Parameter Modes

A parameter can be declared with no mode specification, in which case the default is IN mode. The parameter data type does not require a data type size precision. The following are examples of procedures.

1. A procedure *auto_list* to list the AUTO_MAKE and AUTO_MODEL attribute values of all autos listed in the TENANT_AUTO table that belong to model year 2000 and beyond. This procedure has no parameter.

```
create or replace procedure auto_list is
cursor auto_cursor is
  select auto_make, auto_model
  from tenant_auto
  where auto_year > 1999;
auto_row auto_cursor%rowtype;
begin
open auto_cursor;
loop
 fetch auto_cursor into auto_row;
 exit when auto_cursor%notfound;
 dbms_output.put_line('Make is '||auto_row.auto_make||
                ' and model is '||auto_row.auto_model);
end loop;
close auto_cursor;
end;
```

2. Change the previous *auto_list* procedure to a new procedure *auto_list2*. This procedure has an input parameter for the AUTO_YEAR value, which is used in the search condition of the explicit cursor query.

```
create or replace procedure auto_list2 (year_in in number) is
cursor auto_cursor is
  select auto_make, auto_model
  from tenant_auto
  where auto_year > year_in;
auto_row auto_cursor%rowtype;
begin
open auto_cursor;
loop
 fetch auto_cursor into auto_row;
 exit when auto_cursor%notfound;
 dbms_output.put_line('Make is '||auto_row.auto_make||
                ' and model is '||auto_row.auto_model);
end loop;
```

```
close auto_cursor;
end;
```

3. Now, change the previous *auto_list2* procedure to a new procedure *auto_list3*. This procedure has an input parameter for the AUTO_YEAR value, which is then used in the search condition of the explicit cursor query. The procedure also has two output parameters that will contain the values of the make of the auto and its model from the TENANT_AUTO table.

```
create or replace procedure auto_list3
       (year_in IN number, make_out OUT varchar2,
        model_out OUT varchar2) IS
cursor auto_cursor is
  select auto_make, auto_model
  from tenant_auto
  where auto_year > year_in;
auto_row auto_cursor%rowtype;
begin
for auto_row in auto_cursor
loop
 make_out := auto_row.auto_make;
 model_out := auto_row.auto_model;
 dbms_output.put_line('Make is '||make_out||
                 ' and model is '||model_out);
end loop;
end;
```

4. A procedure *complaint_status* with two input parameters for COMPLAINT_NO and STATUS attribute values. The procedure updates the STATUS attribute value for the input COMPLAINT_NO when the input status value is different from the stored value.

```
create or replace procedure complaint_status (complaint_in IN number,
                      status_in IN varchar2) AS
status_out complaints.status%type;
begin
select status
into status_out
from complaints
where complaint_no = complaint_in;
if status_out = status_in then
dbms_output.put_line('Update not required.');
else
update complaints
set status = status_in
where complaint_no = complaint_in;
dbms_output.put_line('Update completed.');
end if;
commit;
end;
```

Call Procedure from another PL/SQL Program Unit

Procedures communicate with other program units. This communication occurs when a procedure is called from within another procedure or PL/SQL program unit. The call to a procedure from within a PL/SQL program unit involves the name of the procedure and its parameters. The syntax is:

procedure name [(*parameter1 mode datatype, parameter2 mode datatype, ...*)];

It is important that the same number of parameters are included when calling a procedure as in the definition of the procedure. Also, the sequence of the parameter data types during the calling of the procedure should match the sequence of the parameter data types listed in the procedure definition. Figure 3-16 illustrates the concept of PL/SQL procedures interacting with each other.

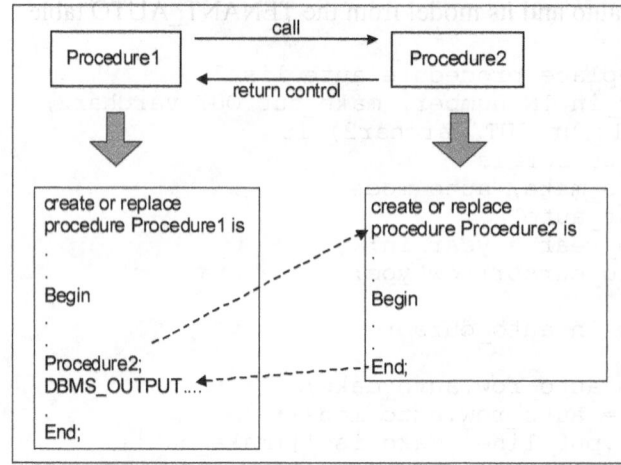

Figure 3-16

For example, the previously defined procedures *auto_list*, *auto_list2*, and *auto_list3* can now be called and executed from the following PL/SQL procedure *calling_procedure*.

```
create or replace procedure calling_procedure IS
auto_out1 tenant_auto.auto_make%type;
auto_out2 tenant_auto.auto_model%type;
begin
dbms_output.put_line('Start auto_list procedure');
auto_list;
dbms_output.put_line('Start auto_list2 procedure');
auto_list2(1999);
dbms_output.put_line('Start auto_list3 procedure');
auto_list3(1999, auto_out1, auto_out2);
dbms_output.put_line('Value of auto_out1 is '||auto_out1);
dbms_output.put_line('Value of auto_out2 is '||auto_out2);
end;
```

Maintain Procedure in SQL Developer

Details on handling procedures in SQL Developer is provided in Appendix E. Procedures can be created (i) directly within SQL Developer, or (ii) in a text editor and thereafter the file opened or copy/pasted in the SQL Worksheet of SQL Developer. A procedure has to be compiled successfully before running it.

A procedure can be executed directly in SQL Developer either through a submenu Run option, or the EXECUTE command with syntax EXECUTE *procedure-name* in the SQL Worksheet. For example, the previous procedure AUTO_LIST2 with input parameter can be run as `execute auto_list(1999);` with "1999" as the input parameter value.

A procedure can be dropped in SQL Developer either through a submenu Drop option, or the DROP PROCEDURE *procedure-name* statement. For example `drop procedure auto_list;`

PL/SQL FUNCTION

A PL/SQL stored function is a named PL/SQL block on the server like a procedure, except that it *returns a single value* that is assigned to a variable in the calling program. It can receive multiple input parameters (values). A function is defined through the header statement attached to a PL/SQL block. The general syntax of a function is:

```
CREATE [OR REPLACE] FUNCTION function-name
            [(parameter1 mode datatype, parameter2 mode datatype, ...)]
            RETURN function return value datatype IS
... declaration statements ...
BEGIN
... pl/sql program statements ...
RETURN return-value;
END;
```

The *function-name* must conform to the Oracle naming standard. The parameter list is optional. The *parameters* can be variables or constants. The parameter *mode* defines how the parameter value can be changed in the program. Like in procedure before, the mode of the parameter can be IN, OUT, or IN OUT. Since a function always returns a value, the usual mode should be IN. If a parameter is declared with no mode specification, the default is IN parameter. The parameter data type does not require a precision or scale value for numeric data type, or the maximum width of a character data type.

Along with the parameter list, the header statement has a RETURN keyword followed by the data type of the return-value that will be returned by the function. There must be at least one RETURN keyword clause in the body of the function that specifies the actual return-value that will be returned.

For example, create a function *tenant_auto* with one input parameter. The input parameter is the TENANT_SS attribute value in TENANT_AUTO table. The function returns the TENANT_NAME value for the input TENANT_SS value.

```
create or replace function tenant_function (ss_in in number)
    return varchar2 IS
name_in tenant.tenant_name%type;
begin
select tenant_name
into name_in
from tenant
where tenant_ss = ss_in;
return name_in;
end;
```

A function is called by another program unit (procedure or function) either (i) using the assignment statement or (ii) anytime a value has to be placed in the calling program unit. The syntax of calling a function using the assignment statement is *variable* := *function-name* [(*parameter1*, ...)];. The syntax of calling a function as a substitute for value is *function-name* [(*parameter1*, ...)]. The number and sequence of the parameter data types during the calling of the function should match the sequence of the parameter data types listed in function definition.

Figure 3-17 illustrates the communication between two program units – procedure and function. The function *xyz_func* has a variable x1 initialized with value 10. It has a numeric input parameter. The function simply adds the input parameter value to the variable x1 and returns the result of the addition. The procedure *xyz_proc* has two statements in its executable section. Both the statements make calls to the function *xyz_func* in ways that illustrate the two ways of communication. The first statement passes an input parameter value of 10 to function *xyz_func* which is then assigned to a variable tcount. The second statement passes the variable tcount to the function *xyz_func* as a substitute for value .

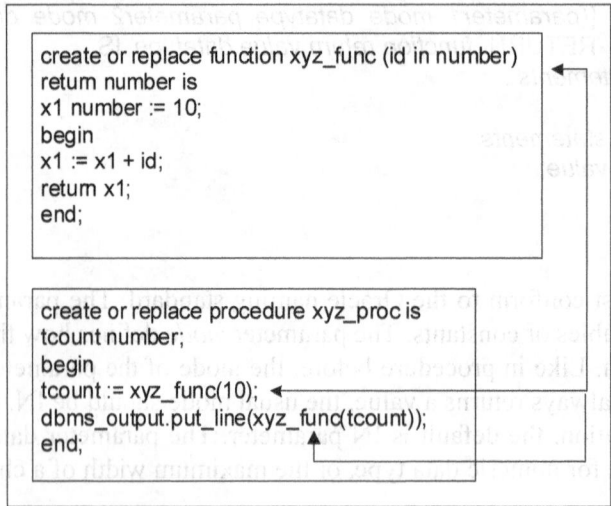

Figure 3-17

For example, create a procedure *auto_tenant_list* that lists the AUTO_MAKE, AUTO_MODEL, and TENANT_NAME attribute values for all cars that belong to model year 2000 and beyond. The procedure has no parameter. The procedure calls the previously defined function *tenant_function* to display the output.

```
CREATE OR REPLACE PROCEDURE auto_tenant_list IS
cursor auto_cursor is
  select auto_make, auto_model, tenant_ss
  from tenant_auto
  where auto_year > 1999;
auto_row auto_cursor%rowtype;
tenant_in tenant.tenant_name%type;
BEGIN
open auto_cursor;
loop
 fetch auto_cursor into auto_row;
 exit when auto_cursor%notfound;
 tenant_in := tenant_function(auto_row.tenant_ss);
 dbms_output.put_line('Make '||auto_row.auto_make|| ' and model ' ||
     auto_row.auto_model || 'is for '|| tenant_in);
end loop;
close auto_cursor;
```

```
    END;
```

Boolean Function

Boolean functions are special type of functions that do not return a value. Instead they return value TRUE or FALSE. The boolean function requires the function header to contain the return datatype as BOOLEAN. Also in the body of the function the RETURN statement should be followed by either TRUE or FALSE keyword. The boolean function syntax is:

CREATE [OR REPLACE] FUNCTION *function-name* [(*parameter1 mode datatype*,
                                 parameter2 mode datatype,...)]
                      RETURN BOOLEAN IS
... *declaration statements* ...
BEGIN
... *pl/sql program statements* ...
RETURN {TRUE | FALSE};
END;

For example, the following program unit is a boolean function that returns true or false depending on whether there is a tenant name in the TENANT table.

```
create or replace function tenant_boolean_func (ss_in IN number)
                    return boolean is
cursor tenant_cursor is
select tenant_name
from tenant
where tenant_ss = ss_in;
tenant_row tenant_cursor%rowtype;
begin
open tenant_cursor;
fetch tenant_cursor into tenant_row;
if tenant_cursor%found then
return true;
else return false;
end if;
close tenant_cursor;
end;
```

Boolean functions are called from other program units through the condition of a selection statement. For example, if the following PL/SQL selection statement is entered in the calling program unit, the condition will be true if the boolean function returns a TRUE value.

```
IF tenant_boolean_func THEN
... pl/sql statements...;
END IF;
```

On the other hand, if the following PL/SQL selection statement is entered in the calling program unit, the condition will be true if the boolean function returns a FALSE value.

```
IF NOT(tenant_boolean_func) THEN
... pl/sql statements...;
END IF;
```

Figure 3-18 illustrates the calling of a boolean function from another program unit.

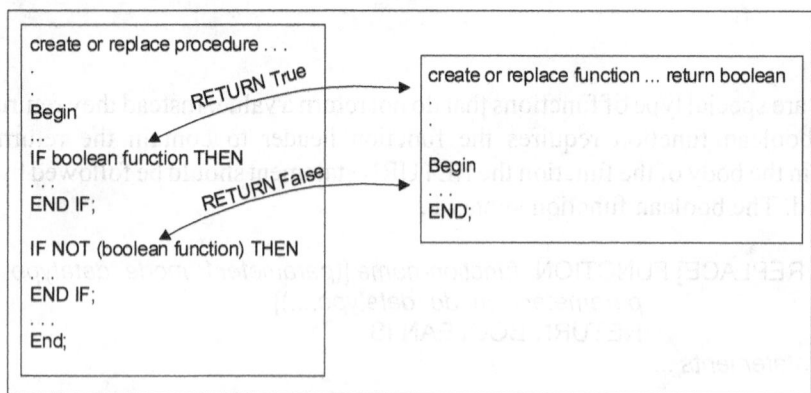

Figure 3-18

For example, the following procedure *check_tenant* calls the previously defined *tenant_boolean_func* function to display a message on whether the tenant exists or not.

```
create or replace procedure check_tenant (ss_in number) IS
begin
if tenant_boolean_func(ss_in) then
dbms_output.put_line('Tenant Exists');
else
dbms_output.put_line('Tenant Does Not Exist');
end if;
end;
```

The execution of procedure *check_tenant* using command `execute check_tenant(333444545)` will display dbms_output message "`Tenant Does Not Exist`," while command `execute check_tenant(123456789)` will display dbms_output message "`Tenant Exists`."

Inline Function

It is possible to use functions directly in SQL query statements. Such functions are referred as **inline functions**. In order to develop inline functions some basic rules have to be followed:

1. The function must use only IN parameter mode.
2. The data types of the function input parameter values, and the function return values must correspond to the Oracle database data type – eg. VARCHAR2, CHAR, NUMBER, DATE, and so on.
3. Function must be stored in the database as a database object.

For example, the following function *age* calculates the age of a person.

```
create or replace function age (input_date in date) return number IS
computed_age number;
begin
```

```
computed_age := TRUNC((SYSDATE - input_date)/365);
RETURN computed_age;
end;
```

The function *age* receives an input parameter of date of birth. It calculates the person's age by subtracting the date of birth from the current system date, and then dividing the result by 365. Since the calculation can contain decimals, the TRUNC SQL function is used. The use of the function in a SQL query statement is as follows:

```
select tenant_name, age(tenant_dob)
from tenant;
```

Maintain Function in SQL Developer

Details on handling functions in SQL Developer is provided in Appendix E. Functions can be created (i) directly within SQL Developer, or (ii) in a text editor and thereafter the file opened or copy/pasted in the SQL Worksheet of SQL Developer. A function has to be compiled successfully before running it. Once created, a function can be tested directly in SQL Developer through a submenu Run option.

A function can be dropped in SQL Developer either through a submenu Drop option, or the DROP FUNCTION *function-name* statement. For example drop function tenant_function;

EXCEPTIONS

Exceptions are optional *runtime* error handling routines defined after the EXCEPTION keyword in the executable section of a PL/SQL program unit. When an error occurs during the execution of a PL/SQL program unit, an exception is *raised*. Immediately, the logic control of the program unit is transferred to the exception section of the program unit.

Exceptions are classified in two broad categories – *system exceptions* and *user-defined exceptions*. Figure 3-19 illustrates the two categories.

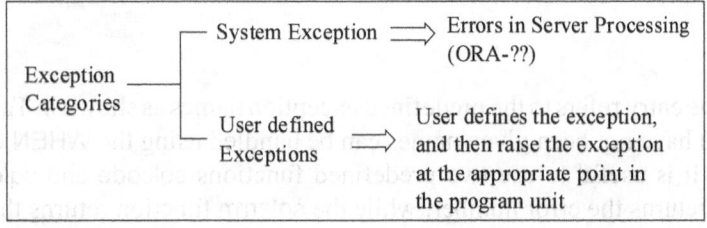

Figure 3-19

System exceptions are raised implicitly (automatically) by the run-time system, and they correspond to errors during database processing. Errors generated by the database server during processing have an ORA prefix. System exceptions are of two types – pre-defined exception and undefined exception. User defined exceptions also work in the same manner, except that the user has to define the exception first, and then utilize a RAISE statement to generate an exception at the appropriate point in the program unit.

Pre-defined Exceptions

Pre-defined exceptions are names (called as *exception name*) given to common server errors that already have been recognized by Oracle. To following Table 3-10 gives a sample list of some of the common server errors and their respective exception names.

Server Error Number	Exception Name	Description
ORA-00001	DUP_VAL_ON_INDEX	Unique constraint on primary key violated.
ORA-01403	NO_DATA_FOUND	Query returns no records.
ORA-01422	TOO_MANY_ROWS	Query returns more rows than expected.
ORA-06502	VALUE_ERROR	Error in truncation, arithmetic, or conversion operation.

Table 3-10: Common Predefined Exception

The syntax for handling pre-defined exceptions within a PL/SQL block is shown in Figure 3-20.

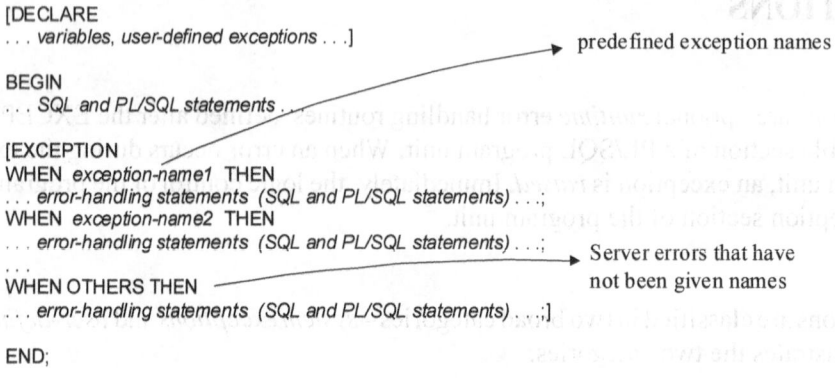

Figure 3-20

The *exception-name* entry refers to the predefined exception names as shown in Table 3-10 above. Oracle database errors that have not been given names can be handled using the WHEN OTHERS clause in the exception section. It is useful to use two predefined functions sqlcode and sqlerrm for this purpose. Function **sqlcode** returns the error number, while the sqlerrm function returns the message description associated with the error. If a SQL statement executes successfully, sqlcode is equal to 0 and sqlerrm contains the string ORA-0000: normal, successful completion.

The following examples show the utilization of pre-defined exception to handle runtime errors in a PL/SQL program unit.

1. A procedure *exception_test1* that inserts a row in STAFF table.

```
create or replace procedure exception_test1 IS
begin
insert into staff (staff_no, first_name, last_name)
values ('SA230', 'Kane', 'Chin');
commit;
dbms_output.put_line('Row Inserted');
end;
```

Since the STAFF_NO (primary key) value is already existing in the STAFF table, an Oracle runtime error occurs. The runtime error is shown below.

```
ORA-00001: unique constraint (PSP4.STAFF_PK) violated
ORA-06512: at "PSP4.EXCEPTION_TEST1", line 3
ORA-06512: at line 1
```

The procedure *exception_test1* is now modified with the exception section as shown below.

```
create or replace procedure exception_test1 IS
begin
insert into staff (staff_no, first_name, last_name)
values ('SA230', 'Kane', 'Chin');
commit;
dbms_output.put_line('Row Inserted');
exception
  when dup_val_on_index then
  dbms_output.put_line('Duplicate Primary Key Value.');
  dbms_output.put_line('Correct Insert Statement.');
end;
```

The execution of the modified *exception_test1* procedure with the use of exception handler now displays the following dbms_output message:

```
Duplicate Primary Key Value.
Correct Insert Statement.
```

2. The procedure *exception_test2* that queries the STAFF table with wrong STAFF_NO value. The example shows the use of SQLERRM function. To use the SQLERRM function, a variable having varchar2 datatype with maximum length of 512 must be declared. This length is necessary, as the maximum length of an Oracle error message is 512.

```
create or replace procedure exception_test2 IS
  staff_in staff.staff_no%type;
  first_in staff.first_name%type;
  last_in staff.last_name%type;
  error_message varchar2(512);
begin
select staff_no, first_name, last_name
into staff_in, first_in, last_in
from staff
where staff_no = 'SA340';
dbms_output.put_line('Row Found');
exception
  when too_many_rows then
  dbms_output.put_line('Too Many Rows.');
  dbms_output.put_line('Correct Query Statement.');
  when others then
  error_message := sqlerrm;
```

```
dbms_output.put_line('Program encountered the following error:');
dbms_output.put_line(error_message);
end;
```

The execution of the procedure *exception_test2* displays the following dbms_output message:

```
Program encountered the following error:
ORA-01403: no data found
```

Undefined Exceptions

Undefined exceptions are those server errors that do not have a pre-defined exception name. To use an undefined exception, the exception must be first defined in the declaration section of the program unit. During this definition process the exception name is associated with a specific server error number. Then the exception can be called in the exception section of the program unit the same way as a pre-defined exception. The syntax to declare an undefined exception in a PL/SQL block is:

```
DECLARE
... variables, ...
exception-name EXCEPTION;
PRAGMA EXCEPTION_INIT( exception-name, Oracle error number );
```

The exception-name is an Oracle variable. The Oracle error number must have the prefix hyphen (-) before the error number. The leading zeros of the error number can be ignored.

The following procedure *exception_test3* inserts a row in the COMPLAINTS table.

```
create or replace procedure exception_test3 IS
error_message varchar2(512);
begin
insert into complaints (complaint_no,complaint_date, rental_no)
values (complaints_sequence.nextval,sysdate,100108);
commit;
dbms_output.put_line('Row Inserted');
exception
  when dup_val_on_index then
  dbms_output.put_line('Duplicate Primary Key Value.');
  dbms_output.put_line('Correct Insert Statement.');
  when others then
  error_message := sqlerrm;
  dbms_output.put_line('Program encountered the following error:');
  dbms_output.put_line(error_message);
end;
```

The execution of the procedure *exception_test3* generates a run time error message due to the wrong foreign key value for the RENTAL_NO attribute. The message through the dbms_output statement in the procedure is:

```
Program encountered the following error:
ORA-02291: integrity constraint (PSP4.COMPLAINTS_FK1) violated - parent
key not found
```

The procedure *exception_test3* is now modified to include the undefined exception to trap the Oracle error number ORA-02291.

```
create or replace procedure exception_test3 IS
e_foreign_key_error EXCEPTION;
PRAGMA EXCEPTION_INIT(e_foreign_key_error, -2291);
error_message varchar2(512);
begin
insert into complaints (complaint_no,complaint_date,rental_no)
values(complaints_sequence.nextval,sysdate,100108);
commit;
dbms_output.put_line('Row Inserted');
exception
when e_foreign_key_error then
dbms_output.put_line('Wrong Foreign Key Value.');
dbms_output.put_line('Correct Insert Statement.');
when dup_val_on_index then
dbms_output.put_line('Duplicate Primary Key Value.');
dbms_output.put_line('Correct Insert Statement.');
when others then
error_message := sqlerrm;
dbms_output.put_line('Program encountered the following error:');
dbms_output.put_line(error_message);
end;
```

The execution of the procedure *exception_test3* with the undefined exception now displays the following dbms_output message:

```
Wrong Foreign Key Value.
Correct Insert Statement.
```

User-Defined Exceptions

User-defined exceptions are those exceptions that are not caused due to server errors, but rather due to non-enforcement of business rules or integrity of the database. User-defined exceptions have to be defined in the declaration section of the program. User-defined exception are declared using the syntax:

    exception-name EXCEPTION;

where exception-name is an Oracle variable. The user-defined exception is raised through the statement RAISE exception-name;.

Once user-defined exceptions are declared, such exceptions are invoked through the PL/SQL selection statements. The syntax of a PL/SQL block with user-defined exception is shown below.

```
DECLARE
. . . variables . . .
exception-name EXCEPTION;
BEGIN
. . . SQL and PL/SQL statements . . .
IF condition THEN
  RAISE exception-name;
END IF;
```

```
[EXCEPTION
WHEN exception-name1 THEN
. . . error-handling statements  (SQL and PL/SQL statements) . . .;
WHEN exception-name2 THEN
. . . error-handling statements  (SQL and PL/SQL statements) . . .;
. . .
WHEN OTHERS THEN
. . . error-handling statements  (SQL and PL/SQL statements) . . .;]

END;
```

The following example creates a procedure *exception_test4*. The procedure updates EMPLOYER_NAME attribute of the TENANT table. The business policy is that a tenant must have an employer. The procedure assigns a null value for the employer_name. Since this violates the business rule, the associated exception (e_employer) is raised.

```
create or replace procedure exception_test4 IS
e_employer_error exception;
employer varchar2(5);
error_message varchar2(512);
begin
update tenant
set employer_name = null
where tenant_ss = 723556089;
select employer_name into employer
from tenant where tenant_ss = 723556089;
if employer is null then
  raise e_employer_error;
else commit;
end if;
exception
  when e_employer_error then
  dbms_output.put_line('A tenant must have an employer.');
  dbms_output.put_line('The Update is void.');
  when others then
  error_message := sqlerrm;
  dbms_output.put_line('Program encountered the following error:');
  dbms_output.put_line(error_message);
end;
```

The execution of the procedure *exception_test4* involving the use of the user-defined exception handler displays the following dbms_output message:

```
A tenant must have an employer.
The Update is void.
```

Exception Usage

Unlike many programming languages where a run-time error such as stack overflow or division by zero stops normal processing and returns control to the operating system, exception handling mechanism in PL/SQL "bulletproofs" the PL/SQL program units in a way that it can continue operating in the presence of errors. This is achieved by placing PL/SQL anonymous block program units inside stored program units as shown in Figure 3-21.

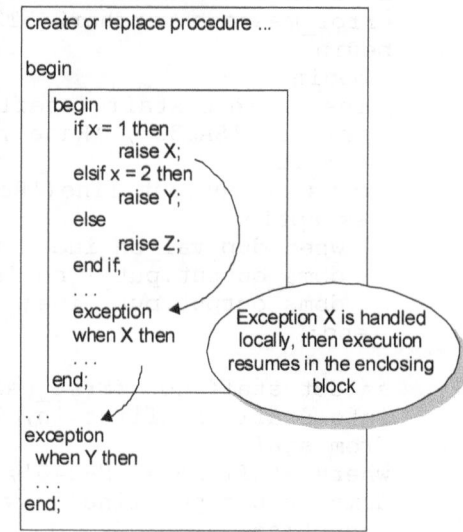

When an exception is raised, PL/SQL looks for the exception handler inside the enclosed anonymous block unit first, closes the current block, and the program continues in the outer block unit from the next statement. If there is no exception handler in the enclosed anonymous block, PL/SQL exits the enclosed block and looks for it in the outer block. That is, the exception reproduces itself in successive **Figure 3-21** enclosing blocks until a handler is found or there are no more blocks to search. In the latter case, PL/SQL returns an unhandled exception error to the host environment.

Using exceptions for error handling has several advantages.

1. Without exception handling, every time a SQL statement is executed, one may have to check for execution errors:

```
BEGIN
SELECT ...
  -- check for 'no data found' error
SELECT ...
  -- check for 'no data found' error
SELECT ...
  -- check for 'no data found' error
```

In this case error processing is not clearly separated from normal processing; nor is it robust.

2. Exceptions improve readability by isolating error-handling routines.

3. Exceptions improve reliability. One need not check for an error at every point it might occur. Just add an exception handler in the PL/SQL block. If the exception is ever raised in that block (or any sub-block), it will be handled.

    For example the following procedure *exception_test5* contains an anonymous block program unit. The anonymous block program unit inserts a row in the STAFF table. During procedure execution, the anonymous block program unit generates a runtime error. The exception handler of anonymous block program unit is executed, and the control is transferred to the statement in the procedure after the anonymous block program unit. The procedure query is thereafter executed and the associated message displayed.

```
create or replace procedure exception_test5 is
staff_in staff.staff_no%type;
first_in staff.first_name%type;
last_in staff.last_name%type;
error_message varchar2(512);
begin
  begin
  insert into staff (staff_no, first_name, last_name)
  values ('SA230', 'Kane', 'Chin');
  commit;
  dbms_output.put_line('Row Inserted');
  exception
    when dup_val_on_index then
    dbms_output.put_line('Duplicate Primary Key Value.');
    dbms_output.put_line('Correct Insert Statement.');
  end;

select staff_no, first_name, last_name
into staff_in, first_in, last_in
from staff
where staff_no = 'SA240';
dbms_output.put_line('Row Found');
exception
when others then
dbms_output.put_line('Program encountered the following error:');
dbms_output.put_line(sqlerrm);
end;
```

The execution of the procedure *exception_test5* displays the following dbms_output message:

```
Duplicate Primary Key Value.
Correct Insert Statement.
Row Found
```

Raise Application Error

RAISE_APPLICATION_ERROR is a procedure in the built-in package DBMS_STANDARD. This procedure allows developers to create meaningful error messages for a specific application. Oracle reserves error codes in the range of -20000 to -20999 for these user-defined errors. The syntax is:

RAISE_APPLICATION_ERROR(*error-number, error-message,* [*keep-errors*]);

Parameter *error-number* is the number of the error that a developer associates with a specific error message. This can be any number between -20999 and -20000. The *error-message* parameter is the text of the error, and it can contain up to 512 characters. The optional parameter *keep-errors* is a boolean parameter. If *keep-errors* is set to TRUE, the new error will be added to the list of errors that has been raised already. If *keep-errors* is set to FALSE, the new error replaces the list of errors that has been raised already. The default value for the parameter *keep-errors* is FALSE. Figure 3-22 illustrates the use of the syntax.

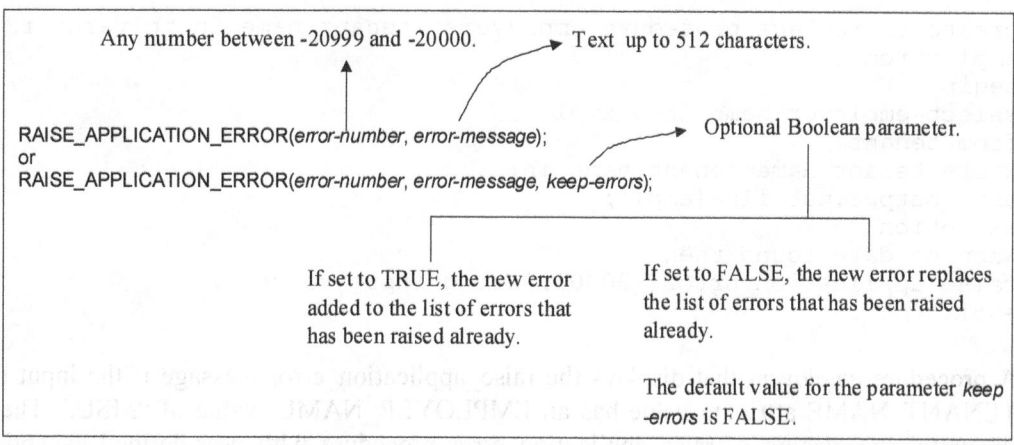

Figure 3-22

The RAISE_APPLICATION_ERROR procedure works with user-defined exceptions. It associates the number of the error with the text of the error. Therefore, as an exception, it does not have a specific name associated with it. Raise_application_error procedure is useful for the following reasons:

1. Ability to provide customized error messages.
2. Ability to transfer error messages just like server errors to third party programs accessing the database (if dbms_output is limited to PL/SQL editors).
3. Ability to invoke error handling from anywhere in the program.
4. Rollback a transaction from a database trigger (explained in the next lesson).

The following examples show the utilization of RAISE_APPLICATION_ERROR procedure within program units.

1. A procedure *cc_count* that displays a count of the number of times a credit card has been used for rental payment. The raise_application_error text is displayed if the procedure is executed with an input parameter value that is not "visa," "mastercard" or "discover."

```
create or replace procedure cc_count (cc_type_in in varchar2) IS
count_in number(3);
begin
if (cc_type_in in ('visa','mastercard','discover')) then
select count(*)
into count_in
from rental_invoice
where cc_type = cc_type_in;
dbms_output.put_line(cc_type_in||' has be used '||count_in||' times.');
else
raise_application_error(-20000,'Wrong input value');
end if;
end;
```

2. A procedure *employers* that displays a specific tenant's EMPLOYER_NAME   value.The raise_application_error message is displayed if the procedure is executed with an input parameter that is not a valid TENANT_NAME attribute value. The example illustrates the placing of raise_application_error procedure within a predefined exception.

```
create or replace procedure employers (tenant_name_in in varchar2) IS
emp1 varchar2(20);
begin
select employer_name into emp1
from tenant
where tenant_name=tenant_name_in;
dbms_output.put_line(emp1);
exception
when no_data_found then
raise_application_error(-20001,'Wrong input value');
end;
```

3. A procedure *employers* that displays the raise_application_error message if the input parameter
   TENANT_NAME attribute value has an EMPLOYER_NAME value of "MSU." The example
   illustrates the placing of raise_application_error procedure with user-defined exception in the
   exception section of the program unit.

```
create or replace procedure employers (tenant_name_in in varchar2) IS
emp1 varchar2(20);
error2 exception;
begin
select employer_name into emp1
from tenant
where tenant_name=tenant_name_in;
dbms_output.put_line(emp1);
if emp1 = 'MSU' then
raise error2;
end if;
exception
when no_data_found then
raise_application_error(-20001,'Wrong input value');
when error2 then
raise_application_error(-20001,'Wrong Employer');
end;
```

CHAPTER SUMMARY

▸ A PL/SQL procedure is a database program unit to perform some task.

▸ A PL/SQL procedure can receive multiple input parameters (values), can return multiple output values, or can return no output values.

▸ PL/SQL procedures are generally stored on database server.

▸ A PL/SQL function is also a database program unit that performs some task except that it returns a single value that is assigned to a variable in the calling program.

▸ A PL/SQL function can also receive multiple input parameters (values).

▸ When inline functions are created, it is possible to use them directly in SQL statements.

▸ Boolean functions are special type of PL/SQL functions that do not return a value. Instead they return status True or False.

▸ PL/SQL program units have EXCEPTION section to handle runtime database errors. During exception handling Oracle server errors or other application errors are mapped to user-friendly explanations or corrective actions.

▸ System exceptions are raised implicitly (automatically) by the PL/SQL engine. System exceptions can be categorized into pre-defined or undefined exceptions.

▸ User-defined exceptions are exceptions that are not caused due to server errors, but rather due to non-enforcement of business rules or integrity of the database. They are raised explicitly by RAISE statements.

▸ Pre-defined exceptions are names (called as *exception name*) to common SQL errors that already have been recognized by Oracle.

▸ Undefined exceptions are those Oracle server errors that do not have a pre-defined exception name.

▸ Undefined exceptions must be first defined as a variable in the declaration section of the program unit with a special data type called EXCEPTION. A pragma exception_init statement then binds an Oracle server error to the exception name variable.

▸ RAISE_APPLICATION_ERROR is a procedure in the built-in package DBMS_STANDARD. It allows developers to create meaningful error messages for a specific application.

▸ Oracle reserves error codes in the range of -20000 to -20999 for RAISE_APPLICATION_ERROR errors.

REVIEW QUESTIONS

1. Define the structure of a PL/SQL procedure.

2. What are the different types of parameter modes in a PL/SQL procedure?

3. Explain the main difference between a PL/SQL procedure and PL/SQL function.

4. What is the difference between a boolean function and an inline function?

5. How can a PL/SQL function be utilized within a SELECT clause of a SQL query.

6. What are exceptions. List their various types?

7. How are undefined exceptions defined?

8. How can one create an undefined exception.

9. What is the relevance of user-defined exception?

10. What is the purpose of raise_application_error?

REVIEW EXERCISES

1. _____ _____ is an integrated, interactive environment to create, execute, and debug PL/SQL programs.

2. A PL/SQL _____ can receive multiple input parameters or can return multiple output values.

3. The parameter mode _____ indicates that the parameter is passed as a read-only (input) value that cannot be changed in the program.

4. The parameter mode _____ indicates that the parameter is passed as a write-only (output) value that can be assigned a value in the program.

5. The following statement is a call to the _____ program.

    ```
    auto_list(1999, 'Jack Model');
    ```

6. The following statement is a call to the _____ program having _____ parameters.

    ```
    auto_list(1999, 'Jack Model');
    ```

7. A PL/SQL _____ can receive multiple input parameters, but must return a single value.

8. The PL/SQL _____ statement that returns a value from a function.

9. Complete the following syntax of a definition line:

```
create function abc (id_in number) _____ varchar2
```

10. The variable id_in is an _____ parameter in following syntax of a definition line.

```
create function abc (id_in number) _____ varchar2;
```

11. Complete the following syntax of a definition line:

```
create function xyz (id_in varchar2) _____ boolean
```

12. A _____ function is a special type of PL/SQL function that does not return a value.

13. A function used in a SQL statement is referred as an _____ function.

14. Exceptions in a PL/SQL program map an Oracle _____ error to error-handling statements.

15. Exception name is a name given to an Oracle _____ error.

16. The entry no_data_found in the following statement is an _____.

```
exception
when no_data_found then
dbms_output.put_line('error has occured');
```

17. The Oracle server error mapped to an exception name is _____.

```
e_xyz exception;
pragma exception_init(e_abc,-2291);
```

18. The entry e_invoice_error in the following statement is an _____.

```
if invoice_no is null then
raise e_invoice_error;
end if;
```

19. RAISE_APPLICATION_ERROR is a _____ exception.

PROBLEM SOLVING EXERCISES

> Run the script file outdoorDB_v4.sql to load the Outdoor Clubs & Product database to complete the following exercises.

Ex3B-1.   Create a procedure "ex3b_membership" that displays membership_id, first_name, last_name, and city attribute values for all customers who have club membership. Save the procedure as a script file with filename ex3b1.

Ex3B-2.   Create a procedure "ex3b_order_details" that displays from the product_order table, order_id, order_date, and total attribute values for an input customer_id value. Include an exception that maps the Oracle server error for an invalid customer_id input, and displays a message "Customer ID not correct. Try again!." Save the procedure as a script file with filename ex3b2.

Ex3B-3.   Create a procedure "ex3b_membership_status" that receives an input Date value and displays from the club_membership table, the membership_id, customer first_name, and customer last_name attribute values along with a *time status* calculated value for the time remaining with respect to the input date, membership_date and duration values. If the input date is beyond the membership time duration, a message should display "Membership has expired." Save the procedure as a script file with filename ex3b3.

Ex3B-4.   Create a procedure "ex3b_membership_duration" that displays membership_id, duration, first_name, last_name, city attribute values for customers who have club membership, along with the name attribute value of the sporting_club. The value of the sporting_club name should be returned by a function "ex3b_club name." Save the procedure as a script file with filename ex3b4_membership, while save the function as ex3b4_clubname.

Ex3B-5.   Add an attribute "qty_ordered" to the product table with data type number(2). Now, create a procedure "ex3b_add_quantities" that adds the quantities that have been ordered for each product so far, and updates those values for the qty_ordered attribute in the product table. For those products that do not yet have an order, the value inserted for the attribute should be zero. At the end of processing display the product_id, qty_ordered values. Save the procedure as a script file with filename ex3b5_qty_ordered.

Ex3B-6.   Create a procedure "ex3b_new_order" with input parameters of customer_id, product_id, quantity, payment_type attribute values to inserts a new order in the product_order table. Use sysdate for order_date attribute value. The ship_date is 5 days after the order_date. Before inserting the new order, the procedure checks a boolean function "ex3b_check_quantity" on whether the quantity ordered is available in stock. If the quantity ordered is more than stock available, the procedure displays a message "Order cannot be accepted." Use the sequence product_order_sequence of the Outdoor Clubs & Product database script file to insert the new order_id value. Include exceptions that map Oracle server errors for invalid inputs of customer_id, product_id, and payment_type. The exception displays different message for each input error. For invalid customer_id the message is "Customer ID not correct. Try again!." For invalid product_id the message is "Product ID not correct. Try again!." For invalid payment_type the message is "Payment Type not correct. Try again!." Save the procedure as a script file with filename ex3b6_new_order, while save the function as ex3b6_check_quantity.

Ex3B-7.   Create a script file ex3b7 that adds an attribute "fee" with data type number(2) to the sporting_clubs table. The fee attribute holds the amount of fee charged per month by a sporting club. Use the following table to update the sporting_clubs table with the fee data.

CLUB_ID	FEE
100	$ 50
110	$ 75
120	$ 85
130	$ 60

Now, create a procedure "ex3b_new_membership" that inserts a new row of club membership. The procedures has input parameters of duration, payment_type, club_id, customer_id attribute values. Use the current date as membership_date attribute value. The new club membership amount attribute value is determined by a call to a function "ex3b_membership_amount." The function uses the fee value in the sporting_clubs table to calculate the amount value. The formula for amount value is "duration * fee." The procedure displays membership_id, membership_date, and amount attribute values.

Include exceptions that map Oracle server errors for invalid inputs of customer_id, club_id, and payment_type. The exception displays different message for each input error. For invalid customer_id the message is "Customer ID not correct. Try again!." For invalid club_id the message is "Club ID not correct. Try again!." For invalid payment_type the message is "Payment Type not correct. Try again!." Save the procedure as a script file with filename ex3b7_new_membership, while save the function as ex3b7_membership_amount.

Ex3B-8.   Create a procedure "ex3b_supplier_update" that contains two input parameters. The first input parameter is a supplier_id attribute value that is used to delete the supplier from the supplier table. The second input parameter is also another supplier_id attribute value that is used to update the deleted supplier entry (of the first input parameter) in the product and purchase_order table with a new supplier value. Create a boolean function "ex3b_supplier_exist" to determine if the supplier_id entered as the first input parameter exists before proceeding with the data manipulations. If the supplier do not exist, then display a message "Invalid Suppliers. Run program unit again!." If the supplier does exist, then after completing the manipulations display the product_id attribute values that have the new updated supplier entry.

Include an exception that maps the Oracle server error for invalid supplier_id input, and displays a message "Supplier ID not correct. Try again!." Save the procedure as a script file with filename ex3b8_supplier_update, while save the function as ex3b8_supplier_exist.

Ex3B-9.   Create a procedure "ex3b_activity_count" with one input parameter. The input parameter is the activity attribute value. The procedure displays the input activity value along with a count of the clubs in the sporting_clubs table that provide the activity. If the input activity is not listed in the club_activity table, the procedure displays a message "Activity not in Database" based on the function "ex3b_activity_check." Create a function "ex3b_activity_check" that checks whether the input activity exists in the database. Save the procedure as a script file with filename ex3b9_activity_count, while save the function as ex3b9_activity_check.

Ex3B-10.   Create a procedure "ex3b_cust_activity" with two input parameters. The input parameters are the attributes first_name and last_name in the customer table. The procedure displays the list of activity values for the sporting club for which the customer has club membership. If the customer name do not have club membership the procedure displays a message "Customer is still not a club member" utilizing the function "ex3b_check_member." Create a function "ex3b_check_member" that checks whether the customer has club membership.

Include an exception that maps the Oracle server error for invalid input, and displays a message "Customer names not correct. Try again!." Save the procedure as a script file with filename ex3b10_cust_activity, while save the function as ex3b10_check_member.

> Run the script file travelDB_v4.sql to load the Travel Anywhere database to complete the following exercises.

Ex3B-11   Create a procedure "ex3b_travel_itin" that generates travel itinerary. The procedure has input parameters of flight org_city, flight dest_city, and airline name attribute values. The procedure will display all flight_no, org_city, dest_city attribute values in proper connection sequence of a travel schedule. The procedure utilizes a function "ex3b_itin_check" to check whether there is a connection between the org_city and dest_city in the flight table. The procedure displays a message "No connection available between the origin city and destination city" if there is no connection between the org_city and dest_city. Save the procedure as a script file with filename ex3b11_travel_itin, while save the function as ex3b11_itin_check.

Ex3B-12   Extend problem exercise Ex3B-11 by creating a procedure "ex3b_lowest_fare" that determines the lowest fare between the org_city and dest_city, and generates a flight ticket for the lowest fare schedule. The modified procedure (i) includes another input parameter for travel_customer customer_id attribute value, (ii) determines the travel itinerary with the lowest overall fare, and (iii) generates a ticket for the input travel_customer customer_id by inserting rows in ticket and flight_ticket tables. The procedure displays the lowest fare flight_no, org_city, dest_city attribute values in proper connection sequence of a travel schedule along with the generated ticket_no attribute value. Use the sequences in the Travel Anywhere database script file during inserting operations. Include an exception that maps the Oracle server error for invalid customer_id input, and displays a message "Customer ID not correct. Try again!." Save the procedure as a script file with filename ex3b12_lowest_fare.

CHAPTER 3
(LESSON C)

PL/SQL Language

- PL/SQL Packages
- Database Triggers
- Dynamic SQL

This lesson introduces additional PL/SQL program units such as PL/SQL packages and database triggers. Nature and working of dynamic SQL is also described.

This lesson utilizes the table structure of Superflex Apartment database to explain examples.

PL/SQL PACKAGES

A PL/SQL package is a collection of logically related procedures and functions. It is like a code library that performs related tasks. A PL/SQL package consists of two separate components – the *package specification*, and *package body*. The package name in the package specification must be the same as the package name in the package body.

Package Specification

The package specification is the public interface of the package. It is also called the package header, and contains definitions of variables, procedures, functions, exceptions, cursors, types that are included in the package. The elements of a package specification (variables, cursors, procedures, functions) can be defined in any order. The syntax of package specification is:

```
CREATE [OR REPLACE] PACKAGE package-name IS
  [... variable declarations ...]
  [... procedure definitions ...]
  [... function definitions ...]
END;
```

The variables in the package specification can be referenced by any program within the package. Variables can also include cursor variables. Variables in a package specification are defined similar to their declaration in a PL/SQL block. For example, `count1 number(2);`.

Cursors in a package specification are defined similar to any explicit cursor declaration in a PL/SQL block. For example,

185

```
cursor package_cursor is
select auto_make, auto_model, auto_year, auto_color
from tenant_auto;
```

Procedure definition in a package involves the listing of the procedure header or definition statement line. For example,

```
PROCEDURE auto_list2 (year_in IN number);
PROCEDURE auto_tenant_list;
```

Function definition in a package involves the listing of the function header or definition statement line. For example,

```
FUNCTION tenant_function (ss_in IN number) RETURN varchar2;
```

The definitions of procedures and functions in a package specification are called *forward declarations*, because the program unit definitions are only declared here. The actual program unit source is described in the package body. Following is a package specification for a package titled *sample_package*.

```
create or replace package sample_package IS
count1 number(2);
cursor package_cursor is
  select auto_make, auto_model, auto_year, auto_color
  from tenant_auto;
procedure auto_list2 (year_in in number);
procedure auto_tenant_list;
function tenant_function (ss_in in number) return varchar2;
end;
```

Package Body

The package body contains the source of the program units declared in the package specification. The package body must be created using the name of an existing package specification. The same name ties the specification and the body units together. In addition, all procedure and function definition statements must match exactly with their corresponding declarations in the package specification. Also package specification should be created before the package body, or an error will occur. The package body is optional, because sometimes a package contains only variable declarations and no other program units. The syntax of package body is:

```
CREATE [OR REPLACE] PACKAGE BODY package-name IS
[... variable declarations ...]
[... cursor definitions ...]
[... named program unit blocks ...]
END;
```

The package-name of the package body must be the same as the package-name used in the package specification. Variables and cursors declared in the beginning of package body are private to the package body program units. Each named program unit like procedure or function can have its own variable or cursor declarations. However such declarations are local to only that program unit. The following is a description of the package body of a package titled *sample_package*. The package specification of *sample_package* has already been defined previously.

```
create or replace package body sample_package is
procedure auto_list2 (year_in in number) is
cursor auto_cursor is
  select auto_make, auto_model from tenant_auto
  where auto_year > year_in;
auto_row auto_cursor%rowtype;
begin
for auto_row in auto_cursor
loop
dbms_output.put_line('Make is '||auto_row.auto_make||
  ' and model is '||auto_row.auto_model);
end loop;
end;

procedure auto_tenant_list is
cursor auto_cursor is
  select auto_make, auto_model, tenant_ss from tenant_auto
  where auto_year > 1999;
auto_row auto_cursor%rowtype;
tenant_in tenant.tenant_name%type;
begin
for auto_row in auto_cursor
loop
tenant_in := tenant_function(auto_row.tenant_ss);
dbms_output.put_line('Make '||auto_row.auto_make|| ' and model ' ||
    auto_row.auto_model || 'is for '|| tenant_in);
end loop;
end;

function tenant_function (ss_in in number) return varchar2 is
name_in tenant.tenant_name%type;
begin
select tenant_name into name_in
from tenant
where tenant_ss = ss_in;
return name_in;
end;
end;
```

Programs within a package are accessed through the convention *package-name.package-specification-program*. For example Figure 3-23 shows a variable tenant_name in a program unit that is assigned the return value of a function tenant_function within the package sample_package.

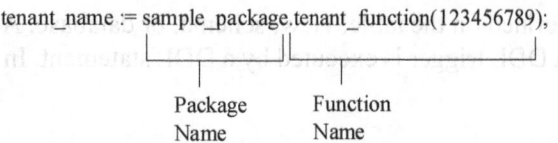

tenant_name := sample_package.tenant_function(123456789);

Package   Function
Name   Name

Figure 3-23

Package program units can have *public* or *private* scope. Any definition declared in the package specification component is considered public, which means that it can be referenced from outside of the package by other program units. On the other hand, definitions are considered private if they can be called only from other program units within the same package. Private scope occurs if a program unit like a function is specified in the package body, but not in the package specification.

Maintain Package in SQL Developer

Details on handling packages in SQL Developer is provided in Appendix E. Packages can be created (i) directly within SQL Developer as package specification and package body program units, or (ii) in a text editor create the two components and thereafter the source file opened or copy/pasted separately in the SQL Worksheet of SQL Developer. Both the package components – package specification and package body have to be separately compiled successfully before running the package.

A package can be executed directly in SQL Developer either through a submenu Run option, or the EXECUTE command with syntax EXECUTE *package-name.package-specification-program* in the SQL Worksheet. For example, to execute the procedure auto_list2 of the package sample_package is `execute sample_package.auto_list2(1999);`

The entire package can be dropped in SQL Developer either through a submenu Drop option, or the DROP PACKAGE *package-name* statement. For example `drop package sample_package;`

It is also possible to drop the package body in SQL Developer either through a submenu Drop option, or the DROP PACKAGE BODY *package-name* statement. For example `drop package body sample_package;`

DATABASE TRIGGERS

A trigger is a named PL/SQL program unit that is stored in the database and executed in response to a specified event. The specified event is associated with either a table, a view, a schema, or the database, and it is one of the following:
- A database manipulation (DML) statement (DELETE, INSERT, or UPDATE).
- A database definition (DDL) statement (CREATE, ALTER, or DROP).
- A database operation (SERVERERROR, LOGON, LOGOFF, STARTUP, or SHUTDOWN).

The trigger is said to be defined on the table, view, schema, or database. A DML trigger is executed by a DML statement, while a DDL trigger is executed by a DDL statement. In this lesson the focus is more on simple DML triggers.

Triggers are quite different from the procedures, functions, or packages that are explicitly called by name for execution. Also unlike the other PL/SQL program units which are independent of database tables, triggers are always associated with database tables. Besides database triggers cannot accept input parameters. The size of the trigger cannot be more than 32K.

Triggers are executed (referred as *fired*) only when the triggering event occurs. When a trigger fires, all operations performed become part of the transaction. A simple trigger can fire at exactly one of the following timing points:
- Before the triggering statement executes.
- After the triggering statement executes.
- Before each row that the triggering statement affects.
- After each row that the triggering statement affects.

For example, if a trigger program unit has been defined to fire before a SQL INSERT statement in the RENTAL table, this trigger fires every time an INSERT operation is performed on the table.

Triggers are used for different purposes like:
- Enforcing referential integrity.
- Enforcing complex business rules that cannot be defined by using integrity constraints.
- Maintaining complex security rules.
- Automatically generating values for derived columns.
- Collecting statistical information on table access.
- Preventing invalid transactions.
- Providing value auditing.

Trigger definition includes specification of the trigger event associated with database table, trigger timing, and trigger levels. Figure 3-24 shows a schematic view of the elements in a trigger definition.

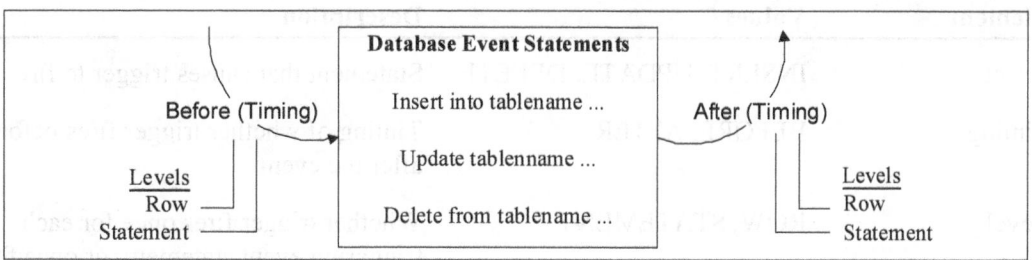

Figure 3-24

In simple DML triggers the database event associates the trigger table with a DML statement. Consequently the trigger is fired (or executed) when these DML statements are executed. One can specify multiple DML statements together in the syntax, or just one.

Trigger timing refers to the time when the execution of the trigger will occur. There are two sets of timings associated with BEFORE and AFTER keywords. The BEFORE timing in the trigger definition implies that the trigger will be fired prior to the completion of the trigger database event (INSERT, UPDATE, or DELETE operation). The AFTER timing in the trigger definition implies that the trigger will be fired after the actual trigger database event (INSERT, UPDATE, or DELETE operation) is completed.

There are two levels of triggers associated with the impact of the trigger on the table. These levels are generally referred as ROW and STATEMENT levels. ROW level trigger fires for each row affected by the associated trigger database event. The STATEMENT trigger fires only once per associated database event.The default is STATEMENT level.

For example, if the trigger is defined as a ROW level trigger, then during the database event associated with say an UPDATE statement, one can have the trigger fire once for each row being updated. So if the update affects 20 rows, the trigger will fire 20 times. On the other hand, if the trigger is defined as a STATEMENT level trigger, then it would fire just once for the UPDATE statement. In other words, if the single update statement is updating 20 rows, the trigger will fire just once. Figure 3-25 provides a schematic view of the difference between a STATEMENT and ROW level triggers.

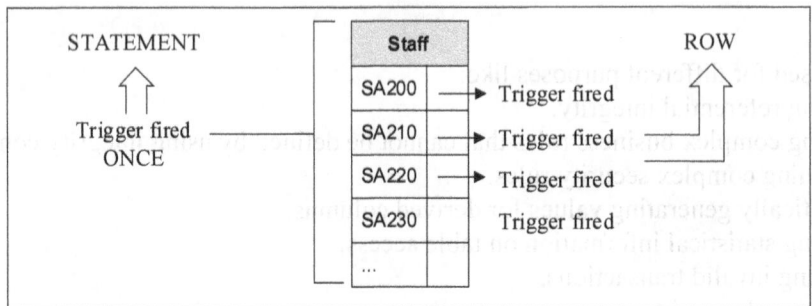

Figure 3-25

Table 3-11 summarizes the elements in trigger definition.

Element	Values	Description
Event	INSERT, UPDATE, DELETE	Statement that causes trigger to fire
Timing	BEFORE, AFTER	Timing of whether trigger fires before or after the event
Level	ROW, STATEMENT	Whether trigger fires once for each triggering event statement, or once for each affected row by the triggering event statement

Table 3-11: Trigger setup details

The general syntax for creating a trigger is:

```
CREATE [OR REPLACE]  TRIGGER trigger-name
[BEFORE | AFTER]
[INSERT | DELETE | UPDATE [OF attribute1 [,attribute2[, ...] ] ] ]
ON tablename
[COMPOUND TRIGGER]
[FOLLOWS trigger-name2]
[ENABLE | DISABLE]
[ REFERENCING    {OLD [AS] old-name [NEW [AS] new-name]
      | NEW [AS] new-name [OLD [AS] old-name] } ]
[FOR EACH ROW]
[WHEN (condition)]
```

```
DECLARE
...
BEGIN
... pl/sql statements ...
END;
```

- The BEFORE keyword implies that the server fires the trigger before executing the triggering event statement, while the AFTER keyword implies that the server fires the trigger after executing the triggering event statement.
- The DELETE keyword indicates that the triggering event is a SQL *delete* statement; the INSERT keyword indicates that the triggering event is a SQL *insert* statement; the UPDATE .. OF keyword indicates that the triggering event is a SQL *update* statement involving the columns or attributes mentioned.
- The *tablename* entry is the name of the table on which the trigger is defined.
- The COMPOUND TRIGGER option allows the trigger to fire at more than one timing point. Compound triggers make it easier to program an approach where you want the actions you implement for the various timing points to share common data. A compound trigger has a declaration section and a section for each of its timing points.
- The FOLLOWS *trigger-name2* clause specifies the relative firing order of triggers of the same type. In essence this clause indicates that the trigger being created should fire after some other *trigger-name2* specified trigger. The *trigger-name2* specified trigger must already exist, must be defined on the same table as the current trigger being created, and must have been successfully compiled. They need not be enabled. The FOLLOWS clause in a way guarantees execution order for triggers defined with the same timing point.
- The ENABLE or DISABLE option explicitly enables or disables a trigger at creation time, with the enabled state as the default. An enabled trigger executes its trigger body if a triggering statement is entered and the trigger restriction (if any) evaluates to TRUE. A disabled trigger does not execute its trigger body, even if a triggering statement is entered and the trigger restriction (if any) evaluates to TRUE. Of course one can also issue an ALTER TRIGGER statement (outlined later in the section) to ENABLE the trigger.
- The REFERENCING keyword indicates correlation names that can be used to refer to the old and new values of the row attributes that are being affected by the trigger.
- FOR EACH ROW clause designates the trigger to be a ROW level trigger. Such a trigger is fired once for each row that is affected by the triggering event. If this clause is omitted, the trigger is a STATEMENT level trigger. A statement trigger is fired only once, when the triggering event is met.
- The WHEN condition clause specifies the trigger restriction. This restriction contains a SQL condition that must be satisfied for the trigger to be fired.
- There are certain restrictions that apply to statements within the execution block of the trigger. Some of these restrictions are:
  - A trigger may not issue transactional control statements like COMMIT, SAVEPOINT, or ROLLBACK. When a trigger fires, all operations performed become part of the transaction.
  - Any function or procedure called by a trigger may not issue a transactional control statement.

In general to reference an attribute value before the triggering event, the prefix OLD can be used like :OLD.attribute_name. For example, an UPDATE or DELETE trigger reference to :old.invoice_due in the RENTAL_INVOICE table is the value of INVOICE_DUE attribute prior to the change (update or delete operation). However the value of :old.invoice_due is NULL for an INSERT trigger on the RENTAL_INVOICE table.

Similarly to reference an attribute value after the triggering event is complete the prefix NEW can be used like :NEW.attribute_name. For example, an UPDATE or INSERT trigger reference to :new.invoice_due in the RENTAL_INVOICE table is the value of INVOICE_DUE attribute after the change (update or insert operation). The value of :new.invoice_due is NULL for a DELETE trigger on the RENTAL_INVOICE table.

However, the NEW or OLD references are only allowed ROW level triggers. They are not allowed in STATEMENT level triggers. Also, the WHEN condition clause does not require the colon (:) prefix for new or old attribute reference.

The following examples illustrate the operation of triggers.

1. A row level trigger *staff_insert_before* that fires before the insert operation associated with the STAFF table occurs. The trigger simply displays the insert attribute values.

    ```
    create or replace trigger staff_insert_before
    before insert
    on staff
    For each row
    Begin
    dbms_output.put_line('before insert of  ' ||:new.first_name||'
    '||:new.last_name);
    end;
    ```

    The trigger can be tested with the following statement:

    ```
    insert into staff (staff_no, first_name, last_name)
    values ('SA400','John','Doe');
    ```

2. A row level trigger *staff_insert_after* that fires after the insert operation associated with the STAFF table occurs. The trigger simply displays the insert attribute values.

    ```
    create or replace trigger staff_insert_after
    after insert
    on staff
    For each row
    Begin
    dbms_output.put_line('after insert of  '||:new.first_name||'
    '||:new.last_name);
    End;
    ```

    The trigger can be tested with the following statement:

    ```
    insert into staff (staff_no, first_name, last_name)
    values ('SA410','Jane','Doe');
    ```

3. A statement level trigger *staff_update_before* that fires before an update operation associated with the STAFF table occurs. The trigger simply displays a text message.

    ```
    create or replace trigger staff_update_before
    before update
    on staff
    begin
    dbms_output.put_line('before updating some staff ');
    end;
    ```

The trigger can be tested with the following statement.

```
update staff set dob = sysdate;
```

The output will show that 7 rows were updated, but still being a statement level trigger the text message will be displayed once.

4. A row level trigger *staff_update_before* that fires before an update operation associated with the STAFF table occurs. The trigger simply displays a text message along with existing attribute value of LAST_NAME and the new DOB attribute value.

```
create or replace trigger staff_update_before
before update
on staff
for each row
begin
dbms_output.put_line('before updating some staff '||
:old.last_name||:new.dob);
end;
```

The trigger can be tested with the following statement.

```
update staff set dob = sysdate;
```

The output will show the dbms_output statement message and values for each row. Notice that the trigger is fired for each row that is updated.

Trigger Exceptions

Triggers become part of the transaction of a statement, which implies that when the transaction raises any exceptions the whole statement is rolled back. In the absence of ROLLBACK statement to block a transaction from completion, RAISE APPLICATION ERROR exceptions are utilized. For example, the following row level update trigger *staff_dob* on the STAFF table prevents any update of DOB attribute value in the staff table.

```
create or replace trigger staff_dob
Before update of dob on staff
For each row
Begin
Raise_application_error(-20000,'cannot change date of birth');
End;
```

Special IF statements

A trigger can determine if it is executing because of an INSERT, UPDATE, or DELETE event with calls to special functions: inserting, updating, and deleting. These functions are declared in package DBMS_STANDARD. The function definition is as follows:

```
create [or replace] package dbms_standard is
   function inserting return boolean;
   function deleting return boolean;
```

```
        function updating return boolean;
        function updating  (column-name varchar2)  return boolean;
        . . .
    end dbms_standard;
```

Inside the PL/SQL block of a trigger one can use the IF statement to determine which statement caused the firing of the trigger. This is especially useful if the trigger is associated with multiple trigger events like INSERT, UPDATE, or DELETE operations in its definition. For example the following trigger *staff_trigger_status* checks the special functions.

```
create or replace trigger staff_trigger_status
before insert or update or delete on staff
for each row
Begin
if inserting then
dbms_output.put_line('inserting person: ' || :new.last_name);
elsif updating then
dbms_output.put_line('updating person: ' ||
:old.last_name || ' to ' || :new.last_name);
elsif deleting then
dbms_output.put_line('deleting person: ' || :old.last_name);
end if;
end;
```

Mutating Tables

Mutating tables is a common error (ORA-4091) if triggers are not managed properly. A mutating table is a table that is being modified by a DML action when a trigger is fired. It is caused by ROW level triggers, because the STATEMENT level trigger occurs in its entirety either before or after the triggering DML statement.

A mutating table occurs when a table which while being modified by a DML statement like UPDATE or DELETE encounters a SELECT or UPDATE statement in the body of the trigger that references the same table. However, there is one exception to table mutation when there is an INSERT event statement that inserts a single row.

The mutating table concept is now explained with the following examples.

1. An UPDATE trigger *staff_read_mutate* on the STAFF table attempts to also query the STAFF table.

```
create or replace trigger staff_read_mutate
after update of dob on staff
for each row
declare
last_name_in staff.last_name%type;
begin
select last_name
into last_name_in
from staff
where staff_no = 'SA200';
dbms_output.put_line(last_name_in);
```

```
end;
```

Now test the trigger with the following statement:

```
update staff
set dob = to_date('1/12/85','mm/dd/yy')
where staff_no = 'SA200';
```

SQL Developer will displays the mutating table error.

```
ORA-04091: table PSP4.STAFF is mutating, trigger/function may not see it'
```

2. An UPDATE trigger *staff_update_mutate* on the STAFF table that also attempts to UPDATE the STAFF table.

```
create or replace trigger staff_update_mutate
after update of dob on staff
for each row
begin
update staff
set salary = 25000
where staff_no = 'SA200';
dbms_output.put_line('Update performed');
end;
```

The trigger generates mutating table error when executing the UPDATE statement like:

```
update staff
set dob = to_date('1/12/85','mm/dd/yy')
where staff_no = 'SA200';
```

3. An INSERT trigger *staff_insert_mutate* on the STAFF table that also attempts to query and UPDATE the STAFF table.

```
create or replace trigger staff_insert_mutate
before insert on staff
for each row
declare
last_name_in staff.last_name%type;
begin
update staff
set dob = to_date('1/12/85','mm/dd/yy')
where staff_no = 'SA200';
select last_name
into last_name_in
from staff
where staff_no = 'SA200';
dbms_output.put_line(last_name_in);
end;
```

Now test the trigger with the following INSERT statement generates the dbms_output message.

```
insert into staff (staff_no, first_name, last_name)
values ('SA330', 'Kane', 'Chin');
```

WORKAROUND FOR TABLE MUTATION

Since it is possible to reference any attribute value within a row of the trigger table using the OLD or NEW prefix, it is possible to have a substitute for the SELECT statement in the trigger. The OLD prefix allows access to row values BEFORE the trigger is fired, while the NEW prefix allows access to row values AFTER the trigger is fired.

For example, the previous UPDATE trigger *staff_read_mutate* on the STAFF table is now modified to access row values from the STAFF table. The trigger will display the dbms_output message during an UPDATE operation.

```
create or replace trigger staff_read_mutate
after update of dob on staff
for each row
declare
last_name_in staff.last_name%type;
begin
--select last_name
--into last_name_in
--from staff
--where staff_no = 'SA200';
dbms_output.put_line(:old.last_name);
end;
```

Similarly any modification of an attribute value within a row can be done through an assignment statement instead of an UPDATE statement.

Once again the previous UPDATE trigger *staff_update_mutate* on the STAFF table is now modified to enable change of SALARY value in the STAFF table. The trigger will display the dbms_output message during an UPDATE operation.

```
create or replace trigger staff_update_mutate
before update of dob on staff
for each row
begin
--update staff
--set salary = 25000
--where staff_no = 'SA200';
:new.salary := 25000;
dbms_output.put_line('Update performed');
dbms_output.put_line('Old Salary '||:old.salary);
dbms_output.put_line('New Salary '||:new.salary);
end;
```

MUTATING TABLES WITH DATABASE RELATIONSHIP

Another situation when table mutating error occurs is if the trigger has statements to change the primary, foreign or unique key columns of the table the trigger is triggering off. In this case the table mutate error is encountered when querying a table other than the table on which the trigger is based. This happens when a foreign key reference is present with an *on-delete-cascade* option.

A row level trigger on the parent table will mutate if the child table is being referred to in the trigger for a delete transaction. This will only happen if the foreign key in the child table is created with the on delete cascade option. No mutation occurs if the parent table is being referred in a trigger in the child table.

Implementing Business Rules through Triggers

Business rules reflect guidelines that affect data during table operations. Triggers are useful in implementing such business rules. Consider the following examples of triggers implementing business rules.

1. An UPDATE trigger *trigger_apartment_bu* on APARTMENT table that is fired every time a change is made from 'V' to 'R' in the value of the APT_STATUS attribute. The trigger checks to see if there are any complaints for the apartment. If any complaint is pending, then the update is cancelled and the raise_application_error message is displayed.

```
create or replace trigger apartment_bu
before update on apartment
for each row
when (old.apt_status='V')
declare
cursor complaint_cursor is
select complaint_no,status
from complaints
where apt_no=:old.apt_no;
complaint_row complaint_cursor%rowtype;
error1 exception;
begin
for complaint_row in complaint_cursor
loop
if complaint_row.status is null then
raise error1;
end if;
end loop;
exception
when no_data_found then
dbms_output.put_line('Update Ok');
when error1 then
raise_application_error(-20100,'Update Cancelled');
end;
```

2. An INSERT trigger *tenant_auto_bi* on TENANT_AUTO table. The trigger checks the implementation of a business rule: if the RENTAL_STATUS for the tenant is "S" then the tenant should not be allowed to have any vehicle registered for parking.

```
create or replace trigger tenant_auto_bi
before insert on tenant_auto
for each row
declare
status_t char(2);
error1 exception;
begin
```

```
select rental.rental_status into status_t
from rental,tenant
where rental.rental_no=tenant.rental_no
and tenant.tenant_ss=:new.tenant_ss;
if status_t = 'S' then
raise error1;
end if;
exception
when error1 then
raise_application_error(-20100,'Insert Cancelled');
end;
```

Relationship Maintenance

Triggers can be utilized for maintaining referential integrity with respect to the cardinality specifications in a data model. The minimum cardinality of any relationship defines how the integrity is maintained. To ensure correct results it is important to utilize the LOCK TABLE statement (to serialize access) with triggers in a multi-user environment.

The following example illustrates the use of triggers in maintaining these relationships. Consider the 1:N relationship with mandatory-to-mandatory minimum cardinality between RENTAL and RENTAL_INVOICE tables (as shown in Figure 1-7). According to the relationship each RENTAL row is associated with at least one RENTAL_INVOICE row. Figure 3-26 illustrates the relationship impact with respect to INSERT and DELETE operations on the two tables.

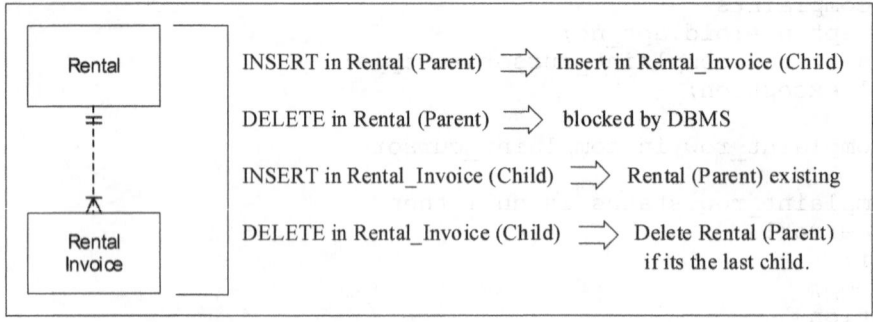

Figure 3-26

Triggers can be utilized such that whenever rental information is inserted in the RENTAL table, related information is also added in the RENTAL_INVOICE table. If RENTAL_INVOICE information is not available, the RENTAL table INSERT operation is not committed. To maintain this mandatory-to-mandatory relationship, two triggers (an INSERT TRIGGER and a DELETE TRIGGER) and a reference table is used. The reference table keeps track of the number of child rows existing for a parent row. The reference table has two attributes: (i) foreign key value in the child table, and (ii) a count of the number of times this value appears in the child table. The syntax for creating such a reference table is as follows:

```
create table rental_invoice_ref
(rental_no number(6) constraint rental_invoice_ref_pk primary key,
tc number(3));
```

The reference table is populated through an insert trigger on the RENTAL_INVOICE table as follows:

```
create or replace trigger rental_invoice_ai
after insert on rental_invoice
for each row
declare
trental_no number(6);
begin
select rental_no into trental_no
from rental_invoice_ref
where rental_no = :new.rental_no;
if trental_no is not null then
update rental_invoice_ref
set tc = tc+1
where rental_no = :new.rental_no;
end if;
exception
when no_data_found then
insert into rental_invoice_ref values(:new.rental_no,1);
end;
```

A delete trigger on RENTAL_INVOICE table then automatically deletes the parent (RENTAL) row when the last related child (RENTAL_INVOICE) row is deleted. The delete trigger is shown below.

```
create or replace trigger rental_invoice_ad
after delete on rental_invoice
for each row
declare
tc_in number(3);
begin
select tc into tc_in
from rental_invoice_ref
where rental_no = :old.rental_no;
if tc_in = 1 then
delete from rental_invoice_ref where rental_no=:old.rental_no;
delete from rental where rental_no=:old.rental_no;
else
update rental_invoice_ref
set tc = tc-1
where rental_no = :old.rental_no;
end if;
end;
```

System Triggers

System triggers refer to triggers that are fired by DDL statements or database system events rather than DML statements. DDL events include statements like CREATE, ALTER, DROP, GRANT, and so on. The database system events include LOGON, LOGOFF, STARTUP, SHUTDOWN, and SERVERERROR. The syntax of system trigger is the same as DML statements triggers with the ON keyword clause now indicating the trigger to be database or schema level trigger.

CREATE [OR REPLACE] TRIGGER *trigger-name*
[BEFORE | AFTER]
[*List of DDL or Database System Events*]
[ON DATABASE | SCHEMA]

```
. . .
BEGIN
. . . pl/sql statements . . .
END;
```

The ON DATABASE option implies that the trigger fires when anyone logs into the database, regardless of the schema. This option can be used to maintain a typical audit of who and when the database has been accessed. The ON SCHEMA option implies that the trigger is specific to the schema in which it is created.

The following trigger *chk_rental_alter* blocks any attempt to execute an ALTER statement in the schema in which the trigger is defined. The trigger will instead display an dbms_output message along with the raise_application_error message.

```
create or replace trigger chk_rental_alter
before alter
on schema
declare
error1 exception;
begin
dbms_output.put_line('System Trigger successful');
raise error1;
exception
when error1 then
raise_application_error(-20100,'Alter Cancelled');
end;
```

Test the *chk_rental_alter* trigger with the following ALTER statements.

```
alter table rental
modify least_type char(3);
alter table apartment
modify flooring char(10);
```

INSTEAD-OF Triggers

Database views have limitations with respect to INSERT, UPDATE, or DELETE statements. These limitations occur especially with views created through the joining of multiple tables. To overcome this limitation, INSTEAD-OF triggers can be defined, which fire when a user issues a DML statement associated with a view. The mechanism of instead-of triggers is that when the user tries to insert, update, or delete a row in a view, the trigger performs the associated insert, update, or delete operation on the table underlying the view.

Instead-of triggers are attached to specific database views. There is no BEFORE or AFTER specification, rather row level operation. The trigger body specifies one or more SQL commands that modify the tables underlying the view. The table attributes to be modified must be contained in the view and are referenced using the OLD qualifier. The following example sequence shows the application of such triggers.

1. Create a view *rental_view* on a SQL query that lists RENTAL_NO, TENANT_NAME, INVOICE_NO and INVOICE_DUE attributes from RENTAL, TENANT, and RENTAL_INVOICE tables.

```
create view rental_view as
select rental.rental_no, tenant_name, invoice_no, invoice_due
from rental, tenant, rental_invoice
where rental.rental_no = rental_invoice.rental_no
and rental.rental_no = tenant.rental_no;
```

2. Create the INSTEAD OF trigger *rental_delete* on *rental_view* view, which deletes a row from RENTAL_INVOICE table.

```
create or replace trigger rental_delete
instead of delete on rental_view
For each row
Begin
delete from rental_invoice
where invoice_no = :old.invoice_no;
end;
```

3. Test the working of the *rental_delete* trigger through a DELETE statement on the *rental_view* view. The DELETE statement will fire the *rental_delete* trigger to delete a row from the RENTAL_INVOICE table.

```
delete from rental_view
where invoice_no = 1006;
```

Maintain Trigger in SQL Developer

Details on handling triggers in SQL Developer is provided in Appendix E. Triggers can be created (i) directly within SQL Developer, or (ii) in a text editor create the trigger source and thereafter the source file is opened or copy/pasted separately in the SQL Worksheet of SQL Developer. The trigger must be compiled successfully before using it.

Triggers can be dropped from the database in SQL Developer either through a submenu Drop Trigger option, or the DROP TRIGGER *trigger-name* statement. For example drop trigger chk_rental_alter;

Triggers can be disabled. Disabling a trigger means that they still exist in the database, but do not fire when the triggering event occurs. Disabling a trigger can be done in SQL Developer either through a submenu Disable option, or the ALTER TRIGGER trigger_name [ENABLE | DISABLE] statement.

Information about triggers can be viewed by querying the USERS_TRIGGERS data dictionary view. For example,

```
select trigger_name, trigger_type, triggering_event
from user_triggers;
```

DYNAMIC SQL

In general SQL statements in a PL/SQL program unit can be categorized as *static* or *dynamic*. Static SQL statements are those where the database objects are validated when the program is compiled. Dynamic SQL statements are SQL queries that are entered as text strings, and then compiled and validated at runtime. The advantage of dynamic SQL is the possibility of structuring SQL query statements dynamically based on user inputs, including DDL statements like CREATE, ALTER, and DROP. This is useful when one wants to create program units that contain SQL queries that use search condition that are based on dynamic conditions, such as attribute name or table name. Also, it provides the ability to create or alter database table structures such as creating a temporary table to generate a report, and then drop the table.

Two methods are available for implementing dynamic SQL within PL/SQL - DBMS_SQL and Native Dynamic SQL. The DBMS_SQL package is a PL/SQL built-in package that offers a programmatic API. Native Dynamic SQL allows the placement of dynamic SQL statements directly into PL/SQL code.

Native Dynamic SQL can be utilized in server-side programs. It has many capabilities compared to DBMS_SQL package. For instance, programming is simpler, because native dynamic SQL is used in the same way that static SQL is used within PL/SQL; supports all of the types, supported by static SQL in PL/SQL, even user-defined types such as user-defined objects, collections and REFs; and, can be utilized for fetching directly into PL/SQL records. In this lesson the native dynamic SQL approach is outlined.

Native Dynamic SQL

Native dynamic SQL (sometimes also referred as embedded dynamic SQL) is performed through the EXECUTE IMMEDIATE statement. Supported statements include DML, DDL, SQL, and PL/SQL anonymous blocks. An extension of EXECUTE IMMEDIATE statement for queries only, involves the use of ref cursors so that a statement may be passed at runtime instead of being given declaratively. The syntax of the native dynamic SQL statement is as follows:

```
EXECUTE IMMEDIATE dynamic-sql-string
    [INTO {define-variable1 [, define-variable2] ... | plsql-record}]
    [USING [IN | OUT | IN OUT] bind-variable1 [,
        [IN | OUT | IN OUT] bind-variable2] ...]
    [{RETURNING | RETURN} INTO bind-variable3 [, bind-variable4] ...];
```

where *dynamic-sql-string* may be any of non-query DML, single row query, anonymous PL/SQL block, call statement, transaction control statement, DDL or session control command.

Define-variables are matched positionally to items in the select list. Where a PL/SQL record is given to retrieve the results of the query, the elements of the record must match the items in the select list as would be the case with a static SQL statement.

Bind-variables can be bound to place holders in a dynamic SQL string. Place holders are indicated by a colon prefix and are matched positionally to variables in the USING clause. Where duplicate place holders are present in a statement, the handling will vary depending on the type of statement involved. If the statement is DML and the same place holder is referenced more than once, then the corresponding *bind-variable* must appear the same number of times in the USING clause. If the statement is a PL/SQL block, then the corresponding *bind-variable* is given only once, its position matching that of the first occurrence of the place holder. However, table or column names cannot be passed as bind variables.

Bind-variables can be IN, OUT or IN OUT depending on their usage. In a standard DML statement all binds will have the default IN mode. However if the statement has a returning clause or is a PL/SQL block or stored program unit call, then the result of the execution may be that bind variables are assigned values. In this case, just as with parameters to a stored procedure or function, it is necessary to indicate the fact by specifying the mode as OUT or IN OUT as appropriate.

An EXECUTE IMMEDIATE statement:

- prepares the given string.
- binds any arguments passed in the USING clause.
- executes the statement.
- when defined as a query, fetches the single row into the define variables or PL/SQL record given in the INTO clause.
- deallocates and clears up as necessary.

If more than one row matches the search criteria a "too_many_rows" exception will be raised. Similarly if no rows are returned the result is a "no_data_found" exception. In these cases the *ref cursor method* should be used instead. The syntax involving ref cursors in dynamic SQL is:

```
OPEN cursor-variable FOR dynamic-query-string
    [USING bind-variable1 [, bind-variable2] ...];
```

where *cursor-variable* is a weakly typed cursor variable. A weakly typed cursor variable is one that is declared without a return type and so may be used with any query. A strongly typed cursor variable has a return record type and may only be used with queries that return records of that type.

Just as with EXECUTE IMMEDIATE, the USING clause maps bind variables positionally to place holders (prefixed by colons) in the query statement. However because the statement must be a query the mode of all bind variables is always IN and so is not specified. Datatype restrictions are the same as for EXECUTE IMMEDIATE.

Fetching Data using the ref cursor is similar to cursor processing. It may include fetch and close statements along with cursor% attributes (notfound, found, rowcount, isopen).

The following are examples involving Dynamic SQL.

1. Executing a DDL CREATE statement that creates a table test1.

```
declare
str varchar2(200);
begin
```

```
str := 'create table test1 (tst varchar2(120))';
execute immediate str;
end;
```

2. Executing a DML INSERT statement that inserts a row into test1 table with bind variables for row attribute values.

```
declare
str varchar2(200);
val1 varchar2(6) := 'hello';
begin
str := 'insert into test1 values (:1)';
execute immediate str using val1;
end;
```

3. Executing a DML INSERT statement that inserts a row into test1 table with attribute values placed directly.

```
declare
str varchar2(200);
--val1 varchar2(6) := 'hello';
begin
str := 'insert into test1 values (''hello2'')';
execute immediate str;
end;
```

4. Executing a DML INSERT statement where the table name is a variable that may not known until runtime.

```
declare
str varchar2(200);
val1 varchar2(6) := 'test1';
begin
str := 'insert into '||val1||' values (''hello3'')';
execute immediate str;
end;
```

5. Retrieving data with a SQL query where the table name is a bind variable.

```
declare
stud varchar2(40);
val1 varchar2(10) := 'customer';
str varchar2(200);
begin
str := 'select last_name from '||val1||' where customer_id = 102';
execute immediate str into stud;
dbms_output.put_line('Last Name is '||stud);
end;
```

6. Retrieving data with a SQL query and an unknown table name involving multiple rows. The anonymous PL/SQL block can also be created as a procedure with an input parameter 'val1.'

```
declare
type my_curs_type is ref cursor;
curs my_curs_type;
t_rec tenant%rowtype;
str varchar2(512);
val1 varchar2(10) := 'tenant';
begin
```

```
str := 'select * from '||val1||'';
open curs for str;
loop
fetch curs into t_rec;
exit when curs%notfound;
dbms_output.put_line(t_rec.tenant_name||' '||t_rec.tenant_dob);
end loop;
close curs;
end;
```

The dbms_output message will be as follows:

```
Jack Robin 21-JUN-60
Mary Stackles 02-AUG-80
Ramu Reddy 11-APR-62
Marion Black 25-MAY-81
Venessa Williams 12-MAR-70
```

7. Retrieving data with unknown table name, attribute name, and condition value involving multiple rows. Procedure *search_db* has input parameters for the unknown entries of the query. It should be noted that the condition value has to be passed as a bind variable.

```
create or replace procedure search_db (table1 varchar2,attr1
varchar2,cond1 varchar2) is
type my_curs_type is ref cursor;
curs my_curs_type;
t_rec tenant%rowtype;
str varchar2(512);
begin
str := 'select * from '||table1||' where '||attr1||' = :j';
open curs for str using cond1;
loop
fetch curs into t_rec;
exit when curs%notfound;
dbms_output.put_line(t_rec.tenant_name);
end loop;
close curs;
end;
```

Test the procedure with the following statement:

```
execute search_db('tenant','employer_name','MSU');
```

The dbms_output message will be as follows:

```
Ramu Reddy
Marion Black
```

CHAPTER SUMMARY

▸ A PL/SQL package is a database program unit that is a collection of logically related procedures and functions.

▸ A PL/SQL package consists of two components – the package specification and package body.

▸ Database triggers are PL/SQL program unit that execute in response to database events like insert, update, or delete.

▸ Triggers can cause table mutation error, where a mutating table is a table that is being modified by a DML action when a trigger is fired.

▸ Triggers are useful to implement business rules.

▸ Triggers are also utilized for maintaining referential integrity in a database.

▸ A special type of trigger referred as system triggers execute in response to DDL statements or database system events rather than DML statements.

▸ INSTEAD-OF triggers are executed when a user issues a DML statement associated with a database view.

▸ The mechanism of instead-of triggers is that when the user tries to insert, update, or delete a row in a view, the trigger performs the associated insert, update, or delete operation on the table underlying the view.

▸ In general SQL statements in a PL/SQL program are categorized as static since database objects are validated when the program is compiled.

▸ Dynamic SQL statements are SQL queries that are entered as text strings, and then compiled and validated at runtime.

▸ The advantage of dynamic SQL is possibility of structuring SQL query statements dynamically based on user inputs, including DDL statements like CREATE, ALTER, and DROP.

▸ Dynamic SQL facilitate SQL queries that use search condition based on dynamic conditions, such as attribute name or table name.

REVIEW QUESTIONS

1. What are the two elements of a package?

2. How is a package referenced by another program?

3. What is the basic purpose of a trigger?

4. Describe the various levels of trigger.

5. Describe the nature of table mutation.

6. In what way can triggers support referential integrity?

7. Describe the difference between the system triggers and DML based triggers.

8. How can triggers be utilized with database views?

9. What is the difference between static SQL and dynamic SQL?

10. Describe the concept of native dynamic SQL.

REVIEW EXERCISES

1. A PL/SQL _____ is a collection of logically related procedures and functions.

2. A PL/SQL package consists of two components _____ and _____.

3. Variables in a _____ can be referenced by any program within the package.

4. The following statement refers to the _____ package.

   ```
   test_all.auto_list(1999);
   ```

5. The entry auto_list(1999) in the following statement refers to a PL/SQL _____.

   ```
   test_all.auto_list(1999);
   ```

6. A PL/SQL _____ is a collection of compiled programs.

7. PL/SQL programs that execute in response to database events like insert, update, and delete are called database _____.

8. A database _____ can fire before or after a triggering event.

9. Database _____ are necessary to enforce referential integrity with respect to cardinality specifications.

10. _____ triggers fire when a user issues a DML statement associated with a view.

11. _____ SQL statements are entered as text strings, which are then compiled and validated at runtime.

12. Native dynamic SQL is performed through the _____ _____ statement.

PROBLEM SOLVING EXERCISES

> Run the script file outdoorDB_v4.sql to load the Outdoor Clubs & Product database to complete the exercises.

Ex3C-1.   Create a package "ex3c_product_category" consisting of two procedures similar to Exercise Ex3A-2 and Ex3A-3 of Chapter 3, Lesson A. Save the package with the same filename as package name.

The first procedure of the package (similar to Ex3A-2) should be named "ex3c_product_price." The second procedure of the package (similar to Ex3A-3) should be named "ex3c_product_count."

Ex3C-2.   Create a package "ex3c_order_member" that has two procedures. The first procedure should be named "ex3c_club_member." This procedure creates a new club membership. It contains input parameters for attributes duration, payment_type, club_id, and customer_id. Club membership is $50 per month. The procedure displays membership_id, membership_date, and amount attribute values. Use the current date for membership_date attribute.

The second procedure named "ex3c_new_order" creates a new product order with a maximum of 3 products in an order. The input parameters for the three products and their respective ordered quantities are referred as product_id1 and quantity1, product_id2 and quantity2, and product_id3 and quantity3. If there are less than 3 products, then NULL should be used for input. The procedure displays order_id, order_date, ship_date, total attribute values. The ship_date attribute value is 5 days after the order_date attribute value. Use the current date for order_date attribute. The procedure inserts a row in product_order table, rows in order_details table, and updates the quantity_in_stock attribute value in the product table.

Save the package with the same file name as the package name.

Ex3C-3.   Create a package "ex3c_membership" that has one procedure and two functions. The procedure is named "ex3c_new_member." It creates a new club membership. The procedure has input parameters for attributes duration, payment_type, name of sporting club, first_name of customer, and last_name of customer. Club membership is $50 per month. The procedure will display membership_id, membership_date, customer_id and amount attribute values. Use the current date for membership_date attribute.

The first function "ex3c_check_club" checks to see if the sporting club exists. If the club does not exist, the membership is denied with a message "This club is not attached to the database."

The second function "ex3c_check_customer" checks to see if the customer exists. If the customer does not exist, a new customer is created to complete the club membership.

Save the package with the same file name as the package name.

Ex3C-4.   Create a package "ex3c_status_check" that has one procedure and one function. The package specification only displays the procedure definition. The procedure is named "product_status" with one input parameter for attribute product_id. The procedure displays product_name, associated supplier name, and a message. The message will either display a total of the quantity ordered for the product, or a text "Not Ordered so far." The value of quantity ordered is determined by a function "product_qty." Create the function product_qty that determines the total quantity ordered for the input product_id attribute value.

Save the package with the same file name as the package name.

Ex3C-5.   Create a trigger "ex3c_product_reorder_au" that is associated with an update operation on the product table. The trigger checks to see whether during the update of the quantity_in_stock attribute, if its value gets lower than the reorder_point attribute value for a product. When this situation occurs, the trigger automatically inserts a new purchase order in the purchase_order table. The new purchase order will use the existing supplier_no attribute value for the product in the product table, and the quantity attribute value will be same as the reorder_qty value for the product in the product table. Save the trigger as a script file having the filename ex3c5_trigger1.

Ex3C-6.   Create a trigger "ex3c_product_order_ai" that is associated with an insert operation on the product_order table. The trigger automatically adds a shipping and handling charge of $ 6 to whatever is the tabulated value of the total attribute. The tabulated value is the sum of (price * quantity) for all products in the product order. Save the trigger as a script file having the filename ex3c6_trigger2.

Ex3C-7.   Create a trigger "ex3c_customer_order_ai" that maintains the relationship between sporting_clubs and club_activity tables with respect to insert operations in both tables. Save the trigger as a script file having the filename ex3c7_trigger3.

Ex3C-8.   Create a trigger "ex3c_product_supp_ai" that maintains the relationship between supplier and product tables with respect to insert operations in both tables. Save the trigger as a script file having the filename ex3c8_trigger4.

Ex3C-9.   Create a trigger "ex3c_product_supp_ad" that maintains the relationship between supplier and product tables with respect to delete operations in both tables. Save the trigger as a script file having the filename ex3c9_trigger5.

Ex3C-10.   Create a database view "product_supp_view" containing product_name, price, supplier name, and supplier city attributes. Save the view definition as a script file having the filename ex3c10_view1. Now create a INSTEAD OF trigger on product_supp_view with respect to insert operation on supplier table. Save the trigger as a script file having the filename ex3c10_trigger6.

Ex3C-11.   Create a view "customer_ord_view" containing first_name, last_name, order_id, product_name, quantity attributes. Save the view definition as a script file having the filename ex3c11_view2. Now create a INSTEAD OF trigger on customer_ord_view with respect to insert and delete operations on customer table. Save the trigger as a script file having the filename ex3c11_trigger7.

Ex3C-12.   Create a procedure "search_info1" that uses a dynamic SQL to find the values pertaining to tables customer or product. The procedure has one input parameter to enter a table name (customer or product). The procedure displays first_name, last_name, and city attribute values if the input parameter is customer table, or product_name and price if the input parameter is product table. Save the procedure as a script file having the filename ex3c12_dynamic1.

Ex3C-13.   Create a procedure "search_info2" that uses a dynamic SQL to find the values pertaining to tables customer or product. The procedure has two input parameters. The first input parameter can be used to enter a table name (customer or product). The second input parameter can be used to enter an attribute name. The possible attribute names are first_name, last_name, and city if the first input parameter table name is customer; or product_name and price attribute names if the first input parameter is product. The procedure should display all the rows for the input attribute name. Save the procedure as a script file having the filename ex3c13_dynamic2.

Ex3C-14.   Create containing a procedure "search_info3" that uses a dynamic SQL to find the values pertaining to tables customer or product. The procedure has three input parameters. The first input parameter can be used to enter a table name (customer or product). The second and third input parameters are supposed to complete a search condition in the SQL query. The second input parameter can be used for an attribute name for the search condition. The third input parameter can be some condition value associated with the attribute name of the second parameter. The conditional operator for the search condition in the query will be = sign. The procedure displays first_name, last_name, and city attribute values if the first input parameter is customer table, or product_name and price if the first input parameter is product table. Save the procedure as a script file having the filename ex3c14_dynamic3.

Ex3C-15.   Create a procedure "insert_info1" that uses a dynamic SQL to insert values pertaining to four input parameters. The first input parameter refers to some table in the database, while the other parameters refer to some attributes of the table. For example, insert first_name, last_name values in customer table. Save the procedure as a script file having the filename ex3c15_dynamic4.

Run the script file travelDB_v4.sql to load the Travel Anywhere database to complete the following exercises.

Ex3C-16.   Create a database trigger "tcust_delete" that maintains database relationship of travel_customer with ticket and hotel_reservation tables. The trigger allows direct deletion of a row in travel_customer by automatically ensuring deletion of travel_customer references in ticket and hotel_reservation tables. Save the trigger as a script file having the filename ex3c11_trigger8.

Ex3C-17.   Create a database trigger "ticket_insert" to enforce a business rule. The rule is that when inserting a new ticket reservation the trigger automatically checks if the travel_customer is also a hotel customer (hotel_reservation table), in which case it automatically provides an additional 10% discount of the quoted fare. Save the trigger as a script file having the filename ex3c11_trigger9.

Ex3C-18.   Create a database trigger "hotel_insert" to enforce a business rule that customers cannot share rooms in a hotel (i.e. one customer per room) . Since during insert of a new hotel_reservation, the insert statement will include the hotel_id, the trigger will check if that hotel_id will be able to implement the business rule. If the hotel does not have rooms then it automatically assigns another hotel in the same city. Save the trigger as a script file having the filename ex3c11_trigger10.

Ex3C-19.   Create a database trigger "hotel_id_update" to enforce a business rule. When updating the hotel_id value in hotel_reservation, if the num_kids value is more than zero, then re-assign a hotel with bed_type DQ in the same city. Save the trigger as a script file having the filename ex3c11_trigger11.

CHAPTER 4
(LESSON A)

Web Application Design with HTML and DOM

- Web Application
- Hypertext Markup Language (HTML)
- Develop Web Site

Web application design is a fusion of two areas: Web layout design and application logic design. The objective of Web application design is to outline how an application will appear over the Web, and specify how users can accomplish application tasks. The basic unit of a Web application is the *Web browser screen*. Web application design consists of:

1. Define the layout and functionality of each screen.
2. Logic of how users will navigate the application.
3. Embed the application (program) logic to control layout format and content.

A Web browser screen displays content through Web pages. Each Web page is a document consisting of text, data, graphics, sound or video, animation, and other emerging types of content. A Web page is created using a special language called HTML (Hypertext Markup Language). Each Web page by default is stored as a file with file type *.html* or *.htm*. Web pages may also have special file types like .asp (for Active Server Pages), .jsp (for Java Server Pages), and so on. A Web application is a collection of one or more Web pages referred as a Web site. A Web site organizes pages in a hierarchical structure as shown in Figure 4-1.

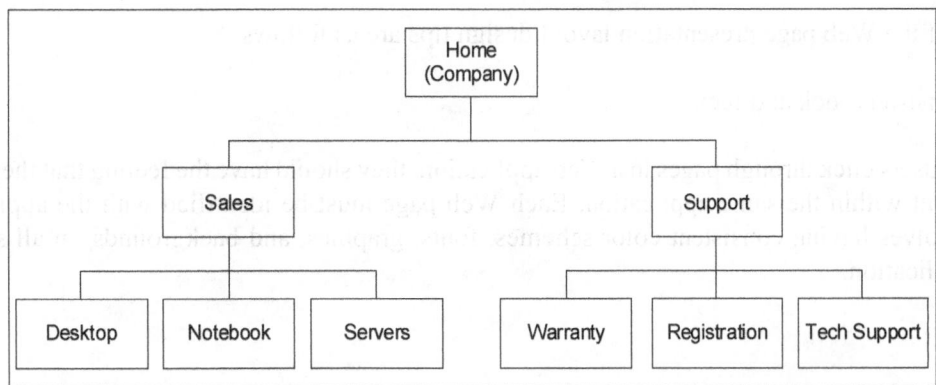

Figure 4-1   Hierarchical Layout of a Web site

The top most Web page of the hierarchy is typically called the *home* page. Home page contains the links to other Web pages of the Web site. The content of each Web page is part of Web design planning. It is possible to have links to all Web pages from the home page or have links to selective Web pages lower in the hierarchy. The home page filename is generally named on the Web server as *default* or *index*.

Designing the layout of a Web page is a very specialized domain. It can affect how users interact with the screen, respond to color schemes and artwork, and how to effectively present information. Web page layout design also includes how users will navigate between screens, as well as create a consistent look and feel across an application.

A typical Web page layout (shown in Figure 4-2) can consist of word processor type margin areas on all four sides of a page. In the middle of the Web page is the area to enter the page content.

The top margin area typically has a *banner* containing the page title. Below the banner there may be a *navigation bar* with links to other pages of the site. Navigation bars may also appear in other margin areas too. Margin areas also have *mail links*, links to external Web sites, or some description text. Entries in the margin areas may remain the same among the Web pages of the site. Also, a Web page may not have all of the margin areas.

Figure 4-2 Web Page Layout

Web Design

Web design in a dynamic page of a Web application consists of two parts – the *presentation part* and the *content part*. The content part is the dynamic part that changes based on data from the database. The nature of content (data) to be displayed in a Web page is often associated with the logic of a program. The presentation part deals with the look and feel of the Web page including its content. The presentation part stays relatively static, even though it is part of the logic of the content.

Some of the Web page presentation layout design tips are as follows:

1. Consistent look and feel.

    As users click through pages in a Web application, they should have the feeling that they are moving about within the same application. Each Web page must be identified with the application. This involves having consistent color schemes, fonts, graphics, and backgrounds on all screens in an application.

2. Text.

    Displaying of text from one side of the screen to the other is sometimes tiring for the eyes. Instead, narrow columns should be used for large blocks of text. This may result in blank spaces on the sides of the column, or stretching the text further down the screen. Also, blank space on a Web page is better than too much clutter. Too much text clutters the screen, and is considered distracting to the reader. Use empty space when possible. Avoid underlining text for emphasis. In a Web page underlined text will be confused with a hyperlink on the Web.

    Further, provide instructions on what the Web Form does. These instructions can be outlined with the form or provide a link to another Web page for instructions.

3. Frames.

    Some designers do not recommend frames. It is considered messy when each frame is displayed with a scroll bar. Also, when a user bookmarks a Web page that uses frames, the original frameset is bookmarked, not the specific combination of frames that the user is seeing.

    However, frames have many helpful uses. It can serve as a tool for navigation from anywhere in an application. Frames are also useful for promoting a consistent look and feel. Further, frames are useful when one part of the Web page must remain stationary, while other part can be scrolled through.

4. Buttons and Links.

    Buttons and links allow users to move through an application. It should be placed in such a way that the user can locate them easily. Generally, buttons should be placed on the same part of every Web page. Provide consistent labels for buttons and links across the Web pages.

5. Horizontal and Vertical Menus.

    A horizontal navigation bar is a collection of links listed across the top or bottom of the Web page. A vertical navigation is a collection of links positioned to the left or right side of the Web page. Typically, the horizontal navigation bar provides links to general areas of the application. This navigation does not change as the user moves through one area or another. The vertical navigation bars change depending on which section of the application the user is in. The options listed in the vertical navigation bar should be specific to the areas that the user is currently visiting. So, when a new area is clicked on the horizontal navigation bar, the vertical navigation bar changes to reflect what is available in the new area.

6. General.

    A Web is a visual medium. A user reads the text but may need information about an image it encounters. In these cases it is important to provide an image label by including an ALT attribute in each image tag. The ALT attribute specifies alternate text that can be displayed or read in place of the image. The use of ALT attribute also helps if the users set their browsers not to display images because of the longer download times required for images.

    Further each Web page should be assigned a title. Since a users will often start with the title of a Web page, so an informative title is extremely helpful.

Web Application Design Methodology

Web application design is an iterative process. A general sequence of steps to design such application are as follows:

1. The first step in Web application design is to identify the users of the application.

2. The next step is to create a *storyboard*. The idea of a storyboard is borrowed from films, where a storyboard is used to map out successive scenes to help plot an entire film. Similarly, during Web design the layout of each Web page must be prepared in detail. This improves communication with

the users as well as helps preparing a blueprint of the application. Storyboard can be created either manually or through a software tool.

3. Create a *prototype* of the application. Prototypes give the users a clearer idea of how the application will work. To ensure that the prototype gives a sense of functionality, embed some dummy data in Web pages. The prototype should be improved based on user interaction, till it is approved by the users. Prototypes can be developed using any Web authoring software like NetObjects Fusion, Dreamweaver, FrontPage, etc.

4. Documentation of each Web page layout including the program logic. Also, explanation of database entity access should be outlined.

HYPERTEXT MARKUP LANGUAGE (HTML)

HTML is the language of the World Wide Web. This lesson provides a brief overview of HTML. HTML is not a programming language, but rather a markup language. A Web page in HTML is a plain text (ASCII) file containing letters, numbers, and other printable characters along with embedded special markup codes. These markup codes are often called as *tags*. HTML tags are used to mark-up HTML elements. Any text editor or word processor can be used to create the HTML layout of a Web page. The Web page (HTML) file has two default file types – .htm or .html.

HTML uses two key symbols for tag specification. These symbols constitute what is often called an angle bracket – less than symbol (<) and greater than symbol (>). All HTML code is enclosed between these two symbols. For example, `<head>` indicates a Web page header tag.

All HTML tags appear in pairs. In between the tag pairs the content is placed. The beginning tag is like <some-tag>, while the closing tag is like </some-tag>. For example `<title>PL/SQL Server Pages</title>` defines the display window title "PL/SQL Server Pages" in the browser. `<title>` marks the beginning of the windows title text, while the `</title>` is the end of the title text. HTML tags are not case-sensitive.

Tags can have attributes. Attributes can provide additional information about the HTML elements on your page. The attributes are placed before the closing bracket of the starting tag. The value of the attribute must be enclosed within double quotation marks. For example, there is a tag `<body>` that defines the body element of a HTML page. With an added bgcolor attribute like `<body bgcolor="red">`, the background color of the Web page in browser becomes red. Another example, consider the `<IMG>` tag that shows an image/video on a Web page. The `<img>` tag can be configured with a number of attributes including the `src` attribute, which specifies the filename of the image file or video clip. The SRC attribute within the `<img>` tag appears as `<img src="mypicture.gif">`. Some of the basic HTML tags are as follows.

Main Elements

Document Type

The document type tag `<!DOCTYPE>` is the very first statement in a Web page. It makes sure the Web site renders correctly in various browsers. The tag tells the browser which HTML or XHTML specification the document uses.

XHTML is the next generation of HTML. It emphasizes writing tags in lower case as well as requiring closing of tag elements.

An HTML document is validated against a Document Type Definition (DTD). Before an HTML file can be properly validated, a correct DTD must be added as the first line of the file. The HTML 4.01 Transitional DTD includes everything in the strict DTD plus deprecated elements and attributes. For example,

```
<!DOCTYPE   HTML   PUBLIC   "-//W3C//DTD   HTML   4.01   Transitional//EN"
"http://www.w3.org/TR/html4/loose.dtd">
```

`<html>` Element

Every Web page must begin and end with the `<html>` element. These are the first and last tags of the document. For example the following is a Web page with only one line "My First Web Page."

```
<html>
My First Web Page.
</html>
```

`<head>` and `<body>` Elements

The HTML statements in a Web page appear in two sections – the head and body. The head part of the page uses `<head>` ... `</head>` tag pairs. The `<head>` tag contains information that is placed at the start of a Web page. It contains general information, also called meta-information, about a document. The tags inside the head element should not be displayed by a browser. Only few tags are legal inside the head section. These are: `<base>`, `<link>`, `<meta>`, `<title>`, `<style>`, and `<script>` as shown in Table 4-1.

HTML Tag	Description
`<title>` ... `</title>`	Defines the Web page title that appears in the browser's title bar.
`<base>` . . . `</ base>`	Defines a base URL for all the links on a page.
`<style>` ... `</style>`	Defines a style sheet.

Table 4-1: Common tags in Head section of a Web page

HTML Tag	Description
`<link> ... </link>`	Defines an external link between the existing Web page and an external source.
`<script> ... </script>`	References embedded scripts.
`<meta> ... </meta>`	Defines Web page document properties.

Table 4-1: Common tags in Head section of a Web page

Following the `<head>` tag is the `<body>` tag that defines the HTML elements that represent the content of the HTML (Web) page. The attributes of the `<body>` tag determines the appearance of an HTML (Web) document. Some of the common attributes of the `<body>` tags are in Table 4-2.

Attribute	Determines
`background`	The background image.
`bgcolor`	The background color.
`text`	Text color.
`link`	The color of an unvisited link.

Table 4-2: Common attributes of Body tag

A simple Web page HTML file is shown below, followed by its appearance in Web browser in Figure 4-1:

```
<html>
<head>
<title>PL/SQL Server Page</title>
</head>
<body>
My First Web Page.
</body>
</html>
```

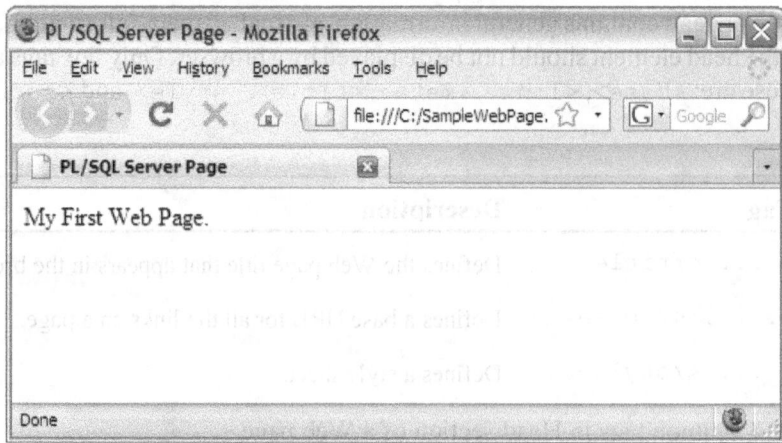

Figure 4-1   Web Page in Browser

Formatting Elements

Headings

Headings are defined with the `<h1>` to `<h6>` tags. `<h1>` defines the largest heading. `<h6>` defines the smallest heading. HTML automatically adds an extra blank line before and after a heading. For example,

```
<h1>This is a heading</h1>
<h2>This is a heading</h2>
<h3>This is a heading</h3>
<h4>This is a heading</h4>
<h5>This is a heading</h5>
<h6>This is a heading</h6>
```

Paragraphs

Paragraphs are defined with the `<p>` tag. HTML automatically adds an extra blank line before and after a paragraph. For example,

```
<p>This is a paragraph</p>
<p>This is another paragraph</p>
```

Line Breaks

The `<br>` tag is used when to end a line, but not to start a new paragraph. The `<br>` tag forces a line break wherever you place it. For example,

```
<p>This <br> is a para<br>graph with line breaks</p>
```

The `<br>` tag is an empty tag. It has no closing tag. In HTML the `<br>` tag has no end tag. In XHTML the `<br>` tag must be properly closed, like `<br />`.

Horizontal Rule

The `<hr>` tag inserts a horizontal rule in the form of a line in the Web page. For example, the following statements in the Web browser will appear as shown in the adjacent box.

```
<p>This is some text before the line.
<hr> This is some text after the line.</p>
```

This is some text before the line.

This is some text after the line.

The <hr> tag is an empty tag. It has no closing tag. In HTML the <hr> tag has no end tag. In XHTML the <hr> tag must be properly closed, like <hr />.

Comments

The <!-> tag is used to insert a comment in the HTML source code. A comment will be ignored by the browser. You can use comments to explain the code, which can help during editing at a later date. For example,

```
<!-- This is a comment -->
```

Text Format

It is not possible to pre-determine how the text is displayed in another browser. Some people have large computer displays, some have small. The text will be reformatted every time the user resizes his window. Never try to format the text in the HTML editor by adding empty lines and spaces to the text. HTML truncates the spaces in the source file. Any number of spaces count as one. Further, a new line counts as one space.

Using empty paragraphs <p> to insert blank lines is a bad habit. Use the <br> tag instead. HTML automatically adds an extra blank line before and after some elements, like before and after a paragraph, and before and after a heading. Table 4-3 is a list of common text formatting tags.

Tag	Description
<b>	Defines bold text
<big>	Defines big text
<em>	Defines emphasized text
<I>	Defines italic text
<small>	Defines small text
<strong>	Defines strong text
<sub>	Defines subscripted text
<sup>	Defines superscripted text

Table 4-3: Text Formatting Tags

Character Entities

Some characters have a special meaning in HTML, like the less than sign (<) that defines the start of an HTML tag. If one wants the browser to actually display these characters one has to insert character entities in the HTML source.

A character entity has three parts: an ampersand (&), an entity name or a # and an entity number, and finally a semicolon (;). For example, to display a less than sign the format is < or < .

The advantage of using a name instead of a number is that a name is easier to remember. The disadvantage is that not all browsers support the newest entity names, while the support for entity numbers is very good in almost all browsers.

List Elements

Unordered Lists

An unordered list is a list of items. The list items are marked with bullets (typically small black circles). An unordered list starts with the `<ul>` tag. Each list item starts with the `<li>` tag. Inside a list item you can put paragraphs, line breaks, images, links, other lists, etc. For example a sample HTML list item statements.

```
<ul>
<li>Coffee</li>
<li>Milk</li></ul>
```

Here is how the above HTML statements look in a Web browser:

- Coffee
- Milk

Ordered Lists

An ordered list is also a list of items. The list items are marked with numbers. An ordered list starts with the `<ol>` tag. Each list item starts with the `<li>` tag. Once again, inside a list item you can put paragraphs, line breaks, images, links, other lists, etc. For example a sample HTML list item statements.

```
<ol>
<li>Coffee</li>
<li>Milk</li></ol>
```

Here is how the above HTML statements it look in a Web browser:

1. Coffee
2. Milk

List tags are summarized in Table 4-4.

Tag	Description
\<ol\>	Defines an ordered list
\<ul\>	Defines an unordered list
\<li\>	Defines a list item
\<dl\>	Defines a definition list
\<dt\>	Defines a definition term
\<dd\>	Defines a definition description

Table 4-4: List Tags

Image Element

Images in a Web page are displayed through the image \<img\> tag and the associated `src` attribute. The \<img\> tag is empty, which means that it contains attributes only and it has no closing tag. To display an image on a page, one needs to use the `src` attribute which is referred as "source". The value of the `src` attribute is the URL of the image you want to display on your page.

The syntax of defining an image is \<img `src="url"`\>. The URL points to the location where the image is stored. An image named "boat.gif" located in the directory "images" on "www.w3schools.com" has the URL http://www.w3schools.com/images/boat.gif.

The browser puts the image where the image tag occurs in the document. If you put an image tag between two paragraphs, the browser shows the first paragraph, then the image, and then the second paragraph.

The Alt Attribute

The `alt` attribute is used to define an "alternate text" for an image. The value of the `alt` attribute is an author-defined text. Example syntax with `alt` attribute is:

```
<img src="boat.gif" alt="Big Boat">.
```

The `alt` attribute tells the reader what he or she is missing on a page if the browser can't load images. The browser will then display the alternate text instead of the image. It is a good practice to include the `alt` attribute for each image on a page, to improve the display and usefulness of your document for people who have text-only browsers. Image tags are summarized in Table 4-5.

Tag	Description
\<img\>	Defines an image
\<map\>	Defines an image map
\<area\>	Defines an area inside an image map

Table 4-5: Image Tags

Hyperlink Element

HTML uses an anchor \<a\> tag to hyperlink to another document on the Web. The hyperlink can point to any resource on the Web like a Web page, an image, a sound file, a movie, and so on. The \<a\> tag can also be utilized to link to other sections of an existing Web page.

The syntax of creating an hyperlink is `<a href="url">Text to be displayed</a>`. The `href` attribute is used to enter the address of the document to link to, and the words between the open and close of the anchor tag will display for the hyperlink in the Web page.

For example, the following syntax defines a link to W3Schools:

```
<a href="http://www.w3schools.com/">Visit W3Schools!</a>
```

The line above will look like this in a Web browser:

Visit W3Schools!

Another attribute in the \<a\> tag called the `target` attribute, one can define where the linked document will be opened. For example, the syntax below will open the document in a new browser window:
```
<a href="http://www.w3schools.com/" target="_blank">Visit W3Schools!</a>
```

Another attribute in the \<a\> tag called the `name` attribute is used to create a named anchor. When using named anchors we can create links that can jump directly into a specific section on a page, instead of letting the user scroll around to find what he/she is looking for. The syntax of a named anchor is `<a name="label">Text to be displayed</a>`.

The name attribute is used to create a named anchor. The name of the anchor can be any text you care to use. For example, `<a name="tips">Tips Section</a>`. To link directly to the "tips" section, add a # sign and the name of the anchor to the end of a URL, like:
```
<a href="http://www.w3schools.com/test.html#tips">Jump to Tips Section</a>.
```

A hyperlink to the Tips Section from WITHIN the file test.html will look like:
```
<a href="#tips">Jump to the Tips Section</a>
```

Always add a trailing slash to subfolder references. For example a link like "`href="http://www.w3schools.com/html`", will generate two HTTP requests to the server, because the server will add a slash to the address and create a new request like "`href="http://www.w3schools.com/html/`"

Named anchors are often used to create "table of contents" at the beginning of a large document. Each chapter within the document is given a named anchor, and links to each of these anchors are put at the top of the document. If a browser cannot find a named anchor that has been specified, it goes to the top of the document. No error occurs.

The following are examples for accessing other URL schemes:

1. Accessing a Newsgroup

    ```
    <a href="news:alt.html">HTML Newsgroup</a>
    ```

2. Downloading with FTP

    ```
    <a href="ftp://www.w3schools.com/ftp/winzip.exe">Download WinZip</a>
    ```

3. Link to mail system

    ```
    <a href="mailto:someone@w3schools.com">someone@w3schools.com</a>
    ```

Table Element

Table consists of horizontal rows and vertical columns (like spreadsheets). The intersection of a row and a column is called a *cell*. HTML uses `<table>` tag pairs to define a table. A HTML table has two additional tags associated with it: `<tr>` for table row, and `<td>` for table data (i.e. information/content in a cell). Each row is enclosed within the `<tr>` tag pair. Each cell content is enclosed with the `<td>` cell pair. The following are the HTML table tags associated with a two-row, two-column table. Table with no border is shown beside the table element syntax.

```
<table>
<tr>
<td> Row 1, Column 1</td>
<td> Row 1, Column 2</td> </tr>
<tr>
<td> Row 2, Column 1</td>
<td> Row 2, Column 2</td> </tr>
</table>
```

Row 1, Column 1	Row 1, Column 2
Row 2, Column 1	Row 2, Column 2

Most of the table appearance properties like background color, alignment, fonts, and so on can be set visually in NetObjects Fusion. However, there are few table properties outlined in Table 4-6 that need to be known for proper display of table contents.

Property	Description
Border	Specify the thickness of lines on the outside edge of the table.
Cell padding	Specify the distance between the cell's content and its border.
Cell spacing	Specify the thickness of the border between the cells.
Alignment	Aligns the content within the cell.

Table 4-6: HTML Table Properties

Table 4-7 is a summary of tags associated with the table element.

Tag	Description
<table>	Defines a table
<th>	Defines a table header
<tr>	Defines a table row
<td>	Defines a table cell
<caption>	Defines a table caption
<colgroup>	Defines groups of table columns
<col>	Defines the attribute values for one or more columns in a table
<thead>	Defines a table head
<tbody>	Defines a table body
<tfoot>	Defines a table footer

Table 4-7: Table Tags

If the border attribute is not specified, the table will be displayed without any borders. Sometimes this can be useful, but most of the time, it may be important to show the borders. The following is an example of table element with borders and headings.

```
<table border="1">
<tr>
<th>Heading</th>
<th>Another Heading</th></tr>
<tr>
<td> Row 1, Column 1</td>
<td> Row 1, Column 2</td> </tr>
<tr>
<td> Row 2, Column 1</td>
<td> Row 2, Column 2</td> </tr>
</table>
```

Heading	Another Heading
Row 1, Column 1	Row 1, Column 2
Row 2, Column 1	Row 2, Column 2

Section Elements

The `<div>` and `<span>` tags are used to define logical sections within a Web page. Such sectioning of a Web page is useful during HTML style definitions as well as document object model (DOM) manipulations. More use of these tags is provided in the Lesson B of this chapter.

The `<div>` tag is a container element that can hold related elements. It also defines a division or section of a Web page. There can be multiple DIV tags in a Web page, wherein each section associated with the tag can be separated through the ID attribute of the tag. For example in the following Web page the `<div>` tag is a collection of `<h1>` and `<p>` tags.

```
<html>
<head>
<title>DOM list</title>
</head>
<body>
<div id="dContain">
<h1>This is a heading</h1>
<p>Sample DOM Paragraph</p> </div>
<h3>End of Page</h3>
</body>
</html>
```

The `<span>` tag makes it possible to separate or section of a bit of inline text from its surroundings. There can be multiple `<span>` tags in a Web page or within a text, wherein each section associated with the tag can be separated through the ID attribute of the tag. For example in the following Web page the `<span>` tag separates the text "DOM" from other text in the `<p>` tag. The span tag does not create a new block of text, but its content can be accessed for manipulation.

```
<html>
<head>
<title>DOM list</title>
</head>
<body>
<div id="dContain">
<h1>This is a heading</h1>
<p>Sample <span id="sid"> DOM </span> Paragraph</p> </div>
<h3>End of Page</h3>
</body>
</html>
```

Web Page Layout

Web page layout generally occurs in the form of a grid. The grid layout mechanism maps a Web page to into virtual rows and columns. Such a mechanism allows placing of content anywhere in the Web page. One very common practice is to use HTML table elements to format the grid layout of a Web page.

HTML Styles

With HTML 4.01 all formatting can be moved out of the HTML document and into a separate style sheet. When a browser reads a style sheet, it will format the document according to it.

There are three ways of inserting a style sheet:

1. *External Style Sheet*

   An external style sheet is ideal when the style is applied to many pages. With an external style sheet, one can change the look of an entire Web site by changing one file. Each page must link to the style sheet using the `<link>` tag. The `<link>` tag goes inside the head section.

   ```
   <head>
   <link rel="stylesheet" type="text/css"
   href="mystyle.css">
   </head>
   ```

2. *Internal Style Sheet*

   An internal style sheet should be used when a single document has a unique style. One can define internal styles in the head section with the `<style>` tag.

   ```
   <head>
   <style type="text/css">
   body {background-color: red}
   p {margin-left: 20px}
   </style>
   </head>
   ```

3. *Inline Styles*

   An inline style should be used when a unique style is to be applied to a single occurrence of an element. To use inline styles utilize the style attribute in the relevant tag. The style attribute can contain any CSS property. The example shows how to change the color and the left margin of a paragraph.

   ```
   <p style="color: red; margin-left: 20px">
   This is a paragraph
   </p>
   ```

WEB PAGE LAYOUT TEMPLATES

The following are three basic Web page layout templates consisting of page titles, banners, navigation bars, and content area. All the templates are text based.

template has provision for page title, text banner, horizontal navigation bar links, and a separator for page content. The template may be modified appropriately.

```
<!DOCTYPE HTML PUBLIC "-//W3C//DTD HTML 4.01 Transitional//EN">
<html>
<head>
<title>Web Page Title</title>
</head>
<body>
<div align="center"><p><h1>Banner Text</h1></p>
<!-- Navigation Bar Links -->
<a href="http://someserver1.com">Link1</a> | <a href="http://someserver2.com"
name="Link2">Link2</a><br>
<hr /></div>
<br> <!-- Start Page Content -->
Main Content Area
Example below displays lists.
<li>list item 1</li><li>list item 2</li>
<ul>
<li>list item 1</li><li>list item 2</li>
</ul>
<ol>
<li>list item 1</li><li>list item 2</li>
</ol> <!-- End Page Content -->
</body>
</html>
```

The view of above template in the Web browser is shown in Figure 5-2.

Banner Text

Link1 | Link2

Main Content Area Example below displays lists.
- list item 1
- list item 2

    - list item 1
    - list item 2

    1. list item 1
    2. list item 2

Figure 4-2   Web Page Layout Template 1

Template 2

This template has provision for page title, text banner, vertical navigation bar links, and content area. The navigation link area is 100 pixels wide, while the content area is 600 pixels wide. The template may be modified appropriately.

```
<!DOCTYPE HTML PUBLIC "-//W3C//DTD HTML 4.01 Transitional//EN">
<html>
<head>
<title>Web Page Title</title>
</head>
<body>
<p><div align="center"><h1>Banner Text</h1></div></p>
<br>
<table summary="" width=700> <!-- Page width -->
<tr>
<td width=100> <!-- Navigation Bar Links -->
<a href="http://someserver1.com">Link 1</a><br>
<a href="http://someserver2.com">Link 2</a>
</td><td width=600> <!-- Start Page Content -->
<p>This is a first paragraph
<li>a1</li><li>a2</li></p>
<p>This is second paragraph
<li>a1</li><li>a2</li></p>
<p>This is the third paragraph.</p> <!-- End Page Content -->
</td></tr>
</table>
</body>
</html>
```

The view of above template in the Web browser is shown in Figure 4-3.

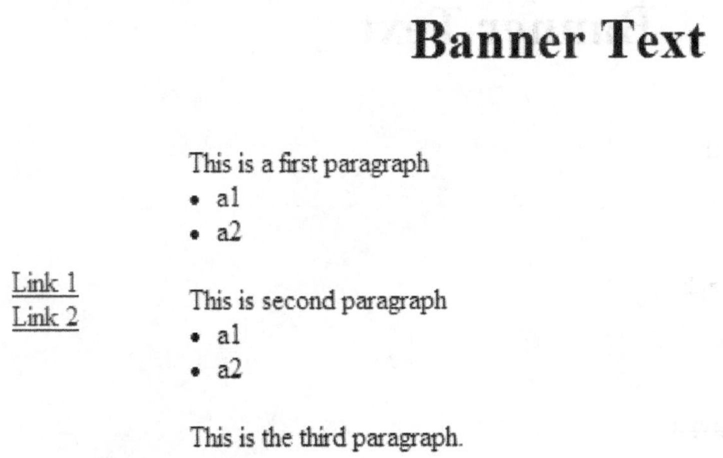

Banner Text

This is a first paragraph
- a1
- a2

Link 1
Link 2

This is second paragraph
- a1
- a2

This is the third paragraph.

Figure 4-3   Web Page Layout Template 2

Template 3

This template is similar to Template 2. It also has provision for page title, text banner, vertical navigation bar links, and content area. However, the navigation link area width is 10% of the screen size, while the content area width is 90% of the screen size. The template may be modified appropriately.

```
<!DOCTYPE HTML PUBLIC "-//W3C//DTD HTML 4.01 Transitional//EN">
<html>
<head>
<title>Web Page Title</title>
</head>
<body>
<p><div align="center"><h1>Banner Text</h1></div></p>
<br>
<table summary="" width=100%> <!-- Page width -->
<tr>
<td width=10%> <!-- Navigation Bar Links -->
<a href="http://someserver1.com">Link 1</a><br>
<a href="http://someserver2.com">Link 2</a>
</td><td width=90%> <!-- Start Page Content -->
<p>This is a first paragraph
<li>a1</li><li>a2</li></p>
<p>This is second paragraph
<li>a1</li><li>a2</li></p>
<p>This is the third paragraph.</p> <!-- End Page Content -->
</td></tr>
</table>
</body>
</html>
```

The view of above template in the Web browser is shown in Figure 4-4.

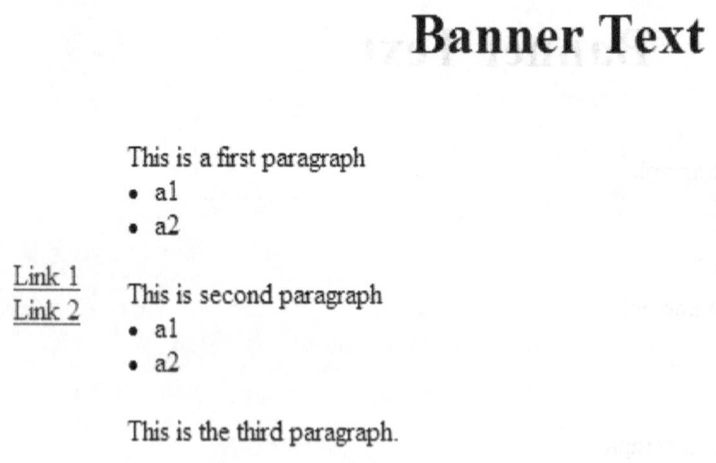

Banner Text

This is a first paragraph
- a1
- a2

Link 1
Link 2

This is second paragraph
- a1
- a2

This is the third paragraph.

Figure 4-4   Web Page Layout Template 3

CHAPTER SUMMARY

▸ Web application design is a fusion of two areas – Web layout design and application logic design.

▸ The objective of Web application design is to specify how application will look over the Web, and how users can accomplish tasks with it.

▸ Dynamic Web page layout design consists of two parts – the presentation part and the content part.

▸ The presentation part deals with the look and feel of the Web page including its content.

▸ The content part is the dynamic part that changes based on data from the database.

▸ The nature of content (data) to be displayed in a Web page is often associated with the logic of a program.

▸ Web pages in a Web site are organized in a hierarchical structure.

▸ The top most Web page of the hierarchy is typically called the home page, which contains the links to other Web pages of the Web site.

▸ A typical Web page layout consists of word processor type margin areas on all four sides which contains banners, navigation bar, mail links etc. In the middle of the Web page is the area to enter the page content.

▸ HTML is not a programming language, but rather a markup language.

▸ A Web page in HTML is a plain text (ASCII) file containing letters, numbers, and other printable characters along with embedded special markup codes.

▸ HTML markup codes are often called as *tags*.

▸ The Web page (HTML) file has two default file types – .htm or .html.

▸ All HTML tags appear in pairs. In between the tag pairs the content is placed.

▸ The beginning tag is like <some-tag>, while the closing tag is like </some-tag>.

▸ Tags can have attributes. Attributes can provide additional information about the HTML elements on your page.

▸ The document type tag <!DOCTYPE> is the very first statement in a Web page.

▸ Every Web page must begin and end with the <HTML> element. These are the first and last tags of the document.

▸ The HTML statements in a Web page appear in two sections – the head and body.

▸ The head part of the page uses <HEAD> ... </HEAD> tag pairs.

- ▸ The <BODY> tag that defines the HTML elements that represent the content of the HTML (Web) page.

- ▸ Headings are defined with the <h1> to <h6> tags.

- ▸ Paragraphs are defined with the <p> tag.

- ▸ The <br> tag is used when to end a line, but not to start a new paragraph.

- ▸ The <!-> tag is used to insert a comment in the HTML source code.

- ▸ An unordered list starts with the <ul> tag. Each list item starts with the <li> tag.

- ▸ An ordered list starts with the <ol> tag. Each list item starts with the <li> tag.

- ▸ Images in a Web page are displayed through the image <img> tag and the associated src attribute.

- ▸ HTML uses an anchor <a> tag to hyperlink to another document on the Web.

- ▸ HTML uses <table> tag pairs to define a table.

- ▸ HTML uses the <div> and <span> tags to create logical sections within a Web page.

- ▸ The <div> and <span> sections can be associated with a style sheet or DOM manipulation.

- ▸ With HTML 4.0 all formatting can be moved out of the HTML document and into a separate style sheet.

REVIEW QUESTIONS

1. What is the structure of a Web site?

2. What are the two parts in designing a dynamic page of a Web application?

3. List some of the Web page presentation layout design tips.

4. What are the steps to facilitate Web application development?

5. List the tags that are essential in every Web page.

6. List some of the formatting tags.

7. List the tags that allow creation of tables in a Web page.

8. What are the features of the tag for hyperlink?

9. What is the general mechanism for Web page layout?

10. What are the different ways to insert HTML styles in a Web page.

_____

REVIEW EXERCISES

1. A Web site is a collection of one or more Web _____.

2. Web pages in a Web site are organized in a _____ structure.

3. The top most Web page in the hierarchy is generally called the _____ page.

4. A typical Web page will consist of _____ areas on all four sides of a page.

5. The Web page title is represented at the top of the Web as a _____.

6. _____ bar contains links to other Web pages in a Web site.

7. Dynamic Web page design consists of _____ part and _____ part.

8. Web application design is a fusion of two areas: _____ and _____.

9. Web pages in a Web site should have a _____ look and feel.

10. One of the steps in Web application design is to create a _____.

11. Headings are defined with the _____ to _____ tags.

12. Paragraphs are defined with the _____ tag.

13. The _____ tag is used when to end a line, but not to start a new paragraph.

14. The _____ tag is used to insert a comment in the HTML source code.

15. An unordered list starts with the _____ tag.

16. Each list item starts with the _____ tag.

17. An ordered list starts with the _____ tag.

18. Images in a Web page are displayed through the image _____ tag.

19. HTML uses an _____ tag to hyperlink to another document on the Web.

20. HTML uses _____ tag pairs to define a table.

PROBLEM SOLVING EXERCISES

Ex4A-1. Create a two page Web site titled "Multimedia."

    1. The home page will have the following text.

        Multimedia is the utilization of different mediums to convey information. The benefits of multimedia can include:

        1.   Improved effectiveness.
        2.   Information clarity.

    2. The second page (titled Computer) will have the following text.

        The computer requirements for multimedia are the following:

        1.   CD-ROM/DVD drive.
        2.   Powerful computer.
        3.   Increased memory.
        4.   Sound card.

    3. Generate the Web site with default.htm as the home page file name.

    4. Open the Web site in the browser and print all the Web pages.

Ex4A-2. Create a Web site titled "ABC Travel" for an online travel agency. The hierarchical site layout is shown below.

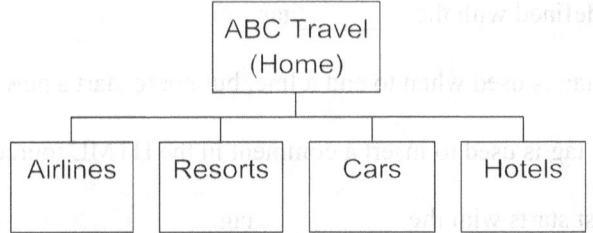

    1. The Home page will have the following text.

Travel with Ease

ABC Travel is a friendly on-line travel agency. ABC Travel makes travel arrangements for airlines, hotels, vacation resorts, and many more. ABC Travel has links with all major international airlines to provide the best deals. ABC guarantees the lowest rate on all bookings.

All reservations pertaining to your travel can be made over here. A credit card payment is necessary to hold the reservations. Receipt of reservations will be e-mailed immediately.

Buttons on the left of the page should be used to make travel arrangements with ABC Travel. New vacation resorts, hotels, and other destination or travel carriers are continuously being added.

---

2. Position an appropriate image on the right of the above text in the Home page.

3. Create the additional Web pages titled Airlines, Hotels, Resorts, Cars.

4. The banner should be titled "ABC Travel." The navigation links should be titled after the page names with the home page titled "Home."

5. Enter the following text for the Airlines page.

Air Travel

The following special deals are currently available:
1.   Low fares between Detroit and New York.
2.   Global Airlines: Special Fares to Europe.
3.   Vacation Fares to Asia.

To check reservations with carriers click here.

---

6. Enter the following text for the Hotels page.

Hotel Arrangements

The following special deals are currently available:
1.   New Orleans French Quarter - The Iberville Suites.
2.   Las Vegas Imperial Palace.
3.   La Quinta : Great rates.

To check reservations with all Hotels click here.

---

7.   Insert the text "**Page Under Construction**" or an appropriate image for Resorts and Cars pages.

8.   Generate the Web site with index.html as the home page file name.

9.   Open the Web site in the browser and print all the Web pages.

Ex4A-3.   Create a sentiment distribution Web site called "Sentiments Anywhere" company.   The hierarchical site layout is shown below.

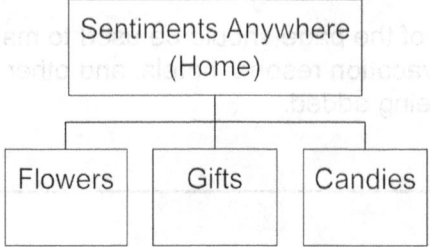

1.   The home page will have the following text.

Sentiments Anywhere provides a range of products like flowers, candies, and gifts to express sentiments.

Customers can purchase products online on this site, as well as through strategic online relationships with such leading Internet service providers like America Online, Microsoft Network, and Yahoo!.

---

2.   Create the additional Web pages titled Flowers, Gifts, and Candies.

3.   The banner should be titled "Sentiment Anywhere." The navigation links should be titled after the page names with the home page titled "Home."

4.   The Flowers Web page will have the following entry:

Express Sentiments with Flowers

Select the flowers that go with the occasion.
- Birthday   • Anniversary • Thank You
- Wedding   • Get Well

---

5.   The Gifts Web page will have the following entry:

Express Sentiments with Gifts

Select the gift that go with the occasion.
- Birthday   • Anniversary   • Thank You
- Wedding   • Get Well

---

6.   The Candies Web page will have the following entry:

Express Sentiments with Candies

Select the candies that go with the occasion.
- Birthday   • Anniversary   • Thank You
- Wedding   • Get Well

---

7.   Generate Web site with default.htm as the home page file name.

8.   Open the Web site in the browser and print all the Web pages.

Ex4A-4.   Create a Web site titled "Travel Anywhere" for an online travel agency. The hierarchical site layout is shown below.

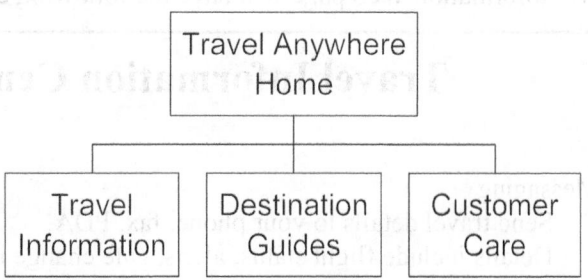

1.   The Home Page will have the following content.

Gateway to the World

Travel Anywhere is a leading on-line travel agency that makes travel arrangements for airlines and hotels. Travel Anywhere has a tradition of excellence and personalized service. Travel Anywhere guarantees the lowest rate on all travel arrangements.

- We offer:
- Lowest available fares
- Computerized reservation system
- Escorted tour packages - cruise packages
- Domestic & international travel
- Boarding passes on most airlines
- Hotel reservations
- 24 HOUR EMERGENCY SERVICE!!
- And of course - friendly service!

Contact us at : (316) 423-8990
               1-800-523-5562

© Copyright 2004 - Travel Anywhere. All rights reserved

---

2. Create the additional Web pages as shown in the Web site hierarchical structure.

3. Generate the Web site with default.htm as the home page file name.

4. The banner should be titled "Travel Anywhere." The navigation links should be titled after the page names with the home page titled "Home."

5. The Travel Information Web page will have the following content.

Travel Information Center

- Messaging   **Setup   Edit**
    - Send travel details to your phone, fax, PDA.
    - Details include flight status, alerts, gate change notification, and much more.
- Tours & Attractions
    - Get a jump on fun by adding theme park tickets, tours, excursions & more to your trip.
    - Include it with your flight or hotel package.
- Airport Shuttle
    - Enjoy the convenience of having a ride waiting upon arrival at your destination.

6. The Destination Guides Web page will have the following content.

Destination Guides

USA

- Lowest Round Trip Fares

St. Louis - New York	Book It
Memphis - Los Angeles	Book It
Los Angeles - New Orleans	Book It

Flight Search

- Special Hotel Rates

Iberville Suites, New Orleans	Book It
Imperial Palace, Las Vegas	Book It

Hotel Reservation

---

7. The Customer Care Web page will have the following content.

Customer FAQ

Question

How much fee is charged for changing my airline ticket?

Answers

Typically, the fee to change a reservation is $100 for domestic and $200 for international itineraries per ticket.

Question

How do I travel with an electronic ticket?

Answers

Electronic tickets allow both the travel agency and the airline you are flying to store your ticket on their respective computer systems. The customer has no need to worry about carrying or possibly losing their tickets. No paper document is issued until you check-in with the airline.

Question

How do I cancel my reservation?

Answers

All airline tickets are subject to the rules and restrictions you agreed to at the time of purchase. Many tickets are non-refundable and have no value for future purchase.

Hotel reservations can be cancelled without any penalty two hours before the expected arrival time on the date of reservation. After the arrival deadline a penalty of $50 per day will be charged.

Question

Do I need to reconfirm my flight before departure?

Answers

It is not required to call to reconfirm your flight with the airline for domestic travel. International travel requires passengers to call and reconfirm your flights with the airline 24 – 72 hours prior to departure.

Still need to contact Customer Service? <u>E-Mail</u> or call 1-800-566-7909

<u>Back to Beginning of Customer Care Questions</u>

---

8.   Open the Web site in the browser and print all the Web pages.

Web Application Design with HTML and DOM

• Document Object Model (DOM)
• DOM Properties and Methods

Document Object Model (DOM) is a World Wide Web Consortium (W3C) defined language-independent standard for representing HTML or XML based documents. DOM is not a programming language. However, DOM provides a standard way for programs like JavaScript to dynamically access and update the content, structure and style of documents.

DOCUMENT OBJECT MODEL (DOM)

DOM represents a HTML Web document in a hierarchical tree like structure (a node tree) with elements, attributes, and text. When a Web page is loaded in a Web browser, the browser uses the DOM to represent the Web page as an object having a hierarchical structure. Once the Web page gets represented as a DOM object, it can then be manipulated through various DOM properties and methods. The DOM concept, its properties and methods are utilized by AJAX to facilitate dynamic interaction with the Web page.

The hierarchical representation of a Web page DOM resembles a family tree. Similar to real family relationships, the DOM tree also uses similar terminology to represent nodes within its tree structure as shown in Figure 4-5. The nodes of the DOM tree are based on the HTML (or XML) tags. The top most node is referred as the "root" node. The DOM tree also uses parent and child terminology to reference nodes. The root node is the parent of the entire DOM tree. The child nodes can also be the parent of nodes below them. There are references to the "first child," "last child," and "siblings" for sequence of children. The order for first child, last child, and sibling references is from left to right. Node types can be element, text, and attribute.

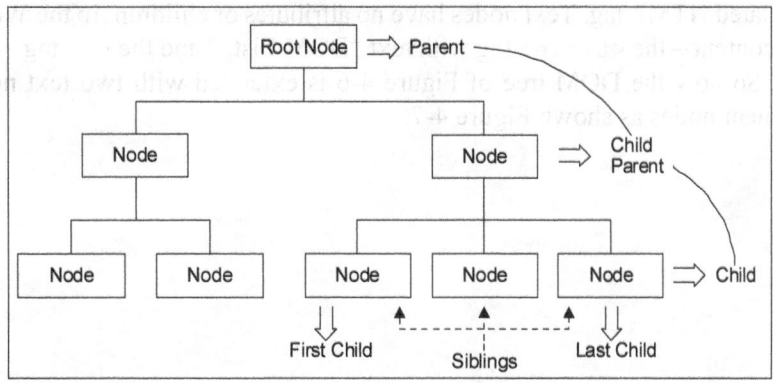

Figure 4-5

241

Element Node

The element nodes are the basic building blocks of a Web page DOM. The hierarchical arrangement of element nodes gives the document its tree structure. The HTML tags provide the name for each element node. For example, the `<html>` tag element node name is *html*, the paragraph `<p>` tag element node name is *p*, and so on. An element node in the DOM tree can contain other element nodes. The `<html>` element node is the root of the DOM tree. For example, consider the following Web page and its DOM tree representations in Figure 4-6 and Figure 4-7 to understand the layout.

```
<html>
<head>
<title>DOM list</title>
</head>
<body>
<p>Sample DOM Paragraph</p>
</body>
</html>
```

Figure 4-6 shows a partial DOM tree with only element nodes. The Web page has two sections `<head>` and `<body>`. Accordingly, in the DOM tree, the root *html* node has two children for these two section tags – *head* node and *body* node. Since the `<head>` tag appears first in the Web page, the *head* node appears on the left side followed by the *body* tag. The sequence of tags in the Web page determines the left-to-right sequence of the child nodes under a parent. There is only one tag `<title>` under the `<head>` tag section. Accordingly, the *title* node appears as a child of *head* node. Similarly there is only one `<p>` tag under the `<body>` tag section. Consequently, the *p* node appears as a child node of *body* node.

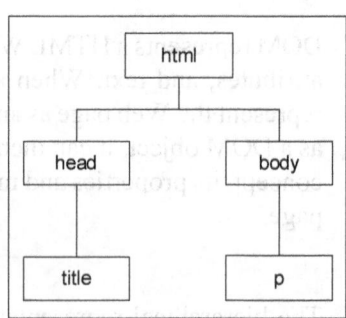

Figure 4-6

Text Node

The text content within a HTML tag is represented as a text node in a DOM tree. The text node is always a child of the associated HTML tag. Text nodes have no attributes or children. In the Web page there are two tags with text content – the `<title>` tag with text "DOM List, " and the `<p>` tag with text "Sample DOM Paragraph." So now the DOM tree of Figure 4-6 is extended with two text nodes under their corresponding element nodes as shown Figure 4-7.

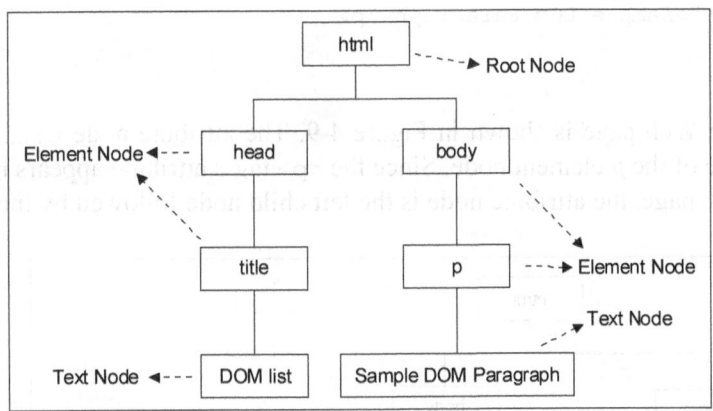

Figure 4-7

To illustrate the DOM tree structure further, consider the following Web page with additional tags in the body section.

```
<html>
<head>
<title>DOM list</title>
</head>
<body>
<h1>This is a heading</h1>
<p>Sample DOM Paragraph</p>
</body>
</html>
```

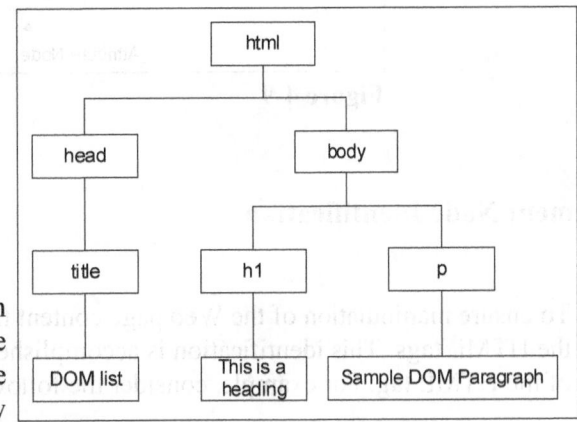

The DOM tree for this Web page is shown in
Figure 4-8. This DOM tree is an extension of the
DOM tree in Figure 4-7. The body section of the
Web page has two tags. Consequently, the body
element node becomes the parent of `<h1>` and **Figure 4-8**
`<p>` tag element nodes. Now, since the `<h1>` tag
appears first followed by the `<p>` tag, consequently the *h1* element node is placed on the left side
followed by the *p* element node.

Attribute Node

A HTML tag attribute and its detail get represented as an attribute node in the DOM tree. Because
attributes are always placed within the opening tag, attribute nodes are always represented as child nodes
under their corresponding HTML tag element node. Consider the following Web page.

```
<html>
<head>
<title>DOM list</title>
</head>
<body>
```

```
<h1>This is a heading</h1>
<p title="paraClass">Sample DOM Paragraph</p>
</body>
</html>
```

The DOM tree for the Web page is shown in Figure 4-9. The attribute node `title="paraClass"` appears as a child node of the *p* element node. Since the `<p>` tag's attribute appears before the `<p>` tag text content in the Web page, the attribute node is the left child node followed by the text node.

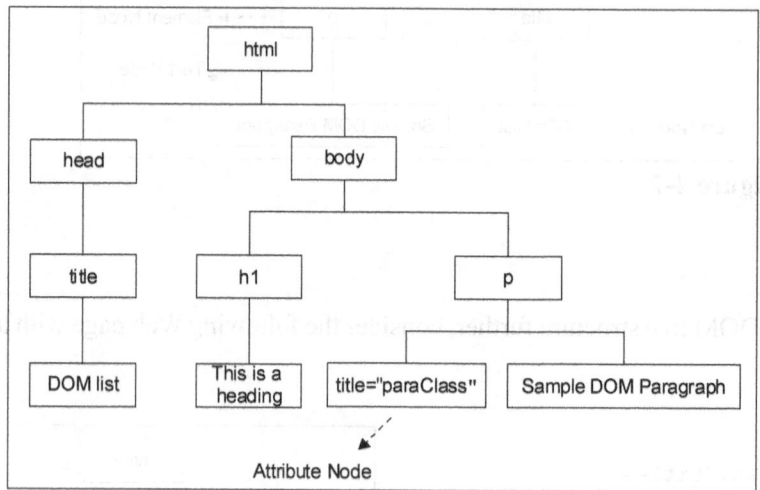

Figure 4-9

Element Node Identification

To ensure manipulation of the Web page content through its DOM structure, it is necessary to identify the HTML tags. This identification is accomplished through the ID attribute and the NAME attributes of the HTML tag. For example, consider the following Web page:

```
<html>
<head>
<title>DOM list</title>
</head>
<body>
<h1 name="hClass">This is a heading</h1>
<p title="paraClass" id="pid">Sample DOM Paragraph</p>
<h3 name="hClass">End of Page</h3>
</body>
</html>
```

In the above Web page, the `<p title="paraClass" id="pid">Sample DOM Paragraph</p>` statement identifies the `<p>` tag with an id "pid," while the `<h1>` tag has a name "h1Class" for reference. Keep in mind that the attribute values are case sensitive.

DOM MANIPULATION

DOM refers to the entire tree of the Web page as a "document object." Once a Web page gets represented as a document object, it is possible to access and modify any node in the tree and its corresponding HTML source. The DOM structured Web page is manipulated through properties and methods attached to the document object. In a way DOM also provides an application programming interface (API) for programming languages to manipulate HTML (and XML) documents within the browser. Tables 4-8 and 4-9 provide a list of some of the DOM properties and methods.

Property Name	Description
attributes	Returns an array of attributes of an element.
childNodes	Returns an array of child nodes of an element.
documentElement	Returns the root node of the document.
document.body	Gives direct access to the `<body>` tag.
firstChild	Returns the first direct child of the current node.
innerHTML	Returns all of the markup and content within a given element. This property is not part of the DOM specification from the W3C. However, most browsers today include support for this property.
lastChild	Returns the last child of the current node.
length	Returns the number of items in a list (e.g. childNodes).
nextSibling	Returns the node immediately following the current one in the tree.
nodeName	Returns the name of the current node. The nodeName property always contains the uppercase tag name of a HTML element. • The nodeName of an element node is the tag name • The nodeName of an attribute node is the attribute name • The name of a text node is always #text • The name of the document node is always #document
nodeType	Returns the type of the current node.
nodeValue	Returns the value of the current node. • On text nodes, the nodeValue property contains the text. • On attribute nodes, the nodeValue property contains the attribute value. • The nodeValue property is not available on document and element nodes.
parentNode	Returns the parent node of the current node.
previousSibling	Returns the node immediately previous to the current one in the tree.
tagName	Returns the name of the element node.

Table 4-8: DOM Properties

Method Name	Description
appendChild	Inserts the specified node into the list of nodes of the current document.
createElement	Creates a floating element node.
createTextNode	Creates a floating text node.
getAttribute	Returns the value of the named attribute on the current node.
getAttributeNode	Returns the attribute of the current element as a separate node.
getElementsById	Returns the element as identified by its ID attribute.
getElementsByTagName	Returns the element as identified by the tag name.
removeAttribute	Removes an attribute from the current element.
removeAttributeNode	Removes the specified attribute from the current element.
removeChild	Removes a child node from the current element.
replaceChild	Replaces one child node of the current element with another.
setAttribute	Adds a new attribute or changes the value of an existing attribute of the current element.
setAttributeNode	Adds a new attribute node to the current element.

Table 4-9: DOM Methods

Explaining the detail working of all DOM methods and properties would be too long. However, a short explanation of how some of the methods and properties work is explained. The AJAX working with JavaScript later in the book has more details on their application. The following Web page is utilized to explain some of the DOM properties and methods. Figure 4-10 shows the DOM tree of the Web page.

```
<html>
<head>
<title>DOM list</title>
</head>
<body>
<div id="container">
<h1 name="hClass" id="hid">This is a heading</h1>
<p title="paraClass" id="pid">Sample DOM Paragraph</p>
<h3 name="hClass">End of Page</h3>
</div>
</body>
</html>
```

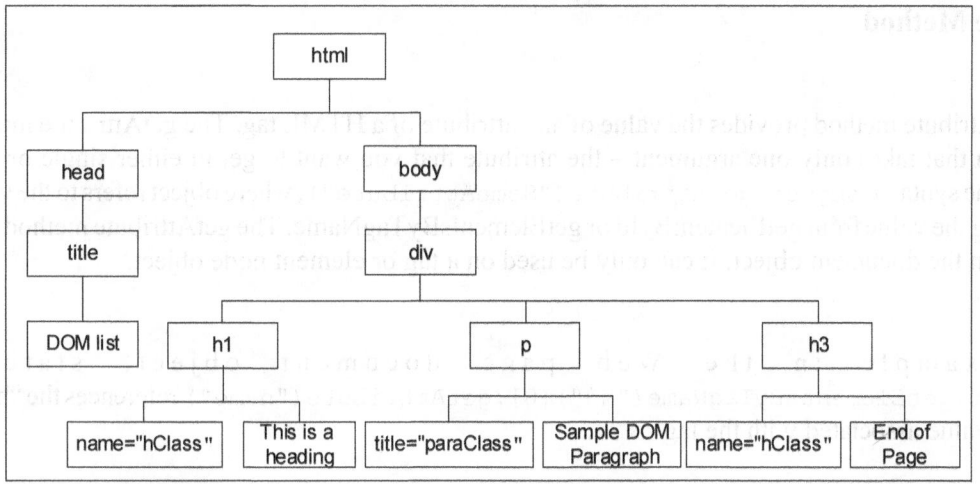

Figure 4-10

getElementById Method

The getElementById method provides the reference to a HTML tag based on its ID attribute. This method is a function that takes just one argument – the ID attribute value of the tag contained in either single or double quotes. The syntax is `document.getElementById("someID")` where document refers to the DOM tree. Using the getElementById method it is possible to reference any HTML tag in the Web page document that has an ID attribute.

For example, in the Web page document object statement `document.getElementById("pid")` references the `<p>` tag associated with the ID"pid."

getElementsByTagName Method

The getElementByTagName method provides reference to HTML tags that don't have unique identifiers (or ID attribute). This method is a function that takes one argument – the name of the tag contained in either single or double quotes. The syntax is `document.getElementsByTagName("someTagName")` where document refers to the DOM tree. It looks very similar to getElementById, but instead of returning a unique value, the method returns an array populated with all the tags having the specified name.

For example in the Web page document object, statement `document.getElementsByTagName("h3")` references the `<h3>` tag.

getAttribute Method

The getAttribute method provides the value of any attribute of a HTML tag. The getAttribute method is a function that takes only one argument – the attribute that you want to get in either single or double quotes. The syntax is `object.getAttribute("SomeAttribute")`, where object refers to the variable containing the value from getElementById or getElementsByTagName. The getAttribute method cannot be used on the document object. It can only be used on a tag or element node object.

For example in the Web page document object, statement `document.getElementsByTagName("h3")[0].getAttribute("name")` references the "hClass" attribute value associated with the tag `<h3>`.

setAttribute Method

The setAttribute method allows change in the value of a HTML tag attribute. It is a function that takes two arguments: attribute name and the new value to be assigned to the attribute. The syntax is `object.setAttribute("SomeAttributeName","SomeValue")`, where object refers to the variable containing the value returned by getElementById or getElementsByTagName. The setAttribute method cannot be used on the document object. It can only be used on a tag or element node object.

For example in the Web page document object, statement `document.getElementsByTagName("h3")[0].setAttribute("name","tClass")` changes the "hClass" attribute value associated with the tag `<h3>` to "tClass."

It's worth noting that, even when a document has been changed by setAttribute, the change won't appear in the view source option of the Web browser. This is because the DOM has dynamically updated the contents of the page after it has loaded. The real power of the DOM is that the contents of a page can be updated without refreshing the page in the browser.

createElement Method

The createElement method creates a new element, which can thereafter be inserted into the existing DOM tree. The syntax is `document.createElement("Some-NodeName")`, where document refers to the DOM tree and Some-NodeName is the name of the HTML tag. Once the element is created, it will exist as a floating node, outside of the existing DOM tree. Consequently, it won't be displayed in the browser immediately. Nonetheless, it has DOM properties, just like any other element node.

For example, the statement `document.createElement("p")` will create a floating `<p>` tag element node.

appendChild Method

The appendChild method inserts a newly created node into the DOM tree. The method appends a new node (created through the createElement method) as a child of an existing node in the document. The syntax is `parent.appendChild(child)`, where "parent" is an existing node in the DOM tree, and "child" is the reference to the node created through the createElement method.

For example, consider the statement `parentID.appendChild(document.createElement("p"))`, where "parentID" refers to a parent node as defined by the statement `document.getElementById("container")`, and `document.createElement("p")` refers to a new node created through the createElement method. The statement adds a new child node within the container element node. Figure 4-11 provides a diagrammatic view of the methods application.

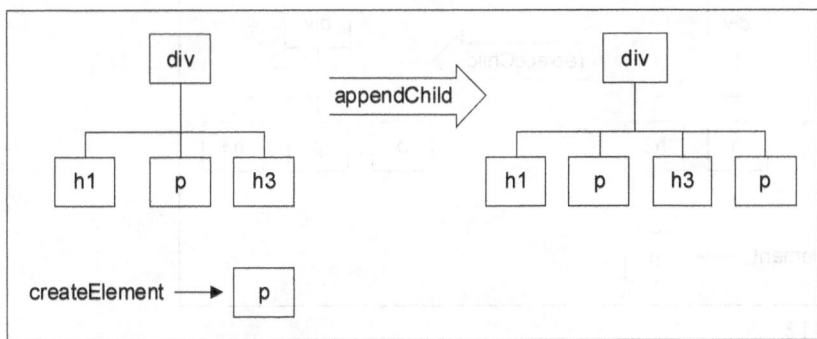

Figure 4-11

createTextNode Method

The createTextNode method creates the text content of some element node. It works best for element nodes created through the createElement method. The syntax is `document.createTextNode("Some-Text")`, where document refers to the DOM tree, while "Some-Text" is the text content that will exist within the text node. Text nodes initially are floating nodes, which thereafter have to be appended to some parent through the appendChild method.

For example, the statement `document.createTextNode("Hello world")` will create a floating text element node.

replaceChild Method

The replaceChild method replaces one child node of a specified parent element node with another node. The syntax is `parentElement.replaceChild(newChild, oldChild)`, where "parentElement" is the parent node whose child will be replaced, the "newChild" refers to an existing node or a new node created with createElement method, while the "oldChild" must be a child node of the parentElement node in the DOM tree. If the new node has any child nodes, they will also be inserted into under the parentElement node. The replaceChild method also works when the newChild is already part of the DOM tree in which case it will first be removed before replacing the oldChild node.

For example, consider the statement `parentID.replaceChild(document.createElement("p"),document.getElementById("hid"))` where "parentID" refers to a parent node as defined by the statement `document.getElementById("container")` and `document.createElement("p")` refers to a new node created through the createElement method, and `document.getElementById("hid")` references the `<h1>` tag associated with the ID "hid." Figure 4-12 provides a diagrammatic view of the methods application.

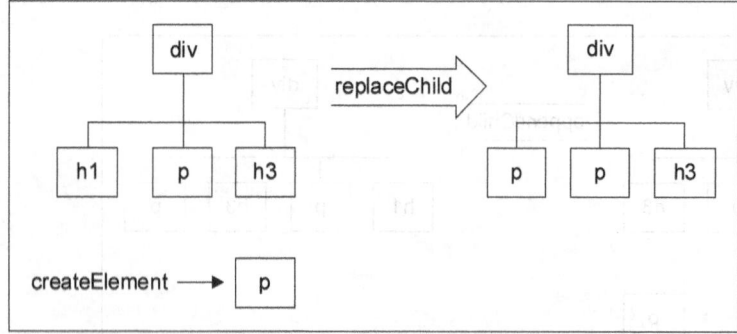

Figure 4-12

innerHTML Property

The innerHTML property returns all the details of a node. For example, the statement `document.getElementById("container").innerHTML` displays the contents of the tree under the `<div id="container">` tag. The displayed contents will be:

```
<h1 name="hClass" id="hid">This is a heading</h1>
<p title="paraClass" id="pid">Sample DOM Paragraph</p>
<h3 name="hClass">End of Page</h3>
```

Similarly, the statement `document.getElementById("pid").innerHTML` will display the contents of the `<p title="paraClass" id="pid">Sample DOM Paragraph</p>` tag.

CHAPTER SUMMARY

▸ The Document Object Model (DOM) is a language-independent standard for representing HTML or XML based documents.

▸ DOM provides a standard way for programs like JavaScript to dynamically access and update the content, structure and style of documents.

▸ DOM represents an HTML Web document in a hierarchical tree like structure (a node tree) with elements, attributes, and text.

▸ When a Web page is loaded in a Web browser, the browser uses the DOM to represent the Web page for manipulation through various DOM properties and methods.

▸ The hierarchical representation of a Web page DOM tree utilizes real family relationships terminology to represent nodes within its tree structure.

▸ The nodes of the DOM tree are based on the HTML (or XML) tags.

▸ The top most node is referred as the root node. The root node is the parent of the entire DOM tree.

▸ The DOM tree also uses parent and child terminology to reference nodes.

▸ Node types can be element, text, and attribute.

▸ The element nodes are the basic building and the hierarchical arrangement of element nodes gives the document its tree structure.

▸ The HTML tags provide the name for each element node.

▸ The text content within a HTML tag is represented as a text node in the DOM tree.

▸ An HTML tag attribute and its detail is represented as an attribute node in the DOM tree.

▸ Manipulation of the Web page content through the DOM structure is accomplished through the ID attribute and NAME attributes of a HTML tag.

▸ The DOM structured Web page is manipulated through properties and methods attached to the document object.

▸ DOM also provides an application programming interface (API) for programming languages to manipulate HTML (or XML) documents within the browser.

REVIEW QUESTIONS

1. Describe the document object model (DOM).

2. Describe the different types of DOM nodes.

3. How are node identified during DOM manipulation.

4. What is the purpose of getElementById DOM method.

5. What is the purpose of getElementByTagName method.

6. What is the purpose of getAttribute method.

7. What is the purpose of setAttribute method.

8. What is the purpose of createElement method.

9. What is the purpose of appendChild method.

10. What is the purpose of createTextNode method.

11. What is the purpose of replaceChild method.

12. What is the purpose of innerHTML property.

REVIEW EXERCISES

1. The Document Object Model (DOM) is a language-independent standard for representing _____ or _____ based documents.

2. DOM represents a Web document in a _____ tree like structure.

3. The HTML tags provide the name for each _____ node.

4. The _____ element node is the root of the DOM tree.

5. The paragraph <p> tag element node name is _____.

6. The text content within a tag is represented as a _____ node in the DOM tree.

7. _____ nodes have no attributes or children.

8. A HTML tag attribute and its detail is represented as an _____ node in the DOM tree.

9. Attribute nodes are always represented as _____ nodes under their corresponding HTML tag element node.

10. Identification of HTML tags is accomplished through the _____ attribute.

11. The _____ method provides the reference to a HTML tag based on its ID attribute.

12. The _____ method provides reference to HTML tags that don't have unique identifiers (or ID attribute).

13. The _____ method provides the value of any attribute associated within a HTML tag.

14. The _____ method allows change in the value of a HTML tag attribute.

15. The _____ method creates a new element, which can thereafter be inserted into the existing DOM tree.

16. The _____ method inserts a newly created node into the DOM tree.

17. The _____ creates the text content of some element node.

18. The _____ method replaces one child node of a specified parent element node with another node.

19. The _____ property returns all the details of a node.

PROBLEM SOLVING EXERCISES

Ex4B-1.   Study the following Web page. Create a DOM tree of the Web page.

```
<html>
<head>
<title>Web Page Title</title>
</head>
<body>
<p id="pid">Main Content Area</p>
<p id="eid">Example below displays lists.</p>
</body>
</html>
```

Ex4B-2.   Study the following Web page. Create a DOM tree of the Web page.

```
<html>
<head>
<title>Web Page Title</title>
</head>
<body>
<p id="pid">Main Content Area</p>
<p id="eid">Example below displays lists.</p>
<table id="tid">
<tr><td>PSP</td></tr>
<tr><td>DOM</td></tr>
</table>
</body>
</html>
```

Ex4B-3.   Study the following Web page. Create a DOM tree of the Web page.

```
<html>
<head>
<title>Web Page Title</title>
</head>
<body>
<p id="pid">Main Content Area</p>
<p id="eid">Example below displays lists.</p>
<li>list item 1</li><li>list item 2</li>
<ul>
<li>list item 1</li><li>list item 2</li>
</ul>
</body>
</html>
```

Ex4B-4.   Study the following Web page. Create a DOM tree of the Web page.

```
<html>
<head>
<title>Web Page Title</title>
</head>
<body>
<div id="blue">
<p id="pid">Main Content Area</p>
<p   title="paraClass"   id="pid">Sample   <span   id="sid">   DOM   </span>
Paragraph</p>
</div>
<table id="tid">
```

```
<tr><td>PSP</td></tr>
<tr><td>DOM</td></tr>
</table>
</body>
</html>
```

Ex4B-5.   Study the following Web page. Create a DOM tree of the Web page.

```
<html>
<head>
<title>Web Page Title</title>
</head>
<body>
<div id="blue">
<p id="pid">Main Content Area</p>
<p  title="paraClass"  id="pid">Sample  <span  id="sid">  DOM  </span>
Paragraph</p>
</div>
<li>list item 1</li>
<li>list item 2</li>
<li><a href="http://missouristate.edu">Home</a></li>
</body>
</html>
```

Ex4B-6.   Extend problem Ex4B-1, by listing the DOM method statements that reference all the tags in `<body>` section of the Web page.

Ex4B-7.   Extend problem Ex4B-4, by listing the DOM method statements that reference all the tags in `<body>` section of the Web page.

Ex4B-2.   Extend problem Ex4B-1, by appending the tag `<h1 name="hClass">This is a heading</h1>` in the Web page DOM tree below the `<p id="eid">Example below displays lists.</p>` tag. List the DOM method statements to accomplish the operation.

Ex4B-9.   Extend problem Ex4B-2, by replacing the `<table id="tid">` tag in the Web page DOM tree with the tag `<h3 name="hClass">Table is replaced</h1>`. List the DOM method statements to accomplish the operation.

Ex4B-10.   Extend problem Ex4B-4, by replacing the `<span id="sid">` tag in the Web page DOM tree with the tag `<h3 name="hClass">Span is replaced</h1>`. List the DOM method statements to accomplish the operation.

Ex4B-11.   Extend problem Ex4B-5, by appending the tag `<p name="pClass">End of table</p>` in the Web page DOM tree below the `<table id="tid">` tag. List the DOM method statements to accomplish the operation.

CHAPTER 5
(LESSON A)

Introduction to PL/SQL Server Pages

- PL/SQL Server Page Statements
- PL/SQL Web Procedure
- Generate PL/SQL Server Page

PL/SQL server pages (PSP) are database driven dynamic Web pages. PSP uses the PL/SQL database language as a scripting language along with HTML to complete the database content and layout of Web pages. In essence PSP = HTML + PL/SQL. Since PL/SQL is optimized for database operations, the resulting Web pages are more efficient in database interactivity. PL/SQL server pages are stored within the Oracle server (DBMS). These pages appear in the Web browser (on the client machine) as plain HTML pages with no special PSP script tags. To enhance the utility of PSP in Web browser, it is possible to include Javascript or other client-side scripting language. PSP supports all browsers, and browser levels equally. It also makes network traffic efficient by minimizing the number of server round trips.

The task of designing the layout of a Web page with regard to the HTML and database content can be quite complex and tedious. Often times in such cases one can lose focus of the database content, and instead get bogged down with HTML layout specifications. Consequently, the focus in this lesson is on simple Web page layouts similar to those provided through templates listed in Chapter 4, Lesson A. Any HTML or Text editor can be utilized to complete the Web pages.

This chapter utilizes the table structure of Outdoor Clubs & Product database to explain examples.

PL/SQL SERVER PAGE STATEMENTS

A PL/SQL server page is a Web document with file extension *.psp*. Each PSP file is loaded into the database server through a utility "loadpsp." Once the PSP file is loaded successfully to the database server, it becomes a PL/SQL procedure on the database server that also contains HTML statements pertaining to the layout of the Web page. PSP generated PL/SQL procedures are referred as PL/SQL Web procedures. The HTML statements within the PL/SQL Web procedure are enclosed within the HTP package string.

PSP statements are also referred as PSP directives. They are categorized according to the different sections of a PL/SQL procedure. All PSP statements/directives are enclosed in special tag symbols <% ... %>. The categorization of PSP statements with respect to a PL/SQL procedure block is shown in Figure 5-1. The statement categories are:

1. *Identification statement* which defines the name of the procedure.
2. *Parameters statements* which lists parameters associated with the procedure.
3. *Declaration statements* which define variables, cursors, and other declarations.
4. *Processing statements* which reflect the logic statements as part of the executable section of a procedure. Such statements can also include the *expression statements* to display any database value.

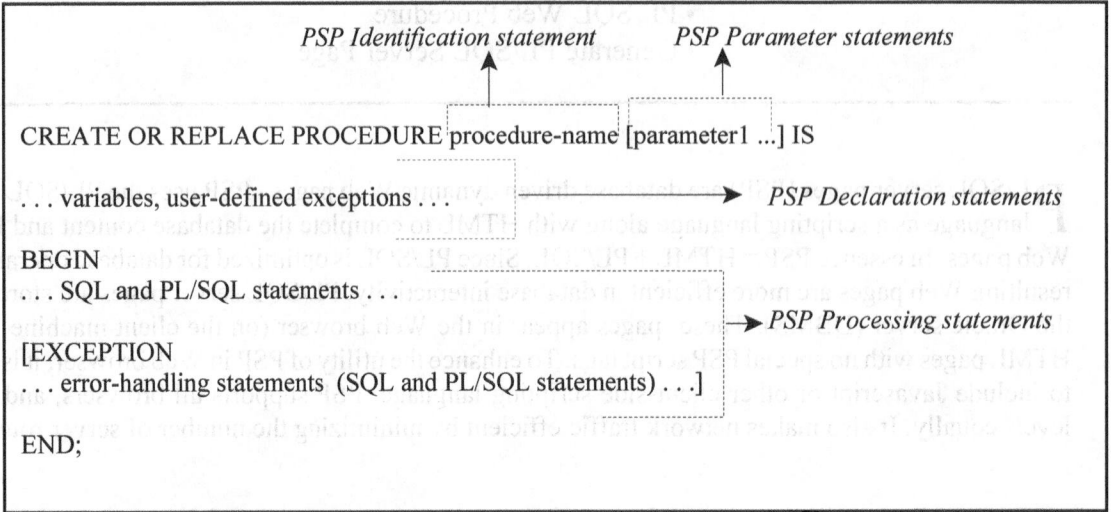

Figure 5-1   PSP Statements association with Procedure Block structure

Even though a PSP eventually becomes a PL/SQL Web procedure, PSP statements can be placed anywhere in a Web page. In other words, it is not necessary to have PSP parameter statements or PSP declaration statements at the beginning of the Web page. The PSP loading utility "loadpsp" automatically transforms the PSP Web page to the PL/SQL procedure block structure by shuffling the PSP statements. For example, if a variable declaration statement is included toward the end of the PSP Web page, or attached with a PL/SQL processing statement, then during the loading process, the loadpsp utility will ensure that all declarations are placed before the BEGIN keyword.

To share procedures, constants, and types across different PL/SQL server pages, compile them into a separate package in the database (not using the PSP technique). Further, to make things easier to maintain, keep declarations together near the beginning of a PSP. The various PSP statements/directives are outlined now.

Page Specification Directive

A necessary statement within the Web page specifying the PL/SQL scripting language. Every PL/SQL server page must have a *page specification* statement. This statement ensures compatibility with other scripting environments. Additionally, the statement also specifies what type of information (MIME type) the Web page produces, as well as any other PSP file to handle all uncaught exceptions.

```
<%@ page [language="PL/SQL"] [contentType="somecontentType string"]
                [errorPage="somefile.psp"] %>
```

The attribute names `contentType` and `errorPage` are case-sensitive. Also there should be no space around the `=` sign.

Procedure Directive

This statement specifies the name of the stored Web procedure produced by the PSP file. By default, the procedure name is the PSP filename without the .psp extension. However, it is a good practice to include this statement to ensure that the procedure is correctly named. Also, there should be no space around the `=` sign.

```
<%@ plsql procedure="procedure-name" %>
```

For example, the following statement specifies the name of the PL/SQL Web procedure in the database as *sample_page*.

```
<%@ plsql procedure="sample_page" %>
```

Parameter Directive

This statement specifies the name, and optionally the type and default, for each parameter expected by the PSP stored Web procedure. The parameters are passed using the CGI protocol, typically from an HTML (Web) form.

```
<%@ plsql parameter="parameter-name" [type="PL/SQL type"] [default="value"] %>
```

By default, parameters are of type VARCHAR2. To use a different type, use the `type="..."` attribute within the statement. To set a default value, so that the parameter becomes optional, include a `default="..."` attribute in the statement. The values of the default attribute is substituted directly into a PL/SQL statement, so any strings must be single-quoted, and one can use special values such as `null`. For example, the following PSP statement defines an input parameter *customer_no_text*.

```
<%@ plsql parameter="customer_no_text" default="null" %>
```

Include Directive

This statement specifies the name of a file to be included at a specific point in the PSP file. The file must have an extension other than .psp. It can contain HTML, PSP script elements, or a combination of both. The name resolution and file inclusion happens when the PSP file is loaded into the database as a stored procedure, so any changes to the file after that are not reflected when the stored procedure is run.

```
<%@ include file="path & name" %>
```

Declaration Directive

This statement declares a set of PL/SQL variables that are available throughout the page. This statement typically spans multiple lines, with individual PL/SQL variable declarations ending with semicolons.

```
<%! PL/SQL declaration;
   [ PL/SQL declaration; ] ... %>
```

All the usual PL/SQL syntax is allowed. The delimiters serve as shorthand, letting you omit the DECLARE keyword. It is possible to specify multiple declaration statements. You can also use explicit DECLARE blocks within the `<% ... %>` delimiters. These declarations are only visible to the following BEGIN/END executable section block. For example, the following PSP statements define two variables.

```
<%! club_no sporting_clubs.club_id%type;
club_name sporting_clubs.name%type; %>
```

Processing Directive

Such statements are PL/SQL statements associated with the execution section of the PL/SQL block. These statements can span multiple lines, with individual PL/SQL statements ending with semicolons. The statements can include complete blocks, or can be the bracketing parts of IF/THEN/ELSE or BEGIN/END blocks. When a code block is split into multiple statements, put HTML tags in the middle, and those pieces are conditionally executed when the stored procedure is run.

```
<% PL/SQL statement; [ PL/SQL statement; ] ... %>
```

For example, the following PSP statement specifies an implicit cursor.

```
<% select club_id, name
   into club_no, club_name
   from sporting_clubs
   where state='NY'; %>
```

Expression Directive

This statement specifies a single PL/SQL expression, such as a string, arithmetic expression, function call, or combination of those things. The result is substituted as a string at that spot in the Web page that is produced by the stored procedure.

```
<%= PL/SQL expression %>
```

Because the result is always substituted in the middle of text or tags, it must be a string value or be able to be cast to a string. For any types that cannot be implicitly casted, such as DATE, pass the value to the PL/SQL TO_CHAR function. The content between the `<%= ... %>` delimiters is processed by the HTP.PRN function, which trims any leading or trailing whitespace and requires that you quote any literal strings. For example, the following PSP statement is a text line with database value as generated by the expression statement.

```
The NY club number <%= club_no%> has name <%= club_name%>
```

Comments in a PSP Script

To put a comment in the HTML portion of a PL/SQL server page, for the benefit of people reading the PSP source code, use the syntax `<%-- Comment text --%>`. These comments do not appear in the HTML output from the PSP.

To create a comment that is visible in the HTML output, place the comment in the HTML portion and use the regular HTML comment syntax `<!-- Comment text -->`.

LOAD PL/SQL SERVER PAGE TO DATABASE

Each PSP file having .psp filetype must be individually loaded to the database server through the utility *loadpsp*. Loadpsp is an Oracle utility that transfers a PSP page to the database server. During this transfer process loadpsp performs two tasks: (i) constructs the PL/SQL Web Procedure from the PSP, and (ii) compile the generated PL/SQL procedure. During the compilation process only the PL/SQL statements are checked. The associated HTML statements are ignored. The syntax for loadpsp utility is:

```
loadpsp [ -replace ] -user username/password[@connect-string]
    [ include-file-name ... ] psp-file-name ...
```

To do a "create and replace" on the stored procedures, include the -replace keyword. The utility logs on to the database using the specified user name, password, and connect string. The stored procedures are created in the corresponding schema. Include the names of all the include files (whose names do not have the .psp extension) before the names of the PL/SQL server pages file.

For example consider the following statement to load PSP file display_order.psp into database.

```
loadpsp -replace -user scott/tiger@webdb c:\sample_page.psp
```

In this example,
- The PSP defined PL/SQL Web procedure is created in the database *webdb*. Webdb is also referred as the connection string. Within the database, the procedure is created in a account with username *scott* and password *tiger*.
- The sample_page.psp file that contains the main source and text of the PSP Web page is stored on the C drive.

Oracle 11g by default creates a connection string named after the server *sid* entry. It is possible to create additional connection strings.

ERRORS DURING THE LOADING PROCESS

If the transfer process compilation is not successful, the loadpsp utility will display the PL/SQL errors. Even though there are compilation errors, loadpsp often times still creates the corresponding PL/SQL Web procedure on the database server.

PL/SQL errors can then be corrected either through a PL/SQL editor like SQL Developer or in the Web page itself. If Web page is modified, the page has to be loaded again. If the errors are caused due to HTML statements, it is better to fix the errors in the Web page. The PSP page has to be successfully compiled for viewing in a Web browser.

PL/SQL WEB PROCEDURE

Since a PSP Web page is stored as a PL/SQL procedure on the database server, it can be viewed by any PL/SQL editor. The HTML statements of the procedure are enclosed within the HTP package string. The HTP package accepts HTML tags as character string. During a request from a Web server to the Web procedure, the HTP package embedded HTML tags become the layout tags of the resulting Web page.

A PSP created PL/SQL Web procedure "sample_page" is shown below. This Web procedure displays a row of output. It wraps the HTP package entry around the HTML layout tags. Later in the chapter a more complete example is provided.

```
CREATE OR REPLACE PROCEDURE SAMPLE_PAGE   AS
make_out tenant_auto.auto_make%type;
model_out tenant_auto.auto_model%type;
  BEGIN NULL;
htp.prn('
');
htp.prn('
<html>
<body>
<br>
');
htp.prn('
');
  select auto_make, auto_model
into make_out,model_out
from tenant_auto
where tenant_ss=173662690;
htp.prn('
The automobile registered for Venessa Williams is ');
htp.prn(make_out);
htp.prn(' model ');
htp.prn(model_out);
htp.prn('
<br>
</body>
</html>
```

```
                         ');
        END;
```

ACCESSING PL/SQL SERVER PAGE

Once the PL/SQL server page has been successfully loaded as a stored procedure, it can be viewed through a URL from a Web browser or other Internet-aware client program. The URL in this case should include the data access descriptor (DAD) of the PL/SQL Web gateway. Also, if the Web page utilizes some additional files like image files or script files to complete the layout, these embedded files have to be stored separately in some virtual folder that is accessible through a relative path specification.

Database Access Descriptor (DAD)

Database access descriptor (DAD) is a mechanism that maps the URL to the correct database schema. All PL/SQL Web applications require a database access descriptor to facilitate their working. Essentially, access to any user's PL/SQL Web procedure is routed through the DAD. For example, if the PSP generated PL/SQL Web procedures are stored in the server account "smiley," the DAD will forward the request from the Web server to this account.

The DAD is setup either with a specific username and password or no username/password. If there is no username assigned to a DAD, visitors to Web pages will have to enter their database username/password to retrieve the Web page. However, if a DAD has been setup with an explicit username/password, then any user can access the account's Web pages. Also, a user wishing to access another user's PL/SQL Web application must receive SQL GRANT EXECUTE privileges for the application.

The database administrator creates the DAD. All three tiers of the Web architecture are involved while accessing the PSP. The communication between the components of the three-tier architecture towards the display of a PL/SQL server page is shown in Figure 5-2.

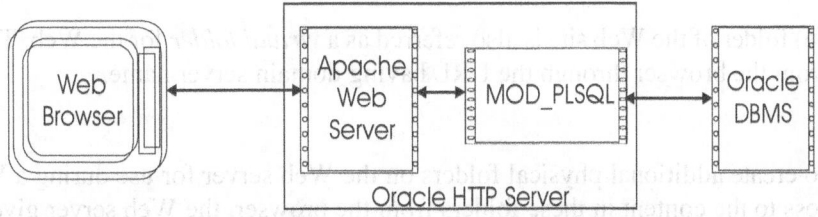

Figure 5-2   PL/SQL Server Page Three-tier Architecture

The details of the interaction between the architecture components are as follows:

1. Web browser sends URL to the DNS server.
2. The DNS server converts the URL to its IP address and sends it back to the Web browser.
3. Using the IP address, the Web browser sends the request to the Oracle HTTP server.
4. The HTTP server directs the request to its PL/SQL module mod_plsql.

5. The mod_plsql module first parses the request and extracts the parameters/header information. Then it queries the database using the database access descriptor (DAD) in the URL address path.
6. The database executes the PL/SQL Web procedure, assembles the Web (HTML) page, and sends it back to the HTTP server.
7. The HTTP server sends it back to the requesting Web browser.
8. The Web browser receives the Web (HTML) pages and begins the request for additional files referred as embedded files.

Embedded files are files that are included in HTML layout specification like Javascript files, image files, and so on. These files are stored on the Web server, and accessed through the concept of virtual folders and access paths.

For example, suppose a DAD named as "classpsp" is created with no username/password. The URL to view the PSP generated PL/SQL Web procedure sample_page is:

> http://server-name/classpsp/cis52899.sample_page

The browser will prompt for cis52899 userid's password.

Details on setting the DAD is provided in Appendix A.

Virtual Folder and Access Paths

Typically a Web Server will have a physical folder assigned for a Web site. For example, www.myserver.com may have physical folder `c:\server55\` assigned to it. This folder is called the "root" folder or "home" folder. When Web developers transfer site files to the Web server, it is actually transferred to the root (home) folder of the Web site. During access of the Web site from the browser, the Web server will map the Web site's URL to its home folder. For example, if user enters the URL `http://www.myserver.com/mypage.html` in the browser, the Web server goes to the home folder for the Web site and fetches the file "mypage.html" for transfer to the browser.

The root (home) folder of the Web site is also referred as a *virtual folder* for the Web. This virtual folder is accessible from the browser through the URL having domain server name.

It is possible to create additional physical folders on the Web server for use during a Web application. To enable access to the content in these folders from the browser, the Web server gives an *alias* name to the physical folders. The convention for creating an alias is /*alias-name*/. So, for example, the physical folder `c:\OAS\MyAcct\` on the Web server is mapped to an alias `/mypsp/`. Now, to access a file flowers.gif in `c:\OAS\MyAcct\` from the browser, the URL should include the `/mypsp/` entry after the Web site name, i.e. `http://www.myserver.com/mypsp/flowers.gif`. This URL is also called as the *absolute path* to access contents of a virtual folder.

Absolute paths are fine for accessing files within a specific Web site. However, this mechanism makes it difficult to port the site to another server. So, if a Web site uses absolute paths for all embedded files, the site's files cannot be moved to another server without having to change each and every path to reflect the new address.

The alternative to enhance portability of a Web site is to use *relative path*. Relative path uses relative pathnames when linking to embedded files within a Web page. There are two types of relative paths: root-relative paths and document-relative paths.

A *root-relative path* always starts with the "/" (a forward slash) and does not include the protocol and domain server name. For example, `/mypsp/flowers.gif` will retrieve the file flowers.gif from the physical folder mapped to `/mypsp/` virtual folder.

The *document-relative path* does begin with "./" (a period and forward slash), and like root-relative path does not include the protocol and domain server name. The starting point is the current document displayed in the browser. Thus these paths are relative to the location of the document. For example `./flowers.gif` will display the flowers.gif file in the Web site's root folder.

If subfolders are created within the physical folders that are mapped to virtual folders, the access path now includes the new subfolder name. So if a new subfolder "images" is created within `/mypsp/` virtual folder (i.e. `c:\OAS\MyAcct\images`), then to access a file petal.gif in this new subfolder the root-relative path will be `/mypsp/images/petal.gif`. The document-relative path to access petal.gif file will be `./images/petal.gif`.

Since the PL/SQL server page is stored on the database server, any embedded files within the Web page will be stored on the Web server instead of the database server. Alternately, it is possible to store images also on the database server, but that approach is not considered in this book. To facilitate retrieval of embedded files needed by PSP, the Web server will have virtual folders setup. *These virtual folders are then accessed by the PSP through the root-relative path mechanism.*

For example, the Web server has a virtual folder called as `/mypsp/` mapped to the physical folder `c:\OAS\MyAcct\`. Now if a PSP utilizes an image file flowers.gif, then (i) this file needs to be transferred to the physical folder aliased as `/mypsp/`, and (ii) within the PSP, the SRC attribute for the `<img>` tag for image should have the root-relative path for the file as `/mypsp/flowers.gif`. For example, `<img src="/mypsp/flowers.gif">`. When the Web server sends the PSP to the browser, it will also send the image file from the virtual folder mapped physical folder.

Virtual folder contents can also contain static Web pages aside from other files. Also the image file of the previous example can also be accessed directly through the browser. For example, suppose the Web server site is `www.myserver.com`. To view the flowers.gif image in the browser, the following URL will now have to be entered.

```
http://www.myserver.com/mypsp/flowers.gif
```

Further, suppose there is a file test1.html in the virtual folder `/myspsp/`. Then the contents of this file can be viewed through the URL `http://www.myserver.com/mypsp/test1.html`.

COMPOSE PL/SQL SERVER PAGE

Composing a PL/SQL server page involves embedding PSP statements within a Web page. Placing of PSP statements is based on the logic of the page. Even though the Web page resides on the database server, the server processes only the PSP defined PL/SQL statements. The server ignores the non-PSP statements that are enclosed within the HTP package string. The statements enclosed within the HTP package string are processed later by the Web browser. During the PL/SQL Web procedure runtime, the PL/SQL statements are executed and based on the logic of the Web page, the results replace the PL/SQL statements. These results can be in the form of a modified page layout and/or display and processing of database values. As PSP statements are essentially associated with database operations, the nature of database interaction through a Web page can be classified into three types:

1. *Display* of database information in a structured (tabular) or unstructured (embed within some narrative text or content) format.
2. *Input* database information.
3. *Modify* existing database information including the successful retrieval of data for such modification.

PSP statements should be placed according to the logic of the Web page. A Web page is interpreted sequentially like a program unit by the database server from beginning to the end, one line at a time. PSP statements can be placed around or within specific HTML tags. For the sake of simplicity, the placement of PSP statements are explained in the following ways:

- Before the tag: which implies the placing of PSP statements before the beginning HTML tag.
- Inside the tag: which implies the placing of PSP statements within the HTML beginning tag so as to set some tag attributes.
- After the tag: which implies the placing of PSP statements after the ending HTML tag.
- Within the tag: which implies the placing of PSP statements between the beginning and ending HTML tags .

The following example illustrates the positioning of PSP statements with respect to HTML tags. Any HTML/Text editor can be utilized to complete the layout of the Web page. Make sure the Web page is saved as a .psp file.

Consider the paragraph HTML tag <p>. Suppose the content to be displayed within the paragraph tag is:

```
<p>Club is good for mountain climbing.</p>
```

The PSP utilizes two variables to hold the database values. The PSP declaration directive statement can be defined as follows:

```
<%!club_name sporting_clubs.name%type;%>
<%!club_state sporting_clubs.state%type;%>
```

Now, a SQL query is executed before this paragraph content. The query fetches a row from the SPORTING_CLUBS table containing the NAME and STATE attribute values from the database, and stores these values in variables club_name and club_state respectively. This query can be positioned before the beginning <p> tag (*before the tag* positioning) as follows:

```
<%select name,state into club_name, club_state from sporting_clubs
where club_id = 120;%>
<p>Club is good for mountain climbing.</p>
```

If the "align" attribute of the <p> tag has to be set according to the result of the query, then the PSP statement to set the attribute should be positioned inside the beginning <p> tag (*inside the tag* positioning) as follows:

```
<%select name,state into club_name,club_state from sporting_clubs
where club_id = 120;%>
<p <%if club_state='MO' then%> align="right" <%else%> align="left"<%end
if;%>>
Club is good for mountain climbing.</p>
```

To display database information as part of the paragraph narrative, the PSP expression directive statement is included within the text content (*within the tag* positioning) as follows:

```
<%select name,state into club_name,club_state from sporting_clubs
where club_id = 120;%>
<p <%if club_state='MO' then%> align="right" <%else%> align="left"<%end
if;%>>
Club <%= club_name%> is good for mountain climbing.</p>
```

where the <%= club_name%> entry displays the database value stored in the variable club_name.

Similarly, if some other PSP statement like a SQL insert statement has to be executed after the paragraph text display, it can be placed after the closing </p> tag (*after the tag* positioning) as follows:

```
<%select name,state into club_name,club_state from sporting_clubs
where club_id = 120;%>
<p <%if club_state='MO' then%> align="right" <%else%> align="left"<%end
if;%>>
Club <%= club_name%> is good for mountain climbing.</p>
<%insert into sporting_clubs (club_id,name)
values (140,'JetBlue Club');%>
```

Since the processing of PSP statements in a Web page is sequential, the processing control of any statement placed after the closing tag will be similar to placing it before the beginning tag of the next HTML tag in page layout.

A complete PSP (filename chapter5_test.psp) based on the above statements using Web Template 1 of Chapter 4, Lesson A is shown below. The additional entries to complete the Web page are PSP page specification statement and PSP procedure statement.

```
<!DOCTYPE HTML PUBLIC "-//W3C//DTD HTML 4.01 Transitional//EN">
<html>
```

```
<%@page language="PL/SQL"%>
<%@plsql procedure="chapter5_test"%>
<%!club_name sporting_clubs.name%type;%>
<%!club_state sporting_clubs.state%type;%>
<head>
<title>PL/SQL Server Page</title>
</head>
<body>
<div align="center"><p><h1>Mountain Climb</h1></p>
<!-- Navigation Bar Links -->

<hr /></div>
<br> <!-- Start Page Content -->
<%select name,state into club_name,club_state from sporting_clubs
    where club_id = 120;%>
<p<%if club_state='MO' then%> align="right" <%else%> align="left"<%end if;%>>
Club <%= club_name%> is good for mountain climbing.</p>
<%insert into sporting_clubs (club_id,name)
    values (140,'JetBlue Club');
    commit;%>
<!-- End Page Content -->
</body>
</html>
```

Save the file, and then load the PSP file through the command prompt window. The command to load the PSP is:

```
loadpsp -replace -user userid/password@connection_string
                drive&path\chapter5_test.psp
```

If there are errors in the page, fix the errors and re-load the page.

After the load operation, the PL/SQL Web procedure for the associated PSP Web page in the database is as follows:

```
CREATE OR REPLACE PROCEDURE CHAPTER5_TEST  AS
club_name sporting_clubs.name%type;
club_state sporting_clubs.state%type;
 BEGIN NULL;
htp.prn('<!DOCTYPE HTML PUBLIC "-//W3C//DTD HTML 4.01 Transitional//EN">
<html>
');
htp.prn('
');
htp.prn('
');
htp.prn('
');
htp.prn('
<head>
<title>PL/SQL Server Page</title>
</head>
<body>
<div align="center"><p><h1>Mountain Climb</h1></p>
<!-- Navigation Bar Links -->

<hr /></div>
<br> <!-- Start Page Content -->
');
select name,state into club_name,club_state from sporting_clubs
    where club_id = 120;
htp.prn('
<p ');
```

```
if club_state='MO' then
htp.prn(' align="right" ');
else
htp.prn(' align="left"');
end if;
htp.prn('>
Club ');
htp.prn( club_name);
htp.prn(' is good for mountain climbing.</p>
');
insert into mountain_clubs (club_id,name)
    values (140,'JetBlue Club');
    commit;
htp.prn('
<!-- End Page Content -->
</body>
</html>
');
 END;
```

The display of chapter5_test PSP Web page in browser is shown in Figure 5-3.

Mountain Climb

Club Cherokee Rafting Club is good for mountain climbing.

Figure 5-3   Chapter5_test PSP Web page in browser

A side-by-side view of the PSP Web page and the associated PL/SQL procedure on the database server is provided in Figure 5-4. The lines shows the relationship between the PSP statements and their associated PL/SQL statements within the PL/SQL Web procedure. Notice that the loadpsp utility places the entire Web page layout within the BEGIN/END section of the procedure. Also the PSP declaration statements are moved to the declaration section of the procedure.

```
<!DOCTYPE HTML PUBLIC "-//W3C//DTD HTML 4.01     CREATE OR REPLACE PROCEDURE
  Transitional//EN">                             CHAPTER5_TEST  AS
<html>                                           club_name sporting_clubs.name%type;
<%@page language="PL/SQL"%>                      club_state sporting_clubs.state%type;
<%@plsql procedure="chapter5_test"%>              BEGIN NULL;
<%!club_name sporting_clubs.name%type;%>         htp.prn('<!DOCTYPE HTML PUBLIC "-
<%!club_state sporting_clubs.state%type;%>       //W3C//DTD HTML 4.01 Transitional//EN">
<head>                                           <html>
<title>PL/SQL Server Page</title>               ');
</head>                                          htp.prn('
<body>                                           ');
<div align="center"><p><h1>Mountain             htp.prn('
Climb</h1></p>                                   ');
<!-- Navigation Bar Links -->                    htp.prn('
                                                 ');
<hr /></div>                                     htp.prn('
<br> <!-- Start Page Content -->                 <head>
<%select name,state into                         <title>PL/SQL Server Page</title>
club_name,club_state from sporting_clubs         </head>
      where club_id = 120;%>                     <body>
<p<%if club_state='MO' then%> align="right"      <div align="center"><p><h1>Mountain
<%else%> align="left"<%end if;%>>                Climb</h1></p>
Club <%= club_name%> is good for mountain         <!-- Navigation Bar Links -->

climbing.</p>                                     <hr /></div>
<%insert into sporting_clubs (club_id,name)       <br> <!-- Start Page Content -->
      values (140,'JetBlue Club');               ');
      commit;%>                                  select name,state into
<!-- End Page Content -->                        club_name,club_state from
</body>                                          sporting_clubs
</html>                                                 where club_id = 120;
                                                 htp.prn('
                                                 <p ');
                                                 if club_state='MO' then
                                                 htp.prn(' align="right" ');
                                                 else
                                                 htp.prn(' align="left"');
                                                 end if;
                                                 htp.prn('>
                                                 Club ');
                                                 htp.prn( club_name);
                                                 htp.prn(' is good for mountain
                                                 climbing.</p>
                                                 ');
                                                 . . .
```

Figure 5-4   PSP Web Page and associated PL/SQL Web Procedure

DEBUG PL/SQL SERVER PAGE

Errors in PSP can be syntactic or runtime. The Oracle database server only generates errors in PL/SQL Web procedures with respect to the PL/SQL statements. The database server does not evaluate the HTML tags for error checking. HTML tag errors will appear in the browser. Keep the following guidelines in mind when encountering problems.

The first set of errors are syntactic. It is important to get all the PL/SQL syntax and PSP directive statements syntax correctly. If there are mistakes in the syntax, the PSP file will not compile at the time of loading to the database server through the loadpsp utility. The syntactic errors can be corrected either on the Web page itself or within the associated PL/SQL Web procedure through a PL/SQL editor. If the syntactic errors are corrected on the Web page, then the page has to be re-loaded to the database server. Some of the common causes for errors at this stage are:

- Missing semicolons to terminate PL/SQL statements where required.
- Mistakes in the PSP directive statement syntax. Check the correct syntax, make sure the directives are closed properly, and that the correct directive is being utilized (declaration, expression, or processing directive) depending on what goes inside it.
- Separation of the tag symbols. Keep the opening tag (<%) and the closing tag (%>) symbols together. Do not enter < symbol on one line and % symbol on next line. It is a good practice to have a space after the opening tag and a space before the closing tag.
- PSP attribute names are case-sensitive. Most are specified in all lowercase; `contentType` and `errorPage` must be specified as mixed-case.

The next set of errors are encountered when a PSP is run by requesting it through a URL in a Web browser. At this stage, it is possible to get an error message HTTP 404 (or "page not found" error) in the browser. The reason for this message is that the database server has encountered some runtime error while executing the PSP based PL/SQL Web procedure. Due to the runtime error, the corresponding Web page is not generated. Consequently the "page not found" error appears in the browser. *To prevent runtime errors, it is recommended that the logic of the PL/SQL program unit associated with the PSP be tested separately.* Error checking at this stage involves:

- Make sure the URL is correct depending on the way the PL/SQL Web gateway is configured. Typically, the path includes the hostname, optionally a port number, the DAD, the schema name (userid), and the name of the stored procedure (with no .psp extension).
- Make sure to request the latest version of the page the next time. The error page might be cached by the browser. You might need to press Shift-Reload in the browser to bypass its cache.

It is possible to display runtime errors in the Web page instead of the HTTP 404 message by using the exception handlers and by printing the debug output as follow:

- Use the EXCEPTION clause in the PSP Web page. In this case, instead of "page not found" message in the browser, the *sqlerrm* function within the exception clause will return the database error in the PL/SQL portion of the Web page. This clause may be inserted in the PSP page anywhere (preferably towards the end of the page) as follows:

```
<%exception
when others then%>
<%= sqlerrm%>
```

Alternately, this clause may also be added within the corresponding PL/SQL Web procedure before the procedure END keyword as:

```
exception
when others then
htp.prn(sqlerrm);
```

Although the loadpsp command reports line numbers correctly when there is a syntax error in the PSP source file, line numbers reported for runtime errors refer to a transformed version of the source and do not match the line numbers in the original source.

Errors associated with Web forms (discussed in later chapters) involve:

- Parameter mismatch. Make sure that the form that calls the response page passes the correct number of parameters, and that the names specified by the NAME attributes on the form match the parameter names in the response page PSP. If the form includes any hidden input fields, or uses the NAME attribute on the Submit or Reset buttons, the response page PSP must declare equivalent parameters.
- If there are a lot of parameter data being passed, such as large strings, one might exceed the volume that can be passed with the GET method form attribute. In such case one should switch to the POST method attribute in the calling form.
- To see exactly what is being passed to the response page, use the GET method attribute form attribute in the calling form so that the parameters are visible in the URL.

TUTORIAL TO GENERATE MULTI-PAGE PSP

The following tutorial is a step-by-step process to create three PSP in the form of a Web site. The hierarchical layout of the site is shown in Figure 5-5. Each PSP file name and their corresponding PL/SQL Web procedure name are similar to the page name shown in the figure. Run the script file outdoorDB_v4.sql to load the Outdoor Clubs & Product Database tables necessary to complete this tutorial.

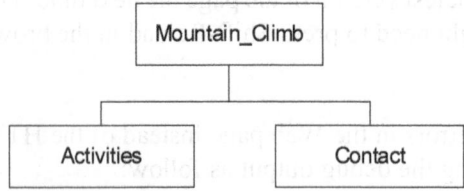

Figure 5-5 Mountain Climb Web Site
Layout

Mountain_Climb Web Page

The home page (Mountain_Climb) will have some narrative text followed by database data. Figure 5-6 shows the layout of the Web page. The PSP will be based on the Web Template 1 (described in Chapter 4, Lesson A). The narrative paragraph will appear within the paragraph <p> tag. The navigation URL will be as follows:

- The URL entered for Home page is `http://server-name/DAD/userid.mountain_climb`
- The URL entered for Activities page is `http://server-name/DAD/userid.activities`
- The URL entered for Contact page is `http://server-name/DAD/userid.contact`

The URL should be modified to suit the existing server configuration in the form of server-name, DAD, and userid.

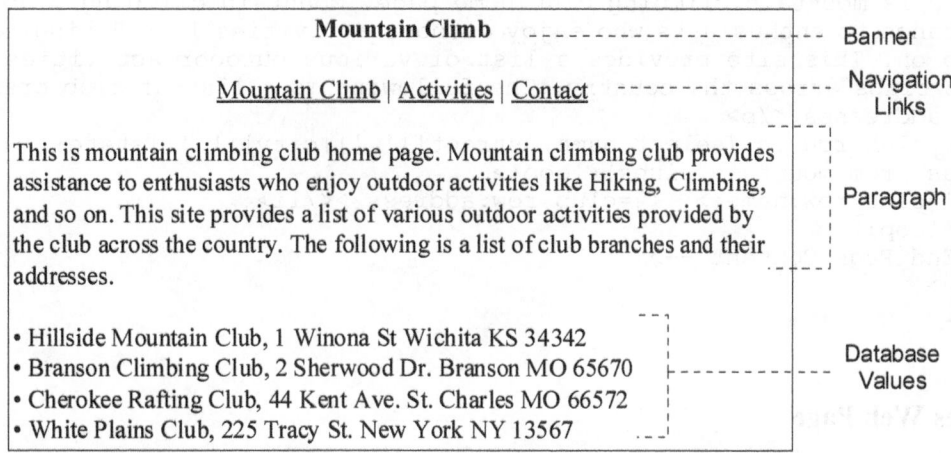

Figure 5-6

The database values pertaining to the club names and their respective addresses can be performed in two steps. The first step is to develop a PL/SQL block that will display this information.

```
begin
for club_row in (select name, street||' '||city||' '||state||' '||zip as
address from mountain_clubs)
loop
dbms_output.put_line(club_row.name||' '||club_row.address);
end loop;
end;
```

The next step is to transfer the PL/SQL block statements to the PSP. In this case the block of PL/SQL statements in the execution section of the PL/SQL block have to be placed in the PSP without the dbms_output.put_line keywords. The "`for club_row in (select name, street||'`
`'||city||' '||state||' '||zip as address from mountain_clubs)loop`" statement
will appear as a PSP processing directive statement. The
`dbms_output.put_line(club_row.name||' '||club_row.address)` statement will utilize
the PSP expression directive statement for displaying the `club_row.name` and `club_row.address`
values without the dbms_output.put_line keywords. The `end loop;` statement also will appear as a
PSP processing directive statement. The complete PSP is shown below.

```
<!DOCTYPE HTML PUBLIC "-//W3C//DTD HTML 4.01 Transitional//EN">
<%@page language="PL/SQL"%>
<%@plsql procedure="mountain_climb"%>
<html>
<head>
<title>Mountain Climb Club</title>
</head>
<body>
<div align="center"><p><h1>Mountain Climb</h1></p>
<!-- Navigation Bar Links -->
<a href="http://server-name/DAD/userid.mountain_climb">Mountain Climb</a> |
<a href="http:/server-name/DAD/userid.Activities">Activities</a>   | <a
href="http://server-name/DAD/userid.Contact">Contact</a><br>
<hr /></div>
<br> <!-- Start Page Content -->
```

```
<!--Main Content Area -->
<p>This is mountain climbing club home page. Mountain climbing club provides
assistance to enthusiasts who enjoy outdoor activities like Hiking, Climbing,
and so on. This site provides a list of various outdoor activities provided
by the clubs across the country. The following is a list of club branches and
their addresses.</p>
<% for club_row in (select name, street||' '||city||' '||state||' '||zip as
address from mountain_clubs) loop%>
<li><%=club_row.name%>  <%=club_row.address%></li>
<%end loop;%>
<!-- End Page Content -->
</body>
</html>
```

Activities Web Page

The activities page will display database information on the activities that the various clubs provide as shown in Figure 5-7.

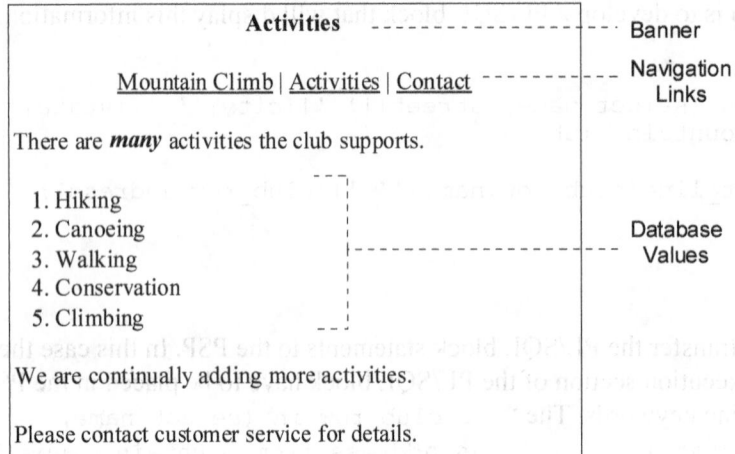

Figure 5-7

The PSP will be based on the Web Template 1 (described in Chapter 4, Lesson A). The narrative paragraph will appear within the paragraph <p> tag. The navigation URL will be similar to Mountain_Climb page. The database values pertaining to the club activities can be performed in two steps. The first step is to develop a PL/SQL block that will display this information.

```
begin
for club_row in (select distinct activity from club_activity)
loop
dbms_output.put_line(club_row.activity);
end loop;
end;
```

The next step is to transfer the PL/SQL block statements to the PSP. Once again the block of PL/SQL statements in the execution section of the PL/SQL block will be placed in the PSP without the dbms_output.put_line keywords. The "`for club_row in (select distinct activity from club_activity)loop`" statement will appear as a PSP processing directive statement. The dbms_output.put_line(club_row.activity) statement will utilize the PSP expression directive statement for displaying the club_row.activity values without the dbms_output.put_line keywords. The end loop; statement also will appear as a PSP processing directive statement. The complete PSP is shown below.

```
<!DOCTYPE HTML PUBLIC "-//W3C//DTD HTML 4.01 Transitional//EN">
<%@page language="PL/SQL"%>
<%@plsql procedure="activities"%>
<html>
<head>
<title>Mountain Climb Club</title>
</head>
<body>
<div align="center"><p><h1>Activities</h1></p>
<!-- Navigation Bar Links -->
<a href="http://server-name/DAD/userid.mountain_climb">Mountain Climb</a> |
<a href="http://server-name/DAD/userid.Activities">Activities</a> | <a
href="http://server-name/DAD/userid.Contact">Contact</a><br>
<hr /></div>
<br> <!-- Start Page Content -->
There are <b><i>many</i></b> activities the club supports.
<ol>
<% for club_row in (select distinct activity from club_activity) loop%>
<li><%=club_row.activity%></li>
<%end loop;%>
</ol>
<p>We are continually adding more activities.</p>
<p>Please contact customer service for details.</p>
<!-- End Page Content -->
</body>
</html>
```

Contact Web Page

The contact page will display static information on the contacts available for the clubs as shown in Figure 5-8.

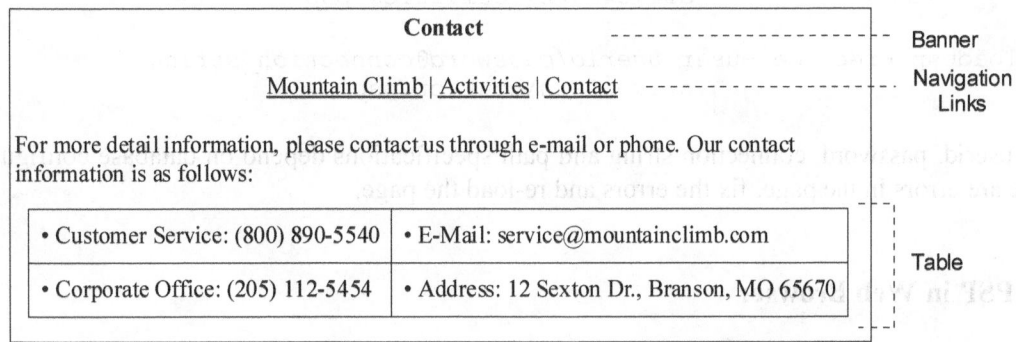

Figure 5-8

The PSP will be based on the Web Template 1 (described in Chapter 4, Lesson A). The narrative paragraph will appear within the paragraph <p> tag. The table entries will utilize the <table> tag. The navigation URL will be similar to Mountain_Climb page. The complete PSP is shown below.

```
<!DOCTYPE HTML PUBLIC "-//W3C//DTD HTML 4.01 Transitional//EN">
<%@page language="PL/SQL"%>
<%@plsql procedure="contact"%>
<html>
<head>
<title>Mountain Climb Club</title>
</head>
<body>
<div align="center"><p><h1>Contact</h1></p>
<!-- Navigation Bar Links -->
<a href="http://server-name/DAD/userid.mountain_climb">Mountain Climb</a> |
<a href="http://server-name/DAD/userid.Activities">Activities</a> | <a
href="http://server-name/DAD/userid.Contact">Contact</a><br>
<hr /></div>
<br> <!-- Start Page Content -->
<p>For more detail information, please contact us through e-mail or phone.
Our contact information is as follows:</p>

<table border="1" cellpadding="0" cellspacing="0">
<thead></thead>
<tr><td><li>Customer Service: (800) 890-5540.</li></td><td><li>E-Mail:
service@mountainclimb.com</li></td></tr>
<tr><td><li>Corporate Office: (205) 112-5454</li></td><td><li>Address: 12
Sexton Dr., Branson, MO 65670</li></td></tr>
</table>
<!-- End Page Content -->
</body>
</html>
```

Load PSP to the Database

Once the PSP have been completed, open the Windows Command Prompt window to execute the loadpsp command for the PSP files. The command to load the PSP will be:

```
loadpsp -replace -user userid/password@connection_string
                    drive&path\mountain_climb.psp

loadpsp -replace -user userid/password@connection_string
                    drive&path\activities.psp

loadpsp -replace -user userid/password@connection_string
                    drive&path\contact.psp
```

The userid, password, connection string and path specifications depend on database configuration. If there are errors in the page, fix the errors and re-load the page.

View PSP in Web Browser

Once the loading is successful type the URL below to retrieve the Web pages from the database. The URL should be modified to suit the existing server configuration in the form of server-name, DAD, and userid.

```
http://server-name/DAD/userid.mountain_climb
```

CHAPTER SUMMARY

▸ PL/SQL server pages (PSP) are Web pages which include PL/SQL language statements.

▸ The PL/SQL language in PSP becomes a server-side scripting language.

▸ As each PSP in browser is a HTML document, the nature of PL/SQL language statements within a PSP are determine the layout logic for the page.

▸ PSP processing is done on the database server rather than the Web server.

▸ The browser receives a plain HTML page with no special PL/SQL script tags.

▸ Some basic knowledge of the HTML makes it easy to understand the positioning of PL/SQL statements within a Web page.

▸ On the database server, a PL/SQL server page (PSP) is a PL/SQL Web procedure that contains HTML tags.

▸ PSP files have the file extension .psp.

▸ Each file is loaded into the database server through a utility "loadpsp."

▸ The PL/SQL language statements are enclosed in special tag symbols <% ... %>.

▸ PSP can include any PL/SQL processing statement within the delimiters <% ... %>.

▸ Page specification directive is a necessary statement within the Web page specifying the PL/SQL scripting language.

▸ Procedure directive statement specifies the name of the stored procedure produced by the PSP file.

▸ Parameter directive statement specifies the name, and optionally the type and default, for each parameter expected by the PSP stored procedure.

▸ Include directive statement specifies the name of a file to be included at a specific point in the PSP file.

▸ Declaration directive statement declares a set of PL/SQL variables that are available throughout the page.

▸ Processing directive statements are PL/SQL statements associated with the execution section of the PL/SQL block.

▸ Expression directive statement specifies a single PL/SQL expression, such as a string, arithmetic expression, function call, or combination of those things.

▸ On the database server, the HTML statements of the procedure are enclosed within the HTP package string.

- ▸ Once the PL/SQL server page has been turned into a stored procedure, it can be displayed through a HTTP URL from a Web browser or other Internet-aware client program.

- ▸ Files (image, script, etc.) included within a PSP page are accessed by the Web server using the concept of virtual folders.

- ▸ Database access descriptor (DAD) is a mechanism that maps the URL to the correct database schema.

- ▸ All PL/SQL Web applications require the a database access descriptor to facilitate their working.

- ▸ Database operations through a Web page can be classified into three types – (i) display of database information in a formatted (tabular) or unformatted (embed with narrative text), (ii) input database information, and (iii) modify existing database information including successful retrieval of data for such modification.

REVIEW QUESTIONS

1. How is a PSP page stored on Oracle database server? Explain.

2. What are PSP statements for declaring local variables?

3. What are PSP statements for input parameters?

4. How is a PSP transferred to the Oracle database server?

5. What is the purpose of DAD?

6. How are images and script files associated with PSP stored on the Web server?

7. What PL/SQL package handles HTML statements. How?

REVIEW EXERCISES

1. A PL/SQL server page is a Web page which includes _____ language statements.

2. The PL/SQL server page uses the PL/SQL language as a _____ scripting language.

3. The PL/SQL language statements in a PL/SQL server page are enclosed within the special tag symbols of _____ and _____.

4. A PL/SQL server page file type is ._____.

5. A PL/SQL server page file is transferred to the database server using the _____ utility.

6. A PL/SQL server page is a PL/SQL _____ in the database server.

7. The HTML tags in a PL/SQL server page are enclosed within the _____ package string within the database server.

8. The database access descriptor maps the _____ to the correct database account/schema.

9. The _____ of a PL/SQL server page based application must include the database access descriptor's name.

10. _____ folders are Web accessible folders mapped to a physical folder on the Web server.

11. The following is an example of _____ virtual path.

    ```
    http://www.studio.com/mywork/getone.htm
    ```

12. The following is an example of _____ virtual path.

    ```
    ./mywork/getone.htm
    ```

13. One of the types of database operations through a Web page can involve _____ of database values in unstructured (narrative text) format.

14. DAD in the following URL is _____.

    ```
    http://www.studio.com/mywork/jack.getone
    ```

PROBLEM SOLVING EXERCISES

Ex5A-1. Run the script file travelDB_v4.sql to load the Travel Anywhere database tables necessary to complete this exercise. Create a single page PSP with the following text containing database values. Optionally, place any relevant clipart in the page (sample shown below).

Air Travel

The following special deals are currently available:
1. Low fares around $ *low_fare_value1* between Detroit and New York.
2. Global Airlines: Special Fares as low as $ *low_fare_value2* to Europe.
3. Vacation Fares to *list_cities* in Asia.

To check reservations with carriers click here.

In the above text, *low_fare_value1*, *low_fare_value2*, and *list_cities* entries are substituted by database values in the browser.

1. Create a procedure Ex5a1a that displays the output of the following queries:
   a. Compute the lowest fare offered by any airline between Detroit and New York..
   b. Compute the lowest fare offered by any airline for any destination in Europe.
   c. List the cities served by airlines in Asia.

   Utilize the queries to complete the Web page as follows:

   • The *low_fare_value1* entry will be the database value based on query (a).
   • The *low_fare_value2* entry will be the database value based on query (b).
   • The *list_cities* entry will be the database values based on query (c).

2. Generate and load PSP Web pages to the Oracle database server. (The instructor will provide the details on the database server accounts).

3. If some clipart is utilized in the Web page, transfer the image to the required virtual folder. (The instructor will provide the necessary instructions on this step).

4. Open the Web page in the browser and print the display.

Ex5A-2. Run the script file travelDB_v4.sql to load the Travel Anywhere database tables necessary to complete this exercise. Create a single page PSP with the following text containing database values. Optionally, place any relevant clipart in the page (sample shown below).

Hotel Arrangements

The following special deals are currently available:
1. New Orleans French Quarter - The Iberville Suites at incredibly low rate of $ *low_rate_value1*.
2. Las Vegas Imperial Palace starting at $ *low_rate_value2*.
3. La Quinta : Great rates from $ *low_rate_value3* to $ *high_rate_value*.

To check reservations with all Hotels click here.

In the above text, *low_rate_value1*, *low_rate_value2*, *low_rate_value3*, and *high_rate_value* entries are substituted by database values in the browser.

1. Create a procedure Ex51b that displays the output of the following queries:
    a. Compute the average rates of Iberville Suites hotel in New Orleans.
    b. Compute the lowest rate of Imperial Palace hotel in Las Vegas.
    c. Compute the lowest rate and the highest rate for La Quinta hotels.

    Utilize the queries to complete the Web page as follows:

    *   The *low_rate_value1* entry will be a database value based on query (a).
    *   The *low_rate_value2* entry will be a database value based on query (b).
    *   The *low_rate_value3* and *high_rate_value* entries will be database values based on query (c).

2. Generate and load PSP Web pages to the Oracle database server. (The instructor will provide the details on the database server accounts).

3. If some clipart is utilized in the Web page, transfer the image to the required virtual folder. (The instructor will provide the necessary instructions on this step).

4. Open the Web page in the browser and print the display.

Ex5A-3. Run the script file travelDB_v4.sql to load the Travel Anywhere database tables necessary to complete this exercise. Extend the problem solving exercise Ex4A-2 of Chapter 4, Lesson A by incorporating PSP Web pages content of Ex5A-1 and Ex5A-2. In the Web site, the content of Ex5A-1 exercise replaces the Airlines Web page, while content of Ex5A-2 exercise replaces the Hotels Web page.

1. Modify the Web pages as PSP. Change the navigation bar links appropriately.

2. Generate and load PSP Web pages to the Oracle database server. (The instructor will provide the details on the database server accounts).

3. Open the Web site in the browser, and print all the pages of the Web site.

Ex5A-4. Run the script file sentimentDB_v4.sql to load the Sentiment Anywhere database tables necessary to complete this exercise. Create a single page PSP with the following text containing database values. Optionally, place any relevant clipart in the page (sample shown below).

Express Sentiments with Flowers

Select the flowers to go with the occasion.
- Birthday (*b_value1* available)   • Anniversary (*a_value1* available)
- Thank You (*t_value1* available)   • Wedding (*w_value1* available)
- Get Well (*g_value1* available)

These flowers range from *low_value1* to *high_value1*.

In the above text, *b_value1, a_value1, t_value1 , w_value1, g_value1, low_value1,* and *high_value1* entries are substituted by database values in the browser.

1. Create a procedure Ex52a that displays the output of the following queries.
    a.   Compute the types of Birthday flowers available.
    b.   Compute the types of Anniversary flowers available.
    c.   Compute the types of Thank You flowers available.
    d.   Compute the types of Wedding flowers available.
    e.   Compute the types of Get Well flowers available.
    f.   Compute the lowest price and the highest price of flowers available.

    Utilize the queries to complete the Web page as follows:

    - The *b_value1* entry will be a database value based on query (a).
    - The *a_value1* entry will be a database value based on query (b).
    - The *t_value1* entry will be a database value based on query (c).
    - The *w_value1* entry will be a database value based on query (d).
    - The *g_value1* entry will be a database value based on query (e).
    - The *low_value1* and *high_value1* entries will be database values based on query (f).

2. Generate and load PSP Web pages to the Oracle database server. (The instructor will provide the details on the database server accounts).

3. If some clipart is utilized in the Web page, transfer the image to the required virtual folder. (The instructor will provide the necessary instructions on this step).

4. Open the Web page in the browser and print the display.

Ex5A-5. Run the script file sentimentDB_v4.sql to load the Sentiment Anywhere database tables necessary to complete this exercise. Create a single page PSP with the following text containing database values. Optionally, place any relevant clipart in the page (sample shown below).

Express Sentiments with Gifts

Select the Gifts to go with the occasion.
- Birthday (*b_value2* available)
- Thank You (*t_value2* available)
- Get Well (*g_value2* available)
- Anniversary (*a_value2* available)
- Wedding (*w_value2* available)

These gifts range from *low_value2* to *high_value2*.

In the above text, *b_value2, a_value2, t_value2, w_value2, g_value2, low_value2,* and *high_value2* entries are substituted by database values in the browser.

1. Create a procedure Ex52b that displays the output of the following queries.
   a. Compute the types of Birthday gifts available.
   b. Compute the types of Anniversary gifts available.
   c. Compute the types of Thank You gifts available.
   d. Compute the types of Wedding gifts available.
   e. Compute the types of Get Well gifts available.
   f. Compute the lowest price and the highest price of gifts available.

   Utilize the queries to complete the Web page as follows:

   - The *b_value2* entry will be a database value based on query (a).
   - The *a_value2* entry will be a database value based on query (b).
   - The *t_value2* entry will be a database value based on query (c).
   - The *w_value2* entry will be a database value based on query (d).
   - The *g_value2* entry will be a database value based on query (e).
   - The *low_value2* and *high_value2* entries will be database values based on query (f).

2. Generate and load PSP Web pages to the Oracle database server. (The instructor will provide the details on the database server accounts).

3. If some clipart is utilized in the Web page, transfer the image to the required virtual folder. (The instructor will provide the necessary instructions on this step).

4. Open the Web page in the browser and print the display.

Ex5A-6. Run the script file sentimentDB_v4.sql to load the Sentiment Anywhere database tables necessary to complete this exercise. Extend the problem solving exercise Ex4A-3 of Chapter 4, Lesson A by incorporating PSP Web pages content of Ex5A-4 and Ex5A-5. In the Web site, the content of Ex5A-4 exercise replaces the Flowers Web page, while content of Ex5A-5 exercise replaces the Gifts Web page.

1. Modify the Web pages as PSP. Change the navigation bar links appropriately.

2. Generate and load PSP Web pages to the Oracle database server. (The instructor will provide the details on the database server accounts).

3. Open the Web site in the browser, and print all the pages of the Web site.

Ex5A-7. Run the script file outdoorDB_v4.sql to load the Outdoor Clubs & Product database tables necessary to complete this exercise. Create a Web site titled "Outdoor Activities" to provide membership in sporting clubs and order outdoor supplies. The hierarchical site layout is shown on the right.

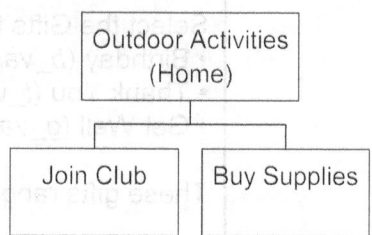

1. The Home page will have the following text.

> Outdoor activities can range from simple hiking to mountain climbing. Such activities require different equipments and supplies to enhance their enjoyment.
>
> We thank you for your visit. Please use the link buttons on the side to explore the site.

2. Position an appropriate image on the right of the above text in the Home page. (optional)

3. Create the additional Web pages titled Join Club, and Buy Supplies.

4. Create a procedure Ex5a7a that displays the output of the following queries.
    a. Compute the number of mountain clubs in the database.
    b. List the names of mountain clubs.

5. Use the queries created in requirement 4 to complete the following text for the Join Club page.

> ## Club Membership
>
> We offer membership to many existing sporting clubs. Currently there are *club_number1* sporting clubs attached to this Site. The fee for membership is $50 per month. The listed sporting clubs are:
> *   *club_name1*
> *   *club_name2*
> .
>
> We welcome new membership. Use the Apply button to join any club.

Note:
*   The *club_number1* will be a database value based on query (a) of requirement (4) above.
*   The *club_name1, club_name2,* ... will be database values based on query (b) of requirement (4) above.

7. Create a procedure Ex5a7b that displays the output of the following queries.
   a. Compute the lowest price and the highest price of products available.
   b. List the names of products available.

8. Use the queries created in requirement 7 to complete the following text for the Buy Supplies page.

Order Supplies

There are many outdoor supplies available. Prices for these supplies range from $ *low_price1* to $ *high_price1*. The list of supplies are:
   • *product_name1*
   • *product_name2*

Please proceed with purchase when ready by using the Buy link button.

Note:
 • The *low_price1* and *high_price1* will be a database values based on the low and high price of products in query (a) of requirement (7) above.
 • The *product_name1, product_name2, ...* will be database values based on query (b) of requirement (7) above.

9. The banner should be titled "Outdoor Activities." The navigation button links should be titled after the page names with the home page titled "Home."

10. Generate and load PSP Web pages to the Oracle database server. (The instructor will provide the details on the database server accounts).

11. If some clipart is utilized in the Web page, transfer the image to the required virtual folder. (The instructor will provide the necessary instructions on this step).

12. Open the Web site in the browser and print the display.

Ex5A-8. Run the script file travelDB_v4.sql to load the Travel Anywhere database tables necessary to complete this exercise. Create a one page Web site titled "Hotel Details" that provides an internal report on hotel features.

1. The banner should be titled "Travel Anywhere." There should not be any navigation link on the Web page.

2. Position an appropriate image on the right of the above text in the Home page. (optional)

3. Create a procedure Ex58a that displays the output of the following queries.
   a. Compute the number of hotels that provide double twins bedrooms.
   b. Compute the number of hotels that provide double queens bedrooms.
   c. Compute the number of hotels in Las Vegas.
   d. Compute the lowest rate and the highest rate of hotels in Las Vegas
   e. Compute the number of hotels in New Orleans.

    f.   Compute the lowest rate and the highest rate of hotels in New Orleans.

    g.   Compute the number of hotels in Orlando.

    h.   Compute the lowest rate and the highest rate of hotels in Orlando.

    i.   Compute the number of hotels in New York.

    j.   Compute the lowest rate and the highest rate of hotels in New York.

    k.   Compute the number of hotel reservations with kids.

4.   The outline of the home page will be as follows:

Hotel Details

Travel Anywhere has the following details on hotels in its database.

- There are *value1* hotels that provide double twins bed rooms.
- There are *value2* hotels that provide double queens bed rooms.
- There are *value3* hotels in Las Vegas with rates from $ *value4* to $ *value5*.
- There are *value6* hotels in New Orleans with rates from $ *value7* to $ *value8*.
- There are *value9* hotels in Orlando with rates from $ *value10* to $ *value11*.
- There are *value12* hotels in New York with rates from $ *value13* to $ *value14*.
- All hotels have baby crib facilities.
- Currently only *value15* reservations have children.

Note:
- The *value1* will be a database value based on query (a) of requirement (3) above.
- The *value2* will be a database value based on query (b) of requirement (3) above.
- The *value3* will be a database value based on query (c) of requirement (3) above.
- The *value4* and *value5* will be database values based on query (d) of requirement (3) above.
- The *value6* will be a database value based on query (e) of requirement (3) above.
- The *value7* and *value8* will be database values based on query (f) of requirement (3) above.
- The *value9* will be a database value based on query (g) of requirement (3) above.
- The *value10* and *value11* will be database values based on query (h) of requirement (3) above.
- The *value12* will be a database value based on query (i) of requirement (3) above.
- The *value13* and *value14* will be database values based on query (j) of requirement (3) above.
- The *value15* will be a database value based on query (k) of requirement (3) above.

5.   Generate and load PSP Web pages to the Oracle database server. (The instructor will provide the details on the database server accounts).

6.   If some clipart is utilized in the Web page, transfer the image to the required virtual folder. (The instructor will provide the necessary instructions on this step).

7.   Open the Web site in the browser and print the display.

Ex5A-9. Run the script file travelDB_v4.sql to load the Travel Anywhere database tables necessary to complete this exercise. Create a one page Web site titled "Air Travel Details" that provides an internal report on air travel.

1. The banner should be titled "Travel Anywhere." There should not be any navigation links on the Web page.

2. Position an appropriate image on the right of the above text in the Home page. (optional)

3. Create a procedure Ex59a that displays the output of the following queries.
   a. Compute the number of destinations in Europe served by both airlines.
   b. List model of the airplane utilized most in air travel.
   c. Compute how many different models of airplanes are used by both airlines.
   d. List the customer first name and last name who has traveled the most number of times.
   e. Compute the number of flight tickets issued for travel with Tranworld airline.
   f. Compute the number of flight tickets issued for travel with Global airline.
   g. Compute how many destination cities served by Global airline in Asia.
   h. Compute how many destination cities served by Tranworld airline in Asia.
   i. List the most common origin city for departures.

4. The outline of the home page will be as follows:

Air Travel Details

Travel Anywhere has the following details on air travel in its database.

- There are *value1* destinations in Europe served by both airlines.
- The *value2* model airplane is utilized most in air travel.
- There are *value3* models of airplane used by both airlines.
- Customer *value4* has traveled most number of times.
- There have been *value5* flight tickets issued for travel with Tranworld airline.
- There have been *value6* flight tickets issued for travel with Global airline.
- Global airline serves *value7* cities in Asia.
- Tranworld airline serves *value8* cities in Asia.
- The most common origin city for departures is *value9*.

Note:
- The *value1* will be a database value based on query (a) of requirement (3) above.
- The *value2* will be a database value based on query (b) of requirement (3) above.
- The *value3* will be a database value based on query (c) of requirement (3) above.
- The *value4* will be a database value based on query (d) of requirement (3) above.
- The *value5* will be a database value based on query (e) of requirement (3) above.
- The *value6* will be a database value based on query (f) of requirement (3) above.
- The *value7* will be a database value based on query (g) of requirement (3) above.
- The *value8* will be a database value based on query (h) of requirement (3) above.
- The *value9* will be a database value based on query (i) of requirement (3) above.

5. Generate and load PSP Web pages to the Oracle database server. (The instructor will provide the details on the database server accounts).

6. If some clipart is utilized in the Web page, transfer the image to the required virtual folder. (The instructor will provide the necessary instructions on this step).

7. Open the Web site in the browser and print the display.

Introduction to PL/SQL Server Pages

• HTML Tables with Database Content
• PL/SQL Server Page with HTML Tables

Tables in Web pages are utilized to structure Web page content in rows and columns. The focus of table use in PSP is only on structuring display of database information. Besides, database information, the contents of a table can include text, image, or another table. The contents can also be hyperlinked.

This chapter utilizes the table structure of Superflex Apartment database to explain examples.

STRUCTURE DATA WITH TABLES

PSP expression statement can be placed inside a HTML table cell (which is represented by the `<td>` tag pair) to display database value. The syntax for displaying such database value in a cell is:

```
<td><%= ..PSP-expression..%></td>
```

To generate rows of values, PSP statements should be positioned around an empty row `<tr>` tag in the form of PL/SQL loop statements. The *before the tag* positioning is accomplished by placing PSP statements before the beginning `<tr>` tag; *inside the tag* positioning is accomplished by placing PSP statements within the beginning `<tr>` tag angle brackets; while, *after the tag* positioning is accomplished by placing PSP statements after the closing `</tr>` tag. The syntax of such placement of PSP statements is as follows:

```
<% ...PSP statements...%>
<tr <% ...PSP statements...%>>
<td><%= ...PSP-expression...%></td>
<td><%= ...PSP-expression...%></td>
</tr>
<% ...PSP statements...%>
```

Additionally, PSP statements can also be positioned around the `<table>` tag in the form of *before the tag* to ensure some database action prior to the display of table values, or *inside the tag* to change some table attribute, or *after the tag* to perform some database action after the table display is complete. The syntax of such placement of PSP statements is as follows:

```
<% ...PSP statements...%>
```

289

```
<table <% ...PSP statements...%>>
<% ...PSP statements...%>
<tr><td><%= ...PSP-expression...%></td>
<td><%= ...PSP-expression...%></td></tr>
<% ...PSP statements...%>
</table>
```

STRUCTURE DATA WITH TABLES TUTORIAL

The following tutorial is a single page PSP that displays a tenant list consisting of tenant social security number, tenant name, and apartment rented (Figure 5-9) with HTML tables. Run the script file superflexDB_v4.sql to load the Superflex Apartments Database tables necessary to complete this tutorial.

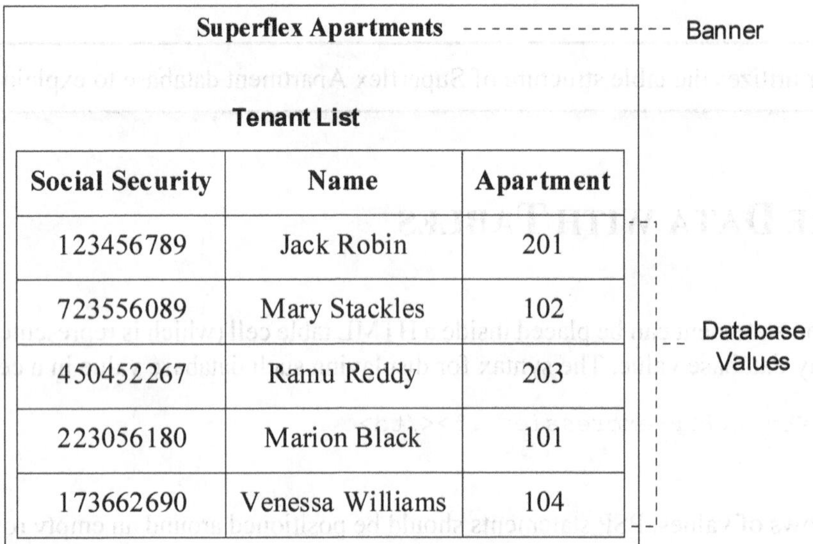

Superflex Apartments			
Tenant List			
Social Security	**Name**	**Apartment**	
123456789	Jack Robin	201	
723556089	Mary Stackles	102	
450452267	Ramu Reddy	203	
223056180	Marion Black	101	
173662690	Venessa Williams	104	

Banner — Superflex Apartments

Database Values

Figure 5-9

The database values pertaining to the club names and their respective addresses can be performed in two steps. The first step is to develop a PL/SQL procedure that will display this information. The PL/SQL procedure ch5_simple_report shows the values of Tenant social security, Tenant name and their apartment number.

```
create or replace procedure ch5_simple_report IS
begin
for list_row in (select tenant_ss,tenant_name,apt_no from tenant,rental
    where tenant.rental_no = rental.rental_no) loop
    dbms_output.put_line('tenant ss '||list_row.tenant_ss||' tenant name '||
    list_row.tenant_name||' apt no '||list_row.apt_no);
end loop;
end;
```

The next step is to transfer the PL/SQL procedure statements to a HTML table structure in a PSP. To complete the transfer, create a table with column headings and an extra row for database output. The cursor processing loop starts before the database output row, and ends after the row as follows:

```
<%for list_row in (select tenant_ss,tenant_name,apt_no from tenant,rental
       where tenant.rental_no = rental.rental_no) loop%>
<tr>
<td><%=list_row.tenant_ss%></td>
<td><%=list_row.tenant_name%></td>
<td><%=list_row.apt_no%></td></tr>
<%end loop;%>
```

The complete PSP (filename tenant_list.psp) using Web Template 1 is as follows:

```
<!DOCTYPE HTML PUBLIC "-//W3C//DTD HTML 4.01 Transitional//EN">
<html>
<%@page language= "PL/SQL"%>
<%@plsql procedure= "tenant_list"%>
<head>
<title>Tenant List</title>
</head>
<body>
<div align="center"><p><h1>Superflex Apartments</h1></p>
<!-- Navigation Bar Links -->
<br>
<hr /></div>
<br> <!-- Start Page Content -->
<table border="0" cellpadding="1" cellspacing="1" summary="">
<tr><td></td><td><b>Tenant List</b></td><td></td></tr>
<tr><th>Social Security</th><th>Name</th><th>Apartment</th></tr>
<%for list_row in (select tenant_ss,tenant_name,apt_no from tenant,rental
where tenant.rental_no = rental.rental_no) loop%>
<tr><td><%=list_row.tenant_ss%></td>
<td><%=list_row.tenant_name%></td>
<td><%=list_row.apt_no%></td></tr>
<%end loop;%>
</table>
<!-- End Page Content -->
</body>
</html>
```

Load PSP to the Database

Once the PSP have been completed, open the Windows Command Prompt window to execute the loadpsp command for the PSP files. The command to load the PSP will be:

```
loadpsp -replace -user userid/password@connection_string
            drive&path\tenant_list.psp
```

The userid, password, connection string and path specifications depend on database configuration. If there are errors in the page, fix the errors and re-load the page.

View PSP in Web Browser

Once the loading is successful type the URL below to retrieve the Web page from the database. The URL should be modified to suit the existing server configuration in the form of server-name, DAD, and userid.

```
http://server-name/DAD/userid.tenant_list
```

CHAPTER SUMMARY

▸ Tables in Web pages are useful in organizing and displaying Web page content in rows and columns.

▸ Tables are also utilized for Web page layout development.

▸ The contents of a table can be text, image, data values or another table. The contents can also be hyperlinked.

▸ The focus of table in PSP is to structure display of database content with HTML tables.

▸ Table consists of horizontal rows and vertical columns (like spreadsheets).

▸ The intersection of a row and a column is called a cell.

▸ HTML uses `<table>` tag pairs to define a table.

▸ PSP statements can be inserted within a cell, or can be used to generate rows of values.

REVIEW QUESTIONS

1. What are the tags for table, rows, and cell contents in HTML?

2. What is meant by cell padding and cell spacing?

3. Where should the PSP statements appear in a table to display rows of values.

REVIEW EXERCISES

1. HTML tables are used to display content as well as design page _____.

2. The intersection of a row and column is called a _____.

3. The HTML tag to define a table is _____.

4. The HTML tag to define a row is _____.

5. The HTML tag to define a cell is _____.

6. The distance between the cell's content and its border is called as cell _____.

7. The thickness of lines on the outside edge of the table is called _____.

8. The thickness of the border between the cells is called cell _____.

9. PSP statements before the table can be placed in the _____ _____ tab of table object HTML window.

10. PSP statements after the table can be placed in the _____ _____ tab of table object HTML window.

PROBLEM SOLVING EXERCISES

Ex5B-1.   Extend the chapter tutorial Web site by adding the following Web page.

1.   A Web page to display (using tables feature) apartments with pending complaints. The table layout is shown below, with attributes from database in italics.

Pending Apartment Complaints			
Complaint#	Apartment#	Apartment Type	Description
complaint_no	*apt_no*	*(Apartment Description)*	*apt_complaint*

Create a PL/SQL procedure "ex5b1_pending_complaints" that displays the data required for the table. Save the procedure as a script file with filename ex5b1. The Apartment Type column should show description like Studio, One-Bedroom, and so on instead of numeric values. Use the procedure code to complete the Web page.

The navigation button/link name for the Web page is "Pending Complaints."

2.   Generate and load PSP Web pages to the Oracle database server. (The instructor will provide the details on the database server accounts).

3.   Open the Web site in the browser and print the display.

Ex5B-2.   Extend the chapter tutorial Web site by adding the following Web page.

1.   A Web page to display (using tables feature) summary of rentals facilitated by staff. The table layout is shown below, with attributes from database in italics.

Staff Rental Summary		
Staff Name	Position	Number of Rentals
first_name last_name	*position*	*staff_rental function value*

Create a PL/SQL procedure "ex5b2_staff_rental_summary" that displays the data required for the table. Save the procedure as a script file with filename ex5b2. Create a function staff_rental that gives a count of the number of rentals facilitated by a staff. Use the function value in Number of Rentals column. Save the function in a file same as function name. Use the procedure code to complete the Web page.

The navigation button/link name for the Web page is "Staff Summary."

2. Generate and load PSP Web pages to the Oracle database server. (The instructor will provide the details on the database server accounts).

3. Open the Web site in the browser and print the display.

Ex5B-3. Extend the chapter tutorial Web site by adding the following Web page.

1. A Web page to display (using tables feature) list of apartments that have been rented by various staff. The Web page either displays for each staff either the apartment number or a message "No Apartment Rented" in case the staff has no associated rental. The table layout is shown below, with attributes from database in italics.

Staff Apartment Details

first_name last_name   *position*

Apartment #

{ *apt_no* | No Apartment Rented }

Create a PL/SQL procedure "ex5b3_staff_apartment_details" that displays the data required for the table. Save the procedure as a script file with filename ex5b3. Use the procedure code to complete the Web page.

The navigation button/link name for the Web page is "Staff Details."

2. Generate and load PSP Web pages to the Oracle database server. (The instructor will provide the details on the database server accounts).

3. Open the Web site in the browser and print the display.

Ex5B-4. Run the script file outdoorDB_v4.sql to load the Outdoor Clubs & Product database tables necessary to complete this exercise. Create a single page PSP with the following content.

1. Display details on products that have been re-ordered so far. The table layout is shown below, with attributes from database in italics.

Reorder List

Product ID	Name	Re-ordered Status
product_id	*product_name*	*ex62_reord_status function value*

Create a PL/SQL procedure "ex5b4_product_reorder_list" that displays the data required for the table. Save the procedure as a script file with filename ex5b4. Create a boolean function ex5b4_reord_status that returns a value on whether a product has been re-ordered so far or not. The Re-ordered Status column will display a 'Yes' or 'No' value based on whether the product has been re-ordered or not. Save the function in a file having the function name. Use the procedure code to complete the Web page.

The navigation button/link name for the Web page is "Reorder List."

2. Generate and load PSP Web pages to the Oracle database server. (The instructor will provide the details on the database server accounts).

3. Open the Web site in the browser and print the display.

Ex5B-5. Run the script file outdoorDB_v4.sql to load the Outdoor Clubs & Product database tables necessary to complete this exercise. Create a single page PSP with the following content.

1. The Product Supplier List Web page displays (using tables feature) count of number of times a product has been ordered from a supplier. The table layout is shown below, with attributes from database in italics.

Product Supplier Details	
supplier_id	*name*
Product Name	**Times Ordered**
product_name	*ex62_time_ord function value*

Create a PL/SQL procedure "ex5b5_product_supplier_details" that displays the data required for the table. Save the procedure as a script file with filename ex5b5. Create a function ex5b5_time_ord that counts the number of times a product has been ordered from a given supplier. Use the function value in Times Ordered column. Save the function in a file having the function name. Use the procedure code to complete the Web page.

The navigation button name for the Web page is "Supplier Summary."

2. Generate and load PSP Web pages to the Oracle database server. (The instructor will provide the details on the database server accounts).

3. Open the Web site in the browser and print the display.

Ex5B-6. Run the script file outdoorDB_v4.sql to load the Outdoor Clubs & Product database tables necessary to complete this exercise. Create a single page PSP with the following content.

1. The Non Membership List Web page displays (using tables feature) customers who do not have club membership so far. The table layout is shown below, with attributes from database in italics.

Membership Status	
Customer Name	Membership Status
first_name last_name	*ex62_cust_status function value*

Create a PL/SQL procedure "ex5b6_membership_status" that displays the data required for the table. Save the procedure as a script file with filename ex5b6. Create a boolean function ex5b6_cust_status that returns a value on whether a customer is a member of a mountain club. The Membership Status column will display a 'Yes' value (if membership exists) or 'No' value (if membership does not exist). Save the function in a file having the function name. Use the procedure code to complete the Web page.

The navigation button/link name for the Web page is "Membership Status."

2. Generate and load PSP Web pages to the Oracle database server. (The instructor will provide the details on the database server accounts).

3. Open the Web site in the browser and print the display.

Ex5B-7. Run the script file outdoorDB_v4.sql to load the Outdoor Clubs & Product database tables necessary to complete this exercise. Create a Web site titled "Outdoor Product Reports" with three Web pages based on the previous problem solving exercises Ex5B-4, Ex5B-5, and Ex5B-6. The structure of Web site hierarchy is shown on the right.

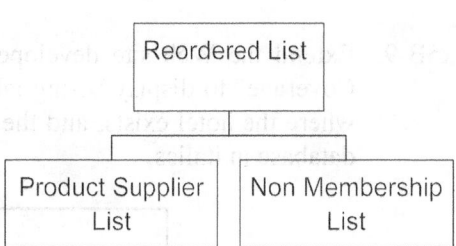

1. The Reordered List Web page is based on Ex5B-4. The Product Supplier List Web page is based on Ex5B-5. The Non Membership List Web page is based on Ex5B-6.

2. Combine the three functions in a package ex5b7_prod_rep_pkg. The procedures for the Web pages above should call their respective functions from the ex5b7_prod_rep_pkg package. Save the package specification as a script file with filename ex5b7a, and package body as a script file with filename ex5b7b.

3. The banner for the Web site should be "Outdoor Product Reports."

4. Generate and load PSP Web pages to the Oracle database server. (The instructor will provide the details on the database server accounts).

5. Open the Web site in the browser and print the display.

Ex5B-8. Run the script file travelDB_v4.sql to load the Travel Anywhere database tables necessary to complete this exercise. Create a one page Web site titled "ABC Travel Details" for an online travel agency. The Web page should display (using tables feature) for each geographic region the flight numbers, the destination, and the associated carrier. The table layout is shown below, with attributes from database in italics.

```
+-----------------------------------------------+
|              Airline Coverage                 |
|                                               |
|  Geographic Region:     region                |
|  _____  |
|                                               |
|     Carrier        Flights    Destination     |
|      name          flight_no    dest_city     |
+-----------------------------------------------+
```

1. Create a PL/SQL procedure "ex5b8_airline_coverage" that displays the data required for the table. Save the procedure as a script file with filename ex5b8. Use the procedure code to complete the Web page.

2. There should be no navigation button on the Web page. The banner for the Web site should be "ABC Travels."

3. Generate and load PSP Web pages to the Oracle database server. (The instructor will provide the details on the database server accounts).

4. Open the Web site in the browser and print the display.

Ex5B-9. Extend the Web site developed in Ex5B-8, by adding another Web page titled "Hotels Coverage" to display (using table feature) for each State, the hotels within the state, cities where the hotel exists, and the rate. The table layout is shown below, with attributes from database in italics.

```
+-----------------------------------------------+
|              Hotels Coverage                  |
|                                               |
|       State:     state                        |
|  _____  |
|                                               |
|     Name           City         Rate          |
|   hotel_name       city        $ rate         |
+-----------------------------------------------+
```

1. Create a PL/SQL procedure "ex5b9_hotels_coverage" that displays the data required for the table. Save the procedure as a script file with filename ex5b9. Use the procedure code to complete the Web page.

2. Add navigation button on the left side of the Web pages (vertical orientation) that will enable viewing of each Web page whenever desired. The banner for the Web site should be "ABC Travels."

3. Generate and load PSP Web pages to the Oracle database server. (The instructor will provide the details on the database server accounts).

4. Open the Web site in the browser and print the display.

Ex5B-10. Run the script file sentimentDB_v4.sql to load the Sentiments Anywhere database tables necessary to complete this exercise. Create a one page Web site titled "Sentiment Details" for an online company offering various sentiments for different occasions. The Web page should display details (using table feature) regarding Flowers type of sentiment. The display should categorize for each occasion, the various sentiments available, their price, and whether that sentiment has been ordered so far. The table layout is shown below, with attributes from database in italics.

```
┌─────────────────────────────────────────────┐
│                 Flower Usage                  │
│                                               │
│   Sentiment Occasion:        occasion         │
│  ───────────────────────────────────────────  │
│                                               │
│   Sentiment Name      Price       Ordered     │
│       name            price    function value │
└─────────────────────────────────────────────┘
```

1. Create a PL/SQL procedure "ex5b10_flower_usage" and a function "ex5b10_flower_ordered" that display the data required for the table. The procedure displays for each occasion the sentiment name and its price. Save the procedure as a script file with filename ex5b10a. The procedure calls the function which determines if the sentiment has been ordered (a 'Yes' value) or not (a 'No' value). Save the function as a script file with filename ex5b10b. If desired use a boolean function to accomplish the task. Use the procedure code to complete the Web page.

2. There should be no navigation button on the Web page. The banner for the Web site should be "Sentiment Anywhere." The home page should be named "Sentiment Use Details."

3. Generate and load PSP Web pages to the Oracle database server. (The instructor will provide the details on the database server accounts).

4. Open the Web site in the browser and print the display.

Ex5B-11. Extend the Web site developed in Ex5B-10, by adding another Web page titled "Gift Details." The Web page should display details (using table feature) regarding Gifts type of sentiment. The display should categorize for each occasion, the various sentiments available, their price, and whether that sentiment has been ordered so far. The table layout is shown below, with attributes from database in italics.

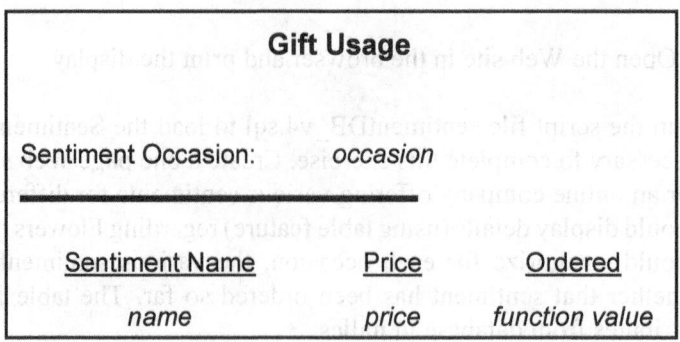

1. Create a PL/SQL procedure "ex5b11_gift_usage" and a function "ex5b11_gift_ordered" that display the data required for the table. The procedure displays for each occasion the sentiment name and its price. Save the procedure as a script file with filename ex5b11a. The procedure calls the function which determines if the sentiment has been ordered (a 'Yes' value) or not (a 'No' value). Save the function as a script file with filename ex5b11b. If desired use a boolean function to accomplish the task. Use the procedure code to complete the Web page.

2. Add navigation button on the left side of the Web pages (vertical orientation) that will enable viewing of each Web page whenever desired. The banner for the Web site should be "Sentiment Anywhere." The Web page should be named "Sentiment Use Details2."

3. Generate and load PSP Web pages to the Oracle database server. (The instructor will provide the details on the database server accounts).

4. Open the Web site in the browser and print the display.

Ex5B-12. Run the script file travelDB_v4.sql to load the Travel Anywhere database tables necessary to complete this exercise. Create a Web site titled "Travel Anywhere Reports" with three Web pages. The banner for the Web site should be "Travel Anywhere Reports." The structure of Web site hierarchy is shown on the right.

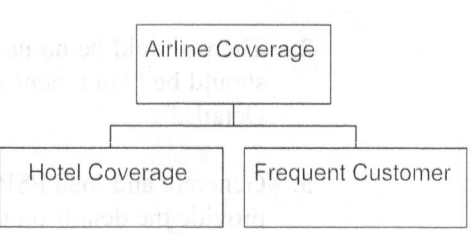

1. The home page should display (using tables feature) cities that are served by both airlines. The table layout is shown below, with attributes from database in italics.

```
┌─────────────────────────────────────────────────────────────┐
│                      Airline Coverage                         │
│                                                               │
│                                                               │
│   airline1 & airline2                                         │
│   ─────────────────────────────────────────                  │
│                                                               │
│                                                               │
│                    Cities                Region               │
│                  dest_city             dest_region            │
│                                                               │
│                                                               │
│   airline3                                                    │
│   ──────────────────────                                      │
│                                                               │
│                                                               │
│                    Cities                Region               │
│                  dest_city             dest_region            │
│                                                               │
└─────────────────────────────────────────────────────────────┘
```

Create a PL/SQL procedure "ex5b12_air_coverage" that displays the data required for the table. The procedure will first display cities that are served by both airlines (airline1 and airline2 value), and then only those cities that are served exclusively by the individual airline (airline3 value). Save the procedure as a script file with filename ex5b12a. Use the procedure code to complete the Web page.

The navigation button name for the Web page is "Airline Coverage."

2. The Hotel Coverage Web page should display (using tables feature) hotels that exist in various cities in the database. The table layout is shown below, with attributes from database in italics.

```
┌─────────────────────────────────────────────────────────┐
│                     Hotel Coverage                        │
│                                                           │
│                                                           │
│   city                                                    │
│   ─────────────────────                                   │
│                                                           │
│                                                           │
│                      Name                 Rate            │
│                   hotel_name            $ rate            │
│                                                           │
└─────────────────────────────────────────────────────────┘
```

Create a PL/SQL procedure "ex5b12_hotel_coverage" that displays the data required for the table. Save the procedure as a script file with filename ex5b12b. Use the procedure code to complete the Web page.

The navigation button name for the Web page is "Hotel Coverage."

3. The Frequent Customer Web page should display (using tables feature) list of customers along with whether they have had a flight or hotel reservation. The table layout is shown below, with attributes from database in italics.

Frequent Customer		
Name	Ticket Reservation	Hotel Reservation
first_name last_name	*ex67_check_air function value*	*ex67_check_hotel function value*

Create a PL/SQL procedure "ex5b12_freq_customer" that displays the data required for the table. Save the procedure as a script file with filename ex5b12c.pls

Create a boolean function ex5b12_check_air that returns a value on whether a customer has a ticket reservation. The Ticket Reservation column will display a 'Yes' value (if reservation exists) or 'No' value (if reservation does not exist). Save the function with the filename same as the function name.

Create a boolean function ex5b12_check_hotel that returns a value on whether a customer has a hotel reservation. The Hotel Reservation column will display a 'Yes' value (if reservation exists) or 'No' value (if reservation does not exist). Save the function with the filename same as the function name. Use the procedure code to complete the Web page.

The navigation button name for the Web page is "Frequent Customer."

4. Combine the procedures and functions in a package ex5b12_cover_pkg. Save the package specification as a script file with filename ex5b12d, and the package body as a script file with filename ex5b12e.

5. Generate and load PSP Web pages to the Oracle database server. (The instructor will provide the details on the database server accounts).

6. Open the Web site in the browser and print the display.

CHAPTER 6
(LESSON A)

Web Forms with PL/SQL Server Pages

- HTML (Web) Form Tags
- Create Web Form
- Input Form with Response Page

Forms in Web pages are essentially utilized to capture user input and transmit it to the database for processing. Typical forms on the Web include order forms, surveys, applications, or gathering search criteria from a user. The database server queries the database using the data gathered in the form, and returns the results to the Web browser. A Web page can have multiple forms. Forms can also be positioned and mixed with the rest of the page content. Figure 6-1 shows the interaction between the Web browser and the database server with respect to Web form.

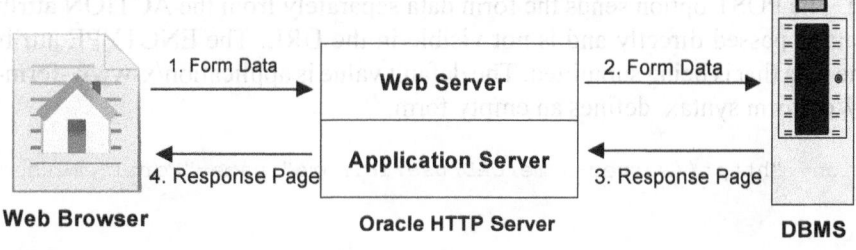

Figure 6-1

This chapter utilizes the table structure of Superflex Apartment database to explain examples.

WEB FORM

Each form is created with the `<form>` and `</form>` tag pair. There can be many forms in a Web page, wherein each form is contained in a separate `<form>` and `</form>` tag pair. However, forms cannot be nested within each other. The form tag has attributes that determine where the form data will be send, as well as other aspects of data submission. Table 6-1 gives the list of attributes and their purpose.

Attribute	Description
action	Specification of the URL to which form data will be submitted.
method	Determines how form data will be submitted.
enctype	Specification of the format of the data being submitted.
target	Specifies the window in which any results returned from the server appears.
name	Define a name for the form.

Table 6-1: HTML Form tag attributes

The ACTION attribute value names the URL where the form data is to be sent. If this attribute is excluded, the data is sent to the Web page URL that contains the form. The form input data is passed through the CGI mechanism. The METHOD attribute provides the mechanism to transfer data. This attribute has two values – GET or POST. The default option is GET, which appends form data to the URL in the ACTION attribute. In this case, the data values are passed in a query string of the URL, separated by "&" characters, with most non-alphanumeric characters in encoded format (such as "%20" for a space). The POST option sends the form data separately from the ACTION attribute URL. In this case, the data is passed directly and is not visible in the URL. The ENCTYPE attribute specifies the format of the data that is being submitted. The default value is application/x-www-form-urlencoded. The following Web form syntax defines an empty form.

```
<form action= "http://server-name/DAD/userid.home" name="Form1" method="POST">

</form>
```

The GET method format is more convenient for debugging and allows visitors to pass exactly the same parameters when they return to the page through a bookmark. The URL in this case looks something like this:

```
http://server-name/DAD/userid.pspname?parmname1=value1&parmname2=value2
```

The POST method format allows a larger volume of parameter data, and is suitable for passing sensitive information that should not be displayed in the URL. (URLs linger on in the browser's history list and in the CGI variables that are passed to the next-visited page.) It is not practical to bookmark pages that are called this way.

Each form can consist of one or more form elements like text box, radio buttons, check box, drop-down list, scrolling list, and multi-line text area (shown in Figure 6-2). Forms can also contain push buttons to perform actions on data in form elements.

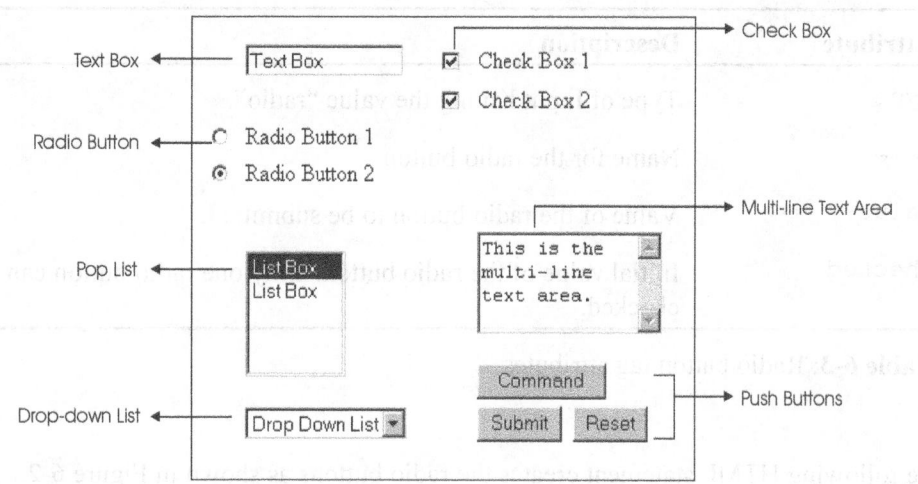

Figure 6-2   HTML Form Elements

Text Box

Text Box is where the user can enter information. The `<input>` tag is used for creating a text box. The attributes associated with the text box tag specification are shown in Table 6-2.

Attribute	Description
type	Type of Input. For text box the value is "text".
name	Name for the text box.
value	Set an initial value.
maxlength	The maximum number of characters that can be entered.
size	Display width of the text box.
readonly	To make text box read only.

Table 6-2: Text box tag attributes

The following HTML statement creates the text box as shown in Figure 6-2.

```
<input type=text name="text1" value="TextBox" size=25 maxlength=20>
```

Radio Button

Radio buttons show choices for selection. These buttons are part of a group. The `<input>` tag is also used for creating radio buttons where the TYPE attribute has the value "radio." All radio buttons in a group should have the same NAME attribute. The attributes associated with the radio button tag specifications are shown in Table 6-3.

Attribute	Description
type	Type of Input having the value "radio".
name	Name for the radio button.
value	Value of the radio button to be submitted.
checked	Initial value of the radio button. Only one radio button can be checked.

Table 6-3: Radio button tag attributes

The following HTML statement creates the radio buttons as shown in Figure 6-2.

```
<input type=radio name="radio1" value="RadioValue 1">Radio Button 1
<input type=radio name="radio1" value="RadioValue 2" checked>Radio Button 2
```

Check Box

Check boxes are used to allow users to include multiple values from a list of items. Check box can be set to yes (checked) or no (unchecked). The `<input>` tag is also used for creating check boxes where the TYPE attribute has the value "checkbox." Each check box can have different NAME/VALUE combination. However, like radio buttons, check boxes can also belong to a group by having the same NAME value, wherein multiple selections can be checked. The attributes associated with the check box tag specifications are shown in Table 6-4.

Attribute	Description
type	Type of Input having the value "checkbox".
name	Name for the check box.
value	Value of the check box to be submitted.
checked	Initial selection of the check box value.

Table 6-4: Check box tag attributes

The following HTML statement creates the check boxes as shown in Figure 6-2.

```
<input type=checkbox name="checkbox1" value="CheckBox 1" checked> Check Box 1
<input type=checkbox name="checkbox2" value="CheckBox 2" checked> Check Box 2
```

Selection List

Selection list shows a list of entries. Each displayed entry has an associated value. The final value of the selection list is the value associated with the selected entry. Selection list can appear as a *pop list* or as a *drop-down list*. Depending on the number of items in the list, a selection list can also include a scroll bar. Selection lists use the `<select> ... </select>` tag pair to display list of values for user to choose from. The attributes associated with the selection list tag specifications are shown in Table 6-5.

Attribute	Description
multiple	Specifies whether the user can select more than one item from the list.
name	Name for the selection list.
size	Specify how many lines of values will be displayed.

Table 6-5: Selection list tag attributes

There is an `<option>` tags inside the `<select>` tag pair to define the items that will appear in the selection list. The attributes within the `<option>` tag pairs are shown in Table 6-6.

Attribute	Description
label	Text to display in the selection list for list values.
value	Value of the text displayed in the list.
selected	Initial selection of a selection list value.

Table 6-6: Selection list OPTION tag attributes

The SIZE attribute determines whether the selection list is a drop-down list or a pop list. If the SIZE attribute is excluded or set to one, then the selection list is a drop-down list. The following HTML statements create the selection list as shown in Figure 6-2. A pop list is created first followed by the drop-down list.

```
<select name="FormsComboBox2" size=5 >
    <option value="1" selected>List Box</option>
    <option value="2">List Box</option>
</select>

<select name="FormsComboBox1" >
    <option value="1" selected>Drop Down List</option>
    <option value="2">Drop Down List</option>
</select>
```

Multi-Line Text Area

Multi-Line text area use the `<textarea> ... </textarea>` tag pair to create an area for user to enter multiple lines of information. The attributes associated with the multiline text area tag specifications are shown in Table 6-7.

Attribute	Description
name	Name for the text area.
col	The number of columns to be displayed in the text area.
rows	The number of rows to be displayed in the text area.

Table 6-7: Multi-Line text area tag attributes

The following HTML statement creates the multi-line text area as shown in Figure 6-2.

```
<testarea name="FormsMultiLine1" rows=4 cols=14 >This is the multi-line text area.
</textarea>
```

Buttons

Buttons in a form can be of different types to perform different functions. A button of SUBMIT type will submit the contents of the form to a Web server. A button of RESET type will reset the existing values in the form to the default values (set at the time of form loading). A button of COMMAND type will perform other functions as coded. The `<input>` tag is used for creating a button. The attributes associated with the button tag specification are shown in Table 6-8.

Attribute	Description
type	Type of Input.
name	Name for the button.
value	Display label on the button.

Table 6-8: Button tag attributes

The following HTML statement creates the *submit* button as shown in Figure 6-2.

```
<input type=submit name="FormsButton1" value="Submit">
```

The following HTML statement creates the *reset* button as shown in Figure 6-2.

```
<input type=reset name="FormsButton2" value="Reset">
```

The following HTML statement creates the *command* button as shown in Figure 6-2.

```
<input type=submit name="FormsButton3" value="Command">
```

It should be noted that unlike other HTML tags, the `<input>` tag is empty, it contains attributes only. Also, the `<input>` tag has no end tag. In XHTML the `<input>` tag must be properly closed like `<input ... />`.

Hidden Field Values

In form processing, when the Submit type button is pressed, the form element values are send to the server. Hidden field values are additional values beside the form element values that need to be also passed to the database server.

Hidden field values can either be static (fixed) values, input parameter values or variable values. To assign variable values to hidden fields, these variables must have their values set before the <FORM> tag is executed. The syntax of hidden input field is:

```
<input type=hidden name="hiddentext1" value="hiddenvalue">
```

TUTORIAL ON INPUT FORM WITH RESPONSE PAGE

The following tutorial creates a two page Web site, with the home page having a Web form. Run the script file superflexDB_v4.sql to load the Superflex Apartments Database tables necessary to complete this tutorial. The outline of the home page with Web form is shown in Figure 6-3.

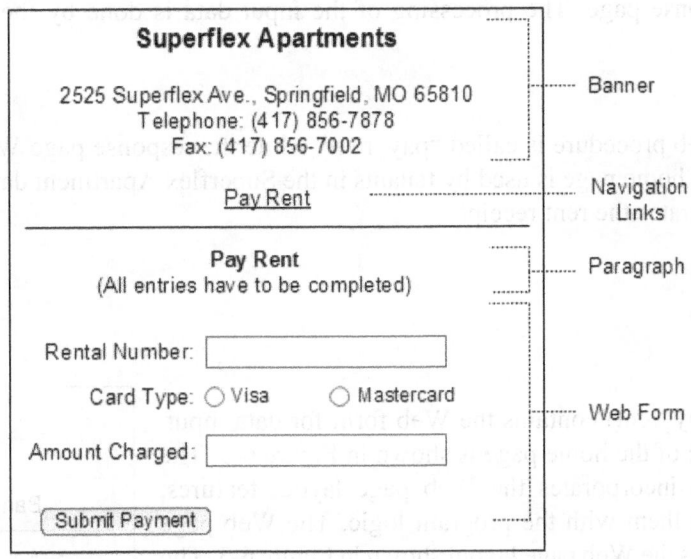

Figure 6-3

The second page serves as the response page. The outline of the response page is shown in Figure 6-4.

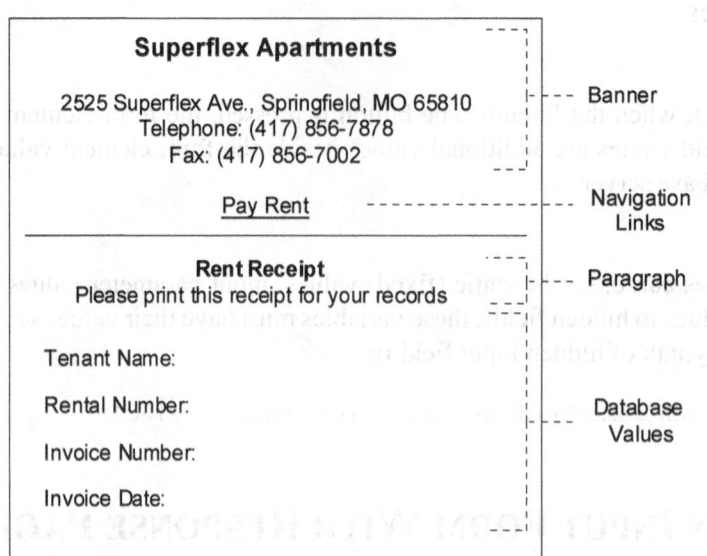

Figure 6-4

In the database, both the Web pages are Web procedures that communicate with each other. Technically the Web (page) procedure with the Web form sends the input data to the Web (page) procedure that serves as the response page. The processing of the input data is done by the Web (page) response procedure.

The home page Web procedure is called "pay_rent" while the response page Web procedure is called "rent_receipt." The home page is used by tenants in the Superflex Apartment database to pay rent. The response page generates the rent receipt.

Pay_Rent Web Page

The home page (pay_rent) contains the Web form for data input. The flowchart logic of the home page is shown in Figure 6-5. The logic diagram also incorporates the Web page layout features, thereby embedding them with the program logic. The Web page logic control follows the Web page layout shown in Figure 6-3. The Web form elements appear in same sequence as shown in the Web page layout after the `<form>` tag. It is important to make a note of the form element names as they would appear in the response page as input parameters.

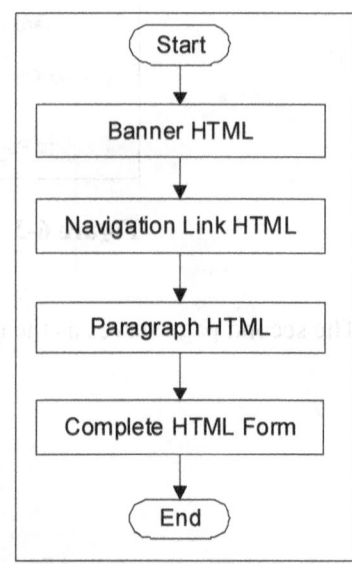

The complete PSP (filename pay_rent.psp) using Web Template 1 is shown below. The navigation URL and the `<form>` tag ACTION attribute URL should be modified to suit the existing server configuration in the form of server-name, DAD, and userid. It is important to include the response page Web procedure name in the `<form>` tag action attribute URL to correctly send the form data to the response page.

Figure 6-5

```
<!DOCTYPE HTML PUBLIC "-//W3C//DTD HTML 4.01 Transitional//EN">
<html>
<%@page language="PL/SQL"%>
<%@plsql procedure="pay_rent"%>
<head>
<title>Pay Rent</title>
</head>
<body>
<div align="center"><p><h2>Superflex Apartments</h2>
2525 Superflex Ave, Springfield, MO 65810<br />
Telephone:(417) 856-7878<br />
Fax: (417) 856-7002</p>
<!-- Navigation Bar Links -->
<a href="http://server-name/DAD/userid.pay_rent">Pay Rent</a><br>
<hr /></div>
<br> <!-- Start Page Content -->
<p><b>Pay Rent</b><br />
(All entries have to be completed)</p>
<form action="http://server-name/DAD/userid.rent_receipt" method="post">
Rental Number: <input type="text" name="rental_no_text" value="" /> <br /><br />
Card Type: <input type="radio" name="cc_type_text" value="Visa"/> Visa
<input type="radio" name="cc_type_text" value="Mastercard"/> Mastercard <br /><br />
Amount Charged: <input type="text" name="invoice_due_text" value="" /><br /><br />
<input type="submit" name="FormsButton1" value="Submit Payment"/>
</form>
<!-- End Page Content -->
</body>
</html>
```

Rent_Receipt Web Page

The response page (rent_receipt) processes the input data sent by the home page, and displays a rent receipt using HTML tables. The flowchart logic of the response page is shown in Figure 6-5. The logic diagram also incorporates the Web page layout features, thereby embedding them with the program logic. The Web page logic control follows the Web page layout shown in Figure 6-6.

The PSP statements first perform the INSERT operation on the RENTAL_INVOICE table based on the data received from the home page through input parameters. The SQL queries thereafter are utilized to complete the receipt. These queries (i) fetch the new INVOICE_NUMBER from the rental_invoice_sequence sequence, and (ii) also fetch the TENANT_NAME attribute value associated with the input RENTAL_NO value. Once all the database information for displaying the receipt is available, the HTML table for rent receipt is completed where the database values are placed as PSP expression statements. The key feature in the database processing performed by the response page is the accurate specification of input parameters.

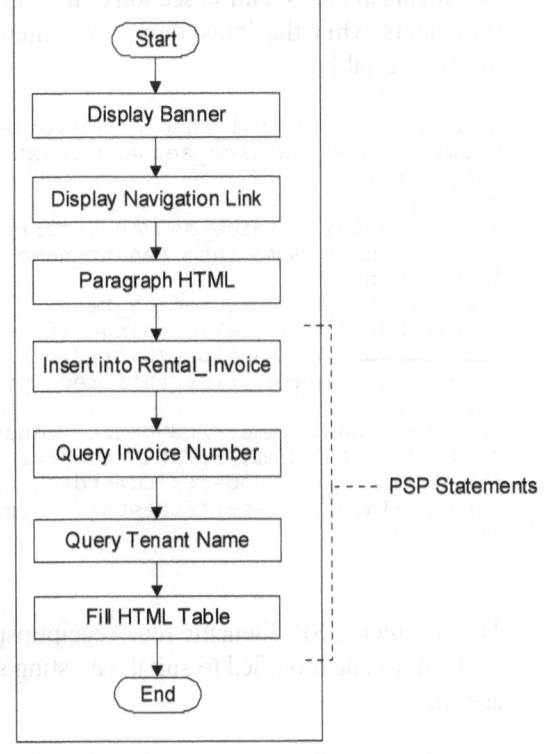

Figure 6-6

To facilitate accuracy and better understanding of the database processing involved in the Web page, a two step approach is outlined. The first step is to develop a focused PL/SQL procedure that concentrates on just the PL/SQL processing aspect of the Web page. In this case, the database values that will be displayed through the Web page are tested through the dbms_output statements. The PL/SQL procedure ch6_rent_receipt outlines the PL/SQL processing aspect of the Web page with the dbms_output statements showing the values that will be displayed as rent receipt. The input parameters of the procedure are named similar to the form element names in the home page (pay_rent) PSP.

```
create or replace procedure ch6_rent_receipt (rental_no_text varchar2,
            cc_type_text varchar2, invoice_due_text varchar2,
            formsbutton1 varchar2) is
tenant_name_text tenant.tenant_name%type;
invoice_no_text rental_invoice.invoice_no%type;
begin
insert into rental_invoice (invoice_no,invoice_date,invoice_due,cc_type,rental_no)
values(rental_invoice_sequence.nextval,sysdate,invoice_due_text,cc_type_text,rental
_no_text);
commit;
select rental_invoice_sequence.currval into invoice_no_text from dual;
select tenant_name into tenant_name_text
from tenant
where rental_no = rental_no_text;
dbms_output.put_line('Tenant Name '||tenant_name_text);
dbms_output.put_line('Rental No '||rental_no_text);||
dbms_output.put_line('Invoice No '||invoice_no_text);
dbms_output.put_line(' Date '||invoice_date_text);
end;
```

The next step is to transfer the PL/SQL procedure statements to the PSP. In this case the block of PL/SQL statements in the execution section of the PL/SQL procedure ch6_rent_receipt appear as PSP processing statements, while the dbms_output statement database values become the PSP expression statements of the HTML table.

```
<% insert into rental_invoice (invoice_no,invoice_date,invoice_due,cc_type,rental_no)
values(rental_invoice_sequence.nextval,sysdate,invoice_due_text,cc_type_text,rental
_no_text);
commit;
select rental_invoice_sequence.currval into invoice_no_text from dual;
select tenant_name into tenant_name_text
from tenant
where rental_no = rental_no_text; %>
<table border="0" cellpadding="1" cellspacing="1" summary="">
<tr><td><b>Rent Receipt</b></td></tr>
<tr><td><i>Please print this receipt for your records.</i></td></tr>
<tr></tr>
<tr><td>Tenant Name:</td><td><%=tenant_name_text%></td></tr>
<tr><td>Rental Number:</td><td><%=rental_no_text%></td></tr>
<tr><td>Invoice Number:</td><td><%=invoice_no_text%></td></tr>
<tr><td>Invoice Date:</td><td><%=sysdate%></td></tr>
</table>
```

The complete PSP (filename rent_receipt.psp) using Web Template 1 is shown below. The navigation URL should be modified to suit the existing server configuration in the form of server-name, DAD, and userid.

```
<!DOCTYPE HTML PUBLIC "-//W3C//DTD HTML 4.01 Transitional//EN">
<html>
<%@page language="PL/SQL"%>
<%@plsql procedure="rent_receipt"%>
<%@plsql parameter="rental_no_text" default="null"%>
<%@plsql parameter="cc_type_text" default="null"%>
```

```
<%@plsql parameter="invoice_due_text" default="null"%>
<%@plsql parameter="formsbutton1" default="null"%>
<%! tenant_name_text tenant.tenant_name%type;
invoice_no_text rental_invoice.invoice_no%type; %>
<head>
<title>Rent Receipt</title>
</head>
<body>
<div align="center"><p><h2>Superflex Apartments</h2>
2525 Superflex Ave, Springfield, MO 65810<br />
Telephone:(417) 856-7878<br />
Fax: (417) 856-7002</p>
<!-- Navigation Bar Links -->
<a href="http://server-name/DAD/userid.pay_rent">Pay Rent</a><br>
<hr /></div>
<br> <!-- Start Page Content -->
<% insert into rental_invoice (invoice_no,invoice_date,invoice_due,cc_type,rental_no)
values(rental_invoice_sequence.nextval,sysdate,invoice_due_text,cc_type_text,rental
_no_text);
commit;
select rental_invoice_sequence.currval into invoice_no_text from dual;
select tenant_name into tenant_name_text
from tenant
where rental_no = rental_no_text; %>
<table border="0" cellpadding="1" cellspacing="1" summary="">
<tr><td><b>Rent Receipt</b></td></tr>
<tr><td><i>Please print this receipt for your records.</i></td></tr>
<tr></tr>
<tr><td>Tenant Name:</td><td><%=tenant_name_text%></td></tr>
<tr><td>Rental Number:</td><td><%=rental_no_text%></td></tr>
<tr><td>Invoice Number:</td><td><%=invoice_no_text%></td></tr>
<tr><td>Invoice Date:</td><td><%=sysdate%></td></tr>
</table>
<!-- End Page Content -->
</body>
</html>
```

Load PSP to the Database

Once the PSP have been completed, open the Windows Command Prompt window to execute the loadpsp command for the PSP files. The command to load the two PSPs will be:

```
loadpsp -replace -user userid/password@connection_string
                    drive&path\pay_rent.psp

loadpsp -replace -user userid/password@connection_string
                    drive&path\rent_receipt.psp
```

The userid, password, connection string and path specifications depend on database configuration. If there are errors in the page, fix the errors and re-load the page.

View PSP in Web Browser

Once the loading is successful type the URL below to retrieve the Web page from the database. The URL should be modified to suit the existing server configuration in the form of server-name, DAD, and userid.

```
http://server-name/DAD/userid.pay_rent
```

A sample runtime of the PSPs in a Web browser is shown in Figure 6-7 for the home page, and Figure 6-8 for the response page.

Superflex Apartments

2525 Superflex Ave, Springfield, MO 65810
Telephone:(417) 856-7878
Fax: (417) 856-7002

Pay Rent

Pay Rent
(All entries have to be completed)

Rental Number: 100101

Card Type: ⊙ Visa   ○ Mastercard

Amount Charged: 500

[Submit Payment]

Figure 6-7

Superflex Apartments

2525 Superflex Ave, Springfield, MO 65810
Telephone:(417) 856-7878
Fax: (417) 856-7002

Pay Rent

Rent Receipt
Please print this receipt for your records.

Tenant Name:	Jack Robin
Rental Number:	100101
Invoice Number:	1028
Invoice Date:	04-JUN-08

Figure 6-8

CHAPTER SUMMARY

▸ Forms in Web pages are essential to capture user input and transmit that information for processing. The database server queries the database using the data gathered in the form, and returns the results to the Web browser.

▸ Typical forms on the Web include order forms, surveys, applications, or gathering search criteria from a user.

▸ A Web page can have multiple forms.

▸ Forms can also be positioned and mixed with the rest of the page contents.

▸ Each form is created within the `<form>` and `</form>` tag pairs.

▸ The `<form>` tag has attributes that determine where the form data will be send, as well as other aspects of data submission.

▸ Each form can consist of one or more form elements like text box, radio buttons, check box, drop-down list, scrolling list, and multi-line text area.

▸ Text Box allow user to enter information directly.

▸ Radio buttons show choices for selection.

▸ Check boxes allow users to include multiple values from a list of items.

▸ Selection list shows a list of entries. Each displayed entry has an associated value. The final value of the selection list is the value associated with the selected entry.

▸ Multi-Line text area provide an area for user to enter multiple lines of information.

▸ Forms also contain push buttons to perform actions on data in form elements.

▸ A form button of SUBMIT type will submit the contents of the form to a Web server.

▸ A form button of RESET type will reset the existing values in the form to the default values (set at the time of form loading).

▸ A form button of COMMAND type will perform other functions as coded.

▸ Forms can also contain hidden fields where additional data besides the form element values can be passed with the form submission.

▸ Major attributes in forms setup include the ACTION attribute where the URL for the Web page (PL/SQL Web procedure) that will receive the form data is specified, and the METHOD specification on the nature of form data submission.

REVIEW QUESTIONS

1. Describe the different form elements.

2. Explain the two ways in which form data can be submitted.

3. What is the purpose of the ACTION attribute in the `<form>` tag?

4. Explain the purpose of three types of form buttons.

5. Why multiple radio buttons are required for a value in a Web form.

6. What is the significance of the response page during input form processing?

7. Explain the purpose of hidden fields.

REVIEW EXERCISES

1. Web forms are used to capture user _____ in a Web page.

2. The HTML tag to define a form is _____.

3. The _____ attribute specifies of the URL to which the form data will be submitted.

4. The _____ attribute indicates how the form data will be submitted.

5. The two methods of submitting form data are _____ and _____.

6. The form element where the user can enter information is _____.

7. The form element that shows choices for selection is _____.

8. Each choice is represented by a single _____.

9. The form element for selection list can appear as _____ list.

10. A radio button label may be different from its assigned _____.

11. A _____ type of button submits the contents of the form to the Web server.

12. A _____ type of button resets the existing values in the form to the default values.

13. A form can have _____ submit and reset type buttons.

14. All submit type of buttons will submit entered form data to the same URL for processing.

15.   During submission of form values to the database server, each form element name becomes a _____ name in the response procedure.

16.   During submission of form values to the database server, each form button name becomes a _____ name in the response procedure.

PROBLEM SOLVING EXERCISES

Ex6A-1.   Run the script file sentimentDB_v4.sql to load the Sentiments Anywhere database tables necessary to complete this exercise. Create a two page Web site titled "Sentiment Order" for an online company offering various sentiments to existing customers for different occasions. The Home Web page should display an input form for users to enter ordering details on the sentiment. The response Web page should check if the sentiment is valid and available, and then display a receipt for printing.

1. The Home page should be titled "Order Sentiment." The response page should be titled "Sentiment Receipt." There should be only one navigation link titled after the Home page. The navigation URL should link to the home page. The banner for both the Web pages should be "Sentiment for Occasion."

2. The Home page input form should use text box form element for Sentiment ID and Quantity corresponding to their respective attributes. The Customer ID form element is a drop-down list where the various customer names and their customer_id attributes appear as Name/Value pair. The default customer name should be "Sania Raina." The Payment Type uses a radio button for the two values of payment_type attribute. The Clear button is of reset type, while the Process Order button is of submit type. The Home page layout is shown below.

3. The response page should either display a text message "The sentiment ordered is not valid!!! Click the Order Sentiment link to place the order again" if the Sentiment ID entered is not valid by checking with the database.

    For valid Sentiment ID, display a table titled Order Receipt as shown below. Include a flat Shipping & Handling fee of $6. The Order Date is the current date, while the Ship Date is 5 days after the Order Date.

Sentiment for Occasion

Order Sentiment

Order Receipt
(Please Print Receipt for your records)
Customer ID:
Customer Name:
Order ID:
Order Date:
Shipping & Handling: $ 6.00
Order Total:
Ship Date:

4. Create a PL/SQL procedure "ex6a1_order_receipt" that completes the processing of the response page in the form of:
   (i) inserting the new order information in sentiment_order and sentiment_details tables.
   (ii) updating the inventory information in the sentiment table.

   The procedure should make provision for the display of text message as well as the completion of application processing and Order Receipt table. Create a sequence "sentiment_order_id_sequence" starting with 1010 to insert order_id attribute value in sentiment_order table. Save the procedure as a script file with filename ex6a1. Use the procedure code to complete the Web page.

5. Generate and load PSP Web pages to the Oracle database server. (The instructor will provide the details on the database server accounts).

6. If some clipart is utilized in the Web page, transfer the image to the required virtual folder. (The instructor will provide the necessary instructions on this step).

7. Open the Web site in the browser and print the display.

Ex6A-2. Extend the Web site developed in Ex6A-1 by creating new PL/SQL program units to further optimize the site. Rename the home page as order_sentiment2, and the response page as sentiment_receipt2.

1. Develop a function "ex6a2_sentiment_shipping" that calculates the shipping cost based on the zip code. The following table can be used to do the calculation.

Zip Codes	Shipping & Handling cost
All zip code having 63 as first two digits	6.00
All zip code having 64 as first two digits	6.00
All zip code having 65 as first two digits	8.50

Save the function as a script file with filename ex6a2a.

2. Extend the previously created procedure ex6a1_order_receipt (rename it as "ex6a2_order_receipt2" with call to function ex6a2_sentiment_shipping. Save the procedure as a script file with filename ex6a2b. Use the procedure code to complete the Web page.

3. Generate and load PSP Web pages to the Oracle database server. (The instructor will provide the details on the database server accounts).

4. If some clipart is utilized in the Web page, transfer the image to the required virtual folder. (The instructor will provide the necessary instructions on this step).

5. Open the Web site in the browser and print the display.

Ex6A-3.   Run the script file outdoorDB_v4.sql to load the Outdoor Clubs & Product database tables necessary to complete this exercise. Create a two page Web site that allows users to join the various sporting clubs. The home page should display an input form for users to enter information for club membership. The response page should display a membership receipt for printing.

1. The home page should be titled "Apply Membership." The response page should be titled "Membership Receipt." There should be only one navigation link titled after the Home page. The navigation URL should link to the home page. The banner for both the Web pages should be "Sporting Clubs."

2. The Home page layout is shown below. It will have an input form that has text box form element for Customer First Name, Customer Last Name, Street, City, Zip Code, and Phone corresponding to their respective attributes. Phone numbers can be entered using either (xxx)xxx-xxxx or (xxx) xxx-xxxx or xxx-xxx-xxxx formats. The State form element is a drop-down list where the various states and their short forms appear as Name/Value pair. The default state should be "Missouri." List at least 5 states. The Sporting Clubs form element is a drop-down list where the various sporting club names and their club_id attributes appear as Name/Value pair. The default sporting club is "Hillside Mountain Club." The Membership Duration form element is a drop-down list where the membership for 2, 4, 5, and 12 months appear as Name/Value pair. The default membership is for 4 months. The Payment Type uses a radio button for the two values of payment_type attribute. The Clear button is of reset type, while the Process Application button is of submit type.

Sporting Clubs

Apply Membership

Membership Form

Customer First Name [   ]

Customer Last Name [   ]

Street [   ]

City [   ]

State [Missouri ▾]

Zip Code [   ]

Phone: [   ]

Sporting Club: [Hillside Mountain Club ▾]

Membership Duration: [4 ▾] months *(Fee is $50 per month)*

Method of Payment: ○ Check ● Credit Card

[Clear]   [Process Application]

3. The response page should display the Membership Receipt table and a thank you text below the receipt. The membership is $50 per month. The layout of the response page is shown below.

Sporting Clubs

Apply Membership

Membership Receipt

Membership ID:

Membership Date:

Duration:

Customer ID:

Customer Name:

Sporting Club:

Thank you for your membership.
We appreciate your business.

4. Create a PL/SQL procedure "ex6a3_membership_receipt" that completes the response page procedure processing. The procedure should complete the database processing required for the page and display the membership receipt values. Create a sequence

"outdoor_cust_id_sequence" starting with 106 to insert customer_id values in customer table. Create another sequence "outdoor_member_id_sequence" starting with 10040 with increments of 10. The outdoor_member_id_sequence should be used to insert membership_id values in club_membership table. Save the procedure as a script file with filename ex6a3. Use the procedure code to complete the Web page.

5. Generate and load PSP Web pages to the Oracle database server. (The instructor will provide the details on the database server accounts).

6. If some clipart is utilized in the Web page, transfer the image to the required virtual folder. (The instructor will provide the necessary instructions on this step).

7. Open the Web site in the browser and print the display.

Ex6A-4.   Run the script file outdoorDB_v4.sql to load the Outdoor Clubs & Product database tables necessary to complete this exercise. Create a two page Web site that creates a new sporting club entry. The Home Web page should display an input form to enter information for the new club. The response Web page should display a message after creating the new club successfully. The Home page layout is shown below.

The layout of the response page is as follows:

1. The home page should be titled "Input Club." The response page should be titled "Create Club." There should be only one navigation link titled after the Home page. The navigation URL should link to the home page. The banner for both the Web pages should be "Sporting Clubs."

2. Create a procedure "ex6a4_create_club" to complete the insertion of new club information in the sporting_clubs table. Use the sequence club_sequence to insert the new club_id. The procedure should display the new club name as well as the generated club_id. Save the procedure as a script file with filename ex6a4. Use the procedure code to complete the response Web page. In the response page the club-name and club-id entries are database values.

3. Generate and load PSP Web pages to the Oracle database server. (The instructor will provide the details on the database server accounts).

4. If some clipart is utilized in the Web page, transfer the image to the required virtual folder. (The instructor will provide the necessary instructions on this step).

5. Open the Web site in the browser and print the display.

Ex6A-5.   Extend the chapter tutorial by changing the rental number input to apartment number input, and also display an error message if the Amount Charged entry is not the same as apt_rent_amt value . Essentially, allow the user to pay rent using their apartment number and some error checking. The modified home page is shown below.

Superflex Apartments

2525 Superflex Ave., Springfield, MO 65810
Telephone: (417) 856-7878
Fax: (417) 856-7002

Pay Rent

Pay Rent
(All entries have to be completed)

Apartment Number: [   ]

Card Type: ○ Visa   ○ Mastercard

Amount Charged: [   ]

[Submit Payment]

---

1. The response page will either display a text message "The amount entered is not correct! Please click Pay Rent to complete payment details!!" or display the rent receipt.

2. The home page should be titled "Pay Rent2." The response page should be titled "Rent Receipt2." There should be only one navigation link titled after the Home page. The navigation URL should link to the home page. The banner for both the Web pages should be "Superflex Apartments."

3. Create a PL/SQL procedure to complete the response page procedure processing. The procedure should be named ex6a5_rent_reciept. The procedure should either display the text message or complete the processing and display the rent receipt database values.

Save the procedure as a script file with filename ex6a5. Use the procedure code to complete the Web page.

4. Generate and load PSP Web pages to the Oracle database server. (The instructor will provide the details on the database server accounts).

5. If some clipart is utilized in the Web page, transfer the image to the required virtual folder. (The instructor will provide the necessary instructions on this step).

6. Open the Web site in the browser and print the display.

Ex6A-6. Run the script file travelDB_v4.sql to load the Travel Anywhere database tables necessary to complete this exercise. Create a two page Web site that searches for available flights between two cities and displays a travel itinerary. The Home page is should be titled "Search Flight." It should display an input form to select the two cities using a drop-down list box. The form layout to is shown on the right.

The response Web page should be titled "Search Results." It should either (i) display a message "There are no flight connections between the Origin City and Destination City. Please go back and try different cities" if there are no connecting flights between the two cities, or (ii) the travel itinerary (layout shown below).

1. There should be only one navigation link titled "Home." The navigation URL should link to the home page. The banner for both the Web pages should be "Travel Anywhere."

2. Create a PL/SQL procedure "ex6a6_search_results" that completes the response page processing. The procedure should either display the text message or complete the processing and display the travel itinerary database values. Save the procedure as a script file with filename ex6a6. Use the procedure code to complete the Web page.

3. Generate and load PSP Web pages to the Oracle database server. (The instructor will provide the details on the database server accounts).

4. If some clipart is utilized in the Web page, transfer the image to the required virtual folder. (The instructor will provide the necessary instructions on this step).

5. Open the Web site in the browser and print the display.

Ex6A-7.   Run the script file travelDB_v4.sql to load the Travel Anywhere database tables necessary to complete this exercise. Create a two page Web site that searches for available flights between two cities to complete the air reservation and generates a ticket receipt. Utilize problem Ex6A-6 to complete the processing. The Home page should be titled "Air Reservations." It should display an input form to enter reservation data. The home page layout is shown on the right.

The response Web page should be titled "Air Receipt." It should either (i) display a message "There are no flight connections between the Origin City and Destination City. Please go back and try different cities" if there are no connecting flights between the two cities, or (ii) a flight ticket receipt along with the travel itinerary (layout shown below).

Travel Anywhere

Home

Flight Ticket Receipt
Ticket Number:
Customer Name:
Issued Date:
Flight Date:
Origin City:
Destination City:
Fare:

Travel Itinerary

Airline	Flight Number	Origin City	Destination City
...	...	...	...

1. There should be only one navigation link titled "Home." The navigation URL should link to the home page. The banner for both the Web pages should be "Travel Anywhere."

2. Create a PL/SQL procedure "ex6a7_air_receipt" that completes the response page procedure processing. Utilize the logic for generating the search results in previous problem solving exercise (Ex6A-6) to complete the travel itinerary. The procedure should either display the text message or complete the processing and display the travel receipt and travel itinerary database values. Save the procedure as a script file with filename ex6a7. Use the procedure code to complete the Web page.

3. Generate and load PSP Web pages to the Oracle database server. (The instructor will provide the details on the database server accounts).

4. If some clipart is utilized in the Web page, transfer the image to the required virtual folder. (The instructor will provide the necessary instructions on this step).

5. Open the Web site in the browser and print the display.

Ex6A-8.   Run the script file travelDB_v4.sql to load the Travel Anywhere database tables necessary to complete this exercise. Create a two page Web site that completes a hotel reservation and generates a reservation receipt. The Home page should be titled "Hotel Reservations." It should display an input form to enter reservation data. The home page layout is shown below.

Travel Anywhere

Home

Hotel Reservation
Hotel Name: Iberville Suites, New Orleans, LA ▼
Arrival Date: [   ] (use mm/dd/yy format)
Departure Date: [   ] (use mm/dd/yy format)
Number of Adults: One ▼
Number of Kids: [   ]
Baby Crib: ○ Yes ○ No
Customer ID: [   ]
[Make Reservation]

The response Web page should be titled "Hotel Receipt." It contains a table that displays the hotel reservation receipt. The response page layout is shown below.

Travel Anywhere

Home

Hotel Reservation Receipt
Reservation Number:
Customer Name:
Reservation Date:
Hotel Name:
Arrival Date:
Departure Date:
Number of Adults:

1. There should be only one navigation link titled "Home." The navigation URL should link to the home page. The banner for both the Web pages should be "Travel Anywhere."

2. Create a PL/SQL procedure "ex6a8_hotel_receipt" that completes the Hotel Receipt page processing. The procedure should complete the database processing required for the page and display the hotel reservation receipt values. Save the procedure as a script file with filename ex6a8. Use the procedure code to complete the Web page.

3. Generate and load PSP Web pages to the Oracle database server. (The instructor will provide the details on the database server accounts).

4. If some clipart is utilized in the Web page, transfer the image to the required virtual folder. (The instructor will provide the necessary instructions on this step).

5. Open the Web site in the browser and print the display.

Ex6A-9.   Run the script file travelDB_v4.sql to load the Travel Anywhere database tables necessary to complete this exercise. Create a Web page that links the Web pages of exercise Ex6A-7 and Ex6A-8. The hierarchical site layout along with page titles is shown on the right.

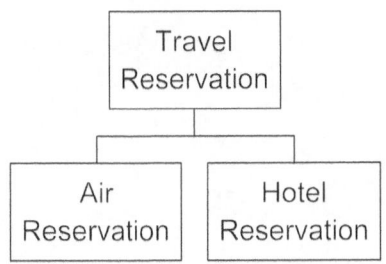

The site now makes travel reservations for both air and hotel. For air reservations, it utilizes the Web site created in the previous problem solving exercise Ex6A-7. For hotel reservations, it utilizes the Web site created in the previous problem solving exercise Ex6A-8.

The home page displays two form areas as shown below. Each form area has only one form button element. The Air Reservation button links to the Air Reservation home page of Ex6A-7, while the Hotel Reservation button links to the Hotel Reservation home page of Ex6A-8.

1. Generate and load PSP Web pages to the Oracle database server. (The instructor will provide the details on the database server accounts).

2. If some clipart is utilized in the Web page, transfer the image to the required virtual folder. (The instructor will provide the necessary instructions on this step).

3.   Open the Web site in the browser and print the display.

Web Forms with PL/SQL Server Pages

- Load Database Values in Web Forms
- Flexible Parameter Passing

Web forms are also utilized for display of previously stored information as well as their modifications in the database. Loading of database data in forms is different from retrieving such data in table or text displays. Loaded database values become the default values of form elements in the browser.

> This chapter utilizes the table structure of Superflex Apartment database to explain examples.

WEB FORM WITH PSP STATEMENTS

Text Box

Loading of database values within a text box is done through a PSP expression statement. The value of the PSP expression is associated with the VALUE attribute of the text box. For example, if *variable_i* is a PL/SQL variable, then the following syntax for the text box tag will display the value of this variable when the PSP expression `<%= variable_i %>` is executed. The value of *variable_i* now becomes the default value when the text box value is loaded in the Web browser.

```
<input type=text name="text1" value="<%= variable_i %>" size=25 maxlength=20>
```

To make a text box read only in browser, extend the associated text box tag with "`readonly`" keyword. For example,

```
<input type=text name="text1" value="<%= variable_i %>" size=25 maxlength=20 readonly>
```

Radio Button

A radio button aside from its assigned value, will either have a checked (or selected) display or an unchecked display. The setting for checked or unchecked display is based on the presence or absence of "checked" attribute in the radio button tag. PSP allows for the correct radio button value to show the associated checked attribute. This is accomplished by embedding each radio button with an IF/THEN PSP statement *inside the tag* to set the "checked" attribute. For example, the following radio button tag

329

syntax shows a checked radio button if some PL/SQL condition is true. The result of PL/SQL statement processing becomes the default setting for the radio button in the Web browser.

```
<input type=radio name="radio1" value="RadioValue 2" <%if ..condition.. then%>checked
<%end if;%>>Radio Button 2
```

Check Box

A check box aside from its assigned value, will either have a checked (or selected) display or an unchecked display. The setting for checked or unchecked display is based on the presence or absence of "checked" attribute in the check box tag. PSP allows for the correct check box value to show the associated checked attribute. This is accomplished by embedding a check box with an an IF/THEN PSP statement *inside the tag* to set the "checked" attribute. For example, the following check box syntax shows a checked check box if some PL/SQL condition is true. The result of PL/SQL statement processing becomes the default setting for the check box in the Web browser.

```
<input type=checkbox name="checkbox2" value="CheckBox 2" <%if ..condition.. then%>
checked <%end if;%>>Check Box 2
```

Selection List

Selection list appears in two styles – drop down menu list or pop list. The PSP statements to load database values for either style is similar. To populate a selection list NAME/VALUE pair values with database values, position a PSP cursor loop statement around the <OPTION> tag, and then use the PSP expression statements for <OPTION> tag name/value pair values. For example, the following syntax shows a pop list tag being populated with database values based on a cursor query. The result of PL/SQL statement processing becomes the default setting for selection list in the Web browser.

```
<select name="FormsComboBox2" size=5 >
    <%for cursor_row in cursor_query loop%>
    <option value="<%=cursor_row.attribute%>"><%=cursor_row.attribute%></option>
    <%end loop;%>
</select>
```

To generate a database generated drop-down list values involving default SELECTED attribute, a PSP IF/THEN statement needs to be embedded for the NAME/VALUE pair values. For example, the following syntax shows a pop list tag being populated with database values wherein the default display value with SELECTED attribute is based on some condition.

```
<select name="FormsComboBox2" size=5 >
    <% for cursor_row in cursor_name loop
    if cursor_row.attribute1 = value1 then %>
    <option value="<%=cursor_row.attribute1%>" selected>
    <%=cursor_row.attribute2%></option>
    <% else %>
    <option value="<%=cursor_row.attribute1%>"><%=cursor_row.attribute2%></option>
    <% end if;
    end loop; %>
</select>
```

Multi-line Text Area

The multi-line text area can display database information by having PSP statements included directly within its tag area. For example, the following multi-line text area tag will display the result of PSP statements processing. These statements must include PSP expression statements to display database values in browser. The result of PL/SQL statement processing becomes the default setting for the multi-line text area in the Web browser.

```
<textarea name="FormsMultiLine1" rows=4 cols=14> <% ..PSP statements..%> </textarea>
```

FLEXIBLE PARAMETER PASSING

In addition to the default (strict) parameter match during the passing of data from Web forms, it is also possible to have a flexible parameter passing approach. Flexible parameter passing allows users to select any number of form elements. It is done by prefixing the procedure name with an exclamation mark (!) in the URL. In flexible parameter passing all parameters are passed through arrays (owa.ident_arr or owa.vc_arr as described in Appendix D) either as a set of two or four parameters. The two parameter interface outlined here provides improved performance, while the four parameter interface is supported for backward compatibility.

The syntax of a procedure definition with two parameter interface is:

```
PROCEDURE procedure-name (name_array  IN  [array_type],
          value_array IN  [array_type]) IS ...
```

where
- name_array is the name from the query string (indexed from 1) in the order submitted (e.g., owa.vc_arr).
- value_array is the values from the query string (indexed from 1) in the order submitted (e.g., owa.vc_arr).
- array_type is the values from the query string (indexed from 1) in the order submitted (e.g., owa.vc_arr).

A sample PSP in two parameter format is:

```
<%@page language="PL/SQL"%>
<%@plsql procedure="flex2psp"%>
<%@plsql parameter="name_array" type="owa_util.vc_arr"%>
<%@plsql parameter="value_array" type="owa_util.vc_arr"%>
<html>
<body>
<p>
<%for i in 1..name_array.count
loop%>
<%=name_array(i)||'='||value_array(i)%></br>
<%end loop;%>
</p>
<%exception
when others then%>
```

```
<%=sqlerrm%>
</body>
</html>
```

To invoke the above procedure the URL is:

```
http://server-name/DAD/!userid.flex2psp?x=john&y=10&z=doe
```

where the name_array values are ('x', 'y', 'z'), while the values_array values are ('john', '10', 'doe').

Overloading and PL/SQL Arrays

PL/SQL allows overloading of packaged subprograms. Stand-alone subprograms cannot be overloaded. Overloading is done in two ways. In the first case parameters exist with similar parameter names, but the data type is owa_util.ident_arr for one procedure and a scalar type for another procedure. For example, consider the following procedures:

```
create or replace package my_pkg as
  procedure my_proc (val in varchar2); -- scalar data type
  procedure my_proc (val in owa_util.ident_arr); -- array data type
end my_pkg;
```

Each of the above procedure has a single parameter of the same name, val. The following URL calls the scalar version of the procedure:

```
http://server-name/DAD/my_proc?val=john
```

The following URL calls the array version of the procedure. In this case, the distinguishing factor is multiple values of val parameter.

```
http://server-name/DAD/my_proc?val=john&val=sally
```

In the second case, the procedure names may be same, but the parameter names are different. For example:

```
create or replace package my_pkg as
  procedure my_proc (valvc2 in varchar2);
  procedure my_proc (valnum in number);
end my_pkg;
```

The URL to invoke the first version of the procedure is:

```
http://server-name/DAD/my_pkg.my_proc?valvc2=john
```

The URL to invoke the second version of the procedure is:

```
http://server-name/DAD/my_pkg.my_proc?valnum=35
```

TUTORIAL ON LOADING FORM WITH DATABASE VALUES

Run the script file superflexDB_v4.sql to load the Superflex
Apartments database tables necessary to complete this tutorial.
The tutorial consists of three PSP pages. The home page
displays a Web form with a drop down list box that displays all
tenant names in the database along with their associated rental
numbers. The user selects a tenant name from the drop-down
list box, and the Web form button submits the selected rental
number value to the second Web page. The second Web page
displays a Web form with attribute values for two attributes
associated with the rental (as submitted by the home page) –
the LEASE_TYPE and APT_NO attribute values. The user can
change these attribute values in the Web form. The changes in

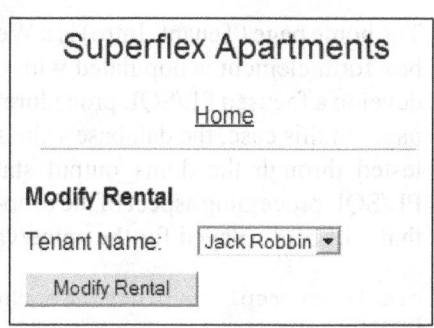

Figure 6-9

the form values are then submitted by the form button to the third Web page, that completes the update
of the attribute values (as entered in the second Web page) and generate a completion message.

The home page is called "Tenant Intro." A sample layout of the home page is shown in Figure 6-9. PSP
statements are utilized to populate the drop down list box LABEL/VALUE option tag attribute pair
entries with database values corresponding to TENANT_NAME/RENTAL_NO values. The Modify
Rental button is a submit type of button. It sends the selected RENTAL_NO value of the drop-down list
box to the second Web page.

The second Web page is called "Tenant Details." A sample
layout of the Web page is shown in Figure 6-10. This page will
have one input parameter for RENTAL_NO value as passed by
the home page. The page has a Web form with four form
elements. First there is a text box containing the RENTAL_NO
value received as an input parameter. Secondly, there is a set of
radio buttons with choices for the two values of LEASE_TYPE
attribute. In the Web form, one of the radio button shows a
checked display depending on the value of the LEASE_TYPE
attribute for the input RENTAL_NO. Third, there is a text box
with APT_NO value associated with the input RENTAL_NO.
The last form element is the submit type button labeled "Modify"
to submit the existing form element values to the third Web page.

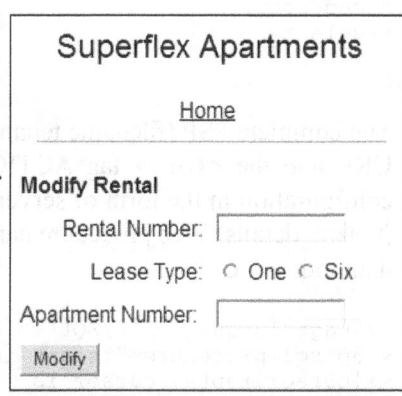

Figure 6-10

The third Web page is called "Tenant Detail Thanks." A sample
layout of the Web page is shown in Figure 6-11. This page will
have four input parameters for RENTAL_NO, LEASE_TYPE,
APT_NO, and submit button (Modify) value as passed by the
second Web page. The page simply updates the database with the
input LEASE_TYPE and APT_NO values for the input
RENTAL_NO value, and displays a "Updates Successful"
message.

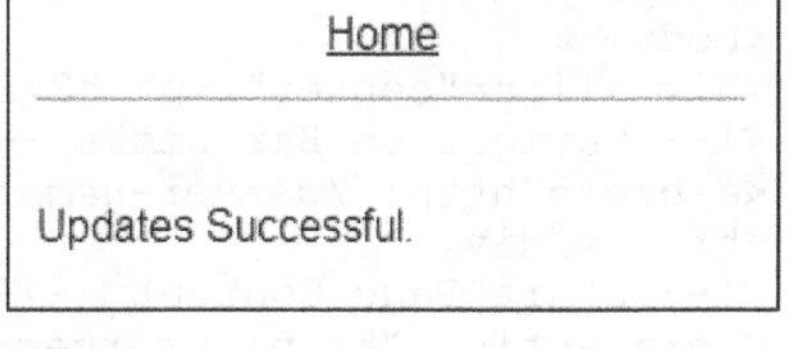

Figure 6-11

Tenant_Intro Web Page

The home page (Tenant_Intro) is a Web page that basically contains one Web form. Since the drop-down box form element is populated with database values, two step approach is outlined. The first step is to develop a focused PL/SQL procedure that concentrates on just the PL/SQL processing aspect of the Web page. In this case, the database values that will be displayed and assigned to the drop-down list box are tested through the dbms_output statements. The PL/SQL procedure ch6_tenant_intro outlines the PL/SQL processing aspect of the drop-down list box with the dbms_output statements showing the values that will be displayed for the name/value pair.

```
create or replace procedure ch6_tenant_intro is
begin
for rental_row in (select tenant_name, rental_no from tenant) loop
dbms_output.put_line('Tenant Name '||rental_row.tenant_name);
dbms_output.put_line('Rental Number '||rental_row.rental_no);
end loop;
end;
```

The next step is to transfer the PL/SQL procedure statements to the PSP. In this case the block of PL/SQL statements in the execution section of the PL/SQL procedure ch6_tenant_intro are embedded as PSP processing statements within the drop-down list box `<select>` tag, while the dbms_output statement database values become the PSP expression statements for the label/value option tag pair.

```
<select name="tenant_name_text">
<%for tenant_row in (select tenant_name from tenant) loop%>
    <option value="<%=tenant_row.tenant_name%>"><%=tenant_row.tenant_name%></option>
<%end loop;%>
</select>
```

The complete PSP (filename tenant_intro.psp) using Web Template 1 is shown below. The navigation URL and the `<form>` tag ACTION attribute URL should be modified to suit the existing server configuration in the form of server-name, DAD, and userid. It is important to include the second PSP (tenant_details) Web procedure name in the `<form>` tag action attribute URL to correctly send the form data to it.

```
<%@page language="PL/SQL"%>
<%@plsql procedure="tenant_intro"%>
<%!cursor rental_cursor is
select tenant_name,rental_no
from tenant;
rental_row rental_cursor%rowtype;%>
<!DOCTYPE HTML PUBLIC "-//W3C//DTD HTML 4.01 Transitional//EN">
<html>
<head>
<title>Tenant Intro</title>
</head>
<body>
<div align="center"><p><h2>Superflex Apartments</h2></p>
<!-- Navigation Bar Links -->
<a href="http://server-name/DAD/userid.tenant_intro">Home</a><br>
<hr /></div>
<!-- Start Page Content -->
<form action="http://server-name/DAD/userid.tenant_details" method="post">
<p><b>Modify Rental</b></p>
Tenant Name: <select name="rental_no_text">
<%for rental_row in rental_cursor loop%>
```

```
<option value="<%=rental_row.rental_no%>"><%=rental_row.tenant_name%></option>
<%end loop;%>
</select> <br /><br />
<input type="submit" name="FormsButton1" value="Modify Rental"/>
</form>
<!-- End Page Content -->
</body>
</html>
```

Tenant_Details Web Page

The second page (Tenant_Details) is a Web page that basically contains one Web form. Since the form element values are populated with database values, two step approach is outlined. The first step is to develop a focused PL/SQL procedure that concentrates on just the PL/SQL processing aspect of the Web page. In this case, the database values that will be assigned to form elements are tested through the dbms_output statements. The PL/SQL procedure ch6_tenant_details outlines the PL/SQL processing with the dbms_output statements showing the database values for the form elements. The input parameters of the procedure are named similar to the form element names in the home page (tenant_intro) PSP.

```
create or replace procedure ch6_tenant_details (rental_no_text varchar2,
        formsbutton1 varchar2) is
apt_no_in rental.apt_no%type;
lease_type_text rental.lease_type%type;
begin
select lease_type,apt_no
into lease_type_text,apt_no_in
from rental
where rental_no = rental_no_text;
dbms_output.put_line('Rental Number '||rental_no_text);
if lease_type_text = 'One' then
dbms_output.put_line('Lease Type '||lease_type_text ||' '||'checked');
end if;
if lease_type_text = 'Six' then
dbms_output.put_line('Lease Type '||lease_type_text ||' '||'checked');
end if;
dbms_output.put_line('Apartment Number '||apt_no_in);
end;
```

The next step is to transfer the PL/SQL procedure statements to the PSP. In this case the block of PL/SQL statements in the execution section of the PL/SQL procedure ch6_tenant_details appear as PSP processing statements within the `<form>` tag, while the dbms_output statement database values become the PSP expression statements of their corresponding form elements. Since the radio button has to display the correct button selection, the IF/THEN statement in the PL/SQL procedure associated with the lease_type attribute is now included within the radio button tag.

```
<form>
<%select lease_type,apt_no
into lease_type_text,apt_no_in
from rental
where rental_no = rental_no_text;%>
Rental Number: <input type="text" name="rental_no_text" value="<%=rental_no_text%>"
/> <br /><br />
Lease Type: <input type="radio" name="lease_type_text" value="One" <%if
lease_type_text = 'One' then %>Checked<%end if;%>/> One
<input type="radio" name="lease_type_text" value="Six" <%if lease_type_text = 'Six'
then%>Checked<%end if;%>/> Six<br /><br />
Apartment Number: <input type="text" name="apt_no_text" value="<%=apt_no_in%>" />
<br /><br />
</form>
```

The complete PSP (filename tenant_intro.psp) using Web Template 1 is shown below. The navigation URL and the <form> tag ACTION attribute URL should be modified to suit the existing server configuration in the form of server-name, DAD, and userid. It is important to include the third PSP (tenant_details_thanks) Web procedure name in the <form> tag action attribute URL to correctly send the form data to it.

```
<%@page language="PL/SQL"%>
<%@plsql procedure="tenant_details"%>
<%@plsql parameter="rental_no_text" default="null"%>
<%@plsql parameter="formsbutton1" default="null"%>
<%!apt_no_text rental.apt_no%type;
lease_type_text rental.lease_type%type;%>
<!DOCTYPE HTML PUBLIC "-//W3C//DTD HTML 4.01 Transitional//EN">
<html>
<head>
<title>Tenant Details Mini</title>
</head>
<body>
<div align="center"><p><h2>Superflex Apartments</h2></p>
<!-- Navigation Bar Links -->
<a href="http://server-name/DAD/userid.tenant_intro">Home</a><br>
<hr /></div>
<!-- Start Page Content -->
<form action="http://server-name/DAD/userid.tenant_details_thanks" method="post">
<p><b>Modify Rental</b></p>
<%select lease_type,apt_no
into lease_type_text,apt_no_text
from rental
where rental_no = rental_no_text;%>
Rental Number: <input type="text" name="rental_no_text" value="<%=rental_no_text%>"
/> <br /><br />
Lease Type: <input type="radio" name="lease_type_text" value="One" <%if
lease_type_text = 'One' then%>Checked<%end if;%>/> One
<input type="radio" name="lease_type_text" value="Six" <%if lease_type_text = 'Six'
then%>Checked<%end if;%>/> Six<br /><br />
Apartment Number: <input type="text" name="apt_no_text" value="<%=apt_no_text%>" />
<br /><br />
<input type="submit" name="FormsButton1" value="Modify"/>
</form>
<!-- End Page Content -->
</body>
</html>
```

Tenant_Details_Thanks Web Page

The third page (Tenant_Details_Thanks) is a Web page that basically performs an update of the RENTAL table and displays a message "Update Successful." Since the page deals with database values, two step approach is again outlined. The first step is to develop a focused PL/SQL procedure that concentrates on just the PL/SQL processing aspect of the Web page. In this case, the update operation and the message displayed through the dbms_output statements. The PL/SQL procedure ch6_tenant_details_thanks outlines the PL/SQL processing with the dbms_output statements showing the message. The input parameters of the procedure are named similar to the form element names in the second page (tenant_details) PSP.

```
create or replace procedure ch6_tenant_details_thanks (rental_no_text varchar2,
     lease_type_text varchar2, apt_no_text varchar2, formsbutton1 varchar2) is
begin
update rental
set lease_type = lease_type_text,
```

```
apt_no = apt_no_text
where rental_no=rental_no_text;
commit;
dbms_output.put_line('Updates Successful');
end;
```

The next step is to transfer the PL/SQL procedure statements to the PSP. In this case the block of PL/SQL statements in the execution section of the PL/SQL procedure ch6_tenant_details_thanks appear as PSP processing statements before the display of the message.

```
<%update rental
set lease_type = lease_type_text,
apt_no = apt_no_text
where rental_no=rental_no_text;
commit;%>
```

The complete PSP (filename tenant_intro.psp) using Web Template 1 is shown below. The navigation URL should be modified to suit the existing server configuration in the form of server-name, DAD, and userid.

```
<%@page language="PL/SQL"%>
<%@plsql procedure="tenant_details_thanks"%>
<%@plsql parameter="rental_no_text" default="null"%>
<%@plsql parameter="lease_type_text" default="null"%>
<%@plsql parameter="apt_no_text" default="null"%>
<%@plsql parameter="formsbutton1" default="null"%>
<%update rental
set lease_type = lease_type_text,
apt_no = apt_no_text
where rental_no=rental_no_text;
commit;%>
<!DOCTYPE HTML PUBLIC "-//W3C//DTD HTML 4.01 Transitional//EN">
<html>
<head>
<title>Tenant Details Thanks Mini</title>
</head>
<body>
<div align="center"><p><h1>Superflex Apartments</h1></p>
<!-- Navigation Bar Links -->
<a href="http://server-name/DAD/userid.tenant_intro">Home</a><br>
<hr /></div>
<br> <!-- Start Page Content -->
<p>Updates Successful.</p>
<!-- End Page Content -->
</body>
</html>
```

Load PSP to the Database

Once the PSP have been completed, open the Windows Command Prompt window to execute the loadpsp command for the PSP files. The command to load the three PSPs will be:

```
loadpsp -replace -user userid/password@connection_string
        drive&path\tenant_intro.psp


loadpsp -replace -user userid/password@connection_string
        drive&path\tenant_details.psp
```

```
loadpsp -replace -user userid/password@connection_string
        drive&path\tenant_details_thanks.psp
```

The userid, password, connection string and path specifications depend on database configuration. If there are errors in the page, fix the errors and re-load the page.

View PSP in Web Browser

Once the loading is successful type the URL below to retrieve the Web page from the database. The URL should be modified to suit the existing server configuration in the form of server-name, DAD, and userid.

```
http://server-name/DAD/userid.tenant_intro
```

A sample runtime of the PSPs in a Web browser is shown in Figure 6-12 for the tenant_intro home page, Figure 6-13 for the tenant_details page, and Figure 6-14 for tenant_details_thanks page.

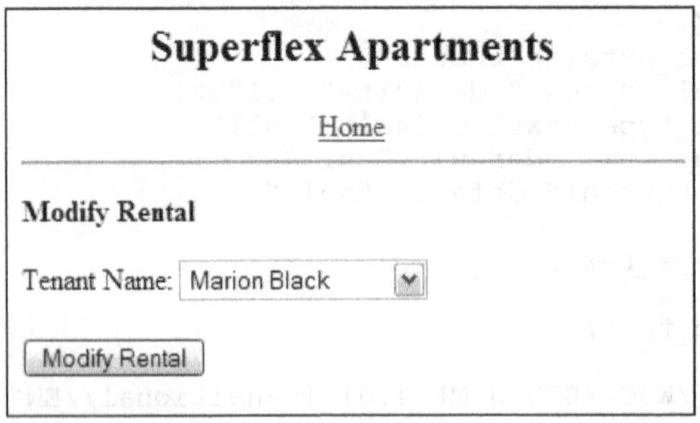

Figure 6-12

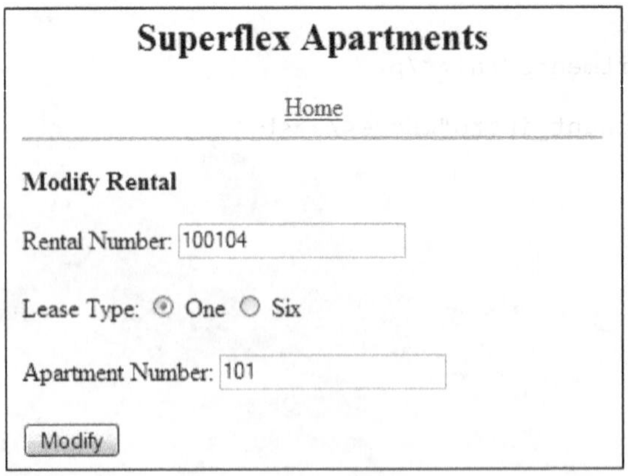

Figure 6-13

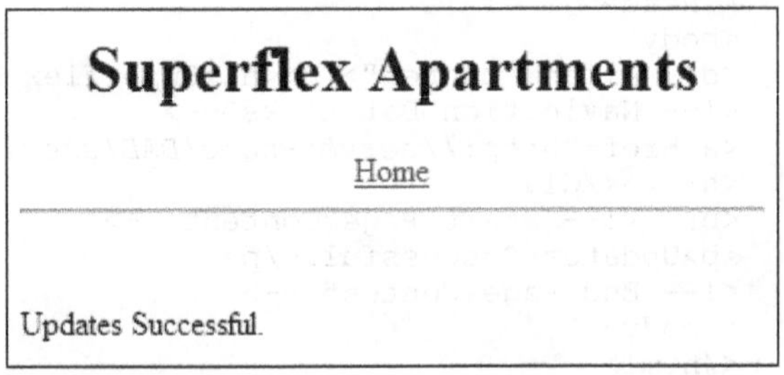

Figure 6-14

CHAPTER SUMMARY

▸ Web (HTML) forms apart from display of stored database information as also utilized for modifications of information.

▸ Loading of database data in various form element is different from using such elements to input database values.

▸ PSP statements to load database values in form elements have to be positioned within or around their corresponding HTML tags.

▸ To load database values in a text box, the VALUE attribute is utilized to enter PSP statements.

▸ Radio buttons are part of a group representing choices. For displaying the correct choice when loading database data, IF/THEN PSP statements utilized to place the CHECKED attribute.

▸ Check box represents values which can be associated with database data. The embedding of PSP statements with check box is similar to radio buttons. For displaying the correct setting when loading database data, IF/THEN PSP statements utilized to place the CHECKED attribute.

▸ Selection Lists can appear in two styles – drop down menu list or pop list. The PSP statements to load the selection list box for either style with database data is through the Label/Value option tag pair containing PSP expression statements within a cursor loop.

▸ Forms multi-line text area show database information by having the PSP statements included directly in its display area.

▸ Once the browser loads the form with database values, the user can modify the displayed values. The modified values are then sent to the database server through a form button of submit type (similar to input of database values based on form settings specifications).

REVIEW QUESTIONS

1. What is the nature of PSP statement needed to load database values in a text box?

2. What is the approach to show the radio button for correct database value?

3. What is the approach to show check box for correct database value?

4. What is the mechanism to make a text box readonly in NetObjects Fusion?

5. Explain the approach to display database values in Multi-line Text area.

REVIEW EXERCISES

1. Display of database values in a Web form requires embedding _____ statements within different form elements.

2. To display value of variable c_name in a text box, the correct PSP statement will be _____.

3. Radio buttons are part of a group representing _____.

4. To display the correct choice when loading database values _____ radio buttons are utilized to represent the same choice.

5. To display the correct choice each radio button's PSP code will exist within a PL/SQL _____ statement.

6. To display database values in selection lists, the Label/Value option tag attribute pair will use PSP _____ statements.

7. _____ field values are additional values aside from form element values that need to be passed to the database server.

8. A _____ type of button submits the modified contents of the form to the Web server.

9. A _____ type of button resets the modified values in the form to the default values.

10. A form can have _____ submit type buttons.

11. All submit type of buttons will submit modified form data to the same URL for processing.

12. During submission of modified form values to the database server, each form element name becomes a _____ name in the response procedure.

13. During submission of modified form values to the database server, each form button name becomes a _____ name in the response procedure.

PROBLEM SOLVING EXERCISES

Ex6B-1.   Run the script file outdoorDB_v4.sql to load the Outdoor Clubs & Product database tables necessary to complete this exercise. Create three PSP pages that allows users to modify details about products.

1.   The first PSP page is the home page and is titled "Get Product." It will have a Web form with the following form elements:

   • A drop-down list box that displays all product_name values in the database along with their associated product_id values. The drop-down list box select tag option tag label/value attribute entries will correspond to product_name/product_id values in the database.
   • A Web form button labeled "Get Details" that will submit the selected product name value to the second Web page.

   The user will select a product_name from the drop-down list box, and the Web form button will submit the associated product_id value to the second Web page.

2.   The second PSP page is titled "Modify Product." It will have a Web form that shows the attribute values in the database associated with the product_name selected in the first Web page. The form elements with attribute values are:

   • A text box that displays the current product_name attribute value.
   • A text box that displays the current product's price attribute value.
   • A set of radio buttons for all the supplier_id attribute values, with the correct supplier_id button checked for the associated product.
   • A text box that displays the current reorder_qty attribute value.
   • A Web form button labeled "Modify" that will submit the form element values to the third Web page.

3.   The third PSP page is titled "Complete Product Change." The page will complete the update of the attribute values (as entered in the second Web page) in the relevant tables and generate a message "Update Successful."

4.   There should be only one navigation link titled after the home page. The navigation URL should link to the home page. The banner for all the Web pages should be "Outdoor Product Update."

5.   Create a PL/SQL procedure "ex6b1_modify_product" that completes the processing of the second Web page. Use the dbms_output statements to display the form element database values. Save the procedure as a script file with filename ex6b1.

6.   Generate and load PSP Web pages to the Oracle database server. (The instructor will provide the details on the database server accounts).

7.   If some clipart is utilized in the Web page, transfer the image to the required virtual folder. (The instructor will provide the necessary instructions on this step).

8.   Open the Web site in the browser and print the display.

Ex6B-2. Run the script file outdoorDB_v4.sql to load the Outdoor Clubs & Product database tables necessary to complete this exercise. Create three PSP pages that allows users to modify details about a sporting club.

1. The first PSP page is the home page and is titled "Get Club." It will have a Web form with the following form elements:

    • A drop-down list box that displays all sporting club names in the database along with their associated club_id values. The drop-down list box select tag option tag label/value attribute entries will correspond to name/club_id values in the database.
    • A Web form button labeled "Get Details" that will submit the selected sporting club name value to the second Web page.

    The user will select a sporting club name from the drop-down list box, and the Web form button will submit the associated club_id value to the second Web page.

2. The second PSP page is titled "Modify Club." It will have a Web form that shows the attribute values in the database associated with the sporting club name selected in the first Web page. The form elements with attribute values are:

    • A text box that displays the current sporting club name attribute value.
    • A text box that displays the current sporting club's phone value.
    • A set of check boxes for all the club activity values, with the correct activity check boxes checked for the associated product.
    • A Web form button labeled "Modify" that will submit the form element values to the third Web page.

3. The third PSP page is titled "Complete Club Change." The page will complete the update of the attribute values (as entered in the second Web page) in the relevant tables and generate a message "Update Successful." Update of club activity will be such that the unchecked activities will be deleted from the club_activity table, while the checked activities if not already existing will be added in the club_activity table.

4. There should be only one navigation link titled after the home page. The navigation URL should link to the home page. The banner for all the Web pages should be "Outdoor Club Update."

5. Create a PL/SQL procedure "ex6b2a_modify_club" that completes the processing of the second Web page. Use the dbms_output statements to display the form element database values. Save the procedure as a script file with filename ex6b2a.

6. Create a PL/SQL procedure "ex6b2b_comp_club_change" that completes the processing of the third Web page. Use the dbms_output statements to display the form element database values. Save the procedure as a script file with filename ex6b2b.

7. Generate and load PSP Web pages to the Oracle database server. (The instructor will provide the details on the database server accounts).

8. If some clipart is utilized in the Web page, transfer the image to the required virtual folder. (The instructor will provide the necessary instructions on this step).

9. Open the Web site in the browser and print the display.

Ex6B-3. Run the script file outdoorDB_v4.sql to load the Outdoor Clubs & Product database tables necessary to complete this exercise. Create two PSP pages that allows user to create a new product order.

1. The first PSP page is the home page and is titled "Enter Order." It will have a Web form with the following form elements:

   - A drop-down list box that displays all customer names (first_name last_name) in the database along with their associated customer_id values. The drop-down list box select tag option tag label/value attribute entries will correspond to customer first_name last_name/customer_id values in the database.
   - A drop-down list box that displays all product_name in the database along with their associated product_id values. The drop-down list box select tag option tag label/value attribute entries will correspond to product_name/product_id values in the database.
   - A text box to enter quantity attribute value.
   - A set of radio buttons for the product_order payment_type attribute values.
   - A Web form button labeled "Checkout" that will submit the form element values to the second Web page.

   The user will select the customer first_name last_name combination, and the product_name from their respective drop-down list boxes, enter a quantity value, and select the payment type radio button. The Web form button will submit the selected customer_id and product_id values from their respective drop-down list boxes, entered quantity value, and the selected payment type values to the second Web page.

2. The second PSP page is titled "Generate Order." The page will complete the generation of the new product order by inserting a row in product_order and order_details tables. The quantity_in_stock value for the product needs to be reduced by the quantity value of the product order. Add a $6 shipping and handling charge to the order amount. At the successful conclusion of the processing, the page will display a message "New product order *order-id* for customer *first-name last-name* for amount *total* has been created." The message entries in italics are database values pertaining to the order.

3. There should be only one navigation link titled after the home page. The navigation URL should link to the home page. The banner for all the Web pages should be "Outdoor Club Update."

4. Create a PL/SQL procedure "ex6b3_generate_order" that completes the processing of the second Web page. Use the dbms_output statements to display the message with database values. Save the procedure as a script file with filename ex6b3.

5. Generate and load PSP Web pages to the Oracle database server. (The instructor will provide the details on the database server accounts).

6. If some clipart is utilized in the Web page, transfer the image to the required virtual folder. (The instructor will provide the necessary instructions on this step).

7. Open the Web site in the browser and print the display.

Ex6B-4.   Run the script file sentimentDB_v4.sql to load the Sentiments Anywhere database tables necessary to complete this exercise. Create three PSP pages that allows users to modify details about sentiments.

1.   The first PSP page is the home page and is titled "Enter Sentiment." It will have a Web form with the following form elements:

   • A text box to enter sentiment_id value.
   • A Web form button labeled "Proceed" that will submit the entered sentiment_id to the second Web page.

2.   The second PSP page is titled "Modify Sentiment." The Web page will either display a message "Sentiment ID is not correct. Please go back and re-enter" when the sentiment_id entered in the home page is invalid, or a Web form with another message at the top of the form.

   The Web form will show the attribute values in the database associated with the sentiment_id entered in the first Web page. The message displayed before the is "Sentiment ID *sentiment-id-text* Details" where the sentiment-id-text is the value of sentiment_id entered in the first Web page. The form elements with attribute values are:

   • A text box that displays the current sentiment name attribute value.
   • A text box that displays the current sentiment price attribute value.
   • A set of radio buttons for all the sentiment type attribute values, with the correct type button checked for the associated sentiment.
   • A drop-down list box that displays all vendor name in the database along with their associated vendor_id values. The drop-down list box select tag option tag label/value attribute entries will correspond to vendor name/vendor_id values in the database. The drop-down list box should be setup in such a way that the current vendor name for the associated sentiment becomes the default display.
   • A Web form button labeled "Modify" that will submit the form element values to the third Web page.

3.   The third PSP page is titled "Confirm Sentiment Change." The page will complete the update of the attribute values (as entered in the second Web page) in the relevant tables and generate a message "Sentiment Update Successful."

4.   There should be only one navigation link titled after the home page. The navigation URL should link to the home page. The banner for all the Web pages should be "Sentiment Anywhere."

5.   Create a PL/SQL procedure "ex6b4_modify_sentiment" that completes the processing of the second Web page. Use the dbms_output statements to display the form element database values. Save the procedure as a script file with filename ex6b4.

6.   Generate and load PSP Web pages to the Oracle database server. (The instructor will provide the details on the database server accounts).

7.   If some clipart is utilized in the Web page, transfer the image to the required virtual folder. (The instructor will provide the necessary instructions on this step).

8.   Open the Web site in the browser and print the display.

Ex6B-5. Run the script file outdoorDB_v4.sql to load the Outdoor Clubs & Product database tables necessary to complete this exercise. Create three PSP pages that allows users to modify details about customer along with creation of a new club membership.

1. The first PSP page is the home page and is titled "Enter Customer." It will have a Web form with the following form elements:

   • A text box to enter customer_id value.
   • A Web form button labeled "Proceed" that will submit the entered customer_id to the second Web page.

2. The second PSP page is titled "Modify Customer." The Web page will either display a message "Customer ID is not correct. Please go back and re-enter" when the customer_id entered in the home page is invalid, or a Web form with another message at the top of the form.

   The Web form will show the attribute values in the database associated with the customer_id entered in the first Web page. The message displayed before the is "Customer ID *customer-id-text* Details" where the customer-id-text is the value of customer_id entered in the first Web page. The form elements with attribute values are:

   • A text box that displays the current customer street attribute value.
   • A text box that displays the current customer city attribute value.
   • A text box that displays the current customer state attribute value.
   • A text box that displays the current customer zip attribute value.
   • A drop-down list box that displays all sporting club names in the database along with their associated club_id values. The drop-down list box select tag option tag label/value attribute entries will correspond to club name/club_id values in the database. The drop-down list should be setup in such a way that the current club name for the associated customer becomes the default display.
   • A set of radio buttons for all the club_membership duration attribute values. Provide a text beside the radio buttons stating "Membership Fee is $50 per month".
   • A set of radio buttons for all the club_membership payment_type attribute values.
   • A Web form button labeled "Modify" that will submit the form element values to the third Web page.

   The Web form performs two roles. First, the data in the form associated with the customer address entries will update the customer table. Secondly, the club_id, duration, and payment_type entries will be used to insert a new row in club_membership table.

3. The third PSP page is titled "Confirm Customer Change." The page will complete the update and insert operation for the attribute values (as entered in the second Web page) in the relevant tables and generate a message "Customer Update Successful."

4. There should be only one navigation link titled after the home page. The navigation URL should link to the home page. The banner for all the Web pages should be "Sentiment Anywhere."

5. Create a PL/SQL procedure "ex6b5_modify_customer" that completes the processing of the second Web page. Use the dbms_output statements to display the form element database values. Save the procedure as a script file with filename ex6b5.

6.   Generate and load PSP Web pages to the Oracle database server. (The instructor will provide the details on the database server accounts).

7.   If some clipart is utilized in the Web page, transfer the image to the required virtual folder. (The instructor will provide the necessary instructions on this step).

8.   Open the Web site in the browser and print the display.

Ex6B-6.   Run the script file superflexDB_v4.sql to load the Superflex Apartments database tables necessary to complete this exercise. Create three PSP pages that allows users to modify details about a tenant.

1.   The first PSP page is the home page and is titled "Rental Input." It will have a Web form with the following form elements:

- A text box to enter rental_no value.
- A Web form button labeled "Get Detail" that will submit the entered rental_no to the second Web page.

2.   The second PSP page is titled "Tenant Modify." The Web page will either display a message "Rental No is not correct. Please go back and re-enter" when the rental_no entered in the home page is invalid, or a Web form.

The Web form will show the attribute values in the database associated with the rental_no entered in the first Web page. The message displayed before the is "Tenant *tenant-name-text* Details" where the tenant-name-text is the value of tenant_name attribute associated with the rental_no entered in the first Web page. The form elements with attribute values are:

- A text box that displays the current tenant employer_name attribute value.
- A text box that displays the current tenant work_phone attribute value.
- A text box that displays the current tenant home_phone attribute value.
- A Web form button labeled "Modify" that will submit the form element values to the third Web page.

The work_phone and home_phone values should be shown in (xxx) xxx-xxxx format.

3.   The third PSP page is titled "Tenant Modify Confirm." The page will complete the update operation for the attribute values (as entered in the second Web page) in the relevant tables and generate a message "Tenant Update Successful."

4.   There should be only one navigation link titled after the home page. The navigation URL should link to the home page. The banner for all the Web pages should be "Sentiment Anywhere."

5.   Create a PL/SQL procedure "ex6b6_modify_tenant" that completes the processing of the second Web page. Use the dbms_output statements to display the form element database values. Save the procedure as a script file with filename ex6b6.

6.   Generate and load PSP Web pages to the Oracle database server. (The instructor will provide the details on the database server accounts).

7. If some clipart is utilized in the Web page, transfer the image to the required virtual folder. (The instructor will provide the necessary instructions on this step).

8. Open the Web site in the browser and print the display.

Ex6B-7. Run the script file superflexDB_v4.sql to load the Superflex Apartments database tables necessary to complete this exercise. Create four PSP pages that allows users to delete or modify details about a tenant's auto details.

1. The first PSP page is the home page and is titled "Auto Input." It will have a Web form with the following form elements:

    • A text box to enter tenant_name value.
    • A Web form button labeled "Get Detail" that will submit the entered tenant_name to the second page.

2. The second PSP page is titled "Auto Modify." The Web page will display a Web form. The form elements with attribute values are:

    • A pop-list box that displays a tenant's auto_model values in the database along with their associated license_no values. The pop-list box select tag option tag label/value attribute entries will correspond to a tenant's auto_model/license_no values in the database.
    • A Web form button labeled "Modify" that will submit the form element values to the third page.
    • A Web form button labeled "Delete" that will also submit the form element values to the third page.

3. The third PSP page is titled "Auto Status." The Web page will either display a display message message "Tenant *tenant-name-text* License Number *license-no-text* Deleted" when the button labeled "Delete" is pressed in the second Web page, or a Web form when the button labeled "Modify" is pressed in the second Web page. The message tenant-name-text is the value of tenant_name attribute, while the license-no-text is the value of the license-no attribute passed on by the second Web page. The form elements with attribute values are:

    • A text box that displays the current tenant auto_make attribute value.
    • A text box that displays the current tenant auto_model attribute value.
    • A text box that displays the current tenant auto_year attribute value.
    • A text box that displays the current tenant auto_color attribute value.
    • A Web form button labeled "Modify" that will submit the form element values to the fourth Web page.

4. The fourth PSP page is titled "Tenant Auto Confirm." The page will complete the update operation for the attribute values (as entered in the third Web page) in the relevant tables and generate a message "Tenant Auto Update Successful."

5. There should be only one navigation link titled after the home page. The navigation URL should link to the home page. The banner for all the Web pages should be "Sentiment Anywhere."

6. Create a PL/SQL procedure "ex6b7_modify_tenant" that completes the processing of the third Web page. Use the dbms_output statements to display the form element database values. Save the procedure as a script file with filename ex6b7.

7. Generate and load PSP Web pages to the Oracle database server. (The instructor will provide the details on the database server accounts).

8. If some clipart is utilized in the Web page, transfer the image to the required virtual folder. (The instructor will provide the necessary instructions on this step).

9. Open the Web site in the browser and print the display.

CHAPTER 7

Oracle XML Essentials

- XML Structure
- XML and DOM
- XML from Database

XML stands for **EX**tensible **M**arkup **L**anguage. It is a markup language like HTML with one major difference. While HTML is designed to focus on page layout, XML is designed to describe data. This chapter introduces the basic syntax and structure of XML, along with its generation from Oracle database tables.

This chapter utilizes the table structure of Superflex Apartment database to explain examples.

Like HTML, the data in XML is defined through the concept of tags (or markup). However, unlike the HTML tags, the XML tags are not predefined. Since XML tags are not predefined, a developer must name the tags to define the content. Figure 7-1 shows the difference in the tags between a Web (HTML) page and a XML document.

Web (HTML) Page

```
<html>
<head>
<title> DOM List </title>
</head>
<body>
<h1> This is a heading </h1>
<p> Sample DOM Paragraph </p>
</body>
</html>
```
→ Pre-defined Tags

XML Document

```
<ROWSET>
  <ROW>
    <RENTAL_NO>100102</RENTAL_NO>
    <RENTAL_DATE>21-MAY-01</RENTAL_DATE>
    <TENANT_NAME>Mary Stackles</TENANT_NAME>
  </ROW>
  <ROW>
    <RENTAL_NO>100105</RENTAL_NO>
    <RENTAL_DATE>15-APR-02</RENTAL_DATE>
    <TENANT_NAME>Venessa Williams</TENANT_NAME>
  </ROW>
</ROWSET>
```
→ User-defined Tags

Figure 7-1

XML uses a Document Type Definition (DTD) or a XML Schema to describe the data. A DTD defines the vocabulary of tags and how they may be used for a specific type of XML document. When a XML document follows all of the rules specified in its corresponding DTD, the XML document is considered "valid."

In general, XML does not do anything by itself. The focus of XML is simply to define the data structure, store the structure, and communicate the structure information. Any type of data – from a purchase order to a stock quote can be represented in XML. One logical unit of data represented in XML is often called a XML "document." When the XML data is moved between systems, the packet of data is often called a XML "datagram." XML data can be stored in either (i) separate XML files in plain text format, (ii) database, or (iii) inside HTML pages as "Data Islands."

In the real world, computer systems and databases contain data in incompatible formats. With XML, data can be exchanged between such systems. Since XML data is expressed in plain text format, XML provides a software- and hardware-independent way of sharing data. XML in a way makes it much easier to create data for different applications to work together.

XML STRUCTURE

XML structure and syntax rules are simple to learn and use. Generally, a XML document has an optional first line followed by its data structure. The first line in the document is a form of XML declaration that defines the XML version and the character encoding used in the document. For example, the statement `<?xml version="1.0" encoding="ISO-8859-1"?>` states that the document conforms to the 1.0 specification of XML and uses the ISO-8859-1 (Latin-1/West European) character set.

The layout of the XML data structure is hierarchical. This layout begins with the second line. The building block of the XML structure is a *XML element*. A XML element is everything from the opening tag to the closing tag, ie. opening tag, content, and closing tag. All XML elements must have a closing tag. For example, `<name>Jack Russell</name>` is a XML element.

XML elements must follow these naming rules:
- Names can contain letters, numbers, and other characters.
- Names must not start with a number or punctuation character.
- Names must not start with the letters xml (or XML, or Xml, etc).
- Names cannot contain spaces.

Any name can be used to define an element name. No words are reserved. However, it is a good idea to give descriptive names. There is no obvious name length limitation. Long names can include an underscore separator. For example `<first_name>` and `<last_name>` are valid element tag names.

Avoid hyphen (-), dot (.), or colon (:) in element names. For example, if an element is named as "first-name," it could be problematic if the software tries to subtract "name" from "first." Similarly if an element is named as "first.name," the software may think that "name" is a property of the object "first."

The colon (:) should not be used in element names because it is reserved for something called *namespaces*.

Since, XML documents often relate to databases, it is a good practice to use the naming rules of the database as the element names within the XML structure. In such cases, the attribute names correspond to the elements names within the XML structure

The XML tags are case sensitive. So, the opening and closing tags must therefore be written in the same case. For example, `<Name>Jack Russell</name>` is incorrect.

XML elements must be properly nested. For example, `<customer><name>Jack Russell</name></customer>` shows a sequence of tags. Since the `<name>` tag appears after the opening `<customer>` tag, its closing tag `</name>` must be before the customer element closing tag `</customer>`.

XML element names can have attributes in the form of name/value pairs within the opening tag. The attribute value must always be quoted. For example, `<name id="102">Jack Russell</name>` has an attribute "id" with value 102. Keep in mind that if attributes are used as containers for data, it is possible to have an XML structure this is difficult to read and maintain. If possible try to use proper element names to describe data. Use of attributes should be restricted only to provide information that is not relevant to the data.

Unlike HTML, a white space in the XML structure is not truncated.

The syntax for writing comments in XML is similar to that of HTML. For example, `<!-- This is a comment -->` statement will indicate a comment in XML document.

A XML document structure must be contained within a single tag pair referred as a *root* element. The hierarchical structure of a XML document starts with the root element and all other elements must be within the root element. An element can have sub elements (child elements). Sub elements must be correctly nested with their parent element. The symbolic layout of XML structure will appear as follows:

```
<root>
  <child>
    <subchild>.....</subchild>
  </child>
</root>
```

The following is an example of an XML structure with three child elements. The Tenant_Details is the root element, while Employer, WorkPhone, and Marital are children of Tenant_Details.

```
<Tenant_Details>
  <Employer>SMSU</Employer>
  <WorkPhone>4178362323</WorkPhone>
  <Marital>M</Marital>
</Tenant_Details>
```

XML Namespace

XML Namespace provides a method to avoid element name conflicts. Since element names in XML are not predefined, a name conflict may occur when two different documents use the same element names.

The XML namespace attribute is placed in the starting tag of an element so that all child elements with the same prefix are associated with the same namespace. For example, the following XML structure carries information about a customer with namespace "f":

```
<f:customer xmlns:f="http://www.w3schools.com/customer">
    <f:name>Jack Russell</f:name>
    <f:state>MO</f:state>
    <f:zip>65807</f:zip>
</f:customer>
```

XML AND DOM

Since the book utilizes XML processing from the perspective of AJAX, the Document Object Model (DOM) for representing the XML structure is important. The hierarchical structure of a XML document is similar conceptually to the DOM hierarchical tree associated with a HTML Web page. The XML DOM characteristics can be listed in nutshell as follows:

- The entire XML document can be referred as a DOM object.
- Every XML tag is a DOM element node.
- The data contained within a XML element is a DOM text node.
- The XML tag attribute is a DOM attribute node.
- The element nodes form a hierarchical relationship (or node tree) with each other, where the top node is called the root. Every node, except the root, has exactly one parent node.
- Similar to DOM, the terms "parent" and "child" can be used to describe the relationship between the element nodes.
- A node can have any number of children. A leaf is a node with no children. Siblings are nodes with the same parent.

Figure 7-2 shows an XML DOM tree structure. Notice the similarity with Chapter 4, Lesson B HTML DOM tree structure of Figure 4-5.

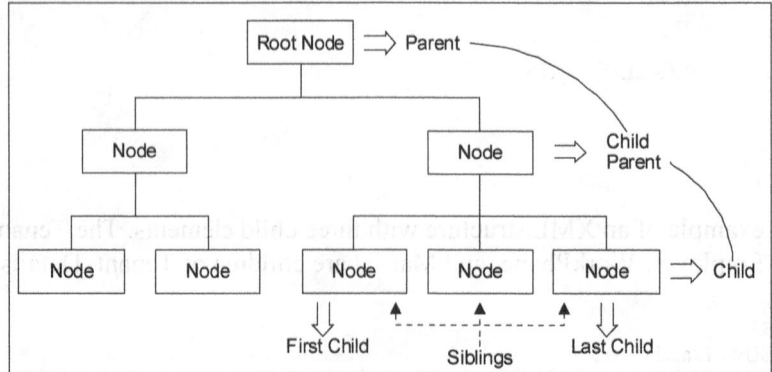

Figure 7-2

Once the XML structure is represented as a DOM tree, it can be traversed with DOM methods and properties. The following is an example of a XML structure with content from the TENANT table followed by its associated DOM tree in Figure 7-3

```
<ROWSET>
  <ROW>
    <RENTAL_NO>100102</RENTAL_NO>
    <RENTAL_DATE>21-MAY-01</RENTAL_DATE>
    <TENANT_NAME>Mary Stackles</TENANT_NAME>
  </ROW>
  <ROW>
    <RENTAL_NO>100105</RENTAL_NO>
    <RENTAL_DATE>15-APR-02</RENTAL_DATE>
    <TENANT_NAME>Venessa Williams</TENANT_NAME>
  </ROW>
</ROWSET>
```

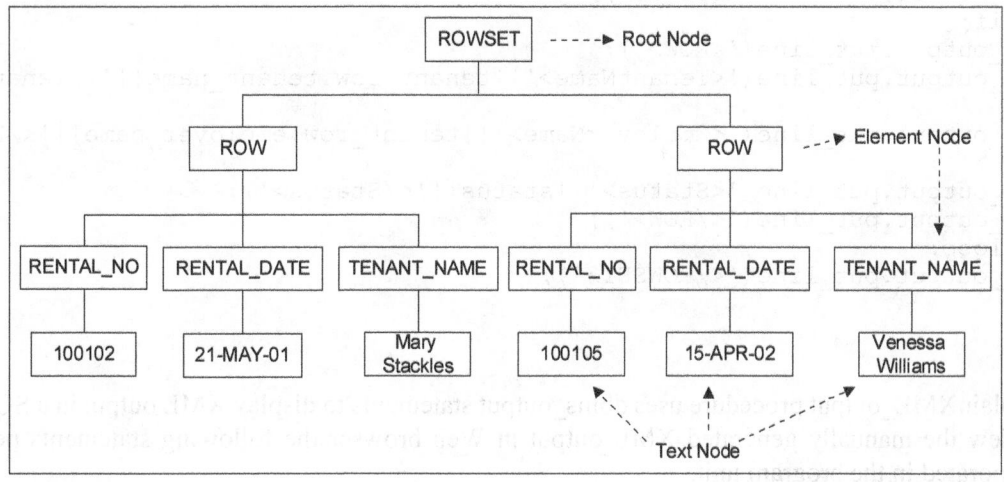

Figure 7-3

GENERATE XML FROM DATABASE

There are many ways to generate XML from Oracle tables. One approach is to manually enter the element names within a program unit along with database data. Another approach is to utilize Oracle XML DB features for generating XML from the database. In this section initially the manual generation of XML is outlined. This is followed by details on two Oracle XML DB features for generating XML: the DBMS_XMLGEN package, and the SQL/XML functions.

Manual XML Generation

Manual generation of XML involves preparing a XML document within a program unit with element names and database data. For example, the following procedure *plainXML_output* displays TENANT_NAME, EMPLOYER_NAME, and a status value (Academic or Professional) based on the EMPLOYER_NAME value in the TENANT table. In this example, beside the database values, a conditional static values is in the XML output. The well-formed XML is manually defined within the procedure, where ROWSET is the root of the structure, and each row of output has the ROW element name. The database and static values have individual element names.

```
create or replace procedure plainXML_output as
cursor tenant_cursor is
select tenant_name, employer_name
from tenant;
tenant_row tenant_cursor%rowtype;
status varchar2(15);
begin
dbms_output.put_line('<ROWSET>');
open tenant_cursor;
loop
fetch tenant_cursor into tenant_row;
exit when tenant_cursor%notfound;
if tenant_row.employer_name = 'MSU' then
status := 'Academic';
else status := 'Professional';
end if;
dbms_output.put_line('<ROW>');
dbms_output.put_line('<TenantName>'||tenant_row.tenant_name||'</TenantName>
');
dbms_output.put_line('<EmployerName>'||tenant_row.employer_name||'</Employe
rName>');
dbms_output.put_line('<Status>'||status||'</Status>');
dbms_output.put_line('</ROW>');
end loop;
dbms_output.put_line('</ROWSET>');
end;
```

The plainXML_output procedure uses dbms_output statements to display XML output in a SQL editor. To view the manually generated XML output in Web browser the following statements need to be incorporated in the program unit.

1. The `owa_util.mime_header('text/xml')` statement.
2. `htp.prn({text|database-value})` package statement where the text could be some static value and the database-value can be some value from the database.

The plainXML_output procedure is now modified as *plainXML_Web* procedure for displaying XML output in the Web browser. The htp.prn statements replace the dbms_output statements. To view the output, the procedure needs to be called from a URL similar to viewing a PL/SQL Server Page.

```
create or replace procedure plainXML_Web as
cursor tenant_cursor is
select tenant_name, employer_name
from tenant;
tenant_row tenant_cursor%rowtype;
status varchar2(15);
begin
owa_util.mime_header('text/xml');
htp.prn('<ROWSET>');
open tenant_cursor;
loop
fetch tenant_cursor into tenant_row;
exit when tenant_cursor%notfound;
if tenant_row.employer_name = 'MSU' then
status := 'Academic';
else status := 'Professional';
```

```
end if;
htp.prn('<ROW>');
htp.prn('<TenantName>'||tenant_row.tenant_name||'</TenantName>');
htp.prn('<EmployerName>'||tenant_row.employer_name||'</EmployerName>');
htp.prn('<Status>'||status||'</Status>');
htp.prn('</ROW>');
end loop;
htp.prn('</ROWSET>');
end;
```

Generating XML with DBMS_XMLGEN

DBMS_XMLGEN is a PL/SQL package supplied with the Oracle database that generates XML as a CLOB or XMLType data. The package creates XML documents from a SQL query. The package is useful for multi-row processing. It uses by default a canonical format to map the SQL query data to XML structure. Oracle's canonical format is:

```
<ROWSET>
  <ROW>
      <attribute_name_1> . . .</attribute_name_1>
      <attribute_name_2> . . .</attribute_name_2>
      <attribute_name_3> . . .</attribute_name_3>
  </ROW>
  <ROW>
      <attribute_name_1> . . .</attribute_name_1>
      <attribute_name_2> . . .</attribute_name_2>
      <attribute_name_3> . . .</attribute_name_3>
  </ROW>
  .
  .
  .
</ROWSET>
```

where
- The ROWSET element name is the root of the overall XML document.
- Each row returned by the SQL query maps to an XML element with the (default) name ROW.
- Each attribute returned by the SQL query maps to a child element of the ROW element.
- The ROW element is repeated for each query row.
- The element names within the ROW element can correspond to actual table attribute names.

The package provides multiple options through its various procedures and functions for customizing the XML output, like changing element names ROWSET or ROW, restrict the number of rows retrieved, and so on. These options are described later when the complete syntax is outlined. To simplify the use of the package, three approaches for XML generation involving the package are outlined.

1. Simple Query Approach

    A simple approach to generate XML from a query. In this approach the output is held in a SELECT clause attribute alias. The syntax is:

    select dbms_xmlgen.getxml('*query*') xml
    from dual;

where *query* represents a SQL query. For example, the following query displays the EMPLOYER_NAME, WORK_PHONE, and MARITAL attribute values from the TENANT table as XML. The XML output follows the query.

```
select dbms_xmlgen.getxml('select employer_name, work_phone, marital
from tenant') xml
from dual;


XML
-------------------------------------------
(CLOB) <?xml version="1.0"?>
<ROWSET>
 <ROW>
  <EMPLOYER_NAME>Kraft Inc.</EMPLOYER_NAME>
  <WORK_PHONE>4173452323</WORK_PHONE>
  <MARITAL>M</MARITAL>
 </ROW>
 <ROW>
  <EMPLOYER_NAME>Kraft Inc.</EMPLOYER_NAME>
  <WORK_PHONE>4175453320</WORK_PHONE>
  <MARITAL>S</MARITAL>
 </ROW>
 <ROW>
  <EMPLOYER_NAME>MSU</EMPLOYER_NAME>
  <WORK_PHONE>4178362323</WORK_PHONE>
  <MARITAL>M</MARITAL>
 </ROW>
 <ROW>
  <EMPLOYER_NAME>MSU</EMPLOYER_NAME>
  <WORK_PHONE>4174257766</WORK_PHONE>
  <MARITAL>S</MARITAL>
 </ROW>
 <ROW>
  <EMPLOYER_NAME>Kraft Inc.</EMPLOYER_NAME>
  <WORK_PHONE>4175557878</WORK_PHONE>
  <MARITAL>M</MARITAL>
 </ROW>
</ROWSET>
```

Another example now shows the query that displays the EMPLOYER_NAME, WORK_PHONE, and MARITAL attribute values from the TENANT table for tenants working in "Kraft Inc." as XML. The XML output follows the query.

```
select dbms_xmlgen.getxml('select employer_name, work_phone, marital
from tenant where employer_name = ''Kraft Inc.''') xml
from dual;

XML
-----------------------------------------------------------------------
(CLOB) <?xml version="1.0"?>
<ROWSET>
 <ROW>
  <EMPLOYER_NAME>Kraft Inc.</EMPLOYER_NAME>
  <WORK_PHONE>4173452323</WORK_PHONE>
  <MARITAL>M</MARITAL>
 </ROW>
 <ROW>
  <EMPLOYER_NAME>Kraft Inc.</EMPLOYER_NAME>
  <WORK_PHONE>4175453320</WORK_PHONE>
```

```
  <MARITAL>S</MARITAL>
 </ROW>
 <ROW>
  <EMPLOYER_NAME>Kraft Inc.</EMPLOYER_NAME>
  <WORK_PHONE>4175557878</WORK_PHONE>
  <MARITAL>M</MARITAL>
 </ROW>
</ROWSET>
```

2. **Implicit Cursor Approach**

   Utilize the simple query approach as an implicit cursor within an anonymous block or program unit. The package generates the XML output as a CLOB data type. The syntax is:

   ```
   declare
   variable1 clob;
   begin
   select dbms_xmlgen.getxml('query') into variable1
   from dual;
   dbms_output.put_line(variable1);
   end;
   ```

   where *query* represents a SQL query. For example, the following query displays the EMPLOYER_NAME, WORK_PHONE, and MARITAL attribute values from the TENANT table as XML. The XML output follows the anonymous block source.

   ```
   declare
   xmlout clob;
   begin
   select dbms_xmlgen.getxml('
   select employer_name, work_phone, marital
   from tenant') into xmlout
   from dual;
   dbms_output.put_line(xmlout);
   end;

   <?xml version="1.0"?>
   <ROWSET>
    <ROW>
     <EMPLOYER_NAME>Kraft Inc.</EMPLOYER_NAME>
     <WORK_PHONE>4173452323</WORK_PHONE>
     <MARITAL>M</MARITAL>
    </ROW>
    <ROW>
     <EMPLOYER_NAME>Kraft Inc.</EMPLOYER_NAME>
     <WORK_PHONE>4175453320</WORK_PHONE>
     <MARITAL>S</MARITAL>
    </ROW>
    <ROW>
     <EMPLOYER_NAME>MSU</EMPLOYER_NAME>
     <WORK_PHONE>4178362323</WORK_PHONE>
     <MARITAL>M</MARITAL>
    </ROW>
    <ROW>
     <EMPLOYER_NAME>MSU</EMPLOYER_NAME>
     <WORK_PHONE>4174257766</WORK_PHONE>
     <MARITAL>S</MARITAL>
    </ROW>
    <ROW>
     <EMPLOYER_NAME>Kraft Inc.</EMPLOYER_NAME>
   ```

```
<WORK_PHONE>4175557878</WORK_PHONE>
<MARITAL>M</MARITAL>
</ROW>
</ROWSET>
```

3. Procedure with Package Options Approach

Utilize the various options of the DBMS_XMLGEN package through a PL/SQL procedure. These option statements can also be embedded within any program unit. The syntax of the DBMS_XMLGEN package is:

```
create or replace procedure xmlProcedure [(parameter1 in number, . . .)] as
variable1 DBMS_XMLGEN.ctxHandle;
variable2 clob;
begin
variable1 := DBMS_XMLGEN.newContext('select . . . [where attribute1= :1 . . .]');
[DBMS_XMLGEN.setbindvalue (variable1, '1', parameter1);]
[DBMS_XMLGEN.setRowSetTag(variable1, 'new-rowset-tag-name');]
[DBMS_XMLGEN.setRowTag(variable1, 'new-row-tag-name');]
[DBMS_XMLGEN.setMaxRows(variable1, no-of-rows);]
[DBMS_XMLGEN.setPrettyPrinting(variable1,{true | false});]
variable2 := DBMS_XMLGEN.getXML(variable1);
DBMS_XMLGEN.closeContext(variable1);
dbms_output.put_line(variable2);
end;
```

where
- *variable1* is a variable with ctxHandle data type. ctxHandle is a number datatype attached to a variable that will hold the XML output. It can be also used to generate a DTD or XML schema.
- newContext(*queryString* IN VARCHAR2) function converts an input query string to XML. Queries with conditions must use the bind variables like :1, :2, etc to assign value later with the setBindValue procedure. The result of this function is assigned to a variable having the ctxHandle datatype.
- setBindValue(*variable* IN ctxHandle, *bindVariableName* IN VARCHAR2, *bindValue* IN VARCHAR2) procedure sets the bind value for the bind variable appearing in the query string associated with the context handle as defined with the newContext function. The query string with bind variables cannot be executed until all the bind variables are set values using the setBindValue() call.
- getXML(*variable* IN ctxHandle, *dtdOrSchema* IN number := NONE) function generates the XML document and returns it as a CLOB. Input variable is the context handle obtained from the newContext() call, and dtdOrSchema(IN) specifies whether we should generate the DTD or Schema.
- closeContext(*variable* IN ctxHandle) procedure closes all resources associated with this handle. Parameter variable is the context handle obtained from the newContext() call to close. After this procedure call one cannot use the handle for any other DBMS_XMLGEN function call.
- setRowTag(*variable* IN ctxHandle, *rowTag* IN VARCHAR2) procedure allows changing the name of the ROW element in XML output.
- setRowSetTag(*variable* IN ctxHandle, *rowSetTag* IN VARCHAR2) procedure allows changing the name of the ROWSET root element in XML output.
- setPrettyPrinting(*variable*,{TRUE |FALSE}) generates XML output in either standard indented format (TRUE argument value) or with all the whitespaces between XML element tags stripped out (FALSE argument value). The FALSE setting is useful when XML output has to be processed in different browsers. The TRUE, FALSE entries are not case sensitive.

• setMaxRows(*variable* IN ctxHandle, *maxRows* IN NUMBER) procedure restricts the number of rows converted to XML.

Figure 7-4 provides guidance on the use of package options in the form of its procedures and functions.

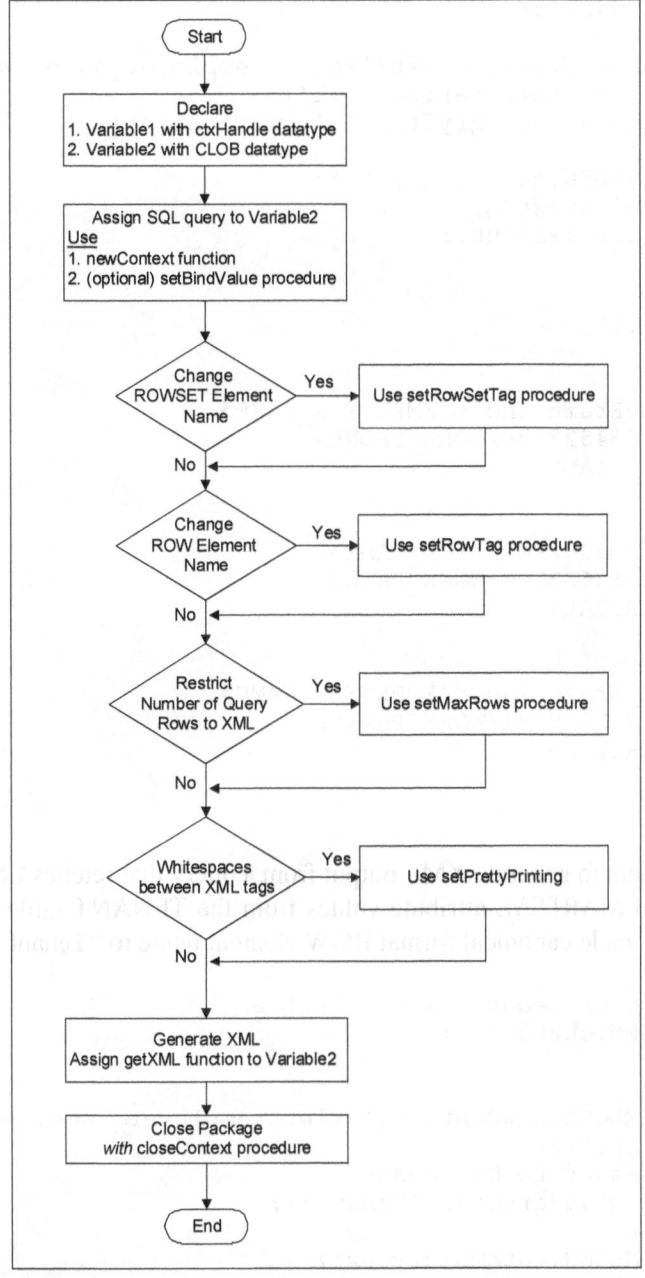

Figure 7-4

View XML in SQL Editor

A series of examples are now provided to illustrate the use of the package with different options in SQL Developer. The DBMS_OUTPUT statement is utilized to view the XML output.

1. A procedure clob_output to generate XML output from a query that fetches EMPLOYER_NAME, WORK_PHONE, and MARITAL attribute values for TENANTs with marital status M. The XML output (shown below the procedure) is in the default Oracle canonical format.

```
create or replace procedure clob_output as
qryCtx DBMS_XMLGEN.ctxHandle;
xmlout clob;
maritalIn varchar2(2) := 'M';
begin
qryCtx := DBMS_XMLGEN.newContext('select employer_name, work_phone,
marital from tenant where marital= :1');
DBMS_XMLGEN.setbindvalue (qryCtx, '1', maritalIn);
-- Get the result
xmlout := DBMS_XMLGEN.getXML(qryCtx);
DBMS_XMLGEN.closeContext(qryCtx);
dbms_output.put_line(xmlout);
end;


<?xml version="1.0"?>
<ROWSET>
 <ROW>
  <EMPLOYER_NAME>Kraft Inc.</EMPLOYER_NAME>
  <WORK_PHONE>4173452323</WORK_PHONE>
  <MARITAL>M</MARITAL>
 </ROW>
 <ROW>
  <EMPLOYER_NAME>MSU</EMPLOYER_NAME>
  <WORK_PHONE>4178362323</WORK_PHONE>
  <MARITAL>M</MARITAL>
 </ROW>
 <ROW>
  <EMPLOYER_NAME>Kraft Inc.</EMPLOYER_NAME>
  <WORK_PHONE>4175557878</WORK_PHONE>
  <MARITAL>M</MARITAL>
 </ROW>
</ROWSET>
```

2. A procedure clob_output to generate XML output from a query that fetches EMPLOYER_NAME, WORK_PHONE, and MARITAL attribute values from the TENANT table. The procedure also modifies the default Oracle canonical format ROW element name to "Tenant."

```
create or replace procedure clob_output as
qryCtx DBMS_XMLGEN.ctxHandle;
xmlout clob;
begin
qryCtx := DBMS_XMLGEN.newContext('select employer_name, work_phone,
marital from tenant');
-- Set the row header to be Tenant
DBMS_XMLGEN.setRowTag(qryCtx, 'Tenant');
-- Get the result
xmlout := DBMS_XMLGEN.getXML(qryCtx);
dbms_output.put_line(xmlout);
DBMS_XMLGEN.closeContext(qryCtx);
end;
```

3. A procedure clob_output to generate XML output from a query that fetches EMPLOYER_NAME, WORK_PHONE, and MARITAL attribute values from the tenant table. The procedure also modifies the default Oracle canonical format ROW element name to "Tenant" and limits the number of rows in the output.

```
create or replace procedure clob_output as
qryCtx DBMS_XMLGEN.ctxHandle;
xmlout clob;
begin
qryCtx := DBMS_XMLGEN.newContext('select employer_name, work_phone,
marital from tenant');
-- Set the row header to be Tenant
DBMS_XMLGEN.setRowTag(qryCtx, 'Tenant');
DBMS_XMLGEN.setMaxRows(qryCtx, 2);
-- Get the result
xmlout := DBMS_XMLGEN.getXML(qryCtx);
dbms_output.put_line(xmlout);
DBMS_XMLGEN.closeContext(qryCtx);
end;
```

4. A procedure clob_output to generate XML output from a query that fetches EMPLOYER_NAME, WORK_PHONE, and MARITAL attribute values from the TENANT table. The procedure also modifies the default Oracle canonical format ROWSET element name to "Root" and the ROW element name to "Tenant."

```
create or replace procedure clob_output as
qryCtx DBMS_XMLGEN.ctxHandle;
xmlout clob;
begin
qryCtx := DBMS_XMLGEN.newContext('select employer_name, work_phone,
marital from tenant');
DBMS_XMLGEN.setRowSetTag(qryCtx, 'Root');
-- Set the row header to be Tenant
DBMS_XMLGEN.setRowTag(qryCtx, 'Tenant');
-- Get the result
xmlout := DBMS_XMLGEN.getXML(qryCtx);
dbms_output.put_line(xmlout);
DBMS_XMLGEN.closeContext(qryCtx);
end;
```

5. A procedure clob_output to generate XML output from a query that fetches EMPLOYER_NAME, WORK_PHONE, and MARITAL attribute values from the tenant table. The procedure also modifies the default Oracle canonical format ROW element name to "Tenant" along with the removal of whitespaces.

```
create or replace procedure clob_output as
qryCtx DBMS_XMLGEN.ctxHandle;
xmlout clob;
begin
qryCtx := DBMS_XMLGEN.newContext('select employer_name, work_phone,
marital from tenant');
-- Set the row header to be Tenant
DBMS_XMLGEN.setRowTag(qryCtx, 'Tenant');
DBMS_XMLGEN.setPrettyPrinting(qryCtx,false);
-- Get the result
xmlout := DBMS_XMLGEN.getXML(qryCtx);
DBMS_XMLGEN.closeContext(qryCtx);
dbms_output.put_line(xmlout);
end;
```

View XML in Web Browser

A series of examples are now provided to illustrate the display of XML output in a Web browser. Once again the `owa_util.mime_header('text/xml')` statement and the `htp.prn({text|database-value})` package statement are utilized to display the XML output.

1. A procedure clob_output that generates XML output for display in Web browser from a query that fetches EMPLOYER_NAME, WORK_PHONE, and MARITAL attribute values from the TENANT table. To view the output, the procedure needs to be called from a URL similar to viewing a PL/SQL Server Page.

```
create or replace procedure clob_output as
xmlout clob;
begin
owa_util.mime_header('text/xml');
select dbms_xmlgen.getxml('
select employer_name, work_phone, marital
from tenant') into xmlout
from dual;
htp.prn(xmlout);
end;
```

2. A procedure clob_output that generates XML output for display in Web browser from a query that fetches EMPLOYER_NAME, WORK_PHONE, and MARITAL attribute values for TENANT_SS 123456789 from the TENANT table. The procedure uses some of the options of the DBMS_XMLGEN package. Once again to view the output, the procedure needs to be called from a URL similar to viewing a PL/SQL Server Page.

```
create or replace procedure clob_output as
qryCtx DBMS_XMLGEN.ctxHandle;
xmlout clob;
tenantNoIn number := 123456789;
begin
owa_util.mime_header('text/xml');
qryCtx := DBMS_XMLGEN.newContext('select employer_name, work_phone,
marital from tenant where tenant_ss= :1');
DBMS_XMLGEN.setbindvalue (qryCtx, '1', tenantNoIn);
xmlout := DBMS_XMLGEN.getXML(qryCtx);
DBMS_XMLGEN.closeContext(qryCtx);
htp.prn(xmlout);
end;
```

3. A PL/SQL Server Page with procedure name clob_output based on a query that fetches EMPLOYER_NAME, WORK_PHONE, and MARITAL attribute values for TENANT_SS 123456789 from the TENANT table. After the page is loaded into the server, the XML output can be viewed in the Web browser. Once again to view the output, the procedure needs to be called from a URL similar to viewing a PL/SQL Server Page.

```
<%@ page language="PL/SQL" contentType="text/xml"%>
<%@ plsql procedure="clob_output" %>
<%! tenantNoIn number := 123456789;
xmlout clob; %>
<% qryCtx := DBMS_XMLGEN.newContext('select employer_name, work_phone,
marital from tenant where tenant_ss= :1');
DBMS_XMLGEN.setbindvalue (qryCtx, '1', tenantNoIn);
xmlout := DBMS_XMLGEN.getXML(qryCtx);
```

```
      DBMS_XMLGEN.closeContext(qryCtx); %>
      <%=xmlout%>
```

Generating XML with SQL/XML Functions

There are many SQL/XML functions that generate XML from database tables. These functions offer flexibility in generating individual XML elements from the database tables. For the sake of simplicity the following functions are outlined:

- XMLElement
- XMLAttributes
- XMLForest
- XMLAGG

XMLElement

The XMLElement function can be used to construct individual XML instances from database tables. It takes as arguments an element name, an optional collection of attributes for the element, and zero or more additional arguments including the other functions that make up the element content. It returns a XMLType instance. The syntax is:

```
select xmlelement("element-name", [attribute-name], {xmlattributes | xmlforest | xmlagg})
from table-name
where condition ...
```

where *element-name* is the name of the beginning element name (it need not be a column name or a column reference); *attribute-name* is an attribute of the table in the query; and xmlattributes, xmlforest, xmlagg are other SQL/XML functions.

For example, the following query generates XML output by retrieving WORK_PHONE and EMPLOYER_NAME attribute values from the TENANT table. Each XML line has set of two element names with data concatenated from two attributes. The opening element name is called "Tenant" followed by another nested element name called "Name." The contents are the concatenated values of work_phone and employer_name attributes. Keep in mind that the first argument is always the element name. XML output follows the query.

```
select xmlelement("Tenant", xmlelement("Name",work_phone,employer_name))
from tenant;

XMLELEMENT("TENANT",XMLELEMENT("NAME",WORK_PHONE,EMPLOYER_NAME))
----------------------------------------------------------------
<Tenant><Name>4173452323Kraft Inc.</Name></Tenant>
<Tenant><Name>4175453320Kraft Inc.</Name></Tenant>
<Tenant><Name>4178362323MSU</Name></Tenant>
<Tenant><Name>4174257766MSU</Name></Tenant>
<Tenant><Name>4175557878Kraft Inc.</Name></Tenant>
```

To generate nested element names with custom names, the previous example can be modified such that each row of the query will be a separate XML statement with custom element names for TENANT_NAME, WORK_PHONE, and EMPLOYER_NAME attribute values. XML output follows the query.

```
select xmlelement("Tenant", xmlelement("Name", tenant_name),
xmlelement("Phone", work_phone), xmlelement("Employer", employer_name))
from tenant;

XMLELEMENT("TENANT",XMLELEMENT("NAME",TENANT_NAME),XMLELEMENT("PHONE",WORK_
PHONE),XMLELEMENT("EMPLOYER",EMPLOYER_NAME))
--------------------------------------------------------------------------
<Tenant><Name>Jack Robin</Name><Phone>4173452323</Phone><Employer>Kraft
Inc.</Employer></Tenant>
<Tenant><Name>Mary Stackles</Name><Phone>4175453320</Phone><Employer>Kraft
Inc.</Employer></Tenant>
<Tenant><Name>Ramu
Reddy</Name><Phone>4178362323</Phone><Employer>MSU</Employer></Tenant>
<Tenant><Name>Marion
Black</Name><Phone>4174257766</Phone><Employer>MSU</Employer></Tenant><Tena
nt><Name>Marion
Black</Name><Phone>4174257766</Phone><Employer>MSU</Employer></Tenant>
<Tenant><Name>Venessa
Williams</Name><Phone>4175557878</Phone><Employer>Kraft
Inc.</Employer></Tenant>
```

XMLAttributes

The XMLAttributes argument within the XMLElement function is used to specify attributes for the XML element name.

The following query lists TENANT_NAME, WORK_PHONE, and EMPLOYER_NAME from the TENANT table as a nested XML output with the TENANT_SS value as an attribute for element name "Tenant." XML output follows the query.

```
select xmlelement("Tenant", XMLAttributes(tenant_ss as "ID"),
xmlelement("Name", tenant_name), xmlelement("Phone", work_phone),
xmlelement("Employer", employer_name))from tenant;

XMLELEMENT("TENANT",XMLATTRIBUTES(TENANT_SSAS"ID"),XMLELEMENT("NAME",TENANT
_NAME),XMLELEMENT("PHONE",WORK_PHONE),XMLELEMENT("EMPLOYER",EMPLOYER_NAME))
--------------------------------------------------------------------------
<Tenant ID="123456789"><Name>Jack
Robin</Name><Phone>4173452323</Phone><Employer>Kraft
Inc.</Employer></Tenant>
<Tenant ID="723556089"><Name>Mary
Stackles</Name><Phone>4175453320</Phone><Employer>Kraft
Inc.</Employer></Tenant>
<Tenant ID="450452267"><Name>Ramu
Reddy</Name><Phone>4178362323</Phone><Employer>MSU</Employer></Tenant>
<Tenant ID="223056180"><Name>Marion
Black</Name><Phone>4174257766</Phone><Employer>MSU</Employer></Tenant>
<Tenant ID="173662690"><Name>Venessa
Williams</Name><Phone>4175557878</Phone><Employer>Kraft
Inc.</Employer></Tenant>
```

XMLForest

The XMLForest function returns a forest of XML elements in a XMLType when given a list of named expressions for the XML elements. Each expression specifies the name of the XML element and its content. This function is useful in generating nested XML elements.

The following query shows the XML output with element names for the attributes WORK_PHONE and EMPLOYER_NAME for each row in the TENANT table. XML output follows the query.

```
select xmlforest(work_phone,employer_name)
from tenant;

XMLFOREST(WORK_PHONE,EMPLOYER_NAME)
-----------------------------------
<WORK_PHONE>4173452323</WORK_PHONE><EMPLOYER_NAME>Kraft Inc.</EMPLOYER_NAME>
<WORK_PHONE>4175453320</WORK_PHONE><EMPLOYER_NAME>Kraft Inc.</EMPLOYER_NAME>
<WORK_PHONE>4178362323</WORK_PHONE><EMPLOYER_NAME>MSU</EMPLOYER_NAME>
<WORK_PHONE>4174257766</WORK_PHONE><EMPLOYER_NAME>MSU</EMPLOYER_NAME>
<WORK_PHONE>4175557878</WORK_PHONE><EMPLOYER_NAME>Kraft Inc.</EMPLOYER_NAME>
```

The XMLForest function can also be used as an argument within the XMLElement function. It then complements the XMLElement function to generate nested element names. The above query is now extended to include XMLElement function and the TENANT_NAME attribute value. XML output follows the query.

```
select xmlelement("Tenant",
xmlforest(tenant_name,work_phone,employer_name))
from tenant;

XMLELEMENT("TENANT",XMLFOREST(TENANT_NAME,WORK_PHONE,EMPLOYER_NAME))
--------------------------------------------------------------------
<Tenant><TENANT_NAME>Jack
Robin</TENANT_NAME><WORK_PHONE>4173452323</WORK_PHONE><EMPLOYER_NAME>Kraft
Inc.</EMPLOYER_NAME></Tenant>
<Tenant><TENANT_NAME>Mary
Stackles</TENANT_NAME><WORK_PHONE>4175453320</WORK_PHONE><EMPLOYER_NAME>Kra
ft Inc.</EMPLOYER_NAME></Tenant>
<Tenant><TENANT_NAME>Ramu
Reddy</TENANT_NAME><WORK_PHONE>4178362323</WORK_PHONE><EMPLOYER_NAME>MSU</E
MPLOYER_NAME></Tenant>
<Tenant><TENANT_NAME>Marion
Black</TENANT_NAME><WORK_PHONE>4174257766</WORK_PHONE><EMPLOYER_NAME>MSU</E
MPLOYER_NAME></Tenant>
<Tenant><TENANT_NAME>Venessa
Williams</TENANT_NAME><WORK_PHONE>4175557878</WORK_PHONE><EMPLOYER_NAME>Kra
ft Inc.</EMPLOYER_NAME></Tenant>
```

XMLAgg

The XMLAgg function is an aggregate function that produces a forest of XML elements from a collection of XML elements, with the option of XML element sorting. XMLAgg aggregates the XML elements pertaining to the attributes within the rows of the table. Useful for generating well formed XML elements with one root.

The following query shows the XML output with element names for attributes TENANT_NAME, WORK_PHONE and EMPLOYER_NAME for each row in the TENANT table. The XML output is now structured to generate a proper XML tree document with the root element name "Rowset." XML output follows the query.

```
select xmlelement("Rowset",xmlagg(xmlelement("Tenant", xmlforest(tenant_name,
work_phone,employer_name)))) from tenant;

XMLELEMENT("ROWSET",XMLAGG(XMLELEMENT("TENANT",XMLFOREST(TENANT_NAME,WORK_P
HONE,EMPLOYER_NAME))))
-----------------------------------------------------------------------
<Rowset>
   <Tenant>
      <TENANT_NAME>Jack Robin</TENANT_NAME>
      <WORK_PHONE>4173452323</WORK_PHONE>
      <EMPLOYER_NAME>Kraft Inc.</EMPLOYER_NAME>
   </Tenant>
   <Tenant>
      <TENANT_NAME>Mary Stackles</TENANT_NAME>
      <WORK_PHONE>4175453320</WORK_PHONE>
      <EMPLOYER_NAME>Kraft Inc.</EMPLOYER_NAME>
   </Tenant>
   <Tenant>
      <TENANT_NAME>Ramu Reddy</TENANT_NAME>
      <WORK_PHONE>4178362323</WORK_PHONE>
      <EMPLOYER_NAME>MSU</EMPLOYER_NAME>
   </Tenant>
   <Tenant>
      <TENANT_NAME>Marion Black</TENANT_NAME>
      <WORK_PHONE>4174257766</WORK_PHONE>
      <EMPLOYER_NAME>MSU</EMPLOYER_NAME>
   </Tenant>
   <Tenant>
      <TENANT_NAME>Venessa Williams</TENANT_NAME>
      <WORK_PHONE>4175557878</WORK_PHONE>
      <EMPLOYER_NAME>Kraft Inc.</EMPLOYER_NAME>
   </Tenant>
</Rowset>
```

CHAPTER SUMMARY

- XML is a markup language designed to describe data.

- Similar to HTML, the data in XML is defined through the concept of tags (or markup).

- XML tags are not predefined like HTML, but rather defined by the developer.

- XML uses a Document Type Definition (DTD) or a XML Schema to describe the data.

- A DTD defines the vocabulary of tags and how they may be used for a specific type of XML document.

- The layout of the XML structure is hierarchical.

- The building block of the XML structure is a XML element.

- A XML element is everything from the opening tag to the closing tag, ie. opening tag, content, and closing tag.

- Any name can be used to define an element name.

- The XML tags are case sensitive and must be properly nested.

- XML element names can have attributes in the form of name/value pairs within the opening tag.

- A XML document structure must be contained within a single tag pair referred as a root element.

- XML Namespace provides a method to avoid element name conflicts.

- The hierarchical structure of a XML document is conceptually similar to the DOM hierarchical tree of a HTML Web page.

- The XML structure once represented as a DOM tree can be traversed with DOM methods and properties.

- Manual generation of XML from Oracle database involves preparing a XML document within a procedure with element names and database data.

- XML output can be viewed in the Web browser by using the `owa_util.mime_header` statement and the `htp.prn` package statements in the procedure.

- DBMS_XMLGEN is a PL/SQL package supplied with Oracle database to generate XML as a CLOB or XMLType data.

- The DBMS_XMLGEN package creates XML documents from a SQL query.

- The DBMS_XMLGEN package is useful for multi-row processing.

- The DBMS_XMLGEN package uses a default canonical format to map the SQL query data to XML.

▸ The Oracle SQL/XML function like XMLElement can be used to construct individual XML instances from database tables.

▸ The Oracle SQL/XML function like XMLForest function returns a forest of XML elements in a XMLType when given a list of named expressions for the XML elements.

▸ The Oracle SQL/XML function like XMLAGG function is an aggregate function that produces a forest of XML elements from a collection of XML elements, with the option of XML element sorting.

REVIEW QUESTIONS

1. Describe the hierarchical structure of XML document.

2. Explain the similarities between XML structure and DOM.

3. What is the purpose of XMLNamespace.

4. What statements are necessary to view XML output in the Web browser.

5. Describe the Oracle canonical format.

6. Describe the features of DBMS_XMLGEN package.

7. Describe the SQL/XML functions.

REVIEW EXERCISES

1. XML is a _____ language for describing data.

2. XML uses a _____ to describe data.

3. The layout of the XML structure is _____ .

4. The building block of an XML structure is _____ _____ .

5. A XML element includes _____ tag, content, and _____ tag.

6. The topmost element in the XML hierarchical structure is the _____ element.

7. To view XML output in a Web browser requires _____ and _____ statements.

8. <apt_no>201_____ is a XML element.

9.   <rental_no><apt_no>201_____ _____ is a XML element.

10. In Oracle canonical format _____ is the root element.

11. The <tenant_name>Jack Robbin</tenant_name> element represented as a DOM tree will show _____ as a element node.

12. The <tenant_name>Jack Robbin</tenant_name> element represented as a DOM tree will show _____ as a text node.

13. In the DOM tree of Oracle canonical format, the table attributes are _____ nodes of _____ element.

14. The XML output is stored as a _____ data type in DBMS_XMLGEN package.

15. The DBMS_XMLGEN package generates XML output in Oracle _____ format.

16. The SQL/XML function _____ can be used to construct individual XML elements.

17. The arguments within a XML element can be specified through the _____ SQL/XML function.

18. The SQL/XML function _____ returns a forest of XML elements.

PROBLEM SOLVING EXERCISES

> Run the script file outdoorDB_v4.sql to load the Outdoor Clubs & Product database to complete the following exercises.

Ex7-1.   Study the following XML document and answer questions pertaining to it.

```
<?xml version="1.0"?>
<ROWSET>
 <ROW>
  <FIRST_NAME>Jack</FIRST_NAME>
  <LAST_NAME>Russell</LAST_NAME>
  <CITY>Springfield</CITY>
 </ROW>
 <ROW>
  <FIRST_NAME>Betty</FIRST_NAME>
  <LAST_NAME>Trumbell</LAST_NAME>
  <CITY>St. Louis</CITY>
 </ROW>
 <ROW>
  <FIRST_NAME>Anil</FIRST_NAME>
  <LAST_NAME>Kaul</LAST_NAME>
  <CITY>Kansas City</CITY>
 </ROW>
</ROWSET>
```

a.   What is the root of the XML document.
b.   What is the element name of the first child of the root node.
c.   What is the node name of the last child of the <ROW> parent.
d.   What is the node name of the first child of the <ROW> parent.
e.   What is the text node of the last child of the <ROW> parent.
f.   What is the text node of the first child of the <ROW> parent.
g.   What are the node names of the <ROW> parent siblings.
h.   How many child nodes exist of the root node.
i.   How many child nodes exist of the <ROW> parent.

Ex7-2.   Study the following XML document and answer questions pertaining to it.

```
<?xml version="1.0"?>
<ROWSET>
 <ROW>
  <NAME>Tiger Mountain</NAME>
  <CITY>Los Angeles</CITY>
  <PRODUCTCOUNT>3</PRODUCTCOUNT>
 </ROW>
 <ROW>
  <NAME>Hillside Ski</NAME>
  <CITY>Los Angeles</CITY>
  <PRODUCTCOUNT>4</PRODUCTCOUNT>
 </ROW>
 <ROW>
  <NAME>Sheraton Recreation</NAME>
  <CITY>New York</CITY>
  <PRODUCTCOUNT>2</PRODUCTCOUNT>
 </ROW>
 <ROW>
  <NAME>Asha Outdoor</NAME>
  <CITY>Chicago</CITY>
```

```
<PRODUCTCOUNT>3</PRODUCTCOUNT>
 </ROW>
</ROWSET>
```

a. What is the root of the XML document.
b. What is the element name of the first child of the root node.
c. What is the node name of the last child of the <ROW> parent.
d. What is the node name of the first child of the <ROW> parent.
e. What is the text node of the last child of the <ROW> parent.
f. What is the text node of the first child of the <ROW> parent.
g. What are the node names of the <ROW> parent siblings.
h. How many child nodes exist of the root node.
i. How many child nodes exist of the <ROW> parent.

Ex7-3.   Study the following XML document and answer questions pertaining to it.

```
<?xml version="1.0"?>
<List>
 <Product>
  <PRODUCT_NAME>Pro Ski Boot</PRODUCT_NAME>
  <ORDERCOUNT>1</ORDERCOUNT>
 </Product>
 <Product>
  <PRODUCT_NAME>Pro Ski Pole</PRODUCT_NAME>
  <ORDERCOUNT>2</ORDERCOUNT>
 </Product>
 <Product>
  <PRODUCT_NAME>Intermediate Ski Boot</PRODUCT_NAME>
  <ORDERCOUNT>3</ORDERCOUNT>
 </Product>
 <Product>
  <PRODUCT_NAME>Mountain Bicycle</PRODUCT_NAME>
  <ORDERCOUNT>1</ORDERCOUNT>
 </Product>
 <Product>
  <PRODUCT_NAME>Water Bottle</PRODUCT_NAME>
  <ORDERCOUNT>3</ORDERCOUNT>
 </Product>
</List>
```

a. What is the root of the XML document.
b. What is the element name of the first child of the root node.
c. What is the node name of the last child of the <ROW> parent.
d. What is the node name of the first child of the <ROW> parent.
e. What is the text node of the last child of the <ROW> parent.
f. What is the text node of the first child of the <ROW> parent.
g. What are the node names of the <ROW> parent siblings.
h. How many child nodes exist of the root node.
i. How many child nodes exist of the <ROW> parent.

Ex7-4.   Generate XML output (use the DBMS_XMLGEN or SQL/XML functions) that lists the product_id, product_name, and price values from the product table where price is greater than 10. Save the source as a script file with filename ex74.

Ex7-5.   Generate XML output (use the DBMS_XMLGEN or SQL/XML functions) that lists the sporting_clubs name, duration, first_name, last_name for customers who have club_membership. Save the source as a script file with filename ex75.

Ex7-6.   Generate XML output (use the DBMS_XMLGEN or SQL/XML functions) that lists the supplier_id, supplier name, and the number of products each supplier has provided. However, only those suppliers who have supplied more than two products should be listed. Save the source as a script file with filename ex76.

Ex7-7.   Generate XML output (use the DBMS_XMLGEN or SQL/XML functions) that lists all products (product_id, product_name) and their remaining stock (quantity_in_stock - reorder_point). List only those rows whose remaining stock is more than the average reorder_qty value. Save the source as a script file with filename ex77.

Ex7-8.   Create a procedure list_clubs that lists the sporting_clubs name, club_membership duration, customer first_name, customer last_name values for those customers who have club membership as XML output (use the DBMS_XMLGEN or SQL/XML functions) in the Web browser. Save the procedure as a script file with filename ex78.

Ex7-9.   Create a procedure list_products that lists all products (product_id, product_name) and their remaining stock (quantity_in_stock - reorder_point) as XML output (use the DBMS_XMLGEN or SQL/XML functions) in the Web browser. List only those rows whose remaining stock is more than the average REORDER_QTY value. Save the procedure as a script file with filename ex79.

Ex7-10.   Create a procedure list_orders that lists order_id, order_date, and shipping time (the number of days it takes to ship order) as XML output (use the DBMS_XMLGEN or SQL/XML functions) in the Web browser. Save the procedure as a script file with filename ex710.

Ex7-11.   Create a procedure membership_details that lists the name of the product (product_name) and a *demand status* text display as XML output in the Web browser. The *demand status* text display is determined by counting the number of times a product has been ordered so far. The *demand status* text display will be either "Low Demand" or "High Demand". Low Demand is displayed if the product has been ordered less than 2 times. High Demand is displayed if the product has been ordered more than 2 times. Save the procedure as a script file with filename ex711.

Ex7-12.   Create a procedure "membership_duration" that displays membership_id, duration, first_name, last_name, city values of customers who have membership, along with the name of the mountain_club as XML output in the Web browser. The value of the mountain club name should be returned by a function "get_club." Create the function get_club that determines the value of the mountain club name. Save the procedure as a script file with filename ex712a. Save the function as a script file with filename ex712b.

Ex7-13.   Create a procedure "product_status" that displays the product_name, associated supplier name, and a message as XML output in the Web browser. The message will either display a total of the quantity ordered for the product, or a text 'Not Ordered so far.' The value of quantity ordered is determined by a function "product_qty." Create the function product_qty that determines the total quantity ordered for the input product_id. Save the procedure as a script file with filename ex713a. Save the function as a script file with filename ex713b.

Ex7-14.   Create a procedure "customer_status" that displays customer first_name, last_name, and a *status* value as XML output in the Web browser. The status value will either display a count of the number of orders placed by the customer or a a text "Not Ordered so far." The value of the number of orders placed by a customer should be determined by a function "customer_count." Create the function customer_count that determines the number of orders placed by a customer. Save the procedure as a script file with filename ex714a. Save the function as a script file with filename ex714b.

CHAPTER 8

Javascript Essentials

- Javascript Structure
- Javascript and DOM Manipulation

Javascript is a client-side scripting language for Web applications. It is an interpreted scripting language. All present-day Web browsers contain a Javascript interpreter. Javascript is generally utilized by Web applications to perform client-side dynamic activity.

Javascript runs under the control of Web browsers where it has access to the browser window and all the embedded objects including the HTML document. It can access and modify any part of a HTML document, thereby making Web applications dynamic. This chapter offers a brief introduction to the essential syntax of Javascript as well as some of the event handlers in the context of DOM manipulations.

JAVASCRIPT STRUCTURE

Unlike many other languages like PL/SQL, *Javascript is case sensitive*. Javascript statements are generally embedded in either the `<head>` section or the `<body>` section of the Web page. Typically the embedded statements within the `<head>` section correspond to functions that are invoked by other statements present in the `<body>` section. Javascript statements are enclosed within the `<script type="text/javascript">` and `</script>` tags.

It is also possible to store the Javascript source in a separate file with file type ".js" in a virtual folder on the Web server or the client machine. The source file should contain only the Javascript statements instead of the `<script>` tag pair. To access the Javascript source in an external file, the SRC attribute of the `<script>` tag is utilized. The SRC attribute value is a text string that references the Javascript file in a URL (virtual folder) or some folder location on the client machine. For example, the tag `<script type="text/javascript" src="/pspweb1/ajax1.js">` references a file ajax1.js stored on the Web server in virtual folder address /pspweb1/.

Variables and Operators

Javascript variable names must begin with uppercase or lowercase ASCII letters, dollar sign ($), or underscore (_). Variable names can include numbers. Reserved words or spaces are not allowed within a variable name. Since Javascript is a case-sensitive language, MYVAR and MyVar are different variable names.

Variables that are declared outside of Javascript program modules like functions have global scope, i.e. their values are available throughout the Web page. Variables declared inside the Javascript program modules have local scope, i.e. their values are only available within the function source.

Javascript supports three primitive data types – number, string, and boolean. Variables in Javascript are dynamically typed, i.e. variables can take values of any data type dynamically. Also variables need not be declared. However, it is good practice to declare variables with keyword `var` as var *variable-name* [*=value*]; with value assigned optionally. For example,

```
var statusIn = "true";
```

It is possible to declare multiple variables with one var keyword. For example,

```
var ctr, index, k=10, customer="Jack Russell";
```

Due to the dynamic typed nature of variable declaration, same variable can take different data type values within the same script. For example,

```
var myVariable = "Hello World"; assigns a literal string.
var myVariable = 100; assigns a numeric value.
```

Javascript support standard arithmetic and string operations including special operation symbols. Numeric operator symbols include increment (++), decrement (--), addition (+), subtraction (-), multiplication (*), and division (/). Some of the common string operators include the concatenation operator denoted by symbol +, toString() method that converts numbers to string, and Number(string) method that converts a string to number.

Objects and Methods

Javascript is also an object-based language. One of the most common object is the Document object referenced within the script as `document`. The Document object represents the content of a browser's window. Any text, graphics, form, or other information displayed in a Web page is part of the Document object. A group of related statements associated with an object that perform some task are called *methods*. There are many methods to manipulate the contents of a Document object. To execute an object's method, the method is appended to the object with a period.

Standard programming logic structures can be implemented through relevant Javascript statements. Such statements consists of selection logic and iteration logic statements. Besides the logic structure statements there are also comment statements, display statements, and arrays. Javascript statements can span many lines, but must terminate with a semi-colon. Any text editor can utilized to compose Javascript statements for a Web page.

Comment Statement

Single line comments in Javascript are preceded by two slashes. For example,

```
<script language="javascript" type="text/javascript">
// Single line comment.
</script>
```

Multiple line comments (block comments) in Javascript are enclosed within /* and */ symbols. For example,

```
<script language="javascript" type="text/javascript">
/*
Line 1 of block comment.
Line 2 of block comment.
*/
</script>
```

Display Statement

Javascript provides many methods to display simple messages containing text or variable values. Some of the common display methods are write() and alert().The write() method displays content within the browser document, while the alert() method shows the message in a pop-up box in the Web browser. For example, the following Web page displays messages consisting of text and variables. The text is enclosed in double quotes. The concatenation symbol + is utilized to combine text and /or variables.

```
<html>
<head>
<script language="javascript" type="text/javascript">
var beginText = "Line continues ", endText = " & ends here.";
var newText = 1;
</script>
</head>
<body>
<script language="javascript">
document.write(beginText);
document.write(endText);
alert("Display " + newText + " window for messages");
</script>
</body>
</html>
```

Selection Logic

The selection logic is a structured programming construct that changes the default sequential processing of statements. In this case, the logic sequences the processing statements based on the result of some condition or decision, based on whether the condition is evaluated as true or false. Javascript provides a IF/ELSE statement that implements the selection logic. The syntax of the selection logic statement is:

```
if (condition) {
  statement(s)
}
[else {
  statement(s)
}]
```

The comparison operators in the condition entry are == (equal), != (not equal), >, <, >=, <=. The following Web page illustrates the use of selection logic through declared variables as condition. The Javascript in the Web page will display a message.

```
<html>
<head>
<script language="javascript" type="text/javascript">
var custNo = 1;
var custName = "Jack Russell";
if (custNo == 1) {
  document.write("Correct");
}
if (custName == 2) {
  document.write("Correct");
}
else {
  document.write(custName);
}
</script>
</head>
<body>
<p> End </p>
</body>
</html>
```

Iteration Logic

Iteration logic is a structured programming construct where one or more action statements are executed repeatedly. These action statements can represent simple sequence logic to more complex logic involving combination of sequence, selection, and even iteration logic. The repetition of action statements within the iteration logic can be for a fixed number of times, or can be based on the result of a condition. In Javascript there are many ways to perform iteration logic. Two mechanisms are outlined below.

1. Use of condition to control the repetition of statements. The syntax is:

    ```
    while (condition) {
      . . . statement(s);
    }
    ```

    The following Web page illustrates the *while* iteration logic through a condition that will cause the repetition of a message 3 times.

    ```
    <html>
    <head>
    <script language="javascript" type="text/javascript">
    var ctr = 3;
    while (ctr < 6) {
      document.write("Value of ctr is " + ctr);
      ctr++;
    }
    ```

```
</script>
</head>
<body>
<p> End </p>
</body>
</html>
```

2. Perform repetition of statements for a fixed number of times.

    for (initialization value; end condition; increment expression) {
        . . . statement(s);
    }

The following Web page illustrates the *for* iteration logic through a condition that will cause the repetition of a message 3 times.

```
<html>
<head>
<script language="javascript" type="text/javascript">
//var ctr = 3;
for (ctr=3; ctr< 6; ctr++) {
  document.write("Value of ctr is " + ctr);
}
</script>
</head>
<body>
<p> End </p>
</body>
</html>
```

Arrays

An arrays contains a set of data represented by a single variable name. Arrays are used to store group of related information. Arrays are declared through the new keyword and the Array() constructor function. The syntax is array-variable = new Array([size]); where array-variable is the name of the variable and size is number of values the variable will hold. Each piece of data contained in an array is called an element.

Data in an array is accessed using an index after the array variable using the syntax array-variable[index], where index value 0 references the first data value, value 1 references the second data value, and so on. For example, the following declaration creates an array multipleValues of size 3.

```
var multipleValues = new Array(3);
```

To access the first data element in multipleValues the syntax is multipleValues[0], the second value is multipleValues[1], and the third value is multipleValues[2]. The following Web page illustrates array variable working through display of array values.

```
<html>
<head>
<script language="javascript" type="text/javascript">
var multipleValues = new Array(3);
multipleValues[0] = "Index 1";
multipleValues[1] = 5;
```

```
multipleValues[2] = "End Element";
document.write(multipleValues[0]);
document.write(multipleValues[2]);
alert("Index 1 Value is " + multipleValues[1]);
</script>
</head>
<body>
<p> Display Array Variable values.</p>
</body>
</html>
```

Setting the size value during declaration of array variable is optional. In this case one can add new elements as necessary. The size of the array can change dynamically. If a value is assigned to an element that has not been created, the element is created automatically, along with the elements that might precede it. For example,

```
var multipleCustomers = new Array();
```

Functions

A function in Javascript is a named block of statements that performs some task and optionally returns a value. The syntax for creating function in Javascript is:

```
function function-name([parameter1, ...]) {
[declarations . . .]
. . . statements . . .
return . . .
}
```

where the function-name is the name of the function. Parameter1 and other parameters are input variables used within the function. Multiple parameters are separated by commas. The function body may consist of one or more statements including variable declarations. Scope of variables declared within a function is limited to the function itself. The function *may* include a return statement which includes the value to be returned by the function.

Functions can be called for value substitution or invoked by Javascript event handlers. The syntax for calling a function is `function-name(([parameter1, ...]);`. The syntax to assign the value returned by a function to a variable is: `variable-name = function-name(([parameter1, ...]);`.

Functions should be created within the `<head>` section of the Web page, while calls to function can occur from the `<head>` or the `<body>` sections of the Web page. The following Web page outlines a function that displays a message.

```
<html>
<head>
<script language="javascript" type="text/javascript">

function testFunction (custName) {
 document.write("testFunction message for " + custName);
}
testFunction("Jack Russell");
```

```
</script>
</head>
<body>
<p> End </p>
</body>
</html>
```

Form Event Handlers

Javascript event handlers are built-in functions that enable interactivity within a Web page or Web application. An event handler executes a segment of a code based on certain events occurring within an application. The syntax of an event handler within an HTML tag is:

```
<HTMLtag eventHandler="Javascript-Function-Name">
```

where HTMLtag is the beginning HTML tag, eventHandler is the name of the event handler and value within quotes is either a Javascript function name or Javascript code. Event handler names are the same as the name of the event itself, but with a prefix *on*. For example, the event handler for the Click event is onClick. There are many event handlers in Javascript. The focus here is on a sample of event handlers that essentially affect HTML forms. Table 8-1 provides a summary of selected event handlers.

Event Handlers	Description
onBlur	The onBlur event occurs when a form element (select, text, or textarea) becomes inactive or the focus of user input moves away from these elements .
onChange	The onChange event occurs when the content of a form element change.
onClick	The onClick event occurs when a form element is clicked once.
onFocus	The onFocus event occurs when a form element (select, text, textarea) becomes active or gets focus.
onSelect	The onSelect event occurs when text is selected in a text or textarea element in the form.
onSubmit	The onSubmit event occurs when the submit button in a form is clicked.

Table 8-1: Javascript Event Handlers

Instead of showing examples of all event handlers, the onClick handler working is illustrated to generalize on how the event handlers work. The following Web page displays a text box and a button, where the user enters some text in the text box. When the user presses the "Click Here" button, the onClick event handler calls a function displayText with one argument. The argument is the text entered by the user. The function displayText uses an alert method to display a message containing the user entered text.

```
<html>
<head>
<script language="javascript" type="text/javascript">
function displayText(input) {
  alert("Hello " + input + "! Welcome");
}
</script>
```

```
</head>
<body>
<h4>Example of onClick Event Handler</h4>
<p>Click on the button after entering your name into the text box:<p>
<form name="form1">
<input type="text" name="CustName" value="" size=10>
<input type="button" value="Click Here"
onClick="displayText(document.form1.CustName.value)">
</form>
</body>
</html>
```

JAVASCRIPT DOM MANIPULATION

The Web browser upon loading a Web page structures the HTML tags as a DOM tree (refer Chapter 4, Lesson B for DOM review). DOM manipulation is accomplished through Javascript. One of the key elements in the manipulation of DOM is the identification of HTML tags through the "id" attribute or tag name. Once the tags have been identified, Javascript allows dynamic manipulation of element or text nodes through DOM properties and methods.

The following examples show how Javascript is facilitating DOM manipulation of Web pages. All the examples use Web form buttons to either change text in a Web page or replace the Web form with some message.

1. Display Element & Text Nodes

    A Web page with four tags (`<div>`, `<h1>`, `<p>`, `<h3>`) and its associated DOM tree is shown in Figure 8-1 (similar to Figure 4-10 in Chapter 4, Lesson B). The Javascript statements display the element nodes and their corresponding text nodes in the `<body>` tag section of the page. The script uses the getElementById and getElementsByTagName methods to identify the tags.

    ```
    <html>
    <head>
    <title>DOM list</title>
    </head>
    <body>
    <div id="container">
    <h1 name="hClass" id="hid">This is a heading</h1>
    <p title="paraClass" id="pid">Sample DOM Paragraph</p>
    <h3 name="hClass">End of Page</h3>
    </div>
    <script language="javascript" type="text/javascript">
    var parentID = document.getElementById("container");
    document.write(parentID.nodeName + "</br>");
    var h1Tag = document.getElementById("hid");
    document.write(h1Tag.nodeName + "</br>");
    document.write(h1Tag.firstChild.nodeValue + "</br>");
    var pTag = document.getElementById("pid");
    document.write(pTag.nodeName + "</br>");
    document.write(pTag.firstChild.nodeValue + "</br>");
    var h3Tag = document.getElementsByTagName("h3");
    document.write(h3Tag[0].nodeName + "</br>");
    document.write(h3Tag[0].firstChild.nodeValue + "</br>");
    </script>
    </body>
    </html>
    ```

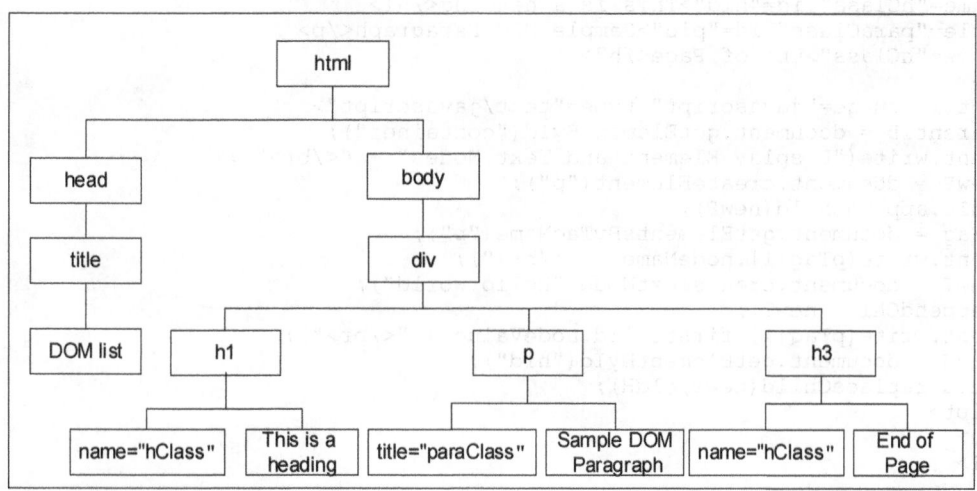

Figure 8-1

2.   Append a New Element and Text Node

Web page of example 1 is extended to now append a new element node <p> with the corresponding text node containing the text "Hello World." The new element node and text node are then displayed.

```
<html>
<head>
<title>DOM list</title>
</head>
<body>
<div id="container">
<h1 name="hClass" id="hid">This is a heading</h1>
<p title="paraClass" id="pid">Sample DOM Paragraph</p>
<h3 name="hClass">End of Page</h3>
</div>
<script language="javascript" type="text/javascript">
var parentID = document.getElementById("container");
document.write("Display Element and Text Nodes" + "</br>");
var newP = document.createElement("p");
parentID.appendChild(newP);
var pTag = document.getElementsByTagName("p");
document.write(pTag[1].nodeName + "</br>");
var newT = document.createTextNode("Hello world");
newP.appendChild(newT);
document.write(pTag[1].firstChild.nodeValue + "</br>");
</script>
</body>
</html>
```

3.   Replace Existing Element Node with a New Element Node

Web page of example 2 is extended to now replace the existing <h1> tag with a new element node <p> and its corresponding text node containing the text "Hello World." The new element node and text node are then displayed.

```
<html>
<head>
<title>DOM list</title>
</head>
<body>
<div id="container">
```

```
<h1 name="hClass" id="hid">This is a heading</h1>
<p title="paraClass" id="pid">Sample DOM Paragraph</p>
<h3 name="hClass">End of Page</h3>
</div>
<script language="javascript" type="text/javascript">
var parentID = document.getElementById("container");
document.write("Display Element and Text Nodes" + "</br>");
var newP = document.createElement("p");
parentID.appendChild(newP);
var pTag = document.getElementsByTagName("p");
document.write(pTag[1].nodeName + "</br>");
var newT = document.createTextNode("Hello world");
newP.appendChild(newT);
document.write(pTag[1].firstChild.nodeValue + "</br>");
var oldH = document.getElementById("hid");
parentID.replaceChild(newP,oldH);
</script>
</body>
</html>
```

4. **Replace Paragraph Node**

    A Web page that shows paragraph content and a HTML form. When the user clicks the Web form button "Test", Javascript replaces the entire paragraph with new content "New Content Replaces Form."

```
<html>
<head>
<script language="javascript" type="text/javascript">
function replaceText(divID,newText) {
document.getElementById(divID).innerHTML=newText;
}
</script>
</head>
<body>
<p id="pid">Old content</p>
<form name="Form1">
<input type="text" name="CustName" value="" size=10>
<input type="button" value="Test" name="Formsbutton1"
onclick="replaceText('pid','New Content Replaces Form')"; >
</form>
</body>
</html>
```

5. **Replace Inline Text**

    A Web page that shows paragraph content and a Web form. When the user clicks the Web form button "Test," Javascript replaces the phrase "an old text" with the phrase "now new text" in the paragraph.

```
<html>
<head>
<script language="javascript" type="text/javascript">

function replaceSpan(enterText,parentID,spanID) {

    var newSpan = document.createElement("span");
    var newText = document.createTextNode(enterText);
    newSpan.appendChild(newText);

    var para = document.getElementById(parentID);
    var spanElm = document.getElementById(spanID);
    para.replaceChild(newSpan,spanElm);
}
</script>
```

```
</head>
<body>
<p id="para1">This is <span id="span1">an old text</span></p> <br>
<form name="Form1">
<input type="button" value="Test" name="Formsbutton1" onclick="replaceSpan('now new
text','para1','span1')"; >
</form>
</body>
</html>
```

6. Replace Web Form

A Web page that shows paragraph content and a Web form. When the user clicks the form button "Modify," Javascript replaces the Web form with the message "The Updates have been applied. Thank You."

```
<html>
<head>
<script language="javascript" type="text/javascript">

function replaceText() {

document.getElementById("main-page").innerHTML = "The Updates have been applied.
Thank You.";

}
</script>
</head>
<body>
<p><b><span id="textToChange">Select tenant and modify other tenant
details</span></b></p>
<div id="main-page"><form name="UpdateForm">
<input type="text" name="CustName" value="" size=10>
<input type=button name="FormsButton1" value="Modify" onClick="replaceText()";>
</form>
</div>
</body>
</html>
```

CHAPTER SUMMARY

▸ Javascript is a client-side scripting language for Web applications.

▸ Javascript is generally utilized by Web applications to perform client-side dynamic activity.

▸ Javascript runs under the control of Web browsers where it has access to the browser window and all the embedded objects including the HTML document.

▸ Javascript is case sensitive.

▸ Javascript statements are generally embedded within a HTML document in either the <head> section or the <body> section.

▸ Javascript statements are enclosed within the <script type="text/javascript"> and </script> tags.

▸ Variables in Javascript are dynamically typed and support three primitive data types – number, string, and boolean.

▸ Javascript is an object-based language.

▸ One of the most common object is the document object that represents the content of a browser's window.

▸ Javascript provides methods to manipulate the contents within a Document object.

▸ A Javascript function is a named block of statements that performs some task and optionally returns a value.

▸ Functions can be called for value substitution or invoked by Javascript event handlers.

▸ Functions should be created within the <head> section of the Web page, while calls to function can occur from the <head> or the <body> sections of the Web page.

▸ Javascript event handlers are built-in functions that enable interactivity within a Web page or Web application.

▸ DOM manipulation is accomplished through Javascript.

▸ Javascript allows dynamic manipulation of element or text nodes through DOM properties and methods.

REVIEW QUESTIONS

1. What is the purpose of Javascript within a Web page?

2. Describe the nature of variables supported by Javascript.

3. Describe how Javascript manipulates the document object.

4. Describe the various program logic control statements available in Javascript.

5. Explain how arrays are handled in Javascript.

6. Explain how Javascript functions are utilized in a Web page.

7. Describe the role of event handlers in Javascript.

8. Describe the various forms of DOM manipulation through Javascript.

REVIEW EXERCISES

1. Javascript is a _____ scripting language for Web applications.

2. Web browsers contain a _____ interpreter.

3. Javascript statements are generally embedded within the _____ section of a Web page.

4. Javascript source can also be stored as a separate file with file type _____.

5. Javascript is _____ sensitive.

6. Variables in Javascript are _____ typed.

7. Javascript provides methods to manipulate the contents of the _____ object.

8. Arrays in Javascript are declared through the _____ keyword.

9. A _____ in Javascript is a named block of statements that performs some task and optionally returns a value.

10. Javascript _____ _____ are built-in functions that enable interactivity within a Web page.

11. Javascript facilitates _____ manipulation of Web pages.

12. Javascript allows dynamic manipulation of _____ or _____ nodes through DOM properties and methods.

PROBLEM SOLVING EXERCISES

Ex8-1.   Study the following Web page. Insert the Javascript script within the Web page that displays all the node names and their corresponding text nodes. Save the Web page with Javascript source with filename ex81.

```
<html>
<head>
<title>Web Page Title</title>
</head>
<body>
<p id="pid">Main Content Area</p>
<p id="eid">Example below displays lists.</p>
</body>
</html>
```

Ex8-2.   Study the following Web page. Insert the Javascript script within the Web page that displays all the node names and their corresponding text nodes. Save the Web page with Javascript source with filename ex82.

```
<html>
<head>
<title>Web Page Title</title>
</head>
<body>
<p id="pid">Main Content Area</p>
<p id="eid">Example below displays lists.</p>
<table id="tid">
<tr><td>PSP</td></tr>
<tr><td>DOM</td></tr>
</table>
</body>
</html>
```

Ex8-3.   Study the following Web page. Insert the Javascript script within the Web page that displays all the node names and their corresponding text nodes. Save the Web page with Javascript source with filename ex83.

```
<html>
<head>
<title>Web Page Title</title>
</head>
<body>
<p id="pid">Main Content Area</p>
<p id="eid">Example below displays lists.</p>
<li>list item 1</li><li>list item 2</li>
<ul>
<li>list item 1</li><li>list item 2</li>
</ul>
</body>
</html>
```

Ex8-4.   Study the following Web page. Insert the Javascript script within the Web page that displays all the node names and their corresponding text nodes. Save the Web page with Javascript source with filename ex84.

```
<html>
<head>
<title>Web Page Title</title>
</head>
```

```
<body>
<div id="blue">
<p id="pid">Main Content Area</p>
<p  title="paraClass"  id="pid">Sample  <span  id="sid">  DOM  </span>
Paragraph</p>
</div>
<table id="tid">
<tr><td>PSP</td></tr>
<tr><td>DOM</td></tr>
</table>
</body>
</html>
```

Ex8-5.   Study the following Web page. Insert the Javascript script within the Web page that displays
         all the node names and their corresponding text nodes. Save the Web page with Javascript
         source with filename ex85.

```
<html>
<head>
<title>Web Page Title</title>
</head>
<body>
<div id="blue">
<p id="pid">Main Content Area</p>
<p  title="paraClass"  id="pid">Sample  <span  id="sid">  DOM  </span>
Paragraph</p>
</div>
<li>list item 1</li>
<li>list item 2</li>
<li><a href="http://missouristate.edu">Home</a></li>
</body>
</html>
```

Ex8-6.   Study the following Web page. Insert the Javascript script within the Web page that displays
         all the node names and their corresponding text nodes. Save the Web page with Javascript
         source with filename ex86.

```
<html>
<head>
<title>Web Page Title</title>
</head>
<body>
<p id="pid">Main Content Area</p>
<p id="eid">Example below displays lists.</p>
<form name="Form1" id="fid">
<input type="text" name="CustName" value="" size=10>
<input type="button" value="Check" name="Formsbutton1">
</form>
</body>
</html>
```

Ex8-7.   Study the following Web page. Insert the Javascript script within the Web page that displays
         all the node names and their corresponding text nodes. Save the Web page with Javascript
         source with filename ex87.

```
<html>
<head>
<title>Web Page Title</title>
</head>
<body>
<div id="blue">
<p id="pid">Main Content Area</p>
<p  title="paraClass"  id="pid">Sample  <span  id="sid">  DOM  </span>
Paragraph</p>
```

```
</div>
<div id="green">
<form name="Form1" id="fid">
<input type="text" name="CustName" value="" size=10>
<input type="button" value="Check" name="Formsbutton1">
</form>
</div>
</body>
</html>
```

Ex8-8.   Extend problem Ex8-1, by including Javascript statements that append the tag `<h1 name="hClass">This is a heading</h1>` in the Web page DOM tree below the `<p id="eid">Example below displays lists.</p>` tag. Save the Web page with Javascript source with filename ex88.

Ex8A-9.   Extend problem Ex8-2, by including Javascript statements that replace the `<table id="tid">` tag in the Web page DOM tree with the tag `<h3 name="hClass">Table is replaced</h1>`. Save the Web page with Javascript source with filename ex89.

Ex8-10.   Extend problem Ex8-4, by including Javascript statements that replace the `<span id="sid">` tag in the Web page DOM tree with the tag `<h3 name="hClass">Span is replaced</h1>`. Save the Web page with Javascript source with filename ex810.

Ex8-11.   Extend problem Ex8-5, by including Javascript statements that append the tag `<p name="pClass">End of table</p>` in the Web page DOM tree below the `<table id="tid">` tag. Save the Web page with Javascript source with filename ex811.

Ex8-12.   Extend problem Ex8-6, by including Javascript statements that replaces the content of the `<p id="eid">Example below displays lists.</p>` tag with the text "Form is below this line." Create a onClick event handler with the form button to accomplish the change. Save the Web page with Javascript source with filename ex812.

Ex8-13.   Extend problem Ex8-7, by including Javascript statements that replaces the content of the `<span id="sid"> DOM </span>` tag with the text "DOM with Form." Create a onClick event handler with the form button to accomplish the change. Save the Web page with Javascript source with filename ex813.

Ex8-14.   Extend problem Ex8-7, by including Javascript statements that replaces the `<form>` tag with the text "Form has been replaced." Create a onClick event handler with the form button to accomplish the change. Save the Web page with Javascript source with filename ex814.

CHAPTER 9
(LESSON A)

AJAX with PL/SQL Server Pages

- AJAX Elements
- AJAX Processing
- Pre-defined Javascript Functions
- Generate Text Data from Database

AJAX stands for asynchronous Javascript and XML. It makes Web applications feel like desktop applications. AJAX enabled Web applications work behind the scenes, getting the data as they need it, and displaying data as desired.

Technically, AJAX changes the traditional approach of round-trip updates of Web pages. With AJAX, a Web page does not have to be completely re-loaded for every data related change or update of its content. It is a technique for dynamic transfer of data from the Web server to the Web page without page re-loading. Besides, this transfer occurs asynchronously, implying that the user can continue using the Web page. Since the entire Web page need not be transferred during content updates, AJAX also reduces data traffic between the Web page and the Web server. This section introduces the concept of AJAX and its working with respect to PL/SQL Server Pages. The examples in this lesson focus on the handling of Text formatted data. The handling of XML formatted data is outlined in the next lesson.

This lesson utilizes the table structure of Superflex Apartment database to explain examples.

AJAX ELEMENTS

There are five elements that make the AJAX environment successful.
1. The client scripting language Javascript.
2. The Web browser.
3. PL/SQL representation of database data in XML or text format.
4. The processing of XML or text formatted data received from the Web server.
5. The HTML document object model (DOM).

The interaction of these elements toward the operationalization of the AJAX environment is outlined now. Unlike the traditional Web application environment where the Web page processing occurs on the Web/Database server, AJAX relies on the client scripting language Javascript to handle the Web page processing tasks. Javascript in AJAX plays a central role in (i) the handling of communication between the Web page and the Web server, and (ii) the updating of Web page content. Hence, instead of using the traditional HTML markup statements (like Submit button) to transfer data, all data needs are serviced by

Javascript. The traditional Submit button can still be used when a complete re-loading of the Web page is desired.

AJAX extends the server-side PL/SQL script with client-side Javascript. The initial loading of the Web page is based on the server-side PL/SQL script. But once the Web page is in the Web browser, Javascript controls further interaction with the Web server for data transfer, unless the entire Web page has to be re-loaded.

The Web browser is the engine that drives AJAX operations. It is the Web browser that facilitates asynchronous interaction of Javascript with the Web server. The asynchronous feature of AJAX is facilitated through a special object called *XMLHttpRequest*. Web browsers like Firefox and Internet Explorer provide this object to facilitate AJAX related asynchronous data transfers.

AJAX focuses only on data returned by the Web/Database server. There are two formats for receiving data from the Web server – text format or XML format. For simple data requests, the Text format may be sufficient. However, for more complex data needs, XML provides a more robust option. Once the data is received (asynchronously) by the Web browser, Javascript utilizes the Web page DOM to update the page content.

There are many possible uses of AJAX framework for Web applications. In this chapter, the focus is on simple updates of a Web page with new data received through asynchronous operations. Also, the trigger of AJAX activity within the Web page will be limited to Web forms.

Figure 9-1 illustrates the AJAX framework. The Web browser loads the Web page containing the AJAX related Javascript. The Web browser connects and fetches the data from the Web/Database server, and thereafter transfers the data to Javascript for page updates. Changes in the Web page are performed by Javascript using the Web page DOM.

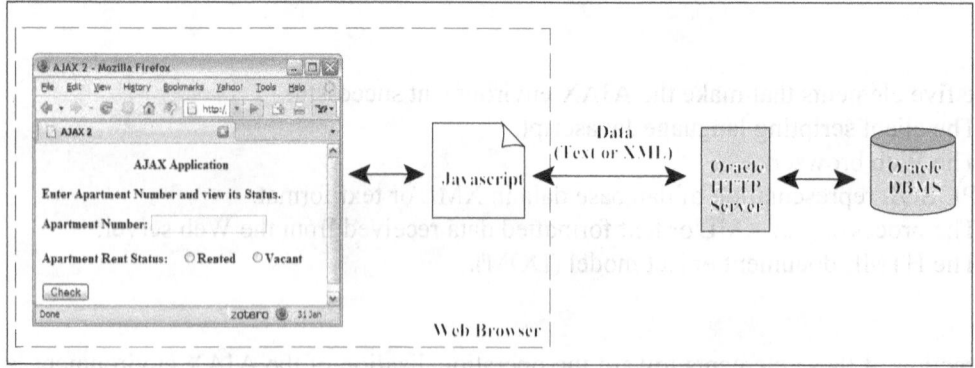

Figure 9-1

AJAX Processing Steps

The steps involved in the processing of AJAX activity including its various elements are outlined now. Each step is associated with a diagram to simplify its understanding.

1. Load PL/SQL server page in Web browser.

    This is the traditional loading of a Web page in Web browser as shown in Figure 9-2. The user enters the URL, and the Web browser connects to the Oracle HTTP (Web) server. The Oracle HTTP Server utilizes the PL/SQL gateway to connect to the Oracle database. The database server processes and transfers the PL/SQL server page to the Web browser.

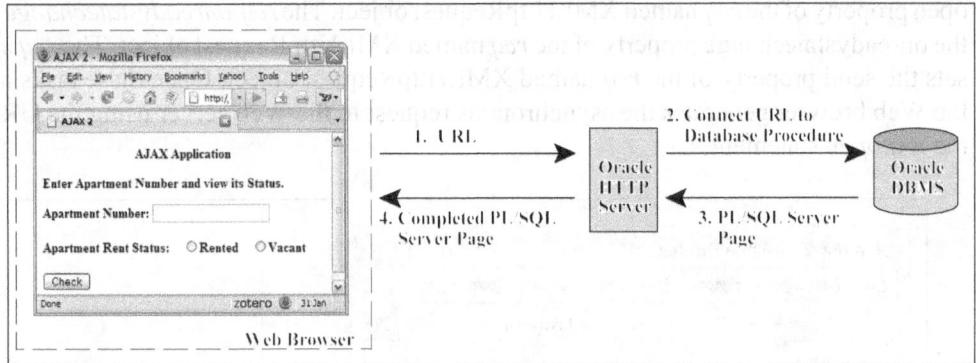

Figure 9-2

2. Initiate AJAX operations.

    AJAX activity is invoked through a Web form element, wherein a Javascript event handler associated with a Web form element calls a Javascript function (referred in this chapter as the *driver* function) to initiate the creation and handling of the XMLHttpRequest object. In Figure 9-3, the onClick event handler associated with HTML command button calls the Javascript driver function getAptStatus.

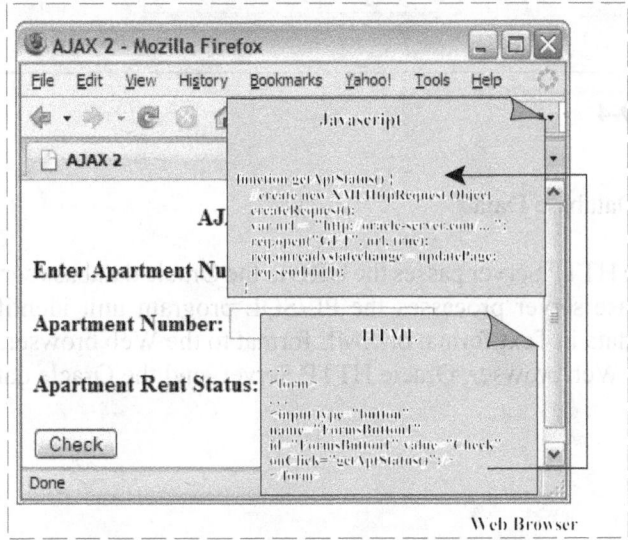

Figure 9-3

3. Perform AJAX operations.

The Javascript driver function performs four tasks associated with AJAX activity. These tasks include (i) the creation of the XMLHttpRequest object, (ii) the setting of the XMLHttpRequest object *open* property that includes the Web server URL and the type of data transfer (GET or POST), (iii) the setting of the *onreadystatechange* property of the XMLHttpRequest object to another Javascript function to handle the data returned by the Web server, and (iv) the setting of the *send* property of the XMLHttpRequest object to enable the Web browser to proceed in making the request for data from the Web server .

The function getAptStatus in figure 9-4 shows the driver function that performs the listed tasks to complete the AJAX operations. The *createRequest()* statement is a call to a standard function that creates the XMLHttpRequest object and assigns it to a variable *req*. The *req.open* statement sets the open property of the *req* named XMLHttpRequest object. The *req.onreadystatechange* statement sets the onreadystatechange property of the *req* named XMLHttpRequest object. The *req.send* statement sets the send property of the *req* named XMLHttpRequest object. Once these tasks are completed, the Web browser generates the asynchronous request to the Web server using the URL specified in the *req.open* statement.

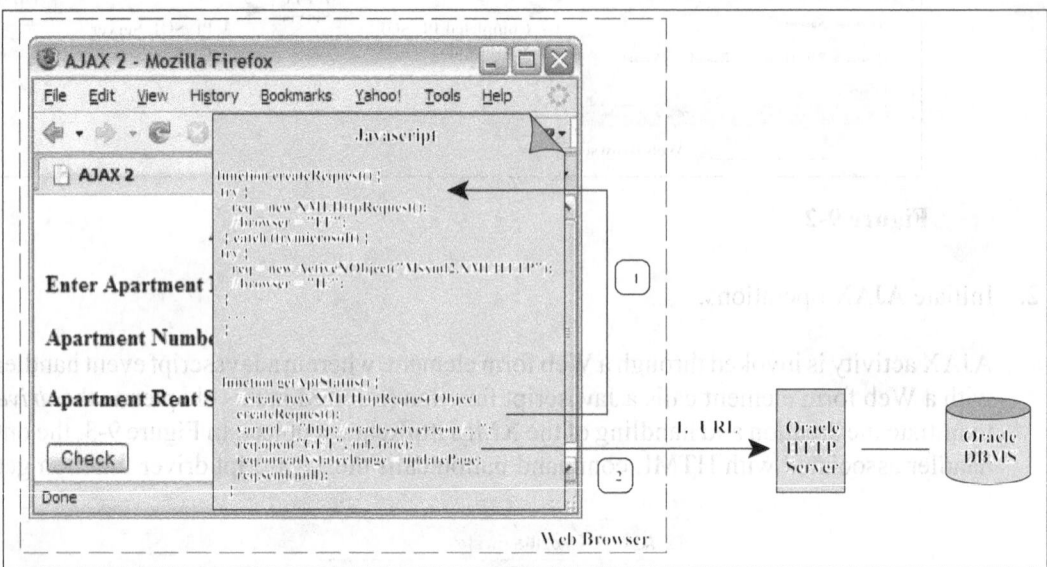

Figure 9-4

4. Generate Database Data

The Oracle HTTP Server passes the URL to the Oracle database server through the PL/SQL gateway. The database server processes the PL/SQL program unit identified in the URL and returns the requested data in Text format or XML format to the Web browser. Figure 9-5 shows the interaction among the Web browser, Oracle HTTP Server, and the Oracle database server.

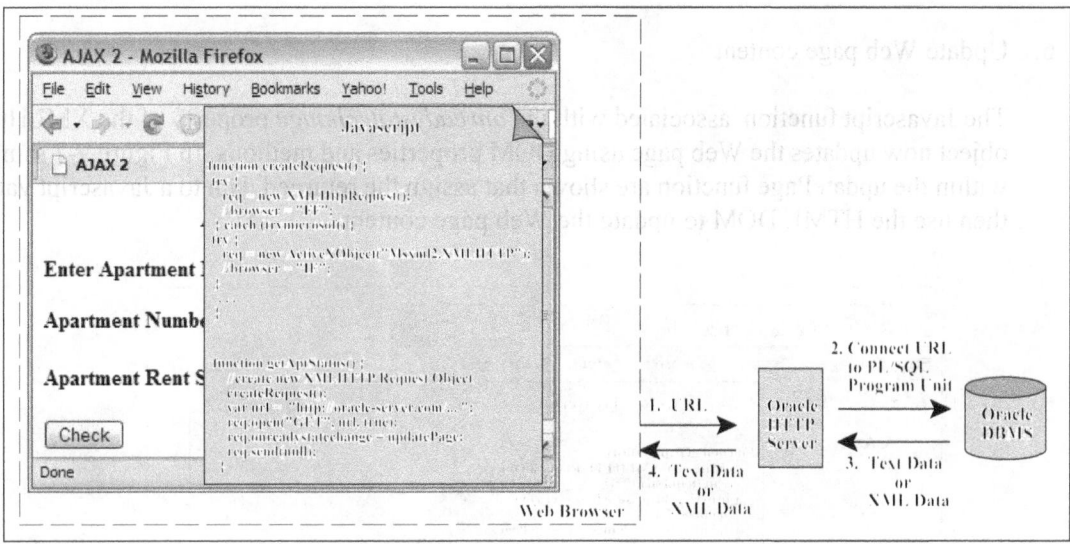

Figure 9-5

5. Processing XML or Text format Data

    Once the XML or Text formatted data is received from the Oracle HTTP server, the Web browser calls the Javascript function previously specified in the *onreadystatechange* property of the XMLHttpRequest object. In other words, the Web browser returns the control back to Javascript once the data is received from the Oracle HTTP server to the function specified in the *onreadystatechange* property of the XMLHttpRequest object. The Web browser stores the text formatted data in the *responseText* property of the XMLHttpRequest object, while the XML data is stored in the *responseXML* property of the XMLHttpRequest object. In Figure 9-6, the Web browser transfers control back to Javascript function updatePage since this function is specified in the onreadystatechange property of *req* named XMLHttpRequest object.

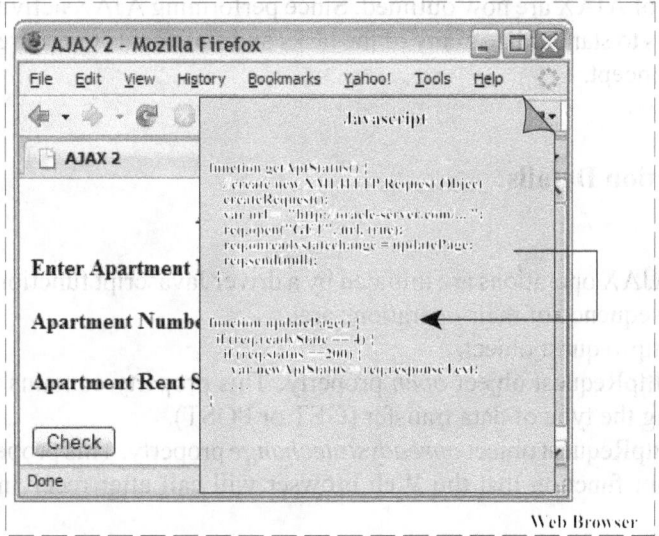

Figure 9-6

6.   Update Web page content

The Javascript function associated with the *onreadystatechange* property of the XMLHttpRequest object now updates the Web page using DOM properties and methods. In Figure 9-7 sample details within the updatePage function are shown that assign the returned data to a Javascript variable, and then use the HTML DOM to update the Web page content.

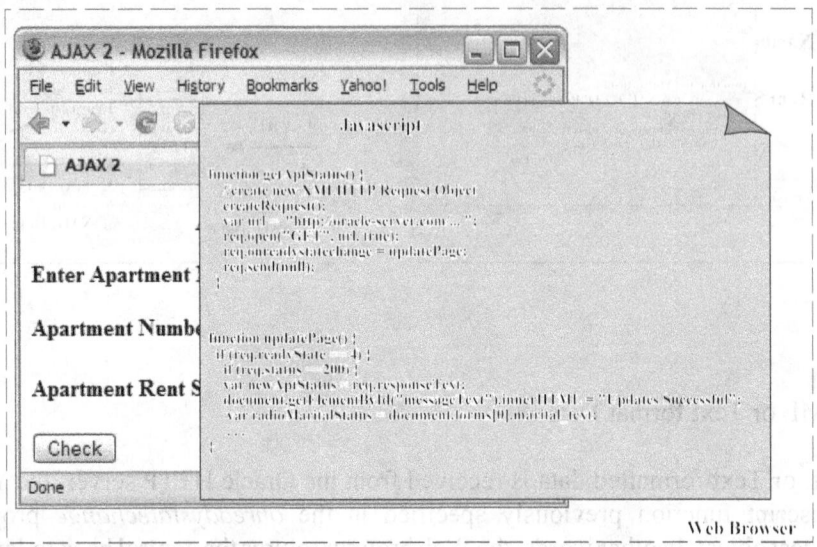

Figure 9-7

AJAX OPERATIONAL DETAILS

The operational details of AJAX are now outlined. Since performing AJAX activity involves Javascript, attempt in this chapter is to standardize many of the tasks and statements to ensure simplicity toward the understanding of the concept.

Javascript Driver Function Details

As mentioned before, AJAX operations are initiated by a driver Javascript function. The tasks performed by this function in the sequence of their operations are:
  i.   Create XMLHttpRequest object.
  ii. Set the XMLHttpRequest object *open* property. This property contains the URL for the Web server including the type of data transfer (GET or POST).
  iii. Set the XMLHttpRequest object *onreadystatechange* property. This property specifies the name of the Javascript function that the Web browser will call after receiving data from the Web server.
  iv. Set the XMLHttpRequest object *send* property. This property makes the request for data from the Web server.

The Javascript driver function is called through Javascript event handlers. For example, suppose getAjaxValue is the driver function. The following syntax shows the use of an *onClick* event handler with a form button or drop-down list selection that calls the driver function getAjaxValue.

```
<input type="button" name="FormsButton1" id="FormsButton1" value="Send"
onClick="getAjaxValue()";/>

<select name="some-name" id="some-name" onChange="getAjaxValue()"; >
```

Figure 9-8 shows the operational steps performed by the Javascript driver function to complete the AJAX operations toward sending data to the Web server.

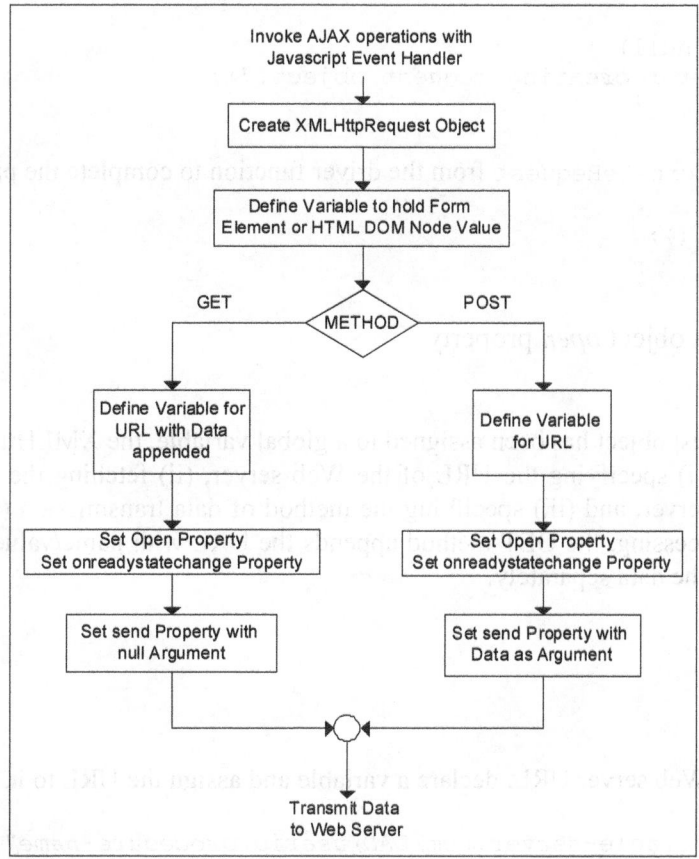

Figure 9-8

Create XMLHttpRequest Object

To create the XMLHttpRequest object, the steps are:

1. Declare a global variable within the script such as `var req = null;`

2. Create a function such as `createRequest` that assigns the XMLHttpRequest object to the global variable. The function statements are standard.

```
function createRequest() {
  try {
```

```
            req = new XMLHttpRequest();
            //browser = "FF";
        } catch (trymicrosoft) {
          try {
            req = new ActiveXObject("Msxml2.XMLHTTP");
            //browser = "IE";
          } catch (othermicrosoft) {
            try {
              req = new ActiveXObject("Microsoft.XMLHTTP");
              //browser = "IE";
            } catch (failed) {
              request = null;
            }
          }
        }

        if (req == null)
          alert("Error creating request object!");
      }
```

3. Call the function `createRequest` from the driver function to complete the process, such as:

```
createRequest();
```

Set the XMLHttpRequest object *open* property

Once the XMLHttpRequest object has been assigned to a global variable, the XMLHttpRequest object open property is set by (i) specifying the URL of the Web server, (ii) fetching the form data to be transmitted to the Web server, and (iii) specifying the method of data transmission (GET or POST). Similar to Web form processing, the GET method appends the URL with name/value pair, while the POST method packages the data separately.

URL Specification:

To ease specification of Web server URL, declare a variable and assign the URL to it. For example,

```
var url="http://oracle-server.com/DAD/userid.procedure-name";
```

where DAD is the database access descriptor of the PL/SQL gateway, the userid is the database server account, and procedure-name is the name of the procedure stored in the specified userid. This URL is similar to accessing any PL/SQL server page from a Web browser. It is also possible to access a procedure within a PL/SQL package using the syntax *package-name.procedure-name*.

Fetch Form Data:

To transmit HTML form data, it is important to define a variable that contains the value of the form element. The value of a HTML form element can be fetched through the DOM property getElementById set on the name of the form element. The following syntax shows the value of some Web form element name assigned to variable varIn.

```
var varIn = document.getElementById("form-element-name").value;
```

Use similar DOM property to fetch other Web form element values.

GET Method:

If the GET method is utilized for sending data, the URL variable is appended as follows:

```
var url="http://oracle-server.com/DAD/userid.procedure-name?varIn=" +
escape(varIn);
```

In the above URL, the varIn is the variable name of some Web form element and `escape(varIn)` is the value of the element. For sending multiple form element values extend the name/value pair in the URL. The following statement shows three form element values (assigned to variables varIn, varIn2, and varIn3) appended to the URL.

```
var url = "http:/oracle-server.com/DAD/userid.procedure-name?varIn=" +
escape(varIn) + "&varIn2=" + escape(varIn2) + "&varIn3=" +
escape(varIn3);
```

The complete statement of the open property of the XMLHttpRequest object with the GET method of transmission is:

```
req.open("GET", url, true);
```

where *req* is the name of the XMLHttpRequest object, the first argument is the GET method, the second argument is the value of the variable `url`, and the third argument entry `true` value makes the request asynchronous. To make the request synchronous, change the third argument entry to `false`. For AJAX asynchronous operations use the `true` value for the third argument.

POST Method:

If the POST method is utilized for sending data, the URL variable stays without any extension as follows:

```
var url="http://oracle-server.com/DAD/userid.procedure-name";
```

The complete statement of the open property of the XMLHttpRequest object with the POST method of transmission is as follows:

```
req.open("POST", url, true);
```

In the above statement, where *req* is the name of the XMLHttpRequest object, the first argument is the POST method, the second argument is the value of the variable `url`, and the third argument entry `true` value makes the request asynchronous. To make the request synchronous, change the third argument entry to `false`. For AJAX asynchronous operations use the `true` value for the third argument.

The data from the Web form that is to be sent to the Web server through the POST method is handled by the *send* property of the XMLHttpRequest object (explained later).

Set the XMLHttpRequest object *onreadystatechange* property

Prior to sending the data from the Web page to the Web server, the Javascript function to which the Web browser will give control once it receives data from the Web/Database server needs to be specified. This specification is done in the *onreadystatechange* property of the XMLHttpRequest object. So, when the Web browser receives the data from the server (XML or Text format), it invokes the Javascript function defined through the onreadystatechange property. For example, the statement below assigns the function updatePage to the onreadystatechange property; so when the Web browser receives data from the Web server it invokes the updatePage function automatically.

```
req.onreadystatechange = updatePage;
```

In the above syntax *req* is the name of the XMLHttpRequest object. Keep in mind that the function name in the above statement should be without the parenthesis.

Set the XMLHttpRequest object *send* property

The *send* property of the XMLHttpRequest object makes the Web browser begin the AJAX operations. In case the GET method of transmission was selected in the XMLHttpRequest object *open* property, the syntax would be:

```
req.send(null);
```

where *req* is the name of the XMLHttpRequest object.

In case the POST method of transmission was selected in the XMLHttpRequest object *open* property, the statement would include the variable names of the Web form element values that need to be transmitted to the Web server.

```
req.send("varIn=" + escape(varIn));
```

In the above statement, *req* is the name of the XMLHttpRequest object, the varIn is the variable name of some Web form element and `escape(varIn)` is the value of the element. In case multiple form element values need to be transmitted, simply extend the name/value pair. The following statement shows three form element values (assigned to variables varIn, varIn2, and varIn3) transmitted to the Web server.

```
req.send("varIn=" + escape(varIn) + "&varIn2=" + escape(varIn2) +
"&varIn3=" + escape(varIn3));
```

Javascript Driver Function Details

The sequence of statements to transmit single form data value to the Web server using the GET method with *req* as the name of the XMLHttpRequest object are as follows:

```
var varIn = document.getElementById("form-element-name1").value;
var   url="http://oracle-server.com/DAD/userid.procedure-name?varIn="   +
escape(varIn);
req.open("GET", url, true);
req.onreadystatechange = updatePage;
req.send(null);
```

The sequence of statements to transmit single form data to the Web server using the POST method with *req* as the name of the XMLHttpRequest object are as follows:

```
var varIn = document.getElementById("form-element-name1").value;
var url="http://oracle-server.com/DAD/userid.procedure-name";
req.open("POST", url, true);
req.onreadystatechange = updatePage;
req.send("varIn=" + escape(varIn));
```

In the above statements, substitute the entries in italics with relevant entries.

Process Web Server Data

Text data returned by the Web server is stored in the *responseText* property of the XMLHttpRequest object. XML data returned by the Web server is stored in the *responseXML* property of the XMLHttpRequest object. This property is referenced by the Javascript function defined through the onreadystatechange property in the AJAX driver function. For example, the following updatePage function utilizes a variable newData to reference the data stored in responseText property.

```
function updatePage() {
   if (req.readyState == 4) {
      if (req.status ==200) {
      var newData = req.responseText;
      document.getElementById("messageText").innerHTML = "The Updates for
" + newData + " have been applied. Thank You.";
      } else
      alert("Processing Error " + req.status);
   }
}
```

In the updatePage function there are two additional properties – *readystate* and *status*. The readystate property gives the state of the request, while the status property gives the status of the request. To ensure proper processing of data by the Web server, these properties are important.

readystate Property

The XMLHttpRequest object has a *ready state* that tells the Web browser about what *state* the request is in. This ready state is like a monitor that informs the Web browser about the stage of processing the request is in, like initialization, processing, completed, etc. Figure 9-9 shows the four ready states that are numbered from 1 to 4.

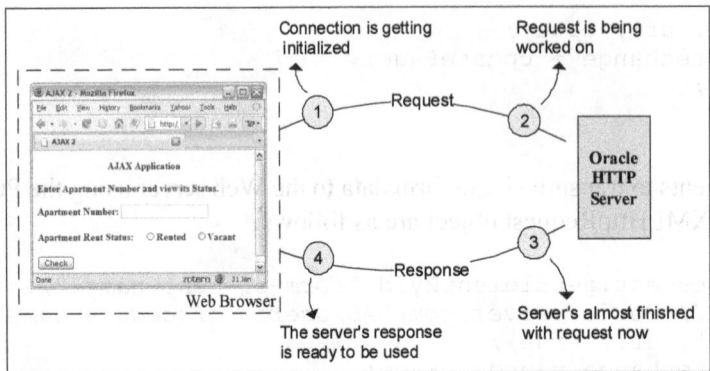

Figure 9-9

These ready states are connected with the XMLHttpRequest object's onreadystatechange property. The Web browser calls the onreadystatechange property function every time the request's ready state changes. In other words, using the above example, the Web browser actually runs the updatePage function every time the ready state changes. So now when the Web server is finished with the request, and the ready state number is "4," the function processing successfully begins. Testing of the readystate property guarantees that the Web server has safely completed the data request.

status Property

The XMLHttpRequest object's status property is the HTTP status code returned from the server. This property informs the status of the request. Even though the readystate of a request may be completed, it doesn't mean that it was successful. To know the success of the request, the status property value should be utilized.

The Web server reports any problem with a request by using a status code. The status code indicates what happened during the request, and whether things went as intended. Hence, even if a request was completed, one still needs to make sure that the status code for the request indicates that everything was alright. There are many status code values, but for simplicity we consider only two values for status code – 200 and 404. These status code values that are returned by the Web server in response to the request through the URL are shown in Figure 9-10.

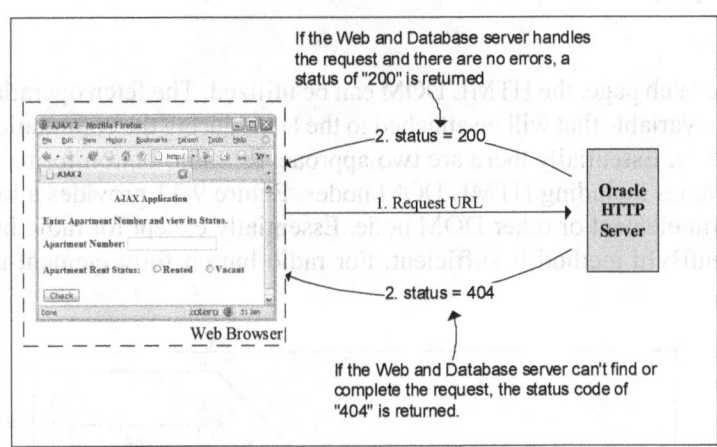

Figure 9-10

Since the Web server return both a readystate and a status code, it is important to test for both these properties before processing any further. The correct readystate value should be 4, while the correct status code should be 200.

In updatePage function described before, variable newData is assigned the data (Text format) received from the server through the statement:

```
var newData = req.responseText;
```

The next statement utilizes the Web page DOM specification to make changes in the Web page.

```
document.getElementById("messageText").innerHTML = "The Updates for " +
newData + " have been applied. Thank You.";
```

In the above statement, a HTML node id attribute value "messageText" is now assigned the value of the return data as part of a message. If this id is associated with the DIV tag, and this tag includes the form tag (`<form>`), then the form is replaced with the new message. Otherwise if the DIV tag includes a paragraph tag (`<p>`), then the new message replaces the content of the paragraph tag. Similar operations can now be performed on individual form element tags.

PRE-DEFINED JAVASCRIPT FUNCTIONS

To ease understanding of AJAX Javascript operations some pre-defined functions have been provided. These functions assist during different stages of AJAX processing. Also, these functions can be modified further due to emerging requirements.

Fetch Data from Web page for Transfer to Web Server

To fetch data from the Web page, the HTML DOM can be utilized. The fetch operations is important for assigning values to the variable that will be attached to the URL during the communication with the Web server (refer Figure 9-4). Essentially there are two approaches: radio button form element values, and other form element values including HTML DOM nodes. Figure 9-11 provides a logic outline on how to fetch data from form element or other DOM node. Essentially except for radio button form element values, the getElementById method is sufficient. For radio button form element use the pre-defined getRadio function.

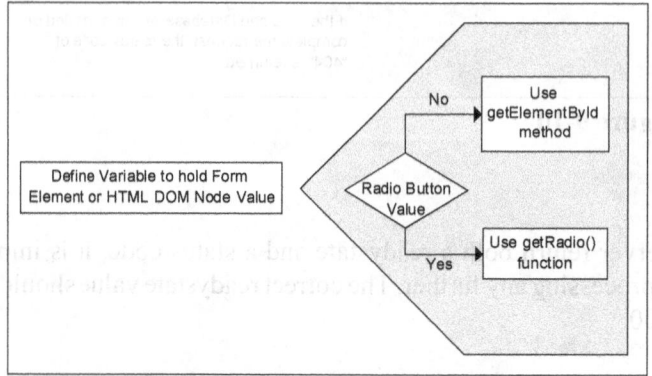

Figure 9-11

To fetch radio button values declare a variable in the driver Javascript function to which the function getRadio is assigned. Essentially the return value from function getRadio gets assigned to this variable. In the statement below, the getAjaxValue is an incomplete driver Javascript function where the variable radioValueIn gets the radio button value from the getRadio function. The syntax of getRadio is also provided. Once the getRadio returns a value, the radioValueIn is now appended to the URL for GET transfer of data to the Web server. In the statement substitute the entries in italics with relevant entries. Similar function can be developed for check box form element.

```
function getAjaxValue() {

var radioValueIn = getRadio();
var url = "http://oracle-server.com/DAD/userid.procedure-
name?radioValueIn " + escape(radioValueIn);
. . .
}

function getRadio() {
  var RadioGroup = document.forms[0].radio-button-name;
  for (i=0; i<RadioGroup.length; i++) {
    if (RadioGroup[i].checked == true) {
      return RadioGroup[i].value;
    }
  }
}
```

To fetch other form element values or HTML DOM node values, the getElementById method can be utilized. In the statement below, the getAjaxValue is an incomplete driver Javascript function where the variable varIn gets its value through the getElementById method. The VarIn variable is now appended to the URL for GET transfer of data to the Web server. In the statement substitute the entries in italics with relevant entries.

```
function getAjaxValue() {

var varIn = document.getElementById("form-element-name1").value;
var url="http://oracle-server.com/DAD/userid.procedure-name?varIn=" +
escape(varIn);
. . .
}
```

Handle Data Returned from the Web Server

The data returned from the Web server is handled by the Javascript function assigned to the onreadystatechange property in the driver Javascript function. This section deals with Text format data returned by the Web server. Since only one string of text data is returned from the Web server, it can contain a single value or set of multiple values. In case of multiple values it is advisable to have some separator among the different values. To ease understanding of the examples a standard function updatePage (set previously through the onreadystatechange property) is again utilized.

Figure 9-12 shows the logic outline for handling Text data returned from the server. Essentially the Text data is assigned to a variable. If the Text data holds multiple values one needs to extract the individual values and store them in separate variables as single values. Once the multiple values are stored as single values in separate variables, it is necessary to check if each of the single value is a radio button value. In case the single value is not a radio button value, it can be directly applied to update a form element value or some HTML DOM node value. However, if the single value is a radio button value, the pre-defined loadRadioButton function can be utilized. In case of loading data in a check box, a function similar to loadRadioButton can be developed.

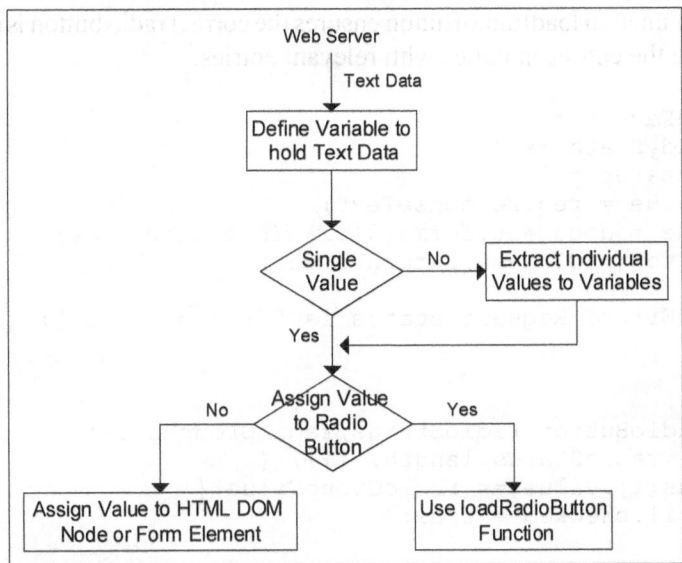

Figure 9-12

The Text format data returned from the server is stored in responseText property of the XMLHttpRequest object. The logic outline is explained through a set of three versions of the updatePage function. The first version shows how to load the responseText property holding single value to single form element (excluding radio button form element). The second version shows how to load the responseText property holding single value to a radio button form element. The third version shows how to extract individual values from responseText property holding multiple value to separate variables.

Load Single Value

This version of updatePage function shows a variable returnValue holding the single value of the responseText property, which is then directly applied to a form element. In the function substitute the entries in italics with relevant entries.

```
function updatePage() {
  if (req.readyState == 4) {
    if (req.status ==200) {
      var returnValue = req.responseText;
      document.getElementById("form-element-name2").value = returnValue;
    } else
      alert("Error! Request status is " + req.status);
  }
}
```

Load Radio Button Value

This version of updatePage function shows how to load the correct radio button value in the existing Web form. The responseText property is assigned to variable returnValue, and the name of the radio button form element is assigned to variable radioName. Then a call is made to another function loadRadioButton to complete the loading. Function loadRadioButton ensures the correct radio button is selected (checked). In the function substitute the entries in italics with relevant entries.

```
function updatePage() {
   if (req.readyState == 4) {
     if (req.status ==200) {
   var returnValue = req.responseText;
   var radioName = document.forms[0].radio-button-name;
   loadRadioButton(radioName,returnValue);
   } else
       alert("Error! Request status is " + req.status);
  }
}

function loadRadioButton(radioStatus,radioGroupValue) {
for (var i=0; i<radioStatus.length; i++) {
 if (radioStatus[i].value == radioGroupValue){
   radioStatus[i].checked = true;
   }
 }
}
```

Load Multiple Values

This version of updatePage function shows a variable returnValue holding the multiple values contained in the responseText property. These multiple values in the example are separated by a comma. If any other separator among values is utilized, the `returnArray = returnValue.split(",");` should be appropriately modified.

The function shows the responseText property holding 4 values. Ignore the first and last value as it may contain unreadable characters. In the example we'll just skip the first value returnValue0. Hence returnValue1 holds the first value, and returnValue2 holds the second value. Depending on how many values returned, define that many variables. Once the individual values contained in responseText property been assigned to separate variables, they can be applied individually to form element values or HTML DOM node values. Keep in mind if a value pertains to radio button element then the function loadRadioButton should be used for updating it. In the function substitute the entries in italics with relevant entries.

```
function updatePage() {
    if (req.readyState == 4) {
      if (req.status ==200) {
    var returnValue = req.responseText;
    returnArray = returnValue.split(",");
    var returnValue0 = returnArray[0].toString();
    var returnValue1 = returnArray[1].toString();
    var returnValue2 = returnArray[2].toString();
    document.getElementById("form-element-name2").value = returnValue1;
    document.getElementById("form-element-name3").value = returnValue2;
    } else
        alert("Error! Request status is " + req.status);
    }
}
```

GENERATE TEXT FORMAT DATA FROM DATABASE

To generate the text data output from the database server simply use the htp.prn package for all output data. The following example is a PSP that generates a single value output. The PSP generates the APT_RENT_AMT attribute value for an input APT_NO value.

```
<%@ page language="PL/SQL"%>
<%@ plsql procedure="load_single_attr"%>
<%@ plsql parameter="aptNoIn" default="null"%>
<%! apt_rent_amt_text apartment.apt_rent_amt%type;%>
<% select apt_rent_amt
into apt_rent_amt_text
from apartment
where apt_no = aptNoIn; %>
<%=apt_rent_amt_text%>
```

The following PSP generates multiple values output separated by comma. The PSP generates an output string with APT_STATUS and APT_UTILITY attribute values based on an input APT_NO value. The output string has additional (repetitious) attribute values in the beginning and end. These additional values at the beginning and end of the output string ensure correct reading of the string by Javascript, since these values will be ignored. When transferring multiple values in a string it is better to place some dummy first and last values.

```
<%@ page language="PL/SQL"%>
<%@ plsql procedure="load_radio_attr"%>
<%@ plsql parameter="aptNoIn" default="null"%>
<%! apt_status_text char(1);
apt_utility_text char(1);
%>
<% select apt_status, apt_utility
into apt_status_text,apt_utility_text
from apartment
where apt_no = aptNoIn; %>
<%=apt_status_text||','||apt_status_text||','||apt_utility_text||','||apt_utilit
y_text%>
```

It is also possible to create a procedure directly within the database server where the Text format output to be sent to the Web browser is enclosed in htp.prn package call. The following example shows the previous PSP Web procedure as a regular procedure in the database.

```
create or replace PROCEDURE load_single_attr (aptNoIn IN VARCHAR2) AS
apt_rent_amt_text apartment.apt_rent_amt%type;
BEGIN NULL;
select apt_rent_amt
into apt_rent_amt_text
from apartment
where apt_no = aptNoIn;
htp.prn(apt_rent_amt_text);
END;
```

Another procedure which generates Web output. The procedure outputs APT_NO attribute value based on two inputs – APT_NO and APT_UTILITY. The procedure updates the APARTMENT table with the input APT_UTILITY value. This procedure is utilized in the tutorial later in the lesson.

```
create or replace procedure update_form (aptNoIn number, radioValueIn varchar2)
as
begin
update apartment
set apt_utility = radioValueIn
where apt_no = aptNoIn;
commit;
htp.prn(aptNoIn);
end;
```

DEBUGGING TIPS

The following tips can assist in the debugging of AJAX related problems.

1. To test values being passed in Web browser use Javascript alert statement.
2. Test procedure on the server separately with dbms_output statement or call directly from Web browser for htp.prn output.
3. Use the else part of the onreadystatechange property function (like UpdatePage function outlined previously) to check the value of status property.

TUTORIAL ON DEVELOPING AJAX WEB PAGES

To explain the working of AJAX, four Web page tutorials are outlined. Each tutorial illustrates a different aspect of AJAX operation.

Tutorial 1: Transfer a single value entered in a textbox form element to update another textbox form element.

In this tutorial, a Web form is displayed with two text boxes – one for Apartment Number and the other for Apartment Rent Amount. The user enters the apartment number value and presses the Send button (Figure 9-13).

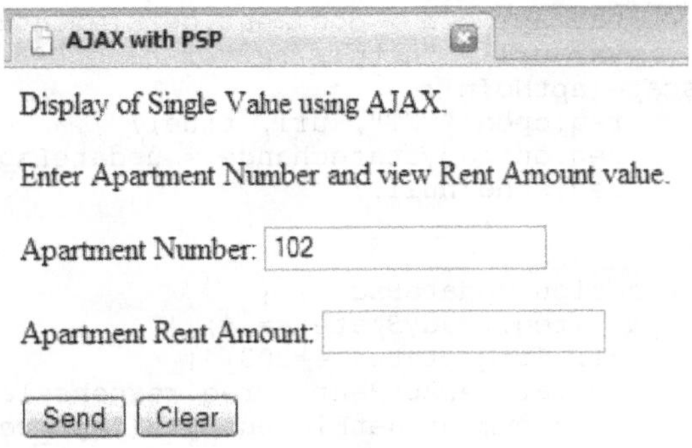

Figure 9-13

The event handler (onClick) associated with the Send button commences AJAX activity with a call to the Javascript function GetAjaxValue. The GET method of transmission is utilized for sending data to the Web/Database server. The Web/Database server executes the procedure load_single_attr (outlined in section Generate Text Format Data from Database), and returns the apartment rent amount as responseText property of the XMLHttpRequest object to the Web browser.

The Web browser calls the Javascript function updatePage (defined with the onreadystatechange property in the function getAjaxValue). The updatePage function initially assigns the responseText property value to a variable newAptRent. The value of variable newAptRent is then assigned to the second text box associated with apartment rent amount in the HTML form (Figure 9-14). The AJAX PSP is provided now. In the PSP, the *url* variable should be modified to suit the existing server configuration in the form of server-name, DAD, and userid.

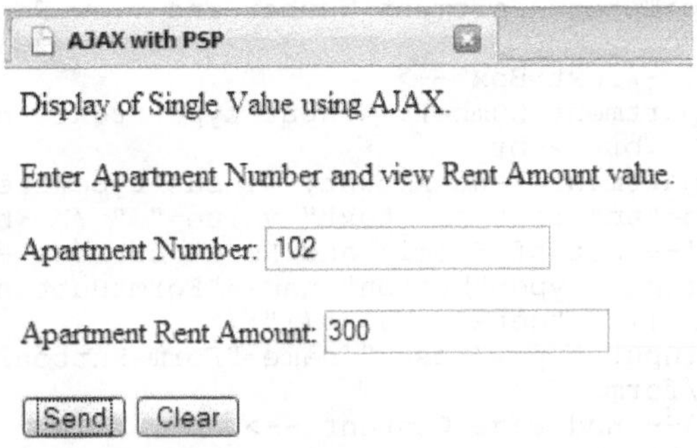

Figure 9-14

```
<%@ page language="PL/SQL"%>
<%@ plsql procedure="text_ajax1"%>
<!DOCTYPE HTML PUBLIC "-//W3C//DTD HTML 4.01 Transitional//EN">
<html>
<head>
<title>AJAX with PSP</title>
<script language="javascript" type="text/javascript">
   var req = null;

   function createRequest() {
     try {
       req = new XMLHttpRequest();
     } catch (ms) {
       try {
```

```
          req = new ActiveXObject("Msxml2.XMLHTTP");
        } catch (otherms) {
          try {
            req = new ActiveXObject("Microsoft.XMLHTTP");
          } catch (failed) {
            request = null;
          }
        }
      }

    if (req == null)
      alert("Error creating request object!");
  }

  function getAjaxValue() {
    createRequest();
    var aptNoIn = document.getElementById("apt_no_text").value;
    var url = "http://server-name/DAD/userid.load_single_attr?aptNoIn=" +
escape(aptNoIn);
    req.open("GET", url, true);
    req.onreadystatechange = updatePage;
    req.send(null);
  }

  function updatePage() {
    if (req.readyState == 4) {
      if (req.status ==200) {
        var newAptRent = req.responseText;
        document.getElementById("apt_rent_amt_text").value = newAptRent;
      } else
        alert("Error! Request status is " + req.status);
    }
  }
</script>
</head>
<body>
<!-- Start Page Content -->
<p>Display of Single Value using AJAX.</p>
<p>Enter Apartment Number and view Rent Amount value.</p>
<form>
<!-- Text Box -->
Apartment Number: <input type="text" name="apt_no_text" id="apt_no_text" value=" "
/> <br /><br />
Apartment Rent Amount: <input type="text" name="apt_rent_amt_text"
id="apt_rent_amt_text" value=" " /> <br /><br />
<!-- Set of Submit and Reset buttons -->
<input type="button" name="FormsButton1" id="FormsButton1" value="Send"
onClick="getAjaxValue()";/>
<input type="reset" name="FormsButton2" id="FormsButton2" value="Clear"/>
</form>
<!-- End Page Content -->
</body>
</html>
```

Tutorial 2: Transfer a single value entered in a textbox form element to update another textbox form element and change the content of a paragraph node.

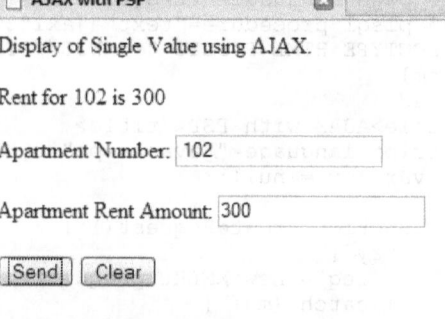

Figure 9-15

This tutorial extends tutorial 1. Essentially the updatePage function after assigning the responseText property value to the variable newAptRent, performs two operations: (i) the value of variable newAptRent is assigned to the second text box associated with apartment rent amount in the Web form, and (ii) a text line associated with the paragraph node "ptext" is replaced with a message containing the apartment number text box input value and the newAptRent value (Figure 9-15). The AJAX PSP is provided now. In the PSP, the *url* variable should be modified to suit the existing server configuration in the form of server-name, DAD, and userid.

```
<%@ page language="PL/SQL"%>
<%@ plsql procedure="text_ajax2"%>
<!DOCTYPE HTML PUBLIC "-/7W3C//DTD HTML 4.01 Transitional//EN">
<html>
<head>
<title>AJAX with PSP</title>
<script language="javascript" type="text/javascript">
   var req = null;

   function createRequest() {
     try {
       req = new XMLHttpRequest();
     } catch (ms) {
       try {
         req = new ActiveXObject("Msxml2.XMLHTTP");
       } catch (otherms) {
         try {
           req = new ActiveXObject("Microsoft.XMLHTTP");
         } catch (failed) {
           request = null;
         }
       }
     }

     if (req == null)
       alert("Error creating request object!");
   }

   function getAjaxValue() {
     createRequest();
     var aptNoIn = document.getElementById("apt_no_text").value;
     var url = "http://server-name/DAD/userid.load_single_attr?aptNoIn=" +
escape(aptNoIn);
     req.open("GET", url, true);
     req.onreadystatechange = updatePage;
     req.send(null);
   }

   function updatePage() {
     if (req.readyState == 4) {
       if (req.status ==200) {
         var newAptRent = req.responseText;
         document.getElementById("apt_rent_amt_text").value = newAptRent;
       var aptNoIn = document.getElementById("apt_no_text").value;
       document.getElementById("ptext").innerHTML = "Rent for " + aptNoIn +" is " +
newAptRent;
       } else
         alert("Error! Request status is " + req.status);
     }
   }
</script>
</head>
<body>
<!-- Start Page Content -->
<p>Display of Single Value using AJAX.</p>
<p id="ptext">Enter Apartment Number and view Rent Amount value.</p>
<form>
<!-- Text Box -->
Apartment Number: <input type="text" name="apt_no_text" id="apt_no_text" value=" "
/> <br /><br />
Apartment Rent Amount: <input type="text" name="apt_rent_amt_text"
id="apt_rent_amt_text" value=" " /> <br /><br />
```

```
<!-- Set of Submit and Reset buttons -->
<input type="button" name="FormsButton1" id="FormsButton1" value="Send"
onClick="getAjaxValue()";/>
<input type="reset" name="FormsButton2" id="FormsButton2" value="Clear"/>
</form>
<!-- End Page Content -->
</body>
</html>
```

Tutorial 3: Transfer two values (text box & radio button) to update database table and display a success message.

In this tutorial, a Web form is displayed with one text box for Apartment Number and a set of radio buttons for representing Apartment Utility Status. The user enters the apartment number value and selects the apartment utility status radio button (Figure 9-16).

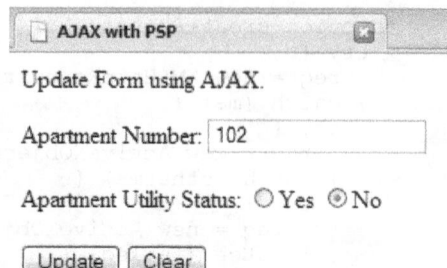

When the Send button is pressed, the associated event handler (onClick) commences AJAX activity with a call to the Javascript function GetAjaxValue. The POST method of transmission is utilized for sending data to the Web/Database

Figure 9-16

server. The Web/Database server executes the procedure update_form (outlined in section Generate Text Format Data from Database), which updates the apartment table with the input apt_utility value for the input apt_no, and returns the apartment number as responseText property of the XMLHttpRequest object to the Web browser.

The Web browser calls the updatePage Javascript function (defined with the onreadystatechange property in the function getAjaxValue). The updatePage function first assigns the responseText property value to a variable newData. The value of variable newData is then used to complete a new message associated with a paragraph node below the HTML form (Figure 9-17). The AJAX PSP is provided now. In the PSP, the *url* variable should be modified to suit the existing server configuration in the form of server-name, DAD, and userid.

Figure 9-17

```
<%@ page language="PL/SQL"%>
<%@ plsql procedure="text_ajax3"%>
<!DOCTYPE HTML PUBLIC "-//W3C//DTD HTML 4.01 Transitional//EN">
<html>
<head>
<title>AJAX with PSP</title>
<script language="javascript" type="text/javascript">
   var req = null;

   function createRequest() {
     try {
       req = new XMLHttpRequest();
     } catch (trymicrosoft) {
       try {
```

```
           req = new ActiveXObject("Msxml2.XMLHTTP");
        } catch (othermicrosoft) {
          try {
            req = new ActiveXObject("Microsoft.XMLHTTP");
          } catch (failed) {
            req = null;
          }
        }
      }

    if (req == null)
      alert("Error creating request object!");
  }

  function getAjaxValue() {
    createRequest();
    var aptNoIn = document.getElementById("apt_no_text").value;
    var radioValueIn = getRadio();
    var url = "http://server-name/DAD/userid.update_form";
    req.open("POST", url, true);
    req.onreadystatechange = updatePage;
    req.send("aptNoIn=" + escape(aptNoIn) + "&radioValueIn=" +
escape(radioValueIn));
  }


  function updatePage() {
    if (req.readyState == 4) {
      if (req.status ==200) {
        var newData = req.responseText;
    document.getElementById("messageText").innerHTML = "The Updates for apartment "
+ newData + " have been applied. Thank You.";
    } else
      alert("Processing Error " + req.status);
  }
}
  function getRadio() {
  var RadioGroup = document.forms[0].apt_utility_text;
  for (i=0; i<RadioGroup.length; i++) {
    if (RadioGroup[i].checked == true) {
      return RadioGroup[i].value;
    }
  }
}

</script>
</head>
<body>
<!-- Start Page Content -->
<p>Update Form using AJAX.</p>
<form>
<!-- Text Box -->
Apartment Number: <input type="text" name="apt_no_text" id="apt_no_text" value=" "
/> <br /><br />
Apartment Utility Status:
<input type="radio" name="apt_utility_text" value="Y">Yes</input>
<input type="radio" name="apt_utility_text" value="N">No</input>
<br /><br />
<!-- Set of Submit and Reset buttons -->
<input type="button" name="FormsButton1" id="FormsButton1" value="Update"
onClick="getAjaxValue()";/>
<input type="reset" name="FormsButton2" id="FormsButton2" value="Clear"/>
</form>
<p id="messageText"></p>
<!-- End Page Content -->
</body>
</html>
```

Tutorial 4: Transfer a single value entered in a textbox form element to update two radio button form elements.

In this example, a HTML form is displayed with one text box for Apartment Number and two sets of radio buttons for Apartment Rent Status and Apartment Utility Status. The user enters the apartment number value and presses the Send button (Figure 9-18).

The event handler (onClick) associated with the Send button commences AJAX activity with a call to the Javascript function GetAjaxValue. The GET method of transmission is utilized for sending data to the Web/Database server. The Web/Database server executes the procedure load_radio_attr (outlined in section Generate Text Format Data from Database), and returns a string of values separated by comma as responseText property of the XMLHttpRequest object to the Web browser.

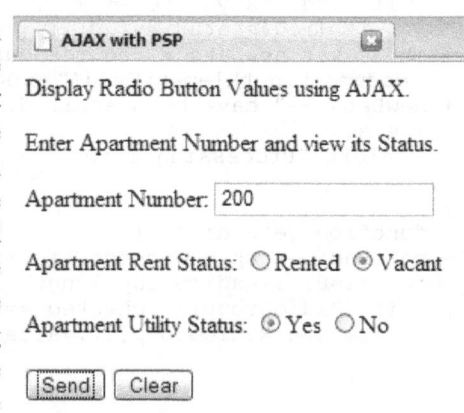

Figure 9-18

The Web browser calls the updatePage Javascript function (defined with the onreadystatechange property in the function getAjaxValue). The updatePage function first assigns the responseText property value to a variable newAptStatus. The value of variable newAptStatus is then split into its individual values and assigned to separate variables radioGroupValue0, radioGroupValue1, and radioGroupValue2. As mentioned before (section ..) ignore the first value assignment to variable radioGroup0. The function then updates the HTML form radio buttons using the loadRadioButton Javascript function (Figure 9-19). The AJAX PSP is provided now. In the PSP, the *url* variable should be modified to suit the existing server configuration in the form of server-name, DAD, and userid.

Figure 9-19

```
<%@ page language="PL/SQL"%>
<%@ plsql procedure="text_ajax4"%>
<!DOCTYPE HTML PUBLIC "-//W3C//DTD HTML 4.01 Transitional//EN">
<html>
<head>
<title>AJAX with PSP</title>
<script language="javascript" type="text/javascript">
   var req = null;

   function createRequest() {
     try {
       req = new XMLHttpRequest();
     } catch (trymicrosoft) {
       try {
         req = new ActiveXObject("Msxml2.XMLHTTP");
       } catch (othermicrosoft) {
         try {
           req = new ActiveXObject("Microsoft.XMLHTTP");
         } catch (failed) {
           req = null;
         }
       }
     }
```

```
      }

    if (req == null)
      alert("Error creating request object!");
  }

  function getAjaxValue() {
    createRequest();
    var aptNoIn = document.getElementById("apt_no_text").value;
    var url = "http://server-name/DAD/userid.load_radio_attr?aptNoIn=" +
escape(aptNoIn);
    req.open("GET", url, true);
    req.onreadystatechange = updatePage;
    req.send(null);
  }

  function updatePage() {
    if (req.readyState == 4) {
      if (req.status ==200) {
        var newAptStatus = req.responseText;
    returnArray = newAptStatus.split(",");
    var radioGroupValue0 = returnArray[0].toString();
    var radioGroupValue1 = returnArray[1].toString();
    var radioGroupValue2 = returnArray[2].toString();
    var radioAptStatus = document.forms[0].apt_status_text;
    var radioUtilityStatus = document.forms[0].apt_utility_text;
    loadRadioButton(radioAptStatus,radioGroupValue1);
    loadRadioButton(radioUtilityStatus,radioGroupValue2);
    } else
        alert("Error! Request status is " + req.status);
  }
}
  function loadRadioButton(radioStatus,radioGroupValue) {
    for (var i=0; i<radioStatus.length; i++) {
    if (radioStatus[i].value == radioGroupValue){
        radioStatus[i].checked = true;
    }
    }
}
</script>
</head>
<body>
<!-- Start Page Content -->
<p>Display Radio Button Values using AJAX.</p>
<p>Enter Apartment Number and view its Status.</p>

<form>
<!-- Text Box -->
Apartment Number: <input type="text" name="apt_no_text" id="apt_no_text" value=" "
/> <br /><br />
Apartment Rent Status:
<input type="radio" name="apt_status_text" value="R">Rented</input>
<input type="radio" name="apt_status_text" value="V">Vacant</input>
<br /><br />
Apartment Utility Status:
<input type="radio" name="apt_utility_text" value="Y">Yes</input>
<input type="radio" name="apt_utility_text" value="N">No</input>
<br /><br />
<!-- Set of Submit and Reset buttons -->
<input type="button" name="FormsButton1" id="FormsButton1" value="Send"
onClick="getAjaxValue()";/>
<input type="reset" name="FormsButton2" id="FormsButton2" value="Clear"/>
</form>
<!-- End Page Content -->
</body>
</html>
```

Note: The traditional form submit button can still be utilized if the entire Web page needs to be changed.

CHAPTER SUMMARY

- AJAX stands for asynchronous Javascript and XML.

- AJAX enabled Web applications work behind the scenes, getting data as they need it, and displaying data as desired.

- AJAX changes the traditional approach of round-trip updates of Web pages.

- An element that make the AJAX environment successful is the client scripting language Javascript.

- An element that make the AJAX environment successful is the Web browser.

- An element that make the AJAX environment successful is the PL/SQL representation of database data in XML or text format.

- An element that make the AJAX environment successful is the HTML document object model (DOM).

- AJAX extends the server-side PL/SQL script with client-side Javascript.

- The Web browser is the engine that drives AJAX operations.

- During AJAX, only data is transferred between the Web browser and the Web server.

- The Web browser facilitates asynchronous interaction of Javascript with the Web server.

- The asynchronous feature of AJAX is facilitated through a special object called XMLHttpRequest.

- The open property of XMLHttpRequest object specifies the Web server URL and the type of data transfer.

- The onreadystatechange property of the XMLHttpRequest object specifies a Javascript function that handles the data returned from the Web server.

- The send property of the XMLHttpRequest object enables the Web browser to proceed with the request for data from the Web server.

REVIEW QUESTIONS

1. What is the role of Javascript in AJAX operations?

2. What is the role of Web browser in AJAX operations?

3. What is the role of PL/SQL Server Page in AJAX operations?

4. What is the role of HTML DOM in AJAX operations?

5. Explain the properties of XMLHttpRequest object.

6. Describe the steps for successful AJAX operation.

REVIEW EXERCISES

1. AJAX stands for asynchronous _____ and _____.

2. AJAX changes the traditional approach of round-trip _____ of Web pages.

3. In AJAX, a Web page does not have to be completely _____ for every data related change or update of its content.

4. AJAX relies on the client scripting language _____ to handle the Web page processing tasks.

5. AJAX extends the server-side _____ script with client-side _____.

6. The Web browser is the _____ that drives AJAX operations.

7. The Web browser facilitates _____ interaction of Javascript with the Web server.

8. The asynchronous feature of AJAX is facilitated through a special object called _____.

9. During AJAX, only _____ is transferred between the Web browser and the Web server.

10. During AJAX, data returned from the Web server can be in _____ or _____ format.

11. During AJAX, Javascript utilizes the HTML _____ to update the page content.

12. The _____ property of XMLHttpRequest object specifies the Web server URL and the type of data transfer.

13. The _____ property of the XMLHttpRequest object specifies a Javascript function that handles the data returned from the Web server.

14. The _____ property of the XMLHttpRequest object enables the Web browser to proceed with the request for data from the Web server.

15. During AJAX, only one string of _____ data is returned by the Web server.

PROBLEM SOLVING EXERCISES

> Run the script file sentimentDB_v4.sql to load the Sentiment Anywhere database to complete the exercises.

Ex9A-1. Create a Web page with a Web form (form layout shown on the right) based on the Sentiment Anywhere database. The user enter the Sentiment ID value, and press the Show button. The Javascript event handler associated with the Show button commences the AJAX activity that (i) displays the Sentiment Name value in the associated text box, and (ii) displays a line "Sentiment Name for ID *sentiment-id* is *sentiment-name*." The sentiment-id and sentiment-name are database values. The Web/database server should return data in text format. Save the Web page with filename ex9a1a. The database procedure utilized for returning data should be saved as a script file with filename ex9a1b.

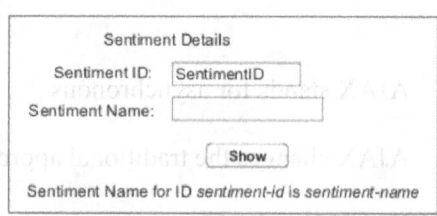

Ex9A-2. Create a Web page with a Web form (form layout shown on the right) based on the Sentiment Anywhere database. The user enter the Sentiment Customer ID value, and press the Show button. The Javascript event handler associated with the Show button commences the AJAX activity that (i) displays the Number of Sentiment Orders value in the associated text box, and (ii) displays a line "Sentiment Customer ID *customer-id* has *order-count* orders." The customer-id and order-count are database values. The Web/database server should return data in text format. Save the Web page with filename ex9a2a. The database procedure utilized for returning data should be saved as a script file with filename ex9a2b.

Ex9A-3. Create a Web page with a Web form (form layout shown on the right) based on the Sentiment Anywhere database. The user enter the Sentiment ID value, and press the Show button. The Javascript event handler associated with the Show button commences the AJAX activity that displays the Sentiment Name and Sentiment Type values in their respective text box. The "Sentiment Details" line is replaced with "Sentiment Details Now Complete." The Web/database server should return data in text format. Save the Web page with filename ex9a3a. The database procedure utilized for returning data should be saved as a script file with filename ex9a3b.

Ex9A-4. Extend exercise Ex9A-3 by allowing the Update button to modify the values in the form. Save the Web page with filename ex9a4a. The database procedure utilized for returning data should be saved as a script file with filename ex9a4b.

Ex9A-5. Create a Web page with a Web form (form layout shown on the right) based on the Sentiment Anywhere database. The user picks a Sentiment Name entry from the drop-down list, and press the Show button. The Javascript event handler associated with the Show button commences the AJAX activity that displays the Sentiment Type and associated Vendor Name values in their respective text box. The "Sentiment Details" line is replaced with "Sentiment Details Now Complete." The Web/database server should return data in text format. Save the Web page with filename ex9a5a. The database procedure utilized for returning data should be saved as a script file with filename ex9a5b.

Ex9A-6. Extend exercise Ex9A-5 by allowing the Update button to modify the values in the form. Save the Web page with filename ex9a6a. The database procedure utilized for returning data should be saved as a script file with filename ex9a6b.

Ex9A-7. Create a Web page with a Web form (form layout shown on the right) based on the Sentiment Anywhere database. The user enter the Sentiment ID value, and press the Show button. The Javascript event handler associated with the Show button commences the AJAX activity that displays the Sentiment Name value and the Sentiment Type values in its radio button. The "Sentiment Details" line is replaced with "Sentiment Details Now Complete." The Web/database server should return data in text format. Save the Web page with filename ex9a7a. The database procedure utilized for returning data should be saved as a script file with filename ex9a7b.

Ex9A-8. Extend exercise Ex9A-7 by allowing the Update button to modify the values in the form. Save the Web page with filename ex9a8a. The database procedure utilized for returning data should be saved as a script file with filename ex9a8b.

CHAPTER 9
(LESSON B)

AJAX with PL/SQL Server Pages

- XML with Javascript
- AJAX with XML

XML facilitates better representation of database data for AJAX processing irrespective of the number of values returned by the Web/Database server. Text formatted data is fine when a single value is returned by the Web/Database server. However when the Web/Database server returns multiple database values, formatting them as XML ensures more transparent representation that the alternative of clubbing database values as a text string with separator symbols. This lesson outlines AJAX operations involving XML formatted data returned from the Web/Database server.

> This lesson utilizes the table structure of Superflex Apartment database to explain examples.

XML WITH JAVASCRIPT

Before going into the details of AJAX operations with XML, a short tutorial on how a XML document can be read within a Web page is provided. Javascript handles the processing of XML data using HTML DOM properties and methods. Since XML is a flexible language with respect to element names, it is important to know the XML document structure prior to its processing. To understand how Javascript reads a XML document, consider a sample XML document in Oracle canonical format shown in Figure 9-20.

```
<ROWSET>
  <ROW>
    <RENTAL_NO>100102</RENTAL_NO>
    <RENTAL_DATE>21-MAY-01</RENTAL_DATE>
    <TENANT_NAME>Mary Stackles</TENANT_NAME>
  </ROW>
  <ROW>
    <RENTAL_NO>100105</RENTAL_NO>
    <RENTAL_DATE>15-APR-02</RENTAL_DATE>
    <TENANT_NAME>Venessa Williams</TENANT_NAME>
  </ROW>
</ROWSET>
```

Figure 9-20

The DOM tree of the XML document is shown in Figure 9-21.

421

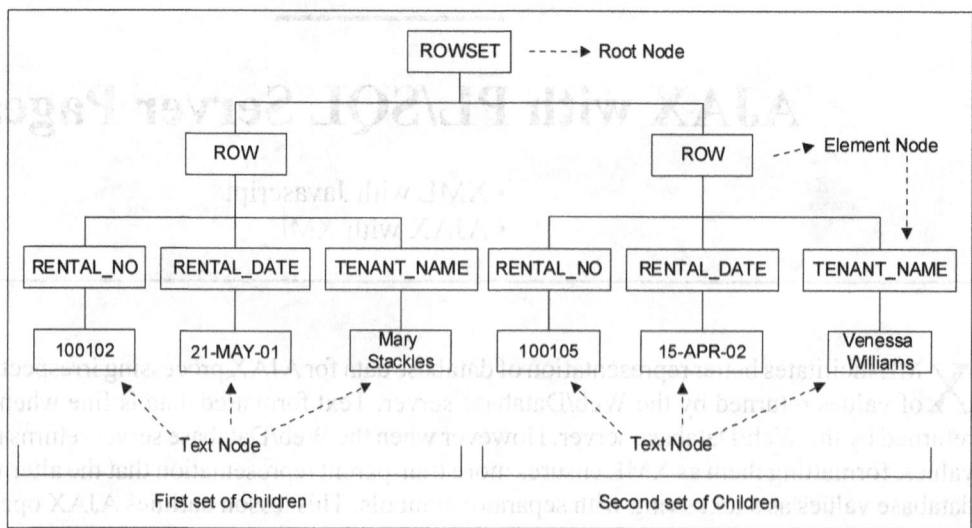

Figure 9-21

There are different ways Javascript can assist in the reading of a XML DOM tree using HTML DOM properties and methods. To initiate any XML processing it is important to first store the XML document as a variable, eg. `var xmlDoc;`. The display of various XML elements in the context of its DOM tree are now outlined. Knowledge of how Javascript can read XML as a DOM tree is important in understanding the associated AJAX operations. The variable names listed below can be modified based on changing requirements.

1. Display the root node of the XML document tree.

    Define a variable "root" that gets the root node for the XML document stored in "xmlDoc" variable. The following line displays the name of the root node.

    ```
    var root = xmlDoc.documentElement;
    document.write("Root Name " + root.nodeName);
    ```

2. Display the number of ROWSET tag pairs in the XML document tree.

    Define a variable "noOfRowSetTags" that gets the length property of the ROWSET tag name within the XML document stored in "xmlDoc" variable. The following line displays the length or number of ROWSET tag pairs.

    ```
    var noOfRowSetTags = xmlDoc.getElementsByTagName("ROWSET").length;
    document.write("ROWSET length " + noOfRowSetTags);
    ```

3. Display the number of ROW tag pairs in the XML document tree.

    Define a variable "noOfRowTags" that gets the length property of the ROW tag name within the XML document stored in "xmlDoc" variable. The following line displays the length or number of ROW tag pairs.

    ```
    var noOfRowTags = xmlDoc.getElementsByTagName("ROW").length;
    ```

```
document.write("ROW length " + noOfRowTags);
```

4. Display the first set of children element node names belonging to the parent ROW element name.

    Define a variable "rows" for the ROW tag name followed by separate variables for the tag names of each children. Since there are three children tag names, there are three corresponding variable names: rental_no1 for tag name RENTAL_NO, rental_date1 for tag name RENTAL_DATE, and tenant_name1 for tag name TENANT_NAME. The node names are then displayed using the nodeName property in the following lines.

```
var rows = xmlDoc.getElementsByTagName("ROW");
var rental_no1 = rows[0].getElementsByTagName("RENTAL_NO");
var rental_date1 = rows[0].getElementsByTagName("RENTAL_DATE");
var tenant_name1 = rows[0].getElementsByTagName("TENANT_NAME");
document.write("Row 1 Name 1 " + rental_no1[0].nodeName);
document.write("Row 1 Name 2 " + rental_date1[0].nodeName);
document.write("Row 1 Name 3 " + tenant_name1[0].nodeName);
```

    Similar variables can be declared for the next set of children for parent ROW.

5. Display the values associated with the first set of children element node names belonging to the parent ROW element name.

    Utilize the variables defined to store the element node names (described in number 4 above).

```
document.write("Row 1 Value 1 " + rental_no1[0].firstChild.nodeValue);
document.write("Row 1 Value 2 " + rental_date1[0].firstChild.nodeValue);
document.write("Row 1 Value 3 " + tenant_name1[0].firstChild.nodeValue);
```

    Similar set of statements can be used to display values associated with variables declared for the next set of children for parent ROW.

XML without Whitespaces

The processing of XML in Internet Explorer and other browsers like Firefox is different. Internet Explorer ignores the whitespaces in the XML document, while Firefox considers them as part of document tree. *To ensure compatibility between browsers, it is better to have a XML format without whitespaces* as follows:

```
<ROWSET><ROW><RENTAL_NO>100102</RENTAL_NO><RENTAL_DATE>21-MAY-01</RENTAL_DATE><T
ENANT_NAME>Mary
Stackles</TENANT_NAME></ROW><ROW><RENTAL_NO>100105</RENTAL_NO><RENTAL_DATE>15-AP
R-02</RENTAL_DATE><TENANT_NAME>Venessa Williams</TENANT_NAME></ROW></ROWSET>
```

The reading of a XML document formatted without whitespaces is more simplified. The following syntax shows the retrieval of data from the first set of children belonging to the ROW element name. Initially define a variable "rows" for the ROW tag name. Then use the DOM properties to access children of the variable rows in the form of tag names and their associated values.

```
var rows = xmlDoc.getElementsByTagName("ROW");
document.write("Row 1 Name 1 " + rows[0].firstChild.nodeName);
document.write("Row 1 Name 2 " + rows[0].firstChild.nextSibling.nodeName);
document.write("Row 1 Value 1 " + rows[0].firstChild.firstChild.nodeValue);
```

```
document.write("Row 1 Value 2 " +
rows[0].firstChild.nextSibling.firstChild.nodeValue);
```

Process XML in Web Page

The following Web page illustrates the syntax outlined above for navigating a XML document. The Web page loads a XML document with the structure described in Figure 9-20 and displays values from its structure (similar to the syntax examples described above). The Web page prompts the user to enter the XML filename before displaying the XML structure values. The output of the Web page in the Web browser is shown in Figure 9-22.

Root Name ROWSET
ROWSET length 1
ROW length 2
Row 1 Name 1 RENTAL_NO
Row 1 Name 2 RENTAL_DATE
Row 1 Name 3 TENANT_NAME
Row 1 Value 1 100102
Row 1 Value 2 21-MAY-01
Row 1 Value 3 Mary Stackles

Figure 9-22

```
<!DOCTYPE HTML PUBLIC "-//W3C//DTD HTML 4.01
Transitional//EN">
<html>
<head>
<title>Navigate XML</title>
<script language="javascript" type="text/javascript">
var xmlDoc;
function loadXML(file)
{
try //IE
  {
  xmlDoc=new ActiveXObject("Microsoft.XMLDOM");
  }
catch(e)
  {
  try //FF
    {
    xmlDoc=document.implementation.createDocument("","",null);
    }
  catch(e)
    {
    alert(e.message);
    return;
    }
  }
xmlDoc.async=false;
xmlDoc.load(file);
}

function readXML(file) {
loadXML(file);
var root = xmlDoc.documentElement;
document.write("Root Name " + root.nodeName + "</br>");

var noOfRowSetTags = xmlDoc.getElementsByTagName("ROWSET").length;
document.write("ROWSET length " + noOfRowSetTags + "</br>");

var noOfRowTags = xmlDoc.getElementsByTagName("ROW").length;
document.write("ROW length " + noOfRowTags + "</br>");

var rows = xmlDoc.getElementsByTagName("ROW");
var rental_no1 = rows[0].getElementsByTagName("RENTAL_NO");
var rental_date1 = rows[0].getElementsByTagName("RENTAL_DATE");
var tenant_name1 = rows[0].getElementsByTagName("TENANT_NAME");
document.write("Row 1 Name 1 " + rental_no1[0].nodeName + "</br>");
document.write("Row 1 Name 2 " + rental_date1[0].nodeName + "</br>");
document.write("Row 1 Name 3 " + tenant_name1[0].nodeName + "</br>");
document.write("Row 1 Value 1 " + rental_no1[0].firstChild.nodeValue + "</br>");
document.write("Row 1 Value 2 " + rental_date1[0].firstChild.nodeValue + "</br>");
document.write("Row 1 Value 3 " + tenant_name1[0].firstChild.nodeValue + "</br>");
```

```
}
</script>
</head>
<body>
<h4>Example of XML Navigation</h4>
<p>Click on the button after entering XML filename into the text box:<p>
<form name="form1">
<input type="text" name="XMLName" value="" size=20>
<input type="button" value="Click Here"
onClick="readXML(document.form1.XMLName.value)">
</form>
</body>
</html>
```

AJAX WITH XML

XML data (document) returned from the Web/Database server is stored in the responseXML property of the XMLHttpRequest object. Similar to the handling of responseText property pertaining to Text data, the responseXML property value is also assigned to a variable.

Read XML Data

The data returned from the Web server is handled by the Javascript function assigned to the onreadystatechange property of the XMLHttpRequest object (as outlined in the driver Javascript function). Once again, to ease understanding of the processing, a standard function called updatePage (set through the onreadystatechange property) is utilized to explain the details.

Figure 9-23 shows the logic outline for handling the XML data returned from the server. It is similar to Figure 9-12 for handling Text data with one major exception – no separation in logic for single and multiple values. Initially the XML data is assigned to a variable. Once stored as a variable, the XML data can now be read by Javascript through HTML DOM properties and methods. To ensure proper reading of XML data, it is necessary to know its structure with respect to the database attributes. To simplify the processing, the default Oracle canonical format is utilized as a standard for explanation.

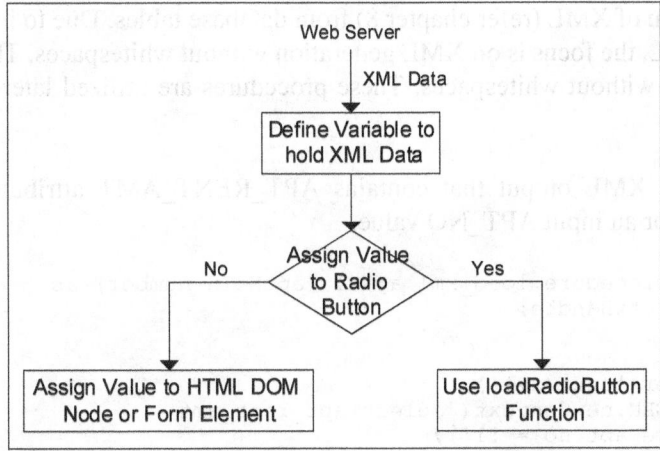

Figure 9-23

The mechanism to fetch a value from the XML tree can be summarized as a three step process. Essentially define variables that will hold the XML data as well as its various elements, and then assign the XML data values to HTML DOM nodes or form elements. These steps with Javascript syntax are explained now.

1. Assign the responseXML property of the XMLHttpRequest object to a variable. In the syntax "req" represents the XMLHttpRequest object.

    ```
    var xmlDoc = req.responseXML;
    ```

2. Assign separate variables to database attributes names that appear as node names. Node-name1, node-name2, and so on are node names in the XML tree representing the database attributes. Substitute the entries in italics with relevant entries.

    ```
    var rows = xmlDoc.getElementsByTagName("ROW");
    var nodeName1 = rows[0].getElementsByTagName("node-name1");
    var nodeName2 = rows[0].getElementsByTagName("node-name2");
    var nodeName3 = rows[0].getElementsByTagName("node-name3");
    . . .
    ```

3. Using the variables (nodeName1, nodeName2, and so on) declared in step 2, new variables (nodeValue1, nodeValue2, and so on) are now declared that fetch the values assigned to the relevant XML node name.

    ```
    var nodeValue1 = nodeName1[0].firstChild.nodeValue;
    var nodeValue2 = nodeName2[0].firstChild.nodeValue;
    var nodeValue3 = nodeName3[0].firstChild.nodeValue;
    . . .
    ```

    Once the data is assigned to these second set of variables, it can then be directly applied to update a form element value or some HTML DOM node value within the Web page. However, if these values needs to be applied to a radio button form element, the pre-defined Javascript function loadRadioButton outlined for Text handling can be utilized.

Generate XML Data

Oracle facilitates generation of XML (refer chapter 8) from database tables. Due to incompatibilities in how browsers process XML, the focus is on XML generation without whitespaces. The following three procedures generate XML without whitespaces. These procedures are utilized later to explain AJAX XML processing tutorial.

1. Procedure to generate XML output that contains APT_RENT_AMT attribute value from the APARTMENT table for an input APT_NO value.

    ```
    create or replace procedure load_xml_ajax1 (aptNoIn number) as
    qryCtx DBMS_XMLGEN.ctxHandle;
    xmlout clob;
    begin
    owa_util.mime_header('text/xml');
    qryCtx := DBMS_XMLGEN.newContext('select apt_rent_amt
    from apartment where apt_no = :1');
    DBMS_XMLGEN.setbindvalue (qryCtx, '1', aptNoIn);
    DBMS_XMLGEN.setPrettyPrinting(qryCtx,false);
    ```

```
xmlout := DBMS_XMLGEN.getXML(qryCtx);
DBMS_XMLGEN.closeContext(qryCtx);
htp.prn(xmlout);
end;
```

2. Procedure to generate XML output that contains APT_STATUS and APT_UTILITY attribute values from the APARTMENT table for an input APT_NO value.

```
create or replace procedure load_xml_ajax2 (aptNoIn number) as
qryCtx DBMS_XMLGEN.ctxHandle;
xmlout clob;
begin
owa_util.mime_header('text/xml');
qryCtx := DBMS_XMLGEN.newContext('select apt_status, apt_utility
from apartment where apt_no = :1');
DBMS_XMLGEN.setbindvalue (qryCtx, '1', aptNoIn);
DBMS_XMLGEN.setPrettyPrinting(qryCtx,false);
xmlout := DBMS_XMLGEN.getXML(qryCtx);
DBMS_XMLGEN.closeContext(qryCtx);
htp.prn(xmlout);
end;
```

3. Procedure to generate XML output that contains AUTO_MAKE, AUTO_MODEL, and AUTO_YEAR attribute values from the TENANT_AUTO for an input TENANT_SS value.

```
create or replace procedure load_xml_ajax3 (tenantNoIn number) as
qryCtx DBMS_XMLGEN.ctxHandle;
xmlout clob;
begin
owa_util.mime_header('text/xml');
qryCtx := DBMS_XMLGEN.newContext('select auto_make, auto_model, auto_year
from tenant_auto where tenant_ss= :1');
DBMS_XMLGEN.setbindvalue (qryCtx, '1', tenantNoIn);
DBMS_XMLGEN.setPrettyPrinting(qryCtx,false);
xmlout := DBMS_XMLGEN.getXML(qryCtx);
DBMS_XMLGEN.closeContext(qryCtx);
htp.prn(xmlout);
exception
when others then
htp.prn(sqlerrm);
end;
```

TUTORIAL ON DEVELOPING XML BASED AJAX WEB PAGES

To explain the working of AJAX, four Web page tutorials are outlined. Each tutorial illustrates a different aspect of AJAX operation with XML.

Tutorial 1: Transfer a single value entered in a textbox form element to update another textbox form element and change the content of a paragraph node.

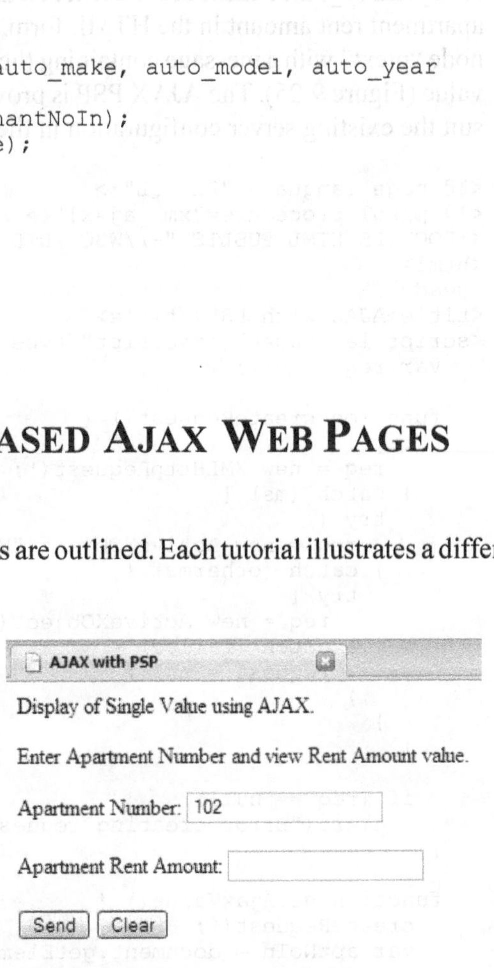

This tutorial is the XML version of the second tutorial outlined in Chapter 9, Lesson A. A Web form is displayed with two text boxes – one for Apartment

Figure 9-24

Number and the other for Apartment Rent Amount. The user enters the apartment number value and presses the Send button (Figure 9-24).

The event handler (onClick) associated with the Send button commences AJAX activity with a call to the Javascript function GetAjaxValue. The GET method of transmission is utilized for sending data to the Web/Database server. The Web/Database server executes the procedure load_xml_ajax1 (outlined in section Generate XML Data). The procedure returns the apartment rent amount as responseXML property of the XMLHttpRequest object to the Web browser.

The Web browser calls the updatePage Javascript function (defined with the onreadystatechange property in the function getAjaxValue). Essentially the updatePage function first assigns the responseXML property value to a variable xmlDoc. The XML document (xmlDoc) contains one value as a child node of the parent ROW element name. The function (i) reads and assigns the XML element name APT_RENT_AMT to a variable AptRentName, (ii) reads and assigns the text value of the element name APT_RENT_AMT to a variable newAptRent, (iii) assigns the text value of element APT_RENT_AMT to the second text box associated with

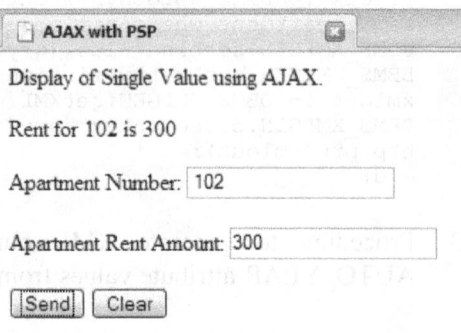

Figure 9-25

apartment rent amount in the HTML form, and (iv) replaces the text line associated with the paragraph node "ptext" with a message containing the apartment number text box input value and the newAptRent value (Figure 9-25). The AJAX PSP is provided now. In the PSP, the *url* variable should be modified to suit the existing server configuration in the form of server-name, DAD, and userid.

```
<%@ page language="PL/SQL"%>
<%@ plsql procedure="xml_ajax1"%>
<!DOCTYPE HTML PUBLIC "-//W3C//DTD HTML 4.01 Transitional//EN">
<html>
<head>
<title>AJAX with PSP</title>
<script language="javascript" type="text/javascript">
   var req = null;

   function createRequest() {
     try {
       req = new XMLHttpRequest();
     } catch (ms) {
       try {
         req = new ActiveXObject("Msxml2.XMLHTTP");
       } catch (otherms) {
         try {
           req = new ActiveXObject("Microsoft.XMLHTTP");
         } catch (failed) {
           request = null;
         }
       }
     }

     if (req == null)
       alert("Error creating request object!");
   }

   function getAjaxValue() {
     createRequest();
     var aptNoIn = document.getElementById("apt_no_text").value;
```

```
         var url = "http://server-name/DAD/userid.load_xml_ajax1?aptNoIn=" +
escape(aptNoIn);
         req.open("GET", url, true);
         req.onreadystatechange = updatePage;
         req.send(null);
    }

    function updatePage() {
      if (req.readyState == 4) {
        if (req.status ==200) {
           var xmlDoc = req.responseXML;
      var rows = xmlDoc.getElementsByTagName("ROW");
      var AptRentName = rows[0].getElementsByTagName("APT_RENT_AMT");
      var newAptRent = AptRentName[0].firstChild.nodeValue;
           document.getElementById("apt_rent_amt_text").value = newAptRent;
      var aptNoIn = document.getElementById("apt_no_text").value;
         document.getElementById("ptext").innerHTML = "Rent for " + aptNoIn +" is " +
newAptRent;
        } else
           alert("Error! Request status is " + req.status);
     }
   }
</script>
</head>
<body>
<!-- Start Page Content -->
<p>Display of Single Value using AJAX.</p>
<p id="ptext">Enter Apartment Number and view Rent Amount value.</p>
<form>
<!-- Text Box -->
Apartment Number: <input type="text" name="apt_no_text" id="apt_no_text" value=" "
/> <br /><br />
Apartment Rent Amount: <input type="text" name="apt_rent_amt_text"
id="apt_rent_amt_text" value=" " /> <br /><br />
<!-- Set of Submit and Reset buttons -->
<input type="button" name="FormsButton1" id="FormsButton1" value="Send"
onClick="getAjaxValue()";/>
<input type="reset" name="FormsButton2" id="FormsButton2" value="Clear"/>
</form>
<!-- End Page Content -->
</body>
</html>
```

Tutorial 2: Transfer a single value entered in a textbox form element to update two radio button form
elements.

This tutorial is the XML version of the fourth tutorial
outlined in Chapter 9, Lesson A. A Web form is displayed
with one text box for Apartment Number and two sets of
radio buttons for Apartment Rent Status and Apartment
Utility Status. The user enters the apartment number value
and presses the Send button (Figure 9-26).

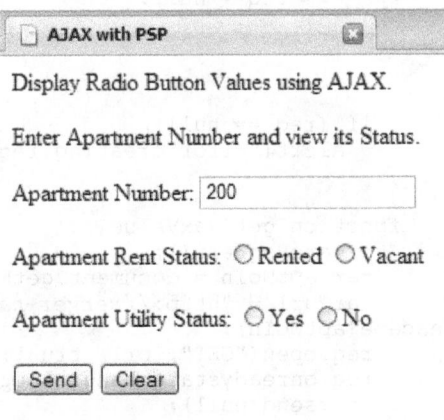

The event handler (onClick) associated with the Send button
commences AJAX activity with a call to the Javascript
function GetAjaxValue. The GET method of transmission
is utilized for sending data to the Web/Database server. The
Web/Database server executes the procedure
load_xml_ajax2 (outlined in section Generate XML Data).

Figure 9-26

The procedure returns the apartment rent status and apartment utility status values as responseXML property of the XMLHttpRequest object to the Web browser.

The Web browser calls the updatePage Javascript function (defined with the onreadystatechange property in the core function getAjaxValue). Essentially the updatePage function first assigns the responseXML property value to a variable xmlDoc. The XML document (xmlDoc) contains two values as child nodes of the parent ROW element name. The function (i) reads and assigns the XML element name APT_STATUS to a variable newAptStatus1, (ii) reads and assigns the XML element name APT_UTILITY to a variable newAptStatus2, (iii) reads and assigns the text value of the element name APT_STATUS to a variable radioGroupValue1, (iv) reads and assigns the text value of the element name APT_UTILITY to a variable radioGroupValue2, (v) assigns the names of the radio button

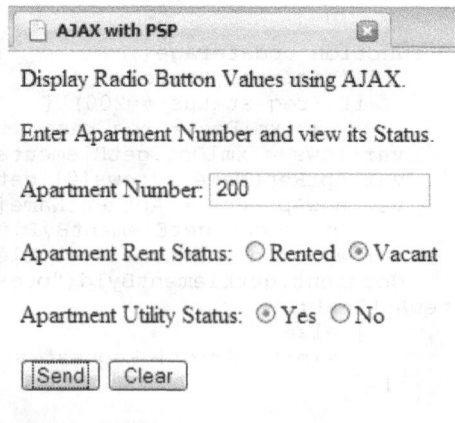

Figure 9-27

groups associated with the first form on the HTML page to variables radioAptStatus and radioUtilityStatus, and (vi) update the HTML form radio buttons using the loadRadioButton Javascript function (Figure 9-27). The AJAX PSP is provided now. In the PSP, the *url* variable should be modified to suit the existing server configuration in the form of server-name, DAD, and userid.

```
<%@ page language="PL/SQL"%>
<%@ plsql procedure="xml_ajax2"%>
<!DOCTYPE HTML PUBLIC "-//W3C//DTD HTML 4.01 Transitional//EN">
<html>
<head>
<title>AJAX with PSP</title>
<script language="javascript" type="text/javascript">
   var req = null;

   function createRequest() {
     try {
       req = new XMLHttpRequest();
     } catch (trymicrosoft) {
       try {
         req = new ActiveXObject("Msxml2.XMLHTTP");
       } catch (othermicrosoft) {
         try {
           req = new ActiveXObject("Microsoft.XMLHTTP");
         } catch (failed) {
           req = null;
         }
       }
     }

     if (req == null)
       alert("Error creating request object!");
   }

   function getAjaxValue() {
     createRequest();
     var aptNoIn = document.getElementById("apt_no_text").value;
     var url = "http://server-name/DAD/userid.load_xml_ajax2?aptNoIn=" +
escape(aptNoIn);
     req.open("GET", url, true);
     req.onreadystatechange = updatePage;
     req.send(null);
   }

   function updatePage() {
```

```
    if (req.readyState == 4) {
      if (req.status ==200) {
        var xmlDoc = req.responseXML;
    var rows = xmlDoc.getElementsByTagName("ROW");
    var newAptStatus1 = rows[0].getElementsByTagName("APT_STATUS");
    var newAptStatus2 = rows[0].getElementsByTagName("APT_UTILITY");
    var radioGroupValue1 = newAptStatus1[0].firstChild.nodeValue;
    var radioGroupValue2 = newAptStatus2[0].firstChild.nodeValue;
    var radioAptStatus = document.forms[0].apt_status_text;
    var radioUtilityStatus = document.forms[0].apt_utility_text;
    loadRadioButton(radioAptStatus,radioGroupValue1);
    loadRadioButton(radioUtilityStatus,radioGroupValue2);
    } else
        alert("Error! Request status is " + req.status);
  }
}
  function loadRadioButton(radioStatus,radioGroupValue) {
    for (var i=0; i<radioStatus.length; i++) {
    if (radioStatus[i].value == radioGroupValue){
        radioStatus[i].checked = true;
    }
    }
}
</script>
</head>
<body>
<!-- Start Page Content -->
<p>Display Radio Button Values using AJAX.</p>
<p>Enter Apartment Number and view its Status.</p>

<form>
<!-- Text Box -->
Apartment Number: <input type="text" name="apt_no_text" id="apt_no_text" value=" "
/> <br /><br />
Apartment Rent Status:
<input type="radio" name="apt_status_text" value="R">Rented</input>
<input type="radio" name="apt_status_text" value="V">Vacant</input>
<br /><br />
Apartment Utility Status:
<input type="radio" name="apt_utility_text" value="Y">Yes</input>
<input type="radio" name="apt_utility_text" value="N">No</input>
<br /><br />
<!-- Set of Submit and Reset buttons -->
<input type="button" name="FormsButton1" id="FormsButton1" value="Send"
onClick="getAjaxValue()";/>
<input type="reset" name="FormsButton2" id="FormsButton2" value="Clear"/>
</form>
<!-- End Page Content -->
</body>
</html>
```

Tutorial 3: Display XML data as HTML table.

This tutorial lists XML details of auto registered for a tenant in the Superflex Apartment database as Web table that replaces the Web form on the Web page. The Web page initially displays a Web form with a dynamic drop-down list of tenant names is displayed as shown in Figure 9-28.

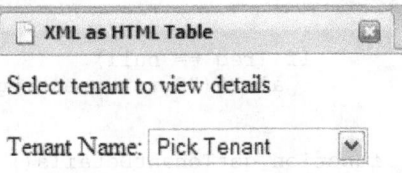

Figure 9-28

The user selects the tenant name, and the event handler (onChange) associated with the drop-down list commences AJAX activity with a call to the Javascript core function getTenantDetails. The POST method of transmission is utilized for sending data to the

Web/Database server. The Web/Database server executes the procedure load_xml_ajax3 (outlined in section Generate XML Data). The procedure returns the auto_make, auto_model, and auto_year values as responseXML property of the XMLHttpRequest object to the Web browser.

The Web browser calls the updatePage Javascript function (defined with the onreadystatechange property in the function getAjaxValue). Essentially the updatePage function first assigns the responseXML property value to a variable xmlDoc. The XML document (xmlDoc) contains multiple ROW element nodes of the root ROWSET element pertaining to the query output rows. The function (i) replaces the text line associated with the paragraph node "ptext" with a message, and (ii) calls a Javascript function replaceForm that generates a dynamic HTML table from XML data, and replaces any existing HTML DOM node with this table as shown in Figure 9-29.

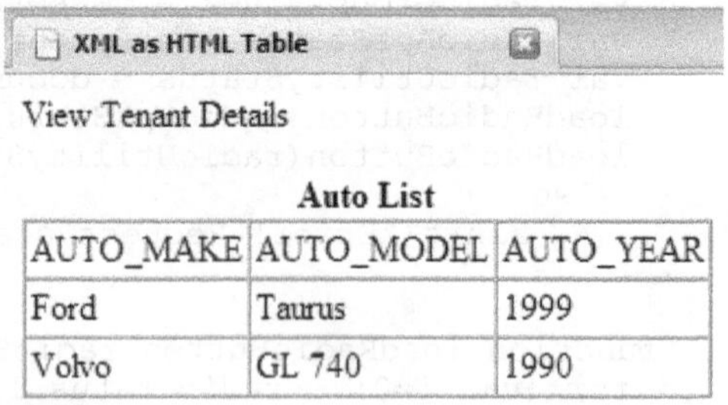

View Tenant Details

Auto List

AUTO_MAKE	AUTO_MODEL	AUTO_YEAR
Ford	Taurus	1999
Volvo	GL 740	1990

Figure 9-29

The replaceForm function has 4 arguments: (i) the parent HTML node id whose child will be replaced, (ii) the child HTML node id that will be replaced by the table, the table title text, and the XML document. In the example, "form1" is the parent DIV tag containing the child form; "UpdateForm" is the tag identifier of the HTML form; "Auto List" is the heading of the table; and xmlDoc is the variable holding the responseXML property value. The AJAX PSP is provided now. In the PSP, the *url* variable should be modified to suit the existing server configuration in the form of server-name, DAD, and userid.

```
<!DOCTYPE HTML PUBLIC "-//W3C//DTD HTML 4.01 Transitional//EN">
<html>
<%@page language="PL/SQL"%>
<%@plsql procedure="xml_ajax3"%>
<head>
<title>XML as HTML Table</title>
<script language="javascript" type="text/javascript">
    var req = null;
    var browser = null;

function createRequest() {
    try {
       req = new XMLHttpRequest();
    } catch (trymicrosoft) {
       try {
          req = new ActiveXObject("Msxml2.XMLHTTP");
       } catch (othermicrosoft) {
          try {
             req = new ActiveXObject("Microsoft.XMLHTTP");
          } catch (failed) {
             req = null;
          }
       }
    }
    if (req == null)
      alert("Error creating request object!");
    }

function getTenantDetails() {
    createRequest();
    var tenantNoIn = document.getElementById("tenant_name_text").value;
    var url = "http://server-name/DAD/userid.load_xml_ajax3";
    req.open("POST", url, true);
    req.onreadystatechange = updatePage;
    req.send("tenantNoIn=" + escape(tenantNoIn));
```

```
        }

function updatePage() {
    if (req.readyState == 4) {
      if (req.status ==200) {
         var xmlDoc = req.responseXML;
         document.getElementById("ptext").innerHTML = "View Tenant Details";
         replaceForm('form1','UpdateForm','Auto List',xmlDoc);
    } else
         alert("Error! Request status is " + req.status);
  }
}

function replaceForm(parentID, formID, THeading, xmlDoc) {

var mainDiv = document.getElementById(parentID);
var orderForm = document.getElementById(formID);

var rootNode = xmlDoc.documentElement;
var noOfROWTags = xmlDoc.getElementsByTagName("ROW").length;
var rows = xmlDoc.getElementsByTagName("ROW");
var cols = rows[0].childNodes.length;

var pTable = document.createElement("table");
var tBody = document.createElement("tbody");

var trow = document.createElement("tr");
var tCaption = document.createElement("caption");
var tBold = document.createElement("strong");
var cellText = document.createTextNode(THeading);
tBold.appendChild(cellText);
tCaption.appendChild(tBold);
pTable.appendChild(tCaption);

for (var i = 0; i < cols; i++) {
 var cell = document.createElement("td");
 var cellText = document.createTextNode(rows[0].childNodes[i].nodeName);
 cell.appendChild(cellText);
 trow.appendChild(cell);
}

tBody.appendChild(trow);

for (var j = 0; j < noOfROWTags; j++) {
  var trow = document.createElement("tr");

  for (var i = 0; i < cols; i++) {
  var cell = document.createElement("td");
  var cellText =
document.createTextNode(rows[j].childNodes[i].firstChild.nodeValue);
  cell.appendChild(cellText);
  trow.appendChild(cell);
 }
  tBody.appendChild(trow); // pTable.appendChild(row);
}

pTable.appendChild(tBody);
pTable.setAttribute("border", "1");
pTable.setAttribute("cellpadding", "2");
pTable.setAttribute("cellspacing", "0");
mainDiv.replaceChild(pTable,orderForm);
}
</script>
</head>
<body>
<p id="ptext">Select tenant to view details</p>
<div id="form1">
<form name="UpdateForm" id="UpdateForm">
Tenant Name: <select name="tenant_name_text" id="tenant_name_text"
onChange="getTenantDetails()";>
```

```
  <option value=" ">Pick Tenant</option>
<%for tenant_row in (select tenant_name,tenant_ss from tenant) loop%>
  <option value="<%=tenant_row.tenant_ss%>"><%=tenant_row.tenant_name%></option>
<%end loop;%> </select><br/><br/>
</form></div>
</body>
</html>
```

CHAPTER SUMMARY

- Javascript handles the processing of XML data using HTML DOM properties and methods.

- To ensure compatibility between browsers, it is better to have XML format without whitespaces.

- XML data returned from the Web/Database server is stored in the responseXML property of the XMLHttpRequest object.

- The XML data returned from the Web server is handled by the Javascript function assigned to the onreadystatechange property of the XMLHttpRequest object.

- To ensure proper reading and processing of XML data, it is necessary to know its structure with respect to the database attributes.

- The mechanism to fetch a value from the XML document tree is facilitated by defining a variable that will hold the XML data.

- To ensure proper reading and processing of XML data, assign separate variables to database attributes names that appear as node names.

REVIEW QUESTIONS

1. How does Javascript handle XML data returned by the Web/Database server?

2. Explain the relevance of formatting XML without whitespaces.

3. What properties of the XMLHttpRequest object are involved in handling XML data returned by the Web/Database server.

4. Describe the steps for successful AJAX operation with XML.

REVIEW EXERCISES

1. Javascript handles the processing of _____ data using HTML DOM properties and methods.

2. XML data returned from the Web/Database server is stored in the _____ property of the XMLHttpRequest object.

3. The XML data returned from the Web/Database server is handled by the Javascript function assigned to the _____ property of the XMLHttpRequest object.

4. To facilitate processing, the _____ property of the XMLHttpRequest object is assigned to a variable.

5. To facilitate processing, separate variables are assigned to database attributes names that appear as _____ names in the XML document.

6. To ensure compatibility between browsers, it is better to format XML format without _____.

7. XML data can be generated through a database _____.

PROBLEM SOLVING EXERCISES

> Run the script file sentimentDB_v4.sql to load the Sentiment Anywhere database to complete the exercises.

Ex9B-1. Create a procedure product_price that lists the product_id, product_name, and price values from the product table where price is greater than 10 as XML output in the Web browser. Save the output as a XML file with filename ex9b1 and also print the XML structure.

Ex9B-2. Create a procedure club_cust_list that lists the sporting_clubs name, duration, first_name, last_name for customers who have club_membership as XML output in the Web browser. Save the output as a XML file with filename ex9b2 and also print the XML structure.

Ex9B-3. Create a procedure list_products that lists all products (product_id, product_name) and their remaining stock (quantity_in_stock - reorder_point) as XML output in the Web browser. List only those rows whose remaining stock is more than the average REORDER_QTY value. Save the output as a XML file with filename ex9b3 and also print the XML structure.

Ex9B-4. Create Web page with a Web form (form layout shown on the right). The user enter the Sentiment ID value, and press the Show button. The Javascript event handler associated with the Show button commences the AJAX activity that (i) displays the Sentiment Name value in the associated text box, and (ii) displays a line "Sentiment Name for ID *sentiment-id* is *sentiment-name*." The sentiment-id and sentiment-name are database values. The Web/database server should return data in XML format. Save the Web page with filename ex9b4a. The database procedure utilized for returning XML data should be saved as a script file with filename ex9b4b.

Ex9B-5. Create Web page with a Web form (form layout shown on the right) . The user enter the Sentiment Customer ID value, and press the Show button. The Javascript event handler associated with the Show button commences the AJAX activity that (i) displays the Number of Sentiment Orders value in the associated text box, and (ii) displays a line "Sentiment Customer ID *customer-id* has *order-count* orders." The customer-id and order-count are database values. The Web/database server should return data in XML format. Save the Web page with filename ex9b5a. The database procedure utilized for returning XML data should be saved as a script file with filename ex9b5b.

Ex9B-6.   Create Web page with a Web form (form layout shown on the right). The user enter the Sentiment ID value, and press the Show button. The Javascript event handler associated with the Show button commences the AJAX activity that displays the Sentiment Name and Sentiment Type values in their respective text box. The "Sentiment Details" line is replaced with "Sentiment Details Now Complete." The Web/database server should return data in XML format. Save the Web page with filename ex9b6a. The database procedure utilized for returning XML data should be saved as a script file with filename ex9b6b.

Ex9B-7.   Extend exercise Ex9B-3 by allowing the Update button to modify the values in the form. Save the Web page with filename ex9b7a. The database procedure utilized for returning XML data should be saved as a script file with filename ex9b7b.

Ex9B-8.   Create Web page with a Web form (form layout shown on the right). The user picks a Sentiment Name entry from the drop-down list, and press the Show button. The Javascript event handler associated with the Show button commences the AJAX activity that displays the Sentiment Type and associated Vendor Name values in their respective text box. The "Sentiment Details" line is replaced with "Sentiment Details Now Complete." The Web/database server should return data in XML format. Save the Web page with filename ex9b8a. The database procedure utilized for returning XML data should be saved as a script file with filename ex9b8b.

Ex9B-9.   Extend exercise Ex9B-5 by allowing the Update button to modify the values in the form. Save the Web page with filename ex9b9a. The database procedure utilized for returning XML data should be saved as a script file with filename ex9b9b.

Ex9B-10.   Create Web page with a Web form (form layout shown on the right). The user enter the Sentiment ID value, and press the Show button. The Javascript event handler associated with the Show button commences the AJAX activity that displays the Sentiment Name value and the Sentiment Type values in its radio button. The "Sentiment Details" line is replaced with "Sentiment Details Now Complete." The Web/database server should return data in XML format. Save the Web page with filename ex9b10a. The database procedure utilized for returning XML data should be saved as a script file with filename ex9b10b.

Ex9B-11.   Extend exercise Ex9B-7 by allowing the Update button to modify the values in the form. Save the Web page with filename ex9b11a. The database procedure utilized for returning XML data should be saved as a script file with filename ex9b11b.

Ex9B-12.   Create Web page with a Web form (form layout shown on the right). The user enter the Sentiment Customer ID value, and press the Show button. The Javascript event handler associated with the Show button commences the AJAX activity that (i) replaces the form with a table showing OrderID, Order Data, and Total Amount value, and (ii) displays a line "Sentiment Customer ID *customer-id* has these orders." The customer-id is the value input in the text box. The Web/database server should return data in XML format. Save the Web page with filename ex9b12a. The database procedure utilized for returning XML data should be saved as a script file with filename ex9b12b.

> Sentiment Customer
>
> Sentiment Customer ID *customer-id* has these orders
>
> Customer ID: CustomerID
>
> Show

Ex9B-13.   Create Web page with a Web form (form layout shown on the right). The user selects the Sentiment Type from the drop-down list, and press the Show button. The Javascript event handler associated with the Show button commences the AJAX activity that (i) replaces the form with a table showing Vendor Name and Vendor City values associated with the sentiment type, and (ii) displays a line "Following is the list of Vendors for *sentiment-type* sentiments." The sentiment-type is the value in the drop-down list. The Web/database server should return data in XML format. Save the Web page with filename ex9b13a. The database procedure utilized for returning XML data should be saved as a script file with filename ex9b13b.

> Sentiment Vendor Details
>
> Following is the list of Vendors for *sentiment-type* sentiments
>
> Sentiment Type: Sentiment Type ⌄
>
> Show

Web Cookies and Locks

- Cookie Structure
- Cookie Actions with Oracle Cookie Package
- Web Page with Cookie Capability

In Web applications, it is often necessary to maintain information about users from one Web page to the next. For example, if a user clicks a link to add an item to a shopping cart, how does the server know whose shopping cart to fill, or how can an application identify and track its users.

Some of this session state information can be passed as parameters to the procedures on the servers. However, passing can become cumbersome when information is needed across an entire Web site – essentially each Web page must have provision of an extra parameter. To overcome this problem, *cookies* can be utilized.

This chapter utilizes the table structure of Superflex Apartment database to explain examples.

A **cookie** is a text string. The string contains a name and a value (name-value pair) that holds information. A cookie is stored and managed by the browser. It is sent to the user's browser by servers. When a server responds to a browser's request by delivering a page to the browser, this response can include a request to set a cookie. If the user's browser is configured to accept cookies, the browser then stores the cookie information including identification of the sending server.

Cookies can be of two types:
- Session-level cookies.
- Persistent cookies.

Session-level cookies are short-term cookies that are held by the browser temporarily, and then deleted when the user exits the browser. Session-level cookies can perform the following:

- Store a session id for a user until the browser is closed.
- Store other data that is temporary until the browser is closed.
- Maintain a shopping cart until the browser is closed.
- Track activity in a single browser session until the browser is closed.

Persistent cookies are cookies saved directly in the computer's file system. These cookie files remain on the computer even after the browser is closed and the power is turned off. A persistent cookie can perform the following:

- Greet a visitor by name when the visitor returns to a Web site the next time using the same computer.
- Compute how many times the user on that specific computer has visited the Web site.
- Provide additional information based on your identity to facilitate additional business.

COOKIE STRUCTURE

A cookie is simply a string of text stored as a single line by the browser. For example, the following is a cookie entry:

```
call_id 225 mysite.edu/ 0 3745294464 29630941 205389344 29629911*
```

The entries for a cookie consists of many parts corresponding to the parameters supplied when setting a cookie. Table 10-1 provides an explanation of the cookie parts.

Cookie Parts	Description
Domain	The Web site server (domain) that set the cookie. This is the domain that will have access to the cookie later. eg. mysite.edu
T/F Flag	A TRUE/FALSE value indicating whether all computers within the domain can access the cookie later. This value is set automatically by the browser unless a value is provided when the cookie is set.
Path	The path within the domain that the cookie is valid for. If / is placed, then all folders in the domain can access the cookie. Otherwise, the default is the current folder and any of its subfolders.
Secure	A TRUE/FALSE value indicating whether a secure protocol such as HTTPS is needed to access the cookie. The word secure must be added to specify that HTTPS is needed.
Expires	Whether this cookie will expire. Expiration date in general are in seconds – the number of seconds since January 1, 1970 (UNIX time).
Name	The name of the cookie. eg. call_id
Value	The value of the cookie. eg. 224

Table 10-1: Parts of a Cookie

When a server sends a cookie, it specifies an expiration date for the cookie. The expiration date determines whether the cookie is a session-level or a persistent cookie. If a cookie is sent with no expiration date, then they are session-level cookies which are held in the browser's memory until the browser is closed. For persistent cookies, most browsers store up to 20 cookies per site.

COOKIE SETUP

Cookies are sent in the HTTP header. Cookies are not part of HTML, but instead part of the HTTP protocol. Each request for a Web page by the browser is returned with a HTTP header. HTTP header is behind-the-scenes means by which the browser communicates with the Web server, and vice-versa. It is through the HTTP header that requests and responses are made. The HTTP header opens with an instruction to open the header. Another instruction closes the header.

Since servers send cookies in the HTTP header, it will not appear in the source of an HTML page in the browser. Also, the HTTP header is not the same as the <HEAD> tag in a Web page. Some of the common variables that are part of HTTP header are:

- SERVER SOFTWARE – name and version of the server software.
- SERVER PROTOCOL – the HTTP version number.
- SERVER NAME – the servers host name.
- SERVER PORT – the port number the server is using for communication.
- REQUEST METHOD – method to request like GET, POST, or HEAD.
- QUERY STRING – the part of query string (if present).

The communication between the browser and a server that wants to set a cookie appears as follows:

1. Browser identifies the server that has the Web page.
2. Browser requests the Web page from the server.
3. Server returns the Web page to the browser for rendering. Included in the HTTP header attached to the Web page may be a request to the browser to set a new cookie.
4. Browser stores any cookies received and renders the Web page.

When the user requests a Web page from the server that placed a cookie previously, the communication between the browser and the server appears as follows:

1. Browser identifies the server that has the Web page.
2. Browser checks for any existing cookies from the server.
3. Browser requests the Web page from the server. Now, the request includes any cookie information previously placed by that server through its HTTP header.
4. Server receives the cookie along with the request for the Web page. The cookie information can now be utilized to complete the Web page for the browser.
5. Server returns the Web page to the browser for rendering. Included in the HTTP header of the Web page may be a request to the browser to set a new cookie.
6. Browser stores any cookies received and renders the Web page.

Browsers offer users options with regard to cookies including the option to completely turn off the cookie functionality. If the cookie feature is turned off by the browser, it is important to inform users to reset the cookie functionality.

COOKIE ACTIONS

There are three main actions necessary with regard to cookie handling.

1. SEND – Send a cookie, or reset the value of an existing cookie.
2. GET – Get or read the value of an existing cookie.
3. DELETE – Delete an expired cookie by setting an expiration date to the past.

Oracle provides a package OWA_COOKIE with procedures to perform each of the cookie actions. The variables and programs in the package are listed below followed by their structure.

*   owa_cookie.send procedure.
*   owa_cookie.cookie datatype.
*   owa_cookie.num_vals variable.
*   owa_cookie.vals(n) variable.
*   owa_cookie.vc_arr variable.
*   owa_cookie.get function.
*   owa_cookie.get_all procedure.
*   owa_cookie.remove procedure.

OWA_COOKIE.SEND(*name, value, expires, path, domain, secure*)

Name is the name of the entry you place in the cookie.

Value is a text string representing the value of the Name entry in the cookie.

Expires is an Oracle DATE data type expiration date for the cookie.

Path is used to specify a path that the cookies are valid for on the server. Specify / so that any branch of URL folder tree can get the cookie. By default the path folder is same as the current folder.

Domain is used to specify a domain that a cookie is valid for on the server. By default, the domain is the current domain, so one can specify NULL.

Secure means that the cookie can only be passed over an Secure Socket Layer (SSL) connection.

OWA_COOKIE.COOKIE

Record type for a cookie. A PL/SQL variable declared with a type of OWA_COOKIE.COOKIE holds the results of a call to the procedure OWA_COOKIE.GET.

OWA_COOKIE.NUM_VALS

A variable that returns the number of values stored in the array.

OWA_COOKIE.VALS(*n*)

A variable that returns the nth value stored in the array. Since the HTTP specification allows multiple values for the same cookie name, the cookie value must be retrieved using this notation.

OWA_COOKIE.VC_ARR

An array to hold multiple values of type varchar2(4096). It is provided as a data type to use when declaring variables to hold results of retrieving all cookies.

OWA_COOKIE.GET(*name*)

Gets a cookie with the specified name. The result of this goes into a variable of the type OWA_COOKIE.COOKIE.

OWA_COOKIE.GET_ALL()

Retrieves all cookies that the server has access to in the order they were sent by the browser.

OWA_COOKIE.REMOVE(*name, value, path*)

Remove the named cookie and its associated value. The path is optional.

To send or remove cookies, the following steps are performed as part of HTTP header.

1. OWA_UTIL.MIME_HEADER(BCLOSE_HEADER=>FALSE);
2. Use OWA_COOKIE.SEND or OWA_COOKIE.REMOVE here.
3. OWA_UTIL.HTTP_HEADER_CLOSE;

The OWA_UTIL.MIME_HEADER procedure structure shown below takes several parameters as part of its structure. These parameters are explained in the Table 10-2.

```
OWA_UTIL.MIME_HEADER(ccontent_type, bclose_header, ccharset);
```

Parameter	Description
ccontent_type	The MIME type for the document being sent. The default value is 'text/html.'
bclose_header	A boolean value. TRUE means the header will be closed immediately. FALSE means that the header remains open until it is explicitly closed with OWA_UTIL.http_header_close.
ccharset	Optioal character set. Default is NULL.

Table 10-2: OWA_UTIL.MIME_HEADER parameters

COOKIE WITH PL/SQL SERVER PAGES

During PSP development, the cookie action *must* be performed before any HTML is generated by the PL/SQL procedure. In other words the HTTP header must be opened and closed before any HTML is generated by the Oracle server. For this reason, *in a PSP, the cookie action statement should be on the first line only*. It is possible to define additional procedures and functions on the server to facilitate cookie actions. However, for reading (or get procedure) the value of a cookie, it is not necessary to put the OWA_COOKIE.GET procedure inside of an HTTP header. The following examples illustrate cookie actions.

1. A procedure to set the cookie name and value.

```
PROCEDURE set_cookie (t_cookie_name in varchar2,
             t_cookie_value in varchar2,
             t_expires in date default null) IS
BEGIN
  owa_util.mime_header(bclose_header=>false);
  owa_cookie.send(t_cookie_name, t_cookie_value, t_expires);
  owa_util.http_header_close;
END;
```

Now a call to this procedure from a PSP to set the cookie is shown below. Note the call to cookie procedure must appear only in the first line of the PSP.

```
<%set_cookie('call_id','672',sysdate+4);%>
<%@page language="PL/SQL"%>
<%@plsql procedure="test_cookie1"%>
<%!t1 char(2);%>
<html>
<body>
<p>PSP Web Page.</p>
<p>Set Cookie.</p>
</body>
</html>
```

To change a cookie value, use the same code but change the value.

2. A function to retrieve the value of a cookie with the name passed in. If no values are found, the function returns a NULL value.

```
FUNCTION get_cookie (t_cookie_name in varchar2) RETURN varchar2 IS
v_cookie owa_cookie.cookie;
BEGIN
v_cookie := owa_cookie.get(t_cookie_name);
if v_cookie.num_vals != 0 then
   return v_cookie.vals(1);
else
   return null;
end if;
END;
```

Now a call to this function from a PSP to retrieve the cookie value is shown below. Note the call to the cookie function must appear in the first line of the PSP.

```
<%g_cookie := get_cookie('call_id');%>
<%!g_cookie number(4);%>
<%@page language="PL/SQL"%>
<%@plsql procedure="test_cookie2"%>
<%!t1 char(2);%>
<html>
<body>
<p>PSP Web Page.</p>
<p>Value of Cookie <%=g_cookie%></p>
</body>
</html>
```

3. A PSP that retrieves all cookie values through the OWA_COOKIE.GET_ALL function. Once again note that the call to the cookie function must appear in the first line of the PSP.

```
<%owa_cookie.get_all(v_cookie_names,v_cookie_values,v_cookie_count);%>
<%@page language="PL/SQL"%>
<%@plsql procedure="test_cookie4"%>
<%!v_cookie_names owa_cookie.vc_arr;
v_cookie_values owa_cookie.vc_arr;
v_cookie_count integer;%>
<html>
<body>
<p>PSP Web Page.</p>
<p>Get Cookie Values.</p>
<p><%for num in 1 .. v_cookie_count loop%>
Cookie # <%=num%>: Name <%=v_cookie_names(num)%>,
        Values=<%=v_cookie_values(num)%><br>
<%end loop;%>
</p>
<%exception when others then%>
Error in get_all_cookies: <%=sqlerrm%>
</body>
</html>
```

4. A function to check whether a cookie exists.

```
FUNCTION cookie_exists (t_cookie_name in varchar2) RETURN boolean IS
v_cookie owa_cookie.cookie;
BEGIN
v_cookie := owa_cookie.get(t_cookie_name);
if v_cookie.num_vals != 0 then
   return true;
else
   return false;
end if;
END;
```

Now a call to this function from a PSP to check whether the cookie exists is shown below. Note again that the call to the cookie function must appear in the first line of the PSP.

```
<%if cookie_exists('session_id') then v_cookie := 'Yes'; else v_cookie :=
'No';end if;%>
<%@page language="PL/SQL"%>
<%@plsql procedure="test_cookie5"%>
<%!v_cookie varchar2(10);%>
<html>
<body>
<p>PSP Web Page.</p>
<p>Check Cookie Exists.</p>
```

```
<p>Cookie Status <%=v_cookie%>
</p>
</body>
</html>
```

TUTORIAL TO SET COOKIE IN WEB APPLICATION

This tutorial extends the two page tutorial of Chapter 6, Lesson A. This time the home page with input form will have the statements to check if a cookie exists for RENTAL_NO. If the cookie is on the computer, it will display a welcome message and automatically insert the RENTAL_NO of the user. If there is no cookie on the computer (for example, the first time the Web page loads in the browser), the input form will have to be filled, and when the response page loads in the browser it will set the cookie for the RENTAL_NO. The home page is called "Pay Rent Cookie" while the response page is called "Rent Receipt Cookie."

To complete this tutorial make sure that the following cookie programs have been setup in your account on the server.
1. procedure set_cookie.
2. function get_cookie.
3. function cookie_exists.

Run the script file superflexDB_v4.sql to load the Superflex Apartments Database tables necessary to complete this tutorial. Make the following modifications to the Web pages of the tutorial.

1. The pay_rent PSP (now saved as filename pay_rent_cookie.psp), modify the page specification and procedure statements along with additional cookie statements as follows. *Make sure these statements start on the first line of the PSP.*

    ```
    <%if cookie_exists('call_id') then g_cookie := get_cookie('call_id'); end if;%>
    <%!g_cookie number(6) :=null;%>
    <%@page language="PL/SQL"%>
    <%@plsql procedure="pay_rent_cookie"%>
    <%!tenant_name_text tenant.tenant_name%type;%>
    ```

    In the body of the Web page, before the input form specification position the following statements to check for the presence of cookie.

    ```
    <%if g_cookie is not null then
       select tenant_name
       into tenant_name_text
       from tenant
       where rental_no=g_cookie;%>
    <p>Welcome <%=tenant_name_text%>.
    Please proceed to complete payment.
    If not <%=tenant_name_text%> please enter your Rental Number.</p><br />
    <%end if;%>
    ```

2. In the rent_receipt PSP (now saved as filename rent_receipt_cookie.psp), modify the page specification and procedure statements along with additional cookie statements as follows. Once again, *make sure these statements start on the first line of the PSP.*

```
<%set_cookie('call_id',rental_no_text,sysdate+5);%>
<%@page language="PL/SQL"%>
<%@plsql procedure="rent_receipt_cookie"%>
```

Load PSP to the Database

Once the PSP have been completed, open the Windows Command Prompt window to execute the loadpsp command for the PSP files. The command to load the two PSPs will be:

```
loadpsp -replace -user userid/password@connection_string
        drive&path\pay_rent_cookie.psp

loadpsp -replace -user userid/password@connection_string
        drive&path\rent_receipt_cookie.psp
```

The userid, password, connection string and path specifications depend on database configuration. If there are errors in the page, fix the errors and re-load the page.

View PSP in Web Browser

Once the loading is successful type the URL below to retrieve the Web page from the database. The URL should be modified to suit the existing server configuration in the form of server-name, DAD, and userid.

```
http://server-name/DAD/userid.pay_rent_cookie
```

Test the working of cookies by opening the home page the second time.

COOKIE EXAMPLES

Cookies store only small pieces of date. However, using cookies in conjunction with database tables makes the cookie much more useful. Statistics about Web traffic are frequently required for Web applications. Cookies can assist in holding this information in the database.

Track Web Traffic

First create a table that will contain data about which pages are visited. A sample syntax of such a table is as follows:

```
CREATE TABLE page_visited
(visitor_id VARCHAR2(200),
ip_address VARCHAR2(20),
browser_type  VARCHAR2(200),
page_requested VARCHAR2(200),
timestamp DATE);
```

Visitor_id is the cookie name retrieved through the get_cookie procedure. Instead of using visitor's name generate a unique identifier for the visitor, which can be maintained incognito from the visitor. The *ip_address* and the *browser_type* values are retrieved from the HTTP header. Information on HTTP header can be retrieved through the OWA_UTIL procedure get_cgi_env (Appendix D). *Page_requested* can be directly inserted from the Web page that was transferred to the browser. *Timestamp* is essentially the sysdate value. An example of a procedure that populates the PAGE_VISIT table in SQL Plus is as follows:

```
create or replace procedure track_page_visit (v_page in varchar2) is
begin
insert into page_visit
     (visitor,
      ip_address,
      browser_type,
      page_requested,
      timestamp)
values (get_cookie('VISITOR'),
        owa_util.get_cgi_env('REMOTE_ADDR'),
        owa_util.get_cgi_env('HTTP_USER_AGENT'),
        v_page,
        sysdate);
end;
```

To call this procedure from any page use the following syntax:

```
track_page_visit(OWA_UTIL.GET_PROCEDURE);
```

The function OWA_UTIL.GET_PROCEDURE above retrieves the name of the current procedure.

Track Web Information

Another use of cookies is to track access to particular information on a Web page by the visitor. For example, besides knowing the page with product information, it would be interesting to know which product was being viewed. To handle this requirement, create a table as follows:

```
CREATE TABLE info_visited
(visitor_id VARCHAR2(200),
ip_address VARCHAR2(20),
browser_type  VARCHAR2(200),
page_requested VARCHAR2(200),
product_id NUMBER,
product_name VARCHAR2(200),
timestamp DATE);
```

Now, the following procedure can be setup to populate the info_visited table.

```
create or replace procedure track_product_visit
                 (v_page in varchar2,
                  v_product_id in number,
                  v_product_name in varchar2) is
begin
insert into track_product_visit
   (visitor,
```

```
        ip_address,
        browser_type,
        page_requested,
        product_id,
        product_name,
        timestamp)
   values (get_cookie('VISITOR'),
           owa_util.get_cgi_env('REMOTE_ADDR'),
           owa_util.get_cgi_env('HTTP_USER_AGENT'),
          v_page,
        v_product_id,
        v_product_name,
           sysdate);
   end;
```

To call this procedure from any page use the following syntax:

```
track_product_visit
   (OWA_UTIL.GET_PROCEDURE,
    v_product_id,
    v_product_name);
```

The function OWA_UTIL.GET_PROCEDURE above retrieves the name of the current procedure. The call to track_product_visit in a Web page is made (i) after access to product details is known, and (ii) before the HTML tag appears and executed.

CHAPTER SUMMARY

- A cookie is a text string.

- The cookie string contains a name and a value (name-value pair) that holds information.

- Cookie are stored and managed by the browser.

- Cookies are sent to the user's browser by servers. When a server responds to a browser's request by delivering a page to the browser, this response can include a request to set a cookie.

- The user's browser should be configured to accept cookies.

- Cookies can be of two types – session-level cookies and persistent cookies.

- Session-level cookies are short-term cookies that are held by the browser temporarily, and then deleted when the user exits the browser.

- Persistent cookies are saved directly in the computer's file system. These cookie files remain on the computer even after the browser is closed and the power is turned off.

- Cookies are sent in the HTTP header. Cookies are not part of HTML, but instead part of the HTTP protocol.

- Each request for a Web page by the browser is returned with HTTP headers that can contain cookies. It is through the HTTP header that requests and responses are made.

- Since servers send cookies in the HTTP header, it will not appear in the source of an HTML page in the browser.

- There are three main actions necessary with regard to cookie handling – SEND, GET, DELETE.

- The SEND action sends a cookie, or reset the value of an existing cookie.

- The GET action gets the existing cookie or read its value.

- The DELETE action deletes an expired cookie by setting an expiration date to the past.

- Oracle provides a package OWA_COOKIE with procedures to perform each of the cookie actions.

- During PL/SQL Server Page development, the cookie action must be performed before any HTML is generated by the PL/SQL procedure.

- For this reason, in a PL/SQL Server Page, the cookie action statement should be on the first line only. It is possible to define additional procedures and functions on the server to facilitate cookie actions.

- Cookies store only small pieces of date. However, using cookies in conjunction with database makes the cookie much more useful for Web application.

REVIEW QUESTIONS

1. Explain the purpose of cookies.

2. Describe briefly the cookie structure.

3. What are session-level cookies?

4. What are persistent cookies?

5. Describe briefly how placement of cookie takes place in Web browser.

6. List the main actions associated with the working of a cookie.

7. What is the Oracle package that enables cookie actions?

8. How and where is cookie action specified in a PL/SQL Server Page?

REVIEW EXERCISES

1. A cookie is a _____ string.

2. A cookie contains a _____ pair that holds information.

3. Cookies are stored and managed by _____.

4. Cookies are of _____ types.

5. _____ cookies are short-term cookies that are held by the browser temporarily.

6. _____ cookies are saved directly in the computer's file system.

7. Cookies are sent in the _____ header.

8. _____ header is behind-the-scenes means by which the browser communicates with the Web server.

9. _____ action sends the cookie or resets the value of an existing cookie.

10. _____ action read the value of an existing cookie.

11. _____ action removes an expired cookie by setting an expiration date to the past.

12. Oracle provides a package _____ with procedures to perform cookie actions.

13. In PL/SQL Server Page the cookie action must be performed before any _____ is generated by its related PL/SQL procedure.

PROBLEM SOLVING EXERCISES

Ex10A-1.   Extend the problem solving exercise Ex6A-3 of Chapter 6, Lesson A with cookie capabilities.

1. Rename the existing home page PSP file as ex10a_apply_membership. The response page PSP should be renamed as file ex10a_membership_receipt.

2. The home page logic should be modified to contain PSP statements to check the existence of a cookie. The cookie value should be utilized (i) to display a welcome message with customer name, and (ii) to populate the Membership Form with values for Customer first_name, last_name, street, city, state, zip, and phone attributes.

3. The response page should set the cookie for the customer id associated with the input customer name value from the home page.

4. Generate and load PSP Web pages to the Oracle database server. (The instructor will provide the details on the database server accounts).

5. If some clipart is utilized in the Web page, transfer the image to the required virtual folder. (The instructor will provide the necessary instructions on this step).

6. Open the Web site in the browser and print the display.

Ex10A-2.   Extend the problem solving exercise Ex6A-7 of Chapter 6, Lesson A with cookie capabilities.

1. Rename the existing home page PSP file as ex10a_air_Reservations. The response page PSP should be renamed as file ex10a_Air_Receipt.

2. The home page logic should be modified to contain PSP statements to check the existence of a cookie. The cookie value should be utilized to display a welcome message with customer name.

3. The response page should set the cookie for the customer_id associated with the input from the home page.

4. Generate and load PSP Web pages to the Oracle database server. (The instructor will provide the details on the database server accounts).

5. If some clipart is utilized in the Web page, transfer the image to the required virtual folder. (The instructor will provide the necessary instructions on this step).

6. Open the Web site in the browser and print the display.

Ex10A-3.   Extend the problem solving exercise Ex6B-5 of Chapter 6, Lesson B with cookie capabilities.

1.   Rename the existing home page PSP as ex10a_enter_customer. The second page PSP should be renamed as file ex10a_modify_customer. The third page PSP will remain the same.

2.   The home page logic should be modified to contain PSP statements to check the existence of a cookie. The cookie value should be utilized to display a welcome message with customer name.

3.   Generate and load PSP Web pages to the Oracle database server. (The instructor will provide the details on the database server accounts).

4.   If some clipart is utilized in the Web page, transfer the image to the required virtual folder. (The instructor will provide the necessary instructions on this step).

5.   Open the Web site in the browser and print the display.

Ex10A-4.   Extend the problem solving exercise Ex6B-6 of Chapter 6, Lesson B with cookie capabilities.

1.   Rename the existing home page PSP as ex10a_rental_input. The second page PSP should be renamed as file ex10a_tenant_modify. The third page PSP will remain the same.

2.   The home page logic should be modified to contain PSP statements to check the existence of a cookie. The cookie value should be utilized to display a welcome message with tenant name.

3.   Generate and load PSP Web pages to the Oracle database server. (The instructor will provide the details on the database server accounts).

4.   If some clipart is utilized in the Web page, transfer the image to the required virtual folder. (The instructor will provide the necessary instructions on this step).

5.   Open the Web site in the browser and print the display.

Web Cookies and Locks

- Web Locking
- Oracle Web Locking Package
- Web Pages with Locking Capability

In traditional database application processing, the application maintains state with the database. This makes it easy to enforce database locking during an application session. Even though PL/SQL is a database language, when generating Web pages with PL/SQL one cannot use the traditional database locking schemes because HTTP is a stateless protocol. The reason being that the Web setup in general does not maintain the state of connectivity with the Web server (the Web doesn't know or care whether or not you're still connected). Hence, conventional database locking schemes cannot be used directly. The result is that users can have lost updates while browsing and updating database information through Web pages.

> This chapter utilizes the table structure of Superflex Apartment database to explain examples.

DATABASE LOCKS FOR WEB APPLICATIONS

Oracle database provides several ways to enforce locking for Web applications. One approach involves the PL/SQL package called OWA_OPT_LOCK that enforces a locking mechanism called *optimistic locking*. It is called *optimistic locking* as the database does not prevent other users from performing updates, but rejects the current update if an intervening update has occurred. The OWA_OPT_LOCK package contains two methods for determining whether the data was changed by another user since it was loaded in the browser. The first method is called the *hidden fields* method, while the second method is called the *checksum* method.

The hidden fields method stores the current values in the hidden form fields in a Web page. Then when the form is submitted with the updates, the procedure checks to see if the values stored in the database still match the hidden field values. This method is implemented through the OWA_OPT_LOCK.STORE_VALUES procedure.

The checksum method performs row checksum at the time the Web page is loaded in the browser, and again as the data is being saved. A checksum is a number calculated from all the bytes stored in the block with a particular rowid. When data is updated, a checksum performed for the same rowid will produce a different result.

To use the checksum method, the checksum value for the affected rowid and the rowid values will be stored in the form hidden fields. When these values are sent to the Web page performing the update, the checksum value is again calculated for the same rowid value. The two checksums (new calculated value and the old checksum value passed to the Web page) are compared to see if the data was changed in the interim. This method is implemented through the OWA_OPT_LOCK.CHECKSUM function.

If either method shows that the values do not match, the procedure could abort the update and notify the user that the data has changed since it was last retrieved.

The variables and programs in the package are:
- vcArray datatype.
- checksum function.
- get_rowid function.
- store_values procedure.
- verify_values function.

VCARRAY

The *vcArray* datatype is a PL/SQL table intended to hold rowid. Rowid is the fastest way to update a row in Oracle. The syntax is:

```
type vcArray is table of varchar2(2000) index by binary_integer;
```

CHECKSUM

The *checksum* function returns a checksum value for a specified string or for a row in a table. For a row in a table, the function calculates the checksum value based on the values of the two columns in the row. This function comes in two versions: (i) return checksum based on the specified string, and (ii) return a checksum based on the values of a row in a table. The syntax is:

```
owa_opt_lock.checksum(t_buff in varchar2) return number;

owa_opt_lock.checksum(
      t_owner in varchar2,
      t_tname in varchar2,
      t_rowid in rowid)
      return number;
```

where t_buff   is the string for which the checksum is to be calculated.
      t_owner   is the owner of the table.
      t_tname   is the table name.
      t_rowid   is the row in t_tname for which the checksum value is to be calculated.

GET_ROWID

The *get_rowid* function returns the rowid datatype from the specified owa_opt_lock.vcArray datatype. The syntax is:

```
owa_opt_lock.get_rowid(t_old_values in vcArray) return rowid;
```

where   t_old_values   is the parameter passed from an HTML form.

STORE_VALUES

The *store_values* procedure stores the column values of the row that is to be updated. The values are stored in hidden fields values of an HTML form. Before the row is updated, these values are compared with the current row values to ensure that the values in the row have not been changed. If the values have changed, users can be informed accordingly. The syntax is:

```
owa_opt_lock.store_values(
     t_owner in varchar2,
     t_tname in varchar2,
     t_rowid in rowid);
```

where   t_owner   is the owner of the table.
        t_tname   is the table name.
        t_rowid   is the row for which you want to store values.

The procedure generates a series of hidden form elements with prefix "old." For example, the name of the owner will be "old_t_owner"; the name of the table is "old_t_tname"; and one element for each column or attribute in the row.

VERIFY_VALUES

The *verify_values* function verifies whether or not values in the specified row have been updated since the last query. This function is used in conjunction with owa_opt_lock.store_values procedure. The syntax is:

```
owa_opt_lock.verify_values(t_old_values in vcArray) return boolean;
```

where   t_old_values   is a PL/SQL table containing the following information:

t_old_values(1) for the owner of the table;
t_old_values(2) for the table name;
t_old_values(3) for the rowid of the row that has to be verified;
remaining indexes contain values for the columns in the table.

Generally this parameter is passed in from the HTML form, from where the owa_opt_lock.store_values procedure was previously called to store the row values in hidden form fields.

TUTORIAL TO ENFORCE WEB DATABASE LOCKS

Run the script file superflexDB_v4.sql to load the Superflex Apartments Database tables necessary to complete this tutorial.

Hidden Fields Method

The tutorial consists of three PSP pages. Web site will have banner entry as "Superflex Apartments." There will be only 1 button in the navigation bar linked to the home (DB_Lock_Input) Web page.

DB_Lock_Input Web Page

The home page (DB_Lock_Input) is a Web page that basically contains one input Web form. The Web form will have one text box form element to input APT_NO value and a submit button labeled "Modify" to submit the form element values to the second PSP (DB_Lock_Modify).

The complete PSP (filename DB_Lock_Input.psp) using Web Template 2 is shown below. The navigation URL and the `<form>` tag ACTION attribute URL should be modified to suit the existing server configuration in the form of server-name, DAD, and userid. It is important to include the second PSP (db_lock_modify) Web procedure name in the `<form>` tag action attribute URL to correctly send the form data to it.

```
<!DOCTYPE HTML PUBLIC "-//W3C//DTD HTML 4.01 Transitional//EN">
<html>
<%@page language="PL/SQL"%>
<%@plsql procedure="db_lock_input"%>
<head>
<title>Web Database Lock</title>
</head>
<body>
<p><div align="center"><h1>Superflex Apartments</h1></div></p>
<br>
<table summary=""width=700> <!-- Page width -->
<tr>
<td width=100> <!-- Navigation Bar Links -->
<a href="http://server-name/DAD/userid.db_lock_input">Enter Apartment</a><br>

</td><td width=600> <!-- Start Page Content -->
<p><b>Modify Apartment</b></p>
<form action="http://server-name/DAD/userid.db_lock_modify" method="post">
Apartment No: <input type=text name="apt_no_text" value=""><br /><br/>
<input type=submit name="FormsButton1" value="Modify">
</form>
<!-- End Page Content -->
</td></tr>
</table>
</body>
</html>
```

DB_Lock_Modify Web Page

The second PSP page (DB_Lock_Modify) is a Web page that basically also contains one Web form, but where the form element values are populated with database values. The Web form will display the input APT_NO value from the home page, besides displaying the associated APT_UTILITY, APT_DEPOSIT_AMT, and APT_RENT_AMT attribute values in their respective text boxes. The a submit button labeled "Submit" will submit the form element values to the third PSP (DB_Lock_Confirm). The second Web page will also have the necessary statements to set the hidden fields pertaining to the form update with respect to associated APARTMENT table row id used to populate the form elements. These statements are specified within the form.

The complete PSP (filename DB_Lock_Modify.psp) using Web Template 2 is shown below. The navigation URL and the <form> tag ACTION attribute URL should be modified to suit the existing server configuration in the form of server-name, DAD, and userid. It is important to include the third PSP (db_lock_confirm) Web procedure name in the <form> tag action attribute URL to correctly send the form data to it.

```
<!DOCTYPE HTML PUBLIC "-//W3C//DTD HTML 4.01 Transitional//EN">
<html>
<%@page language="PL/SQL"%>
<%@plsql procedure="db_lock_modify"%>
<%@plsql parameter="apt_no_text" default="null"%>
<%@plsql parameter="formsbutton1" default="null"%>
<%!t_row_id rowid;
t_apt_utility apartment.apt_utility%type;
t_apt_deposit_amt apartment.apt_deposit_amt%type;
t_apt_rent_amt apartment.apt_rent_amt%type;%>
<head>
<title>Web Database Lock</title>
</head>
<body>
<p><div align="center"><h1>Superflex Apartments</h1></div></p>
<br>
<table summary=""width=700> <!-- Page width -->
<tr>
<td width=100> <!-- Navigation Bar Links -->
<a href="http://server-name/DAD/userid.db_lock_input">Enter Apartment</a><br>

</td><td width=600> <!-- Start Page Content -->
<p><b>Modify Apartment</b></p>
<form action="http://server-name/DAD/userid.db_lock_confirm" method="post">
<input type=hidden name="apt_no_text" value="<%=apt_no_text%>">
<%select rowid,apt_utility,apt_deposit_amt,apt_rent_amt
into t_row_id,t_apt_utility,t_apt_deposit_amt,t_apt_rent_amt
from apartment
where apt_no = apt_no_text;
owa_opt_lock.store_values('userid','apartment',t_row_id);%>
Apartment No: <%=apt_no_text%><br /><br/>
Utility Available: <input type=text name="apt_utility_text"
    value="<%=t_apt_utility%>"><small>(Y for Yes, N for No)</small><br /><br/>
Deposit Amount: <input type=text name="apt_deposit_amt_text"
    value="<%=t_apt_deposit_amt%>"><br /><br/>
Rent Amount: <input type=text name="apt_rent_amt_text" value="<%=t_apt_rent_amt%>">
    <br /><br/>
<input type=submit name="FormsButton1" value="Submit">
</form>
<!-- End Page Content -->
</td></tr>
</table>
</body>
</html>
```

DB_Lock_Confirm Web Page

The third PSP page (DB_Lock_Confirm) performs the hidden field check prior to updating. If the row has not been changed since the last access, the Web page proceeds with the update of the APARTMENT table attributes passed as input parameters from the second page, and displays a success message. Otherwise it avoids the update and displays another message.

The complete PSP (filename db_lock_confirm.psp) using Web Template 2 is shown below. The navigation URL should be modified to suit the existing server configuration in the form of server-name, DAD, and userid.

```
<!DOCTYPE HTML PUBLIC "-//W3C//DTD HTML 4.01 Transitional//EN">
<html>
<%@page language="PL/SQL"%>
<%@plsql procedure="db_lock_confirm"%>
<%@plsql parameter="apt_no_text" default="null"%>
<%@plsql parameter="formsbutton1" default="null"%>
<%@plsql parameter="apt_utility_text" default="null"%>
<%@plsql parameter="apt_deposit_amt_text" default="null"%>
<%@plsql parameter="apt_rent_amt_text" default="null"%>
<%@plsql parameter="old_apartment" type="owa_opt_lock.vcArray"%>
<%!curr_rowid rowid;
lock_check char(5);%>
<head>
<title>Web Database Lock</title>
</head>
<body>
<p><div align="center"><h1>Superflex Apartments</h1></div></p>
<br>
<table summary=""width=700> <!-- Page width -->
<tr>
<td width=100> <!-- Navigation Bar Links -->
<a href="http://server-name/DAD/userid.db_lock_input">Enter Apartment</a><br>

</td><td width=600> <!-- Start Page Content -->
<%curr_rowid := owa_opt_lock.get_rowid(old_apartment);
if (owa_opt_lock.verify_values(old_apartment)) then
lock_check := 'true';
else lock_check := 'false';
end if;
if lock_check = 'true' then
update apartment
set apt_utility = apt_utility_text,
apt_deposit_amt = apt_deposit_amt_text,
apt_rent_amt = apt_rent_amt_text
where apt_no = apt_no_text;
commit;%>
<P>Updates have been applied successfully.</P>
<P>Thanks.</P>
<%end if;%>

<%if lock_check = 'false' then%>
<P>The updates cannot be applied, as the row has been changed since the initial
request.</P>
<%end if;%>
<!-- End Page Content -->
</td></tr>
</table>
</body>
</html>
```

Load PSP to the Database

Once the PSP have been completed, open the Windows Command Prompt window to execute the loadpsp command for the PSP files. The command to load the three PSPs will be:

```
loadpsp -replace -user userid/password@connection_string
        drive&path\db_lock_input.psp
```

```
loadpsp -replace -user userid/password@connection_string
             drive&path\db_lock_modify.psp

loadpsp -replace -user userid/password@connection_string
             drive&path\db_lock_confirm.psp
```

The userid, password, connection string and path specifications depend on database configuration. If there are errors in the page, fix the errors and re-load the page.

View PSP in Web Browser

Once the loading is successful type the URL below to retrieve the Web page from the database. The URL should be modified to suit the existing server configuration in the form of server-name, DAD, and userid.

```
http://server-name/DAD/userid.db_lock_input
```


Test the working of the owa_opt_lock package by opening the Web site through another browser window simultaneously. Then make modifications in the second browser window to see the effect of the modifications in the first browser window.

Checksum Method

Modify the Hidden Fields Method tutorial. The layout of the Web pages is similar to the previous tutorial. The Web site will have banner entry as "Superflex Apartments." There will be only 1 button in the navigation bar linked to the home (DB_Lock_Input2) Web page.

DB_Lock_Input2 Web Page

The home page (DB_Lock_Input2) is a Web page that basically contains one input Web form. The Web form will have one text box form element to input APT_NO value and a submit button labeled "Modify" to submit the form element values to the second PSP (DB_Lock_Modify2).

The complete PSP (filename DB_Lock_Input2.psp) using Web Template 2 is shown below. The navigation URL and the `<form>` tag ACTION attribute URL should be modified to suit the existing server configuration in the form of server-name, DAD, and userid. It is important to include the second PSP (db_lock_modify2) Web procedure name in the `<form>` tag action attribute URL to correctly send the form data to it.

```
<!DOCTYPE HTML PUBLIC "-//W3C//DTD HTML 4.01 Transitional//EN">
<html>
<%@page language="PL/SQL"%>
<%@plsql procedure="db_lock_input2"%>
<head>
<title>Web Database Lock</title>
</head>
<body>
<p><div align="center"><h1>Superflex Apartments</h1></div></p>
```

```
<br>
<table summary=""width=700> <!-- Page width -->
<tr>
<td width=100> <!-- Navigation Bar Links -->
<a href="http://server-name/DAD/userid.db_lock_input2">Enter Apartment</a><br>

</td><td width=600> <!-- Start Page Content -->
<p><b>Modify Apartment</b></p>
<form action="http://server-name/DAD/userid.db_lock_modify2" method="post">
Apartment No: <input type=text name="apt_no_text" value=""><br /><br/>
<input type=submit name="FormsButton1" value="Modify">
</form>
<!-- End Page Content -->
</td></tr>
</table>
</body>
</html>
```

DB_Lock_Modify2 Web Page

The second PSP page (DB_Lock_Modify2) is a Web page that basically also contains one Web form, but where the form element values are populated with database values. The Web form will display the input APT_NO value from the home page, besides displaying the associated APT_UTILITY, APT_DEPOSIT_AMT, and APT_RENT_AMT attribute values in their respective text boxes. The a submit button labeled "Submit" will submit the form element values to the third PSP (DB_Lock_Confirm). The second Web page will also have the necessary statements to set the checksum as a hidden field pertaining to the form update with respect to associated APARTMENT table row id used to populate the form elements. These statements are specified within the form.

The complete PSP (filename DB_Lock_Modify2.psp) using Web Template 2 is shown below. The navigation URL and the `<form>` tag ACTION attribute URL should be modified to suit the existing server configuration in the form of server-name, DAD, and userid. It is important to include the third PSP (db_lock_confirm2) Web procedure name in the `<form>` tag action attribute URL to correctly send the form data to it.

```
<!DOCTYPE HTML PUBLIC "-//W3C//DTD HTML 4.01 Transitional//EN">
<html>
<%@page language="PL/SQL"%>
<%@plsql procedure="db_lock_modify2"%>
<%@plsql parameter="apt_no_text" default="null"%>
<%@plsql parameter="formsbutton1" default="null"%>
<%!t_row_id rowid;
t_apt_utility apartment.apt_utility%type;
t_apt_deposit_amt apartment.apt_deposit_amt%type;
t_apt_rent_amt apartment.apt_rent_amt%type;%>
<%select rowid,apt_utility,apt_deposit_amt,apt_rent_amt
into t_row_id,t_apt_utility,t_apt_deposit_amt,t_apt_rent_amt
from apartment
where apt_no = apt_no_text;%>
<head>
<title>Web Database Lock</title>
</head>
<body>
<p><div align="center"><h1>Superflex Apartments</h1></div></p>
<br>
<table summary=""width=700> <!-- Page width -->
<tr>
<td width=100> <!-- Navigation Bar Links -->
<a href="http://server-name/DAD/userid.db_lock_input2">Enter Apartment</a><br>
```

```
</td><td width=600> <!-- Start Page Content -->
<p><b>Modify Apartment</b></p>
<form action="http://server-name/DAD/userid.db_lock_confirm2" method="post">
<input type=hidden name="apt_no_text" value="<%=apt_no_text%>">
<input type=hidden name="p_checksum"
    value="<%=owa_opt_lock.checksum('userid','apartment',t_row_id)%>">
<input type=hidden name="p_rowid" value="<%=t_row_id%>">

Apartment No: <%=apt_no_text%><br /><br/>
Utility Available: <input type=text name="apt_utility_text"
    value="<%=t_apt_utility%>"><small>(Y for Yes, N for No)</small><br /><br/>
Deposit Amount: <input type=text name="apt_deposit_amt_text"
    value="<%=t_apt_deposit_amt%>"><br /><br/>
Rent Amount: <input type=text name="apt_rent_amt_text" value="<%=t_apt_rent_amt%>">
    <br /><br/>
<input type=submit name="FormsButton1" value="Submit">
</form>
<!-- End Page Content -->
</td></tr>
</table>
</body>
</html>
```

DB_Lock_Confirm2 Web Page

The third PSP page (DB_Lock_Confirm2) performs the hidden field check prior to updating. If the row has not been changed since the last access, the Web page proceeds with the update of the APARTMENT table attributes passed as input parameters from the second page, and displays a success message. Otherwise it avoids the update and displays another message.

The complete PSP (filename db_lock_confirm2.psp) using Web Template 2 is shown below. The navigation URL should be modified to suit the existing server configuration in the form of server-name, DAD, and userid.

```
<!DOCTYPE HTML PUBLIC "-//W3C//DTD HTML 4.01 Transitional//EN">
<html>
<%@page language="PL/SQL"%>
<%@plsql procedure="db_lock_confirm2"%>
<%@plsql parameter="apt_no_text" default="null"%>
<%@plsql parameter="formsbutton1" default="null"%>
<%@plsql parameter="apt_utility_text" default="null"%>
<%@plsql parameter="apt_deposit_amt_text" default="null"%>
<%@plsql parameter="apt_rent_amt_text" default="null"%>
<%@plsql parameter="p_checksum" type="number"%>
<%@plsql parameter="p_rowid" type="rowid"%>
<%!curr_rowid rowid;
lock_check char(5);%>
<head>
<title>Web Database Lock</title>
</head>
<body>
<p><div align="center"><h1>Superflex Apartments</h1></div></p>
<br>
<table summary=""width=700> <!-- Page width -->
<tr>
<td width=100> <!-- Navigation Bar Links -->
<a href="http://server-name/DAD/userid.db_lock_input2">Enter Apartment</a><br>

</td><td width=600> <!-- Start Page Content -->
<%if p_checksum = owa_opt_lock.checksum('pspclass1','apartment',p_rowid) then
lock_check := 'true';
```

```
else lock_check := 'false';
end if;
if lock_check = 'true' then
update apartment
set apt_utility = apt_utility_text,
apt_deposit_amt = apt_deposit_amt_text,
apt_rent_amt = apt_rent_amt_text
where apt_no = apt_no_text;
commit;%>
<P>Updates have been applied successfully.</P>
<P>Thanks.</P>
<%end if;%>

<%if lock_check = 'false' then%>
<P>The updates cannot be applied, as the row has been changed since the initial
request.</P>
<%end if;%>
<!-- End Page Content -->
</td></tr>
</table>
</body>
</html>
```

Load PSP to the Database

Once the PSP have been completed, open the Windows Command Prompt window to execute the loadpsp command for the PSP files. The command to load the three PSPs will be:

```
loadpsp -replace -user userid/password@connection_string
            drive&path\db_lock_input2.psp

loadpsp -replace -user userid/password@connection_string
            drive&path\db_lock_modify2.psp

loadpsp -replace -user userid/password@connection_string
            drive&path\db_lock_confirm2.psp
```

The userid, password, connection string and path specifications depend on database configuration. If there are errors in the page, fix the errors and re-load the page.

View PSP in Web Browser

Once the loading is successful type the URL below to retrieve the Web page from the database. The URL should be modified to suit the existing server configuration in the form of server-name, DAD, and userid.

```
http://server-name/DAD/userid.db_lock_input2
```

Test the working of the owa_opt_lock package by opening the Web site through another browser window simultaneously. Then make modifications in the second browser window to see the effect of the modifications in the first browser window.

CHAPTER SUMMARY

▸   In traditional database application processing, the application maintains state with the database. This makes it easy to enforce database locking during application session.

▸   Since HTTP is a stateless protocol, one cannot use the traditional database locking schemes.

▸   The reason Web does not maintain the state is because the Web doesn't know or care whether or not you're still connected when the requested Web page (PL/SQL Web procedure) specified in the URL is done.

▸   The result is that users can have lost updates problems while browsing and updating database information through Web pages.

▸   Oracle provides several ways to enforce locking for Web applications.

▸   One approach involves the PL/SQL package called OWA_OPT_LOCK that enforces a locking mechanism called optimistic locking.

▸   It is called optimistic locking as the database does not prevent other users from performing updates, but rejects the current update if an intervening update has occurred.

▸   The OWA_OPT_LOCK package provides two methods for determining whether the data was changed by another user since it was loaded in the browser.

▸   The first method is called the hidden fields method, while the second method is called the checksum method.

▸   If either method shows that the values do not match, the procedure could abort the update and notify the user that the data has changed since the data was last retrieved.

REVIEW QUESTIONS

1.   Explain briefly why the traditional locking schemes do not work for Web applications.

2.   What is the Oracle package that enforces locking for Web applications?

3.   What is optimistic locking mechanism?

4.   What are the two methods to enforce Web database locking?

5.   Explain the checksum method to enforce Web database locking.

REVIEW EXERCISES

1. In traditional database application processing, the application maintains _____ with the database.

2. HTTP is a _____ protocol.

3. The Web does not maintain the _____ when the requested Web page has been rendered.

4. Users can have _____ updates while browsing and updating database information through Web page.

5. Oracle provides a PL/SQL package called _____ that enforces Web locking mechanism.

6. _____ locking does not prevent other users from performing updates, but rejects the current update if an intervening update occurs.

7. There are _____ methods by which Oracle performs locking.

8. The _____ method stores the current values in the hidden form fields in the Web page.

9. The _____ method performs row checksum at the time the Web page is loaded in the browser and when the data is saved.

10. The store_values procedure enforces the _____ fields method.

PROBLEM SOLVING EXERCISES

Ex10B-1.   Modify the problem solving exercise Ex6B-2 of Chapter 6, Lesson B with Web locking capabilities. Choose appropriate locking method. The "Complete_Club_Change" PSP should either display a message "The Updates cannot be applied, as the row has been changed since the initial request" if row has been changed or "Update Successful" message otherwise.

Ex10B-2.   Modify the problem solving exercise Ex6B-4 of Chapter 6, Lesson B with Web locking capabilities. Choose appropriate locking method. The "Confirm_Sentiment_Change" PSP should either display a message "The Updates cannot be applied, as the row has been changed since the initial request" if row has been changed or "Sentiment Update Successful" message otherwise.

Ex10B-3.   Modify the problem solving exercise Ex6B-5 of Chapter 6, Lesson B with Web locking capabilities. Choose appropriate locking method. The "Confirm_Customer_Change" PSP should either display a message "The Updates cannot be applied, as the row has been changed since the initial request" if row has been changed or "Customer Update Successful" message otherwise.

Ex10B-4.   Modify the problem solving exercise Ex6B-6 of Chapter 6, Lesson B with Web locking capabilities. Choose appropriate locking method. The "Tenant_Modify_Confirm" PSP should either display a message "The Updates cannot be applied, as the row has been changed since the initial request" if row has been changed or "Tenant Update Successful" message otherwise.

APPENDIX A

Database Access Descriptor

ENABLE HTTP SERVER

Oracle 11g includes an embedded XML DB HTTP server. To start HTTP server, login SQL Plus with DBA privileges (SYS or SYSTEM userid) and enter the following command:

```
EXEC DBMS_XDB.SETHTTPPORT(port-number);
commit;
```

where port-number is the assigned port to be used with the URL to access PL/SQL server pages in the browser. For example, the following statement starts HTTP server for port 7777.

```
EXEC DBMS_XDB.SETHTTPPORT(7777);
commit;
```

SET DATABASE ACCESS DESCRIPTOR

The setting and administration of Database Access Descriptor (DAD) is performed using the DBMS_EPG package. This package has procedures to enable various DAD features like create DAD, delete DAD, allow authorized access, and so on. To set DAD features, login SQL Plus with DBA privileges (SYS or SYSTEM userid).

1. Create a new DAD:

   The CREATE_DAD procedure is used to create a DAD. It requires two parameters – one for DAD name, and the other for associated virtual path. For example the following PL/SQL anonymous block create a DAD named "classpsp" and its associated virtual path as follows:

   ```
   begin
   DBMS_EPG.create_dad('classpsp','/classpsp/*');
   end;
   /
   ```

   To access a PL/SQL server page from the browser, with a DAD "classpsp" the URL will be:

   ```
   http://host-name:port/classpsp/userid.PSP-ProcedureName
   ```

   The browser by default will prompt for userid password.

471

2. Enable static authentication:

    Static authentication is a way to avoid login prompts in browser while accessing Web pages. The AUTHORIZE_DAD procedure authorizes DAD to invoke procedures with database user's privileges. The procedure has two input parameters of which the – one for the DAD name and the other for the userid. For example, the following PL/SQL anonymous block allow the "classpsp" DAD access to a user "sam" account. *The userid must be entered in uppercase.*

    ```
    begin
    DBMS_EPG.authorize_dad('classpsp','SAM');
    end;
    /
    ```

3. Assign DAD attribute value:

    The SET_DAD_ATTRIBUTE procedure assigns a value for various DAD attributes. The procedure has three input parameters – (i) a DAD name, (ii) an attribute name, and (iii) attribute value. For example, the following PL/SQL anonymous block has "classpsp" as DAD name, "authentication-mode" as attribute name, and "Basic" as attribute value.

    ```
    begin
    DBMS_EPG.set_dad_attribute('classpsp', 'authentication-mode', 'Basic');
    end;
    /
    ```

    Table A-1 provides mapping of some of the mod_plsql attributes with embedded XML DB (PL/SQL Gateway) DAD attributes.

mod_plsql DAD Attribute	XML DB DAD Attribute	Allows Multiple Occurrences	Possible Values
PlsqlAuthenticationMode	authentication-mode	No	Basic, SingleSignOn, GlobalOwa, CustomOwa, PerPackageOwa
PlsqlDatabaseUsername	database-username	No	String
PlsqlDefaultPage	default-page	No	String
PlsqlDocumentPath	document-path	No	String
PlsqlDocumentProcedure	document-procedure	No	String
PlsqlDocumentTablename	document-table-name	No	String
PlsqlMaxRequestsPerSession	max-requests-per-session	No	Unsigned integer
PlsqlPathAlias	path-alias	No	String
PlsqlSessionCookieName	session-cookie-name	No	String

Table A-1: Mapping Between mod_plsql and XML DB DAD Attributes

4. Drop a DAD

The DROP_DAD procedure can be used to remove an unwanted DAD. All the virtual-path mappings of the DAD will be dropped also. For example, the following PL/SQL anonymous block drop the "classpsp" DAD.

```
begin
DBMS_EPG.drop_dad('classpsp');
end;
/
```

CREATE VIRTUAL (WEB) FOLDER

To enable viewing of images in a PSP through the browser create a virtual (Web) folder and then access those images through absolute path specifications. *The virtual (Web) folder name as well as file names are case sensitive.*

1. Go to My Network Places and start the "Add Network Place Wizard." Figure A-1 opens.

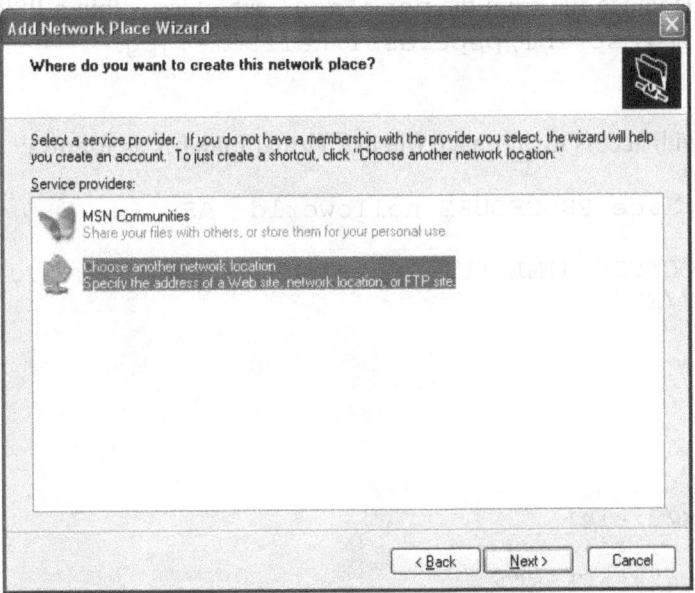

Figure A-1

2.   Select "Choose another network location", then

3.   Click "Next" and follow the Wizard's prompts.

4.   When prompted for an "Internet or network address", enter the URL of the HTTP server name including the port number assigned during the Enable HTTP Server section. For example, the URL http://missouristate.edu:7777/ opens virtual folder assigned to this URL at port 7777.

        Continue to follow the Wizard's prompts. The system will prompt for username and password. Enter the SYSTEM userid and its corresponding password.

Towards the end of wizard, enter a name to identify this virtual folder, eg. WEBSPACE.

5.   Once the Wizard is finished, the "My Network Places" window will contain a Web folder WEBSPACE. To access WEBSPACE folder initially the system may prompt for DBA type userid and password.

6.   Now, within the home virtual folder, *create a subfolder*. Move files from hard drive to this new subfolder, and then access them directly through the browser or PSP procedure.

For example, create a subfolder `pspweb1`, and paste an image file HalfDome.jpg in it.

To access this image file from the browser enter the URL `http://missouristate.edu:7777/pspweb1/HalfDome.jpg`.

To access this image file from the `pspweb1` subfolder within a PSP procedure, the absolute path will be `/pspweb1/HalfDome.jpg`.

If another subfolder `pspclass1` is created inside `pspweb1`, and the image file HalfDome.jpg is pasted inside it, then to access the image from the browser, the URL is `http://missouristate.edu:8080/pspweb1/pspclass1/HalfDome.jpg`.

Now, to access this image file from the `pspclass1` subfolder within a PSP procedure, the absolute path will be `/pspweb1/pspclass1/HalfDome.jpg`.

A sample PSP procedure with access to an image file in a virtual folder is as follows:

```
create or replace PROCEDURE helloworld  AS
 BEGIN NULL;
htp.prn('<!DOCTYPE HTML PUBLIC "-//W3C//DTD HTML 4.0
Transitional//EN">
');
htp.prn('
');
htp.prn('
<html>
<head>
<title>Hello</title>
</head>
<body bgcolor="#FFFFFF">
<img src="/pspweb1/pspclass1/HalfDome.jpg">
<p>Hello World</p>
</body>
</html>');
 END;
```

APPENDIX B

Portable Applications

Oracle provide a mechanism to generate portable PL/SQL applications through a Wrap Utility. This utility is a stand-alone programming utility that encrypts PL/SQL source code. The utility uses human-readable PL/SQL source code as input, and writes out portable binary object code. The binary code can be distributed without fear of exposing the proprietary algorithms and methods. Oracle will still understand and know how to execute the code. Keep note of the fact that once the PL/SQL source code is wrapped, it cannot be unwrapped.

By hiding application internals, the Wrap Utility prevents
- misuse of your application by other developers
- exposure of your algorithms to business competitors

Wrapped code makes the application portable. The PL/SQL compiler recognizes and loads wrapped compilation units automatically. Other advantages include
- platform independence – no need to deliver multiple versions of the same compilation unit.
- dynamic loading – users need not shut down and re-link to add a new feature.
- dynamic binding – external references are resolved at load time.
- strict dependency checking – invalidated program units are recompiled automatically.
- normal importing and exporting – the Import/Export utility accepts wrapped files.

The Wrap Utility is upward-compatible with Oracle. So, for example, it is possible to load wrapped files processed by Oracle 10g into Oracle 11g. However, the Wrap Utility is not downward-compatible. Hence it is not possible to load wrapped files processed by Oracle 11g Wrap Utility into a Oracle 10g Oracle database.

When wrapping a package or object type, wrap only the body, not the spec. That way, other developers see the information they need to use the package or type, but they do not see its implementation.

Like all encrypted files, wrapped files cannot be edited. To revise a wrapped file, you must revise and re-wrap the underlying source code. So, do not wrap a subprogram, package, or object type until it is ready for shipment to end-users.

Running the Wrap Utility

To run the Wrap Utility, enter the wrap command at your operating system prompt using the following syntax:

```
wrap iname=input_file [oname=output_file]
```

Leave no space around the equal signs because spaces delimit individual arguments.

The wrap command requires only one argument, which is `iname=input_file`, where input_file is the name of the Wrap Utility input file. It is not necessary to specify the file extension if it is .sql. Optionally, the wrap command takes a second argument, which is `oname=output_file` where output_file is the name of the Wrap Utility output file. You need not specify the output file because its name defaults to that of the input file and its extension defaults to plb (PL/SQL binary). Generally, the output file is much larger than the input file. For example,

```
C:\>wrap iname=c:\oracle_wrap_utility\load_xml_ajax2.sql oname=c:\oracle_wrap_ut
ility\load_xml_ajax2.plb
```

Also the following commands are equivalent:

```
C:\>wrap iname=c:\oracle_wrap_utility\load_xml_ajax2.sql
C:\>wrap iname=c:\oracle_wrap_utility\load_xml_ajax2.sql oname=c:\oracle_wrap_ut
ility\load_xml_ajax2.plb
```

The input file can contain any combination of SQL statements. However, the Wrap Utility encrypts only the following CREATE statements, which define subprograms, packages, or object types:

```
CREATE [OR REPLACE] FUNCTION function_name
CREATE [OR REPLACE] PROCEDURE procedure_name
CREATE [OR REPLACE] PACKAGE package_name
CREATE [OR REPLACE] PACKAGE BODY package_name
CREATE [OR REPLACE] TYPE type_name ... OBJECT
CREATE [OR REPLACE] TYPE BODY type_name
```

All other SQL statements are passed intact to the output file. Comment lines are deleted unless they appear inside a subprogram, package, or object type.

When encrypted, a subprogram, package, or object type has the form

```
<header> wrapped <body>
```

where header begins with the reserved word CREATE and ends with the name of the subprogram, package, or object type, and body is an intermediate form of object code. The word wrapped tells the PL/SQL compiler that the subprogram, package, or object type was encrypted by the Wrap Utility.

Loading the wrap files in Oracle Database

In SQL Developer, go to the File Menu, Open option, and select the .plb file from the folder. The source will not be displayed. Compile the file for use.

APPENDIX C

Oracle Web Utilities

Oracle has provided many Web utilities in the form of pre-defined packages. Some of these utilities are briefly outlined in this appendix.

OWA_UTIL Package

The owa_util package contains utility programs that perform various Web related tasks. It contains three types of utility programs. Summary of such utility programs are described in Table D-1.

1. Dynamic SQL Utilities to produce pages with dynamically generated SQL code.

2. HTML utilities to retrieve the values of CGI environment variables and perform URL redirects.

3. Date utilities to enable correct date-handling. Date values are simple strings in HTML, but are treated as a data type by the Oracle database.

OWA_UTIL utilities	Description
owa_util.bind_variables	Function that prepares a SQL query and binds variables to it.
owa_util.calendarprint	Procedure that prints a calendar.
owa_util.cellsprint	Procedure that prints the contents of a query in a HTML table.
owa_util.choose_date	Procedure that generates HTML form elements that allow the user to select a date.
owa_util.dateType	A data type to hold date information.
owa_util.get_cgi_env	Function that returns the value of the specified CGI environment variable.
owa_util.get_owa_service_path	Function that returns the full virtual path for the PL/SQL Gateway.
owa_util.get_procedure	Function that returns the name of the procedure that is invoked by the PL/SQL Gateway.
owa_util.http_header_close	Procedure that closes the HTTP header.
owa_util.ident_arr	A data type that stores an array of form element values.
owa_util.ip_address	A data type used by the owa_sec.get_client_ip function.

Table D-1: OWA_UTL utility programs

OWA_UTIL utilities	Description
owa_util.listprint	Procedure that generates a HTML form element containing data from a query.
owa_util.mime_header	Procedure that generates the Content-type line in the HTTP header.
owa_util.print_cgi_env	Procedure that generates a list of all CGI environment variables and their values.
owa_util.redirect_url	Procedure that generates the Location line in the HTTP header.
owa_util.showpage	Procedure that prints a page generated by the htp and htf packages in SQL*Plus.
owa_util.showsource	Procedure that prints the source for the specified subprogram.
owa_util.signature	Procedure that prints a line that says that the page is generated by the PL/SQL Agent.
owa_util.status_line	Procedure that generates the Status line in the HTTP header.
owa_util.tablePrint	Function that prints the data from a table in the database as an HTML table.
owa_util.todate	Function that converts dateType data to the standard PL/SQL date type.
owa_util.who_called_me	Procedure that returns information on the caller of the procedure.

Table D-1: OWA_UTL utility programs

Define OWA_UTIL.IDENT_ARR

This utility defines an array datatype for a procedure parameter. It is defined as:

```
type ident_arr is table of varchar2(30) index by binary_integer;
```

In PSP, it is used for form pages that have multiple instances of similar form elements with the same name. It is declared in a PSP as:

```
<%@ plsql parameter="parameter-name" type="owa_util.ident_arr"%>
```

It should be noted that unlike other types of scalar parameters, owa_util.ident_arr declared parameters may not have `default="null"` extensions to their declaration. The parameter-name entry can refer to multiple instances of similar form element. For example, the following HTML statements in a form area defines four text box form elements with the same name "v1" having different values. To reference different values of "v1" in the response PSP, it should be declared as a parameter of datatype owa_util.ident_arr.

```
<input type=text name="v1" value="value1">
<input type=text name="v1" value="value2">
```

```
<input type=text name="v1" value="value3">
<input type=text name="v1" value="value4">
```

Another variation of array datatype similar to OWA_UTIL.IDENT_ARR is OWA_UTIL.VC_ARR.

Return Value of a CGI Environment Variable

The OWA_UTIL.GET_CGI_ENV function returns the value of a specified CGI environment variable. If the variable is not defined, the function returns a NULL value. The full syntax of owa_util.get_cgi_env is as follows:

OWA_UTIL.GET_CGI_ENV(*parameter-name* IN VARCHAR2) RETURN VARCHAR2;

where the *parameter-name* is the name of the CGI environment variable. The parameter details are listed in Table D-2.

CGI Environment Variable	Description	Example
gateway_interface	The name and version of the gateway being used. The gateway interface name and version are separated by a forward slash with no spaces.	CGI/1.1
http_user_agent	The name of the browser and operating system the user is using.	Mozilla/5.0 (Windows; U; Windows NT 5.0; en-US; rv:1.6) Gecko/20040113
path_info	Path information as it was passed to the server in the URL.	/pspclass1.test_owa_util3
path_translated	Extra path information. Contains the physical path name obtained in the path_info environment variable.	
remote_addr	The IP address of the client that made the request.	172.16.1.35
remote_host	The name or IP address of the remote computer that made the request.	
script_name	The name of the script involved. For PSP, it is the PL/SQL agent name.	/pls/classpsp
server_name	The domain name of the computer that is running the server software.	psp_server

Table D-2: CGI Envirnoment Variable Parameters

CGI Environment Variable	Description	Example
server_port	The TCP port number on which the server is operating. 80 is the default HTTP port number.	7778
server_protocol	The name and version of the protocol the server is using.	HTTP/1.1
server_software	The name of the server handling the request.	Oracle HTTP Server Powered by Apache/1.3.22 (Win32) mod_plsql/3.0.9.8.3b mod_ssl/2.8.5 OpenSSL/0.9.6b mod_fastcgi/2.2.12 mod_oprocmgr/1.0 mod_perl/1.25

Table D-2: CGI Envirnoment Variable Parameters

An example of a PSP using the CGI environment variables is shown below.

```
<%@page language="PL/SQL"%>
<%@plsql procedure="test_owa_util1"%>
<%!environ1 varchar(120);%>
<html>
<body>
<p>PSP Web Page.</p>
<p>Test for OWA_UTIL Variables</p>
<%environ1 := owa_util.get_cgi_env('http_user_agent');%>
<p>HTTP User Agent is <%=environ1%></p>
</body>
</html>
```

Return Names and Values of all CGI Environment Variables

The OWA_UTIL.PRINT_CGI_ENV procedure generates all the CGI environment variables and their values made available by the PL/SQL agent to a PL/SQL procedure. The syntax is as follows:

OWA_UTIL.PRINT_CGI_ENV;

This procedure receives no parameters and generates a list of all environment variables. An example of a PSP that displays OWA_UTIL variables is as follows:

```
<%@page language="PL/SQL"%>
<%@plsql procedure="test_all_util1"%>
<html>
<body>
<p>PSP Web Page.</p>
<p>Test for Printing all OWA_UTIL Variables</p>
<%owa_util.print_cgi_env;%>
</body>
</html>
```

Return the name of the Procedure invoked by PL/SQL Gateway

The OWA_UTIL.GET_PROCEDURE function returns the name of the procedure that is being invoked by the PL/SQL agent. The syntax of the function definition is as follows:

OWA_UTIL.GET_PROCEDURE RETURN VARCHAR2;

This function receives no parameters and returns the name of the procedure, including the package name if the procedure is defined in the package. An example of the PSP using the function is as follows:

```
<%@page language="PL/SQL"%>
<%@plsql procedure="test_get_util1"%>
<%!environ1 varchar(120);%>
<html>
<body>
<p>PSP Web Page.</p>
<p>Test for OWA_UTIL Variables</p>
<%environ1 := owa_util.get_procedure;%>
<p>Procedure is <%=environ1%></p>
</body>
</html>
```

Return Information about the Calling PL/SQL Code Unit

The OWA_UTIL.WHO_CALLED_ME procedure returns information (in the form of output parameters) about the PL/SQL code unit that invoked it. This procedure is useful to track Web traffic hits to Web pages. The syntax is as follows:

```
OWA_UTIL.WHO_CALLED_ME(
    owner OUT VARCHAR2,
    name OUT VARCHAR2,
    lineno OUT VARCHAR2,
    caller_t OUT VARCHAR2);
```

Owner is the name of the owner of the program unit. *Name* is the name of the program unit. *Lineno* is the line number within the program unit where the call was made. *Caller_t* is the type of program unit that made the call. Possible types are package body, anonymous block function, and procedure.

For example we will create two PSP that call each other. The first PSP "test_who_util1" is shown below:

```
<%@page language="PL/SQL"%>
<%@plsql procedure="test_who_util1"%>
<html>
<body>
<p>PSP Web Page.</p>
<p>Test for OWA_UTIL Variables</p>
<%test_who_util2;%>
<p>Call is completed.</p>
</body>
</html>
```

The second PSP "test_who_util2" is as follows:

```
<%@page language="PL/SQL"%>
<%@plsql procedure="test_who_util2"%>
<%!t_owner varchar(40);
t_name varchar(40);
t_lineno number;
t_caller_t varchar(40);%>
<html>
<body>
<p>Inside Called PSP Web Page.</p>
<%owa_util.who_called_me(t_owner,t_name,t_lineno,t_caller_t);%>
<p>Owner is <%=t_owner%></p>
<p>Name is <%=t_name%></p>
<p>Line Number is <%=t_lineno%></p>
<p>Caller is <%=t_caller_t%></p>
</body>
</html>
```

The first program test_who_util1 calls the second program test_who_util2. The owa_util function is inside the second program.

View the source code of a Procedure in the Web Browser

The OWA_UTIL.SHOWSOURCE procedure displays the source of the specified package, procedure, or function. The syntax of the procedure is as follows:

OWA_UTIL.SHOWSOURCE(*cname* IN VARCHAR2);

where *cname* refers to function, procedure, or package.

It is possible to use owa_util.showsource directly in the browser to view the source code. The URL in this case will be:

```
http://server-name/DAD/owa_util.sourcename?cname=value
```

However, by default an error will occur with the message "You don't have permission to access /pls/dad/owa_util.showsource on this server." The reason for the error is the server security that secure packages installed under the SYS schema. "owa_util" is one of these packages. DBA permission may be necessary to make the changes for this procedure to work.

UTL_SMTP Package

You can send e-mail from a PL/SQL program unit or stored subprogram with the UTL_SMTP package. *Prior to using the UTL_SMTP package it is important to configure the Access Control List (ACL) in the database*. ACL is part of the Oracle security setup and is a Oracle XML DB functionality.

The following procedure send_test_email uses the SMTP package to send a simple e-mail message.

```
CREATE OR REPLACE PROCEDURE send_test_email IS
  mailhost    VARCHAR2(64) := 'mailhost.domain.com';
  sender      VARCHAR2(64) := 'myname@mydomain.com';
  recipient   VARCHAR2(64) := 'you@somedomain.com';
  mail_conn   UTL_SMTP.CONNECTION;
BEGIN
  mail_conn := UTL_SMTP.OPEN_CONNECTION(mailhost, 25); -- 25 is the port
  UTL_SMTP.HELO(mail_conn, mailhost);
  UTL_SMTP.MAIL(mail_conn, sender);
  UTL_SMTP.RCPT(mail_conn, recipient);

  UTL_SMTP.OPEN_DATA(mail_conn);
  UTL_SMTP.WRITE_DATA(mail_conn, 'This is a test message.' || chr(13));
  UTL_SMTP.WRITE_DATA(mail_conn, 'This is line 2.' || chr(13));
  UTL_SMTP.CLOSE_DATA(mail_conn);

  -- If message were in single string, open_data(), write_data(),
  -- and close_data() could be in a single call to data().

  UTL_SMTP.QUIT(mail_conn);
EXCEPTION
  WHEN OTHERS THEN
    -- Insert error-handling code here
    NULL;
END;
```

UTL_HTTP Package

The UTL_HTTP package allows PL/SQL to read Web pages like a text-only browser. It reads the HTML into a PL/SQL table or a VARCHAR2 variable. Once the browser content has been transferred it can then be analyzed. *Prior to using the UTL_SMTP package it is important to configure the Access Control List (ACL) in the database.* ACL is part of the Oracle security setup and is a Oracle XML DB functionality.

The package has two functions REQUEST and REQUEST_PIECES. The function RETURN returns a string of 4000 charcters. The REQUEST_PIECES returns a varchar2 PL/SQL table (array) of 2000 bytes. In order to use REQUEST_PIECES one must first define a PL/SQL table in which to receive the result. The syntax is:

```
UTL_HTTP.REQUEST('www.some-site.com ');
UTL_HTTP.REQUEST_PIECES('www.some-site.com ');
```

For example, the following PSP retrieves the contents of some Web site.

```
<%@page language="PL/SQL"%>
<%@plsql procedure="test_utl_http1"%>
<%!t_html_table utl_http.html_pieces;%>
<html>
<body>
<p>PSP Web Page.</p>
<p>Test for OWA_HTTP</p>
<%t_html_table := utl_http.request_pieces('http://www.some-site.com');%>
<p>UTL_HTTP Result</p>
<%for i in 1 .. t_html_table.count
loop%>
```

```
<%=t_html_table(i)%>
<%end loop;%>
</body>
</html>
```

The REQUEST_PIECES function accepts optional input parameters, aside from the mandatory URL. Some of the parameters are:

- MAX_PIECES to specify the maximum number of pieces (array records) the function returns before truncating the page. The default is 32K.
- PROXY value to inform UTL_HTTP the IP address or domain of your proxy server. The default is NULL, which indicates none is required.

There are two exceptions that can be declared when using UTL_HTTP package. These exceptions avoid the ORA-06510 error. The syntax of the exceptions is:

```
DECLARE
INIT_FAILED EXCEPTION;
REQUEST_FAILED EXCEPTION;
```

The init_failed exception occurs when initialization of HTTP callout subsystem fails. The request_failed exception occurs if the site doesn't respond or is down.

There can be numerous possible uses of UTL_HTTP, like:

- track stock prices.
- intelligence tool to gather information from competitors Web site.
- call other CGI programs.
- read templates.
- perform load testing.

OWA_SEC Package

Generally when a DAD is configured, PL/SQL Web procedures are executed either without any authentication (if the Web procedures are in the DAD specified userid schema) or with authentication of database userid and password. There is another method for authentication provided by utility OWA_SEC. OWA_SEC package provides security to the Web procedures in the form of an authorization check before allowing access to the procedure. It checks username, password, IP address, and hostname from the client that is making a request to the server. The package components are listed in Table D-3.

Program	Description
GET_CLIENT_HOSTNAME (function)	This function returns the hostname of the client as varchar2 data type. Syntax: owa_sec.get_client_hostname return varchar2;
GET_CLIENT_IP (function)	This function returns the IP address of the client in the form of a PL/SQL table with four rows corresponding to the four elements of the IP address. Syntax: owa_sec.get_client_ip return owa_util.ip_address;
GET_PASSWORD (function)	This function returns the password the user used to logon. Syntax: owa_sec.get_password return varchar2;
GET_USER_ID (function)	This function returns the userid that was used to logon. Syntax: owa_sec.get_user_id return varchar2;
SET_AUTHORIZATION (procedure)	This procedure is used with the OWA_CUSTOM package to set the mode of authentication. Syntax: owa_sec.set_authorization(scheme in integer);
SET_PROTECTION_REALM (procedure)	This procedure sets the realm of the page that is returned to the user. The user must enter the userid and login that already exists in the realm of authorization to succeed. Syntax: owa_sec.set_protection_realm(realm in varchar2);

Table D-3: OWA_SEC Package Programs

The OWA_SEC package must be called by a procedure that is performing authentication. If OWA_SEC is called outside of the procedure performing authentication, the return value is NULL. Further, the authentication mode must be configured correctly in the DAD to use OWA_SEC successfully.

Each package in the DAD that the user calls must have a function called AUTHORIZE. Within this function, the logic must indicate whether the userid and password supplied by the user are valid. The function will return a boolean value of true or false.

File Upload and Download

Oracle provide a mechanism to upload and download files directly from the database using a Database Access Descriptor (DAD). The steps to setup the upload/download capability are as follows:

1. Create a account that will be used for storing the files in the database. For example, userid "utils" with password also "utils."

2. In the *utils* account create the following *documents* table. This table will hold the uploaded file.

```
CREATE TABLE documents
  (name           VARCHAR2(256) UNIQUE NOT NULL,
   mime_type      VARCHAR2(128),
   doc_size       NUMBER,
   dad_charset    VARCHAR2(128),
   last_updated   DATE,
   content_type   VARCHAR2(128),
   blob_content   BLOB);
```

3. In the *utils* account create the following package specification *document_api* followed by the corresponding package body.

```
CREATE OR REPLACE PACKAGE document_api AS
procedure upload;
procedure upload (file in varchar2);
procedure download;
procedure download (file in varchar2);
END;


CREATE OR REPLACE PACKAGE BODY document_api AS

PROCEDURE upload AS
  l_real_name  VARCHAR2(1000);
BEGIN
  htp.htmlopen;
  htp.headopen;
  htp.title('Test Upload');
  htp.headclose;
  htp.bodyopen;
  htp.header(1, 'Test Upload');
    htp.print('<form enctype="multipart/form-data" action="document_api.upload"
method="post">');
  htp.print(' File to upload: <input type="file" name="file"><br />');
  htp.print(' <input type="submit" value="Upload">');
  htp.print('</form>');
  htp.bodyclose;
  htp.htmlclose;
END upload;

PROCEDURE upload (file  IN  VARCHAR2) AS
  l_real_name  VARCHAR2(1000);
BEGIN
  htp.htmlopen;
  htp.headopen;
```

487

```
      htp.title('File Uploaded');
      htp.headclose;
      htp.bodyopen;
      htp.header(1, 'Upload Status');
      l_real_name := SUBSTR(file, INSTR(file, '/') + 1);

      BEGIN
         -- Delete any existing document to allow update.
         DELETE FROM documents
         WHERE   name = l_real_name;

         -- Update the prefixed name with the real file name.
         UPDATE documents
         SET     name = l_real_name
         WHERE   name = file;

         htp.print('Uploaded ' || l_real_name || ' successfully.');
      EXCEPTION
         WHEN OTHERS THEN
            htp.print('Upload of ' || l_real_name || ' failed.');
            htp.print(SQLERRM);
      END;
      htp.br;

      -- Create some links to demonstrate URL downloads.
      htp.br;
      htp.print('URL Downloads:');
      htp.br;
      FOR cur_rec IN (SELECT name FROM documents) LOOP
        htp.anchor('docs/' || cur_rec.name, 'docs/' || cur_rec.name);
        htp.br;
      END LOOP;

      -- Create some links to demonstrate direct downloads.
      htp.br;
      htp.print('Direct Downloads:');
      htp.br;
      FOR cur_rec IN (SELECT name FROM documents) LOOP
                  htp.anchor('document_api.download?file='    ||    cur_rec.name,
   'document_api.download?file=' || cur_rec.name);
         htp.br;
      END LOOP;

      htp.bodyclose;
      htp.htmlclose;
   END upload;

   PROCEDURE download IS
     l_filename   VARCHAR2(255);
   BEGIN
     l_filename := SUBSTR(OWA_UTIL.get_cgi_env('PATH_INFO'), 2);
     WPG_DOCLOAD.download_file(l_filename);
   EXCEPTION
     WHEN OTHERS THEN
        htp.htmlopen;
        htp.headopen;
        htp.title('File Downloaded');
        htp.headclose;
        htp.bodyopen;
        htp.header(1, 'Download Status');
        htp.print('Download of ' || l_filename || ' failed.');
        htp.print(SQLERRM);
        htp.bodyclose;
        htp.htmlclose;
   END download;


   PROCEDURE download (file  IN  VARCHAR2) AS
     l_blob_content   documents.blob_content%TYPE;
     l_mime_type      documents.mime_type%TYPE;
```

```
BEGIN
  SELECT blob_content,
         mime_type
  INTO   l_blob_content,
         l_mime_type
  FROM   documents
  WHERE  name = file;

  OWA_UTIL.mime_header(l_mime_type, FALSE);
  htp.p('Content-Length: ' || DBMS_LOB.getlength(l_blob_content));
  OWA_UTIL.http_header_close;

  WPG_DOCLOAD.download_file(l_blob_content);
EXCEPTION
  WHEN OTHERS THEN
    htp.htmlopen;
    htp.headopen;
    htp.title('File Downloaded');
    htp.headclose;
    htp.bodyopen;
    htp.header(1, 'Download Status');
    htp.print(SQLERRM);
    htp.bodyclose;
    htp.htmlclose;
END download;

END;
```

4. Create a database access descriptor (DAD). For example, create a DAD "utils."

5. Set the following DAD attributes using anonymous PL/SQL block in SQL Plus:

```
begin
DBMS_EPG.set_dad_attribute('classpsp','authentication-mode','Basic');
end;
/

begin
DBMS_EPG.set_dad_attribute('classpsp','document-table-name','utils.documents');
end;
/

begin
DBMS_EPG.set_dad_attribute('classpsp','document-path','docs');
end;
/

begin
DBMS_EPG.set_dad_attribute('classpsp','document-
procedure','document_api.download');
end;
/
```

Note: DAD is case sensitive.

A file can be uploaded by using the following URL format:

```
http://server-name:port/DAD/document_api.upload
```

For example, the URL http://missouristate.edu:7777/utils/document_api.upload will display a text box and a button to select the file. Once the file is uploaded the system displays the stored files for viewing or download.

A file can be directly downloaded by using the following format:

```
http://server-name:port/DAD/document_api.download?file=filename
```

where filename is the full filename including its file type.

For example, http://missouristate.edu:7777/utils/document_api.download?file=bw.doc will download the file bw.doc.

The upload and download Web pages can be modified through the Upload and Download Web procedures.

Store and Download Database Information as Text File

The following steps show how to store database information as a text file and then download it through the Web using the document_api package. The file is initially saved as a text file through UTL_FILE utility on the server or network space and then transferred to the *documents* table as a BLOB.

1. Create a Oracle directory object using the syntax:

    create directory *dir-name* as *path*;

    For example, `create directory OUT_DIR as 'C:\utl_test\';`

2. In the account that is used to upload/download files (eg. utils) create a procedure *transfer_file* with one input parameter. The input parameter contains the name of the file that will be inserted into the *documents* table.

    ```
    create or replace
    PROCEDURE transfer_file (file_input in varchar2) AS

    BEGIN
    insert into documents (name, mime_type, dad_charset, content_type)
    values(file_input,'application/force-download','ascii','BLOB');
    END;
    ```

3. In the account that is used to upload/download files (eg. utils), grant execute on the *upload_file* procedure to another account so that any text file can be transferred to the documents table.

    For example, `grant execute on transfer_file to userid;`

4. In another account, create the following procedure *generate_csv* that takes a line of table row and creates/appends to a text file.

    ```
    create or replace
    PROCEDURE GENERATE_CSV
    ( path IN VARCHAR2,
    filename IN VARCHAR2,
    line IN VARCHAR2) AS
    output_file  utl_file.file_type;

    BEGIN
    output_file := utl_file.fopen (path,filename, 'A');
    ```

```
utl_file.put_line (output_file, line);
utl_file.fclose(output_file);
END GENERATE_CSV;
```

5. Create a procedure *export_row* that retrieves data from database tables (eg. customer table in the procedure), and transfers each row to the *generate_csv* procedure. The procedure then calls the *transfer_file* procedure described previously with the filename that needs to be stored in the *documents* table.

```
create or replace
PROCEDURE EXPORT_ROW (filename in varchar2) AS
cursor cust_cur is
select customer_id, first_name, last_name, city
from customer;
cust_row cust_cur%rowtype;
str varchar2(2000);
BEGIN
for cust_row in cust_cur
loop
str :=
(cust_row.customer_id||','||cust_row.first_name||','||cust_row.last_name||','||c
ust_row.city);
generate_csv('OUT_DIR',filename,str);
end loop;
utils.transfer_file(filename);
END EXPORT_ROW;
```

Once the file is in the *documents* table, it can be downloaded from the Web using the document_api package.

APPENDIX E

SQL Developer

SQL Developer is a free SQL and PL/SQL editor available on the Oracle Web site. Figure E-1 shows the main interface screen of SQL Developer. SQL Developer window generally utilizes the left side for navigation to find and select objects, while the right side displays information about selected objects.

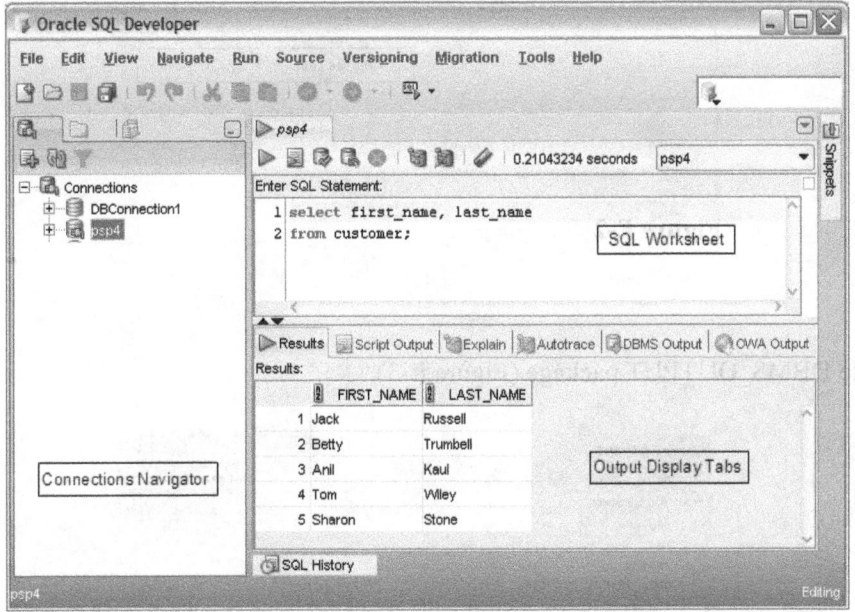

Figure E-1

Create at least one database connection in the Connections Navigator pane to work with database objects. To create a new database connection, right-click the Connections node in the Connections navigator, select New Connection, and complete the required entries in the ensuing dialog box. The right side of the SQL Developer window has tabs and panes for objects that you select or open. Also, on the right side, the SQL Worksheet is utilized to enter and execute SQL, PL/SQL, and SQL*Plus statements. The Output Display Tabs area shows the result of SQL Worksheet command execution.

HANDLING ANONYMOUS PL/SQL PROGRAM UNIT

The following figures outline steps in executing, displaying output, and runtime error display of an anonymous PL/SQL program unit in SQL Developer.

1. Run anonymous PL/SQL program unit (Figure E-2).

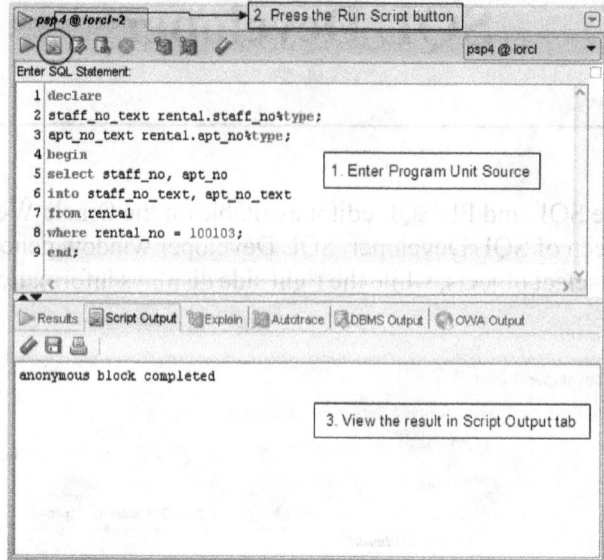

Figure E-2

2. Enable DBMS_OUTPUT package (Figure E-3).

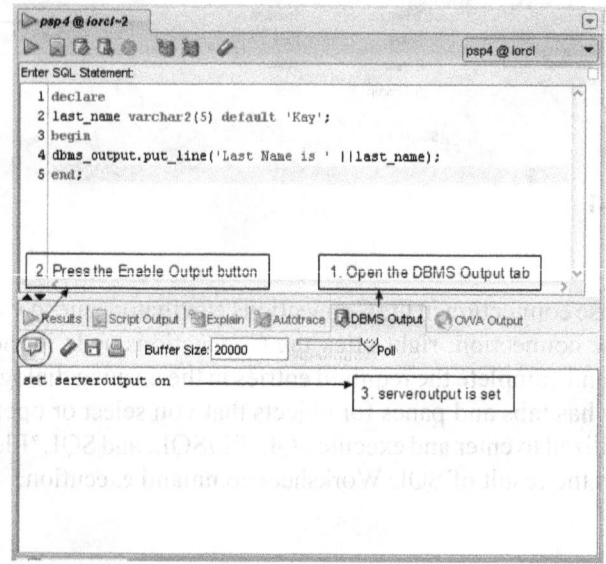

Figure E-3

3. Display output with DBMS_OUTPUT package (Figure E-4).

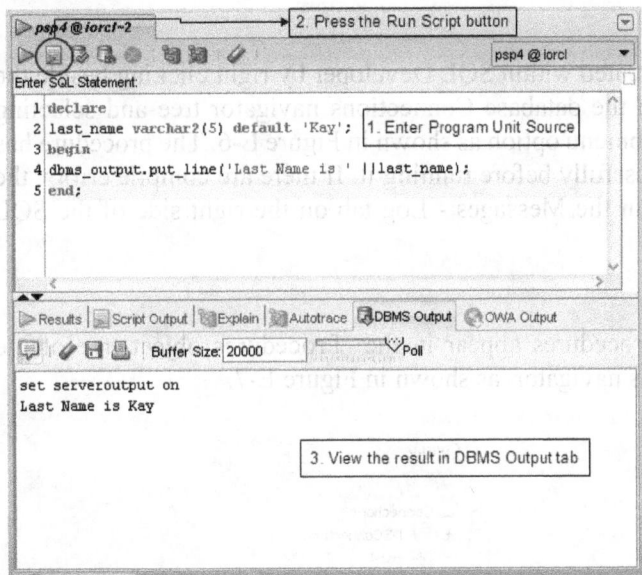

Figure E-4

4. Program unit runtime error (Figure E-5).

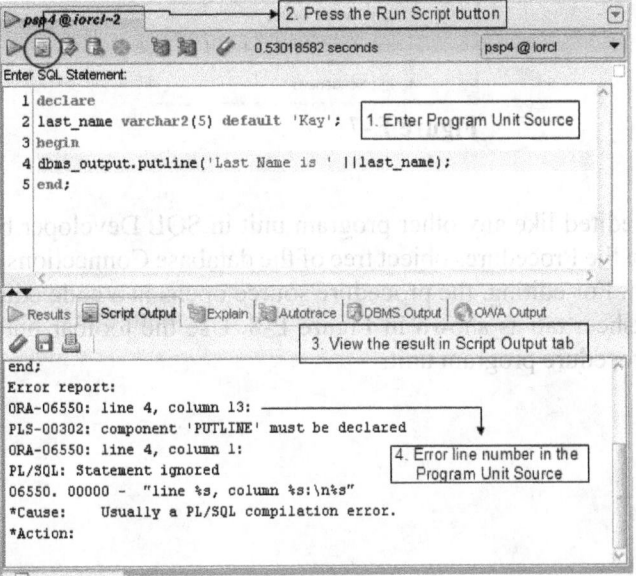

Figure E-5

HANDLING PROCEDURES

Procedures can be created within SQL Developer by right clicking beside the Procedures object in the database Connections navigator tree and selecting "New Procedure" submenu option as shown in Figure E-6. The procedure has to be compiled successfully before running it. If there are compile errors, the error details appear in the Messages - Log tab on the right side of the SQL Developer window.

Figure E-6

Once created, the procedures appear in the Procedures object tree of the database Connections navigator as shown in Figure E-7.

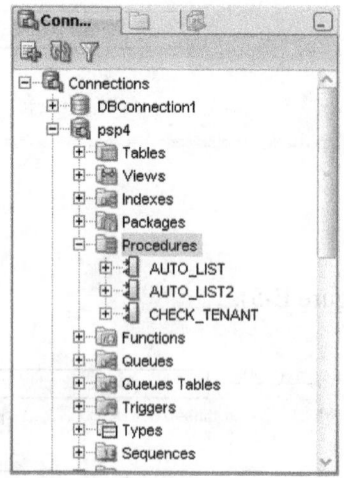

Figure E-7

A procedure can be edited like any other program unit in SQL Developer by right clicking beside the procedure name from the Procedures object tree of the database Connections navigator and selecting the Edit submenu option. For editing, the procedure source opens in a code editing window as a tab along with the SQL Worksheet tab as shown in Figure E-8. Use the toolbar buttons to compile as well as execute (Run) the procedure program unit.

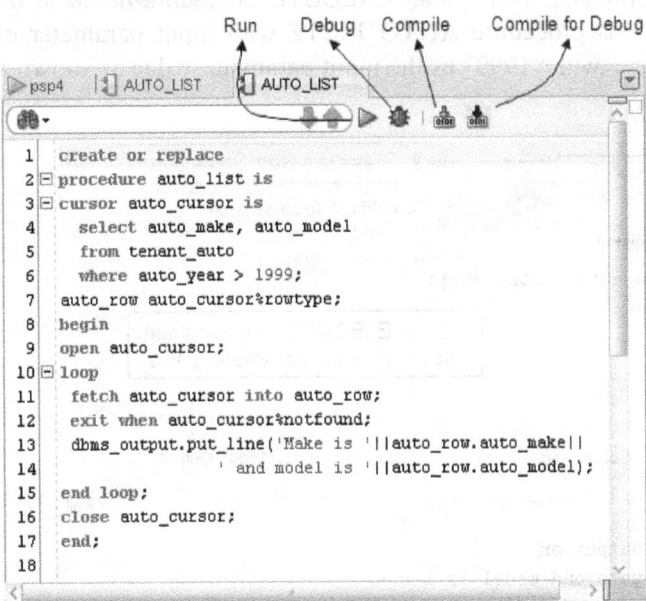

Figure E-8

A procedure can be executed directly in SQL Developer by in two ways:

1. Right click beside the procedure name in the Procedures object tree (Figure E-7) and select the Run submenu option. A Run PL/SQL window opens (Figure E-9), where a PL/SQL anonymous block program unit appears that executes the procedure. If the procedure has input parameters, enter the input values for the parameter names in the Executable section of the PL/SQL anonymous block program unit, and press the OK button to run the procedure.

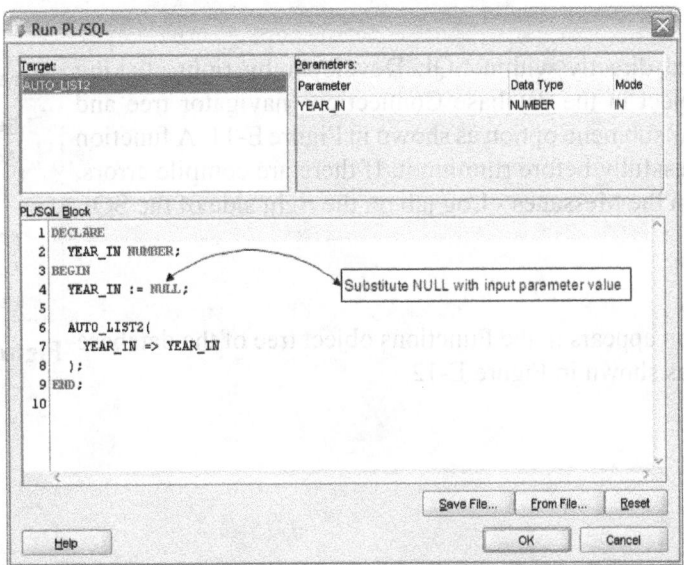

Figure E-9

2. The EXECUTE command with syntax EXECUTE *procedure-name* in the SQL Worksheet. For example, the previous procedure AUTO_LIST2 with input parameter can be run as `execute auto_list(1999);` with "1999" as the input parameter value as shown in Figure E-10.

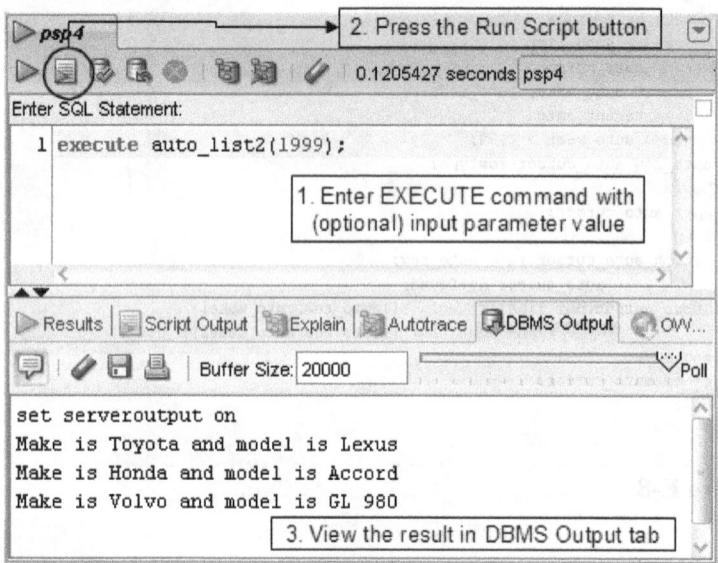

Figure E-10

A procedure can be dropped by right clicking beside the procedure name in the Procedures object tree (Figure E-7) and selecting the Drop submenu option, or executing the statement DROP PROCEDURE *procedure-name*. For example `drop procedure auto_list;`

HANDLING FUNCTIONS

Functions can be created directly within SQL Developer by right clicking beside the Functions object in the database Connections navigator tree and selecting "New Function" submenu option as shown in Figure E-11. A function has to be compiled successfully before running it. If there are compile errors, the error details appear in the Messages - Log tab on the right side of the SQL Developer window.

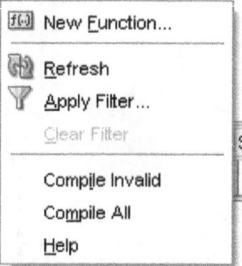

Once created, the function appears in the Functions object tree of the database **Figure E-11**
Connections navigator as shown in Figure E-12.

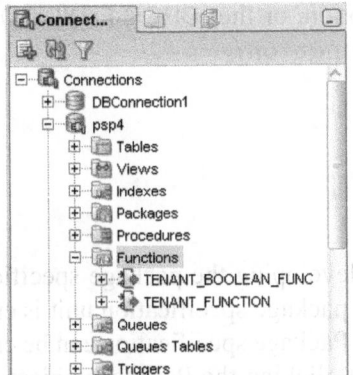

Figure E-12

A function can be edited like any other program unit in SQL Developer by right clicking beside the function name from the Functions object tree of the database Connections navigator and selecting the Edit option. For editing the function source opens in a code editing window as a tab along with the SQL Worksheet tab as shown in Figure E-8. Use the toolbar buttons to compile as well as execute (Run) the function program unit.

A function can be tested directly in SQL Developer by right clicking beside function name in the Functions object tree and selecting the Run submenu option. The Run PL/SQL window opens (Figure E-13), where a PL/SQL anonymous block program unit appears that has a statement that calls the function. If the function has input parameters, enter the input values for the parameter names in the Executable section of the PL/SQL anonymous block program unit, and press the OK button. The function is executed, and its return value displayed in a DBMS_OUTPUT statement.

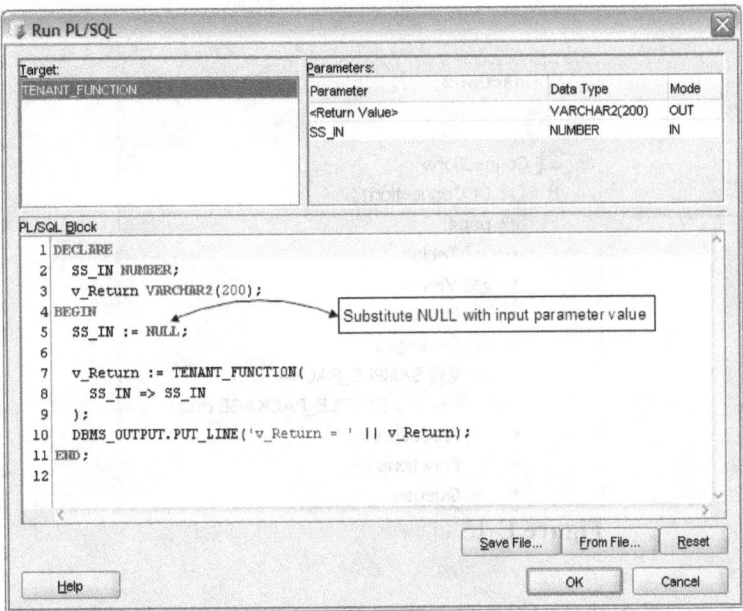

Figure E-13

A function can be dropped by right clicking beside the function name in the Functions object tree (Figure E-12) and select the Drop submenu option, or the DROP FUNCTION *function-name* statement. For example `drop function tenant_function;`

HANDLING PACKAGES

Creating a PL/SQL package involves developing the package specification and package body units separately. The package specification unit is created first followed by the package body unit. Package specification can be created directly within SQL Developer by right clicking the Packages object in the database Connections navigator tree and selecting the "New Package" submenu option as shown in Figure E-14. A "Create PL/SQL Package" dialog box opens to enter the package name, followed by the code editing window (similar to Figure E-8) to complete the package specification details. The package specification unit has to be compiled successfully. If there are compile errors, the error details appear in the Messages - Log tab on the right side of the SQL Developer window.

Figure E-14

Once the package specification unit has been successfully created, it appears in the Packages object tree of the database Connections navigator. To create the package body unit, right-click the package specification unit in the Package object of the database Connections navigator tree and select the "Create Body" submenu option. Complete the source of the package unit in the ensuing code editing window (similar to Figure E-8). Once again, the package body unit has to be compiled successfully. If there are compile errors, the error details appear in the Messages - Log tab on the right side of the SQL Developer window. The completed package specification unit and the package body unit appear in the Packages object tree of the database Connections navigator as shown in Figure E15.

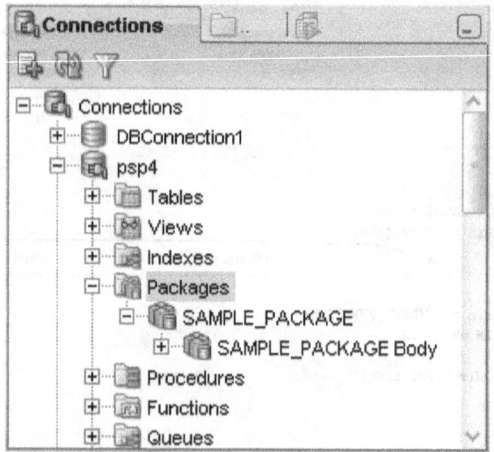

Figure E-15

A package can be tested directly in SQL Developer by right clicking beside the package specification name in the Packages object tree, and selecting the Run submenu option A package can be dropped by right clicking beside the package name in the Packages object tree and selecting the Drop Package submenu option, or executing the statement DROP PACKAGE *package-name* in the SQL worksheet. For example `drop package sample_package;`

HANDLING TRIGGERS

Triggers can be created directly within SQL Developer by right clicking beside the Triggers object in the database Connections navigator tree and selecting "New Trigger" submenu option. A "Create Trigger" dialog box opens to enter the trigger definition details (Figure E-16), followed by the code editing window (similar to Figure E-8) to complete the trigger source. A trigger has to be compiled successfully before running it. If there are compile errors, the error details appear in the Messages - Log tab on the right side of the SQL Developer window. Once created, the trigger appears in the Triggers object tree of the database Connections navigator.

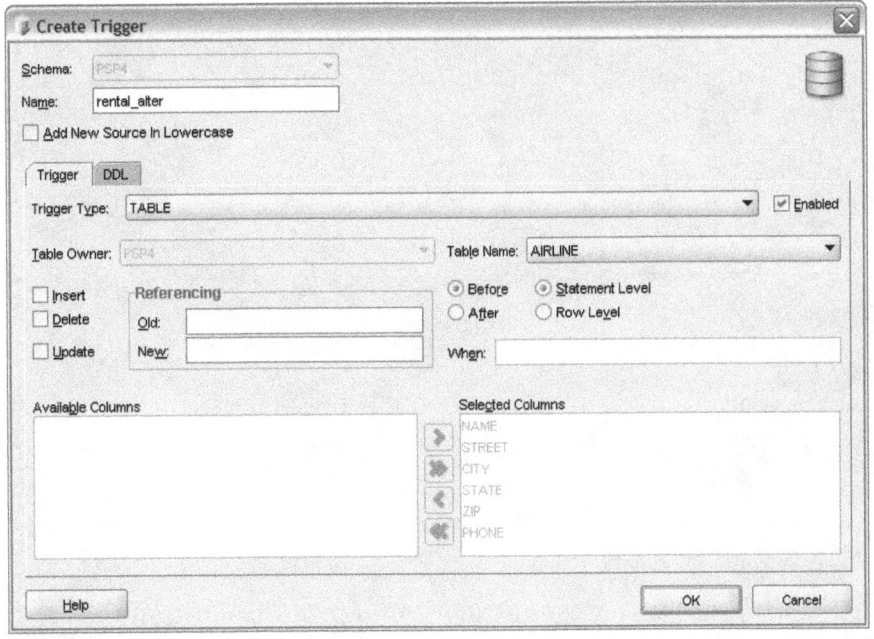

Figure E-16

A trigger can be dropped by right clicking beside the trigger name in the Triggers object tree and selecting the "Drop Trigger" submenu option, or executing the statement DROP TRIGGER *trigger-name* in the SQL worksheet. For example `drop trigger product_supp_ai;`

HANDLING PSP

PL/SQL server pages once loaded to the Oracle database appear within SQL Developer as procedures. Hence they can be edited like traditional procedures. However, to run PSP based Web procedures either use the Web browser or within SQL Developer utilize the OWA Output tab.

The OWA Output tab enables you to see the HTML output of PSP based Web procedures that have been executed as PL/SQL anonymous block in the SQL Worksheet. The tab contains icons for the following operations:

- Enable/Disable OWA Output: Enables and disables the checking of the OWA output buffer and the display of OWA output to the pane.
- Clear: Erases the contents of the pane.
- Save: Saves the contents of the pane to a file that you specify.
- Print: Prints the contents of the pane.

INDEX